Edited by PAUL ESCHHOLZ
and ALFRED ROSA
University of Vermont

W9-BRX-062

Outlooks
and Insights

A READER FOR COLLEGE WRITERS

Fourth Edition

St. Martin's Press / New York

Editor: Edward Hutchinson
Managing editor: Patricia Mansfield-Phelan
Project editor: Alda D. Trabucchi
Production supervisor: Alan Fischer
Cover design: Sheree Goodman
Cover art: "Girl in Kimono Looking Through Window," 1980
          © 1994 George Segal/VAGA, New York

Library of Congress Catalog Card Number: 94-65176
Copyright © 1995 by St. Martin's Press, Inc.
All rights reserved. No part of this book may be reproduced, stored in a retrieval system, or transmitted by any form or by any means, electronic, mechanical, photocopying, recording, or otherwise, except as may be expressly permitted by the applicable copyright statutes or in writing by the Publisher.
Manufactured in the United States of America.
9 8 7 6 5
f e d c b a

For information, write:
St. Martin's Press, Inc.
175 Fifth Avenue
New York, NY 10010

ISBN: 0-312-10110-4

Acknowledgments

"The Language of Prejudice," originally titled Chapter 11 (Linguistic Factors), by Gordon Allport, *The Nature of Prejudice* (pp. 178–188), © 1979 by Addison-Wesley Publishing Company, Inc. Reprinted by permission of the publisher.

"On Power" from *The Habit of Loving* by Barbara Ascher. Copyright © 1986, 1987, 1989 by Barbara Lazear Ascher. Reprinted by permission of Random House, Inc.

"The Unknown Citizen" from *Collected Poems* by W. H. Auden. Copyright © 1940 and renewed 1968 by W. H. Auden. Reprinted by permission of Random House, Inc.

"What Is the Truth About Global Warming?" by Robert James Bidinotto. Reprinted with permission from the February 1990 Reader's Digest. Copyright © 1990 by The Reader's Digest Assn., Inc.

"College Is a Waste of Time and Money" from *The Case Against College*, 1975. Reprinted by permission of Caroline Bird.

"Defining the 'American Indian:' A Case Study in the Language of Suppression" by Haig A. Bosmajian, *The Speech Teacher*, March 1973.

"Rite of Passage" by Anthony Brandt. Originally published in *Atlantic Monthly*, February 1981. Reprinted by permission of the author.

"Angels on a Pin" by Alexander Calandra. Originally appeared in the *Saturday Review*, December 1968.

Acknowledgments and copyrights are continued at the back of the book on pages 632–634, which constitute an extension of the copyright page.

It is a violation of the law to reproduce these selections by any means whatsoever without the written permission of the copyright holder.

Preface

The fourth edition of *Outlooks and Insights*, like the first three, is an exciting yet practical, classroom-tested solution to an old problem: how best to use readings to help students improve their writing. Most teachers of writing, and indeed most writers, would agree that reading supports writing in many ways. A fine essay can serve as an example of masterful writing and also of mature thought and insight; such examples can give inexperienced writers a sense of what is possible and inspire them to aim high. An essay can also provide students with information and ideas for use in their writing, or it may stimulate them to pursue new lines of inquiry and to write on new topics of their own. And, of course, an essay can illustrate the effective use of rhetorical strategies and techniques. The readings collected here will serve all of these familiar purposes. But *Outlooks and Insights* has an additional dimension: It provides students with explicit guidance—through discussion, examples, and exercises—in reading well and in using their reading in their writing.

This guidance is provided, first of all, in our introduction "On Reading and Writing." Here we offer well-grounded, sympathetic, and practical instruction to students on how to become more active and accurate readers and how to turn what they read to effective use in their compositions. We acknowledge that different people respond differently to the same text, and also that one reader may use different reading strategies at different times according to his or her particular purpose in reading the piece. But we also insist that any interpretation of a text should be supported by evidence drawn from the words on the page, so that diverse readers can find common ground for discussion and agreement. To this end we offer criteria and a set of questions designed to help students respond fully to what they read and to help them distinguish between a purely personal response and a reasoned understanding.

Many students are unaware of the choices they have available to them when they are required to write about something they have read. To help them better understand these options, "On Reading and Writing" offers not only advice but full-length examples of three different kinds of papers that composition students are frequently required to write: the paper that analyzes a reading, the expository or argumentative essay on a topic derived from the reading, and the personal experience essay. All three essays were written in response to the same selection, George Orwell's "A Hanging." The first analyzes some aspects of Orwell's rhetoric, showing how he uses certain details to support his thesis. The second argues in support of capital punishment, engaging Orwell's topic but taking an independent position on it. The third recounts a personal experience in which the student writer discovered her own capacity for thoughtless cruelty. Taken together, these compositions suggest the wide range of original responses that are possible in college writing assignments.

New to the introduction is a section called "Writing the Documented Paper." Here we offer advice on note-taking, integrating source materials into an essay, in-text citation of sources, and compiling a list of works cited. Both MLA and APA styles are discussed. This section concludes with a documented student essay analyzing John Updike's short story "A Sense of Shelter."

The heart of any anthology is, of course, the selections it contains. The readings in this new edition of *Outlooks and Insights* are both numerous and fresh. We have chosen 58 essays, ten short stories, and eight poems, offering instructors a large variety of options for making individual assignments and for organizing the course. The readings are grouped in eight thematic units, beginning with themes of personal experiences and relationships, continuing with such aspects of our lives as education, work, language, and culture, and finally arriving at an examination of eight contemporary social issues and ethical questions and the presentation of seven classic statements on the relationship of the individual and society. As in the third edition, we have subsections within most of the thematic units. The subsections are designed to concentrate classroom discussion and student writing on well-defined issues, concerns, and questions. For example, in the thematic unit "Family and Friends" there are subsections on "Family Ties," "The Troubled American Family," and "What Are Friends?" In the thematic unit CAMPUS LIFE are the subsections "Teaching and Learning" and "Campus Issues of the 1990s," and in "Language of America" are "Language, Prejudice, and Sexism" and "Language and Persuasion." The selections in each subsection play off one another and encourage stimulating debate and controversy in the classroom, while helping to focus and direct student writing. Because we have used these selections in our own classrooms, we know that each subsection provides a manageable and balanced assignment for a college composition class. Of special note in this edition are two new thematic units. "Cultural Encounters" presents five writers with different racial and ethnic backgrounds who explore what happens when cultures collide. In "Contemporary Issues," eight writers examine such topics as illiteracy, violence, animal rights, global warming, extinction and endangered species, and euthanasia. We trust that you will find these new sections as provocative and engaging as our students have.

There are thirty-five new readings in this edition. Each has been chosen to be challenging but not baffling, and we have sought to appeal to students' interests and concerns as well as to broaden them. The selections are a mixture of the new and the familiar—familiar to composition instructors, that is, for few first-year students will have read even such durable pieces as Zora Neale Hurston's "How It Feels to Be Colored Me," E. B. White's "Once More to the Lake," and George Orwell's "Politics and'the English Language," essays that have earned their places in the canon of essential readings for composition classes. In particular, we have been careful to choose readings that are provocative or have an argumentative bent, and that contain information that students can use to effect in their own writing.

Most of the essays in *Outlooks and Insights* were written in the last decade or two, but we have seasoned them with a few selections from classic authors: Jefferson, Thoreau, Chopin, Dickinson, Scudder, and Frost. In most sections we have included a poem and a story that can be used effectively in a composition class. Any writer can learn from the meticulously sustained irony of Auden's "The Unknown Citizen" as well as from Dick Gregory's "Shame," from the controlled and modulated prose style of a Welty, Vonnegut, or Oates story as well as from that of a Steinem or Steele essay. The questions and writing suggestions for the stories and poems are much like those supplied for the essays, with minimal attention to questions of literary form. In "On Reading and Writing," however, we do alert students to some important genre differences, so that they will not read stories and poems in exactly the same way they read essays.

The questions and writing topics supplied for each selection further develop and exploit the advice and instruction given in "On Reading and Writing." The study questions about each essay, story, and poem, like the general questions in the introduction, help students to test and increase their understanding of what they have read, and may also help them gather material for analytical papers. The assignments, which are called "Writing Topics," focus the students' attention on the central issues and questions of the thematic units. Often we use these topics to generate classroom discussion and debate before we ask our students to write. We find that such discussions coax students to develop their own lines of thinking and to articulate clearly their views on a specific issue. The writing topics suggest ways that students may use a reading in their writing, and they are designed to elicit results ranging from autobiographical essays to research papers.

Each thematic section begins with epigraphs that highlight the issues of that section. These epigraphs may find use in their own right as objects of discussion and sources of writing assignments. Each selection is provided with a biographical headnote that sets the piece in the context of the author's work and where necessary supplies information about the author's original audience and purpose. To make *Outlooks and Insights* still more flexible and useful, there is a rhetorical table of contents that classifies the selections by type and by principle of organization, as well as a glossary that will help students understand rhetorical and literary terms in the questions without having to refer to other sources.

In working on the fourth edition of *Outlooks and Insights* we have benefited inestimably from the observations and suggestions of our fellow teachers from across the country: Norbert Artzt, Miami-Dade Community College; Nancy Barbieri, University of Wisconsin–Milwaukee; Robinson Blann, Trevecca Nazarene College; Bege K. Bowers, Youngstown State University; William Clarke, Cypress College; Keith DeFolo, College of San Mateo; Ronald Dwelle, Grand Valley State University; Carol Anne Eby, Trevecca Nazarene College; Linda Ellis, Iona College; Nancy Gibson, Memphis State University; Jitske Hart, Gonzaga University, Whitworth College; Carol Hovanec, Ramapo College of New Jersey; Chandice Johnson, North Dakota State University; Myrl Guy Jones, Radford University; Philip A. Keith, Michigan State University; Ira Jean Kragthorpe, Moorpark College; Jay Losey, Baylor University; Virginia Mellor, Temple University; Rachel H. Moore, Baylor University; Mary Anne Nunn, Wake Forest University; Michael Pulley, Ozarks Technical Community College; Peter Reska, Central Connecticut State University; Cynthia Rickettson, Central Piedmont Community College; Noel Sipple, Northern Virginia Community College; Patricia Sullivan, St. John's University; Dianne Sutton, Ohio State University; Mary Tiryak, Temple University; and Michael Young, University of Nebraska.

We are grateful to our editor, Edward Hutchinson, for his insightful assistance and encouragement and to the other folks at St. Martin's Press—Karen Allanson, Sam Potts, and Alda Trabucchi—for their efforts on behalf of this project. Our colleagues at the University of Vermont helped us by assigning George Orwell's "A Hanging" to their composition classes and providing us with student papers for the introduction. To Chris and Karen Bellitto, for their work on the instructor's manual that accompanies *Outlooks and Insights*, our special thanks. Finally, we want particularly to acknowledge the contribution of our students, who teach us something new every day.

Paul Eschholz

Alfred Rosa

Contents

6   Cultural Encounters   467

7   Contemporary Issues   503

8   The Individual and Society: Some Classic Statements   557

Rhetorical Table of Contents

The selections in *Outlooks and Insights* are arranged in eight sections according to their themes. The following list of contents, which is certainly not exhaustive, first classifies many of the essays according to the rhetorical strategies they exemplify. It then classifies selections by genre—for example, public documents and speeches, poems, and short stories.

Argument and Persuasion

Cause and Effect

Comparison and Contrast

Definition

Description

Classification and Division

Illustration

Narration

Process Analysis

Public Documents and Speeches

Poems

Short Stories

Introduction: On Reading and Writing

People read for many different reasons, and they read in different ways as well. They may read for enjoyment, or to improve themselves, or to gather information, or to obtain an education or do a job; sometimes their reading benefits them in several ways at once, and in ways they did not expect. Sometimes they read with painstaking care, while at other times they may skip and skim, or even begin reading in the middle or at the end, all depending on what they are reading and what they want from it. But whatever the reason and whatever the method, reading is most rewarding when it is done actively, in a thoughtful spirit and with an inquiring mind.

Many people believe that the right way to read is passively, taking in what they read and storing it away for later use. But this kind of reading is seldom either fulfilling or useful. Unless you bring to bear on your reading what you know and believe, testing what you read and allowing it to test you, you will seldom find the experience particularly rewarding, and you may have some trouble even remembering much of what you have read. Active reading is like conversation: You give as well as take. You examine and question the author's claims, you remember and ponder ideas and information that relate to your reading, you even laugh at the jokes—at least the good ones. By responding so fully, you are taking possession of what you read, making it your own and getting it ready for use—in discussions with your friends, classmates, and teachers, for example, or in writing of your own.

Unquestionably, one of the benefits of active reading is that it can help you become a better writer. Reading can provide you with information and ideas for use in your writing, and often with subjects to write about. Moreover, it can provide you with examples to learn from. Writing is a skill that can be learned, like playing tennis or playing the piano, and one of the best ways to improve your writing is by observing how accomplished writers get their results. As you read you can see for yourself what a writer's strategies are, analyze how they work, and then adapt them to your own writing purposes. By experiencing and discussing the ideas and techniques of many different writers and incorporating them into your writing, you can develop your writing skills and explore the dimensions of your own personal style.

In using *Outlooks and Insights,* you will learn to read as a writer. To read as a writer, you must be able to discover what is going on in any essay, to figure out the writer's reasons for shaping the essay in a particular way, to decide whether the result works well or poorly—and why. Like writing itself, analytical reading is a skill that takes time to acquire. But the skill is necessary if you are to understand the craft of a piece of writing. Perhaps the most important reason to master the skills of analytical reading is that, for everything you write, you will be your own first reader and critic. How well you are able to analyze your own drafts will powerfully affect how well you revise them; and revising well is crucial to writing well. So reading others' writings analytically is useful and important practice.

Outlooks and Insights is a reader for writers, as the subtitle says. The selections in this book can entertain you, inform you, and even contribute to your self-awareness and understanding of the world around you. The writers included here are among the most skillful of their time, many of them well known and widely published. From their work you can learn important and useful writing strategies and skills. Most are contemporary, writing on issues of our own day for readers like us, but some great writers of the past are here as well. The idealism of a Henry David Thoreau, the moral indignation of an Elizabeth Cady Stanton, the noble vision of a Martin Luther King, Jr., continue to move readers despite the intervening years.

Outlooks and Insights is an anthology of writings arranged according to their subjects and themes. The first of its eight sections includes narratives and discussions of personal experiences and relationships, while the following sections broaden to increasingly wide frames of reference, finally arriving at themes concerning our society and, ultimately, all humanity. Each section begins with several aphorisms that highlight the issues addressed and serve as topics for thought, discussion, and writing. Within each section, every piece has its own brief introduction providing information about the author and often about the selection's original purpose and audience. After each piece comes "Questions for Study and Discussion," an aid to active reading. These questions ask you to analyze what you have just read to discover, or rediscover, important points about its content and its writing. In addition, each selection has two or more "Writing Topics."

Although intended primarily to stimulate writing, these suggested writing topics may be used as a starting point for your own thoughts or for class discussion.

Getting the Most Out of What You Read

What does it mean, to understand a piece of writing—an essay, for example? It means, of course, that you comprehend all the words in it. It also means that you have enough background knowledge to grasp its subject matter; a discussion of Brownian motion would mean little to someone who knew no physics, nor would an analysis of Elizabethan metrics enlighten someone unfamiliar with sixteenth-century English poetry. You have only understood the essay if you have grasped it as a whole, so that you can summarize and explain its chief points in your own words and show that each part contributes to the whole.

As you read, you absorb the essay part by part. You cannot "read" the whole all at once, as you can take in a building or a face, but must hold most of the essay in your memory and form your impression of it bit by bit as you read. How this works—what the mind does—is not fully understood, and different readers may well have different ways of doing it. That could be yet another reason why a single piece can evoke so many diverse responses. But there are some guidelines that can help you achieve an understanding of what you read.

UNDERSTANDING THE PARTS OF AN ESSAY

As you progress through an essay, word by word and sentence by sentence, keep the following guidelines in mind to help you think critically about what you are reading:

- *Make sure you understand what each word means. If a word is new to you and the context does not make its meaning clear, don't guess—look it up.*
- *Stay sensitive to connotations, the associations words carry with them. The words falsehood and fib mean about the same thing, but they convey quite different attitudes and feelings.*
- *Watch for allusions and try to interpret them. If the author refers to "the patience of Job," you don't really understand the passage unless you know how patient Job was. If you don't understand the allusion, check standard reference works such as dictionaries, encyclopedias, and books of quotations, or ask someone you think might know the answer.*

- Be on the alert for key words and ideas. The two often go together. Key words in this introduction, for example, are reading and writing; their repetition points up the key idea that these activities are really inseparable and mutually beneficial. A key idea within an essay is normally developed at some length in one or more paragraphs, and it may be stated directly at the beginning or end of a paragraph.
- Be a critical thinker. Use your knowledge and your common sense to test what you read. Is each "fact" true, as far as you know (or can find out)? Is the author's reasoning logical?
- Interpret figures of speech. When George Orwell speaks of a writer who "turns as it were instinctively to long words and exhausted idioms, like a cuttlefish squirting out ink," you must not only know or find out what a cuttlefish is but also find out how and why it squirts ink and judge how well the image expresses the author's idea.
- Pay attention to where you are in the essay. Note where the introduction ends and the body of the essay begins, and where the body gives way to the conclusion. Note where the author turns, let us say, from personal narrative to a series of arguments, or where those arguments are succeeded by refutation of other people's views. And be on the alert for the point at which you discover what the essay is really about—the point where it "makes its move," like a chess player going on the attack or a basketball forward streaking toward the basket. Often the essay's purpose and main idea are clear from the beginning, but sometimes the author withholds or even conceals them until much later.

UNDERSTANDING THE WHOLE ESSAY

As you read, you are constantly creating and re-creating your idea of the essay as a whole. At the end you will have reached some conclusions about it. Here, again, are some points to keep in mind while reading:

- Look for the main idea of the essay—what is often called the thesis. Sometimes the main idea is directly stated, either in the introduction or later on; sometimes it is not stated but can be inferred from the essay as a whole. Define the thesis of an essay as narrowly and specifically as you can while still taking the whole of the essay into account.
- Determine the author's purpose. Is it to persuade you to a point of view? To explain a subject to you? The author may directly state his or her purpose, or it may be clearly implied by the thesis.
- Analyze the relation between the whole and its parts. How does the main idea of each paragraph relate to the thesis? Does the information supplied in the body of the essay support the thesis—make it more persuasive or easier to understand? Does the author ever seem to get away from the main point, and if so, why?
- Be sure that the author's thinking is both reasonable and complete. Has the author left out any information that you think might be relevant to the thesis? Does he or she fail to consider any important views—including perhaps your

own view? Does the author assume anything without supporting the assumption or even stating it? How important are the omissions—do they lessen the clarity or the persuasiveness of the essay?

- *Evaluate the essay. Whether or not you like the essay or agree with it is important, but don't stop there; ask yourself why. Test its reasoning for errors and omissions. Test its explanation for clarity and completeness. Consider the author's style, whether it is suitable to the subject, agreeable or powerful in itself, and consistently maintained. In short, assess all the strengths and weaknesses.*

Some Tips and Techniques for Reading an Essay

Each essay offers its own distinctive challenges and rewards, but there are some reading techniques that you can use successfully with all of them in your quest for understanding. Here are some tips on reading.

Prepare Yourself. Before you plunge into reading the essay itself, form some expectations of it. Ponder the title: What does it tell you about the essay's subject matter? About its tone? Think about the author: Have you read anything else by him or her? If so, what do you know about the author's attitudes and style that may help prepare you now? If any materials accompany the essay, like the introductions in *Outlooks and Insights,* read them. These preparations will help you put yourself into an alert, ready frame of mind.

Read and Reread. You should read the selection at least twice, no matter how long or short it is. Very few essays yield their full meaning on first reading, and their full meaning is what you should be aiming to extract.

The first reading is for getting acquainted with the essay and forming your first impressions of it. The essay will offer you information, ideas, and arguments you did not expect, and as you read you will find yourself continually modifying your sense of its purpose, its strategy, and sometimes even what it is about or what point it is intended to make. (This is especially true when the author delays starting the thesis—or makes no thesis statement at all.) Only when you have finished your first reading can you be confident that you have then really begun to understand the piece as a whole.

The second reading is quite different from the first. You will know what the essay is about, where it is going, and how it gets there; now you can relate the parts more accurately to the whole. You can work at the difficult passages to make sure you fully understand what they mean. You can test your first impressions against the words on the page, developing and deepening your sense of the essay's core meaning—or possibly changing your mind about it. And as a writer, you can now pay special attention to the author's purpose and means of achieving that purpose, looking for features of organization and style that you can learn from and adapt to your own work.

Ask Yourself Questions. As you probe the essay, focus your attention by asking yourself some basic questions about it. Here are some you may find useful:

1. Do I like the essay or not? What, for me, are the most interesting parts of it? What parts do I find least interesting or hardest to understand?

2. What is the essay's main idea? What are the chief supporting ideas, and how do they relate to the main idea?

3. What is the author's attitude toward the essay's subject? What is the author's purpose? What readers was the author apparently writing for, and what is his or her attitude toward them? How am I part of the intended audience—if I am?

4. How is the essay structured? How does its organization relate to its main idea and to the author's purpose?

5. Can I follow the essay's line of reasoning? Is its logic valid, however complex, or are there mistakes and fallacies? If the reasoning is flawed, how much damage does this do to the essay's effect?

6. Does the author supply enough information to support the essay's ideas, and enough details to make its descriptions precise? Is all of the information relevant and, as far as I know, accurate? Are all of the details convincing? What does the author leave out, and how do these omissions affect my response to the essay?

7. What are the essay's basic, underlying assumptions? Which are stated and which are left unspoken? Are they acceptable, or do I challenge them? If I do, and I am right, how does this affect the essay's main idea?

8. Do all the elements of the essay relate, directly or indirectly, to its main idea? Can I explain how they relate? If any do not, what other purposes do they serve, if any?

9. Where do I place this essay in the context of my other reading? In the context of my life and thought? What further thoughts, and further reading, does it incite me to? Would I recommend it to anyone else to read? To whom, and why?

Each selection in *Outlooks and Insights* is followed by a set of questions, similar to the ones just suggested but usually more specific, which should help you in your effort to understand the piece. All of these questions work best when you try to answer them as fully as you can, remembering and considering many details from the selection to support your answers. Most of the questions are variations on these three basic ones: "What's going on here?" and "Why?" and "What do I think about it?"

Make Notes. Keep a pencil in hand and use it. Some readers like to write in their books, putting notes and signals to themselves in the margins and underlining key passages; others keep notebooks and jot their responses down there.

There is no all-purpose, universal method for annotating a text; what you write will depend on the details of the work at hand and how you respond. But you may find these tips useful:

- *Keep track of your responses. Jot down ideas that come to mind whether or not they seem directly relevant to what you are reading. If you think of a fact or example that supports the author's ideas, or disproves them, make a note. If a passage impresses or amuses you, set it off with an exclamation point in the margin. Converse with the text. Write* yes *or* no *or* why? *or* so what? *in response to the author's ideas and arguments.*

- *Mark words or passages you don't understand at first reading. A question mark in the margin may do the job, or you may want to circle words or phrases in the text. During the second reading you can look up the words and allusions and puzzle out the more difficult passages.*

- *Mark key points. Underline or star the main idea, or write it down in your notebook. Mark off the selection into its main sections, so that you can better see the essay's organization and understand the sequence of the author's thoughts.*

When annotating your text, don't be timid. Mark up your book as much as you please. Above all, don't let annotating become burdensome; it's an aid, not a chore. A word or phrase will often serve as well as a sentence. You may want to delay much of your annotating until your second reading, so that the first reading can be fast and free.

Using Your Reading in the Writing Process

What does analytical reading have to do with your own writing? Reading is not simply an end in itself; it is also a means to help you become a better writer. In *Outlooks and Insights* we are concerned with both the content and the form of an essay—that is, with what an essay has to say and with the strategies used to say it. All readers pay attention to content, to the substance of what an author is saying. Far fewer, however, notice the strategies that authors use to organize their writing, to make it understandable and effective. Yet using these strategies is an essential element of the writer's craft, an element that must be mastered if one is to write well.

There is nothing difficult about the strategies themselves. When you want to tell a story about being unemployed, for example, you naturally use the strategy called *narration.* When you want to show the differences between families in the 1940s and families today, you naturally *compare and contrast* representative families of the two eras. When you want to explain how toxins enter the food chain, you fall automatically into the strategy called *process analysis.* And when you want to determine the reasons for the disaster at the Chernobyl nuclear plant, you use *cause and effect analysis.* These and other strategies are ways we think about the world and our experiences in it and come to an understanding of them. What makes them sometimes seem difficult, especially in writing, is that most people use them more or less unconsciously, with little awareness that they're doing so. Critical thinking, especially in writing, does not come from simply using these structures—everyone does that—but from using them with purpose and thoughtfulness.

At the simplest level, reading can provide you with information and ideas both to give authority to your writing and to enliven it. Moreover, your reading often provides you with subjects to write about. For example, one of our students, after reading James Rachels's "Active and Passive Euthanasia" (p. ooo), wrote an essay analyzing the strengths and weaknesses of the author's argument. Another student read Charlotte Perkins Gilman's short story "The Yellow Wallpaper" (p. ooo) and used it as a springboard to her essay defining "anxiety." In a more subtle way, analytical reading can increase your awareness of how the writing of others affects you, and thus make you more sensitive to how your own writing will affect your readers. If you've ever been irritated by an article that makes an outrageous claim without a shred of supporting evidence, you might be more likely to back up your own claims more carefully. If you've been delighted by a happy turn of phrase or absorbed by a new idea, you might be less inclined to feed your own readers on clichés and platitudes. You will begin to consider in more detail how your own readers are likely to respond.

Analytical reading of the kind you'll be encouraged to do in this text will help you master important strategies of critical thinking and writing that you can use very specifically throughout the writing process. During the early stages of your writing you will need to focus on the large issues of choosing a subject, gathering information, planning the strategies suited to your purpose, and organizing your ideas. As you move from a first draft through further revisions, your concerns will begin to narrow. In conference with your instructor you may discover a faulty beginning or ending, or realize that your tone is inappropriate, or see that the various parts of your essay are not quite connected, or notice awkward repetitions in your choice of words and phrases. Analytical reading can lead you to solutions for such problems at every stage of your writing, from selecting a subject to revising and editing your final draft.

Reading George Orwell's "A Hanging": A Case Study

Some writers, and some essays, become classics—people continue to read them for decades or centuries. Such a writer is George Orwell, the English author best known for his novel *1984*, a vivid and terrifying evocation of life in a totalitarian state. But that was his last major work. One of his first works was an essay, "A Hanging," which he wrote in 1931 (he was then twenty-eight) about one of his experiences as a police official in Burma, where he had served from 1922 to 1927. "A Hanging" was published in *The Adelphi*, a socialist literary magazine whose readers would have been sympathetic to Orwell's attitudes.

As you read "A Hanging," note your own questions and responses in the margins or in your notebook. At the end of the essay you will find one reader's notes to which you can compare your responses.

A Hanging

GEORGE ORWELL

It was in Burma, a sodden morning of the rains. A sickly light, like   1
yellow tinfoil, was slanting over the high walls into the jail yard. We were
waiting outside the condemned cells, a row of sheds fronted with double
bars, like small animal cages. Each cell measured about ten feet by ten and
was quite bare within except for a plank bed and a pot for drinking water.
In some of them brown silent men were squatting at the inner bars, with
their blankets draped around them. These were the condemned men, due
to be hanged within the next week or two.

One prisoner had been brought out of his cell. He was a Hindu, a   2
puny wisp of a man, with a shaven head and vague liquid eyes. He had a
thick, sprouting moustache, absurdly too big for his body, rather like the
moustache of a comic man on the films. Six tall Indian warders were
guarding him and getting him ready for the gallows. Two of them stood by
with rifles and fixed bayonets, while the others handcuffed him, passed a
chain through his handcuffs and fixed it to their belts, and lashed his arms
right to his sides. They crowded very close about him, with their hands
always on him in a careful, caressing grip as though all the while feeling
him to make sure he was there. It was like men handling a fish which is
still alive and may jump back into the water. But he stood quite unresist-
ing, yielding his arms limply to the ropes, as though he hardly noticed
what was happening.

Eight o'clock struck and a bugle call, desolately thin in the wet air,   3
floated from the distant barracks. The superintendent of the jail, who was
standing apart from the rest of us, moodily prodding the gravel with his
stick, raised his head at the sound. He was an army doctor, with a gray
toothbrush moustache and a gruff voice. "For God's sake hurry up, Francis," he said irritably. "The man ought to have been dead by this time.
Aren't you ready yet?"

Francis, the head jailer, a fat Dravidian in a white drill suit and gold   4
spectacles, waved his black hand. "Yes sir, yes sir," he bubbled. "All iss
satisfactorily prepared. The hangman iss waiting. We shall proceed."

"Well, quick march, then. The prisoners can't get their breakfast till   5
this job's over."

We set out for the gallows. Two warders marched on either side of   6
the prisoner, with their rifles at the slope; two others marched close against
him, gripping him by arm and shoulder, as though at once pushing and
supporting him. The rest of us, magistrates and the like, followed behind.
Suddenly, when we had gone ten yards, the procession stopped short

without any order or warning. A dreadful thing had happened—a dog, come goodness knows whence, had appeared in the yard. It came bounding among us with a loud volley of barks, and leapt round us wagging its whole body, wild with glee at finding so many human beings together. It was a large woolly dog, half Airedale, half pariah. For a moment it pranced round us, and then, before anyone could stop it, it had made a dash for the prisoner and, jumping up, tried to lick his face. Everyone stood aghast, too taken aback even to grab at the dog.

"Who let that bloody brute in here?" said the superintendent angrily. 7 "Catch it, someone!"

A warder, detached from the escort, charged clumsily after the dog, 8 but it danced and gamboled just out of his reach, taking everything as part of the game. A young Eurasian jailer picked up a handful of gravel and tried to stone the dog away, but it dodged the stones and came after us again. Its yaps echoed from the jail walls. The prisoner, in the grasp of the two warders, looked on incuriously, as though this was another formality of the hanging. It was several minutes before someone managed to catch the dog. Then we put my handkerchief through its collar and moved off once more, with the dog still straining and whimpering.

It was about forty yards to the gallows. I watched the bare brown 9 back of the prisoner marching in front of me. He walked clumsily with his bound arms, but quite steadily, with that bobbing gait of the Indian who never straightens his knees. At each step his muscles slid neatly into place, the lock of hair on his scalp danced up and down, his feet printed themselves on the wet gravel. And once, in spite of the men who gripped him by each shoulder, he stepped slightly aside to avoid a puddle on the path.

It is curious, but till that moment I had never realized what it means 10 to destroy a healthy, conscious man. When I saw the prisoner step aside to avoid the puddle I saw the mystery, the unspeakable wrongness, of cutting a life short when it is in full tide. This man was not dying, he was alive just as we are alive. All the organs of his body were working—bowels digesting food, skin renewing itself, nails growing, tissues forming—all toiling away in solemn foolery. His nails would still be growing when he stood on the drop, when he was falling through the air with a tenth of a second to live. His eyes saw the yellow gravel and the gray walls, and his brain still remembered, foresaw, reasoned—reasoned even about puddles. He and we were a party of men walking together, seeing, hearing, feeling, understanding the same world; and in two minutes, with a sudden snap, one of us would be gone—one mind less, one world less.

The gallows stood in a small yard, separate from the main grounds 11 of the prison, and overgrown with tall prickly weeds. It was a brick erection like three sides of a shed, with planking on top, and above that two beams and a crossbar with the rope dangling. The hangman, a gray-haired convict in the white uniform of the prison, was waiting beside his machine. He greeted us with a servile crouch as we entered. At a word from Francis the two warders, gripping the prisoner more closely than ever, half led half pushed him to the gallows and helped him clumsily up the ladder. Then the hangman climbed up and fixed the rope round the prisoner's neck.

We stood waiting, five yards away. The warders had formed in a rough circle round the gallows. And then, when the noose was fixed, the prisoner began crying out to his god. It was a high, reiterated cry of "Ram! Ram! Ram! Ram!"[1] not urgent and fearful like a prayer or cry for help, but steady, rhythmical, almost like the tolling of a bell. The dog answered the sound with a whine. The hangman, still standing on the gallows, produced a small cotton bag like a flour bag and drew it down over the prisoner's face. But the sound, muffled by the cloth, still persisted, over and over again: "Ram! Ram! Ram! Ram!"

The hangman climbed down and stood ready, holding the lever. Minutes seemed to pass. The steady, muffled crying from the prisoner went on and on, "Ram! Ram! Ram!" never faltering for an instant. The superintendent, his head on his chest, was slowly poking the ground with his stick; perhaps he was counting the cries, allowing the prisoner a fixed number—fifty, perhaps, or a hundred. Everyone had changed color. The Indians had gone gray like bad coffee, and one or two of the bayonets were wavering. We looked at the lashed, hooded man on the drop, and listened to his cries—each cry another second of life, the same thought was in all our minds: oh, kill him quickly, get it over, stop that abominable noise!

Suddenly the superintendent made up his mind. Throwing up his head he made a swift motion with his stick. "Chalo!"[2] he shouted almost fiercely.

There was a clanking noise, and then dead silence. The prisoner had vanished, and the rope was twisting on itself. I let go of the dog, and it galloped immediately to the back of the gallows; but when it got there it stopped short, barked, and then retreated into a corner of the yard, where it stood among the weeds, looking timorously out at us. We went round the gallows to inspect the prisoner's body. He was dangling with his toes pointed straight downward, very slowly revolving, as dead as a stone.

The superintendent reached out with his stick and poked the bare brown body: it oscillated slightly. "*He's* all right," said the superintendent. He backed out from under the gallows, and blew out a deep breath. The moody look had gone out of his face quite suddenly. He glanced at his wrist watch. "Eight minutes past eight. Well, that's all for this morning, thank God."

The warders unfixed bayonets and marched away. The dog, sobered and conscious of having misbehaved itself, slipped after them. We walked out of the gallows yard, past the condemned cells with their waiting prisoners, into the big central yard of the prison. The convicts, under the command of warders armed with lathis,[3] were already receiving their break-

12

13

14

15

16

17

---

[1]In the Hindu religion, Rama is the incarnation of the god Vishnu.
[2]*"Let go,"* in Hindi.
[3]Wooden batons.

fast. They squatted in long rows, each man holding a tin pannikin, while two warders with buckets marched round ladling out rice; it seemed quite a homely, jolly scene, after the hanging. An enormous relief had come upon us now that the job was done. One felt an impulse to sing, to break into a run, to snigger. All at once everyone began chattering gaily.

The Eurasian boy walking beside me nodded toward the way we had come, with a knowing smile: "Do you know, sir, our friend [he meant the dead man] when he heard his appeal had been dismissed, he pissed on the floor of his cell. From fright. Kindly take one of my cigarettes, sir. Do you not admire my new silver case, sir? From the boxwalah, two rupees eight annas.⁴ Classy European style." 18

Several people laughed—at what, nobody seemed certain. 19

Francis was walking by the superintendent, talking garrulously: "Well, sir, all hass passed off with the utmost satisfactoriness. It was all finished—flick! like that. It iss not always so—oah, no! I have known cases where the doctor was obliged to go beneath the gallows and pull the prissoner's legs to ensure decease. Most disagreeable!" 20

"Wriggling about, eh? That's bad," said the superintendent. 21

"Ach, sir, it iss worse when they become refractory! One man, I 22 recall, clung to the bars of hiss cage when we went to take him out. You will scarcely credit, sir, that it took six warders to dislodge him, three pulling at each leg. We reasoned with him. 'My dear fellow,' we said, 'think of all the pain and trouble you are causing to us!' But no, he would not listen! Ach, he wass very troublesome!"

I found that I was laughing quite loudly. Everyone was laughing. 23 Even the superintendent grinned in a tolerant way. "You'd better all come out and have a drink," he said quite genially. "I've got a bottle of whisky in the car. We could do with it."

We went through the big double gates of the prison into the road. 24 "Pulling at his legs!" exclaimed a Burmese magistrate suddenly, and burst into a loud chuckling. We all began laughing again. At that moment Francis' anecdote seemed extraordinarily funny. We all had a drink together, native and European alike, quite amicably. The dead man was a hundred yards away.

One Reader's Notes

Here are the notes one reader made in his notebook during and after his first reading of "A Hanging." They include personal comments, queries concerning the meaning of words and details, and some reflections on the piece and its subject. The numbers in parentheses indicate which paragraphs the notes refer to.

---

⁴Indian currency worth less than 50 cents. *Boxwalah:* in Hindi, a seller of boxes.

NOTES MADE DURING THE READING

(2) puny prisoner, 6 tall guards, handcuffs, rope, chains. handled "like a fish"—cells like animal cages. suggests prisoner thought less than human.

(4) natives do dirty work, Brits stand around supervising. what's a Dravidian?

(6) dog—half Airedale, half pariah, like prison staff a mixture of Brits and natives. prisoner its favorite person. why? pet?

(10) main idea (?): "I saw the mystery, the unspeakable wrongness, of cutting a life short when it is in full tide."

But what was the man's crime? might have been a murderer or terrorist. Does O. mean that *all* cap. pun. is wrong?

Dog incident—dog recog. prisoner's humanity, behaves naturally, O. claims the execution is unnatural.

(11) hangman a convict, not an official. yard overgrown—significance?

(12) what god is Ram? prisoner a Hindu.

(13) why everyone transfixed? more than surprise? "kill him quickly"—selfish.

(15) the dog again. What was O. doing there anyway? all he does is hold dog. observer from P.D.?

(17) what's a lathi? or lathis? dog "conscious of having misbehaved"—how does O. know?

(18) prisoner afraid before, found courage to face death—humanizes him. what's a boxwalah?

Anticlimax from here on. prisoners impassive, officials near hysteria. again, why such a big deal, if they do executions often (other condemned men there). take O's word that this time was different. laughing it off, life goes on, etc.

(24) Euros and natives on same side, against prisoners. still nothing about dead man's crime, but can't have been so bad given everyone's reactions—? nobody says it's what he deserved.

NOTES MADE AFTER FINISHING THE READING

did this really happen? seems too pat, with dog and all, and O. hanging around doing nothing instead of whatever he usually did. Could have happened, maybe that's enough.

no argument against cap. pun., just personal insight from personal experience. can't make laws that way. no reasons pro or con except O. thinks it unnatural, with dog's behavior as the proof.

form—chron. narration, no gaps or flashbacks. intro para 1, sets scene. climax: the hanging. conclusion starts para 17 (?), winds story down.

style clear, direct, not fancy, strong words, lots of detail and color, etc. good writing obviously, but he doesn't persuade me about cap. pun.

Looking over this reader's shoulder, you can see that he gets increasingly skeptical about Orwell's thesis statement, and you may guess that he himself supports capital punishment—or at least sees some point in it. The reader has noted a good deal of what Orwell put into the essay, such as who does what at the prison; perhaps on the second reading he will get more out of the essay's concluding paragraphs, which are skimmed over in his notes. And the reader has also noticed some of the things Orwell left out, such as the nature of the prisoner's offense. He has begun to find relations between the details and the whole, notably by thinking about the significance of the dog's behavior. All in all, he has made a good beginning at understanding "A Hanging."

From Reading to Writing

In many college courses you will be required to discuss your reading in some writing of your own. In composition courses, such writing assignments often take these forms:

1. An analysis of the reading's content, form, or both.
2. An original composition on the topic of the reading, or on a related topic.
3. An original composition on a topic of your choice, inspired in some way by the reading but not bound by its subject matter.

Which kind of paper you write may be specified by your instructor, or the choice may be left to you.

Three Student Essays in Response to George Orwell's "A Hanging"

In the following pages you will find an analytical essay, an argumentative essay, and a narrative essay; each is a response to Orwell's "A Hanging" and each is typical of how students write for their composition courses.

An Analytical Essay

When you write an analysis of something you have read, your purpose is to show that you have understood the work and to help your readers increase their understanding of it, too. You do this by drawing attention to aspects of its meaning, structure, and style that are important but not obvious. Such an analysis grows directly out of your reading, and more specifically out of the notes you made during your first and subsequent readings of the text.

When planning your analytical paper, start by considering what point you most want to make—what your thesis will be. If you can think of several possible theses for your paper, and you often will be able to, select the one that seems to you the most important—and that you think you can support and defend most strongly and effectively using evidence from the piece you are writing about. Many different theses would be possible for an analytical paper about Orwell's "A Hanging." Here are a few:

> In "A Hanging," George Orwell carefully selects details to persuade us that capital punishment is wrong.

> "A Hanging" reveals how thoroughly the British had imposed their laws, customs, and values on colonial Burma.

> Though "A Hanging" appeals powerfully to the emotions, it does not make a reasoned argument against capital punishment.

> In "A Hanging," George Orwell employs metaphor, personification, and dialogue to express man's inhumanity to other men.

This last is the thesis of the student paper that follows, "The Disgrace of Man."

Think, too, about your audience. Who will read your paper? Will they know the work you are analyzing? If not, then you need to supply enough information about the work so that your readers can understand you. But if you expect your essay to be read by your instructor and classmates, and if it is about an assigned reading, you can usually assume that they know the work and need no summary of it, though they may need clear reminders of specific details and passages that you analyze closely and that may have escaped their attention.

Students writing papers for their courses have a special problem: What can they say that their readers, especially their instructors, do not already know? This is a problem all writers face, including instructors themselves when writing professional articles, and the answer is always the same: Write honestly about what you see in the work and what you think about it. Because all readers respond differently to the same text, any one of them—including you—may notice details or draw conclusions that others miss. Teachers may be experienced, knowledgeable readers, but they do not know everything. Some might not have noticed that Orwell excludes from "A Hanging" any hint of the prisoner's crime, yet this omission is important because it reinforces Orwell's main point: Capital punishment is always wrong, no matter what the circumstances. And even if you think you have no such discoveries to offer, your individual point of view and response to the text will lend your writing originality and interest. As the poet James Stephens once wrote, "Originality does not consist in saying what no one has said before, but in saying exactly what you think yourself."

The following student essay, "The Disgrace of Man," is original in Stephens's sense, and the student has also discovered something in "A Hanging" that other readers might well have missed, something about Orwell's way of telling his story that contributes, subtly but significantly, to its effect.

The Disgrace of Man

George Orwell's "A Hanging" graphically depicts the execution of a prisoner in a way that expresses a universal tragedy. He artfully employs metaphor, personification, and dialogue to indicate man's inhumanity toward other men, and to prompt the reader's sympathy and self-examination.

Orwell uses simile and metaphor to show that the prisoner is treated more like an animal than like a human being. The cells of the condemned men, "a row of sheds . . . quite bare within," are "like small animal cages." The warders grip the prisoner "like men handling a fish." Though they refer to the prisoner as "the man" or "our friend," the other characters view him as less than human. Even his cry resounds like the "tolling of a bell" rather than a human "prayer or cry for help," and after he is dead the superintendent pokes at the body with a stick. These details direct the reader's attention to the lack of human concern for the condemned prisoner.

In contrast, Orwell emphasizes the "wrongness of cutting a life short" by representing the parts of the prisoner's body as taking on human behavior. He describes the lock of hair "dancing" on the man's scalp, his feet "printing themselves" on the gravel, all his organs "toiling away" like a team of laborers at some collective project. In personifying these bodily features, Orwell forces the reader to see the prisoner's vitality, his humanity. The reader, in turn, associates each bodily part with himself; he becomes highly aware of the frailty of life. As the author focuses on how easily these actions can be stopped, in any human being, "with a sudden snap," the reader feels the "wrongness" of the hanging as if his own life were threatened.

In addition to creating this sense of unmistakable life, Orwell uses the dog as a standard for evaluating the characters' appreciation of human life. The dog loves people—he is "wild with glee to find so many human beings together"—and the person he loves the most is the prisoner, who has been treated as less than human by the jail attendants. When the prisoner starts to pray, the other people are silent, but the dog answers "with a whine." Even after the hanging, the dog runs directly to the gallows to see the prisoner again. The reader is forced to reflect on his own reaction: Which is more shocking, the dog's actions or the observers' cold response?

Finally, Orwell refers to the characters' nationalities to stress that this insensitivity extends to all nationalities and races. The hanging takes place in Burma, in a jail run by a European army doctor and a native of southern India. The warders are also Indians, and the hangman is actually a fellow prisoner. The author calls attention to each of these participants and implies that each one of them might have halted the brutal proceedings. He was there too and could have intervened when he suddenly realized that killing the prisoner would be wrong. Yet the "formality of the hanging" goes on.

As he reflects on the meaning of suddenly destroying human life, Orwell emphasizes the similarities among all men, regardless of nationality. Before the hanging, they are "seeing, hearing, feeling, understanding the same world," and afterward there would be "one mind less, one world less." Such feelings do not affect the other characters, who think of the hanging not as killing but as a job to be done, a job made unpleasant by those reminders (the incident of the dog, the prisoner's praying) that they are dealing with a human being. Orwell uses dialogue to show how selfish and callous the observers are. Though they have different accents—the superintendent's "for God's sake hurry up," the Dravidian's "It was all finished"—they think and feel the same. Their words, such as *"He's* all right," show that they are more concerned about their own lives than the one they are destroying.

Although George Orwell sets his story in Burma, his point is universal; although he deals with capital punishment, he implies other questions of life and death. We are all faced with issues such as capital punishment, abortion, and euthanasia, and sometimes we find ourselves directly involved, as Orwell did. "A Hanging" urges us to examine ourselves and to take very seriously the value of a human life.

Most teachers would consider "The Disgrace of Man" a fine student essay. It is well organized, stating its thesis early, supporting it effectively, and sticking to the point. The discussion is clear and coherent, and it is firmly based on Orwell's text—the student author has understood the core meaning of "A Hanging." She has also noticed many details that express Orwell's attitude toward the hanging and toward his imperial colleagues, and she has interpreted them so that her readers can plainly see how those details contribute to the total effect of "A Hanging." How many would have observed that Orwell actually personifies the parts of the prisoner's body? How many, having noticed it, would have grasped the relation of this detail to Orwell's point? That's accurate, active reading.

An Argumentative Essay

Perhaps you recall the annotations of "A Hanging" on pages 13–14. The writer of those notes was attentive to the meaning of the text, but as he read he found himself disagreeing with Orwell's view that taking human life is always unspeakably wrong. He might have gone on to analyze "A Hanging," as he was obviously capable of doing, but he did not. Instead, given the opportunity to choose his own topic, he decided to present his own views on Orwell's subject: capital punishment.

The writer began by exploring the topic, jotting down notes on what he knew and believed. He also went to the library to look up recent research into the effects of capital punishment, but found that authorities still cannot agree on whether the death penalty deters crime or protects society, so his efforts led only to a few sentences in his first paragraph. Why go to so much trouble for a short writing assignment? Evidently the writer cared enough about his topic to want to do it justice, not just for the assignment's sake but for his own. As the English philosopher John Stuart Mill wrote, "If the cultivation of the understanding consists in one thing more than in another, it is surely in learning the grounds of one's own opinions." The author of "For Capital Punishment" knew what he believed, and he used the occasion of a writing assignment to work out a rationale for that belief.

For Capital Punishment

The debate on capital punishment goes on and on. Does the death penalty deter people from committing murder? Does it protect us from criminals who would murder again if they were returned to society? These questions have not yet been answered beyond any doubt, and maybe they never will be. But is the death penalty cruel and unnatural? This is a different kind of question, having to do with the nature of the punishment itself, and it can be answered. I think the answer is no, and that capital punishment has a place in a civilized society. I also feel that it should be imposed as the penalty for the worst crimes.

In the United States this is a constitutional issue, because the Bill of Rights does not allow cruel and unusual punishment. The Supreme Court has interpreted these words not to include capital punishment, and there is a basis in the Constitution for their decision: The fifth amendment says that "no person shall . . . be deprived of life, liberty, or property, without due process of law," which means that a person can be deprived of life if due process has been observed. The Court did find some years ago that the death penalty was being imposed much more often on poor black people than on any others, and suspended capital punishment throughout the nation because due process was obviously *not* being observed, but when the Court considered that that situation had been corrected it permitted execution to resume in 1977, with the death of Gary Gilmore.

But beyond the constitutionality of capital punishment there is the deeper question of whether it is morally wrong. We accept some punishments as just, while others seem barbaric. The difference, I think, has to do with what the condemned man is made to suffer. The lightest punishments take away some of his money or restrict his freedom of movement in society; some examples are fines, probation, and work-release programs. Then there are punishments that remove the criminal from society, such as imprisonment and deportation. The kind of punishment we do not accept, though it is still used in some countries, is the kind that is meant to do physical harm: beating, maiming, torture. The death penalty is a special case. It removes criminals from society permanently and economically, but it also involves physical harm. It is in the balance between the two effects, I think, that we can find out whether capital punishment is morally acceptable.

If we condemned people to death because we wanted them to suffer, you would expect that methods of execution would have been made more painful and frightening over the years. Instead, the opposite has happened. Traitors used to be tortured to death before screaming mobs, but now the condemned man dies in private as painlessly as possible; Texas now uses chemical injections that are apparently almost painless. It must be, then, that the reason for execution is not physical harm but removal from society, which is a widely accepted purpose for judicial punishment.

But why, then, would not life imprisonment serve the same purpose just as well? There are two main reasons why it does not. First, "life imprisonment" does not mean what it says; most lifers are considered for parole after fifteen years or less, even monsters like Charles Manson and Sirhan Sirhan. It's true that these two have not been released, but they might be at any time their California parole board changes its mind. So life imprisonment does not insure that the worst criminals will be removed from society permanently. Second, as long as a criminal stays in prison he is a burden on the very society he has offended against, costing society tens of thousands of dollars each year to keep him secure and healthy. There is also a real question in mind whether caging a prisoner for life, if it actually is for life, is any more merciful than putting him to death. The conditions in American prisons, where the inmates are often brutalized and degraded by each other and even by their guards, must often seem a "fate worse than death."

Most nations of the world, and most states in the United States, have legalized capital punishment and used it for many years. They—we—are not bloodthirsty monsters, but ordinary people seeking safety and justice under the law. Maybe the time will come when the death penalty is no longer needed or wanted, and then it will be abolished. But that time is not yet here.

The writer of "For Capital Punishment" has taken on a large subject, on which many books have been written and many more will be. When discussing a controversial topic of wide interest, many people tend to parrot back uncritically the opinions they have read and heard, which is easy to do but does not add much to what everyone knows. This writer has escaped that temptation and thought this subject through, in the process working out reasoned and partly original arguments of his own to support his view. His discussion is clear and well organized; he states his thesis at the end of the first paragraph and supports it with evidence and reasoning throughout the paper. Of course many reasonable people will disagree with his support of capital punishment, just as he disagrees with Orwell's opposition to it. But most composition teachers, even those who do not share this writer's views, would consider "For Capital Punishment" a good student paper.

A Narrative Essay

In "A Hanging," George Orwell writes about an incident that brought him to an important insight. The author of the following essay did the same. Reading Orwell brought back to mind a childhood experience that has made her aware of the potential for thoughtless violence that lies within us all. Part of Orwell's influence on her is revealed by her choice of subject—the heedless killing of three helpless nestlings. But she also follows Orwell in her choice of a writing strategy; like him she narrates a personal experience that illustrates a general moral principle.

Killing for Fun

Every summer my family returns to our ancestral home, which is in a community where the same families have lived generation after generation. There are tennis courts, a golf course, boats, and other occupations to help pass the long, hot days. This all sounds very enjoyable, and it usually was, but sometimes it got very boring. Spending every summer with the same gang and doing the same things, under the same grown-ups' noses, began to seem dull, and by the time I was thirteen I was ready to experience the thrill of the forbidden.

One afternoon in July, I was supposed to sail in some races with my best friend Mitchell, but the air was so thick and heavy that we decided not to go. We sat around his house all day, waiting for his brother to bring back the family power boat so that we could water ski. Thinking back to that summer, I remember how frustrated and irritable we were, our pent-up energy ready to explode. We roamed his house searching for something—anything—to do, but we only succeeded in making one mess after another and angering his mother. Finally we hit on something. We were eating lunch on Mitchell's back porch when we both noticed his father's rifle propped in a corner.

Now Mitchell's father has often warned all of us that his rifle was strictly off limits. The rifle itself was not very dangerous, as it was only an air gun that shot small pellets, but he was afraid of its being misused and hurting someone. He himself used it to scare off stray dogs and was usually very careful to put it away, but for some reason on that particular day he had forgotten. We decided that it would be fun to take the rifle out in the nearby woods and shoot at whatever we found there.

We had to be very careful not to be seen by the borough residents as they all knew us. For most parents, kids heading for the woods meant trouble. So Mitchell and I sneaked out of his house with the gun and went slinking through some old horse stables on our way to the woods. By the time we arrived at the edge of the woods we felt like spies. There was a caretaker's cottage there, and the caretaker was forever on the lookout for what he thought were troublesome kids. When we successfully passed the cottage our spirits were high, as we had gotten safely through the danger zone on the way to our forbidden project.

As we went into the woods we began to find some animals and birds to use as targets, but try as we might, we could not hit anything. Our pellets seemed to disappear in flight, not even giving us the satisfaction of hitting a tree and making a noise. Our mission was not succeeding, and we decided to look for an easier target.

Finally we startled a mother bird, who flew away leaving her nest behind. We thought the nest would make a fine target, stationary as it was and with live creatures inside. We took turns shooting at in an attempt to knock it out of the tree, intoxicated with our power and carried away by the thrill of it all. Mitchell was the one to knock it down. It tottered, and after a little rustling a small object fell out, and the nest followed, landing upside down.

Mitchell ran up and excitedly turned it over. The sight was horribly repulsive. Underneath lay three naked pink corpses, staring up at us silently with wide dark eyes and wide, underdeveloped, faintly yellow beaks. They looked as if they had been savagely strangled one by one, except for the small pellet holes in each tiny body. A few feet away a slight movement caught my eye. The object that had fallen first was a fourth baby bird. It had survived the shooting and the fall and was flopping around, mutilated as it was. I poked Mitchell, who was staring at the massacre underneath the nest, and directed his attention to the desperately flapping pink lump a few feet away.

I could see that Mitchell was repulsed by the sight, but being a thirteen-year-old boy he refused to show it. He made an attempt to maintain a hunter's attitude, and fiercely drove pellet after pellet into the injured bird. We tried to joke about it, and as soon as we were out of sight of the nest we broke into hysterically uncontrollable laughter, trying to avoid thinking about what we had done. On the way home we avoided talking about it, and I felt relieved to part company with Mitchell when we got home.

That incident shocked me into thinking about the results of my actions. Mitchell and I were not inhuman monsters, determined to massacre baby birds; we were just bored kids looking for an adventure and not thinking about the consequences. I wonder how much unhappiness and even crime comes from young people acting selfishly and thoughtlessly, out for a thrill. If they had to see the suffering they cause, they would surely think harder before they act.

The author of "Killing for Fun" tells her story well. She describes her experience vividly, with much closely observed detail, and builds suspense to hold her readers' attention. What makes "Killing for Fun" not just a story but a personal essay is the last paragraph, where she turns her experience into an observation about life. The observation may not be brand new, but then it needn't be—few important truths are. George Orwell was certainly not the first to oppose capital punishment. In both narrative essays it is the authors' personal experiences, honestly and precisely recounted, that give their general observations force.

These three essays, each different from the other two and from Orwell's, illustrate but a few of the many ways different people can respond to their reading and use their responses in their writing. Each paper also shows how a student, working under the limitations of an assigned reading and a specific writing assignment, can create an interesting and original piece of writing by analyzing the reading carefully, or exploring his or her own beliefs, or drawing on personal experience. Each of the selections in *Outlooks and Insights* provides you with opportunities to do the same.

Some Notes on Fiction and Poetry

The poems and short stories in *Outlooks and Insights* explore many of the same themes the essays do, and can serve your writing purposes in similar ways. A story or a poem may give you ideas for your writing; and even though you may never write poetry or fiction, you can still learn much about structure and style from reading literature. These selections will be most useful to you, however, if you know about the basic elements of fiction and poetry. The following pages provide a brief, highly selective introduction to some of their most important qualities and forms.

READING SHORT STORIES

Short stories look much like essays, and the two forms are similar in other ways as well. Both are written in prose; some essays, like nearly all stories, are narratives; both may contain dialogue. And certainly a reader can learn from fiction as well as from nonfiction about the ways other people think, feel, and behave, and how they deal with ethical problems. But stories also differ from essays in fundamental respects, and call for different expectations and responses from their readers.

Though a short story may incorporate materials from real life, including places and even characters and incidents, it is essentially the product of the author's imagination. Eudora Welty says that she got the idea for her short story "A Worn Path" (p. 129) from watching an old woman walking slowly across a winter country landscape, but that the rest of the story was pure invention. In an essay, on the other hand, we expect the events and characters to be rendered accurately from real life. Part of the force of George Orwell's "A Hanging" comes from our belief that he is reporting a personal experience—that he did indeed attend a hanging at which the events he narrates actually took place.

Both essays and stories can make points about life, but each type does so differently. An essay normally states its main idea or *thesis* openly and explains or argues that idea at length in a direct and orderly way. A story, however, does not tell—it shows. Its main idea, called its *theme,* is not so much discussed as embodied in the characters and action, and is seldom presented openly—each reader has to discover a story's theme for himself or herself. As Eudora Welty puts it, "A narrative line is in its deeper sense . . . the tracing out of a meaning"—which is the story's theme. Theme is not the same as subject. The subject of "A Worn Path" is an old woman's long, wearying trip to town to get medicine for her ill grandson—a trip which she has made many times before and will make again. The story's theme, however, is the general observation it illustrates and embodies. Different readers may put the theme of "A Worn Path" into different words. Welty says it this way: "The habit of love cuts through confusion and stumbles or contrives its way out of difficulty, it remembers the way even when it forgets, for a dumbfounded moment, its reason for being." This is the story's true meaning and encompasses all of its details, right down to the path itself, worn by the old woman's often-repeated errand of love. As this suggests, a story's theme reveals the unity of the whole work—or can even be said to give the work its unity.

Most short stories have other elements in common that are seldom found in nonfiction writing. The action in a short story, called its *plot,* typically unfolds in a pattern consisting of a series of stages that can be diagrammed in this way:

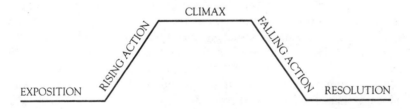

The *exposition* sets the scene, describes the situation, and begins to introduce some of the characters. The *rising action* (sometimes called the *complication*) sets the characters into conflict—with each other or within themselves—and the conflict rises in tension and complexity. At the *climax* the tension and complexity reach their peaks, and the central character takes an action or undergoes an experience that is the turning point of the story. After the climax comes the *falling action,* in which the tension slackens and the story moves toward its conclusion. The end of the story is the *resolution,* in which the conflict of the plot gives way to a new stability. "A Worn Path" follows this pattern. Its exposition consists of the first two paragraphs. The rising action, beginning in paragraph 3, builds to a climax when Phoenix meets the hunter. After the falling action, in which she makes her way into town, the resolution begins in paragraph 70 when she arrives at the doctor's office. These conventions of plot have served countless writers for more than two thousand years with no loss in effectiveness and vitality, and still provide the structure for novels, short stories, plays—even movies and television dramas.

How we take in the events of the plot is determined by the author's use of a narrative *point of view*. Sometimes the story is told by one of the characters, as in Charlotte Perkins Gilman's "The Yellow Wallpaper" (p.). This is called *first-person point of view* because the narrator often uses the first-person pronoun *I*. When the story is told by a narrator standing somewhere outside the events of the story, this is called *third-person point of view* because the narrator uses the third-person pronouns *he, she,* and *they*. "A Worn Path" is told from the third-person point of view; the narrator, like a movie camera's eye, tracks old Phoenix Jackson all the way to town, reporting on her doings from outside the story.

The third-person point of view has two main forms: *omniscient* and *limited*. If the narrator tells us what all the characters are doing, wherever they are, and even what they are thinking and feeling, the author is using the third-person omniscient point of view. An example is Katherine Anne Porter's "Rope" (p. 230). In "A Worn Path," on the other hand, the narrator tells us only what Phoenix Jackson does, says, hears, and sees; we can only infer what the characters are thinking from what they say and do.

READING POEMS

Almost anything can be subject matter for poetry, and the range of poetic styles and forms is enormous: Sharon Olds's "On the Subway" (p.), for example, uses poetic devices such as metaphor and juxtaposition, while Robert Frost's "The Road Not Taken" (p. 97) seems as plain as prose. But even the plainest poetry should never be read merely to understand its message, for that would be to ignore the special delights and the special kinds of meaning that only poetry can convey.

Let's look at one poem as an active reader would, trying to respond not only to its literal meaning but also to its special qualities as a poem. The poem is by William Shakespeare:

That time of year thou may'st in me behold
When yellow leaves, or none, or few, do hang
Upon those boughs which shake against the cold,
Bare ruined choirs where late the sweet birds sang.
In me thou seest the twilight of such day

5

As after sunset fadeth in the west,
Which by and by black night doth take away,
Death's second self that seals up all in rest.
In me thou seest the glowing of such fire
That on the ashes of his youth doth lie,   10
As the deathbed whereon it must expire,
Consumed with that which it was nourished by.
   This thou perceiv'st, which makes thy love more strong,
   To love that well which thou must leave ere long.

One of the first things a reader would notice about this poem is that it conveys its meaning in a special way. The speaker of the poem says, in effect, that he is old, but he only tells us so indirectly. He compares his time of life with a season, a time of day, and a stage in the life of a fire, and these three images evoke our own experience so that we understand what he means. In autumn the days grow shorter and colder, at twilight the day's heat and light are going fast, and the embers of a dying fire grow dimmer and cooler with every minute; so too with advancing age, when the vigor and passions of earlier years have faded and death is soon to come. The images also reinforce each other, each describing a natural process that cannot be avoided or stopped and evoking the same progression from warmth to cold, from light to dark. And there is a progression from one image to the next: Autumn, a span of months and days, is succeeded by twilight, a matter of an hour or less, and last comes fire, which can rise and go out in a few minutes. This speeding up of time prepares for the last line's suggestion that death will come "ere long." Images such as these, which occur only occasionally in prose, can often be a poem's chief means of conveying its meaning.

Another resource that prose writers use sparingly but that is vital to poetry is the *sound* of the language—its vowels and consonants, and the rhythms of words and phrases. Tradition has it that poetry began as song, and poets often choose their words not only to convey meaning but to make a kind of music through planned patterns of verbal sounds. To hear and appreciate that music to the fullest, it's a good idea to read a poem aloud, listening for those patterns. And even if you can't read aloud (for example, if you are in a library reading room or on the bus), try to "hear" the poem in your imagination.

Even on first reading "That Time of Year" you probably noticed that Shakespeare has written his poem with not only its sense but its sound in mind. The rhythm is regular, as each of the fourteen lines has exactly ten syllables, and those syllables alternate regularly between weak and strong stress: "That *time* of *year* thou *may'st* in *me* behold." Shakespeare's skill is such that to achieve this musical effect he never needs to sacrifice clarity, and indeed he rarely departs from natural phrasing. There is evidence, too, that Shakespeare has coordinated the vowel and consonant sounds of his poem.

For one thing, he rhymes his lines in a complex but regular pattern. For another, two particular consonants, *l* and *s,* recur throughout the poem. They are most conspicuous in phrases like "second self that seals" (line 8) and "*leave ere long*" (line 14), which are examples of alliteration, but on closer examination you will find that one or both sounds appear, usually more than once, in each line of the poem, and help to give it its special music.

Shakespeare's use of rhyme deserves special attention, because it fits perfectly the meaning and even the grammar of his poem. Each of the three images is expressed in a single sentence that takes up four lines, and those lines are rhymed in an interlocking pattern that makes the image, and the sentence, seem all the more self-contained. The arrival of a new image brings the beginning not only of a new sentence but also of a new and different set of rhymes. The last two lines of the poem are not an image but a direct statement, and they have a rhyme pattern of their own using *strong* and *long.* Some readers may even notice in this last rhyme a distant echo of *hang* and *sang* from the beginning of the poem.

Shakespeare's rhyme scheme fits the meaning of his poem so closely that you might think he had invented both as part of the same creative act. In this fact this is not so. He wrote 153 other poems in exactly the same form, which is sometimes called the Shakespearean sonnet in his honor. Moreover, Shakespeare did not invent the form, which had existed for forty years and been used by many poets before he took it up. Here we have a strange thing: Maybe the form itself gave Shakespeare ideas for poems, or at least set him challenges that heated rather than cooled his imagination. How versatile the sonnet form was in Shakespeare's hands you can see from the following, which has exactly the same structure as "That Time of Year" but a very different theme:

My mistress' eyes are nothing like the sun;
Coral is far more red than her lips' red;
If snow be white, why then her breasts are dun;
If hairs be wires, black wires grow on her head.
I have seen roses damasked, red and white,   5
But no such roses see I in her cheeks;
And in some perfumes is there more delight
Than in the breath that from my mistress reeks.
I love to hear her speak; yet well I know
That music hath a far more pleasing sound: 10
I grant I never saw a goddess go;
My mistress, when she walks, treads on the ground.
   And yet, by heaven, I think my love as rare
   As any she belied with false compare.

Writing the Documented Paper

A documented paper is not unlike the other writing that you will do in your college writing course. You will find yourself drawing heavily on what you learned about writing essays earlier in this introduction (pp. 7–22). First you determine what you want to say, then you decide on a purpose, develop a thesis, consider your audience, collect your evidence, write a first draft, revise and edit, and prepare a final version. What differentiates the documented paper from other kinds of papers is your research and how you acknowledge it.

In this section you will learn how to take useful notes on sources, how to summarize, paraphrase, and quote your sources, how to integrate your notes into your paper, how to acknowledge your sources, and how to avoid plagiarism. Finally, we have provided a sample documented paper by a student that illustrates the various facets of this type of writing.

A good place to begin is to select a story or article from *Outlooks and Insights* that suggests something you wish to write about. After reading your selection and doing a search for relevant materials (books, journal articles, and reviews) in the library, you will be in a good position to decide on a topic and to develop a preliminary thesis—the main idea for your paper. At this point you will be ready to begin carefully rereading the source materials that directly relate to your topic.

Note-Taking

As you read source material, take notes. You're looking for ideas, facts, opinions, statistics, examples, and evidence that you think will be useful in writing your paper. As you work through your sources, look for recurring themes and notice where the writers and critics are in agreement and where they differ in their views. Try to remember that the effectiveness of your paper is largely determined by the quality—not necessarily the quantity—of your evidence. The purpose of a research paper is not to present a collection of quotations that show you have read all the material and can report what others have said about your topic. Instead, your goal is to analyze, evaluate, and synthesize the information you collect—in other words, to enter into the discussion of the issues and thereby take ownership of your topic. You want to view the results of your research from your own perspective and arrive at an informed opinion of your topic.

Now for some practical advice on taking notes: First and foremost, be systematic in your note-taking. As a rule, write one note on a card, and use cards of uniform size—preferably 4″ × 6″ cards because they are large enough to accommodate even a long note on a single card, yet small enough to be easily handled and conveniently carried. More importantly, when you get to planning and writing your paper, you will be able to sequence your notes according to the plan you have envisioned for your paper. Furthermore, should you decide to alter your organizational plan, you can easily reorder your cards to reflect revisions.

Try not to take too many notes. One good way to help decide whether to take a note is to ask yourself, "How exactly does this material help prove or disprove my thesis?" You might even try envisioning where you could use the information in your paper. If it does not seem relevant to your thesis, don't bother to take a note.

Once you decide to take a note, you must decide whether to summarize, paraphrase, or quote directly. The approach that you take is largely determined by the content of the passage in the source material and the way you intend to use it in your paper. The following examples used to illustrate the note-taking process and documentation are all based on K. C. Roberts's work on John Updike's story "A Sense of Shelter" (pp. 64–73). Her final essay appears on pages 36–42.

SUMMARY

When you **summarize** material from a source, you capture in condensed form the essential idea of a passage, entire chapter, or article. Summaries are particularly useful when you are working with lengthy, detailed arguments or long passages of narrative or descriptive background information, and the details are not germane to the overall thrust of your paper: You simply want to capture the essence of the passage while dispensing with the details because you are confident that your readers will readily understand the point being made or do not need to be convinced about the validity of the point. Because you are distilling information, a summary is always shorter than the original; often a chapter or more can be reduced to a paragraph, or several paragraphs to a sentence or two. Remember, in writing a summary you should use your own words, but do not forget to include bibliographic information for the source on your card.

Consider the following passage from Elizabeth A. Hait's article "John Updike's 'A Sense of Shelter' ":

> The phrase "the ugly, humiliated, educable self" is significant because here, for the first time in the story, the narrator actually states that two sides of William's personality are being examined and that a choice between them is being made. If William does change at the end of the story, then his young, immature self, sheltered by home, school, and mother, should be the self that is shut away in the locker. But if William remains static, then the self that made the feeble proposal to Mary Landis, that made the unsuccessful attempt to enter the world of mature, adult experience, is the self that William should hide away.

Roberts, wishing to capture Hait's point without repeating her detailed account, wrote the following summary.

Summary Note Card

locker scene

Hait contends that the locker scene is helpful in determining how to interpret the conclusion of the story because in slamming his locker shut, he symbolically closes the door on one of his selves.

Hait, 555

PARAPHRASE

When you **paraphrase** a source you restate the information in your own words instead of quoting directly. Unlike a summary, which gives a brief overview of the essential information in the original, a paraphrase seeks to maintain the same level of detail as the original to aid readers in understanding and believing the information presented. A paraphrase presents the original information in approximately the same number of words, but in your own style of wording. In other words, your paraphrase should closely parallel the presentation of ideas in the original, but should not use the same words or sentence structure as the original. Even though you are using your own words when paraphrasing, it is important to remember that you are borrowing ideas and therefore must acknowledge the source of these ideas with a citation.

How would you paraphrase the following passage from Hait's article?

The choice for William, then, involves whether to continue with his life as it is, developing intellectually but not emotionally and socially, or to leave the shelter of his intellectual superiority and take the risk of emotional and social development.

The following note card illustrates how K. C. Roberts, the writer of the sample paper at the end of this section, paraphrased the passage from Hait.

Paraphrase Note Card

William's Choice
William must decide between the security
of the academic world that he currently
wallows in and the uncertainty and perhaps
rewards of social and emotional involvement.

Hait, 555

In most cases it is better to summarize or paraphrase material—which by definition means using your own words—instead of quoting verbatim (word for word). To capture an idea in your own words ensures that you have thought about it and understand what your source is saying. But be sure to identify the source in your notes, so that you will remember and be able to cite the source when writing your essay.

DIRECT QUOTATION

When you directly **quote** a source, you copy the words of your source exactly, putting all quoted material in quotation marks. When you make a quoted note card, carefully check for accuracy, including punctuation and capitalization. Be selective about what you choose to quote; reserve direct quotation for important ideas stated memorably, for especially clear explanations by authorities, and for arguments or assertions in the exact words of those individuals putting them forth. Consider, for example, the following conclusion that Robert Detweiler draws in his book *John Updike:*

He is only trading the "sense of shelter" that the Olinger schools and classmates have provided for a thoroughly planned, totally orthodox and secure professional career.

Quotation Note Card

William's secure Career
"He is only trading the 'sense of shelter' that the Olinger schools and Classmates have provided for a thoroughly planned, totally orthodox and secure professional Career."

Detweiler, 59-60

As on other types of note cards, include bibliographic information for the source.

On occasion, you'll find a useful passage with some memorable wording in it. Avoid the temptation to quote the whole passage; instead you can combine a summary or paraphrase with a direct quotation. Consider the following paragraphs from Alice and Kenneth Hamilton's *The Elements of John Updike*:

> It is the cold outside meeting the warmth inside that stirs his imagination to thoughts of kingship. But he is unwilling to go outside into the cold. He prefers the coziness of the basement study room where he prepares for his future as an academic. . . .
>   Thus his future is to be one insulated from outside troubles, quiet and enclosed.

In the following note card, notice how Roberts was careful to put quotation marks around all words that she borrowed directly from the source.

Summary and Quotation Note Card

---

borders
This border is not only between two places
but represents the decision William must
make later in the short story to live a life
of risk or one "insulated from outside
troubles."

Hamilton and Hamilton, 113

Integrating Quotations into Your Text

Whenever you want to use borrowed material, be it a summary, para-phrase, or quotation, it is best to introduce the material with a signal phrase—a phrase that alerts the reader that borrowed information is going to come. A signal phrase usually consists of the author's name and a verb. Well-chosen signal phrases help you to integrate quotations, paraphrases, and summaries into the flow of your paper. In addition, signal phrases let your reader know who is speaking and, in the case of summaries and paraphrases, exactly where your ideas end and someone else's begin. Never confuse your reader by having a quotation appear suddenly without introduction in your paper.

UNANNOUNCED QUOTATION

William's behavior is contrasted with that of the character he loves, Mary, who is more adventurous. "On each of the three occasions she appears, Updike presents her *going away* from William's world, away from the classroom, out of the soda bar and finally out of the school itself" (Edwards 467).

INTEGRATED QUOTATION

William's behavior is contrasted with that of the character he loves, Mary, who is more adventurous. As A. S. G. Edwards, professor of

English at the University of Victoria, points out, "On each of the three occasions she appears, Updike presents her *going away* from William's world, away from the classroom, out of the soda bar and finally out of the school itself" (467).

How well you integrate a quotation, paraphrase, or summary into your paper depends partly on varying your signal phrases, and in particular choosing a verb for the signal phrase that accurately conveys the tone and intent of the writer. If a writer is arguing, use the verb *argues* (or *asserts, claims,* or *contends*); if the writer is contesting a particular position or fact, use the verb *contests* (or *denies, disputes, refutes,* or *rejects*). In using verbs that are specific to the situation in your paper, you bring your readers into the intellectual debate as well as avoid the monotony of repeating such all-purpose verbs as *says* and *writes.* The following are just a few examples of how you can vary signal phrases to add interest to your paper:

> *Robert Detweiler contends that . . .*
>
> *According to critic Elizabeth A. Hait, . . .*
>
> *As Alice and Kenneth Hamilton have observed, . . .*
>
> *R. W. Reising of the University of South Florida emphasizes . . .*
>
> *John Updike himself rejects the widely held belief that . . .*

Other verbs that you should keep in mind when constructing signal phrases include the following:

acknowledges	compares	grants	reasons
adds	confirms	implies	reports
admits	declares	insists	responds
believes	endorses	points out	suggests

Documenting Your Sources

Whenever you summarize, paraphrase, or quote a person's thoughts and ideas, or use facts or statistics that are not commonly known or believed, you must properly acknowledge the source of your information. These acknowledgments are called *citations.* Your citations must consistently follow either Modern Language Association (MLA) or American Psychological Association (APA) style. The MLA documentation system is used in English and the humanities, while the APA system is used throughout the social sciences. (Your instructor will tell you which system to use.)

There are two components of documentation in a research paper: the **in-text citation,** placed in the body of your paper, and the **list of works cited,** which provides complete publication data for your sources and is placed at the end of your paper.

IN-TEXT CITATIONS

Most in-text citations consist only of the author's last name and a page reference. Usually the author's name is given in an introductory or signal phrase at the beginning of the borrowed material and the page reference is given in parentheses at the end. If the author's name is not given in the signal phrase, put it in the parentheses along with the page reference. The parenthetical reference signals the end of the borrowed material and directs your reader to the list of works cited should he or she want to pursue a source. Consider the following examples of in-text citations from K. C. Roberts' paper.

MLA *Style*

```
        In the wake of Mary's spurning,
William returns to the warmth of the
school, a world that he understands,
and goes to his locker. Hait contends
that the locker scene is helpful in de-
termining how to interpret the conclu-
sion of the story because in slamming
his locker shut, he symbolically closes
the door on one of his selves (555). He
decides, in the end, to remain shel-
tered; in the opinion of one critic,
"he is only trading the 'sense of shel-
ter' that the Olinger schools and class-
mates have provided for a thoroughly
planned, totally orthodox and secure
professional career" (Detweiler 60).
```

APA *Style*

```
        In the wake of Mary's spurning,
William returns to the warmth of the
```

```
school, a world that he understands,
and goes to his locker. Hait (1989) con-
tends that the locker scene is helpful
in determining how to interpret the con-
clusion of the story because in slam-
ming his locker shut, he symbolically
closes the door on one of his selves
(p. 555). He decides, in the end, to re-
main sheltered; in the opinion of one
critic, "he is only trading the 'sense
of shelter' that the Olinger schools
and classmates have provided for a thor-
oughly planned, totally orthodox and se-
cure professional career" (Detweiler,
1984, p. 60).
```

LIST OF WORKS CITED

MLA Style

Detweiler, Robert. *John Updike.* Rev. ed. Boston: Twayne Publishers, 1984.
Hait, Elizabeth A. "John Updike's 'A Sense of Shelter.' " *Studies in Short Fiction*
Fall 1989: 555–57.

APA Style

Detweiler, R. (1984). *John Updike.* Boston: Twayne Publishers.
Hait, E. A. (1989). John Updike's a sense of shelter. *Studies in Short Fiction, 26,*
555–557.
A sample list of works cited according to MLA style can be found at the
conclusion of the student paper, on page 41. For a complete discussion of the
documentation systems recommended by the Modern Language Association
(MLA) and the American Psychological Association (APA), consult the
MLA Handbook for Writers of Research Papers, third edition, 1988, or the
Publication Manual of the American Psychological Association, third edition,
1983.

A Note on Plagiarism

The important of honesty and accuracy in doing library research can't
be stressed enough. Any material borrowed word for word must be placed

within quotation marks and be properly cited; any idea, explanation, or argument you have paraphrased or summarized must be documented, and it must be clear where the paraphrased material begins and ends. In short, to use someone else's ideas, whether in their original form or in an altered form, without proper acknowledgment is to be guilty of **plagiarism.** And plagiarism is plagiarism, even if it is accidental.

A little attention and effort at the note-taking stage can go a long way toward eliminating the possibility of inadvertent plagiarism. Check all direct quotations against the wording of the original, and double-check your paraphrases to be sure that you have not used the writer's wording or sentence structure. It is easy to forget to put quotation marks around material taken verbatim or to use the same sentence structure and most of the same words— substituting a synonym here and there—and record it as a paraphrase. In working closely with the ideas and words of others, intellectual honesty demands that we distinguish between what we borrow—and therefore acknowledge in a citation—and what is our own.

While writing your paper, be careful whenever you incorporate one of your notes into it; make sure that you put quotation marks around material taken verbatim, and double-check your text against your note card—or better yet, the original if you have it on hand—to make sure again that your quotation is accurate. When paraphrasing or summarizing, make sure you haven't inadvertently borrowed key words or sentence structures from the original.

Finally, as you proofread your final draft, check all your citations one last time. If at any time while taking notes or writing a paper you have a question about plagiarism, consult your instructor for clarification and guidance before proceeding.

A Student's Documented Essay in Response to John Updike's "A Sense of Shelter"

Title and author are centered on separate lines.

> ## The Role of Setting in John Updike's
> ## "A Sense of Shelter"
>
> ### K. C. Roberts

Roberts presents her thesis that setting is integral to the story's meaning.

> An author can use several techniques to describe the characters in a short story. Direct physical descriptions are often employed to

depict a character, along with the actions the character takes and what characters say about each other, especially the main character. In John Updike's short essay "A Sense of Shelter," however, the author chooses to describe the central character, William, and the secondary character, Mary, by setting detailed scenes that illustrate how they see their world and where they fit in it. In this way, the setting enhances the narrative, the characterization, and the story's central theme.

William's world revolves around his school, which for him is a safe haven. Updike paints his picture vividly from the first paragraph, when he contrasts the warm classroom with the cold, snowy weather outside the classroom.[1] According to literary critics Alice and Kenneth Hamilton this comparison is a "boundary line" (112). As William looks out the window and sharpens his pencils,

> Raised number 1 (superscript) indicates that there is an informational note at the end of the paper (an endnote as opposed to a footnote).

> his knuckles came within a fraction of an inch of the tilted glass, and the faint chill this proximity breathed on them sharpened his already acute sense of shelter. . . . The feeling the gloom gave him was not gloomy, it was joyous: he felt they were all sealed in, safe. (Updike 83–84)

> Indent a long quotation ten spaces and double-space within. Only retain quotation marks in original. Citation in parentheses follows end punctuation in a long, set-off quotation.

In-text citation of summary with direct quotation. Author's name in signal phrase and page number in parentheses.

Roberts smoothly integrates Updike quotations.

The Hamiltons contend that this border is not only between two places, but represents the decision William must make later in the short story either to live a life of risk or one "insulated from outside troubles" (113).

As William goes through the school day, the idea of the school as a comfort zone is emphasized. Using almost poetic language, Updike describes "the snug sense of his work done, of the snow falling, of the warm minutes that walked through their shelter so slowly" (91). In addition, he calls the school a "closed world of closed surfaces," and describes how even the radiators seem to protect William from the cold (98).

A school is often full of life when there are noisy students around. Ironically, William finds it most comforting when classes are over and the rooms and hallways are nearly empty. The narrator tells us that William "felt reluctant to leave" the school because "this building was as much his home. He knew all its nooks" (93). In fact, he has his own inner sanctum within this shelter: a small, isolated boys' bathroom that provides a "feeling of secrecy" (93–94). The stairwell, too, "felt more secret than the hall" (96).

Once the author has vividly

painted a picture of a setting that is safe and unchallenged, the reader can more easily understand where characters stand within that setting. Fearing rejection from his fellow high school seniors, for example, William chooses to sit with the more accepting juniors, who tend to look up to him as the older student (88). William's behavior is contrasted with that of the character he loves, Mary, who is more adventurous, as A. S. G. Edwards points out.

Signal phrase introduces long, set-off quotation.

> On each of the three occasions she appears, Updike presents her going away from William's world, away from the classroom, out of the soda bar and finally out of the school itself. This final encounter effectively dramatizes the nature of the contrasting characters: Mary's steady progression through and finally away from the school out into the cold world more appropriate to her greater experience and maturity is set against William's hurried retreat into the womb-like warmth of the school. (467)

As Updike allows his characters to act, react, and change throughout the story, he enlarges the significance and meaning of setting of the story, especially as it

Paraphrase of a secondary source with author's name in signal phrase and page number in parentheses.

concerns William's future. Notice
what happens, for example, when
William decides to take a risk by
telling Mary that he has always loved
her. William must leave the security
of his shelter in order to speak with
Mary after she steps away from his
attempt to kiss her. William follows
Mary when she abruptly exits the warm
school into the snow and slush. "Cold
water gathered on the back of
[William's] shirt," Updike writes.
"He put his hands in his pockets and
pressed his arms against his sides to
keep from shivering" (99). There is
more to this physical act than simply
moving from warmth to the cold. As
Elizabeth A. Hait observes, William
must decide between the security of
the academic world that he currently
wallows in and the uncertainty and
perhaps rewards of social and
emotional involvement (555).

Summary of source
with author's name
in signal phrase
and page number
in parentheses.
Direct quotation of
secondary source
with author's name
in signal phrase
and page number
in parentheses.

This encounter ends with Mary
turning her back on William, causing
his sense of security to be
transformed, at least briefly.
Whereas before the warm school had
given him pleasure, now it almost
smothers and confines him. In the wake
of Mary's spurning, William returns
to the warmth of the school, a world
that he understands, and goes to his
locker. Hait contends that the locker

scene is helpful in determining how to interpret the conclusion of the story because in slamming his locker shut, he symbolically closes the door on one of his selves (555). He decides, in the end, to remain sheltered; in the opinion of critic Robert Detweiler, "he is only trading the 'sense of shelter' that the Olinger schools and classmates have provided for a thoroughly planned, totally orthodox and secure professional career" (60).[2]

By painting a picture of a comfortable atmosphere inside the school and a challenging one outside, Updike permits the reader not only to appreciate the choice William makes but, in a way, to experience it as well. Many authors simply use setting to establish an initial tone and then allow the story to unfold. Updike, in contrast, uses the setting and atmosphere that grows from it to dramatize the issues at stake in William's decision.

In her conclusion, Roberts returns to her thesis and gives a more detailed account of the setting's importance.

Notes

The heading "Notes" is centered.

[1] For a fuller discussion of the "inside—outside" contrast, see Alice and Kenneth Hamilton (106—18).

Information notes provide additional material or sources.

Notes appear on a separate numbered page following the text and before the list of works cited.

Double-space throughout note entries; leave a space but do not put a period after the superscript number.

[2] Not all critics agree on this point. Two, in fact, take opposing points of view. R. W. Reising interprets the last scene in the short story as a representation of William learning how to take future risks (651–52). A. S. G. Edwards believes it shows "a rejection of even the possibility of experience" (468).

The heading "Works Cited" is centered.

Works Cited

The list of works cited begins on a new page. Each entry begins at the left margin. Subsequent lines are indented five spaces. Double-space throughout.

Detweiler, Robert. John Updike. Rev. ed. Boston: Twayne Publishers, 1984.

Edwards, A. S. G. "Updike's 'A Sense of Shelter.' " Studies in Short Fiction Summer 1971: 467–68.

Hait, Elizabeth A. "John Updike's 'A Sense of Shelter.' " Studies in Short Fiction Fall 1989: 555–67.

Hamilton, Alice and Kenneth. The Elements of John Updike. Grand Rapids, Michigan: William B. Eerdmans, 1970.

Reising, R. W. "Updike's 'A Sense of Shelter.' " Studies in Short Fiction Fall 1970: 651–52.

Updike, John. Pigeon Feathers and Other Stories. New York: Alfred A. Knopf, 1962.

I

Private Lives

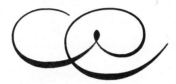

Our entire life, with our fine moral code and our precious freedom, consists ultimately in accepting ourselves as we are.
—JEAN ANOUILH

All the miseries of mankind come from one thing: not knowing how to remain alone.
—BLAISE PASCAL

We are great fools. "He has spent his life in idleness," we say; "I have done nothing." What, have you not lived?
—MICHEL DE MONTAIGNE

A Sense of Self

DICK GREGORY

Dick Gregory was one of the angry African-American comics who emerged at the beginning of the 1960s who, as entertainers, could speak of racial injustice to audiences that would not listen to other African-American leaders. A contemporary of Martin Luther King, Jr., and Malcom X, Gregory played a significant part in the civil rights movement of the sixties with his comedy, his political advocacy and his writing. His books include *From the Back of the Bus* (1962), *Nigger* (1964), and *Dick Gregory's Political Primer* (1972). After having lost a tremendous amount of weight, Gregory has in recent years turned to counseling people whose lives are threatened by obesity. His experimental approaches to diet, weight, and self-esteem have received much public notice, and he has written *Dick Gregory's Natural Diet for Folks Who Eat: Cookin' with Mother Nature* (1973).

Gregory's childhood was hard. He was born in the Depression year of 1932 in the segregated state of Missouri, and grew up burdened by deprivations of all kinds. The following excerpt from his autobiography, *Nigger*, gives a hint of what his early years were like, describing a childhood experience that made him aware of how others saw him—and of the meaning of shame.

Shame

I never learned hate at home, or shame. I had to go to school for that. I was about seven years old when I got my first big lesson. I was in love with a little girl named Helene Tucker, a light-complected little girl with pigtails and nice manners. She was always clean and she was smart in school. I think I went to school then mostly to look at her. I brushed my hair and even got me a little old handkerchief. It was a lady's handkerchief, but I didn't want Helene to see me wipe my nose on my hand. The pipes were frozen again, there was no water in the house, but I washed my socks and shirt every night. I'd get a pot, and go over to Mister Ben's grocery store, and stick my pot down into his soda machine. Scoop out some chopped ice. By evening the ice melted to water for washing. I got sick a lot that winter because the fire would go out at night before the clothes were dry. In the morning I'd put them on, wet or dry, because they were the only clothes I had.

Everybody's got a Helene Tucker, a symbol of everything you want. I   2
loved her for her goodness, her cleanness, her popularity. She'd walk down
my street and my brothers and sisters would yell, "Here comes Helene," and
I'd rub my tennis sneakers on the back of my pants and wish my hair wasn't
so nappy and the white folks' shirt fit me better. I'd run out on the street. If I
knew my place and didn't come too close, she'd wink at me and say hello.
That was a good feeling. Sometimes I'd follow her all the way home, and
shovel the snow off her walk and try to make friends with her Momma and
her aunts. I'd drop money on her stoop late at night on my way back from
shining shoes in the taverns. And she had a Daddy, and he had a good job.
He was a paper hanger.

I guess I would have gotten over Helene by summertime, but some-   3
thing happened in that classroom that made her face hang in front of me for
the next twenty-two years. When I played the drums in high school it was for
Helene and when I broke track records in college it was for Helene and when
I started standing behind microphones and heard applause I wished Helene
could hear it too. It wasn't until I was twenty-nine years old and married and
making money that I finally got her out of my system. Helene was sitting in
that classroom when I learned to be ashamed of myself.

It was on a Thursday. I was sitting in the back of the room, in a seat   4
with a chalk circle drawn around it. The idiot's seat, the troublemaker's seat.

The teacher thought I was stupid. Couldn't spell, couldn't read,   5
couldn't do arithmetic. Just stupid. Teachers were never interested in finding
out that you couldn't concentrate because you were so hungry, because you
hadn't had any breakfast. All you could think about was noontime, would it
ever come? Maybe you could sneak into the cloakroom and steal a bite of
some kid's lunch out of a coat pocket. A bite of something. Paste. You can't
really make a meal of paste, or put it on bread for a sandwich, but sometimes
I'd scoop a few spoonfuls out of the big paste jar in the back of the room.
Pregnant people get strange tastes. I was pregnant with poverty. Pregnant
with dirt and pregnant with smells that made people turn away, pregnant
with cold and pregnant with shoes that were never bought for me, pregnant
with five other people in my bed and no Daddy in the next room, and
pregnant with hunger. Paste doesn't taste too bad when you're hungry.

The teacher thought I was a troublemaker. All she saw from the front   6
of the room was a little black boy who squirmed in his idiot's seat and made
noises and poked the kids around him. I guess she couldn't see a kid who
made noises because he wanted someone to know he was there.

It was on a Thursday, the day before the Negro payday. The eagle   7
always flew on Friday. The teacher was asking each student how much his
father would give to the Community Chest. On Friday night, each kid would
get the money from his father, and on Monday he would bring it to the
school. I decided I was going to buy a Daddy then. I had money in my pocket

from shining shoes and selling papers, and whatever Helene Tucker pledged for her Daddy I was going to top it. And I'd hand the money right in. I wasn't going to wait to Monday to buy me a Daddy.

I was shaking, scared to death. The teacher opened her book and started calling out names alphabetically. 8

"Helene Tucker?" 9

"My Daddy said he'd give two dollars and fifty cents." 10

"That's very nice, Helene. Very, very nice indeed." 11

That made me feel pretty good. It wouldn't take too much to top that. I had almost three dollars in dimes and quarters in my pocket. I stuck my hand in my pocket and held onto the money, waiting for her to call my name. But the teacher closed her book after she called everybody else in the class. 12

I stood and raised my hand. 13

"What is it now?" 14

"You forgot me." 15

She turned toward the blackboard. "I don't have time to be playing with you, Richard." 16

"My Daddy said he'd . . ." 17

"Sit down, Richard, you're disturbing the class." 18

"My Daddy said he'd give . . . fifteen dollars." 19

She turned around and looked mad. "We are collecting this money for you and your kind, Richard Gregory. If your Daddy can give fifteen dollars you have no business being on relief." 20

"I got it right now, I got it right now, my Daddy gave it to me to turn in today, my Daddy said . . ." 21

"And furthermore," she said, looking right at me, her nostrils getting big and her lips getting thin and her eyes opening wide. "We know you don't have a Daddy." 22

Helene Tucker turned around, her eyes full of tears. She felt sorry for me. Then I couldn't see her too well because I was crying, too. 23

"Sit down, Richard." 24

And I always thought the teacher kind of liked me. She always picked me to wash the blackboard on Friday, after school. That was a big thrill, it made me feel important. If I didn't wash it, come Monday the school might not function right. 25

"Where are you going, Richard?" 26

I walked out of school that day, and for a long time I didn't go back very often. There was shame there. 27

Now there was shame everywhere. It seemed like the whole world had been inside that classroom, everyone had heard what the teacher had said, everyone had turned around and felt sorry for me. There was shame in going to the Worthy Boys Annual Christmas Dinner for you and your kind, because everyone knew what a worthy boy was. Why couldn't they just call it 28 the Boys Annual Dinner, why'd they have to give it a name? There was shame in wearing the brown and orange and white plaid mackinaw the welfare gave to 3,000 boys. Why'd it have to be the same for everybody so when you walked down the street the people could see you were on relief? It was a nice warm mackinaw and it had a hood, and my Momma beat me and called me a little rat when she found out I stuffed it in the bottom of a pail full of garbage way over on Cottage Street. There was shame in running over to Mister Ben's at the end of the day and asking for his rotten peaches, there was shame in asking Mrs. Simmons for a spoonful of sugar, there was shame in running out to meet the relief truck. I hated that truck, full of food for you and your kind. I ran into the house and hid when it came. And then I started to sneak through alleys, to take the long way home so the people going into White's Eat Shop wouldn't see me. Yeah, the whole world heard the teacher that day, we all know you don't have a Daddy.

It lasted for a while, this kind of numbness. I spent a lot of time   29 feeling sorry for myself. And then one day I met this wino in a restaurant. I'd been out hustling all day, shining shoes, selling newspapers, and I had googobs of money in my pocket. Bought me a bowl of chili for fifteen cents, and a cheeseburger for fifteen cents, and a Pepsi for five cents, and a piece of chocolate cake for ten cents. That was a good meal. I was eating when this old wino came in. I love winos because they never hurt anyone but themselves.

The old wino sat down at the counter and ordered twenty-six cents   30 worth of food. He ate it like he really enjoyed it. When the owner, Mister Williams, asked him to pay the check, the old wino didn't lie or go through his pocket like he suddenly found a hole.

He just said: "Don't have no money."   31

The owner yelled: "Why in hell you come in here and eat my food if   32 you don't have no money? That food cost me money."

Mister Williams jumped over the counter and knocked the wino off his   33 stool and beat him over the head with a pop bottle. Then he stepped back and watched the wino bleed. Then he kicked him. And he kicked him again.

I looked at the wino with blood all over his face and I went over.   34 "Leave him alone, Mister Williams. I'll pay the twenty-six cents."

The wino got up, slowly, pulling himself up to the stool, then up to the   35 counter, holding on for a minute until his legs stopped shaking so bad. He looked at me with pure hate. "Keep your twenty-six cents. You don't have to pay, not now. I just finished paying for it."

He started to walk out, and as he passed me, he reached down and   36 touched my shoulder. "Thanks, sonny, but it's too late now. Why didn't you pay before?"

I was pretty sick about that. I waited too long to help another man.   37

Questions for Study and Discussion   •

1. What does Gregory mean by *shame?* What precisely was he ashamed of, and what in particular did he learn from the incident at school?

2. What is the teacher's attitude toward Gregory? Consider her own words and actions as well as Gregory's opinion in arriving at your answer.

3. What role does money play in Gregory's narrative? How does it relate to his sense of shame?

4. Gregory's use of details—his description of Helene Tucker's manners or his plaid mackinaw, for example—does more than merely make his narrative vivid and interesting. Cite several other specific details he gives, and consider the effect each has on your response to the story.

5. What effect does Gregory's repetition of the word *shame* have on you? Does Gregory repeat any other words or phrases? If so, with what effect?

Writing Topics

1. Write an essay in which you describe an event in your life that made you sharply aware of how other people see you. How did you feel—surprised, ashamed, angry, proud, or something else? Why? Do you still feel the same way?

2. Social institutions and organizations help to shape our self-esteem, as they did with Dick Gregory. In an essay, discuss the effect one such institution or organization has had on you. How did it influence you? Did it help or hinder you in developing a positive image of yourself?

3. Gregory's work with overweight people has not been restricted to diet but has included improving their self-esteem. Write an essay in which you explore the relationship between appearance (such as dress, behavior, weight, height, hairstyle) and self-image. It may be useful to discuss those factors that affect self-image with your friends before you begin to write.

GEORGE ORWELL

George Orwell (1903–1950) was one of the most brilliant social critics of our time. He was born in Bengal, India, but grew up in England and received a traditional education at the prestigious school of Eton. Instead of going on to a university, he joined the civil service and was sent to Burma at nineteen as an assistant superintendent of police. Disillusioned with British imperialism, Orwell resigned in 1929 and began a decade of studying social and political issues firsthand and then writing about them in such works as *Down and Out in Paris and London* (1933) and *The Road to Wigan Pier* (1937). His most famous books are *Animal Farm* (1945), a satire of the Russian Revolution, and *1984* (1949), a chilling novel set in an imagined totalitarian state of the future.

"Shooting an Elephant" was published in the British magazine *New Writing* in 1936. Hitler, Mussolini, and Stalin were in power, building the "younger empires" Orwell refers to in his second paragraph, and the old British Empire was soon to decline, as Orwell predicted. In this essay, Orwell tells of a time when, in a position of authority, he found himself compelled to act against his convictions.

Shooting an Elephant

In Moulmein, in lower Burma, I was hated by large numbers of 1 people—the only time in my life that I have been important enough for this to happen to me. I was sub-divisional police officer of the town, and in an aimless, petty kind of way anti-European feeling was very bitter. No one had the guts to raise a riot, but if a European woman went through the bazaars alone somebody would probably spit betel juice over her dress. As a police officer I was an obvious target and was baited whenever it seemed safe to do so. When a nimble Burman tripped me upon the football field and the referee (another Burman) looked the other way, the crowd yelled with hideous laughter. This happened more than once. In the end the sneering yellow faces of young men that met me everywhere, the insults hooted after me when I was at a safe distance, got badly on my nerves. The young Buddhist priests were the worst of all. There were several thousands of them in the town and none of them seemed to have anything to do except stand on street corners and jeer at Europeans.

All this was perplexing and upsetting. For at that time I had already 2 made up my mind that imperialism was an evil thing and the sooner I chucked up my job and got out of it the better. Theoretically—and secretly, of course—I was all for the Burmese and all against their oppressors, the

British. As for the job I was doing, I hated it more bitterly than I can perhaps make clear. In a job like that you see the dirty work of Empire at close quarters. The wretched prisoners huddling in the stinking cages of the lock-ups, the gray, cowed faces of the long-term convicts, the scarred buttocks of the men who had been flogged with bamboos—all these oppressed me with an intolerable sense of guilt. But I could get nothing into perspective. I was young and ill educated and I had had to think out my problems in the utter silence that is imposed on every Englishman in the East. I did not even know that the British Empire is dying, still less did I know that it is a great deal better than the younger empires that are going to supplant it. All I knew was that I was stuck between my hatred of the empire I served and my rage against the evil-spirited little beasts who tried to make my job impossible. With one part of my mind I thought of the British Raj as an unbreakable tyranny, as something clamped down, in *saecula saeculorum,* upon the will of prostrate peoples; with another part I thought that the greatest joy in the world would be to drive a bayonet into a Buddhist priest's guts.¹ Feelings like these are the normal by-products of imperialism; ask any Anglo-Indian official, if you can catch him off duty.

One day something happened which in a roundabout way was enlight- 3
ening. It was a tiny incident in itself, but it gave me a better glimpse than I had had before of the real nature of imperialism—the real motives for which despotic governments act. Early one morning the sub-inspector at a police station the other end of the town rang me up on the 'phone and said that an elephant was ravaging the bazaar. Would I please come and do something about it? I did not know what I could do, but I wanted to see what was happening and I got on a pony and started out. I took my rifle, an old .44 Winchester and much too small to kill an elephant, but I thought the noise might be useful *in terrorem.* Various Burmans stopped me on the way and told me about the elephant's doings. It was not, of course, a wild elephant, but a tame one which had gone "must."² It had been chained up, as tame elephants always are when their attack of "must" is due, but on the previous night it had broken its chain and escaped. Its mahout, the only person who could manage it when it was in that state, had set out in pursuit, but had taken the wrong direction and was now twelve hours' journey away, and in the morning the elephant had suddenly reappeared in the town. The Burmese population had no weapons and were quite helpless against it. It had already destroyed somebody's bamboo hut, killed a cow and raided some fruit-stalls and devoured the stock; also it had met the municipal rubbish van and, when the driver jumped out and took to his heels, had turned the van over and inflicted violences upon it.

---

¹Raj: rule, especially in India. *Saecula saeculorum:* from time immemorial.

²That is, gone into an uncontrollable frenzy.

The Burmese sub-inspector and some Indian constables were waiting   4
for me in the quarter where that elephant had been seen. It was a very poor
quarter, a labyrinth of squalid bamboo huts, thatched with palm-leaf, winding all over a steep hillside. I remember that it was a cloudy, stuffy morning
at the beginning of the rains. We began questioning the people as to where
the elephant had gone and, as usual, failed to get any definite information.
That is invariably the case in the East; a story always sounds clear enough at
a distance, but the nearer you get to the scene of events the vaguer it
becomes. Some of the people said that the elephant had gone in one direction, some said that he had gone in another, some professed not even to have
heard of any elephant. I had almost made up my mind that the whole story
was a pack of lies, when we heard yells a little distance away. There was a
loud, scandalized cry of "Go away, child! Go away this instant!" and an old
woman with a switch in her hand came round the corner of a hut, violently
shooing away a crowd of naked children. Some more women followed,
clicking their tongues and exclaiming; evidently there was something that
the children ought not to have seen. I rounded the hut and saw a man's dead
body sprawling in the mud. He was an Indian, a black Dravidian coolie,
almost naked, and he could not have been dead many minutes. The people
said that the elephant had come suddenly upon him round the corner of the
hut, caught him with its trunk, put its foot on his back and ground him into
the earth. This was the rainy season and the ground was soft, and his face
had scored a trench a foot deep and a couple of yards long. He was lying on
his belly with arms crucified and head sharply twisted to one side. His face
was coated with mud, the eyes wide open, the teeth bared and grinning with
an expression of unendurable agony. (Never tell me, by the way, that the
dead look peaceful. Most of the corpses I have seen looked devilish.) The
friction of the great beast's foot had stripped the skin from his back as neatly
as one skins a rabbit. As soon as I saw the dead man I sent an orderly to a
friend's house nearby to borrow an elephant rifle. I had already sent back to
the pony, not wanting it to go mad with fright and throw me if it smelt the
elephant.

The orderly came back in a few minutes with a rifle and five cartridges,   5
and meanwhile some Burmans had arrived and told us that the elephant was
in the paddy fields below, only a few hundred yards away. As I started forward
practically the whole population of the quarter flocked out of the houses and
followed me. They had seen the rifle and were all shouting excitedly that I
was going to shoot the elephant. They had not shown much interest in the
elephant when he was merely ravaging their homes, but it was different now
that he was going to be shot. It was a bit of fun to them, as it would be to an
English crowd; besides they wanted the meat. It made me vaguely uneasy. I
had no intention of shooting the elephant—I had merely sent for the rifle to
defend myself if necessary—and it is always unnerving to have a crowd
following you. I marched down the hill, looking and feeling a fool, with the

rifle over my shoulder and an ever-growing army of people jostling at my heels. At the bottom, when you got away from the huts, there was a metalled road and beyond that a miry waste of paddy fields a thousand yards across, not yet ploughed but soggy from the first rains and dotted with coarse grass. The elephant was standing eight yards from the road, his left side toward us. He took not the slightest notice of the crowd's approach. He was tearing up bunches of grass, beating them against his knees to clean them, and stuffing them into his mouth.

I had halted on the road. As soon as I saw the elephant I knew with 6 perfect certainty that I ought not to shoot him. It is a serious matter to shoot a working elephant—it is comparable to destroying a huge and costly piece of machinery—and obviously one ought not to do it if it can possibly be avoided. And at that distance, peacefully eating, the elephant looked no more dangerous than a cow. I thought then and I think now that his attack of "must" was already passing off; in which case he would merely wander harmlessly about until the mahout came back and caught him. Moreover, I did not in the least want to shoot him. I decided that I would watch him for a little while to make sure that he did not turn savage again, and then go home.

But at that moment I glanced round at the crowd that had followed 7 me. It was an immense crowd, two thousand at the least and growing every minute. It blocked the road for a long distance on either side. I looked at the sea of yellow faces above the garish clothes—faces all happy and excited over this bit of fun, all certain that the elephant was going to be shot. They were watching me as they would watch a conjurer about to perform a trick. They did not like me, but with the magical rifle in my hands I was momentarily worth watching. And suddenly I realized that I should have to shoot the elephant after all. The people expected it of me and I had got to do it; I could feel their two thousand wills pressing me forward, irresistibly. And it was at this moment, as I stood there with the rifle in my hands, that I first grasped the hollowness, the futility of the white man's dominion in the East. Here was I, the white man with his gun, standing in front of the unarmed native crowd—seemingly the leading actor of the piece; but in reality I was only an absurd puppet pushed to and fro by the will of those yellow faces behind. I perceived in this moment that when the white man turns tyrant it is his own freedom that he destroys. He becomes a sort of hollow, posing dummy, the conventionalized figure of a sahib. For it is the condition of his rule that he shall spend his life in trying to impress the "natives," and so in every crisis he has got to do what the "natives" expect of him. He wears a mask, and his face grows to fit it. I had got to shoot the elephant. I had committed myself to doing it when I sent for the rifle. A sahib has got to act like a sahib; he has got to appear resolute, to know his own mind and do definite things. To come all that way, rifle in hand, with two thousand people marching at my heels, and then to trail feebly away, having done nothing—no, that was impossible. The crowd would laugh at me. And my whole life, every white man's life in the East, was one long struggle not to be laughed at.

But I did not want to shoot the elephant. I watched him beating his   8
bunch of grass against his knees with that preoccupied grandmotherly air that elephants have. It seemed to me that it would be murder to shoot him. At that age I was not squeamish about killing animals, but I had never shot an elephant and never wanted to. (Somehow it always seems worse to kill a *large* animal.) Besides, there was the beast's owner to be considered. Alive, the elephant was worth at least a hundred pounds; dead, he would only be worth the value of his tusks, five pounds, possibly.[3] But I had got to act quickly. I turned to some experienced-looking Burmans who had been there when he arrived, and asked them how the elephant had been behaving. They all said the same thing; he took no notice of you if you left him alone, but he might charge if you went too close to him.

It was perfectly clear to me what I ought to do. I ought to walk up to   9
within, say, twenty-five yards of the elephant and test his behavior. If he charged, I could shoot; if he took no notice of me, it would be safe to leave him until the mahout came back. But also I knew that I was going to do no such thing. I was a poor shot with a rifle and the ground was soft mud into which one would sink at every step. If the elephant charged and I missed him, I should have about as much chance as a toad under a steam-roller. But even then I was not thinking particularly of my own skin, only of the watchful yellow faces behind. For at that moment, with the crowd watching me, I was not afraid in the ordinary sense, as I would have been if I had been alone. A white man mustn't be frightened in front of "natives"; and so, in general, he isn't frightened. The sole thought in my mind was that if anything went wrong those two thousand Burmans would see me pursued, caught, trampled on, and reduced to a grinning corpse like that Indian up the hill. And if that happened it was quite probable that some of them would laugh. That would never do. There was only one alternative. I shoved the cartidges into the magazine and lay down on the road to get a better aim.

The crowd grew very still, and a deep, low, happy sigh, as of people   10
who see the theater curtain go up at last, breathed from innumerable throats. They were going to have their bit of fun after all. The rifle was a beautiful German thing with cross-hair sights. I did not even know that in shooting an elephant one would shoot to cut an imaginary bar running from ear-hole to ear-hole. I ought, therefore, as the elephant was sideways on, to have aimed straight at his ear-hole; actually I aimed several inches in front of this, thinking the brain would be further forward.

When I pulled the trigger I did not hear the bang or feel the kick—one   11
never does when a shot goes home—but I heard the devilish roar of glee that

---

[3]The British pound would have been worth five dollars at the time.

went up from the crowd. In that instant, in too short a time, one would have thought, even for the bullet to get there, a mysterious, terrible change had come over the elephant. He neither stirred nor fell, but every line of his body had altered. He looked suddenly stricken, shrunken, immensely old, as though the fruitful impact of the bullet had paralyzed him without knocking him down. At last, after what seemed a long time—it might have been five seconds, I dare say—he sagged flabbily to his knees. His mouth slobbered. An enormous senility seemed to have settled upon him. One could have imagined him thousands of years old. I fired again into the same spot. At the second shot he did not collapse but climbed with desperate slowness to his feet and stood weakly upright, with legs sagging and head drooping. I fired a third time. That was the shot that did for him. You could see the agony of it jolt his whole body and knock the last remnant of strength from his legs. But in falling he seemed for a moment to rise, for as his hind legs collapsed beneath him he seemed to tower upward like a huge rock toppling, his trunk reaching skyward like a tree. He trumpeted, for the first and only time. And then down he came, his belly toward me, with a crash that seemed to shake the ground even where I lay.

I got up. The Burmans were already racing past me across the mud. It 12 was obvious that the elephant would never rise again, but he was not dead. He was breathing very rhythmically with long rattling gasps, his great mound of a side painfully rising and falling. His mouth was wide open—I could see far down into caverns of pale pink throat. I waited a long time for him to die, but his breathing did not weaken. Finally, I fired two remaining shots into the spot where I thought his heart must be. The thick blood welled out of him like red velvet, but still he did not die. His body did not even jerk when the shots hit him, the tortured breathing continued without a pause. He was dying, very slowly and in great agony, but in some world remote from me where not even a bullet could damage him further. I felt that I had got to put an end to that dreadful noise. It seemed dreadful to see the great beast lying there, powerless to move and yet powerless to die, and not even to be able to finish him. I sent back for my small rifle and poured shot after shot into his heart and down his throat. They seemed to make no impression. The tortured gasps continued as steadily as the ticking of a clock.

In the end I could not stand it any longer and went away. I heard later 13 that it took him half an hour to die. Burmans were bringing dahs[4] and baskets even before I left, and I was told they had stripped his body almost to the bones by the afternoon.

Afterwards, of course, there were endless discussions about the shoot- 14 ing of the elephant. The owner was furious, but he was only an Indian and could do nothing. Besides, legally I had done the right thing, for a mad

---

[4]Heavy knives.

elephant has to be killed, like a mad dog, if its owner fails to control it. Among the Europeans opinion was divided. The older men said I was right, the younger men said it was a damn shame to shoot an elephant for killing a coolie, because an elephant was worth more than any damn Coringhee coolie. And afterwards I was very glad that the coolie had been killed; it put me legally in the right and it gave me a sufficient pretext for shooting the elephant. I often wondered whether any of the others grasped that I had done it solely to avoid looking a fool.

Questions for Study and Discussion

1. Why is the setting of this narrative significant? What is imperialism, and what does Orwell's essay say about it?

2. Why, according to Orwell, did he shoot the elephant? Do you find his interpretation convincing? Why, or why not?

3. What do you think was Orwell's purpose in telling this story? Cite evidence from the essay that indicates to you that purpose. Does he accomplish his purpose?

4. What part of the essay struck you most strongly? The shooting itself? Orwell's feelings? The descriptions of the Burmans and their behavior? Or something else? Can you identify anything about Orwell's prose that enhances the impact of that passage? Explain.

5. What is Orwell doing in the final paragraph? How does that paragraph affect your response to the whole essay?

Writing Topics

1. Consider situations in which you have been a leader, like Orwell, or part of a crowd, like the Burmans. As a leader, what was your attitude toward your followers? As a follower, what did you feel toward your leader? From these experiences, what conclusions can you draw? Write an essay about the relationship between leaders and followers.

2. Tell of a situation in which you felt compelled to act against your convictions. What arguments can justify your action? How much freedom of choice did you actually have, and what were the limits on your freedom? On what basis can you refuse to subordinate your convictions to others', or to society's?

3. Orwell has shown one of the ironies of imperialism, that colonial officers are ruled by those they govern, or, to put it another way, that the rulers are ruled by the ruled. What are some other criticisms of imperialism? Using library sources, write an essay on the differing views of imperialism, from the perspective of the imperial power and from that of the people subject to the power.

ZORA NEALE HURSTON

Zora Neale Hurston (1901–1960) was raised in the rural South and grew up to become one of the stars of the Harlem Renaissance. Her work as an anthropologist, folklorist, and novelist has centered on maintaining and sharing her cultural heritage. Her works include a collection of folktales, numerous short stories and magazine articles, an autobiography, and five novels, most notable among them her masterwork, *Their Eyes Were Watching God: A Novel* (1937).

In the following essay, taken from *I Love Myself When I Am Laughing* (1979), Hurston expresses an enthusiastic pride in having grown up "colored" in a white world.

How It Feels to Be Colored Me

I am colored but I offer nothing in the way of extenuating circum- 1
stances except the fact that I am the only Negro in the United States whose grandfather on the mother's side was *not* an Indian chief.

I remember the very day that I became colored. Up to my thirteenth 2
year I lived in the little Negro town of Eatonville, Florida. It is exclusively a colored town. The only white people I knew passed through the town going to or coming from Orlando. The native whites rode dusty horses, the North-ern tourists chugged down the sandy village road in automobiles. The town knew the Southerners and never stopped cane chewing when they passed. But the Northerners were something else again. They were peered at cau-tiously from behind curtains by the timid. The more venturesome would come out on the porch to watch them go past and got just as much pleasure out of the tourists as the tourists got out of the village.

The front porch might seem a daring place for the rest of the town, but 3
it was a gallery seat for me. My favorite place was atop the gate-post. Proscenium box for a born first-nighter. Not only did I enjoy the show, but I didn't mind the actors knowing that I liked it. I usually spoke to them in passing. I'd wave at them and when they returned my salute, I would say something like this: "Howdy-do-well-I-thank-you-where-you-goin'?" Usually

automobile or the horse paused at this, and after a queer exchange of compliments, I would probably "go a piece of the way" with them, as we say in farthest Florida. If one of my family happened to come to the front in time to see me, of course negotiations would be rudely broken off. But even so, it is clear that I was the first "welcome-to-our-state" Floridian, and I hope the Miami Chamber of Commerce will please take notice.

During this period, white people differed from colored to me only in   4
that they rode through town and never lived there. They liked to hear me "speak pieces" and sing and wanted to see me dance the parse-me-la, and gave me generously of their small silver for doing such things, which seemed strange to me for I wanted to do them so much that I needed bribing to stop. Only they didn't know it. The colored people gave no dimes. They deplored any joyful tendencies in me, but I was their Zora nevertheless. I belonged to them, to the nearby hotels, to the county—everybody's Zora.

But changes came in the family when I was thirteen, and I was sent to   5
school in Jacksonville. I left Eatonville, the town of the oleanders, as Zora. When I disembarked from the river-boat at Jacksonville, she was no more. It seemed that I had suffered a sea change. I was not Zora of Orange County any more, I was now a little colored girl. I found it out in certain ways. In my heart as well as in the mirror, I became a fast brown—warranted not to rub nor run.

But I am not tragically colored. There is no great sorrow dammed up in   6
my soul, nor lurking behind my eyes. I do not mind at all. I do not belong to the sobbing school of Negrohood who hold that nature somehow has given them a lowdown dirty deal and whose feelings are all hurt about it. Even in the helter-skelter skirmish that is my life, I have seen that the world is to the strong regardless of a little pigmentation more or less. No, I do not weep at the world—I am too busy sharpening my oyster knife.

Someone is always at my elbow reminding me that I am the grand-   7
daughter of slaves. It fails to register depression with me. Slavery is sixty years in the past. The operation was successful and the patient is doing well, thank you. The terrible struggle that made me an American out of a potential slave said "On the line!" The Reconstruction said "Get set!"; and the generation before said "Go!" I am off to a flying start and I must not halt in the stretch to look behind and weep. Slavery is the price I paid for civilization, and the choice was not with me. It is a bully adventure and worth all that I have paid through my ancestors for it. No one on earth ever had a greater chance for glory. The world to be won and nothing to be lost. It is thrilling to think—to know that for any act of mine, I shall get twice as much praise or twice as much blame. It is quite exciting to hold the center of the national stage, with the spectators not knowing whether to laugh or to weep.

The position of my white neighbor is much more difficult. No brown   8
specter pulls up a chair beside me when I sit down to eat. No dark ghost
thrusts its leg against mine in bed. The game of keeping what one has is
never so exciting as the game of getting.

I do not always feel colored. Even now I often achieve the unconscious   9
Zora of Eatonville before the Hegira. I feel most colored when I am thrown
against a sharp white background.

For instance at Barnard. "Besides the waters of the Hudson" I feel my   10
face. Among the thousand white persons, I am a dark rock surged upon, and
overswept, but through it all, I remain myself. When covered by the waters,
I am; and the ebb but reveals me again.

Sometimes it is the other way around. A white person is set down in   11
our midst, but the contrast is just as sharp for me. For instance, when I sit in
the drafty basement that is The New World Cabaret with a white person, my
color comes. We enter chatting about any little nothing that we have in
common and are seated by the jazz waiters. In the abrupt way that jazz
orchestras have, this one plunges into a number. It loses no time in circumlo-
cutions, but gets right down to business. It constricts the thorax and splits
the heart with its tempo and narcotic harmonies. This orchestra grows
rambunctious, rears on its hind legs and attacks the tonal veil with primitive
fury, rending it, clawing it until it breaks through to the jungle beyond. I
follow those heathen—follow them exultingly. I dance wildly inside myself;
I yell within, I whoop; I shake my assegai above my head, I hurl it true to the
mark *yeeeeooww!* I am in the jungle and living in the jungle way. My face is
painted red and yellow and my body is painted blue. My pulse is throbbing
like a war drum, I want to slaughter something—give paid, give death to
what, I do not know. But the piece ends. The men of the orchestra wipe
their lips and rest their fingers. I creep back slowly to the veneer we call
civilization with the last tone and find the white friend sitting motionless in
his seat, smoking calmly.

"Good music they have here," he remarks, drumming the table with   12
his fingertips.

Music. The great blobs of purple and red emotion have not touched   13
him. He has only heard what I felt. He is far away and I see him but dimly
across the ocean and the continent that have fallen between us. He is so pale
with his whiteness then and I am *so* colored.

At certain times I have no race, I am *me*. When I set my hat at a   14
certain angle and saunter down Seventh Avenue, Harlem City, feeling as
snooty as the lions in front of the Forty-Second Street Library, for instance.
So far as my feelings are concerned, Peggy Hopkins Joyce on the Boule
Mich with her gorgeous raiment, stately carriage, knees knocking together

in a most aristocratic manner, has nothing on me. The cosmic Zora emerges. I belong to no race nor time. I am the eternal feminine with its string of beads.

I have no separate feeling about being an American citizen and col-   15 ored. I am merely a fragment of the Great Soul that surges within the boundaries. My country, right or wrong.

Sometimes, I feel discriminated against, but it does not make me angry.   16 It merely astonishes me. How *can* any deny themselves the pleasure of my company? It's beyond me.

But in the main, I feel like a brown bag of miscellany propped against a   17 wall. Against a wall in company with other bags, white, red and yellow. Pour out the contents, and there is discovered a jumble of small things priceless and worthless. A first-water diamond, an empty spool, bits of broken glass, lengths of string, a key to a door long since crumbled away, a rusty knife-blade, old shoes saved for a road that never was and never will be, a nail bent under the weight of things too heavy for any nail, a dried flower or two still a little fragrant. In your hand is the brown bag. On the ground before you is the jumble it held—so much like the jumble in the bags, could they be emptied, that all might be dumped in a single heap and the bags refilled without altering the contents of any greatly. A bit of colored glass more or less would not matter. Perhaps that is how the Great Stuffer of Bags filled them in the first place—who knows?

Questions for Study and Discussion

1. What does Hurston mean when she says she remembers the day she became "colored"? How does she contrast her "colored" self with her "no race" self?

2. Many African-American and other minority writers convey attitudes ranging from rage, to despair, to resignation at the way that they are discriminated against by whites. Hurston is different. How would you characterize her attitude? What does it tell you about the kind of person she is? What in Hurston's choice of words and images led you to your conclusion?

3. In your own words, what are the "brown specter" and the "dark ghost" that Hurston refers to in paragraph 8? How do these images relate to her statement that "the game of keeping what one has is never so exciting as the game of getting"? Do you agree or disagree with this statement? Explain.

4. What cultural stereotype does Hurston claim with pride in paragraph 11? What image of whites does it evoke? How does her contrasting of blacks and whites strike you? Is it fair? Explain.

5. Hurston concludes her essay with an analogy. What is that analogy, and how well does it work? What does it reveal to the reader about the author's view of citizenship and humankind? Does her vision of humankind and citizenship strike you as realistic?

Writing Topics

1. Reread Dick Gregory's essay "Shame" in the beginning of this section. Write an essay in which you discuss the ways his attitude toward being "different" contrasts with Hurston's. Note how the two authors use word choice and tone to convey their self-image.

2. Hurston grew up in a world in which most blacks were discriminated against and made to feel inferior to whites. What do you suppose were some of the influences that enabled Hurston to maintain such a positive self-image? Do you think these influences can counteract discrimination not only against race, but against sex, age, or some other trait perceived as limiting? In your essay be sure to discuss the ways in which certain influences can nurture or destroy a child's positive self-image.

3. Although Hurston has a positive attitude toward being "colored," she is nevertheless aware that not all blacks do. Think of some trait of yours such as race, national origin, sex, or a limiting physical condition that has been a concern in your life. Write an essay in which you reflect on this concern. To what extent have you been successful in maintaining a positive self-image in the face of discrimination and self-doubt?

EMILY DICKINSON

Emily Dickinson (1830–1886), hailed as one of the greatest American poets, was born in Amherst, Massachusetts, into a Calvinist household. Her father was a lawyer prominent in civic affairs, affording her the opportunity to meet many of the history-making personalities of the day. Nevertheless, by the time she was thirty, Dickinson had become a virtual recluse in her father's home. She renounced her family's religion, yet continued to mourn the loss of the spiritual refuge it offered. This tension in her own nature likened her to such contemporary poets as Ralph Waldo Emerson and Henry David Thoreau, who perceived a universe at once beautiful and cold and saw its fulfillment in the reconciling of those dualities.

Dickinson's great reputation is based upon 1,775 poems that are read and enjoyed, and studied and analyzed, by those of all ages around the world. All the more startling, then, is the fact that she saw only eleven of those poems published in her lifetime. For her, anonymity was not an altogether undesirable state, however, as she reveals in "I'm Nobody! Who Are You?"

I'm Nobody! Who Are You?

I'm nobody! Who are you?
Are you nobody, too?
Then there's a pair of us—don't tell!
They'd banish us, you know.

How dreary to be somebody!
How public, like a frog,
To tell your name the livelong day
To an admiring bog!

Questions for Study and Discussion

1. Why do you suppose the speaker of the poem does not want you to reveal you are a nobody? To whom does "they" refer in the fourth line? Why does the speaker think "They'd banish us"?

2. Why does the speaker think it "dreary to be somebody" and "To tell your name the livelong day / To an admiring bog"?

3. This poem is often included in collections of children's poetry. Aside

from its rather simple and accessible diction, what makes the poem particularly apt for young readers?

4. How would you describe Dickinson's tone in this poem? Is she resigned, angry, defiant, or something else? How well does her tone suit her meaning?

Writing Topics

1. How important is fame to you? Would you like to become famous one day? Why? In what way would you like to be well known? How do you measure fame? Would you consider yourself "a nobody" if you never became famous? Why, or why not? Write an essay in which you examine fame and its benefits and drawbacks. Draw from your own experience, your reading, and what you learn from the media for examples to illustrate your ideas.

2. Think of a goal you have attained and another goal that you have not been able to reach. Write an essay in which you compare and contrast your feelings about the two experiences. How was the contemplation of success sweeter than its achievement? How was it more bitter?

3. Look further into the life of Emily Dickinson, particularly at the question of her attempts to become a published poet. She has been the subject of a number of biographies, among them a particularly good one by Richard Sewell. Write an essay in which you examine the question of why she was not published more often and what effect that might have had on her poetry and her reputation.

JOHN UPDIKE

John Updike was born in 1932 and grew up in Shillington, Pennsylvania, a small town where his father taught high school. His childhood, described in a sketch called "The Dogwood Tree" (1965), was much like that of millions of other middle-class Americans, and these are typically the characters of his short stories and novels. Like the young man in the following story, Updike carried a rubber-lined bookbag, which from time to time was stolen by girls, one of whom he loved "deeply, but ineffectually." Updike went to Harvard, where he became editor of its undergraduate humor magazine, *The Lampoon*. Later he spent a year at Oxford University in England. Updike has published many short stories, as well as poems, plays, and novels. Four of his best-known novels are about Harry "Rabbit" Angstrom: *Rabbit, Run* (1960), *Rabbit Redux* (1971), *Rabbit Is Rich* (1981), and *Rabbit at Rest* (1990).

"A Sense of Shelter" is from the short story collection *Pigeon Feathers* (1962).

A Sense of Shelter

Snow fell against the high school all day, wet big-flaked snow that did 1
not accumulate well. Sharpening two pencils, William looked down on a parking lot that was a blackboard in reverse; car tires had cut smooth arcs of black into its white, and where the school buses had backed around, there were handsome pairs of arabesque V's. The snow, though at moments it whirled opaquely, could not quite bleach these scars away. The temperature must be exactly 32°. The window was open a crack, and a canted pane of glass lifted outdoor air into his face, coating the cedarwood smell of pencil shavings with the transparent odor of the wet window sill. With each revolution of the handle his knuckles came within a fraction of an inch of the tilted glass, and the faint chill this proximity breathed on them sharpened his already acute sense of shelter.

The sky behind the shreds of snow was stone-colored. The murk inside 2
the high classroom gave the air a solidity that limited the overhead radiance to its own vessels; six globes of dull incandescence floated on the top of a thin sea. The feeling the gloom gave him was not gloomy, it was joyous: he felt they were all sealed in, safe; the colors of cloth were dyed deeper, the sound of whispers was made more distinct, the smells of tablet papers and wet shoes and varnish and face powder pierced him with a vivid sense of posses-

sion. These were his classmates sealed in, his, the stupid as well as the clever, the plain as well as the lovely, his enemies as well as his friends, his. He felt like a king and seemed to move to his seat between the bowed heads of subjects that loved him less than he loved them. His seat was sanctioned by tradition; for twelve years he had sat at the rear of classrooms, William Young, flanked by Marsha Wyckoff and Andy Zimmerman. Once there had been two Zimmermans, but one went to work in his father's greenhouse, and in some classes—Latin and Trig—there were none, and William sat at the edge of the class as if on the lip of a cliff, and Marsha Wyckoff became Marvin Wolf or Sandra Wade, but it was always the same desk, whose surface altered from hour to hour but from whose blue-stained ink-hole his mind could extract, like a chain of magician's handkerchiefs, a continuity of years. As a senior he was a kind of king, and as a teacher's pet another kind, a puppet king, who had gathered in appointive posts and even, when the moron vote split between two football heroes, some elective ones. He was not popular, he had never had a girl, his intense friends of childhood had drifted off into teams and gangs, and in large groups—when the whole school, for instance, went in the fall to the beautiful, dung-and-cotton-candy-smelling county fair—he was always an odd man, without a seat on the bus home. But exclusion is itself a form of inclusion. He even had a nickname: Mip, because he stuttered. Taunts no longer much frightened him; he had come late into his inheritance of size, but this summer it had arrived, and he at last stood equal with his enormous, boisterous parents, and had to unbutton his shirt cuffs to get his wrists through them, and discovered he could pick up a basketball with one hand. So, his long legs blocking two aisles, he felt regal even in size and, almost trembling with happiness under the high globes of light beyond whose lunar glow invisible snowflakes were drowning on the gravel roof of his castle, believed that the long delay of unpopularity had been merely a consolidation, that he was at last strong enough to make his move. Today he must tell Mary Landis he loved her.

He had loved her since, a fat-faced toughie with freckles and green 3 eyes, she deftly stole his rubber-lined schoolbag on the walk back from second grade along Jewett Street and outran him—simply had better legs. The superior speed a boy was supposed to have failed to come; his kidneys burned with panic. In front of the grocery store next to her home she stopped and turned. She was willing to have him catch up. This humiliation on top of the rest was too much to bear. Tears broke in his throat; he spun around and ran home and threw himself on the floor of the front parlor, where his grandfather, feet twiddling, perused the newspaper and soliloquized all morning. In time the letter slot rustled, and the doorbell rang, and his mother and Mary exchanged the schoolbag and polite apologies. Their gentle voices had been to him, lying there on the carpet with his head wrapped in his arms, indistinguishable. Mother had always liked Mary. From when she had been a tiny girl dancing along the hedge on the end of an older sister's arm, Mother had liked her. Out of all the children that flocked, similar as pigeons, around the neighborhood, Mother's heart had reached out with claws and fastened on Mary. He never took the schoolbag to school again, had refused to touch it. He supposed it was still in the attic, still faintly smelling of pink rubber.

The buzzer sounded the two-minute signal. In the middle of the class- 4 room Mary Landis stood up, a Monitor badge pinned to her belt. She wore a lavender sweater with the sleeves pushed up to expose her forearms, a deli-cately cheap effect. Wild stories were told about her; perhaps it was merely his knowledge of these that put the hardness in her face. Her eyes in their shape seemed braced for squinting and their green was frosted. Her freckles had faded. William thought she laughed less this year; now that she was in the Secretarial Course and he in the College Preparatory, he saw her in only one class a day, this one, English. She stood a second, eclipsed at the thighs by Jack Stephens' shoulders, looking back at the room with a stiff glance, as if she had seen the same faces too many times before. Her habit of perfect posture emphasized the angularity she had grown into; there was a nervous edge, a boxiness in her bones, that must have been waiting all along under the childish fat. Her eye sockets were deeply indented and her chin had a prim square set that seemed defiant to him. Her brown skirt was snug and straight; she had less hips than bosom, and thin, athletic legs. Her prolonged chest poised, she sauntered up the aisle and encountered a leg thrown in her path. She stared down until it withdrew; she was used to such attentions. As she went out the door, somebody she saw in the hall made her smile, a wide smile full of warmth and short white teeth, and love scooped at his heart. He would tell her.

In another minute, the second bell rasped. Shuffling through the per- 5 fumed crowds to his next class, he crooned to himself, in the slow, over-enunciated manner of the Negro vocalist who had brought the song back this year,

Lah-vender blue, dilly dilly,
Lavendih green-een;
Eef I were king, dilly dilly,
You would: be queen.

The song gave him an exultant sliding sensation that intertwined with 6 the pleasures of his day. He knew all the answers, he had done all the work, the teachers called upon him only to rebuke the ignorance of the others. In Trig and Soc Sci both it was this way. In gym, the fourth hour of the morning, he, who was always picked near the last, startled his side by excelling at volleyball, leaping like a madman, shouting like a bully. The ball felt light as a feather against his big bones. His hair wet from the shower, he walked in the icy air to Luke's Luncheonette, where he ate three hamburg-ers in a booth with three juniors. There was Barry Kruppman, a tall, thyroid-eyed boy who came on the school bus from the country town of Bowsville and was an amateur hypnotist and occultist; he told them about a Portland, Oregon, businessman who under hypnosis had been taken back through sixteen reincarnations to the condition of an Egyptian concubine in the household of a high priest of Isis. There was his friend Lionel Griffin, a pudgy simp whose blond hair stood out above his ears in two slick waxed wings. He was supposed to be a fairy, and in fact did seem most excited by the transvestite aspect of the soul's transmigration. And there was Lionel's girl, Virginia, a drab little mystery who chain-smoked Herbert Tareytons and never said anything. She had sallow skin, and Lionel kept jabbing her and shrieking. William would rather have sat with members of his own class, who filled the other booths, but he would have had to force himself on them. These juniors admired him and welcomed his company. He asked, "Wuh-well, was he ever a c-c-c-cockroach, like Archy?"

Kruppman's face grew intense; his furry lids drooped down over the bulge of his eyes, and when they drew back, his pupils were as small and hard as BBs. "That's the really interesting thing. There was this gap, see, between his being a knight under Charlemagne and then a sailor on a ship putting out from Macedonia—that's where Yugoslavia is now—in the time of Nero; there was this gap when the only thing the guy would do was walk around the office snarling and growling, see, like this." Kruppman worked his blotched ferret face up into a snarl and Griffin shrieked. "He tried to bite one of the assistants and they think that for six hundred years"—the uncanny, unhealthy seriousness of his whisper hushed Griffin momentarily—"for six hundred years he just was a series of wolves. Probably in the German forests. You see, when he was in Macedonia"—his whisper barely audible—"he murdered a woman." 7

Griffin squealed with pleasure and cried, "Oh, Kruppman! Kruppman, how you do go on!" and jabbed Virginia in the arm so hard a Herbert Tareyton jumped from her hand and bobbled across the Formica table. 8

The crowd at the soda bar had thinned and when the door to the outside opened he saw Mary come in and stand there for a second where the smoke inside and the snow outside swirled together. The mixture made a kind of— Kruppman's ridiculous story had put the phrase in his head—wolf-weather, and she was just a gray shadow against it. She bought a pack of cigarettes from Luke and went out again, a kerchief around her head, the pneumatic thing above the door hissing behind her. For a long time, always in fact, she had been at the center of whatever gang was the best one: in the second grade the one that walked home up Jewett Street together, and in the sixth grade the one that went bicycling as far away as the quarry and the Rentschler estate and played touch football Saturday afternoons, and in the ninth grade the one that went rollerskating at Candlebridge Park with the tenth-grade boys, and in the eleventh grade the one that held parties lasting past midnight and that on Sundays drove in caravans as far as Philadelphia and back. And all the while there had been a succession of boy friends, first Jack Stephens and Fritz March 9 in their class and then boys a grade ahead and then Barrel Lord, who was a senior when they were sophomores and whose name was in the newspapers all football season, and then this last summer someone out of the school alto-gether, a man she met while working as a waitress in the city of Alton. So this year her weekends were taken up, and the party gang carried on as if she had never existed, and nobody saw her much except in school and when she stopped by in Luke's to buy a pack of cigarettes. Her silhouette against the big window had looked wan, her head hooded, her face nibbled by light, her fingers fiddling on the glass counter with her coins. He yearned to reach out, to comfort her, but he was wedged deep in the shrill booths, between the jingling guts of the pinball machine and the hillbilly joy of the jukebox. The impulse left him with a disagreeable feeling. He had loved her too long to want to pity her; it endangered the investment of worship on which he had not yet realized any return.

The two hours of the school afternoon held Latin and a study hall. In   10
study hall, while the five people at the table with him played tick-tack-toe and sucked cough drops and yawned, he did all his homework for the next day. He prepared thirty lines of Vergil, Aeneas in the Underworld. The study hall was a huge low room in the basement of the building; its coziness crept into Tartarus. On the other side of the fudge-colored wall the circular saw in the woodworking shop whined and gasped and then whined again; it bit off pieces of wood with a rising, terrorized inflection—*bzzzzzup!* He solved ten problems in trigonometry. His mind cut nearly through their knots and separated them, neat stiff squares of correctness, one by one from the long but finite plank of problems that connected Plane with Solid Geometry. Lastly, as the snow on a ragged slant drifted down into the cement pits outside the steel-mullioned windows, he read a short story by Edgar Allan Poe. He closed the book softly on the pleasing sonority of its final note of horror, gazed at the red, wet, menthol-scented inner membrane of Judy Whipple's yawn, rimmed with flaking pink lipstick, and yielded his con-science to the snug sense of his work done, of the snow falling, of the warm minutes that walked through their shelter so slowly. The perforated acoustic tiling above his head seemed the lining of a long tube that would go all the way: high school merging into college, college into graduate school, graduate school into teaching at a college—section man, assistant, associate, *full* professor, possessor of a dozen languages and a thousand books, a man bril-liant in his forties, wise in his fifties, renowned in his sixties, revered in his seventies, and then retired, sitting in a study lined with acoustical books until the time for the last transition from silence to silence, and he would die, like Tennyson, with a copy of "Cymbeline" beside him on the moon-drenched bed.

After school he had to go to Room 101 and cut a sports cartoon into a   11
stencil for the school paper. He liked the building best when it was nearly empty. Then the janitors went down the halls sowing seeds of red wax and

making an immaculate harvest with broad brooms, gathering all the fluff and hairpins and wrappers and powder that the animals had dropped that day. The basketball team thumped in the hollow gymnasium; the cheerleaders rehearsed behind drawn curtains on the stage. In Room 101 two giggly typists with stripes bleached into their hair banged away between mistakes. At her desk Mrs. Gregory, the faculty sponsor, wearily passed her pencil through misspelled news copy. William took the shadow box from the top of the filing cabinet and the styluses and shaders from their drawer and the typed stencils from the closet where they hung, like fragile blue scarves, on hooks. "B-BALLERS BOW, 57-42," was the headline. He drew a tall b-baller bowing to a stumpy pagan idol, labeled "W" for victorious Weiserton High, and traced it in the soft blue wax with a fine loop stylus. His careful breath grazed his fingers. His eyebrows frowned while his heart throbbed happily on the giddy prattle of the typists. The shadow box was simply a plastic frame holding a pane of glass and lifted at one end by two legs so the light bulb, fitted in a tin tray, could slide under; it was like a primitive lean-to sheltering a fire. As he worked, his eyes smarting, he mixed himself up with the light bulb, felt himself burning under a slanting roof upon which a huge hand scratched. The glass grew hot; the danger in the job was pulling the softened wax with your damp hand, distorting or tearing the typed letters. Sometimes the center of an o stuck to your skin like a bit of blue confetti. But he was expert and cautious. He returned the things to their places feeling airily tall, heightened by Mrs. Gregory's appreciation, which she expressed by keeping her back turned, in effect saying that other staff members were undependable but William did not need to be watched.

In the hall outside Room 101 only the shouts of a basketball scrimmage reverberated; the chant of the cheerleaders had been silenced. Though he had done everything, he felt reluctant to leave. Neither of his parents would be home yet. Since the death of his grandfather, both worked in Alton, and this building was as much his home. He knew all its nooks. On the second floor of the annex, beyond the art room, there was a strange, narrow boys' lavatory that no one ever seemed to use. It was here one time that Barry Kruppman tried to hypnotize him and thus cure his stuttering. Kruppman's voice purred and his irises turned tiny in the bulging whites, and for a moment William felt himself lean backward involuntarily, but he was distracted by the bits of bloodshot pink in the corners of these portentous eyes, the folly of giving up his will to an intellectual inferior occurred to him; he refused to let go and go under, and perhaps therefore his stuttering had continued.

The frosted window at the end of the long room cast a watery light on the green floor and made the porcelain urinals shine like slices of moon. The semiopacity of this window gaze great denseness to the room's feeling of secrecy. William washed his hands with close attention, enjoying the lavish amount of powdered soap provided for him in this castle. He studied his face in the mirror, making infinitesimal adjustments to attain the absolutely most flattering angle, and then put his hands below his throat to get their strong, long-fingered beauty into the picture. As he walked toward the door he sang, closing his eyes and gasping as if he were a real Negro whose entire career depended upon this recording.

Who—told me so, dilly dilly,
Who told me soho?
Aii told myself, dilly dilly,
I told: me so.

When he emerged into the hall it was not empty: one girl walked down its varnished perspective toward him, Mary Landis, in a heavy brown coat, with a scarf on her head and books in her arms. Her locker was up here, on the second floor of the annex. His own was in the annex basement. A ticking sensation that existed neither in the medium of sound nor of light crowded against his throat. She flipped the scarf back from her hair and in a conversational voice that carried well down the clean panes of the hall said, "Hi, Billy." The name came from way back, when they were both children, and made him feel small but brave.

"Hi. How are you?"

"Fine." Her smile broadened.

What was so funny? Was she really, as it seemed, pleased to see him? "Du-did you get get through cheer-cheer-cheerleading?"

"Yes. Thank God. *Oh* she's so awful. She makes us do the same stupid locomotives for every cheer; I told her, no wonder nobody cheers any more."

"This is M-M-Miss Potter?" He blushed, feeling that he made an ugly face in getting past the "M." When he got caught in the middle of a sentence the constriction was somehow worse. He admired the way words poured up her throat, distinct and petulant.

"Yes, Potbottom Potter," she said. "She's just aching for a man and takes it out on us. I wish she would get one. Honestly, Billy, I have half a mind to quit. I'll be so glad when June comes, I'll never set foot in this idiotic building again."

Her lips, pale with the lipstick worn off, crinkled bitterly. Her face, foreshortened from the height of his eyes, looked cross as a cat's. He was a little shocked that poor Miss Potter and this kind, warm school stirred her to what he had to take as actual anger; this grittiness in her was the first abrasive texture he had struck today. Couldn't she see around teachers, into their fatigue, their poverty, their fear? It had been so long since he had spoken to her, he didn't know how insensitive she had become. "Don't quit," he brought out of his mouth at last. "It'd be n-n-nuh—it'd be nothing without you."

He pushed open the door at the end of the hall for her and as she passed under his arm she looked up and said, "Why, aren't you sweet."

The stair well, all asphalt and iron, smelled of galoshes. It felt more   23
private than the hall, more specially theirs; there was something magical in
its shifting multiplicity of planes as they descended that lifted the spell on his
tongue, so that words came as quickly as his feet pattered on the steps.

"No, I mean it," he said, "you're really a beautiful cheerleader. But   24
then you're beautiful period."

"I have skinny legs."   25

"Who told you that?"   26

"Somebody."   27

"Well, *he* wasn't very sweet."   28

"No."   29

"Why do you hate this poor old school?"   30

"Now, Billy. You know you don't care about this junky place any more   31
than I do."

"I love it. It breaks my heart to hear you say you want to get out,   32
because then I'll never see you again."

"You don't care, do you?"   33

"Why *sure* I care you *know*"—their feet stopped; they had reached the   34
bottom, the first-floor landing, two brass-barred doors and a grimy radiator—
"I've always li-loved you."

"You don't mean that."   35

"I do too. It's ridiculous but there it is. I wanted to tell you today and   36
now I have."

He expected her to go out of the door in derision but instead she   37
showed a willingness to discuss this awkward matter. He should have realized
before this that women enjoy being talked to. "It's a very silly thing to say,"
she asserted tentatively.

"I don't see why," he said, fairly bold now that he couldn't seem more   38
ridiculous, and yet picking his words with a certain strategic care. "It's not
that silly to love somebody, I mean what the hell. Probably what's silly is not
to do anything about it for umpteen years but then I never had an opportunity, I thought."

He set his books down on the radiator and she set hers down beside his.   39
"What kind of opportunity were you waiting for?"

"Well, see, that's it; I didn't know." He wished, in a way, she'd go out   40
the door. But she had propped herself against the wall and plainly expected
him to keep talking. "Yuh-you were such a queen and I was such a nothing
and I just didn't really want to presume." It wasn't very interesting; he was
puzzled that she seemed to be interested. Her face had grown quite stern, the
mouth very small and thoughtful, and he made a gesture with his hands
intended to release her from the bother of thinking about it; after all, it was
just a disposition of his heart, nothing permanent or expensive; maybe it was
just his mother's idea anyway. Half in impatience to close the account, he
asked, "Will you marry me?"

"You don't want to marry me," she said. "You're going to go on and be a   41
great man."

He blushed in pleasure; is this how she saw him, is this how they all   42
saw him, as worthless now but in time a great man? "No, I'm not," he said,
"but anyway, you're great now. You're so pretty, Mary."

"Oh, Billy," she said, "if you were me for just one day you'd hate it."   43

She said this rather blankly, watching his eyes; he wished her voice had   44
shown more misery. In his world of closed surfaces a panel, carelessly pushed,
had opened, and he hung in this openness paralyzed, unable to think what to
say. Nothing he could think of quite fitted the abruptly immense context.
The radiator cleared its throat; its heat made, in the intimate volume just on
this side of the doors on whose windows the snow beat limply, a provocative
snugness; he supposed he should try, and stepped forward, his hands lifting
toward her shoulders. Mary side-stepped between him and the radiator and
put the scarf back on, lifting the cloth like a broad plaid halo above her head
and then wrapping it around her chin and knotting it so she looked, in her
red galoshes and bulky coat, like a peasant woman in a European movie.
With her thick hair swathed, her face seemed pale and chunky, and when
she recradled the books in her arms her back bent humbly under the point of
the kerchief. "It's too hot in here," she said. "I have to wait for somebody."
The disconnectedness of the two statements seemed natural in the fragmented atmosphere his stops and starts had produced. She bucked the brass
bar with her shoulder and the door slammed open; he followed her into the
weather.

"For the person who thinks your legs are too skinny?"   45

"Uh-huh." As she looked up at him a snowflake caught on the lashes of   46
one eye. She jerkily rubbed that cheek on the shoulder of her coat and
stamped a foot, splashing slush. Cold water gathered on the back of his shirt.
He put his hands in his pockets and pressed his arms against his sides to keep
from shivering.

"Thuh-then you wo-wo-won't marry me?" His wise instinct told him   47
the only way back was by going forward, through absurdity.

"We don't know each other," she said.   48

"My God," he said. "Why not? I've known you since I was two."   49

"What do you know about me?"   50

This awful seriousness of hers; he must dissolve it. "That you're not a   51
virgin." But instead of making her laugh, this made her face go dead and
turned it away. Like beginning to kiss her, it had been a mistake; in part, he felt
grateful for his mistakes. They were like loyal friends, who are nevertheless
embarrassing. "What do you know about *me*?" he asked, setting himself up for
a finishing insult but dreading it. He hated the stiff feel of his smile between
his cheeks; glimpsed, as if the snow were a mirror, how hateful he looked.

"That you're basically very nice."   5

Her returning good for evil blinded him to his physical discomfort, set   53
him burning with regret. "Listen," he said, "I did love you. Let's at least get
that straight."

"You never loved anybody," she said. "You don't know what it is."   54
"O.K.," he said. "Pardon me."   55
"You're excused."   56
"You better wait in the school," he said. "He's-eez-eez going to be a   57
long time."

She didn't answer and walked a little distance, toeing out in the   58
childish way common to the women of the county, along the slack cable that
divided the parking lot from the softball field. One bicycle, rusted as if it had
been there for years, leaned in the rack, its fenders supporting thin crescents
of white.

The warmth inside the door felt heavy, like a steamed towel laid   59
against his face. William picked up his books and ran his pencil along the
black ribs of the radiator before going down the stairs to his locker in the
annex basement. The shadows were thick at the foot of the steps; suddenly it
felt late, he must hurry and get home. He had the irrational fear they were
going to lock him in. The cloistered odors of paper, sweat, and, from the
woodshop at the far end of the basement hall, sawdust were no longer
delightful to him. The tall green double lockers appeared to study him
through the three air slits near their tops. When he opened his locker, and
put his books on his shelf, below Marvin Wolf's, and removed his coat from
his hook, his self seemed to crawl into the long dark space thus made vacant,
the ugly, humiliated, educable self. In answer to a flick of his great hand the
steel door weightlessly slammed shut, and through the length of his body he
felt so clean and free he smiled. Between now and the happy future predicted
for him he had nothing, almost literally nothing to do.

Questions for Study and Discussion

1. How does William see himself—what kind of person does he think he
is? Use specific details from the story to support your answer.
2. What kind of person is Mary Landis? Is she as William sees her? What
is it about Mary that attracts him to her? Why does William feel that he must tell
her he loves her?
3. Look back at the conversation between Mary and William. What is
each thinking at each point in the conversation? How do you know? Are there
any points where you cannot interpret their thoughts?
4. Updike tells his story from William's point of view, but in the third
person. What is the advantage of this narrative strategy? Could Updike have
used a different strategy as effectively? For example, could he have used the first-
person point of view? Why, or why not?

5. Consider the story's title, "A Sense of Shelter." How does it fit the story? Who is being sheltered, by what, and from what?

6. In the last paragraph we are given William's response to his conversation with Mary. What is his response?

Writing Topics

1. William Young's attitude toward school embodies his attitude toward life and his plans for the future. How do your feelings toward school and your classmates relate to your ambitions and your view of life?

2. What is love? Use whatever examples you like in your definition, whether from your own experience or from psychology, literature, or some other field.

3. The years of adolescence are a crucial period in the development of one's personality, and they have been much studied by psychologists. Consulting a textbook in the psychology of adolescence if you like, choose an expert of the subject that interests you and investigate what psychologists have to say about it.

Turning Points

LANGSTON HUGHES

Langston Hughes was born in 1902 in Joplin, Missouri, and though he began
writing poetry at an early age, he was at first unable to get his work published
and supported himself by traveling about the country, doing whatever work he
could find. He was working as a busboy when his poetry was discovered in 1925
by Vachel Lindsay, a famous poet of the time. A year later Hughes published his
first book of poems, *The Weary Blues,* and entered Lincoln University in
Pennsylvania. He graduated in 1929 and set about making his way as a writer.
Hughes's work focuses on African-American life, often incorporating dialect and
jazz rhythms. His writings include novels, plays, and a popular series of newspaper
sketches, but his reputation rests most solidly on his poems. Much of his finest
poetry has been collected as *Selected Poems* (1959). He died in 1967.

In this selection taken from his autobiography, *The Big Sea* (1940), Hughes
narrates his experiences at a church revival meeting he attended when he was
twelve years old.

Salvation

I was saved from sin when I was going on thirteen. But not really saved.   1
It happened like this. There was a big revival at my Auntie Reed's church.
Every night for weeks there had been much preaching, singing, praying, and
shouting, and some very hardened sinners had been brought to Christ, and
the membership of the church had grown by leaps and bounds. Then just
before the revival ended, they held a special meeting for children, "to bring
the young lambs to the fold." My aunt spoke of it for days ahead. That night
I was escorted to the front row and placed on the mourners' bench with all
the other young sinners, who had not yet been brought to Jesus.

My aunt told me that when you were saved you saw a light, and   2
something happened to you inside! And Jesus came into your life! And God
was with you from then on! She said you could see and hear and feel Jesus in
your soul. I believe her. I have heard a great many old people say the same
thing and it seemed to me they ought to know. So I sat there calmly in the
hot, crowded church, waiting for Jesus to come to me.

The preacher preached a wonderful rhythmical sermon, all moans and   3
shouts and lonely cries and dire pictures of hell, and then he sang a song
about the ninety and nine safe in the fold, but one little lamb was left out in
the cold. Then he said: "Won't you come? Won't you come to Jesus? Young
lambs, won't you come?" And he held out his arms to all us young sinners
there on the mourners' bench. And the little girls cried. And some of them
jumped up and went to Jesus right away. But most of us just sat there.

A great many old people came and knelt around us and prayed, old   4
women with jet-black faces and braided hair, old men with work-gnarled
hands. And the church sang a song about the lower lights are burning some
poor sinners to be saved. And the whole building rocked with prayer and
song.

Still I kept waiting to *see* Jesus.   5

Finally all the young people had gone to the altar and were saved, but   6
one boy and me. He was a rounder's son named Westley. Westley and I were
surrounded by sisters and deacons praying. It was very hot in the church, and
getting late now. Finally Westley said to me in a whisper: "God damn! I'm
tired o' sitting here. Let's go up and be saved." So he got up and was saved.

Then I was left all alone on the mourners' bench. My aunt came and   7
knelt at my knees and cried, while prayers and songs swirled all around me in
the little church. The whole congregation prayed for me alone, in a mighty
wail of moans and voices. And I kept waiting serenely for Jesus, waiting,
waiting—but he didn't come. I wanted to see him, but nothing happened to
me. Nothing! I wanted something to happen to me, but nothing happened.

I heard the songs and the minister saying: "Why don't you come? My   8
dear child, why don't you come to Jesus? Jesus is waiting for you. He wants
you. Why don't you come? Sister Reed, what is this child's name?"

"Langston," my aunt sobbed.   9

"Langston, why don't you come? Why don't you come and be saved?   10
Oh, Lamb of God! Why don't you come?"

Now it was really getting late. I began to be ashamed of myself, holding   11
everything up so long. I began to wonder what God thought about Westley,
who certainly hadn't seen Jesus either, but who was now sitting proudly on
the platform, swinging his knickerbockered legs and grinning down at me,
surrounded by deacons and old women on their knees praying. God had not
struck Westley dead for taking his name in vain or for lying in the temple. So
I decided that maybe to save further trouble, I'd better lie, too, and say that
Jesus had come, and get up and be saved.

So I got up.   12

Suddenly the whole room broke into a sea of shouting, as they saw me   13
rise. Waves of rejoicing swept the place. Women leaped in the air. My aunt
threw her arms around me. The minister took me by the hand and led me to
the platform.

When things quieted down, in a hushed silence, punctuated by a few   14 ecstatic "Amens," all the new young lambs were blessed in the name of God. Then joyous singing filled the room.

That night, for the last time in my life but one—for I was a big boy 15 twelve years old—I cried. I cried, in bed alone, and couldn't stop. I buried my head under the quilts, but my aunt heard me. She woke up and told my uncle I was crying because the Holy Ghost had come into my life, and because I had seen Jesus. But I was really crying because I couldn't bear to tell her that I had lied, that I had deceived everybody in the church, that I hadn't see Jesus, and that now I didn't believe there was a Jesus any more, since he didn't come to help me.

Questions for Study and Discussion

1. Why does the young Langston expect to be saved at the revival meeting? Once the children are in church, what appeals are made to them to encourage them to seek salvation?

2. Trace the various pressures working on Hughes that lead to his decision to "get up and be saved." What important realization finally convinces him to lie about being saved?

3. Even though Hughes's account of the events at the revival is at points humorous, the experience was nonetheless painful for him. Why does he cry on the night of his "salvation"? Why does his aunt think he is crying? What significance is there in the disparity between their views?

4. What paradox or apparent contradiction does Hughes present in the first two sentences of the narrative? Why do you suppose he uses this device?

5. What is the function of the third sentence, "It happened like this"?

6. Hughes consciously varies the structure and length of his sentences to create different effects. What effect does he create through the short sentences in paragraph 2 and 3 and the long sentence that concludes the final paragraph? How do the short, one-sentence paragraphs aid him in telling his story?

7. Although Hughes tells most of his story himself, he allows Auntie Reed, the minister, and Westley to speak for themselves. What does Hughes gain by having his characters speak for themselves?

8. How does Hughes's choice of words help to establish a realistic atmosphere for a religious revival meeting? Does he use any traditional religious figures of speech?

9. Why does Hughes italicize the word *see* in paragraph 5? What do you think he means by *see*? What do you think his aunt means by *see*? Explain.

Writing Topics

1. Like the young Langston Hughes, we sometimes find ourselves in situations in which, for the sake of conformity, we do things we do not believe in.

Consider one such experience you have had. What is it about human nature that makes us occasionally act in ways that contradict our inner feelings?

2. In the end of his essay Langston Hughes suffers alone. He cannot bring himself to talk about his dilemma with other people. Why can it be so difficult to seek the help of others? Consider examples from your experience and what you have seen and read about other people.

3. Sometimes the little, insignificant, seemingly trivial experiences in our daily lives can provide the material for narratives that reveal something about ourselves and the world we live in. Select one seemingly trivial event in your life, and write an essay in which you narrate that experience and explain its significance.

E. B. WHITE

Master essayist, storyteller, and poet, Elwyn Brooks White (1899–1985) was born in Mount Vernon, New York, lived some years in New York City, and for many years made his home on a saltwater farm in Maine. After studying at Cornell University, he joined the staff of *The New Yorker* in 1926, where he wrote essays, editorials, anonymous fillers, and even cartoon captions that helped to establish the magazine's and his own reputation for witty and graceful prose. A selection of his essays is available in *The Essays of E. B. White* (1977). He is the author of the classic children's stories *Stuart Little* (1945), *Charlotte's Web* (1952), and *The Trumpet of the Swan* (1970), and he revised William Strunk's celebrated work *The Elements of Style* several times beginning in 1959. "Once More to the Lake," first published in *Harper's* in 1941, is a loving account of a trip White took with his son to the site of his own childhood vacations.

Once More to the Lake

One summer, along about 1904, my father rented a camp on a lake in Maine and took us all there for the month of August. We all got ringworm from some kittens and had to rub Pond's Extract on our arms and legs night and morning, and my father rolled over in a canoe with all his clothes on; but outside of that the vacation was a success and from then on none of us ever thought there was any place in the world like that lake in Maine. We returned summer after summer—always on August 1st for one month. I have since become a salt-water man, but sometimes in summer there are days when the restlessness of the tides and the fearful cold of the sea water and the incessant wind which blows across the afternoon and into the evening make me wish for the placidity of a lake in the woods. A few weeks ago this feeling got so strong I bought myself a couple of bass hooks and a spinner and returned to the lake where we used to go, for a week's fishing and to revisit old haunts.

I took along my son, who had never had any fresh water up his nose and who had seen lily pads only from train windows. On the journey over to the lake I began to wonder what it would be like. I wondered how time would have marred this unique, this holy spot—the coves and streams, the hills that the sun set behind, the camps and the paths behind the camps. I

79

was sure that the tarred road would have found it out and I wondered in what other ways it would be desolated. It is strange how much you can remember about places like that once you allow your mind to return into the grooves which lead back. You remember one thing, and that suddenly reminds you of another thing. I guess I remembered clearest of all the early mornings, when the lake was cool and motionless, remembered how the bedroom smelled of the lumber it was made of and of the wet woods whose scent entered through the screen. The partitions in the camp were thin and did not extend clear to the top of the rooms, and as I was always the first up I would dress softly so as not to wake the others, and sneak out into the sweet outdoors and start out in the canoe, keeping close along the shore in the long shadows of the pines. I remembered being very careful never to rub my paddle against the gunwale for fear of distrubing the stillness of the cathedral.

The lake had never been what you would call a wild lake. There were   3
cottages sprinkled around the shores, and it was in farming country although the shores of the lake were quite heavily wooded. Some of the cottages were owned by nearby farmers, and you would live at the shore and eat your meals at the farmhouse. That's what our family did. But although it wasn't wild, it was a fairly large and undisturbed lake and there were places in it which, to a child at least, seemed infinitely remote and primeval.

I was right about the tar: it led to within half a mile of the shore. But   4
when I got back there, with my boy, and we settled into a camp near a farmhouse and into the kind of summertime I had known, I could tell that it was going to be pretty much the same as it had been before—I knew it, lying in bed the first morning, smelling the bedroom and hearing the boy sneak quietly out and go off along the shore in a boat. I began to sustain the illusion that he was I, and therefore, by simple transposition, that I was my father. This sensation persisted, kept cropping up all the time we were there. It was not an entirely new feeling, but in this setting it grew much stronger. I seemed to be living a dual existence. I would be in the middle of some simple act, I would be picking up a bait box or laying down a table fork, or I would be saying something, and suddenly it would be not I but my father who was saying the words and making the gesture. It gave me a creepy sensation.

We went fishing the first morning. I felt the same damp moss covering   5
the worms in the bait can, and saw the dragonfly alight on the tip of my rod as it hovered a few inches from the surface of the water. It was the arrival of this fly that convinced me beyond any doubt that everything was as it always had been, that the years were a mirage and there had been no years. The small waves were the same, chucking the rowboat under the chin as we fished at anchor, and the boat was the same boat, the same color green and the ribs broken in the same places, and under the floor-boards the same freshwater leavings and débris—the dead helgramite, the wisps of moss, the rusty discarded fishhook, the dried blood from yesterday's catch. We stared silently at the tips of our rods, at the dragonflies that came and went. I

lowered the tip of mine into the water, tentatively, pensively dislodging the fly, which darted two feet away, poised, darted two feet back, and came to rest again a little farther up the rod. There had been no years between the ducking of this dragonfly and the other one—the one that was part of memory. I looked at the boy, who was silently watching his fly, and it was my hands that held his rod, my eyes watching. I felt dizzy and didn't know which rod I was at the end of.

We caught two bass, hauling them in briskly as though they were   6
mackerel, pulling them over the side of the boat in a businesslike manner without any landing net, and stunning them with a blow on the back of the head. When we got back for a swim before lunch, the lake was exactly where we had left it, the same number of inches from the dock, and there was only the merest suggestion of a breeze. This seemed an utterly enchanted sea, this lake you could leave to its own devices for a few hours and come back to, and find that it had not stirred, this constant and trustworthy body of water. In the shallows, the dark, water-soaked sticks and twigs, smooth and old, were undulating in clusters on the bottom against the clean ribbed sand, and the track of the mussel was plain. A school of minnows swam by, each minnow with its small individual shadow, doubling the attendance, so clear and sharp in the sunlight. Some of the other campers were in swimming, along the shore, one of them with a cake of soap, and the water felt thin and clear and unsubstantial. Over the years there had been this person with the cake of soap, this cultist, and here he was. There had been no years.

Up to the farmhouse to dinner through the teeming, dusty field, the   7
road under our sneakers was only a two-track road. The middle track was missing, the one with the marks of the hooves and the splotches of dried flaky manure. There had always been three tracks to choose from in choosing which track to walk in; now the choice was narrowed down to two. For a moment I missed terribly the middle alternative. But the way led past the tennis court, and something about the way it lay there in the sun reassured me; the tape had loosened along the backline, the alleys were green with plantains and other weeds, and the net (installed in June and removed in September) sagged in the dry noon, and the whole place steamed with midday heat and hunger and emptiness. There was a choice of pie for dessert, and one was blueberry and one was apple, and the waitresses were the same country girls, there having been no passage of time, only the illusion of it as in a dropped curtain—the waitresses were still fifteen; their hair had been washed, that was the only difference—they had been to the movies and seen the pretty girls with the clean hair.

Summertime, oh summertime, pattern of life indelible, the fade-proof   8
lake, the woods unshatterable, the pasture with the sweetfern and the juniper forever and ever, summer without end; this was the background, and the life along the shore was the design, the cottages with their innocent and tranquil design, their tiny docks with the flagpole and the American flag

floating against the white clouds in the blue sky, the little paths over the roots of the trees leading from camp to camp and the paths leading back to the outhouses and the can of lime for sprinkling, and at the souvenir counters at the store the miniature birch-bark canoes and the post cards that showed things looking a little better than they looked. This was the American family at play, escaping the city heat, wondering whether the newcomers in the camp at the head of the cove were "common" or "nice," wondering whether it was true that the people who drove up for Sunday dinner at the farmhouse were turned away because there wasn't enough chicken.

It seemed to me, as I kept remembering all this, that those times and 9 those summers had been infinitely precious and worth saving. There had been jollity and peace and goodness. The arriving (at the beginning of August) had been so big a business in itself, at the railway station the farm wagon drawn up, the first smell of the pine-laden air, the first glimpse of the smiling farmer, and the great importance of the trunks and your father's enormous authority in such matters, and the feel of the wagon under you for the long ten-mile haul, and at the top of the last long hill catching the first view of the lake after eleven months of not seeing this cherished body of water. The shouts and cries of other campers when they saw you, and the trunks to be unpacked, to give up their rich burden. (Arriving was less exciting nowadays, when you sneaked up in your car and parked it under a tree near the camp and took out the bags and in five minutes it was all over, no fuss, no loud wonderful fuss about trunks.)

Peace and goodness and jollity. The only thing that was wrong now, 10 really, was the sound of the place, an unfamiliar nervous sound of the outboard motors. This was the note that jarred, the one thing that would sometimes break the illusion and set the years moving. In those other summertimes all motors were inboard; and when they were at a little distance, the noise they made was a sedative, an ingredient of summer sleep. They were one-cylinder and two-cylinder engines, and some were make-and-break and some were jump-spark, but they all made a sleepy sound across the lake. The one-lungers throbbed and fluttered, and the twin-cylinder ones purred and purred, and that was a quiet sound too. But now the campers all had outboards. In the daytime, in the hot mornings, these motors made a petulant, irritable sound; at night, in the still evening when the afterglow lit the water, they whined about one's ears like mosquitoes. My boy loved our rented outboard, and his great desire was to achieve singlehanded mastery over it, and authority, and he soon learned the trick of choking it a little (but not too much), and the adjustment of the needle valve. Watching him I would remember the things you could do with the old one-cylinder engine with the heavy flywheel, how you could have it eating out of your hand if you got really close to it spiritually. Motor boats in those days didn't have clutches, and you would make a landing by shutting off the motor at the proper time and coasting in with a dead rudder. But there was a way of reversing them, if you learned the trick, by cutting the switch and putting it on again exactly on the final dying revolution of the flywheel, so that it would kick back against compression and begin reversing. Approaching a dock in a strong following breeze, it was difficult to slow up sufficiently by the ordinary coasting method, and if a boy felt he had complete mastery over his motor, he was tempted to keep it running beyond its time and then reverse it a few feet from the dock. It took a cool nerve, because if you threw the switch a twentieth of a second too soon you could catch the flywheel when it still had speed enough to go up past center, and the boat would leap ahead, charging bull-fashion at the dock.

We had a good week at the camp. The bass were biting well and the 11 sun shone endlessly, day after day. We would be tired at night and lie down in the accumulated heat of the little bedrooms after the long hot day and the breeze would stir almost imperceptibly outside and the smell of the swamp drift in through the rusty screens. Sleep would come easily and in the morning the red squirrel would be on the roof tapping out his gay routine. I kept remembering everything, lying in bed in the mornings—the small steamboat that had a long rounded stern like the lip of a Ubangi,[1] and how quietly she ran on the moonlight sails, when the older boys played their mandolins and the girls sang and we ate doughnuts dipped in sugar, and how sweet the music was on the water in the shining night, and what it had felt like to think about girls then. After breakfast we would go up to the store and the things were in the same place—the minnows in a bottle, the plugs and spinners disarranged and pawed over by the youngsters from the boys' camp, the fig newtons and the Beeman's gum. Outside, the road was tarred and cars stood in front of the store. Inside, all was just as it had always been, except there was more Coca-Cola and not so much Moxie and root beer and birch beer and sarsaparilla. We would walk out with a bottle of pop apiece and sometimes the pop would backfire up our noses and hurt. We explored the streams, quietly, where the turtles slid off the sunny logs and dug their way into the soft bottom; and we lay on the town wharf and fed worms to the tame bass. Everywhere we went I had trouble making out which was I, the one walking at my side, the one walking in my pants.

One afternoon while we were there at that lake a thunderstorm came 12 up. It was like the revival of an old melodrama that I had seen long ago with childish awe. The second-act climax of the drama of the electrical disturbance over a lake in America had not changed in any important respect. This was the big scene, still the big scene. The whole thing was so familiar, the first feeling of oppression and heat and a general air around camp of not wanting to go very far away. In midafternoon (it was all the same) a curious darkening of the sky, and a lull in everything that had made life tick; and then the way the boats suddenly swung the other way at their moorings with

---

[1] A member of an African tribe whose lower lip is stretched around a wooden, platelike disk.

the coming of a breeze out of the new quarter, and the premonitory rumble. Then the kettle drum, then the snare and then the bass drum and cymbals, then crackling light against the dark, and the gods grinning and licking their chops in the hills. Afterward the calm, the rain steadily rustling in the calm lake, the return of light and hope and spirits, and the campers running out in joy and relief to go swimming in the rain, their bright cries perpetuating the deathless joke about how they were getting simply drenched, and the children screaming with delight at the new sensation of bathing in the rain, and the joke about getting drenched linking the generations in a strong indestructible chain. And the comedian who waded in carrying an umbrella.

When the others went swimming my son said he was going in too. He   13 pulled his dripping trunks from the line where they had hung all through the shower, and wrung them out. Languidly, and with no thought of going in, I watched him, his hard little body, skinny and bare, saw him wince slightly as he pulled up around his vitals the small, soggy, icy garment. As he buckled the swollen belt suddenly my groin felt the chill of death.

Questions for Study and Discussion

1. The first three paragraphs introduce White's essay. Taken together, how do they prepare for what follows? What does each paragraph contribute?

2. White returns to the lake wondering whether it will be as he remembers it from his childhood vacations. What remains the same? What significance does White attach to the changes in the road, the waitresses, and the outboard motorboats?

3. In paragraph 4 White tells us, "I began to sustain the illusion that [my son] was I, and therefore, by simple transposition, that I was my father." What first prompts this "illusion"? Where else does White refer to it? How does it affect your understanding of what the week at the lake means to White?

4. In paragraph 12 White describes a late afternoon thunderstorm at the lake. How does White organize his description? What does the metaphor of the old melodrama contribute to that description?

5. What is the tone of this essay, and what does it reveal about White's attitude toward his experience? Has he undergone a process of self-discovery? Give examples to support your answer.

6. The closing sentence takes many readers by surprise. Why did White feel the "chill of death"? Has he prepared for this surprise earlier in the essay? If so, where?

Writing Topics

1. Have you ever returned to a place you once knew well but have not seen in years—a house or a city where you once lived, a school you once

attended, a favorite vacation spot? What memories did the visit bring back? Did you, like White, find that little had changed and feel that time had stood still, or were there many changes? If possible, you might make such a visit, to reflect on what has happened to the place—and to you—since you were last there.

2. What, for you, is the ideal vacation? Where would you go and what would you do? What do you hope and expect that a good vacation will do for you?

3. Write an essay in which you discuss death and when you first became aware of your own mortality.

Actor, radio announcer, humorist, and writer, Jean Shepherd was born in 1929 in Chicago. As an actor he has had four one-man shows and has appeared in off-Broadway plays, and as an announcer he has worked for radio stations in Cincinnati, Philadelphia, and New York. Shepherd has also contributed columns to the *Village Voice* (1960–1967) and to *Car and Driver* (1968–1977), as well as prize-winning fiction to *Playboy*. His published works include *The America of George Ade* (1961); *In God We Trust: All Others Pay Cash* (1967); *Wanda Hickey's Night of Golden Memories and Other Disasters* (1972); *The Ferrari in the Bedroom* (1973); *The Phantom of the Open Hearth* (1977); and *A Fistful of Fig Newtons* (1981).

In the following essay, Shepherd takes us along as he relives a not-so-easily forgotten blind date. In telling his story he displays his considerable talent for evoking a sense of drama, pathos, and humor.

The Endless Streetcar Ride into the Night and the Tinfoil Noose

Mewling, puking babes. That's the way we all start. Damply clinging to   1
someone's shoulder, burping weakly, clawing our way into life. *All* of us.
Then gradually, surely, we begin to divide into two streams, all marching
together up that long yellow brick road of life, but on opposite sides of the
street. One crowd goes on to become the Official people, peering out at us
from television screens, magazine covers. They are forever appearing in
newsreels, carrying attaché cases, surrounded by banks of microphones while
the world waits for their decisions and statements. And the rest of us go on to
become . . . just us.

They are the Prime Ministers, the Presidents, Cabinet Members, Stars,   2
dynamic Molders of the Universe, while we remain forever the onlookers,
the applauders of their real lives.

Forever down in the dark dungeons of our souls we ask ourselves: 3

"How did they get away from me? When did I make that first misstep   4
that took me forever to the wrong side of the street, to become eternally part
of the accursed, anonymous Audience?"

It seems like one minute we're all playing around back of the garage,   5
kicking tin cans and yelling at girls, and the next instant you find yourself
doomed to exist as an office boy in the Mail Room of Life, while another ex-

mewling, puking babe sends down Dicta, says "No comment" to the Press, and lives a real, genuine *Life* on the screen of the world.

Countless sufferers at this hour are spending billions of dollars and endless man hours lying on analysts' couches, trying to pinpoint the exact moment that they stepped off the track and into the bushes forever. 6

It all hinges on one sinister reality that is rarely mentioned, no doubt due to its implacable, irreversible inevitability. These decisions cannot be changed, no matter how many brightly cheerful, buoyantly optimistic books on HOW TO ACHIEVE A RICHER, FULLER, MORE BOUNTIFUL LIFE or SEVEN MAGIC GOLDEN KEYS TO INSTANT DYNAMIC SUCCESS or THE SECRET OF HOW TO BECOME A BILLIONAIRE we read, or how many classes are attended for instruction in handshaking, back slapping, grinning, and making After-Dinner speeches. Joseph Stalin was not a Dale Carnegie graduate. He went all the way. It is an unpleasant truth that is swallowed, if at all, like a rancid, bitter pill. A star is a star; a numberless cipher is a numberless cipher. 7

Even more eerie a fact is that the Great Divide is rarely a matter of talent or personality. Or even luck. Adolf Hitler had a notoriously weak handshake. His smile was, if anything, a vapid mockery. But inevitably his star zoomed higher and higher. Cinema luminaries of the first order are rarely blessed with even the modicum of Talent, and often their physical beauty leaves much to be desired. What is the difference between Us and Them, We and They, the Big Ones and the great, teeming rabble? 8

There are about four times in a man's life, or a woman's, too, for that matter, when unexpectedly, from out of the darkness, the blazing carbon lamp, the cosmic searchlight of Truth shines full upon them. It is how we react to those moments that forever seals our fate. One crowd simply puts on its sunglasses, lights another cigar, and heads for the nearest plush French restaurant in the jazziest section of town, sits down and orders a drink, and ignores the whole thing. While we, the Doomed, caught in the brilliant glare of illumination, see ourselves inescapably for what we are, and from that day on skulk in the weeds, hoping no one else will spot us. 9

Those moments happen when we are least able to fend them off. I caught the first one full in the face when I was fourteen. The fourteenth summer is a magic one for all kids. You have just slid out of the pupa stage, leaving your old baby skin behind, and have not yet become a grizzled, hardened tax-paying beetle. At fourteen you are made of cellophane. You curl easily and everyone can see through you. 10

When I was fourteen, Life was flowing through me in a deep, rich torrent of Castoria. How did I know that the first rocks were just ahead, and I was about to have my keel ripped out on the reef? Sometimes you feel as though you are alone in a rented rowboat, bailing like mad in the darkness with a leaky bailing can. It is important to know that there are at least two billion other ciphers in the same boat, bailing with the same leaky can. They all think they are alone and are crossed with an evil star. They are right. 11

I'm fourteen years old, in my sophomore year at high school. One day   12
Schwartz, my purported best friend, sidled up to me edgily outside of school
while we were waiting on the steps to come in after lunch. He proceeded to
outline his plan:

"Helen's old man won't let me take her out on a date on Saturday night   13
unless I get a date for her girlfriend. A double date. The old coot figures, I
guess, that if there are four of us there won't be no monkey business. Well, how
about it? Do you want to go on a blind date with this chick? I never seen her."

Well. For years I had this principle—absolutely *no* blind dates. I was a   14
man of perception and taste, and life was short. But there is a time in your
life when you have to stop taking and begin to give just a little. For the first
time the warmth of sweet Human Charity brought the roses to my cheeks.
After all, Schwartz was my friend. It was little enough to do, have a blind
date with some no doubt skinny, pimply girl for your best friend. I would do
it for Schwartz. He would do as much for me.

"Okay. Okay, Schwartz."   15

Then followed the usual ribald remarks, feckless boasting, and dirty   16
jokes about dates in general and girls in particular. It was decided that next
Saturday we would go all the way. I had a morning paper route at the time,
and my life savings stood at about $1.80. I was all set to blow it on one big
night.

I will never forget that particular Saturday as long as I live. The air was   17
as soft as the fines of spun silk. The scent of lilacs hung heavy. The catalpa
trees rustled in the early evening breeze from off the Lake. The inner Me
itched in that nameless way, that indescribable way that only the fourteen-
year-old Male fully knows.

All that afternoon I had carefully gone over my wardrobe to select the   18
proper symphony of sartorial brilliance. That night I set out wearing my
magnificent electric blue sport coat, whose shoulders were so wide that they
hung out over my frame like vast, drooping eaves, so wide I had difficulty
going through an ordinary door head-on. The electric blue sport coat that
draped voluminously almost to my knees, its wide lapels flapping soundlessly
in the slightest breeze, My pleated gray flannel slacks began just below my
breastbone and indeed chafed my armpits. High-belted, cascading down
finally to grasp my ankles in a vise-like grip. My tie, indeed one of my most
prized possessions, had been a gift from my Aunt Glenn upon the state
occasion of graduation from eighth grade. It was of a beautiful silky fabric,
silvery pearly colored, four inches wide at the fulcrum, and of such a length
to endanger occasionally my zipper in moments of haste. Hand-painted upon
it was a magnificent blood-red snail.

I had spent fully two hours carefully arranging and rearranging my great   19
mop of wavy hair, into which I had rubbed fully a pound and a half of Greasy
Kid Stuff.

Helen and Schwartz waited on the corner under the streetlight at the   20
streetcar stop near Junie Jo's home. Her name was Junie Jo Prewitt. I won't

forget it quickly, although she has, no doubt, forgotten mine. I walked down the dark street alone, past houses set back off the street, through the darkness, past privet hedges, under elm trees, through air rich and ripe with promise. Her house stood back from the street even farther than the others. It sort of crouched in the darkness, looking out at me, kneeling. Pregnant with Girldom. A real Girlfriend house.

The first faint touch of nervousness filtered through the marrow of my skullbone as I knocked on the door of the screen-enclosed porch. No answer. I knocked again, louder. Through the murky screens I could see faint lights in the house itself. Still no answer. Then I found a small doorbell button buried in the sash. I pressed. From far off in the bowels of the house I heard two chimes "Bong" politely. It sure didn't sound like our doorbell. We had a real ripper that went off like a broken buzz saw, more of BRRRAAAAKKK than a muffled Bong. This was a rich people's doorbell.   21

The door opened and there stood a real, genuine, gold-plated Father: potbelly, underwear shirt, suspenders, and all.   22

"Well?" he asked.   23

For one blinding moment of embarrassment I couldn't remember her name. After all, she was a blind date. I couldn't just say: 24

"I'm here to pick up some girl."   25

He turned back into the house and hollered: 26

"JUNIE JO! SOME KID'S HERE!"   27

"Heh, heh. . . ." I countered.   28

He led me into the living room. It was an itchy house, sticky stucco walls of a dull orange color, and all over the floor this Oriental rug with the design crawling around, making loops and sworls. I sat on an overstuffed chair covered in stiff green mohair that scratched even through my slacks. Little twisty bridge lamps stood everywhere. I instantly began to sweat down the back of my clean shirt. Like I said, it was a very itchy house. It had little lamps sticking out of the walls that looked like phony candles, with phony glass orange flames. The rug started moaning to itself.   29

I sat on the edge of the chair and tried to talk to this Father. He was a Cub fan. We struggled under water for what seemed like an hour and a half, when suddenly I heard someone coming down the stairs. First the feet; then those legs, and there she was. She was magnificent! The greatest-looking girl I ever saw in my life! I have hit the double jackpot! And on a blind date! Great Scot!   30

My senses actually reeled as I clutched the arm of that bilge-green chair for support. Junie Jo Prewitt made Cleopatra look like a Girl Scout!   31

Five minutes later we are sitting in the streetcar, heading toward the bowling alley. I am sitting next to the most fantastic creation in the Feminine department known to Western man. There are the four of us in that long, yellow-lit streetcar. No one else was aboard; just us four. I, naturally, being a trained gentleman, sat on the aisle to protect her from candy wrappers and cigar butts and such. Directly ahead of me, also on the aisle, sat   32

Schwartz, his arm already flung affectionately in a death grip around Helen's neck as we boomed and rattled through the night.

I casually flung my right foot up onto my left knee so that she could see   33
my crepe-soled, perforated, wind-toed, Scotch bluchers with the two-toned laces. I started to work my famous charm on her. Casually, with my practiced offhand, cynical, cutting sardonic humor I told her about how my Old Man had cracked the block in the Oldsmobile, how the White Sox were going to have a good year this year, how my kid brother wet his pants when he saw a snake, how I figured it was going to rain, what a great guy Schwartz was, what a good second baseman I was, how I figured I might go out for football. On and on I rolled, like Old Man River, pausing significantly for her to pick up the conversation. Nothing.

Ahead of us Schwartz and Helen were almost indistinguishable one   34
from the other. They giggled, bit each other's ears, whispered, clasped hands, and in general made me itch even more.

From time to time Junie Jo would bend forward stiffly from the waist   35
and say something I could never quite catch into Helen's right ear.

I told her my great story of the time that Uncle Carl lost his false teeth   36
down the airshaft. Still nothing. Out of the corner of my eye I could see that she had her coat collar turned up, hiding most of her face as she sat silently looking forward past Helen Weathers into nothingness.

I told her about this old lady on my paper route who chews tobacco and   37
roller skates in the backyard every morning. I still couldn't get through to her. Casually I inched my right arm up over the back of the seat behind her shoulders. The acid test. She leaned forward, avoiding my arm, and stayed that way.

"Heh, heh, heh. . . ."   38

As nonchalantly as I could, I retrieved it, battling a giant cramp in my   39
right shoulder blade. I sat in silence for a few seconds, sweating heavily as ahead Schwartz and Helen are going at it hot and heavy.

It was then that I became aware of someone saying something to me. It   40
was an empty car. There was no one else but us. I glanced around, and there it was. Above us a line of car cards looked down on the empty streetcar. One was speaking directly to me, to me alone.

DO YOU OFFEND?

Do I *offend?!*   41

With no warning, from up near the front of the car where the motor-   42
man is steering I see this thing coming down the aisle directly toward *me*. It's coming closer and closer. I can't escape it. It's this blinding, fantastic brilliant, screaming blue light. I am spread-eagled in it. There's a pin sticking through my thorax. I see it all now.

I AM THE BLIND DATE!   43

ME!!   44

I'M the one they're being nice to!   45

I'm suddenly getting fatter, more itchy. My new shoes are like bowling   46
balls with laces; thick, rubber-crepe bowling balls. My great tie that Aunt
Glenn gave me is two feet wide, hanging down to the floor like some crinkly
tinfoil noose. My beautiful hand-painted snail is seven feet high, sitting up
on my shoulder, burping. Great Scot! It is all clear to me in the searing white
light of Truth. My friend Schwartz, I can see him saying to Junie Jo:

"I got this crummy fat friend who never has a date. Let's give him a   47
break and. . . ."

I AM THE BLIND DATE!   48

They are being nice to *me!* She is the one who is out on a Blind Date.   49
A Blind Date that didn't make it.

In the seat ahead, the merriment rose to a crescendo. Helen tittered;   50
Schwartz cackled. The marble statue next to me stared gloomily out into the
darkness as our streetcar rattled on. The ride went on and on.

I AM THE BLIND DATE!   51

I didn't say much the rest of the night. There wasn't much to be said.   52

Questions for Study and Discussion

1. Shepherd develops his long narrative to illustrate his point about turning points in life. What exactly is his point, and where is it stated? In what way is
the blind date episode a moment of truth?

2. Where does Shepherd's narrative begin?

3. What distinction does Shepherd draw between "Official people" and
"just us"? Do you agree with his assessment? Explain.

4. For whom has Shepherd written this essay? How do you know?

5. What event triggers the narrator's moment of insight?

6. Explain Shepherd's title. What is the "tinfoil noose"?

7. What do you know of the narrator from the story he tells? What do you
learn of his appearance? His personality?

8. To what extent does Shepherd use figurative language in his essay? Cite
several examples of metaphors and similes. What do these figures add to his
style?

Writing Topics

1. Shepherd believes that people on average experience four moments of
truth in a lifetime. Moreover, he states that "it is how we react to those moments
that forever seals our fate." From your own experiences, recount one such
moment in your life and how you dealt with it. In retrospect, how do you think
you handled the situation?

2. Write an essay in which you argue for or against Shepherd's assertion
that "Official people" are insensitive to or can simply ignore moments of truth.

SAMUEL H. SCUDDER

Samuel H. Scudder (1837–1911) was a graduate of Williams College and Harvard University and was a university professor and leading scientist of his day. His special field of study was butterflies, grasshoppers, and crickets, and in 1888–1889 he published the results of his thirty years of research on butterflies in *The Butterflies of the Eastern United States and Canada with Special Reference to New England.*

Although the following article about the famous zoologist and geologist Louis Agassiz was first published in 1874, the approach Agassiz took with Scudder and the lesson he imparted to him are as valid for us today as when Scudder first met his great teacher.

Learning to See

It was more than fifteen years ago that I entered the laboratory of Professor Agassiz, and told him I had enrolled my name in the Scientific School as a student of natural history. He asked me a few questions about my object in coming, my antecedents generally, the mode in which I afterwards proposed to use the knowledge I might acquire, and, finally, whether I wished to study any special branch. To the latter I replied that, while I wished to be well grounded in all departments of zoology, I purposed to devote myself specially to insects.

"When do you wish to begin?" he asked.

"Now," I replied.

This seemed to please him, and with an energetic "Very well!" he reached from the shelf a huge jar of specimens in yellow alcohol.

"Take this fish," he said, "and look at it; we call it a haemulon; by and by I will ask what you have seen."

With that he left me, but in a moment returned with explicit instructions as to the care of the object entrusted to me.

"No man is fit to be a naturalist," said he, "who does not know how to take care of specimens."

I was to keep the fish before me in a tin tray, and occasionally moisten the surface with alcohol from the jar, always taking care to replace the stopper tightly. Those were not the days of ground-glass stoppers and elegantly shaped exhibition jars; all the old students will recall the huge neckless glass bottles with their leaky, wax-besmeared corks, half eaten by insects, and begrimed with cellar dust. Entomology was a cleaner science than ichthyology, but the example of the Professor, who had unhesitatingly plunged to the bottom of the jar to produce the fish, was infectious; and though this alcohol had a "very ancient and fishlike smell," I really dared not to show any aversion within these sacred precincts, and treated the alcohol as though it were pure water. Still I was concious of a passing feeling of disappointment, for gazing at a fish did not commend itself to an ardent entomologist. My friends at home, too, were annoyed when they discovered that no amount of eau-de-Cologne would drown the perfume which haunted me like a shadow.

In ten minutes I had seen all that could be seen in that fish, and started 9 in search of the Professor—who had, however, left the Museum; and when I returned, after lingering over some of the odd animals stored in the upper apartment, my specimen was dry all over. I dashed the fluid over the fish as if to resuscitate the beast from a fainting-fit, and looked with anxiety for a return of the normal sloppy appearance. This little excitement over, nothing was to be done but to return to a steadfast gaze at my mute companion. Half an hour passed—an hour—another hour; the fish began to look loathsome. I turned it over and around; looked it in the face—ghastly, from behind, beneath, above, sideways, at a three-quarters' view—just as ghastly. I was in despair; at an early hour I concluded that lunch was necessary; so, with infinite relief, the fish was carefully placed in the jar, and for an hour I was free.

On my return, I learned that Professor Agassiz had been at the Mu- 10 seum, but had gone, and would not return for several hours. My fellow-students were too busy to be disturbed by continued conversation. Slowly I drew forth that hideous fish, and with a feeling of desperation again looked at it. I might not use a magnifying glass; instruments of all kinds were interdicted. My two hands, my two eyes, and the fish; it seemed a most limited field. I pushed my finger down its throat to feel how sharp the teeth were. I began to count the scales in the different rows, until I was convinced that that was nonsense. At last a happy thought struck me—I would draw the fish; and now with surprise I began to discover new features in the creature. Just then the Professor returned.

"That is right," said he, "a pencil is one of the best eyes. I am glad to 11 notice, too, that you keep your specimen wet, and your bottle corked."

With these encouraging words, he added: 12

"Well, what is it like?" 13

He listened attentively to my brief rehearsal of the structure of parts 14 whose names were still unknown to me: the fringed gill-arches and movable operculum; the pores of the head, fleshy lips and lidless eyes; the lateral line, the spinous fins and forked tail; the compressed and arched body. When I had finished, he waited as if expecting more, and then with an air of disappointment:

"You have not looked very carefully; why," he continued more ear-   15
nestly, "you haven't even seen one of the most conspicuous features of the animal, which is as plainly before your eyes as the fish itself; look again, look again!" and he left me to my misery.

I was piqued; I was mortified. Still more of that wretched fish! But now   16
I set myself to my task with a will, and discovered one new thing after another, until I saw how just the Professor's criticism had been. The after-noon passed quickly; and when, toward its close, the Professor inquired:

"Do you see it yet?"   17

"No," I replied, "I am certain I do not, but I see how little I saw   18
before."

"That is the next best," said he, earnestly, "but I won't hear you now;   19
put away your fish and go home; perhaps you will be ready with a better answer in the morning. I will examine you before you look at the fish."

This was disconcerting. Not only must I think of my fish all night,   20
studying, without the object before me, what this unknown but most visible feature might be; but also, without my discoveries, I must give an exact account of them the next day. I had a bad memory; so I walked home by Charles River in a distracted state, with my two perplexities.

The cordial greeting from the Professor the next morning was reassur-   21
ing; here was a man who seemed to be quite as anxious as I that I should see for myself what he saw.

"Do you perhaps mean," I asked, "that the fish has symmetrical sides   22
with paired organs?"

His thoroughly pleased "Of course! Of course!" repaid the wakeful   23
hours of the previous night. After he had discoursed most happily and enthusiastically—as he always did—upon the importance of this point, I ventured to ask what I should do next.

"Oh, look at your fish!" he said, and left me again to my own devices.   24
In a little more than an hour he returned, and heard my new catalogue.

"That is good, that is good!" he repeated; "but that is not all; go on";   25
and so for three long days he placed that fish before my eyes, forbidding me to look at anything else, or to use any artificial aid. "Look, look, look," was his repeated injunction.

The fourth day, a second fish of the same group was placed beside the   26
first, and I was bidden to point out the resemblances and differences between the two; another and another followed, until the entire family lay before me, and a whole legion of jars covered the table and surrounding shelves; the odor had become a pleasant perfume; and even now, the sight of an old, six-inch, worm-eaten cork brings fragrant memories.

The whole group of haemulons was thus brought in review; and, 27
whether engaged upon the dissection of the internal organs, the preparation
and examination of the body framework, or the description of the various
parts, Agassiz's training in the method of observing facts and their orderly
arrangement was ever accompanied by the urgent exhortation not to be
content with them.

"Facts are stupid things," he would say, "until brought into connection 28
with some general law."

At the end of eight months, it was almost with reluctance that I left 29
these friends and turned to insects; but what I had gained by this outside
experience has been of greater value than years of later investigation in my
favorite groups.

This was the best entomological lesson I ever had—a lesson whose 30
influence has extended to the details of every subsequent study; a legacy the
Professor has left me, as he has left it to many others, of inestimable value,
which we could not buy, with which we cannot part.

A year afterward, some of us were amusing ourselves with chalking 31
outlandish beasts on the Museum blackboard. We drew prancing starfishes;
frogs in mortal combat; hydra-headed worms; stately crawfishes, standing on
their tails, bearing aloft umbrellas; and grotesque fishes with gaping mouths
and staring eyes. The Professor came in shortly after, and was as amused as
any at our experiments. He looked at the fishes.

"Haemulons, every one of them," he said; "Mr.——— drew them." 32

True; and to this day, if I attempt a fish, I can draw nothing but 33
haemulons.

Questions for Study and Discussion

1. What important lesson does Scudder learn from his experience with
Professor Agassiz? Where is the lesson referred to in the essay?

2. Briefly describe Professor Agassiz's teaching technique or method.
What about his style made it effective with Scudder? Would it be as effective
today? Explain.

3. How much time did Scudder spend studying haemulons? Was it necessary to spend this amount of time? Could the process have been speeded up with
the use of lectures or textbooks? Explain.

4. How did Scudder happen to draw the fish? How did his drawing the fish
help him better to understand or know the fish? What does Agassiz mean when
he says "a pencil is one of the best eyes"?

5. What in Scudder's diction indicates his attitude toward the experience?
What in Scudder's style and diction shows that this essay was written in the
nineteenth century and not the twentieth?

6. What did Agassiz mean when he said, "Facts are stupid things until
brought into connection with some general law"?

Writing Topics

1. Using Scudder's essay as a model, write about a teacher who had a significant impact or influence on you and your education. What was there in the way this particular teacher approached learning that has stayed with you?

2. Professor Agassiz's comment "a pencil is one of the best eyes" has been echoed by many writers over the years. For example, Anne Morrow Lindbergh has said, "I think best with a pencil in my hand." What for you is the relationship between writing, thinking, and learning? Does your understanding of a subject increase when you write about it? Do you see relationships or connections that you didn't see when reading and talking about a subject?

3. In education, how important do you think it is to find good answers to other people's questions, and how important to learn to ask good questions yourself? Where has the emphasis been in your education so far? Can good question-asking be taught and learned? If so, how? If not, why not?

ROBERT FROST

Robert Frost (1874–1963) was born in San Francisco but moved with his family to Massachusetts when he was eleven, and he became a New Englander through and through. He attended Dartmouth and Harvard briefly, spent some time as a millworker and schoolteacher, and in 1900 moved to a farm in New Hampshire, where he lived most of the rest of his life. From 1912 to 1915 he lived in England, where he published two books of poems that brought him his first critical recognition. He returned to the United States a popular poet and soon became a highly influential one. He taught at Amherst, Dartmouth, Harvard, and the University of Michigan and was awarded several Pulitzer Prizes as well as numerous honors. Among his most celebrated poems are "The Tuft of Flowers" (1913), "Birches" (1916), and "Fire and Ice" (1923); they can be found in *The Poetry of Robert Frost* (1969).

Completed in 1916, "The Road Not Taken" has become a cultural symbol of the difficulty and consequences of making a choice in life. Ostensibly about the choice between two roads that diverge in the woods, the poem, of course, implies much more. As Frost himself said, "I'm always saying something that's just the edge of something more."

The Road Not Taken

Two roads diverged in a yellow wood,
And sorry I could not travel both
And be one traveler, long I stood
And looked down one as far as I could
To where it bent in the undergrowth; 5

Then took the other, as just as fair,
And having perhaps the better claim,
Because it was grassy and wanted wear;
Though as for that the passing there
Had worn them really about the same, 10

And both that morning equally lay
In leaves no step had trodden black.
Oh, I kept the first for another day!
Yet knowing how way leads on to way,
I doubted if I should ever come back. 15

I shall be telling this with a sigh
Somewhere ages and ages hence:

Two roads diverged in a wood, and I—
I took the one less traveled by,
And that has made all the difference.   20

Questions for Study and Discussion

1. Why did the speaker in the poem make the decision that he did? Was it a difficult choice to make? What things did the speaker consider when making his decision?
2. Can the speaker in the poem really tell that he made the right decision? Explain.
3. Metaphorically, what do the roads and the yellow wood signify?
4. What, if anything, does Frost's poem reveal about turning points, those significant decisions that alter the course of our lives?

Writing Topics

1. Compare the sentiments expressed in Frost's twenty-line poem to those expressed in Langston Hughes's autobiographical essay "Salvation" (pp. 75–77). In what ways are they similar; in what ways different?
2. By the time you enter college you have been exposed to poetry and have formed an opinion about it—you either like it, dislike it, or are merely indifferent to it. What is it in poetry, or your own attitudes, that causes you to respond to it as you do?
3. Write an essay in which you examine a choice or decision you made some time ago. Would you make the same choice again? What do you know now that you didn't know then?

KATE CHOPIN

Kate Chopin (1851–1904) was born in St. Louis, Missouri, of Creole-Irish descent. After her marriage she lived in Louisiana where she acquired the intimate knowledge of Creole-Cajun culture that provided the impetus for much of her writing and earned her a reputation as a local colorist. However, her first novel, *The Awakening* (1899), generated scorn and outrage for its explicit depiction of a Southern woman's sexual awakening. Only recently has Chopin been recognized for her literary talent and independence of style and feeling. Besides the novel, her works include two collections of short fiction, *Bayou Folk* (1894) and *A Night in Acadie* (1897). In 1969, *The Complete Works of Kate Chopin* was published by Louisiana State University Press.

"The Story of an Hour" describes the tragic consequences of a woman's feelings of unexpected joy at the news of her husband's death.

The Story of an Hour

Knowing that Mrs. Mallard was afflicted with a heart trouble, great   1
care was taken to break to her as gently as possible the news of her husband's death.

It was her sister Josephine who told her, in broken sentences; veiled   2
hints that revealed in half concealing. Her husband's friend Richards was there, too, near her. It was he who had been in the newspaper office when intelligence of the railroad disaster was received, with Brently Mallard's name leading the list of "killed." He had only taken the time to assure himself of its truth by a second telegram, and had hastened to forestall any less careful, less tender friend in bearing the sad message.

She did not hear the story as many women have heard the same, with a   3
paralyzed inability to accept its significance. She wept at once, with sudden, wild abandonment, in her sister's arms. When the storm of grief had spent itself she went away to her room alone. She would have no one follow her.

There stood, facing the open window, a comfortable, roomy armchair.   4
Into this she sank, pressed down by a physical exhaustion that haunted her body and seemed to reach into her soul.

She could see in the open square before her house the tops of trees that   5
were all aquiver with the new spring life. The delicious breath of rain was in

the air. In the street below a peddler was crying his wares. The notes of a distant song which some one was singing reached her faintly, and countless sparrows were twittering in the eaves.

There were patches of blue sky showing here and there through the 6 clouds that had met and piled one above the other in the west facing her window.

She sat with her head thrown back upon the cushion of the chair, quite 7 motionless, except when a sob came up into her throat and shook her, as a child who has cried itself to sleep continues to sob in its dreams.

She was young, with fair, calm face, whose lines bespoke repression 8 and even a certain strength. But now there was a dull stare in her eyes, whose gaze was fixed away off yonder on one of those patches of blue sky. It was not a glance of reflection, but rather indicated a suspension of intelligent thought.

There was something coming to her and she was waiting for it, fear- 9 fully. What was it? She did not know; it was too subtle and elusive to name. But she felt it, creeping out of the sky, reaching toward her through the sounds, the scents, the color that filled the air.

Now her bosom rose and fell tumultuously. She was beginning to recog- 10 nize this thing that was approaching to possess her, and she was striving to beat it back with her will—as powerless as her two white slender hands would have been.

When she abandoned herself a little whispered word escaped her 11 slightly parted lips. She said it over and over under her breath: "free, free, free!" The vacant stare and the look of terror that had followed it went from her eyes. They stayed keen and bright. Her pulses beat fast, and the coursing blood warmed and relaxed every inch of her body.

She did not stop to ask if it were or were not a monstrous joy that held 12 her. A clear and exalted perception enabled her to dismiss the suggestion as trivial.

She knew that she would weep again when she saw the kind, tender 13 hands folded in death; the face that had never looked save with love upon her, fixed and gray and dead. But she saw beyond that bitter moment a long procession of years to come that would belong to her absolutely. And she opened and spread her arms out to them in welcome.

There would be no one to live for her during those coming years; she 14 would live for herself. There would be no powerful will bending hers in that blind persistence with which men and women believe they have a right to impose a private will upon a fellow-creature. A kind intention or a cruel intention made the act seem no less a crime as she looked upon it in that brief moment of illumination.

And yet she had loved him—sometimes. Often she had not. What did 15 it matter! What could love, the unsolved mystery, count for in face of this possession of self-assertion which she suddenly recognized as the strongest impulse of her being!

"Free! Body and soul free!" she kept whispering. 16

Josephine was kneeling before the closed door with her lips to the 17
keyhole, imploring for admission. "Louise, open the door! I beg; open the door—you will make yourself ill. What are you doing, Louise? For heaven's sake open the door."

"Go away. I am not making myself ill." No; she was drinking in a very 18
elixir of life through that open window.

Her fancy was running riot along those days ahead of her. Spring days, 19
and summer days, and all sorts of days that would be her own. She breathed a quick prayer that life might be long. It was only yesterday she had thought with a shudder that life might be long.

She arose at length and opened the door to her sister's importunities. 20
There was a feverish triumph in her eyes, and she carried herself unwittingly like a goddess of Victory. She clasped her sister's waist and together they descended the stairs. Richards stood waiting for them at the bottom.

Some one was opening the front door with a latchkey. It was Brently 21
Mallard who entered, a little travel-stained, composedly carrying his gripsack and umbrella. He had been far from the scene of accident, and did not even know there had been one. He stood amazed at Josephine's piercing cry; at Richards' quick motion to screen him from the view of his wife.

But Richards was too late. 22

When the doctors came they said she had died of heart disease—of joy 23
that kills.

Questions for Study and Discussion

1. What assumption do Mrs. Mallard's relatives and friends make about her feelings toward her husband? How would you describe her true feelings? What evidence does the author give to bring you to your conclusion?

2. Chopin uses language to create a sensual expression for her feelings. Choose examples of this sensuality from the text and explain the senses they appeal to and in what way. How do these impressions add or detract from the story?

3. Why do you suppose Mrs. Mallard fights her feeling of freedom, however briefly?

4. Chopin could have written an essay detailing the sense of oppression some women feel within the confines of marriage, yet she chose a narrative form. What advantages does Chopin gain in her use of the narrative?

5. For most of the story we know the heroine of the tale only as "Mrs. Mallard." Why has the author chosen not to mention her first name sooner? How does this omission suit the point of the story?

6. What is the final irony of Chopin's story?

7. The entire action of this story takes place in an hour. Why has the author selected this title for her story? What is the significance of the short period?

Writing Topics

1. Chopin's story describes feelings of oppression and near-hatred of a spouse that might be hard for a college student to comprehend, especially in a time when women are moving closer to controlling their own destinies. The fact is that Chopin, writing in the late 1890s, was a staunch feminist who used the story form to eloquently and poignantly describe the life and feelings of wives during that era.

Write an essay describing how you reacted to this story. Do you think that women of the 1990s experience the same kinds of feelings toward their husbands?

2. Toward the end of the story, Chopin describes Mrs. Mallard's feelings of love and hate toward her husband. Is it possible to love and hate someone at the same time? In an essay, recall a close relationship you have been in that encompassed both these feelings.

II

Family and Friends

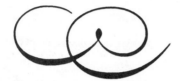

All happy families resemble each other; each unhappy family is unhappy in its own way.
—LEO TOLSTOY

God gives us relatives; thank God, we can choose our friends.
—ADDISON MIZNER

Family Ties

S. I. HAYAKAWA

He was president of San Francisco State College and a U.S. senator, but Samuel Ichiyé Hayakawa (1906–1992) was most influential as a scholar and teacher of general semantics, the study of the meanings of words and how they influence our lives. Born in Vancouver, Canada, Hayakawa attended the University of Manitoba, McGill University, and the University of Wisconsin before beginning a career as a professor of English. He wrote several books, including *Language in Thought and Action* (1941), which has been widely used as a textbook. He also wrote many articles on a wide range of social and personal issues, making frequent reference to the use of general semantics in everyday life.

   This is one of those articles. It was written for *McCall's* magazine. Some of his readers were no doubt faced with the same dilemma as the Hayakawas, whose son Mark was born with Down's syndrome, a form of retardation. What happened next, and why, is the subject of "Our Son Mark."

Our Son Mark

It was a terrible blow for us to discover that we had brought a retarded   1
child into the world. My wife and I had had no previous acquaintance with
the problems of retardation—not even with the words to discuss it. Only
such words as imbecile, idiot, and moron came to mind. And the prevailing
opinion was that such a child must be "put away," to live out his life in an
institution.

   Mark was born with Down's syndrome, popularly known as mongol-   2
ism. The prognosis for his ever reaching anything approaching normality was
hopeless. Medical authorities advised us that he would show some mental
development, but the progress would be painfully slow and he would never
reach an adolescent's mental age. We could do nothing about it, they said.
They sympathetically but firmly advised us to find a private institution that
would take him. To get him into a public institution, they said, would
require a waiting period of five years. To keep him at home for this length of
time, they warned, would have a disastrous effect on our family.

   That was twenty-seven years ago. In that time, Mark has never been   3 "put away." He has lived at home. The only institution he sees regularly is the workshop he attends, a special workshop for retarded adults. He is as much a part of the family as his mother, his older brother, his younger sister, his father, or our longtime housekeeper and friend, Daisy Rosebourgh.

Mark has contributed to our stability and serenity. His retardation has 4 brought us grief, but we did not go on dwelling on what might have been, and we have been rewarded by finding much good in things the way they are. From the beginning, we have enjoyed Mark for his delightful self. He has never seemed like a burden. He was an "easy" baby, quiet, friendly, and passive; but he needed a baby's care for a long time. It was easy to be patient with him, although I must say that some of his stages, such as his love of making chaos, as we called it, by pulling all the books he could reach off the shelves, lasted much longer than normal children's.

Mark seems more capable of accepting things as they are than his 5 immediate relatives; his mental limitation has given him a capacity for contentment, a focus on the present moment, which is often enviable. His world may be circumscribed, but it is a happy and bright one. His enjoyment of simple experiences—swimming, food, birthday candles, sports-car rides, and cuddly cats—has that directness and intensity so many philosophers recommend to all of us.

Mark's contentment has been a happy contribution to our family, and 6 the challenge of communicating with him, of doing things we can all enjoy, has drawn the family together. And seeing Mark's communicative processes develop in slow motion has taught me much about the process in all children.

Fortunately Mark was born at a time when a whole generation of 7 parents of retarded children had begun to question the accepted dogmas about retardation. Whatever they were told by their physicians about their children, parents began to ask: "Is that so? Let's see." For what is meant by "retarded child"? There are different kinds of retardation. Retarded child No. 1 is not retarded child No. 2, or 3, or 4. Down's syndrome is one condition, while brain damage is something else. There are different degrees of retardation, just as there are different kinds of brain damage. No two retarded children are exactly alike in all respects. Institutional care *does* turn out to be the best answer for some kinds of retarded children or some family situations. The point is that one observes and reacts to the *specific* case and circumstances rather than to the generalization.

This sort of attitude has helped public understanding of the nature and 8 problems of retardation to become much deeper and more widespread. It's hard to believe now that it was "definitely known" twenty years ago that institutionalization was the "only way." We were told that a retarded child could not be kept at home because "it would not be fair to the other children." The family would not be able to stand the stress. "Everybody" believed these things and repeated them, to comfort and guide the parents of the retarded.

We did not, of course, lightly disregard the well-meant advice of univer- 9
sity neurologists and their social-worker teams, for they had had much experience and we were new at this shattering experience. But our general semantics, or our parental feelings, made us aware that their reaction to Mark was to
a generalization, while to us he was an individual. They might have a valid
generalization about statistical stresses on statistical families, but they knew
virtually nothing about our particular family and its evaluative processes.

Mark was eight months old before we were told he was retarded. Of 10
course we had known that he was slower than the average child in smiling,
in sitting up, in responding to others around him. Having had one child who
was extraordinarily ahead of such schedules, we simply thought that Mark
was at the other end of the average range.

In the course of his baby checkups, at home and while traveling, we 11
had seen three different pediatricians. None of them gave us the slightest
indication that all was not well. Perhaps they were made uncertain by the
fact that Mark, with his part Japanese parentage, had a right to have "mongo-
lian" features. Or perhaps this news is as hard for a pediatrician to tell as it is
for parents to hear, and they kept putting off the job of telling us. Finally,
Mark's doctor did suggest a neurologist, indicating what his fears were, and
made an appointment.

It was Marge who bore the brunt of the first diagnosis and accompany- 12
ing advice, given at the university hospital at a time when I had to be out of
town. Stunned and crushed, she was told: "Your husband is a professional
man. You can't keep a child like this at home."

"But he lives on love," she protested. 13

"Don't your other children live on love, too?" the social worker asked. 14

Grief-stricken as she was, my wife was still able to recognize a non 15
sequitur. One does not lessen the love for one's children by dividing it among
several.

"What can I read to find out more about his condition and how to take 16
care of him?" Marge asked.

"You can't get help from a book," answered the social worker. "You 17
must put him away."

Today this sounds like dialogue from the Dark Ages. And it *was* the 18
Dark Ages. Today professional advice runs generally in the opposite direction: "Keep your retarded child at home if it's at all possible."

It was parents who led the way: They organized into parents' groups; 19
they pointed out the need for preschools, schools, diagnostic centers, work-
training centers, and sheltered workshops to serve the children who were
being cared for at home; they worked to get these services, which are now
being provided in increasing numbers. But the needs are a long way from
being fully met.

Yet even now the cost in money—not to mention the cost in human 20
terms—is much less if the child is kept at home than if he is sent to the

institutions in which children are put away. And many of the retarded are living useful and independent lives, which would never have been thought possible for them.

But for us at that time, as for other parents who were unknowingly 21
pioneering new ways for the retarded, it was a matter of going along from day to day, learning, observing, and saying, "Let's see."

There was one more frightening hurdle for our family to get over. On 22
that traumatic day Marge got the diagnosis, the doctor told her that it was too risky for us to have any more children, that there was a fifty percent chance of our having another mongoloid child. In those days, nothing was known of the cause of mongolism. There were many theories. Now, at least, it is known to be caused by the presence of an extra chromosome, a fault of cell division. But the question "Why does it happen?" had not yet been answered.

Today, genetic counseling is available to guide parents as to the proba- 23
bilities of recurrence on a scientific basis. We were flying blind. With the help of a doctor friend, we plunged into medical books and discovered that the doctor who gave us the advice was flying just as blind as we were. No evidence could be found for the fifty percent odds. Although there did seem to be some danger of recurrence, we estimated that the probabilities were with us. We took the risk and won.

Our daughter, Wynne, is now twenty-five. She started as Mark's baby 24
sister, passed him in every way, and really helped bring him up. The fact that she had a retarded brother must have contributed at least something to the fact that she is at once delightfully playful and mature, observant, and understanding. She has a fine relationship with her two brothers.

Both Wynne and Alan, Mark's older brother, have participated, with 25
patience and delight, in Mark's development. They have shown remarkable ingenuity in instructing and amusing him. On one occasion, when Mark was not drinking his milk, Alan called him to his place at the table and said, "I'm a service station. What kind of car are you?" Mark, quickly entering into the make-believe, said, "Pord."

Alan: "Shall I fill her up?" 26
Mark: "Yes." 27
Alan: "Ethyl or regular?" 28
Mark: "Reg'lar." 29
Alan (bringing the glass to Mark's mouth): "Here you are." 30
When Mark finished his glass of milk, Alan asked him, "Do you want 31
your windshield cleaned?" Then, taking a napkin, he rubbed it briskly across Mark's face, while Mark grinned with delight. This routine became a regular game for many weeks.

Alan and Wynne interpret and explain Mark to their friends, but never 32
once have I heard them apologize for him or deprecate him. It is almost as if

they judge the quality of other people by how they react to Mark. They think he is "great," and expect their friends to think so too.

Their affection and understanding were shown when Wynne flew to Oregon with Mark to visit Alan and his wife, Cynthea, who went to college there. Wynne described the whole reunion as "tremendous" and especially enjoyed Mark's delight in the trip. 33

"He was great on the plane," she recalls. "He didn't cause any trouble except that he rang the bell for the stewardess a couple of times when he didn't need anything. He was so great that I was going to send him back on the plane alone. He would have enjoyed that." But she didn't, finally, because she didn't trust others to be able to understand his speech or to know how to treat him without her there to give them clues. 34

Mark looks reasonably normal. He is small for his age (about five feet tall) and childlike. Anyone who is aware of these matters would recognize in him some of the characteristic symptomatic features, but they are not extreme. His almost incomprehensible speech, which few besides his family and teachers can understand, is his most obvious sign of retardation. 35

Mark fortunately does not notice any stares of curiosity he may attract. To imagine how one looks in the eyes of others takes a level of awareness that appears to be beyond him. Hence he is extremely direct and totally without self-consciousness. 36

I have seen him come into our living room, walk up to a woman he has never seen before, and kiss her in response to a genuinely friendly greeting. Since few of us are accustomed to such directness of expression—especially the expression of affection—the people to whom this has happened are deeply moved. 37

Like other children, Mark responds to the evaluation of others. In our family, he is accepted just as he is. Because others have always treated him as an individual, a valued individual, he feels good about himself, and, consequently, he is good to live with. In every situation between parent and child or between children, evaluations are involved—and these interact on each other. Certainly, having Mark at home has helped us be more aware and be more flexible in our evaluations. 39

This kind of sensitivity must have carried over into relations between the two normal children, because I cannot remember a single real fight or a really nasty incident between Alan and Wynne. It's as if their readiness to try to understand Mark extended into a general method of dealing with people. And I think Marge and I found the same thing happening to us, so that we became more understanding with Alan and Wynne than we might otherwise have been. If we had time and patience for Mark, why not for the children who were quick and able? We knew we could do serious damage to Mark by expecting too much of him and being disappointed. But how easy it is to expect too much of bright children and how quickly they feel your disappoint- 39 ment! Seeing Mark's slow, slow progress certainly gave us real appreciation of the marvelous perception and quick learning processes of the other two, so that all we had to do was open our eyes and our ears, and listen and enjoy them.

I don't want to sound as if we were never impatient or obtuse as 40 parents. We were, of course. But parents need to be accepted as they are, too. And I think our children—bless their hearts—were reasonably able to do so.

With Mark, it was easy to feel surprise and delight to any of his 41 accomplishments. He cannot read and will never be able to. But he can pick out on request almost any record from his huge collection—Fleetwood Mac, or the Rolling Stones, or Christmas carols—because he knows so well what each record looks like. Once we were discussing the forthcoming marriage of some friends of ours, and Mark disappeared into his playroom to bring out, a few minutes later, a record with a song "A House, a Car, and a Wedding Ring."

His love of music enables him to figure out how to operate almost any 42 record changer or hi-fi set. He never tries to force a piece of machinery because he cannot figure out how it works, as brighter people often do. And in a strange hotel room, with a TV set of unknown make, it is Mark—not Marge or I—who figures out how to turn it on and get a clear picture. As Alan once remarked: "Mark may be retarded, but he's not stupid!"

Of course, it has not all been easy—but when has easiness been the 43 test of the value of anything? To us, the difficult problems that must be faced in the future only emphasize the value of Mark as a person.

What does that future hold for Mark? 44

He will never be able to be independent; he will always have to live in 45 a protected environment. His below-50 IQ reflects the fact that he cannot cope with unfamiliar situations.

Like most parents of the retarded, we are concentrating on providing 46 financial security for Mark in the future, and fortunately we expect to be able to achieve this. Alan and his wife and Wynne have all offered to be guardians for Mark. It is wonderful to know they feel this way. But we hope that Mark can find a happy place in one of the new residence homes for the retarded.

The residence home is something new and promising and it fills an 47 enormous need. It is somewhat like a club, or a family, with a house-mother or manager. The residents share the work around the house, go out to work if they can, share in recreation and companionship. Away from their families, who may be overprotective and not aware of how much the retarded can do for themselves (are we not guilty of this, too!), they are able to live more fully as adults.

An indication that there is still much need for public education about 48 the retarded here in California is that there has been difficulty in renting decent houses for this kind of home. Prospective neighbors have objected. In some ways the Dark Ages are still with us; there are still fear and hostility where the retarded are concerned.

Is Mark able to work? Perhaps. He thrives on routine and enjoys things others despise, like clearing the table and loading the dishwasher. To Mark, it's fun. It has been hard to develop in him the idea of work, which to so many of us is "doing what you don't want to do because you have to." We don't know yet if he could work in a restaurant loading a dishwasher. In school, he learned jobs like sorting and stacking scrap wood and operating a delightful machine that swoops the string around and ties up a bundle of wood to be sold in the supermarket. That's fun, too. 49

He is now in a sheltered workshop where he can get the kind—the one kind—of pleasure he doesn't have much chance for. That's the pleasure of contributing something productive and useful to the outside world. He does various kinds of assembling jobs, packaging, sorting, and simple machine operations. He enjoys getting a paycheck and cashing it at the bank. He cannot count, but he takes pride in reaching for the check in a restaurant and pulling out his wallet. And when we thank him for dinner, he glows with pleasure. 50

It's a strange thing to say, and I am a little startled to find myself saying it, but often I feel that I wouldn't have had Mark any different. 51

Questions for Study and Discussion

1. The Hayakawas were warned that Mark, if kept at home, would have a "disastrous effect" on the family. Why? What effect did Mark actually have on his parents, his brother, and his sister?

2. What do you believe was Hayakawa's purpose in writing this essay? Apart from what the essay says about Mark, and about Down's syndrome, what important point does it make?

3. How did the Hayakawas' sensitivity to the uses and misuses of language affect their responses to professional advice about Mark?

4. Several times Hayakawa refers to the Dark Ages. What were the Dark Ages? Why are they relevant to Hayakawa's account?

5. Are there any suggestions in this essay that the Hayakawas may at times have found Mark's behavior irritating, or worse? How does this affect your response to the essay?

Writing Topics

1. Sometimes it is wise to accept and follow expert advice. At other times it may be necessary to disregard such advice and make one's own decision. Have you or another member of your family ever deliberately gone against an authorita-

tive opinion? Recount the episode, and say whether on reflection you think the decision was a good one.

2. What is now known about Down's syndrome—its cause, its treatment, its risks?

3. According to many books, magazine articles, and television documentaries, the American family is "in trouble." Do you agree? What exactly does such a statement mean to you? Is it a meaningful statement at all?

ANTHONY BRANDT

Anthony Brandt was born in Cranford, New Jersey, in 1936 and studied at Princeton and Columbia. After a brief career in business, he became a freelance writer and has contributed essays and poems to such magazines as the *Atlantic Monthly*, *Prairie Schooner*, and the *New York Quarterly*. He published *Reality Police: The Experience of Insanity in America* in 1975 and is presently at work on a book about the American dream, which he says will attempt to define that dream and trace its origins and development.

As a young boy, Brandt was forced to watch his beloved grandmother slowly lose her grip on reality and gradually slide into senility. Thirty years later his mother, too, had to be consigned to a nursing home, no longer able to take care of herself. In the following memoir, first published in the *Atlantic Monthly*, Brandt describes the two cases and what they have meant to him.

My Grandmother: A Rite of Passage

Some things that happen to us can't be borne, with the paradoxical 1 result that we carry them on our backs the rest of our lives. I have been half obsessed for almost thrity years with the death of my grandmother. I should say with her dying: with the long and terrible changes that came at the worst time for a boy of twelve and thirteen, going through his own difficult changes. It felt like and perhaps was the equivalent of a puberty rite: dark, frightening, aboriginal, an obscure emotional exchange between old and young. It has become part of my character.

I grew up in New Jersey in a suburban town where my brother still lives 2 and practices law. One might best describe it as quiet, protected, and green; it was no preparation for death. Tall, graceful elm trees lined both sides of the street where we lived. My father's brother-in-law, a contractor, built our house; we moved into it a year after I was born. My grandmother and grandfather (my mother's parents; they were the only grandparents who mattered) lived up the street "on the hill"; it wasn't much of a hill, the terrain in that part of New Jersey being what it is, but we could ride our sleds down the street after it snowed, and that was hilly enough.

Our family lived, or seemed to a young boy to live, in very stable, very 3 ordinary patterns. My father commuted to New York every day, taking the

Jersey Central Railroad, riding in cars that had windows you could open, getting off the train in Jersey City and taking a ferry to Manhattan. He held the same job in the same company for more than thirty years. The son of Swedish immigrants, he was a funny man who could wiggle his ears without raising his eyebrows and made up the most dreadful puns. When he wasn't being funny he was quiet, the newspaper his shield and companion, or the *Saturday Evening Post,* which he brought home without fail every Wednesday evening, or *Life,* which he brought home Fridays. It was hard to break through the quiet and the humor, and after he died my mother said, as much puzzled as disturbed, that she hardly knew him at all.

She, the backbone of the family, was fierce, stern, the kind of person   4 who can cow you with a glance. My brother and I, and my cousins, were all a little in awe of her. The ruling passion in her life was to protect her family; she lived in a set of concentric circles, sons and husbands the closest, then nieces, nephews, brothers, parents, then more distant relatives, and outside that a few friends, very few. No one and nothing else existed for her; she had no interest in politics, art, history, or even the price of eggs. "Fierce" is the best word for her, or single-minded. In those days (I was born in 1936) polio was every parent's bugbear; she, to keep my brother and me away from places where the disease was supposed to be communicated, particularly swimming pools, took us every summer for the entire summer to the Jersey shore, first to her parent's cottage, later to a little cottage she and my father bought. She did that even though it meant being separated from my father for nearly three months, having nobody to talk to, having to handle my brother and me on her own. She hated it, she told us years later, but she did it: fiercely. Or there's the story of one of my cousins who got pregnant when she was sixteen or seventeen; my mother took her into our house, managed somehow to hide her condition from the neighbors, then, after the birth, arranged privately to have the child adopted by a family the doctor recommended, all this being done without consulting the proper authorities, and for the rest of her life never told a single person how she made these arrangements or where she had placed the child. She was a genuine primitive, like some tough old peasant woman. Yet her name was Grace, her nickname Bunny; if you saw through the fierceness, you understood that it was a version of love.

Her mother, my grandmother, seemed anything but fierce. One of our   5 weekly routines was Sunday dinner at their house on the hill, some five or six houses from ours. When I was very young, before World War II, the house had a mansard roof, a barn in the back, lots of yard space, lots of rooms inside, and a cherry tree. I thought it was a palace. Actually it was rather small, and became smaller when my grandmother insisted on tearing down the mansard roof and replacing it with a conventional peaked roof; the house lost three attic rooms in the process. Sunday dinner was invariably roast beef or chicken or leg of lamb with mashed potatoes and vegetables, standard American fare but cooked by my grandparents' Polish maid, Josephine, not by my grandmother. Josephine made wonderful pies in an old cast-iron coal stove and used to let me tie her string to the kitchen sink. My grandfather was a gentle man who smoked a pipe, had a bristly reddish moustache, and always seemed to wind up paying everybody else's debts in the family; my mother worshipped him. There were usually lots of uncles at these meals, and they were a playful bunch. I have a very early memory of two of them tossing me back and forth between them, and another of the youngest, whose name was Don, carrying me on his shoulders into the surf. I also remember my grandmother presiding at these meals. She was gray-haired and benign.

Later they sold that house. My benign grandmother, I've been told since, was in fact a restless, unsatisfied woman; changing the roof line, moving from house to house, were her ways of expressing that dissatisfaction. In the next house, I think it was, my grandfather died; my grandmother moved again, then again, and then to a house down the street, at the bottom of the hill this time, and there I got to know her better. I was nine or ten years old. She let me throw a tennis ball against the side of the house for hours at a time; the noise must have been terribly aggravating. She cooked lunch for me and used to make pancakes the size of dinner plates, and corn fritters. She also made me a whole set of yarn figures a few inches long, rolling yarn around her hand, taking the roll and tying off arms, legs, and a head, then sewing a face onto the head with black thread. I played with these and an odd assortment of hand-me-down toy soldiers for long afternoons, setting up wars, football games, contests of all kinds, and designating particular yarn figures as customary heroes. Together we played a spelling game: I'd be on the floor playing with the yarn figures, she'd be writing a letter and ask me to spell "appreciate" (it was always that word), and I'd spell it for her while she pretended to be impressed with my spelling ability and I pretended that she hadn't asked me to spell that same word a dozen times before. I was good, too, at helping her find her glasses.

One scene at this house stands out. My uncle Bob came home from the war and the whole family, his young wife, other uncles, my mother and father and brother and I, gathered at the house to meet him, and he came in wearing his captain's uniform and looking to me, I swear it, like a handsome young god. In fact he was an ordinary man who spent the rest of his life selling insurance. He had been in New Guinea, a ground officer in the Air Corps, and the story I remember is of the native who came into his tent one day and took a great deal of interest in the scissors my uncle was using. The native asked in pidgin English what my uncle would require for the scissors in trade, and he jokingly said, well, how about a tentful of bananas. Sure enough, several days later two or three hundred natives came out of the jungle, huge bunches of bananas on their soldiers, and filled my uncle's tent.

Things went on this way for I don't know how long, maybe two years, maybe three. I don't want to describe it as idyllic. Youth has its problems.

6

7

8

But this old woman who could never find her glasses was wonderful to me, a grandmother in the true likeness of one, and I couldn't understand the changes when they came. She moved again, against all advice, this time to a big, bare apartment on the other side of town. She was gradually becoming irritable and difficult, not much fun to be around. There were no more spelling games; she stopped writing letters. Because she moved I saw her less often, and her home could no longer be a haven for me. She neglected it, too; it grew dirtier and dirtier, until my mother eventually had to do her cleaning for her.

Then she began to see things that weren't there. A branch in the back yard became a woman, I remember, who apparently wasn't fully clothed, and a man was doing something to her, something unspeakable. She developed diabetes and my mother learned to give her insulin shots, but she wouldn't stop eating candy, the worst thing for her, and the diabetes got worse. Her face began to change, to slacken, to lose its shape and character. I didn't understand these things; arteriosclerosis, hardening of the arteries, whatever the explanation, it was only words. What I noticed was that her white hair was getting thinner and harder to control, that she herself seemed to be shrinking even as I grew, that when she looked at me I wasn't sure it was me she was seeing anymore.

After a few months of this, we brought her to live with us. My mother was determined to take care of her, and certain family pressures were brought to bear too. That private man my father didn't like the idea at all, but he said nothing, which was his way. And she was put in my brother's bedroom over the garage, my brother moving in with me. It was a small house, six rooms and a basement, much too small for what we had to face.

What we had to face was a rapid deterioration into senile dementia and the rise from beneath the surface of this smiling, kindly, white-haired old lady of something truly ugly. Whenever she was awake she called for attention, calling, calling a hundred times a day. Restless as always, she picked the bedclothes off, tore holes in sheets and pillows, took off her nightclothes and sat naked talking to herself. She hallucinated more and more frequently, addressing her dead husband, a dead brother, scolding, shouting at their apparitions. She became incontinent and smeared feces on herself, the furniture, the walls. And always calling—"Bunny, where are you? Bunny, I want you!"—scolding, demanding; she could seldom remember what she wanted when my mother came. It became an important event when she fell asleep; to make sure she stayed asleep the radio was kept off, the four of us tiptoed around the house, and when I went out to close the garage door, directly under her window (it was an overhead door and had to be pulled down), I did it so slowly and carefully, half an inch at a time, that it sometimes took me a full fifteen minutes to get it down.

That my mother endured this for six months is a testimony to her strength and determination, but it was really beyond her and almost destroyed her health. My grandmother didn't often sleep through the night; she would wake up, yell, cry, a creature of disorder, a living *memento mori*,[1] and my mother would have to tend to her. The house began to smell in spite of all my mother's efforts to keep my grandmother's room clean. My father, his peace gone, brooded in his chair behind his newpaper. My brother and I fought for *Lebensraum*,[2] each of us trying to grow up in his own way. People avoided us. My uncles were living elsewhere—Miami, Cleveland, Delaware. My grandmother's two surviving sisters, who lived about ten blocks away, never came to see her. Everybody seemed to sense that something obscene was happening, and stayed away. Terrified, I stayed away, too. I heard my grandmother constantly, but in the six months she lived with us I think I went into her room only once. That was as my mother wished it. She was a nightmare, naked and filthy without warning.

After six months, at my father's insistence, after a night nurse had been hired and left, after my mother had reached her limits and beyond, my parents started looking for a nursing home, anyplace they could put her. It became a family scandal; the two sisters were outraged that my mother would consider putting her own mother in a home, there were telephone calls back and forth between them and my uncles, but of course the sisters had never come to see her themselves, and my mother never forgave them. One of my uncles finally came from Cleveland, saw what was happening, and that day they put my grandmother in a car and drove her off to the nearest state mental hospital. They brought her back the same day; desperate as they were, they couldn't leave her in hell. At last, when it had come time to go to the shore, they found a nursing home in the middle of the Pine Barrens, miles from anywhere, and kept her there for a while. That, too, proving unsatisfactory, they put her in a small nursing home in western New Jersey, about two hours away by car. We made the drive every Sunday for the next six months, until my grandmother finally died. I always waited in the car while my mother visited her. At the funeral I refused to go into the room for one last look at the body. I was afraid of her still. The whole thing had been a subtle act of violence, a violation of the sensibilities, made all the worse by the fact that I knew it wasn't really her fault, that she was a victim of biology, of life itself. Hard knowledge for a boy just turned fourteen. She became the color of all my expectations. 13

Life is savage, then, and even character is insecure. Call no man happy until he be dead, said the Greek lawgiver Solon. But what would a wise man say to this? In that same town in New Jersey, that town I have long since abandoned as too flat and too good to be true, my mother, thirty years older 14

---

[1]A rememberance of death, usually a work of art with symbols of death or mortality, such as a skull.

[2]Living space, room for growth, development, or the like.

now, weighing in at ninety-two pounds, incontinent, her white hair wild about her head, sits strapped into a chair in another nursing home talking incoherently to her fellow patients and working her hands at the figures she thinks she sees moving around on the floor. It's enough to make stones weep to see this fierce, strong woman, who paid her dues, surely ten times over, reduced to this.

Yet she is *cheerful.* This son comes to see her and she quite literally   15 babbles with delight, introduces him (as her father, her husband—the connections are burnt out) to the aides, tells him endless stories that don't make any sense at all, and *shines,* shines with a clear light that must be her soul. Care and bitterness vanish in her presence. Helpless, the victim of numerous tiny strokes—"shower strokes," the doctors call them—that are gradually destroying her brain, she has somehow achieved a radiant serenity that accepts everything that happens and incorporates and transforms it.

Is there a lesson in this? Is some pattern larger than life working itself   16 out; is this some kind of poetic justice on display, a mother balancing a grandmother, gods demonstrating reasons beyond our comprehension? It was a bitter thing to put her into that place, reeking of disinfectant, full of senile, dying old people, and I used to hate to visit her there, but as she has deteriorated she has also by sheer force of example managed to change my attitude. If she can be reconciled to all this, why can't I? It doesn't last very long, but after I've seen her, talked to her for half an hour, helped feed her, stroked her hair, I walk away amazed, as if I had been witness to a miracle.

Questions for Study and Discussion

1. What, for Brandt, is the meaning of his experiences with his grandmother and mother? How have those experiences affected his attitude toward life?

2. A "rite of passage" is a ritual associated with an important change in one's life. Brandt finds an analogy between his experiences with his grandmother and the frightening ritual in primitive societies by which the elders formally initiate the young into adulthood. How are Brandt's experiences like an initiation? How do they differ?

3. Are there any other "rites of passage" (besides Brandt's own) in the essay? Who changes, and how? What rituals, if any, are involved?

4. How much time passes between the onset of the grandmother's senility and her death? How does Brandt indicate this passage of time? As you read, did you feel that events were moving more quickly or slowly than that? Why do you suppose Brandt handles time the way he does?

5. What part of this essay struck you most forcefully? Examine the writing of that passage. Can you identify any specific elements that seem to affect the total impact of the passage?

6. Brandt writes in paragraph 13, "The whole thing had been a subtle act

of violence, a violation of the sensibilities." What does he mean? You may find it helpful to look up the word *sensibility* in your desk dictionary.

Writing Topics

1. Anthony Brandt describes his grandmother as an elderly, loving, playful companion. What have your grandparents been to you? What do you think a grandparent's role should be?

2. Old age may be a time of great achievement, as it was for the cellist Pablo Casals or the artist Georgia O'Keeffe demonstrated, or it may bring senility, as it did to Anthony Brandt's grandmother. What is your conception of old age? Describe the people you know, or know about, who are examples of that conception.

KAREN P. ENGELHARDT

Karen P. Engelhardt graduated from Pace University in White Plains, New York, with an English and communications major and a philosophy minor. She currently works with the elderly as a social worker in a New York City nursing home and continues to write essays and fiction. This reflective article originated as a remembrance of her grandmothers, who passed away within a few months of each other.

A Tale of Two Gravies

"Come on kids! We're going to Grandma's."   1

"Which one?"   2

During my childhood, these words were typical in my home almost   3
every Saturday and Sunday afternoon. On Saturday, we'd go a few blocks to Grandma Ruth's, my father's mother; on Sunday, my mother would answer, "Grandma Meatball," her mom, and we'd drive to the suburbs. Each of those visits was enormously different, at least from the eyes of the little girl I was. I always wondered then why Grandma Ruth's "gravy" was thick and brown and poured over mashed potatoes, but Grandma Meatball's was tomato sauce that she ladled over macaroni, sausage, and beef. As I grew up, however, I began to understand that Grandma Ruth and Grandma Meatball, who came from entirely diverse worlds, were more alike than I ever imagined.

"Come on kids. We're going to Grandma's."   4

"Which one?"   5

It was Saturday. "Grandma Ruth's." She lived only five minutes away,   6
in an apartment building off Allerton Avenue in the Bronx. When she knew we were coming she would poke her head out the window so she could point out the best parking space when we got closer to the apart-

ment. The building was old and there was no elevator. We climbed the five flights of stairs that led to my Grandma's apartment, for some still unknown reason marked "2E."

The doorbell was much higher than my reach and my dad would lift me   7
up so I could ring it. The kitchen was about three feet from the door, so it wasn't long before Grandma Ruth came rushing out. She wasn't that tall, only about five-four, and slender, but she still smothered me and my sister, Tami. Looking at pictures of her when she was younger you'd say she never changed. She had begun to gray when she was only sixteen and the years in between made her wispy hair bright white. Grandma Ruth, in my mind's eye, will always be one of those young old people: young in mind and spirit with a body that just couldn't keep up.

Grandma Ruth was born in New York and was a city girl her whole life.   8
She had three raucous boys. Grandma Ruth loved to talk and laugh; she was always having "company" over. My father remembers sitting at the kitchen table stuffing fund-raising envelopes she'd brought home from work so they could make a little extra money. Grandma Ruth would tell him stories of her family picnics in upstate New York. These became family lore for me, too.

Grandma Ruth's Saturday meals were spectacular. The smells coming   9
from the kitchen made the two hours before dinner almost unbearable. Roast beef with gravy, mashed potatoes, creamed onions, mashed turnips, and string beans were the usuals. The roast beef was sometimes replaced by a roast pork or leg of lamb. Whatever the main course, it was meat, and there was always bread and butter. The weekend after Grandma Ruth died, my mother made this exact meal. It was our way of saying good-bye—and thanks.

Years ago, while we waited for her dinner, we'd get bored with the   10
grown-up conversation. I would sit at my grandmother's desk by the phone and play secretary with her datebook. She had a desk set of those marble pen holders where the pen is attached by a chain. This became my telephone since I wasn't allowed to use the real one. When even this got boring, I would begin to wander around the house looking for the next thing to keep my interest. The dining room had all kinds of cool stuff in it so I would usually end up there. Trinkets and books lined long shelves that spanned one entire wall of the room; there was plenty to explore and keep my imagination busy.

The dining room table was set with white dishes with green flowers on   11
the edges. Even the glasses were frosted white with matching green flowers. The kiddy bridge table was just off to the left, but it was set the same way so we wouldn't feel left out. The adults drank wine; we drank Hoffman's lemon soda. It always amazed me how much the adults could talk while they ate, though my mother told me not to talk when we chewed. The laughter and chatter never ceased. After dinner, my folks would sprawl out on her bed and take a nap. My sister and I would look out the window, just like Grandma.

"Come on kids, we're going to Mass, then we're going to Grandma's."   12

"Which one?"   13

Sunday: "Grandma Meatball."   14

After ten o'clock Mass we'd pile into my father's long, tired Pontiac for   15
the forty-five-minute trip to Long Island. For as long as I could remember,
Grandma Meatball and Grandpa lived in Uncle Vinny's basement apartment. In marked contrast to Grandma Ruth, Grandma Meatball was very
Old World Italian. She was a quiet woman who spoke more with the smiling
silence of her eyes; her house was filled with religious paintings and statues.
When she did talk, she'd amaze us with her stories of Arthur Avenue, a noisy
Italian section of town, where she and Grandpa raised a brood of seven
children in a three-room apartment. She'd remember life in the Italian
countryside before she came to America. Simply thinking that this wise old
woman was once a little girl, like me, who barely knew English was not
something I could picture.

When we arrived, stir crazy from the long trip, Tami and I would swing   16
around to the backyard of the house where Grandpa was fussing with his
vegetable garden. He knew we were coming and he wanted to have a bag of
tomatoes ready to go home with us. Then we'd go down the concrete steps to
the basement where Grandma was standing by the stove stirring her "gravy."
The minute we'd walk in, she'd say hello with her quiet eyes; we'd literally
get lost in her round hugs, stronger than a man's. After the long greeting—
she never let go easily, even years later as she lay in her hospital bed—she'd
lead us over to the stove where the bowl of meatballs was waiting for us.
Grandma would always fry extra meatballs for us to eat when we got there.
She had to make a double batch, because half went into the gravy and the
rest got eaten one by one by whomever walked into the kitchen.

Macaroni didn't have to get thrown in until the last minute before we   17
ate, so we were basically waiting for the gravy meat to cook. While Grandma
put out bread, cheese, wine, and fruit to pick at before dinner, my cousins
came down from upstairs and we played. Grandma's basement apartment was
perfect for hide and seek: there were nooks and crannies all over the place.
The closets were enough to keep us busy until we were called to eat, but the
laundry room was off limits ever since my cousin John got thrown in the
dryer by his brothers. It was on at the time.

There wasn't enough room for everyone to eat downstairs, so we would   18
carry the meal up to Aunt Mary and Uncle Vinny's kitchen because it was
bigger. I had five aunts and uncles all together, so if everyone was on Long
Island at once there was absolutely no way we could fit everyone, even in the
larger kitchen. The kids would be in the living room sitting at the bridge
table. There was no room for us to make our own plate, so each mother
would make one up for her kids. We didn't feel left out because we were in
the other room. Everyone talked so loudly we were able to contribute from
where we were.

The autumn my grandmothers died, I thought often about those big   19 weekend dinners. When I was a kid, all I was able to see were the differences between these women. Looking back, I realize that the cultural, emotional, even personal disparity fascinated me at that time. But as I grew and learned more about their lives, I came to understand that Grandma Ruth and Grandma Meatball were much more alike than I had ever imagined.

They loved and protected their children and grandchildren passion- 20
ately. The good family values that are so often missing from today's world were daily lessons in their homes: they taught my mother and father to keep a family together, to put each other and their children first, and to under-stand that a family that stuck together no matter what could never be poor. By educating my parents, each of my grandmothers, unique as they were, contributed to my growth as a young woman in these same ways. They each loved me in their own language and expressed that love on their own terms. Their separate worlds merged together to make me the whole that I am. They taught me that where I stand depends on where they stood before me. A little girl sees the old-fashioned ways of her grandmothers. The young woman understands the underlying importance, even timeliness, of their commitment to be matriarchs to their families. To remember their stories and pass them on to my own family, then, is to honor them. That is their legacy, and my responsibility.

Questions for Study and Discussion

1. How were Engelhardt's grandmothers alike? How were they different? Are the differences or the similarities more important to Engelhardt?

2. What is the importance of gravy for Engelhardt in this sketch of her two grandmothers?

3. What does the ritual of visiting the grandmothers say about Engel-hardt's mother's and father's sense of obligation to their parents? What was shared besides the ritual of the food that Engelhardt remembers so well?

4. What does Engelhardt see as the lasting contribution of her grandmoth-ers to her development?

Writing Topics

1. Write an essay in which you analyze the rituals that your family ob-serves, from eating to family gatherings, churchgoing, watching television, play-ing sports, and shopping. What is the importance of such rituals? What func-tions do they serve?

2. Read Anthony Brandt's article "My Grandmother: A Rite of Passage" (pp. 113–118). Write an essay in which you compare Engelhardt's essay with Brandt's for what light you can shed on the way we come to know our grandpar-ents and the ways that they are remembered and change over time.

ROBERT HAYDEN

The black experience is the source of some of Robert Hayden's best poetry, from his dramatic evocation of the slave trade in "Middle Passage" to his elegy for Malcolm X in "El-Hajj Malik El-Shabazz." Alongside these, however, are many other poems about his own particular roots, "Pennsylvania gothic, Kentucky homespun, Virginia baroque," and a great-grandmother who was "a Virginia freedman's Indian bride," as he says in "Beginnings." Hayden was born in Detroit in 1913 and went to college there at Wayne State University. He lived in Nashville from 1946 to 1969 and then returned to his native state, where he taught at the University of Michigan until his death in 1980. In his last years he was named consultant in poetry to the Library of Congress. His own selection of his best poems was published in 1975 as *Angle of Ascent*.

One of Hayden's first published poems, "Obituary," was about his father. Twenty years later, when he was nearly fifty and was himself a parent, he reflected once again on his father in "Those Winter Sundays." One hears often of labors of love; here, Hayden tells of a love that could express itself only through labor.

Those Winter Sundays

Sundays too my father got up early
and put his clothes in the blueback cold,
then with cracked hands that ached
from labor in the weekday weather made
banked fires blaze. No one ever thanked him.   5

I'd wake and hear the cold splintering, breaking.
When the rooms were warm, he'd call,
and slowly I would rise and dress,
fearing the chronic angers of that house,

Speaking indifferently to him,   10
who had driven out the cold
and polished my good shoes as well.
What did I know, what did I know
of love's austere and lonely offices?

Questions for Study and Discussion

1. What does the speaker of the poem now realize about his father that he did not realize at an earlier age? Why do those "winter Sundays" stand out in his memory?

2. What might Hayden mean when he refers to "the chronic angers of that house"?

3. Does the poem suggest something about the relationship that often exists between parents and children? If so, what?

4. How does the speaker of the poem now view his behavior as a child? How does he feel about it? What lines indicate his feeling?

5. What is the tone of the poem? How would you describe Hayden's diction? What effect does it create?

6. What does Hayden mean by "love's austere and lonely offices"? State the meaning of the phrase in your own words and explain how it applies to the rest of the poem.

Writing Topics

1. In the last line of the poem, Hayden writes of "love's austere and lonely offices." How can a person know that an action is motivated by love if it is not done in a clearly loving way? Do actions really speak louder than words? Call on your own experience to support your answer in an essay.

2. Hayden refers to the "chronic angers" in the household in which he grew up. What are some of the effects such a situation has on children? Besides your own experience and that of people you know, you may want to consult sources in psychiatry or developmental psychology before writing an essay on this topic.

LINDA HOGAN

Poet, novelist, short story writer, and playwright, Linda Hogan was born in Denver, Colorado, in 1947 and grew up in Oklahoma. In 1978 she earned her master's degree in English and creative writing from the University of Colorado at Boulder. Since 1984 Hogan has been an associate professor of American Studies and American Indian Studies at the University of Minnesota. Hogan's writing reflects her interest in what for her are "the deepest questions, those of spirit, of shelter, of growth and movement toward liberation, inner and outer." She has published four collections of poetry, including *Calling Myself Home* (1979), *Daughters, I Love You* (1981), *Eclipse* (1983), and *Seeing Through the Sun* (1985), which won the 1986 American Book Award from the Before Columbus Foundation. In addition, she has two collections of short fiction, *That Horse* (1985) and *The Big Woman* (1987), a novel, *Mean Spirit* (1989), and a three-act play, *A Piece of the Moon* (1981). Hogan says that her current interest is "in wildlife rehabilitation and studying the relationship between humans and other species, and trying to create world survival skills out of what I learn from this." In that spirit she is at work on a collection of essays on human–animal relations.

In "Heritage," first published in her collection *Calling Myself Home* (1979), Hogan, a Chickasaw, reflects on her family and the cultural heritage that they passed down to her. She carefully describes the good as well as the bad things she inherited from her family.

Heritage

From my mother, the antique mirror
where I watch my face take on her lines.
She left me the smell of baking bread
to warm fine hairs in my nostrils,
she left the large white breasts that weigh down
my body.   5

From my father I take his brown eyes,
the plague of locusts that leveled our crops,
they flew in formations like buzzards.

From my uncle the whittled wood   10
that rattles like bones
and is white
and smells like all our old houses
that are no longer there. He was the man
who sang old chants to me, the words   15
my father was told not to remember.

From my grandfather who never spoke
I learned to fear silence.
I learned to kill a snake
when you're begging for rain.   20

And grandmother, blue-eyed woman
whose skin was brown,
she used snuff.
When her coffee can full of black saliva
spilled on me   25
it was like the brown cloud of grasshoppers
that leveled her fields.
It was the brown stain
that covered my white shirt,
my whiteness a shame.   30
That sweet black liquid like the food
she chewed up and spit into my father's mouth
when he was an infant.
It was the brown earth of Oklahoma
stained with oil.   35
She said tobacco would purge your body of poisons.
It has more medicine than stones and knives
against your enemies.

That tobacco is the dark night that covers me.

She said it is wise to eat the flesh of deer   40
so you will be swift and travel over many miles.
She told me how our tribe has always followed a stick
that pointed west
that pointed east.
From my family I have learned the secrets   45
of never having a home.

Questions for Study and Discussion

1. The speaker says that she has inherited things from her mother, father, uncle, grandfather, and grandmother. To which person does she appear to be most indebted? Explain.

2. What are the things that the speaker seems happy to inherit? What is she unhappy to inherit? Are there any things about which you are not quite sure how she feels? Explain.

3. What does the speaker mean when she says her father was told not to remember the words of the chants her uncle sang to her?

4. In line 30 the speaker tells us that her whiteness was a "shame." What does she mean?

5. Why do you suppose line 39 stands by itself? In what ways does it serve to summarize and conclude the speaker's story about her grandmother's snuff, the coffee can accident, and the associations made between the "black saliva" and her heritage? Explain.

6. How would you describe the speaker's tone in this poem? Is she proud of her heritage? How do you think she feels about having "learned the secrets / of never having a home"? Explain.

Writing Topics

1. Write an essay in which you discuss the importance of family for you. What are the benefits that your family gives you? What contributions to your family do you make in return? Use specific examples from your own family experience to illustrate the points of your essay.

2. Write an essay (or perhaps a poem) about your heritage. You may find it helpful to start by listing all your relatives that you have known and noting what you have received from each. Be as specific as you can in making notes about memorable—both good and bad—childhood experiences.

3. How does your lifestyle compare with that of your parents and/or grandparents? What values, customs, and beliefs do you share? On what family issues do you have a difference of opinion? Write an essay in which you discuss the importance of family in preserving a culture's values, customs, and beliefs.

EUDORA WELTY

The American South has brought forth more than its share of fine writers, and Eudora Welty holds an honored place among them. She was born in 1909 in Jackson, Mississippi, and that is where she has lived for most of her life. Her father was president of an insurance company, and she was able to go away to the University of Wisconsin and then to take a postgraduate course in advertising at Columbia University's business school. During the Great Depression, jobs in advertising were scarce, so Welty returned home to Jackson and began to write. Her published works include many short stories, now available as her *Collected Stories* (1980), five novels, and a collection of her essays, *The Eye of the Story* (1975). Welty's *One Writer's Beginnings* (1987) recounts the events in childhood that influenced her development as a writer. In "A Worn Path" we meet one of Welty's memorable characters, old Phoenix Jackson, on her way to town on a vital errand.

A Worn Path

It was December—a bright frozen day in the early morning. Far out in 1 the country there was an old Negro woman with her head tied in a red rag, coming along a path through the pinewoods. Her name was Phoenix Jackson. She was very old and small and she walked slowly in the dark pine shadows, moving a little from side to side in her steps, with the balanced heaviness and lightness of a pendulum in a grandfather clock. She carried a thin, small cane made from an umbrella, and with this she kept tapping the frozen earth in front of her. This made a grave and persistent noise in the still air, that seemed meditative like the chirping of a solidarity little bird.

She wore a dark striped dress reaching down to her shoe tops, and an 2 equally long apron of bleached sugar sacks, with a full pocket: all neat and tidy, but every time she took a step she might have fallen over her shoelaces, which dragged from her unlaced shoes. She looked straight ahead. Her eyes were blue with age. Her skin had a pattern all its own of numberless branching wrinkles and as though a whole little tree stood in the middle of her forehead, but a golden color ran underneath, and the two knobs of her cheeks were illumined by a yellow burning under the dark. Under the red rag her hair came down on her neck in the frailest of ringlets, still black, and with an odor like copper.

Now and then there was a quivering in the thicket. Old Phoenix said, 3 "Out of my way, all you foxes, owls, beetles, jack rabbits, coons and wild animals! . . . Keep out from under these feet, little bob-whites. . . . Keep the big wild hogs out of my path. Don't let none of those come running my direction. I got a long way." Under her small black-freckled hand her cane, limber as a buggy whip, would switch at the brush as if to rouse up any hiding things.

On she went. The woods were deep and still. The sun made the pine 4 needles almost too bright to look at, up where the wind rocked. The cones dropped as light as feathers. Down in the hollow was the mourning dove—it was not too late for him.

The path ran up a hill. "Seem like there is chains about my feet, time I 5 get this far," she said, in the voice of argument old people keep to use with themselves. "Something always take a hold of me on this hill—pleads I should stay."

After she got to the top she turned and gave a full, severe look behind 6 her where she had come. "Up through pines," she said at length. "Now down through oaks."

Her eyes opened their widest, and she started down gently. But before 7 she got to the bottom of the hill a bush caught her dress.

Her fingers were busy and intent, but her skirts were full and long, so 8 that before she could pull them free in one place they were caught on another. It was not possible to allow the dress to tear. "I in the thorny bush," she said. "Thorns, you doing your appointed work. Never want to let folks pass, no sir. Old eyes thought you was a pretty little green bush."

Finally, trembling all over, she stood free, and after a moment dared to 9 stoop for her cane.

"Sun so high!" she cried, leaning back and looking, while the thick 10 tears went over her eyes. "The time getting all gone here."

At the foot of this hill was a place where a log was laid across the creek. 11

"Now comes the trial," said Phoenix. 12

Putting her right foot out, she mounted the log and shut her eyes. 13 Lifting her skirt, leveling her cane fiercely before her, like a festival figure in some parade, she began to march across. The she opened her eyes and she was safe on the other side.

"I wasn't as old as I thought," she said. 14

But she sat down to rest. She spread her skirts on the bank around her 15 and folded her hands over her knees. Upon above her was a tree in a pearly cloud of mistletoe. She did not dare to close her eyes and when a little boy brought her a plate with a slice of marble-cake on it she spoke to him. "That would be acceptable," she said. But when she went to take it there was just her own hand in the air.

So she left that tree, and had to go through a barbed-wire fence. There 16 she had to creep and crawl, spreading her knees and stretching her fingers like a baby trying to climb the steps. But she talked loudly to herself: she could not let her dress be torn now; so late in the day, and she could not pay for having her arm or her leg sawed off if she got caught fast where she was.

At last she was safe through the fence and risen up out in the clearing. 17 Big dead trees, like black men with one arm, were standing in the purple stalks of the withered cotton field. There sat a buzzard.

"Who you watching?" 18

In the furrow she made her way along. 19

"Glad this not the season for bulls," she said, looking sideways, "and 20 the good lord made his snakes to curl up and sleep in the winter. A pleasure I don't see no two-headed snake coming around that tree, where it come once. It took a while to get by him, back in the summer."

She passed through the old cotton and went into a field of dead corn. It 21 whispered and shook and was taller than her head. "Through the maze now," she said, for there was no path.

Then there was something tall, black, and skinny there, moving before 22 her.

At first she took it for a man. It could have been a man dancing in the 23 field. But she stood still and listened, and it did not make a sound. It was as silent as a ghost.

"Ghost," she said sharply, "who be you the ghost of? For I have heard of 24 nary death close by."

But there was no answer—only the ragged dancing in the wind. 25

She shut her eyes, reached out her hand, and touched a sleeve. She 26 found a coat and inside that an emptiness, cold as ice.

"You scarecrow," she said. Her face lighted. "I ought to be shut up for 27 good," she said with laughter. "My senses is gone. I too old. I the oldest people I ever know. Dance, old scarecrow," she said, "while I dancing with you."

She kicked her foot over the furrow, and with mouth drawn down, 28 shook her head once or twice in a little strutting way. Some husks blew down and whirled in streamers about her skirts.

Then she went on, parting her way from side to side with the cane, 29 through the whispering field. At last she came to the end, to a wagon track where the silver grass blew between the red ruts. The quail were walking around like pullets, seeming all dainty and unseen.

"Walk pretty," she said. "This the easy place. This the easy going." 30

She followed the track, swaying through the quiet bare fields, through 31 the little strings of trees silver in their dead leaves, past cabins silver from weather, with the doors and windows boarded shut, all like old women under a spell sitting there. "I walking in their sleep," she said, nodding her head vigorously.

In a ravine she went where a spring was silently flowing through a 32 hollow log. Old Phoenix bent and drank. "Sweetgum makes the water sweet," she said, and drank more. "Nobody know who made this well, for it was here when I was born."

The track crossed a swampy part where the moss hung as white as lace from every limb. "Sleep on, alligators, and blow your bubbles." Then the track went into the road. 33

Deep, deep the road went down between the high green-colored banks. Overhead the live-oaks met, and it was as dark as a cave. 34

A black dog with a lolling tongue came up out of the weeds by the ditch. She was meditating, and not ready, and when he came at her she only hit him a little with her cane. Over she went in the ditch, like a little puff of milkweed. 35

Down there, her senses drifted away. A dream visited her, and she reached her hand up, but nothing reached down and gave her a pull. So she lay there and presently went to talking. "Old woman," she said to herself, "that black dog came up out of the weeds to stall you off, and now there he sitting on his fine tail, smiling at you." 36

A white man finally came along and found her—a hunter, a young man, with his dog on a chain. 37

"Well, Granny!" he laughed. "What are you doing there?" 38

"Lying on my back like a June-bug waiting to be turned over, mister," she said, reaching up her hand. 39

He lifted her up, gave her a swing in the air, and set her down. "Anything broken, Granny?" 40

"No sir, them old dead weeds is springy enough," said Phoenix, when she had got her breath. "I thank you for your trouble." 41

"Where do you live, Granny?" he asked, while the two dogs were growling at each other. 42

"Away back yonder, sir, behind the ridge. You can't even see it from here." 43

"On your way home?" 44

"No sir, I going to town." 45

"Why, that's too far! That's as far as I walked when I come out myself, and I get something for my trouble." He patted the stuffed bag he carried, and there hung down a little closed claw. It was one of the bob-whites, with its beak hooked bitterly to show it was dead. "Now you go on home, Granny!" 46

"I bound to go to town, mister," said Phoenix. "The time come around." 47

He gave another laugh, filling the whole landscape. "I know you odd colored people! Wouldn't miss going to town to see Santa Claus!" 48

But something held old Phoenix very still. The deep lines in her face went into a fierce and different radiation. Without warning, she had seen with her own eyes a flashing nickel fall out of the man's pocket onto the ground. 49

"How old are you, Granny?" he was saying.   50

"There is no telling, mister," she said, "no telling."   51

Then she gave a little cry and clapped her hands and said, "Git on   52
away from here, dog! Look! Look at that dog!" She laughed as if in admiration. "He ain't scared of nobody. He a big black dog." She whispered, "Sic
him!"

"Watch me get rid of that cur," said the man. "Sic him, Pete! Sic him!"   53

Phoenix heard the dogs fighting, and heard the man running and   54
throwing sticks. She even heard a gunshot. But she was slowly bending
forward by that time, further and further forward, the lids stretched down
over her eyes, as if she were doing this in her sleep. Her chin was lowering
almost to her knees. The yellow palm of her hand came out from the fold of
her apron. Her fingers slid down and along the ground under the piece of
money with the grace and care they would have in lifting an egg from under
a setting hen. Then she slowly straightened up, she stood erect, and the
nickel was in her apron pocket. A bird flew by. Her lips moved. "God
watching me the whole time. I come to stealing."

The man came back, and his own dog panted about them. "Well I   55
scared him off that time," he said, and then he laughed and lifted his gun and
pointed it at Phoenix.

She stood straight and faced him.   56

"Doesn't the gun scare you?" he said, still pointing it.   57

"No sir, I seen plenty go off closer by, in my day, and for less than what 58
I done," she said, holding utterly still.

He smiled, and shouldered the gun. "Well, Granny," he said, "you   59
must be a hundred years old, and scared of nothing. I'd give you a dime if I
had any money with me. But you take my advice and stay home, and
nothing will happen to you."

"I bound to go on my way, mister," said Phoenix. She inclined her head   60
in the red rag. Then they went in different directions, but she could hear the
gun shooting again and again over the hill.

She walked on. The shadows hung from the oak trees to the road like   61
curtains. Then she smelled wood-smoke, and smelled the river, and she saw
a steeple and the cabins on their steep steps. Dozens of little black children
whirled around her. There ahead was Natchez shining. Bells were ringing.
She walked on.

In the paved city it was Christmas time. There were red and green   62
electric lights strung and crisscrossed everywhere, and all turned on in the
daytime. Old Phoenix would have been lost if she had not disturbed her
eyesight and depended on her feet to know where to take her.

She paused quietly on the sidewalk where people were passing by. A   63
lady came along in the crowd, carrying an armful of red, green, and silver-
wrapped presents; she gave off perfume like the red roses in hot summer, and
Phoenix stopped her.

"Please, missy, will you lace up my shoe?" she held up her foot. 64
"What do you want, Grandma?" 65
"See my shoe," said Phoenix. "Do all right for out in the country, but 66 wouldn't look right to go in a big building."
"Stand still then, Grandma," said the lady. She put her packages down 67 on the sidewalk beside her and laced and tied both shoes tightly.
"Can't lace 'em with a cane," said Phoenix. "Thank you, missy. I 68 doesn't mind asking a nice lady to tie up my shoe, when I gets out on the street."
Moving slowly and from side to side, she went into the big building, 69 and into a tower of steps, where she walked up and around and around until her feet knew to stop.
She entered a door, and there she saw nailed up on the wall the 70 documents that had been stamped with the gold seal and framed in the gold frame, which matched the dream that was hung up in her head.
"Here I be," she said. There was a fixed and ceremonial stiffness over 71 her body.
"A charity case, I suppose," said an attendant who sat at the desk 72 before her.
But Phoenix only looked above her head. There was sweat on her face, 73 the wrinkles in her skin shone like a bright net.
"Speak up, Grandma," the woman said. "What's your name? We must 74 have your history, you know. Have you been here before? What seems to be the trouble with you?"
Old Phoenix only gave a twitch to her face as if a fly were bothering 75 her.
"Are you deaf?" cried the attendant. 76
But then the nurse came in. 77
"Oh, that's just old Aunt Phoenix," she said. "She doesn't come for 78 herself—she has a little grandson. She makes these trips just as regular as clockwork. She lives away back of the Old Natchez Trace." She bent down. "Well, Aunt Phoenix, why don't you just take a seat? We won't keep you standing after your long trip." She pointed.
The old woman sat down, bolt upright in the chair. 79
"Now, how is the boy?" asked the nurse. 80
Old Phoenix did not speak. 81
"I said, how is the boy?" 82
But Phoenix only waited and stared ahead, her face very solemn and 83 withdrawn into rigidity.
"Is his throat any better?" asked the nurse. "Aunt Phoenix, don't you 84 hear me? Is your grandson's throat any better since the last time you came for the medicine?"
With her hands on her knees, the old woman, silent, erect, and mo- 85 tionless, just as if she were in armor.

"You mustn't take up our time this way, Aunt Phoenix," the nurse said. 86
"Tell us quickly about your grandson, and get it over. He isn't dead, is he?"

At last there came a flicker and then a flame of comprehension across 87
her face, and she spoke.

"My grandson. It was my memory had left me. There I sat and forgot 88
why I made my long trip."

"Forgot?" The nurse frowned. "After you came so far?" 89

Then Phoenix was like an old woman begging a dignified forgiveness 90
for waking up frightened in the night. "I never did go to school, I was too old
at the Surrender," she said in a soft voice. "I'm an old woman without an
education. It was my memory fail me. My little grandson, he is just the same,
and I forgot it in the coming."

"Throat never heals, does it?" said the nurse, speaking in a loud, sure 91
voice to old Phoenix. By now she had a card with something written on it, a
little list. "Yes. Swallowed lye. When was it?—January—two-three years
ago—"

Phoenix spoke unasked now. "No, missy, he not dead, he just the 92
same. Every little while his throat begin to close up again, and he not able to
swallow. He not get his breath. He not able to help himself. So the time
come around, and I go on another trip for the soothing medicine."

"All right. The doctor said as long as you come to get it, you could 93
have it," said the nurse. "But it's an obstinate case."

"My little grandson, he sit up there in the house all wrapped up, 94
waiting by himself," Phoenix went on. "We is the only two left in the world.
He suffer and it don't seem to put him back at all. He got a sweet look. He
going to last. He wear a little patch quilt and peep out holding his mouth
open like a little bird. I remembers so plain now. I not going to forget him
again, no, the whole enduring time. I could tell him from all the others in
creation."

"All right." The nurse was trying to hush her now. She brought her 95
bottle of medicine. "Charity," she said, making a check mark in a book.

Old Phoenix held the bottle close to her eyes, and then carefully put it 96
into her pocket.

"I thank you," she said. 97

"It's Christmas time, Grandma," said the attendant. "Could I give you 98
a few pennies out of my purse?"

"Five pennies is a nickel," said Phoenix stiffly. 99

"Here's a nickel," said the attendant. 100

Phoenix rose carefully and held out her hand. She received the nickel 101
and then fished the other nickel out of her pocket and laid it beside the new
one. She stared at her palm closely, with her head on one side.

Then she gave a tap with her cane on the floor. 102

"This is what come to me to do," she said. "I going to the store and buy 103
my child a little windmill they sells, made out of paper. He going to find it

hard to believe there such a thing in the world. I'll march myself back where he waiting, holding it straight up in his hand."

She lifted her free hand, gave a little nod, turned around, and walked   10 out of the doctor's office. Then her slow step began on the stairs, going down.

Questions for Study and Discussion

1. Why is Old Phoenix going to Natchez? Who does she tell, and why?
2. What obstacles does Phoenix meet on the way? How, emotionally, does she cope with those obstacles? What does this reveal about her character?
3. How does Phoenix get the money she plans to spend at the end of the story? What will she be bringing home to her grandson? What is the significance of this gift?
4. What is the nature of the relationship between Phoenix and her grandson?
5. In paragraph 90 Phoenix says, "I never did go to school, I was too old at the Surrender." What does this mean?
6. Welty uses many figurative comparisons in this story—for example, "Over she went in the ditch, like a little puff of milkweed." Collect some other examples of metaphor and simile, and explain what each means. Do all of them have something in common? If so, what significance do you find in that?
7. What does the title of the story mean to you? Does it have any metaphorical meaning? Explain.
8. After reading this story, many people have asked: "Is Phoenix Jackson's grandson really dead?" Did this question occur to you? Is an answer to this question important to an understanding of Welty's story? Explain.

Writing Topics

1. Write a character sketch of an old person you know well. If you like, you can organize your sketch by showing your subject engaged in some typical activity.
2. Family obligations can be tiresome chores, or willing acts of love, or even both. What family obligations do you have—or do others have toward you? How do you feel about these obligations? Write an essay in which you explain your thoughts on these obligations.
3. Though brought up in a time and place where racial discrimination and hatred were widespread, Eudora Welty writes of Phoenix Jackson with understanding and love. Is this typical of her? Read some of her other works—perhaps the story "Powerhouse" or the essay "A Pageant of Birds"—and then write an essay in which you assess the image of African-Americans in her work.

The Troubled American Family

MARGARET MEAD

With the publication of *Coming of Age in Samoa* in 1928, Margaret Mead (1901–1978) began a career that would establish her as one of the world's leading cultural anthropologists. During her lifetime she studied in various fields—family structures, primitive societies, ecology, cultural traditions, and mental health. She was curator of ethnology at the American Museum of Natural History and director of Columbia University's Research on Contemporary Cultures. After she retired, she became a contributing editor for *Redbook*, where the following article appeared in 1977. In this essay she examines the problems besetting the contemporary American family. Despite the grim picture she paints, Mead remains essentially optimisitic. She believes that we can help each other make the family viable for ourselves and future generations.

Can the American Family Survive?

All over the United States, families are in trouble. It is true that there 1
are many contented homes where parents are living in harmony and raising
their children responsibly, and with enjoyment in which the children share.
Two out of three American households are homes in which a wife and
husband live together, and almost seven out of ten children are born to
parents living together in their first marriage.

However, though reassuring, these figures are deceptive. A great many 2
of the married couples have already lived through one divorce. And a very
large number of the children in families still intact will have to face the
disruption of their parents' marriage in the future. The numbers increase
every year.

It is also true that the hazards are much greater for some families than 3
for others. Very young couples, the poorly educated, those with few skills and
a low income, Blacks and members of other minority groups—particularly if
they live in big cities—all these are in danger of becoming high-risk families
for whose children a family breakdown is disastrous.

But no group, whatever its status and resources, is exempt. This in 4 itself poses a threat to all families, especially those with young children. For how can children feel secure when their friends in other families so like their own are conspicuously lost and unhappy? In one way or another we all are drawn into the orbit of families in trouble.

Surely it is time for us to look squarely at the problems that beset 5 families and to ask what must be done to make family life more viable, not only for ourselves now but also in prospect for all the children growing up who will have to take responsibility for the next generation.

The Grim Picture

There are those today—as at various times in the past—who doubt 6 that the family can survive, and some who believe it should not survive. Indeed, the contemporary picture is grim enough.

- *Many young marriages entered into with love and high hopes collapse before* 7 *the first baby is weaned. The very young parents, on whom the whole burden of survival rests, cannot make it entirely on their own, and they give up.*
- *Families that include several children break up and the children are uprooted* 8 *from the only security they have known. Some children of divorce, perhaps the majority, will grow up as stepchildren in homes that, however loving, they no longer dare to trust fully. Many—far too many—will grow up in single-parent homes. Still others will be moved, rootless as rolling stones, from foster family to foster family until at last they begin a rootless life on their own.*
- *In some states a family with a male breadwinner cannot obtain welfare, and* 9 *some fathers, unable to provide adequately for their children, desert them so that the mothers can apply for public assistance. And growing numbers of mothers, fearful of being deserted, are leaving their young families while, as they hope and believe, they still have a chance to make a different life for themselves.*
- *As divorce figures have soared—today the proportion of those currently di-* 10 *vorced is more than half again as high as in 1960, and it is predicted that one in three young women in this generation will be divorced—Americans have accepted as a truism the myth that from the mistakes made in their first marriage women and men learn how to do it better the second time around. Sometimes it does work. But a large proportion of those who have resorted to divorce once choose this as the easier solution again and again. Easily dashed hopes become more easily dashed.*
- *At the same time, many working parents, both of whom are trying hard to care* 11 *for and keep together the family they have chosen to bring into being, find that there is no place at all where their children can be cared for safely and gently and responsibly during the long hours of their own necessary absence at their jobs. They have no relatives nearby and there is neither a daycare center nor afterschool care for their active youngsters. Whatever solution they find, their children are likely to suffer.*

The Bitter Consequences

The consequences, direct and indirect, are clear. Thousands of young   12
couples are living together in some arrangement and are wholly dependent
on their private, personal commitment to each other for the survival of their
relationship. In the years from 1970 to 1975 the number of single persons in
the 25-to-34-year age group has increased by half. Some couples living
together have repudiated marriage as a binding social relationship and have
rejected the family as an institution. Others are delaying marriage because
they are not sure of themselves or each other; still others are simply responding to what they have experienced of troubled family life and the effects of
divorce.

At the end of the life span there are the ever-growing numbers of   13
women and men, especially women, who have outlived their slender family
relationships. They have nowhere to turn, no one to depend on but strangers
in public institutions. Unwittingly we have provided the kind of assistance
that, particularly in cities, almost guarantees such isolated and helpless old
people will become the prey of social vultures.

And at all stages of their adult life, demands are made increasingly on   14
women to earn their living in the working world. Although we prefer to
interpret this as an expression of women's wish to fulfill themselves, to have
the rights that go with money earned and to be valued as persons, the
majority of women who work outside their homes do so because they must. It
is striking that ever since the 1950s a larger proportion of married women
with children than of married but childless women have entered the labor
force. According to recent estimates some 14 million women with children—four out of ten mothers of children under six years of age and more
than half of all mothers of school-age children—are working, the great
majority of them in full-time jobs.

A large proportion of these working women are the sole support of   15
their families. Some 10 million children—more than one in six—are living
with only one parent, generally with the mother. This number has doubled
since 1960.

The majority of these women and their children live below the poverty   16
level, the level at which the most minimal needs can be met. Too often the
women, particularly the younger ones, having little education and few skills,
are at the bottom of the paid work force. Though they and their children are
in great need, they are among those least able to demand and obtain what
they require merely to survive decently, in good health and with some hope
for the future.

But the consequences of family trouble are most desperate as they affect   17
children. Every year, all over the country, over 1 million adolescents, nowadays principally girls, run away from home because they have found life with
their families insupportable. Some do not run very far and in the end a great

many come home again, but by no means all of them. And we hear about only a handful whose terrifying experiences or whose death happens to come into public view.

In homes where there is no one to watch over them, elementary school   18 children are discovering the obliterating effects of alcohol; a growing number have become hard-case alcoholics in their early teens. Other young girls and boys, wanderers in the streets, have become the victims of corruption and sordid sex. The youngsters who vent their rage and desperation on others by means of violent crimes are no less social victims than are the girls and boys who are mindlessly corrupted by the adults who prey on them.

Perhaps the most alarming symptom of all is the vast increase in child   19 abuse, which, although it goes virtually unreported in some groups, is not limited to any one group in our population. What seems to be happening is that frantic mothers and fathers, stepparents or the temporary mates of parents turn on the children they do not know how to care for, and beat them—often in a desperate, inarticulate hope that someone will hear their cries and somehow bring help. We know this, but although many organizations have been set up to help these children and their parents, many adults do not know what is needed or how to ask for assistance or whom they may expect a response from.

And finally there are the children who end their own lives in absolute   20 despair. Suicide is now third among the causes of death for youngsters 15 to 19 years old.

What Has Gone Wrong?

In recent years, various explanations have been suggested for the break-   21 down of family life.

Blame has been placed on the vast movement of Americans from rural   22 areas and small towns to the big cities and on the continual restless surge of people from one part of the country to another, so that millions of families, living in the midst of strangers, lack any continuity in their life-style and any real support for their values and expectations.

Others have emphasized the effects of unemployment and under-   23 employment among Blacks and other minority groups, which make their families peculiarly vulnerable in life crises that are exacerbated by economic uncertainty. This is particularly the case where the policies of welfare agencies penalize the family that is poor but intact in favor of the single-parent family.

There is also the generation gap, particularly acute today, when parents   24 and their adolescent children experience the world in such very different ways. The world in which the parents grew up is vanishing, unknown to their children except by hearsay. The world into which adolescents are growing is in many ways unknown to both generations—and neither can help the other very much to understand it.

Then there is our obvious failure to provide for the children and young 25 people whom we do not succeed in educating, who are in deep trouble and who may be totally abandoned. We have not come to grips with the problems of hard drugs. We allow the courts that deal with juveniles to become so overloaded that little of the social protection they were intended to provide is possible. We consistently underfund and understaff the institutions into which we cram children in need of re-education and physical and psychological rehabilitation, as if all that concerned us was to get them—and keep them—out of our sight.

Other kinds of explanations also have been offered. 26

There are many people who, knowing little about child development, 27 have placed the principle blame on what they call "permissiveness"—on the relaxing of parental discipline to include the child as a small partner in the process of growing up. Those people say that children are "spoiled," that they lack "respect" for their parents or that they have not learned to obey the religious prohibitions that were taught to their parents, and that all the troubles plaguing family life have followed.

Women's Liberation, too, has come in for a share of the blame. It is 28 said that in seeking self-fulfillment, women are neglecting their homes and children and are undermining men's authority and men's sense of responsibility. The collapse of the family is seen as the inevitable consequence.

Those who attribute the difficulties of troubled families to any single 29 cause, whether or not it is related to reality, also tend to advocate panaceas, each of which—they say—should restore stability to the traditional family or, alternatively, supplant the family. Universal day care from birth, communal living, group marriage, contract marriage and open marriage all have their advocates.

Each such proposal fastens on some trouble point in the modern 30 family—the lack of adequate facilities to care for the children of working mothers, for example, or marital infidelity, which, it is argued, would be eliminated by being institutionalized. Others, realizing the disastrous effects of poverty on family life, have advocated bringing the income of every family up to a level at which decent living is possible. Certainly this must be one of our immediate aims. But it is wholly unrealistic to suppose that all else that has gone wrong will automatically right itself if the one—but very complex— problem of poverty is eliminated.

A Look at Alternatives

Is there, in fact, any viable alternative to the family as a setting in which 31 children can be successfully reared to become capable and responsible adults, relating to one another and a new generation of children as well as to the world around them? Or should we aim at some wholly new social invention?

Revolutionaries have occasionally attempted to abolish the family, or   32
at least to limit its strength by such measures as arranging for marriages without binding force or for rearing children in different kinds of collectives. But as far as we know, in the long run such efforts have never worked out satisfactorily.

The Soviet Union, for instance, long ago turned away from the flexi-   33
ble, impermanent unions and collective child-care ideals of the early revolutionary days and now heavily emphasizes the values of a stable family life. In Israel the kibbutz, with its children's house and carefully planned, limited contract between parents and children, is losing out to social forms in which the family is both stronger and more closely knit. In Scandinavian countries, where the standards of child care are very high, serious efforts have been made to provide a viable situation for unmarried mothers and the children they have chosen to bring up alone; but there are disturbing indices of trouble, expressed, for example, in widespread alcoholism and a high rate of suicide.

Experience suggests that we would do better to look in other directions.   34
Two approaches may be rewarding. First we can look at other kinds of societies—primitive societies, peasant societies and traditional complex but unindustrialized societies (prerevolutionary China, for example)—to discover whether there are ways in which families are organized that occur in all societies. This can give us some idea of needs that must be satisfied for families to survive and prosper.

Second we can ask whether the problems that are besetting American   35
families are unique or are instead characteristic of families wherever modern industrialization, a sophisticated technology and urban living are drawing people into a new kind of civilization. Placing our own difficulties within a wider context can perhaps help us to assess what our priorities must be as we attempt to develop new forms of stability in keeping with contemporary expressions of human needs.

Looking at human behavior with all that we know—and can infer—   36
about the life of our human species from earliest times, we have to realize that the family, as an association between a man and a woman and the children she bears, has been universal. As far as we know, both primitive "group" marriage and primitive matriarchy are daydreams—or nightmares, depending on one's point of view—without basis in historical reality. On the contrary, the evidence indicates that the couple, together with their children, biological or adopted, are everywhere at the core of human societies, even though this "little family" (as the Chinese called the nuclear family) may be embedded in joint families, extended families of great size, clans, manorial systems, courts, harems or other institutions that elaborate on kin and martial relations.

Almost up to the present, women on the whole have kept close to   37
home and domestic tasks because of the demands of pregnancy and the
nursing of infants, the rearing of children and the care of the disabled and
the elderly. They have been concerned primarily with the conservation of
intimate values and human relations from one generation to another over
immense reaches of time. In contrast, men have performed tasks that require
freer movement over greater distances, more intense physical effort and
exposure to greater immediate danger; and everywhere men have developed
the formal institutions of public life and the values on which these are based.
However differently organized, the tasks of women and men have been
complementary, mutually supportive. And where either the family or the
wider social institutions have broken down, the society as a whole has been
endangered.

In fact, almost everywhere in the world today societies *are* endangered.   38
The difficulties that beset families in the United States are by no means
unique. Families are in trouble everywhere in a world in which change—
kinds of change that in many cases we ourselves proudly initiated—has been
massive and rapid, and innovations have proliferated with only the most
superficial concern for their effect on human lives and the earth itself. One
difference between the United States and many other countries is that,
caring so much about progress, Americans have moved faster. But we may
also have arrived sooner at a turning point at which it becomes crucial to
redefine what we most value and where we are headed.

Looking to the past does not mean that we should return to the past or   39
that we can undo the experiences that have brought us where we are now.
The past can provide us only with a base for judging what threatens sound
family life and for considering whether our social planning is realistic and
inclusive enough. Looking to the past is not a way of binding ourselves but of
increasing our awareness, so that we are freer to find new solutions in
keeping with our deepest human needs.

So the question is not whether women should be forced back into their   40
homes or should have an equal say with men in the world's affairs. We
urgently need to draw on the talents women have to offer. Nor is there any
question whether men should be deprived of a more intimate family role. We
have made a small beginning by giving men a larger share in parenting, and I
believe that men and children have been enriched by it.

What we need to be sure of is that areas of caretaking associated in the   41
past with families do not simply drop out of our awareness so that basic
human needs go unmet. All the evidence indicates that this is where our
greatest difficulties lie. The troubles that plague American families and
families all over the industrialized world are symptomatic of the breakdown
of the responsible relationship between families and the larger communities
of which they are part.

For a long time we have worked hard at isolating the individual family.   42

This has increased the mobility of individuals; and by encouraging young families to break away from the older generation and the home community, we have been able to speed up the acceptance of change and the rapid spread of innovative behavior. But at the same time we have burdened every small family with tremendous responsibilities once shared within three generations and among a large number of people—the nurturing of small children, the emergence of adolescents into adulthood, the care of the sick and disabled and the protection of the aged. What we have failed to realize is that even as we have separated the single family from the larger society, we have expected each couple to take on a range of obligations that traditionally have been shared within a larger family and a wider community.

So all over the world there are millions of families left alone, as it were, each in its own box—parents faced with the specter of what may happen if either one gets sick, children fearful that their parents may end their quarrels with divorce, and empty-handed old people without any role in the life of the next generation.   43

Then, having pared down to almost nothing the relationship between families and the community, when families get into trouble because they cannot accomplish the impossible we turn their problems over to impersonal social agencies, which can act only in a fragmented way because they are limited to patchwork programs that often are too late to accomplish what is most needed.   44

Individuals and families do get some kind of help, but what they learn and what those who work hard within the framework of social agencies convey, even as they try to help, is that families should be able to care for themselves.   45

What Can We Do?

Can we restore family stability? Can we establish new bonds between families and communities? Perhaps most important of all, can we move to a firm belief that living in a family is worth a great effort? Can we move to a new expectation that by making the effort, families can endure? Obviously the process is circular. Both optimism and action are needed.   46

We shall have to distinguish between the things that must be done at once and the relations between families and communities that can be built up only over time. We shall have to accept willingly the cost of what must be done, realizing that whatever we do ultimately will be less costly than our present sorry attempts to cope with breakdown and disaster. And we shall have to care for the failures too.   47

In the immediate future we shall have to support every piece of Federal legislation through which adequate help can be provided for families, both   48 single-parent families and intact poor families, so that they can live decently and safely and prepare their children for another kind of life.

We shall have to support Federal programs for day care and after-school 49 care for the children of working mothers and working parents, and for facilities where in a crisis parents can safely leave their small children for brief periods; for centers where the elderly can be cared for without being isolated from the rest of the world; for housing for young families and older people in communities where they can actually interact as friendly grandparents and grandchildren might; and for a national health program that is concerned not with fleecing the Government but with health care. And we must support the plea of Vice-President Walter F. Mondale, who, as chairman of the Senate Subcommittee on Children and Youth, called for "family impact" statements requiring Government agencies to account for what a proposed policy would do for families—make them worse off or better able to take care of their needs.

Government-funded programs need not be patchwork, as likely to 50 destroy as to save. We need to realize that problems related to family and community life—problems besetting education, housing, nutrition, health care, child care, to name just a few—are interlocked. To solve them, we need awareness of detail combined with concern for the whole, and a wise use of tax dollars to accomplish our aims.

A great deal depends on how we see what is done—whether we value it 51 because we are paying for it and because we realize that the protection given families in need is a protection for all families, including our own. Committing ourselves to programs of care—instead of dissociating ourselves from every effort—is one step in the direction of reestablishing family ties with the community. But this will happen only if we accept the idea that each of us, as part of a community, shares in the responsibility for everyone, and thereby benefits from what is done.

The changes that are needed cannot be accomplished by Federal legisla- 52 tion alone. Over a longer time we must support the design and building of communities in which there is housing for three generations, for the fortunate and the unfortunate, and for people of many backgrounds. Such communities can become central in the development of the necessary support system for families. But it will take time to build such communities, and we cannot afford just to wait and hope they will happen.

Meanwhile we must act to interrupt the runaway belief that marriages 53 must fail, that parents and children can't help but be out of communication, that the family as an institution is altogether in disarray. There still are far more marriages that succeed than ones that fail; there are more parents and children who live in trust and learn from one another than ones who are out of touch; there are more people who care about the future than we acknowledge.

What we need, I think, is nationwide discussion—in magazines, 54 in newspapers, on television panel shows and before Congressional committees—of how people who are happily married can help those who are not, how people who are fortunate can help those who are not and how people who have too little to do can help those who are burdened by too much.

Out of such discussions can come a heightened awareness and perhaps   55
some actual help, but above all, fresh thought about what must be done and the determination to begin to do it.

It is true that all over the United States families are in trouble. Realiz-   56
ing this should not make us cynical about the family. It should start us working for a new version of the family that is appropriate to the contemporary world.

Questions for Study and Discussion

1. What types of families, according to Mead, are more prone to breakdown? Why do you suppose this is true? What effect does this breakdown have on the children of so-called secure families?

2. In paragraph 6 Mead draws a grim picture of the contemporary American family. In her analysis of the situation what does she see as the major effects on adults? On children?

3. What for Mead is the "most alarming symptom" of family trouble? What explanation does she offer for why it occurs so often?

4. What according to Mead are the explanations that have been suggested for the breakdown of family life? Which ones do you find most plausible?

5. Mead suggests that it is sometimes helpful to look to the past. Does she advocate returning to the past? Explain.

6. What does Mead mean when she states in paragraph 41, "The troubles that plague American families and families all over the industrialized world are symptomatic of the breakdown of the responsible relationship between families and the larger communities of which they are part"?

7. Paragraphs 1 through 5 introduce Mead's essay. What would be gained or lost had Mead combined these paragraphs into a single paragraph?

8. What solutions to the problem of family breakdown does Mead offer? Do you agree with her on any of these solutions? Wouldn't the dissolution of the family structure be a much easier solution? Does Mead see this as a viable alternative?

Writing Topics

1. Write an essay in which you argue for one or more innovative alternatives to the family as a traditional social unit.

2. Write an essay in which you explore the importance of family for you. What benefits do you derive from your family? What do you give your family in return? Do you think the American family is in trouble? Why or why not?

MICHAEL REESE and PAMELA ABRAMSON

In the last few years, the spread of AIDS has heightened public awareness of the homosexual lifestyle. Nevertheless, most parents still react with anger and denial at the news of their child's homosexuality. In the following selection, Michael Reese and Pamela Abramson chronicle the reactions of each member of the Chronister family to just such news. And while the parents' negative reaction to their son Kelly's homosexuality may be expected, what is surprising is that Kelly also experienced feelings of guilt, shame, and anxiety. The story, which is at once objective and sensitive, first ran as a cover story for a January 1986 issue of *Newsweek*.

Homosexuality: One Family's Affair

It was the hardest question she'd ever had to ask. "Are you gay?" Joan   1
Chronister finally blurted out to her son, Kelly, who was fidgeting at the other end of the sofa. When he begrudgingly, almost bitterly, replied yes, Joan immediately felt her tears and disgust dissolve into detachment. After 22 years of nursing him through mumps and measles, tending his cuts and bruises and applauding his football feats and straight-A report cards, Joan suddenly saw her son as a stranger. *He's my child,* she thought as he walked out the door. *And I don't even know him.*

That afternoon Joan sat and sobbed, unsure whether she was crying   2
for Kelly or the family's dashed expectations. He had been named after K. O. Kelly, Brenda Starr's rough-and-tough comic-strip boyfriend, because his father wanted him to be "tough as hell." But expectations die hard, and if Paul Chronister was disappointed that Kelly hadn't always been his idea of tough, it was nothing compared with the betrayal he felt when he learned his son was homosexual. It was, he says bitterly, like "the son I knew had died, and a new one was born." Four years have passed, and the Chronisters are still trying to cope with that jarring midlife adjustment. It's been both an individual and a family struggle—and has coincided with the nation's heightened awareness of homosexuality because of the AIDS

health crisis. What the Chronisters have learned is that there is no easy way for an American family to confront homosexuality. Joan has taped a saying to her refrigerator door to remind herself of that. "Be into acceptance," it says. "Not understanding."

The Chronisters' entire notion of homosexuality had been shaped by stereotypes: effeminate men with limp wrists. But Kelly wasn't like that. His preppy good looks, athletic prowess and All-American demeanor never foretold that today, at 26, he would be living with his lover, Randy Ponce, in a fashionable brownstone in a gay enclave of northwestern Portland, Ore. It's just 15 miles south of his parents' tidy ranch house in Vancouver, Wash., but it might as well be a foreign country. Though Joan was raised in a tolerant rural Canadian family and Paul broke early from his own Pentecostal upbringing, they have remained conservative in their social values—clinging to tenets that took them from being penniless newlyweds to life as owners of three successful pizza franchises in Washington state.

Paul was proud of his own aggressive instincts in business but thought them lacking in his son. "If we could just get him to be a little meaner," Paul would say, "he could go as far as he wanted to go." That wasn't Kelly. He could be competitive, playing a hard game of street hockey or starring as first-string tackle on his high-school football team. But he was always hardest on himself, a perfectionist who still remembers a B in seventh-grade science as a crushing defeat. Even at home Kelly was almost *too* good, always eager to fix dinners and do the laundry. "Odd that a teen-age boy wants to help his mom," Joan remembers thinking. Both she and Paul came to regard Kelly's perfectionism as his greatest fault. "Everyone is looking for the perfect kid," sighs Paul. "Then you have one and you wish they'd be a little bit ornery."

On the Fringe

Kelly saw his perfectionism as a way of hiding from himself and from others. By always being the teacher's pet, by being a hustler in football practice and by being a fringe member of many social groups but the leader of none, Kelly managed to mask his insecurities. Despite his achievements, he had long felt himself an outsider, separate from his peers. He remembers vague sexual feelings as early as the age of seven, when he would linger in the boys' showers after swimming lessons. When his feelings blossomed in his early teens, Kelly had no point of reference and no one he felt comfortable talking to. The only person he even suspected might be gay was a coach whom all the other boys laughed at when they caught him eyeing them in the showers. And though Kelly knew he was only looking for guys when he peeked at his father's girlie magazines, it confused him when he once saw a pornographic picture of a man putting on nylons. "That isn't me," he thought.

It was easier for Kelly to know what he wasn't. He wasn't comfortable   6
when his footbal buddies told faggot jokes; he knew he might betray himself
by not laughing, so he even told a few himself. He wasn't able to join in their
postgame drinking and picking-up-girls sprees: he was afraid that if he got
drunk the truth might slip out. Most of all, he wasn't interested in girls. He
came up with lame excuses for those bold enough to ask him out. When that
failed, he made up an imaginary girlfriend who lived out of town and to
whom he loudly professed he would always remain loyal.

At home, Kelly's cover-ups were just as elaborate. He refused to ask his   7
parents to buy him a coat and tie for his senior yearbook photo session
because he was afraid they would expect him to wear the new clothes to a
dance or on a date. Then, when his father inevitably asked why he wasn't
going to the senior prom, Kelly could shrug and say he had nothing to wear.
The ruse seemed to work. His parents never suspected that their son might
be homosexual. That was something entirely beyond their realm of experience; Kelly, they assured each other, was simply shy and would "come out of
his shell" in college. But Kelly knew all along that he was postponing the
crisis. He saw college as his only escape.

After a few months at Eastern Washington University near Spokane,   8
Kelly began to feel despair. There was no one on campus he even remotely
thought might be gay. Then one fall day Kelly found himself on the athletic
field staring at another student; the young man returned Kelly's stare, came
over and struck up a conversation. That night Kelly agonized over the
overture: *Maybe he's gay. Maybe it'll finally happen.* But Kelly still wasn't sure,
even when they met again the next day on the athletic field and exchanged
an awkward touch. Finally, a few weeks later, they moved into a private
music room, where Kelly listened for hours while his friend played the piano.
There Kelly had his first sexual experience with another man.

It left him scared, happy but even more confused than before. "What's   9
going to happen to me? What kind of a life will I have?" he kept asking
himself between encounters with his friend that continued sporadically for
the next four years. "Why do I feel this way?" There were few places to turn
for answers. At that time the gay community at Eastern Washington was
virtually invisible. There was not—as there is now—a Gay Students' Union
or places that openly offered counseling to gay students. His sexual contact
throughout college was restricted to that single relationship. Kelly channeled
his energy into his business studies and long, lonely bicycle rides along the
wheat fields near campus. He sometimes rode a hundred miles a day, as if just
by pedaling hard enough and fast enough he could push away his feelings.

Knowing what he now knew about himself, Kelly couldn't face long   10
family visits or summers working for his father at the pizza parlor. Instead, he
moved from the dorms into an apartment of his own, immersed himself in
classes and timidly continued his sexual education. He went to the campus
bookstore, furtively browsing through gay psychology texts he was too afraid

to buy. Through the mail he ordered a "gay guide" of Spokane but couldn't work up the nerve to go into the three gay bars that were listed. Finally, one Thanksgiving, he imploded. After fixing himself Cornish game hens, mashed potatoes, gravy and pumpkin pie, he went for along walk in the snow. *I know what I am*, he thought, *but why me? Why was I dealt this?* He began to cry. *I'm alone*, he sobbed, *and it's because I'm gay that I'm alone.*

Kelly's fear of rejection meant he could share his secret with no one,   11
especially not his family. When his parents called and teased him about girls, he always responded with a curt "Leave me alone." That's just Kelly's way, they told themselves, glad that at least he seemed to be doing well in school. And when he graduated with high honors in business management, they proudly drove the six hours to Spokane thinking their son's future was made—that surely a wife and grandchildren would soon follow. But Paul never made it to the ceremonies. After suffering chest pains, he was rushed by air ambulance back to Portland for open-heart surgery. Kelly, who had made no firm postgraduation plans, suddenly found himself back in Vancouver watching TV and helping to run the pizza parlors.

He could stand it only for so long. Soon he was back on his bicycle—   12
speeding across the river to Portland, a gay-bar guide tucked in his back pocket. Still too scared to go inside, Kelly usually ended up alone in some shopping-mall restaurant, drinking coffee. That's where he met David, whom Kelly, despite his apprehension, accompanied to his first gay bar, The Rafters. It was not at all what he had imagined. Instead of being dark and ominous, it was bright and friendly; instead of aging drag queens and tough guys in leather, the bar was filled with good-looking young men dancing and having a good time. *They're just average Joes!* Kelly thought. *Guys just like me.*

Kelly didn't feel that way about David, who was loud, flamboyant and   13
sissified in his dress—not at all the sort Kelly wanted his parents to meet. Or did he? To this day, Kelly isn't sure whether he wasn't trying to make a statement the one time he brought David home—or whether he really wanted to slip him out before Joan, eager to meet the first friend Kelly had brought home in years, confronted them at the front door. Joan took one look and went pale. "Oh, my God," she said to Paul after they had left. "That boy with Kelly is queer."

A Secret Search

She tried to make sense of it. She looked back on Kelly's mood swings,   14
his long, unexplained bike rides into Portland and his almost giddy excitement about going to a Halloween party; that wasn't like Kelly, especially staying out all night with the excuse he'd had too much to drink. But Joan needed proof. Shaking with guilt and apprehension, she steamed open a letter, and searched through his dresser drawers, where she found a scrap of

paper. Written on it was the title of a book: "Young, Gay and Proud." "He's queer! He's queer!" she screamed, running hysterically into the arms of her husband, who held her and tried to tell her it was going to be OK.

When Joan confronted Kelly the next day, Paul decided to get "the hell   15
out of the house." Unable to face Kelly or more of Joan's tears, Paul beat a hasty overnight retreat to one of his pizza parlors; he felt he needed to be alone with his anger, sadness and confusion. He tried not to place blame, but the thoughts came anyway: "Jesus, Joan was more domineering than I was." He felt anger toward Kelly: "He can't cope with the ladies. He's taking the easy way out." He wondered whether they should send him to a psychiatrist: "You have a flat tire, you fix it." Finally, alone in a motel room, Paul broke down and cried, an uncharacteristic release for a man who always held everything inside. But it didn't help: that night Paul suffered a mild heart attack.

With Paul sick and uneager to talk about Kelly, Joan had no one to   16
share her own quandry. Finally she looked in the Yellow Pages under "H" for homosexuals and then under "G," where she found a listing for a gay-crisis hot line. She was trembling when she picked up the phone, and her voice cracked when she first heard herself say the words out loud: "My son is gay." The hot line put her in touch with another mother, who listened to Joan's story and promised to send her a pamphlet about a support group for friends and parents of gay people. She invited Joan to a Gay Men's Chorus Christmas performance. Joan, accompanied by Kelly's older sister, Rhonda, was overwhelmed to see hundreds of gay men, so many of them just like Kelly. She asked them questions: "Where do you work?" "Where do you live?" "Do your parents accept you?" But most of all she kept asking, "Are you happy?"

Icy Stares

Joan realized she'd been closed off from Kelly's world and she wanted to   17
make up for lost time. But she had to do it on her own. Paul was in retreat, refusing to talk about it or even to acknowledge Kelly when he came home to pick up some of his possessions; he had moved in with a man in Portland. Kelly continued to keep his mother at arm's length; their phone calls and visits consisted of monosyllables and icy stares. Finally, while Paul slumped silently in his chair in the family room, Joan attended a monthly support-group meeting. It took her months to choke out the words: "I'm Joan Chronister and I have a gay son."

She listened and learned, quickly realizing that Kelly was not going to   18
change and that no one was to blame. She started manning the hot line and joining excursions to Portland's gay bars. She talked with all kinds of people—from drag queens and lesbians to other parents of gays—and if she couldn't completely understand, at least she was beginning to accept. One

June day she attended Portland's Gay Pride Day parade. As she watched the curious crowd go by, Joan noticed a lone man holding a sign, "Parents and Friends of Lesbians and Gay Men." Overcome with emotion, she stepped out into the street and joined him.

Paul never marched or went to a support-group meeting. Instead, he stayed at home and hoped time would work its wonders. For a while he thought Kelly might come home lisping and limp-wristed; when he didn't Paul breathed a sigh of relief and decided it was enough to accept what he'd accepted that first night in his motel room: that as much as he hated Kelly's homosexuality, he could never close the door on his own son. He still doesn't want to know what Kelly's gay life and friends are like, or to imagine what he does inside his bedroom. Joan's transformation into self-proclaimed gay-rights activist sometimes creates a strain. "I don't want to hash it over all the time," says Paul. "But she has the need, an exceptional need." 19

Stable Relationship

It's also hard on Kelly, who is still trying to find a comfortable way to express his sexuality. He's come a long way since he and a boyfriend showed up at Rhonda's wedding wearing identical blazers and pink shirts. Now Kelly tries to make a softer statement by inviting his parents to dinner and letting his relationship with Randy speak for itself. They met more than two years ago through a mutual friend; they found they shared a distaste for the bar scene and a desire for a stable relationship. Since then they've exchanged identical gold rings, furnished a home together and worked side by side at a suburban Portland video store; with their joint savings account, they now plan to go back to college and maybe start a business. And if Paul still can't bring himself to refer to Randy as his sons "lover," Kelly understands. He knows by the way his father teases and firmly shakes Randy's hand that Paul is, in his own way, making an effort to accept them both. 20

It is problematic whether the fractures Kelly's homosexuality has opened in the Chronister family will ever completely heal. Paul continues to struggle with his inner anguish and could not bring himself to accompany his wife to the Portland Gay Pride Day parade, where she spoke last June ("My name is Joan Chronister and I'm proud my child is homosexual"). Joan for her part blames her husband for not being more understanding. Both are trying to reach some sort of common ground between themselves. 21

And for Kelly there remains detachment from his parents and uncertainty about the future. He was all of 10 when the gay-rights movement was born with the 1969 Stonewall Inn riot. And though he has never been inside a bathhouse or slipped into the boozy world of obsessive sex, he knows that AIDS—not cries of liberation—is the historical force shaping his generation of gay men. He hears evangelists call the epidemic divine retribution for 22 crimes against nature and he fears the political backlash that might come. But he has no illusions about changing society—or changing himself. Says Kelly, "It's part of my being."

Questions for Study and Discussion

1. When Kelly's mother learned of her son's homosexuality she said, "He's my child. And I don't even know him." His father said, "The son I knew had died, and a new one was born." Based on comments they made later, what do you suppose they meant by these remarks?

2. Why was it easier for Kelly when he was young to know what he "wasn't" rather than what he "was"?

3. Although Kelly is a homosexual, he harbored many stereotypical attitudes of his own against gay men. What were some of these stereotypes? What were some of the "truths" he learned about gay men?

4. What devices did Kelly employ to hide his insecurities from himself and from others?

5. How was the anguish of Kelly's homosexuality similar for him and for his parents? How was it different? How has each of them chosen to deal with it? How realistic do you think their various choices are?

6. The title suggests that the authors will present the attitudes of each member of the Chronister family. What of the authors' attitudes toward their subjects? Do the authors' tones vary from section to section as they deal with different members of the family? Do they present one or another of the family members more favorably? Cite examples of diction and tone to support your answer.

7. The members of the Chronister family ask themselves many questions. What are some of these questions? Why do you suppose they are left unanswered? Choose one or two and answer them yourself.

Writing Topics

1. After reading about the Chronister family, how would you describe each of them? How do you feel about each of them? Is anyone more or less sympathetic? What reasons can you offer for your opinion?

2. Imagine that you have to tell your parents something about yourself that you expect they will find deeply disturbing, such as that you are gay, or marrying someone they will object to, or changing your religion. In an essay describe how you would tell them. How do you think they would receive the news?

JANE HOWARD

Jane Howard was born in Springfield, Illinois, in 1935. After graduating from the University of Michigan, she went to work for *Life* magazine, first as a reporter, then as an editor, and finally as a staff reporter. Later she taught courses in writing at the University of Georgia, Yale University, the State University of New York at Albany, and Southampton College. From 1974 to 1983 she served as the book critic for *Mademoiselle*. Her published works include *Please Touch: A Guided Tour of the Human Potential Movement* (1970), *A Different Woman* (1973), *Families* (1978), and *Margaret Mead: A Life* (1984).

The following selection is from *Families*, about which the *New York Review of Books* critic Diane Johnson wrote, "All in all, there's comfort in Howard's book for everyone who worries about his family arrangements—that is, for 83.7 percent of us. It's reassuring to read about people who are weirder than you are, and inspiring to read about people who are better."

All Happy Clans Are Alike: In Search of the Good Family

Call it a clan, call it a network, call it a tribe, call it a family. Whatever 1 you call it, whoever you are, you need one. You need one because you are human. You didn't come from nowhere. Before you, around you, and presumably after you, too, there are others. Some of these others must matter a lot—to you, and if you are very lucky, to one another. Their welfare must be nearly as important to you as your own. Even if you live alone, even if your solitude is elected and ebullient, you still cannot do without a clan or a tribe.

The trouble with the clans and tribes many of us were born into is not 2 that they consist of meddlesome ogres but that they are too far away. In emergencies we rush across continents and if need be oceans to their sides, as they do to ours. Maybe we even make a habit of seeing them, once or twice a year, for the sheer pleasure of it. But blood ties seldom dictate our addresses. Our blood kin are often too remote to ease us from our Tuesdays to our Wednesdays. For this we must rely on our families of friends. If our relatives are not, do not wish to be, or for whatever reasons cannot be our friends, then by some complex alchemy we must try to transform our friends into our relatives. If blood and roots don't do the job, then we must look to water and branches, and sort ourselves into new constellations, new families.

These new families, to borrow the terminology of an African tribe (the 3

154

Bangwa of the Cameroons), may consist either of friends of the road, as-cribed by chance, or friends of the heart, achieved by choice. Ascribed friends are those we happen to go to school with, work with, or live near. They know where we went last weekend and whether we still have a cold. Just being around gives them a provisional importance in our lives, and us in theirs. Maybe they will still matter to us when we or they move away; quite likely they won't. Six months or two years will probably erase us from each other's thoughts, unless by some chance they and we have become friends of the heart.

Wishing to be friends, as Aristotle wrote, is quick work, but friendship 4 is a slowly ripening fruit. An ancient proverb he quotes in his *Ethics* had it that you cannot know a man until you and he together have eaten a peck of salt. Now a peck, a quarter of a bushel, is quite a lot of salt—more, perhaps, than most pairs of people ever have occasion to share. We must try though. We must sit together at as many tables as we can. We must steer each other through enough seasons and weathers so that sooner or later it crosses our minds that one of us, God knows which or with what sorrow, must one day mourn the other.

We must devise new ways, or revive old ones, to equip ourselves with 5 kinfolk. Maybe such an impulse prompted whoever ordered the cake I saw in my neighborhood bakery to have it frosted to say "HAPPY BIRTHDAY SURRO-GATE." I like to think that this cake was decorated not for a judge but for someone's surrogate mother or surrogate brother: Loathsome jargon, but admirable sentiment. If you didn't conceive me or if we didn't grow up in the same house, we can still be related, if we decide we ought to be. It is never too late, I like to hope, to augment our families in ways nature neglected to do. It is never too late to choose new clans.

The best-chosen clans, like the best friendships and the best blood 6 families, endure by accumulating a history solid enough to suggest a future. But clans that don't last have merit too. We can lament them but we shouldn't deride them. Better an ephemeral clan or tribe than none at all. A few of my life's most totally joyous times, in fact, have been spent with people whom I have yet to see again. This saddens me, as it may them too, but dwelling overlong on such sadness does no good. A more fertile exercise is to think back on those times and try to figure out what made them, for all their brevity, so stirring. What can such times teach us about forming new and more lasting tribes in the future?

New tribes and clans can no more be willed into existence, of course, 7 than any other good thing can. We keep trying, though. To try, with gritted teeth and girded loins, is after all American. That is what the two Helens and I were talking about the day we had lunch in a room up in a high-rise motel near the Kansas City airport. We had lunch there at the end of a two-day conference on families. The two Helens were social scientists, but I liked them even so, among other reasons because they both objected to that motel's coffee shop even more than I did. One of the Helens, from Virginia, disliked it so much that she had brought along homemade whole wheat bread, sesame butter, and honey from her parents' farm in South Dakota, where she had visited before the conference. Her picnic was the best thing that happened, to me at least, those whole two days.

"If you're voluntarily childless and alone," said the other Helen, who   8 was from Pennsylvania by way of Puerto Rico, "it gets harder and harder with the passage of time. It's stressful. That's why you need support systems." I had been hearing quite a bit of talk about "support systems." The term is not among my favorites, but I can understand its currency. Whatever "support systems" may be, the need for them is clearly urgent, and not just in this country. Are there not thriving "megafamilies" of as many as three hundred people in Scandinavia? Have not the Japanese for years had an honored, enduring—if perhaps by our standards rather rigid—custom of adopting nonrelatives to fill gaps in their families? Should we not applaud and maybe imitate such ingenuity?

And consider our own Unitarians. From Santa Barbara to Boston they   9 have been earnestly dividing their congregations into arbitrary "extended families" whose members are bound to act like each other's relatives. Kurt Vonnegut, Jr., plays with a similar train of thought in his fictional *Slapstick*. In that book every newborn baby is assigned a randomly chosen middle name, like Uranium or Daffodil or Raspberry. These middle names are connected with hyphens to numbers between one and twenty, and any two people who have the same middle name are automatically related. This is all to the good, the author thinks, because "human beings need all the relatives they can get—as possible donors or receivers not of love but of common decency." He envisions these extended families as "one of the four greatest inventions by Americans," the others being *Robert's Rules of Order*, the Bill of Rights, and the principles of Alcoholics Anonymous.

This charming notion might even work, if it weren't so arbitrary.   10 Already each of us is born into one family not of our choosing. If we're going to devise new ones, we might as well have the luxury of picking the members ourselves. Clever picking might result in new families whose benefits would surpass or at least equal those of the old. As a member in reasonable standing of six or seven tribes in addition to the one I was born to, I have been trying to figure which characteristics are common to both kinds of families.

1. Good families have a chief, or a heroine, or a founder—someone   11 around whom others cluster, whose achievements, as the Yiddish word has it, let them *kvell*, and whose example spurs them on to like feats. Some blood dynasties produce such figures regularly; others languish for as many as five generations between demigods, wondering with each new pregnancy whether this, at last, might be the messianic baby who will redeem them. Look, is there not something gubernatorial about her footstep, or musical about the way he bangs with his spoon on his cup? All clans, of all kinds,

need such a figure now and them. Sometimes clans based on water rather than blood harbor several such personages at one time. The Bloomsbury Group in London six decades ago was not much hampered by its lack of a temporal history.

2. Good families have a switchboard operator—someone who cannot help but keep track of what all the others are up to, who plays Houston Mission Control to everyone else's Apollo. This role is assumed rather than assigned. The person who volunteers for it often has the instincts of an archivist, and feels driven to keep scrapbooks and photograph albums up to date, so that the clan can see proof of its own continuity.   12

3. Good families are much to all their members, but everything to none. Good families are fortresses with many windows and doors to the outer world. The blood clans I feel most drawn to were founded by parents who are nearly as devoted to what they do outside as they are to each other and their children. Their curiosity and passion are contagious. Everybody, where they live, is busy. Paint is spattered on eyeglasses. Mud lurks under fingernails. Person-to-person calls come in the middle of the night from Tokyo and Brussels. Catcher's mitts, ballet slippers, overdue library books, and other signs of extrafamilial concerns are everywhere.   13

4. Good families are hospitable. Knowing that hosts need guests as much as guests need hosts, they are generous with honorary memberships for friends, whom they urge to come early and often and to stay late. Such clans exude a vivid sense of surrounding rings of relatives, neighbors, teachers, students, and godparents, any of whom at any time might break or slide into the inner circle. Inside that circle a wholesome, tacit emotional feudalism develops: you give me protection, I'll give you fealty. Such pacts begin with, but soon go far beyond, the jolly exchange of pie at Thanksgiving or cake on a birthday. They mean that you can ask me to supervise your children for the fortnight you will be in the hospital, and that however inconvenient this might be for me, I shall manage to do so. It means I can phone you on what for me is a dreary, wretched Sunday afternoon and for you is the eve of a deadline, knowing you will tell me to come right over, if only to watch you type. It means we need not dissemble. ("To yield to seeming," as Martin Buber wrote, "is man's essential cowardice, to resist it is his essential courage . . . one must at times pay dearly for life lived from the being, but it is never too dear.")   14

5. Good families deal squarely with direness. Pity the tribe that doesn't have, and cherish, at least one flamboyant eccentric. Pity too the one that supposes it can avoid for long the woes to which all flesh is heir. Lunacy, bankruptcy, suicide, and other unthinkable fates sooner or later afflict the noblest of clans with an undertow of gloom. Family life is a set of givens, someone once told me, and it takes courage to see certain givens as blessings rather than as curses. It surely does. Contradictions and inconsistencies are givens, too. So is the battle against what the Oregon patriarch Kenneth   15

Babbs calls malarkey. "There's always malarkey lurking, bubbles in the cess-pool, fetid bubbles that pop and smell. But I don't put up with malarkey, between my stepkids and my natural ones or anywhere else in the family."

6. Good families prize their rituals. Nothing welds a family more than these. Rituals are vital especially for clans without histories, because they evoke a past, imply a future, and hint at continuity. No line in the seder service at Passover reassures more than the last: "Next year in Jerusalem!" A clan becomes more of a clan each time it gathers to observe a fixed ritual (Christmas, birthdays, Thanksgiving, and so on), grieves at a funeral (any-one may come to most funerals; those who do declare their tribalness), and devises a new rite of its own. Equinox breakfasts can be at least as welding as Memorial Day parades. Several of my colleagues and I used to meet for lunch every Pearl Harbor Day, preferably to eat some politically neutral fare like smorgasbord, to "forgive" our only ancestrally Japanese friend, Irene Kubota Neves. For that and other things we became, and remain, a sort of family.

"Rituals," a California friend of mine said, "aren't just externals and holidays. They are the performances of our lives. They are a kind of short-hand. They can't be decreed. My mother used to try to decree them. She'd make such a goddamn fuss over what we talked about at dinner, aiming at Topics of Common Interest, topics that celebrated our cohesion as a family. These performances were always hollow, because the phenomenology of the moment got sacrificed for the *idea* of the moment. Real rituals are discovered in retrospect. They emerge around constitutive moments, moments that only happen once, around whose memory meanings cluster. You don't choose those moments. They choose themselves." A lucky clan includes a born mythologizer, like my blood sister, who has the gift for apprehending such a moment when she sees it, and who cannot help but invent new rituals everywhere she goes.

7. Good families are affectionate. This of course is a matter of style. I know clans whose members greet each other with gingerly handshakes or, in what pass for kisses, with hurried brushes of jawbones, as if the object were to touch not the lips but the ears. I don't see how such people manage. "The tribe that does not hug," as someone who has been part of many *ad hoc* families recently wrote to me, "is no tribe at all. More and more I realize that everybody, regardless of age, needs to be hugged and comforted in a brotherly or sisterly way now and then. Preferably now."

8. Good families have a sense of place, which these days is not achieved easily. As Susanne Langer wrote in 1957, "Most people have no home that is a symbol of their childhood, not even a definite memory of one place to serve that purpose . . . all the old symbols are gone." Once I asked a roomful of supper guests if anyone felt a strong pull to any certain spot on the face of the earth. Everyone was silent, except for a visitor from Bavaria. The rest of us seemed to know all too well what Walker Percy means in *The Moviegoer* when he tells of the "genie-soul of a place, which every place has

or else is not a place [and which] wherever you go, you must meet and master or else be met and mastered." All that meeting and mastering saps plenty of strength. It also underscores our need for tribal bases of the sort which soaring real estate taxes and splintering families have made all but obsolete.

So what are we to do, those of us whose habit and pleasure and doom is   20
our tendency, as a Georgia lady put it, to "fly off at every other whipstitch?" Think in terms of movable feasts, that's what. Live here, wherever here may be, as if we were going to belong here for the rest of our lives. Learn to hallow whatever ground we happen to stand on or land on. Like medieval knights who took their tapestries along on Crusades, like modern Afghanis with their yurts, we must pack such totems and icons as we can to make short-term quarters feel like home. Pillows, small rugs, watercolors can dispel much of the chilling anonymity of a motel room or sublet apartment. When we can, we should live in rooms with stoves or fireplaces or at least candlelight. The ancient saying is true: Extinguished hearth, extinguished family.

Round tables help too, and as a friend of mine once put it, so do "too   21
many comfortable chairs, with surfaces to put feet on, arranged so as to encourage a maximum of eye contact." Such rooms inspire good talk, of which good clans can never have enough.

9. Good families, not just the blood kind, find some way to connect   22
with posterity. "To forge a link in the humble chain of being, encircling heirs to ancestors," as Michael Novak has written, "is to walk within a circle of magic as primitive as humans knew in caves." He is talking of course about babies, feeling them leap in wombs, giving them suck. Parenthood, however, is a state which some miss by chance and others by design, and a vocation to which not all are called. Some of us, like the novelist Richard P. Brickner, look on as others "name their children and their children in turn name their own lives, devising their own flags from their parents' cloth." What are we who lack children to do? Build houses? Plant trees? Write books or symphonies or laws? Perhaps, but even if we do these things, there should be children on the sidelines if not at the center of our lives.

It is a sadly impoverished tribe that does not allow access to, and make   23
much of, some children. Not too much, of course; it has truly been said that never in history have so many educated people devoted so much attention to so few children. Attention, in excess, can turn to fawning, which isn't much better than neglect. Still, if we don't regularly see and talk to and laugh with people who can expect to outlive us by twenty years or so, we had better get busy and find some.

10. Good families also honor their elders. The wider the age range,   24
the stronger the tribe. Jean-Paul Sartre and Margaret Mead, to name two spectacularly confident former children, have both remarked on the central importance of grandparents in their own early lives. Grandparents are now in much more abundant supply than they were a generation or two ago, when old age was more rare. If actual grandparents are not at hand, no family

should have too hard a time finding substitute ones to whom to pay un-feigned homage. The Soviet Union's enchantment with day-care centers, I have heard, stems at least in part from the state's eagerness to keep children away from their presumably subversive grandparents. Let that be a lesson to clans based on interest as well as to those based on genes.

Of courses there are elders and elders. Most people in America, as   25
David T. Bazelon has written, haven't the slightest idea of what to do with the extra thirty years they have been given to live. Few are as briskly secure as Alice Roosevelt Longworth, who once, when I visited her for tea, showed a recent photograph and asked whether I didn't think it made her look like "a malevolent Eurasian concubine—an *aged* malevolent Eurasian concu-bine." I admitted that it did, which was just what she wanted to hear. But those of us whose fathers weren't Presidents may not grow old, if at all, with such style.

Sad stories abound. The mother of one friend of mine languished for   26
years, never far from a coma, in a nursing home. Only when her husband and children sang one of her favorite old songs, such as "Lord Jeffrey Am-herst," would a smile fleet across her face. But a man I know of in New Jersey, who couldn't stand the state of Iowa or babies, changed his mind on both counts when his daughter, who lived in Iowa, had a baby. Suddenly he took to inventing business trips to St. Louis, by way of Cedar Rapids, phoning to say he would be at the airport there at 11:31 P.M. and "Be sure to bring Jake!" That cheers me. So did part of a talk I had with a woman in Albuquerque, whom I hadn't seen since a trip some years before to the Soviet Union.

"Honey," she said when I phoned her during a short stopover and asked   27
how she was, "if I were any better I'd blow up and *bust!* I can't *tell* you how *neat* it is to put some age on! A lot of it, of course, has to do with going to the shrink, getting uncorked, and of course it doesn't hurt to have money—no, we *don't* have a ranch; it's only 900 acres, so we call it a farm. But every year, as far as age is concerned, I seem to get better, doing more and more stuff I love to do. The only thing I've ever wanted and don't have is a good marriage. Nothing I do ever pleases the men I marry. The only reason I'm still married now is it's too much trouble not to be. But my girls are growing up to be just *neat* humans, and the men they're sharing their lives with are too. They pick nice guys, my girls. I wish I could say the same. But I'm a lot better off than many women my age. I go to parties where sixty-year-olds with blue bouffant hairdos are still telling the same jokes they told twenty-five or thirty years ago. Complacent? No, that's not it, exactly. What they are is sad—sad as the dickens. They don't seem to be *connected*."

Some days my handwriting resembles my mother's, slanting hopefully   28
and a bit extravagantly eastward. Other days it looks more like my father's: resolute, vertical, guardedly free of loops. Both my parents will remain in my nerves and muscles and mind until the day I die, and so will my sister, but

they aren't the only ones. If I were to die tomorrow, the obituary would note that my father and sister survived me. True, but not true enough. Like most official lists of survivors, this one would be incomplete.

Several of the most affecting relationships I have ever known of, or been part of, have sprung not from genes or contracts but from serendipitous, uncanny bonds of choice. I don't think enough can be said for the fierce tenderness such bonds can generate. Maybe the best thing to say is nothing at all, or very little. Midwestern preachers used to hold that "a heavy rain doesn't seep into the ground but rolls off—when you preach to farmers, your sermon should be a drizzle instead of a downpour." So too with any cause that matters: shouting and lapel-grabbing and institutionalizing can do more harm than good. A quiet approach works better.   29

"I wish it would hurry up and get colder," I said one warm afternoon several Octobers ago to a black man with whom I was walking in a park.   30

"Don't worry," he told me. "Like my grandmother used to say when I was a boy, 'Hawk'll be here soon enough.' "   31

"What did she mean by 'hawk'?"   32

"Hawk meant winter, cold, trouble. And she was right: the hawk always came."   33

With regard to families, many would say that the hawk has long been here, hovering. "I'd rather put up with being lonely now than have to put up with being still more lonely in the future," says a character in Natsume Soseki's novel *Kokoro*. "We live in an age of freedom, independence, and the self, and I imagine this loneliness is the price we have to pay for it." Seven decades earlier, in *Either/Or*, Sören Kierkegaard had written, "Our age has lost all the substantial categories of family, state, and race. It must leave the individual entirely to himself, so that in a stricter sense he becomes his own creator."   34

If it is true that we must create ourselves, maybe while we are about it we can also devise some new kinds of families, new connections to supplement the old ones. The second verse of a hymn by James Russell Lowell says,   35

New occasions bring new duties;
Time makes ancient good uncouth.

Surely one outworn "good" is the maxim that blood relatives are the only ones who can or should greatly matter. Or look at it another way: go back six generations, and each one of us has sixty-four direct ancestors. Go back twenty—only four or five centuries, not such a big chunk of human history—and we each have more than a million. Does it not stand to reason, since the world population was then so much smaller, that we all have a lot more cousins—though admittedly distant ones—than we were brought up to suspect? And don't these cousins deserve our attention?

One day after lunch at a friend's apartment I waited in his lobby while he collected his mail. Out of the elevator came two nurses supporting a   36 wizened, staring woman who couldn't have weighed much more than seventy pounds. It was all the woman could do to make her way down the three steps to the sidewalk and the curb where a car was waiting. Those steps must have been to that woman what a steep mountain trail would be to me. The nurses guided her down them with infinite patience.

"Easy, darlin'," one nurse said to the woman.   37

"That's a good girl," said the other. The woman, my friend's doorman   38
told us, was ninety. That morning she had fallen and hurt herself. On her forehead was something which, had it not been a bruise, we might have thought beautiful: a marvel of mauve and lavender and magenta. This woman, who was then being taken to a nursing home, had lived in my friend's apartment for forty years. All her relatives were dead, and her few surviving friends no longer chose to see her.

"But how can that be?" I asked my friend. "*We* could never be that   39
alone, could we?"

"Don't be so sure," said my friend, who knows more of such matters   40
than I do. "Even if we were to end up in the same nursing home, if I was in markedly worse shape than you were, you might not want to see me, either."

"But I can't imagine not wanting to see you."   41

"It happens," my friend said.   42

Maybe we can keep it from happening. Maybe the hawk can be kept at   43
bay, if we give more thought to our tribes and our clans and our several kinds of families. No aim seems to me more urgent, nor any achievement more worthy of a psalm. So *hosanna in excelsis,* and blest be the tie that binds. And please pass the salt.

Questions for Study and Discussion

1. As Howard's subtitle indicates, this essay attempts to describe and enumerate the characteristics of the good family. According to Howard, what is it that all good families have in common?

2. How does Howard organize her essay?

3. What are "friends of the road"? How do they differ from "friends of the heart"?

4. What are some of the problems, difficulties, or shortcomings of contemporary life that prompt Howard to search for the "good family"? Why can people no longer count on their biological families?

5. Howard uses a wide variety of examples to support and illustrate her points. What types of examples has she used? Which examples do you find most effective? Explain.

6. In paragraph 4, Howard refers to an ancient proverb that Aristotle quotes in *Ethics:* "You cannot know a man until you and he together have eaten a peck of salt." How do you interpret this proverb?

Writing Topics

1. Howard says that she belongs to six or seven tribes in addition to her biological family. Write an essay in which you discuss one or more of the "tribes" of which you are a member.

2. Howard believes that "good families prize their rituals." What are some of the rituals that you and your family share? What personal needs do these rituals serve for you? Write an essay in which you argue for the preservation of rituals in the family setting.

WILLA CATHER

Born in Gore, Virginia, Willa Cather (1873–1947) moved with her family to Red Cloud, Nebraska, when she was nine years old. After graduating from the University of Nebraska in 1895, she took a job as a newspaper reporter and later as a high school English and Latin teacher in Pittsburgh, Pennsylvania. During these years Cather started to experiment with poetry and short fiction, culminating in the publication of a collection of poems, *April Twilights* (1903), and a collection of short stories, *The Troll Garden* (1905). After seeing her work, S. S. McClure, the editor of *McClure's Magazine,* persuaded her to leave Pittsburgh and come to New York to join the magazine's staff. With the publication of *Alexander's Bridge* in 1912, Cather's career as a novelist was launched. *O Pioneers!* (1913), *The Song of the Lark* (1915), and *My Ántonia* (1918), three novels concerned with her experiences growing up on the prairie, followed in quick succession. She won the Pulitzer Prize in 1922 for *One of Ours.* Cather's other novels include *The Professor's House* (1925), *Death Comes for the Archbishop* (1927), and *Shadows on the Rock* (1931).

"Paul's Case" was first published in 1905 in *The Troll Garden.* Still one of her best-known and best-liked stories, "Paul's Case" tells of a misunderstood high school boy's futile attempts to break out of the routines of his everyday existence and follow the promptings of his heart.

Paul's Case

It was Paul's afternoon to appear before the faculty of the Pittsburgh High School to account for his various misdemeanors. He had been suspended a week ago, and his father had called at the Principal's office and confessed his perplexity about his son. Paul entered the faculty room suave and smiling. His clothes were a trifle outgrown, and the tan velvet on the collar of his open overcoat was frayed and worn; but for all that there was something of the dandy about him, and he wore an opal pin in his neatly knotted black four-in-hand, and a red carnation in his buttonhole. This latter adornment the faculty somehow felt was not properly significant of the contrite spirit befitting a boy under the ban of suspension.

Paul was tall for his age and very thin, with high, cramped shoulders and a narrow chest. His eyes were remarkable for a certain hysterical brilliancy, and he continually used them in a conscious, theatrical sort of way, peculiarly offensive in a boy. The pupils were abnormally large, as though he were addicted to belladonna, but there was a glassy glitter about them which that drug does not produce.

When questioned by the Principal as to why he was there, Paul stated, politely enough, that he wanted to come back to school. This was a lie, but

Paul was quite accustomed to lying; found it, indeed, indispensable for overcoming friction. His teachers were asked to state their respective charges against him, which they did with such a rancor and aggrievedness as evinced that this was not a usual case. Disorder and impertinence were among the offenses named, yet each of his instructors felt that it was scarcely possible to put into words the real cause of the trouble, which lay in a sort of hysterically defiant manner of the boy's; in the contempt which they all knew he felt for them, and which he seemingly made not the least effort to conceal. Once, when he had been making a synopsis of a paragraph at the blackboard, his English teacher had stepped to his side and attempted to guide his hand. Paul had started back with a shudder and thrust his hands violently behind him. The astonished woman could scarcely have been more hurt and embarrassed had he struck at her. The insult was so involuntary and definitely personal as to be unforgettable. In one way and another, he had made all his teachers, men and women alike, conscious of the same feeling of physical aversion. In one class he habitually sat with his hand shading his eyes; in another he always looked out of the window during the recitation; in another he made a running commentary on the lecture, with humorous intent.

His teachers felt this afternoon that his whole attitude was symbolized 4 by his shrug and his flippantly red carnation flower, and they fell upon him without mercy, his English teacher leading the pack. He stood through it smiling, his pale lips parted over his white teeth. (His lips were continually twitching, and he had a habit of raising his eyebrows that was contemptuous and irritating to the last degree.) Older boys than Paul had broken down and shed tears under that ordeal, but his set smile did not once desert him, and his only sign of discomfort was the nervous trembling of the fingers that toyed with the buttons of his overcoat, and an occasional jerking of the other hand which held his hat. Paul was always smiling, always glancing about him, seeming to feel that people might be watching him and trying to detect something. This conscious expression, since it was as far as possible from boyish mirthfulness, was usually attributed to insolence or "smartness."

As the inquisition proceeded, one of his instructors repeated an imperti- 5 nent remark of the boy's, and the Principal asked him whether he thought that a courteous speech to make to a woman. Paul shrugged his shoulders slightly and his eyebrows twitched.

"I don't know," he replied. "I didn't mean to be polite or impolite, 6 either. I guess it's a sort of way I have, of saying things regardless."

The Principal asked him whether he didn't think that a way it would be 7 well to get rid of it. Paul grinned and said he guessed so. When he was told that he could go, he bowed gracefully and went out. His bow was like a repetition of the scandalous red carnation.

His teachers were in despair, and his drawing master voiced the feeling 8 of them all when he declared there was something about the boy which none of them understood. He added "I don't really believe that smile of his comes altogether from insolence; there's something sort of haunted about it. The boy is not strong, for one thing. There is something wrong about the fellow."

The drawing master had come to realize that, in looking at Paul, one saw only his white teeth and the forced animation of his eyes. One warm afternoon the boy had gone to sleep at his drawing board, and his master had noted with amazement what a white, blue-veined face it was; drawn and wrinkled like an old man's about the eyes, the lips twitching even in his sleep. 9

His teachers left the building dissatisfied and unhappy; humiliated to have felt so vindictive toward a mere boy, to have uttered this feeling in cutting terms, and to have set each other on, as it were, in the gruesome game of intemperate reproach. One of them remembered having seen a miserable street cat set at bay by a ring of tormentors. 10

As for Paul, he ran down the hill whistling the Soldiers' Chorus from *Faust,* looking wildly behind him now and then to see whether some of his teachers were not there to witness his light-heartedness. As it was now late in the afternoon and Paul was on duty that evening as usher at Carnegie Hall, he decided that he would not go home to supper. 11

When he reached the concert hall the doors were not yet open. It was chilly outside, and he decided to go up into the picture gallery—always deserted at this hour—where there were some of Raffaëlli's gay studies of Paris streets and an airy blue Venetian scene or two that always exhilarated him. He was delighted to find no one in the gallery but the old guard, who sat in the corner, a newspaper on his knee, a black patch over one eye and the other closed. Paul possessed himself of the place and walked confidently up and down, whistling under his breath. After a while he sat down before a blue Rico and lost himself. When he bethought him to look at his watch, it was after seven o'clock, and he rose with a start and ran downstairs, making a face at Augustus Caesar, peering out from the cast-room, and an evil gesture at the Venus of Milo as he passed her on the stairway. 12

When Paul reached the ushers' dressing-room half a dozen boys were there already, and he began excitedly to tumble into his uniform. It was one of the few that at all approached fitting, and Paul thought it very becoming— though he knew the tight, straight coat accentuated his narrow chest, about which he was exceedingly sensitive. He was always excited while he dressed, twanging all over to the tuning of the strings and preliminary flourishes of the horns in the music-room; but tonight he seemed quite beside himself, and he teased and plagued the boys until, telling him that he was crazy, they put him down on the floor and sat on him. 13

Somewhat calmed by his suppression, Paul dashed out to the front of the house to seat the early comers. He was a model usher. Gracious and smiling he ran up and down the aisles. Nothing was too much trouble for him; he carried messages and brought programs as though it were his greatest pleasure in life, and all the people in his section thought him a charming 14 boy, feeling that he remembered and admired them. As the house filled, he grew more and more vivacious and animated, and the color came to his cheeks and lips. It was very much as though this were a great reception and Paul were the host. Just as the musicians came out to take their places, his English teacher arrived with checks for the seat which a prominent manufacturer had taken for the season. She betrayed some embarrassment when she handed Paul the tickets, and a *hauteur* which subsequently made her feel very foolish. Paul was startled for a moment and had the feeling of wanting to put her out; what business had she here among all these fine people and gay colors? He looked her over and decided that she was not appropriately dressed and must be a fool to sit downstairs in such togs. The tickets had probably been sent her out of kindness, he reflected, as he put down a seat for her, and she had about as much right to sit there as he had.

When the symphony began Paul sank into one of the rear seats with a   15
long sigh of relief, and lost himself as he had done before the Rico. It was not that symphonies, as such, meant anything in particular to Paul, but the first sigh of the instruments seemed to free some hilarious spirit within him; something that struggled there like the Genius in the bottle found by the Arab fisherman. He felt a sudden zest for life; the lights danced before his eyes and the concert hall blazed into unimaginable splendor. When the soprano soloist came on, Paul forgot even the nastiness of his teacher's being there, and gave himself up to the peculiar intoxication such personages always had for him. The soloist chanced to be a German woman, by no means in her first youth, and the mother of many children; but she wore a satin gown and a tiara, and she had that indefinable air of achievement, the world-shine upon her, which always blinded Paul to any possible defects.

After a concert was over, Paul was often irritable and wretched until he   16
got to sleep—and tonight he was even more than usually restless. He had the feeling of not being able to let down; of its being impossible to give up this delicious excitement which was the only thing that could be called living at all. During the last number he withdrew and, after hastily changing his clothes in the dressing-room, slipped out to the side door where the singer's carriage stood. Here he began pacing rapidly up and down the walk, waiting to see her come out.

Over yonder the Schenley, in its vacant stretch, loomed big and square   17
through the fine rain, the windows of its twelve stories glowing like those of a lighted cardboard house under a Christmas tree. All the actors and singers of any importance stayed there when they were in the city, and a number of the big manufacturers of the place lived there in the winter. Paul had often hung about the hotel, watching the people go in and out, longing to enter and leave schoolmasters and dull care behind him forever.

At last the singer came out, accompanied by the conductor, who   18
helped her into her carriage and closed the door with a cordial *auf Weidersehen*,—which set Paul to wondering whether she were not an old

sweetheart of his. Paul followed the carriage over to the hotel, walking so rapidly as not to be far from the entrance when the singer alighted and disappeared behind the swinging glass doors which were opened by a Negro in a tall hat and a long coat. In the moment that the door was ajar, it seemed to Paul that he, too, entered. He seemed to feel himself go after her up the steps, into the warm, lighted building, into an exotic, a tropical world of shiny, glistening surfaces and basking ease. He reflected upon the mysterious dishes that were brought into the dining-room, the green bottles in buckets of ice, as he had seen them in the supper party pictures of the Sunday supplement. A quick gust of wind brought the rain down with sudden vehemence, and Paul was startled to find that he was still outside in the slush of the gravel driveway; that his boots were letting in the water and his scanty overcoat was clinging wet about him; that the lights in front of the concert hall were out, and that the rain was driving in sheets between him and the orange glow of the windows above him. There it was, what he wanted—tangibly before him, like the fairy world of Christmas pantomime; as the rain beat in his face, Paul wondered whether he were destined always to shiver in the black night outside, looking up at it.

He turned and walked reluctantly toward the car tracks. The end had to come some time; his father in his night-clothes at the top of the stairs, explanations that did not explain, hastily improvised fictions that were forever tripping him up, his upstairs room and its horrible yellow wallpaper, the creaking bureau with the greasy plush collar-box, and over his painted wooden bed the pictures of George Washington and John Calvin, and the framed motto, "Feed my Lambs," which had been worked in red worsted by his mother, whom Paul could not remember.

Half an hour later, Paul alighted from the Negley Avenue car and went slowly down one of the side streets off the main thoroughfare. It was a highly respectable street, where all the houses were exactly alike, and where business men of moderate means begot and reared large families of children, all of whom went to Sabbath-school and learned the shorter catechism, and were interested in arithmetic; all of whom were as exactly alike as their homes, and of a piece with the monotony in which they lived. Paul never went up Cordelia Street without a shudder of loathing. His home was next to the house of the Cumberland minister. He approached it tonight with the nerveless sense of defeat, the hopeless feeling of sinking back forever into ugliness and commonness that he had always had when he came home. The moment he turned into Cordelia Street he felt the waters close above his head. After each of these orgies of living, he experienced all the physical depression which follows a debauch; the loathing of respectable beds, of common food, of those permeated by kitchen odors; a shuddering repulsion for the flavorless, colorless mass of everyday existence; a morbid desire for cool things and soft lights and fresh flowers.

The nearer he approached the house, the more absolutely unequal Paul felt to the sight of it all; his ugly sleeping chamber, the cold bathroom with the grimy zinc tub, the cracked mirror, the dripping spiggots; his father, at the top of the stairs, his hairy legs sticking out from his nightshirt, his feet thrust into carpet slippers. He was so much later than usual that there would certainly be inquiries and reproaches. Paul stopped short before the door. He felt that he could not be accosted by his father tonight; that he could not toss again on that miserable bed. He would not go in. He would tell his father that he had no car fare, and it was raining so hard he had gone home with one of the boys and stayed all night.

Meanwhile, he was wet and cold. He went around to the back of the house and tried one of the basement windows, found it open, raised it cautiously, and scrambled down the cellar wall to the floor. There he stood, holding his breath, terrified by the noise he had made; but the floor above him was silent, and there was no creak on the stairs. He found a soap-box, and carried it over to the soft ring of light that streamed from the furnace door, and sat down. He was horribly afraid of rats, so he did not try to sleep, but sat looking distrustfully at the dark, still terrified lest he might have awakened his father. In such reactions, after one of the experiences which made days and nights out of the dreary blanks of the calendar, when his senses were deadened, Paul's head was always singularly clear. Suppose his father had heard him getting in at the window and had come down and shot him for a burglar? Then, again, suppose his father had come down, pistol in hand, and he had cried out in time to save himself, and his father had been horrified to think how nearly he had killed him? Then, again, suppose a day should come when his father would remember that night, and wish there had been no warning cry to stay his hand? With this last supposition Paul entertained himself until daybreak.

The following Sunday was fine; the sodden November chill was broken by the last flash of autumnal summer. In the morning Paul had to go to church and Sabbath-school, as always. On seasonable Sunday afternoons the burghers of Cordelia Street usually sat out on their front "stoops," and talked to their neighbors on the next stoop, or called to those across the street in neighborly fashion. The men sat placidly on gay cushions placed upon the steps that led down to the sidewalk, while the women, in their Sunday "waists," sat in rockers on the cramped porches, pretending to be greatly at their ease. The children played in the streets; there were so many of them that the place resembled the recreation grounds of a kindergarten. The men on the steps—all in their shirt sleeves, their vests unbuttoned—sat with their legs well apart, their stomachs comfortably protruding, and talked of the prices of things, or told anecdotes of the sagacity of their various chiefs and overlords. They occasionally looked over the multitude of squabbling children, listened affectionately to their high-pitched, nasal voices, smiling to see their own proclivities reproduced in their offspring, and interspersed their legends of the iron kings with remarks about their sons' progress at school, their grades in arithmetic, and the amounts they had saved in their toy banks. On this last Sunday of November, Paul sat all the afternoon on the lowest step of his "stoop," staring into the street, while his sisters, in their rockers, were talking to the minister's daughters next door about how many shirtwaists they had made in the last week, and how many waffles someone had eaten in the last church supper. When the weather was warm, and his father was in a particularly jovial frame of mind, the girls made lemonade, which was always brought out in a red-glass pitcher, ornamented with forget-me-nots in blue enamel. This the girls thought very fine, and the neighbors joked about the suspicious color of the pitcher.

Today Paul's father, on the top step, was talking to a young man who   24
shifted a restless baby from knee to knee. He happened to be the young man who was daily held up to Paul as a model, and after whom it was his father's dearest hope that he would pattern. This young man was of a ruddy complexion, with a compressed, red mouth, and faded, near-sighted eyes, over which he wore thick spectacles, with gold bows that curved about his ears. He was clerk to one of the magnates of a great steel corporation, and was looked upon in Cordelia Street as a young man with a future. There was a story that, come five years ago—he was now barely twenty-six—he had been a trifle 'dissipated,' but in order to curb his appetites and save the loss of time and strength that a sowing of wild oats might have entailed, he had taken his chief's advice, oft reiterated to his employees, and at twenty-one had married the first woman whom he could persuade to share his fortunes. She happened to be an angular school mistress, much older than he, who also wore thick glasses, and who had now borne him four children, all nearsighted, like herself.

The young man was relating how his chief, now cruising in the Mediter-   25
ranean, kept in touch with all the details of the business, arranging his office hours on his yacht just as though he were at home, and "knocking off work enough to keep two stenographers busy." His father told, in turn, the plan his corporation was considering, of putting in an electric railway plant at Cairo. Paul snapped his teeth; he had an awful apprehension that they might spoil it all before he got there. Yet he rather liked to hear these legends of the iron kings, that were told and retold on Sundays and holidays; these stories of palaces in Venice, yachts on the Mediterranean, and high play at Monte Carlo appealed to his fancy, and he was interested in the triumphs of cash boys who had become famous, though he had no mind for the cash-boy stage.

After supper was over, and he had helped to dry the dishes, Paul   26
nervously asked his father whether he could go to George's to get some help in his geometry, and still more nervously asked for car fare. This latter request he had to repeat, as his father, on principle, did not like to hear requests for money, whether much or little. He asked Paul whether he could not go to some boy who lived nearer, and told him that he ought not to leave

his school work until Sunday; but he gave him the dime. He was not a poor man, but he had a worthy ambition to come up in the world. His only reason for allowing Paul to usher was that he thought a boy ought to be earning a little.

Paul bounded upstairs, scrubbed the greasy odor of the dishwater from his hands with the ill-smelling soap he hated, and then shook over his fingers a few drops of violet water from the bottle he kept hidden in his drawer. He left the house with his geometry conspicuously under his arm, and the moment he got out of Cordelia Street and boarded a downtown car, he shook off the lethargy of two deadening days, and began to live again.

The leading juvenile of the permanent stock company which played at one of the downtown theaters was an acquaintance of Paul's, and the boy had been invited to drop in at the Sunday night rehearsals whenever he could. For more than a year Paul had spent every available moment loitering about Charley Edwards's dressing-room. He had won a place among Edwards's following not only because the young actor, who could not afford to employ a dresser, often found him useful, but because he recognized in Paul something akin to what churchmen term "vocation."

It was at the theater and at Carnegie Hall that Paul really lived; the rest was but a sleep and a forgetting. This was Paul's fairy tale, and it had for him all the allurement of a secret love. The moment he inhaled the gassy, painty, dusty odor behind the scenes, he breathed like a prisoner set free, and felt within him the possibility of doing or saying splendid, brilliant things. The moment the cracked orchestra beat out the overture from *Martha*, or jerked at the serenade from *Rigoletto*, all stupid and ugly things slid from him, and his senses were deliciously, yet delicately fired.

Perhaps it was because, in Paul's world, the natural nearly always wore the guise of ugliness, that a certain element of artificiality seemed to him necessary in beauty. Perhaps it was because his experience of life elsewhere was so full of Sabbath-school picnics, petty economies, wholesome advice as to how to succeed in life, and the unescapable odors of cooking, that he found this existence so alluring, these smartly-clad men and women so attractive, that he was so moved by these starry apple orchards that bloomed perennially under the limelight.

It would be difficult to put it strongly enough how convincingly the stage entrance of that theater was for Paul the actual portal of Romance. Certainly none of the company ever suspected it, least of all Charley Edwards. It was very like the old stories that used to float about London of fabulously rich Jews, who had subterranean halls, with palms, and fountains, and soft lamps and richly apparelled women who never saw the disenchanting light of London day. So, in the midst of that smoke-palled city, enamored of figures and grimy toil, Paul had his secret temple, his wishing-carpet, his bit of blue-and-white Mediterranean shore bathed in perpetual sunshine.

Several of Paul's teachers had a theory that his imagination had been perverted by garish fiction; but the truth was, he scarcely ever read at all. The books at home were not such as would either tempt or corrupt a youthful mind, and as for reading the novels that some of his friends urged upon him—well, he got what he wanted much more quickly from music; any sort of music, from an orchestra to a barrel organ. He needed only the spark, the indescribable thrill that made his imagination master of his senses, and he could make plots and pictures enough of his own. It was equally true that he was not stage-struck—not, at any rate, in the usual acceptation of that expression. He had no desire to become an actor, any more than he had to become a musician. He felt no necessity to do any of these things; what he wanted was to see, to be in the atmosphere, float on the wave of it, to be carried out, blue league after blue league, away from everything.

After a night behind the scenes, Paul found the school-room more   33 than ever repulsive; the bare floors and naked walls; the prosy men who never wore frock coats, or violets in their buttonholes; the women with their dull gowns, shrill voices, and pitiful seriousness about prepositions that govern the dative. He could not bear to have the other pupils think, for a moment, that he took these people seriously; he must convey to them that he considered it all trivial, and was there only by way of a joke, anyway. He had autograph pictures of all the members of the stock company which he showed to classmates, telling them the most incredible stories of his familiarity with these people, of his acquaintance with the soloists who came to Carnegie Hall, his suppers with them and the flowers he sent them. When these stories lost their effect, and his audience grew listless, he would bid all the boys good-by, announcing that he was going to travel for a while; going to Naples, to California, to Egypt. Then, next Monday, he would slip back, conscious and nervously smiling; his sister was ill, and he would have to defer his voyage until spring.

Matters went steadily worse with Paul at school. In the itch to let his   34 instructors know how heartily he despised them, and how thoroughly he was appreciated elsewhere, he mentioned once or twice that he had no time to fool with theorems; adding—with a twitch of the eyebrows and a touch of that nervous bravado which so perplexed them—that he was helping the people down at the stock company; they were old friends of his.

The upshot of the matter was, that the Principal went to Paul's father,   35 and Paul was taken out of school and put to work. The manager at Carnegie Hall was told to get another usher in his stead; the doorkeeper at the theater was warned not to admit him to the house; and Charley Edwards remorsefully promised the boy's father not to see him again.

The members of the stock company were vastly amused when some of   36 Paul's stories reached them—especially the women. They were hardworking women, most of them supporting indolent husbands or brothers, and they laughed rather bitterly at having stirred the boy to such fervid and florid inventions. They agreed with the faculty and with his father, that Paul's was a bad case.

The east-bound train was plowing through a January snowstorm; the dull dawn was beginning to show gray when the engine whistled a mile out of Newark. Paul started up from the seat where he had lain curled in uneasy slumber, rubbed the breath-misted window glass with his hand, and peered out. The snow was whirling in curling eddies above the white bottom lands, and the drifts lay already deep in the fields and along the fences, while here and there the long dead grass and dried weed stalks protruded black above it. Lights shone from the scattered houses, and a gang of laborers who stood beside the track waved their lanterns. 37

Paul had slept very little, and he felt grimy and uncomfortable. He had made the all-night journey in a day coach because he was afraid if he took a Pullman he might be seen by some Pittsburgh business man who had noticed him in Denny & Carson's office. When the whistle woke him, he clutched quickly at his breast pocket, glancing about him with an uncertain smile. But the little, clay-bespattered Italians were still sleeping, the slatternly women across the aisle were in open-mouthed oblivion, and even the crumby, crying babies were for the nonce stilled. Paul settled back to struggle with his impatience as best he could. 38

When he arrived at the Jersey City station, he hurried through his breakfast, manifestly ill at ease and keeping a sharp eye about him. After he reached the Twenty-third Street Station, he consulted a cabman, and had himself driven to a men's furnishing establishment which was just opening for the day. He spent upward of two hours there, buying with endless reconsidering and great care. His new street suit he put on in the fitting-room; the frock coat and dress clothes he had bundled into the cab with his new shirts. Then he drove to a hatter's and a shoe house. His next errand was at Tiffany's, where he selected silver-mounted brushes and a scarf-pin. He would not wait to have his silver marked, he said. Lastly, he stopped at a trunk shop on Broadway, and had his purchases packed into various traveling bags. 39

It was a little after one o'clock when he drove up to the Waldorf, and, after settling with the cabman, went into the office. He registered from Washington; said his mother and father had been abroad, and that he had come down to await the arrival of their steamer. He told his story plausibly and had no trouble, since he offered to pay for them in advance, in engaging his rooms; a sleeping-room, sitting room and bath. 40

Not once, but a hundred times Paul had planned this entry into New York. He had gone over every detail of it with Charley Edwards, and in his scrap book at home there were pages of description about New York hotels, cut from the Sunday pages. 41

When he was shown to his sitting room on the eighth floor, he saw at a glance that everything was as it should be; there was but one detail in his mental picture that the place did not realize, so he rang for the bell boy and sent him down for flowers. He moved about nervously until the boy returned, putting away his new linen and fingering it delightedly as he did so. When the flowers came, he put them hastily into water, and then tumbled into a hot bath. Presently he came out of his white bathroom, resplendent in his new silk underwear, and playing with the tassels of his red robe. The snow was whirling so fiercely outside his windows that he could scarcely see across the street; but within, the air was deliciously soft and fragrant. He put the violets and jonquils on the tabouret beside the couch, and threw himself down with a long sigh, covering himself with a Roman blanket. He was thoroughly tired; he had been in such haste, he had stood up to such a strain, covered so much ground in the last twenty-four hours, that he wanted to think how it had all come about. Lulled by the sound of the wind, the warm air, and the cool fragrance of the flowers, he sank into deep, drowsy retrospection. 42

It had been wonderfully simple; when they had shut him out of the theater and concert hall, when they had taken away his bone, the whole thing was virtually determined. The rest was a mere matter of opportunity. The only thing that at all surprised him was his own courage—for he realized well enough that he had always been tormented by fear, a sort of apprehensive dread that, of late years, as the meshes of the lies he had told closed about him, had been pulling the muscles of his body tighter and tighter. Until now, he could not remember a time when he had not been dreading something. Even when he was a little boy, it was always there—behind him, or before, or on either side. There had always been the shadowed corner, the dark place into which he dared not look, but from which something seemed always to be watching him—and Paul had done things that were not pretty to watch, he knew. 43

But now he had a curious sense of relief, as though he had at last thrown down the gauntlet to the thing in the corner. 44

Yet it was but a day since he had been sulking in the traces; but yesterday afternoon that he had been sent to the bank with Denny & Carston's deposit, as usual—but this time he was instructed to leave the book to be balanced. There was above two thousand dollars in checks, and nearly a thousand in the bank notes which he had taken from the book and quietly transferred to his pocket. At the bank he had made out a new deposit slip. His nerves had been steady enough to permit of his returning to the office, where he had finished his work and asked for a full day's holiday tomorrow, Saturday, giving a perfectly reasonable pretext. The bank book, he knew, would not be returned before Monday or Tuesday, and his father would be out of town for the next week. From the time he slipped the bank notes into his pocket until he boarded the night train for New York, he had not known a moment's hesitation. 45

How astonishingly easy it had all been; here he was, the thing done; 46
and this time there would be no awakening, no figure at the top of the stairs.
He watched the snowflakes whirling by his window until he fell asleep.

When he awoke, it was four o'clock in the afternoon. He bounded up 47
with a start; one of his precious days gone already! He spent nearly an hour in
dressing, watching every stage of his toilet carefully in the mirror. Everything
was quite perfect; he was exactly the kind of boy he had always wanted to be.

When he went downstairs,, Paul took a carriage and drove up Fifth 48
Avenue toward the Park. The snow had somewhat abated; carriages and
tradesmen's wagons were hurrying soundlessly to and fro in the winter twilight; boys in woolen mufflers were shoveling off the doorsteps; the avenue
stages made fine spots of color against the white street. Here and there on the
corners whole flower gardens blooming behind glass windows, against which
the snow flakes stuck and melted; violets, roses, carnations, lilies of the
valley—somehow vastly more lovely and alluring that they blossomed thus
unnaturally in the snow. The Park itself was a wonderful stage winter-piece.

When he returned, the pause of the twilight had ceased, and the tune 49
of the streets had changed. The snow was falling faster, lights streamed from
the hotels that reared their many stories fearlessly up into the storm, defying
the raging Atlantic winds. A long, black stream of carriages poured down the
avenue, intersected here and there by other streams, tending horizontally.
There were a score of cabs about the entrance of his hotel, and his driver had
to wait. Boys in livery were running in and out of the awning stretched across
the sidewalk, up and down the red velvet carpet laid from the door to the
street. Above, about, within it all, was the rumble and roar, the hurry and
toss of thousands of human beings as hot for pleasure as himself, and on
every side of him towered the glaring affirmation of the omnipotence of
wealth.

The boy set his teeth and drew his shoulders together in a spasm of 50
realization; the plot of all dramas, the text of all romances, the nerve-stuff of
all sensations was whirling about him like the snowflakes. He burnt like a
faggot in a tempest.

When Paul came down to dinner, the music of the orchestra floated up 51
the elevator shaft to greet him. As he stepped into the thronged corridor, he
sank back into one of the chairs against the wall to get his breath. The lights,
the chatter, the perfumes, the bewildering medly of color—he had, for a
moment, the feeling of not being able to stand it. But only for a moment;
these were his own people, he told himself. He went slowly about the
corridors, through the writing-rooms, smoking-rooms, reception-rooms, as
though he were exploring the chambers of an enchanted palace, built and
peopled for him alone.

When he reached the dining room he sat down at a table near a 52
window. The flowers, the white linen, the many-colored wine glasses, the
gay toilettes of the women, the low popping of corks, the undulating repeti-

tions of the *Blue Danube* from the orchestra, all flooded Paul's dream with bewildering radiance. When the roseate tinge of his champagne was added—that cold, precious, bubbling stuff that creamed and foamed in his glass—Paul wondered that there were honest men in the world at all. This was what all the world was fighting for, he reflected; this was what all the struggle was about. He doubted the reality of his past. Had he ever known a place called Cordelia Street, a place where fagged-looking business men boarded the early car? Mere rivets in a machine they seemed to Paul— sickening men, with combings of children's hair always hanging to their coats, and the smell of cooking in their clothes. Cordelia Street—Ah, that belonged to another time and country! Had he not always been thus, had he not sat here night after night, from as far back as he could remember, looking pensively over just such shimmering textures, and slowly twirling the stem of a glass like this one between his thumb and middle finger? He rather thought he had.

He was not in the least abashed or lonely. He had no special desire to 53 meet or to know any of these people; all he demanded was the right to look on and conjecture, to watch the pageant. The mere stage properties were all he contended for. Nor was he lonely later in the evening, in his loge at the Opera. He was entirely rid of his nervous misgivings, of his forced aggressiveness, of the imperative desire to show himself different from his surroundings. He felt now that his surroundings explained him. Nobody questioned the purple; he had only to wear it passively. He had only to glance down at his dress coat to reassure himself that here it would be impossible for anyone to humiliate him.

He found it hard to leave his beautiful sitting room to go to bed that 54 night, and sat long watching the raging storm from his turret window. When he went to sleep, it was with the lights turned on in his bedroom; partly because of his old timidity, and partly so that, if he should wake in the night there would be no wretched moment of doubt, no horrible suspicion of yellow wall-paper, or of Washington and Calvin above his bed.

On Sunday morning the city was practically snow-bound. Paul break- 55 fasted late, and in the afternoon he fell in with a wild San Francisco boy, a freshman at Yale, who said he had run down for a "little flyer" over Sunday. The young man offered to show Paul the night side of the town, and the two boys went off together after dinner, not returning to the hotel until seven o'clock the next morning. They had started out in the confiding warmth of a champagne friendship, but their parting in the elevator was singularly cool. The freshman pulled himself together to make his train, and Paul went to bed. He woke at two o'clock in the afternoon, very thirsty and dizzy, and rang for ice water, coffee, and the Pittsburgh papers.

On the part of the hotel management, Paul excited no suspicion. 56 There was this to be said for him, that he wore his spoils with dignity and in no way made himself conspicuous. His chief greediness lay in his ears and eyes, and his excesses were not offensive ones. His dearest pleasures were the gray winter twilights in his sitting room; his quiet enjoyment of his flowers, his clothes, his wide divan, his cigarette and his sense of power. He could not remember a time when he had felt so at peace with himself. The mere release from the necessity of petty lying, lying every day and every day, restored his self-respect. He had never lied for pleasure, even at school; but to make himself noticed and admired, to assert his difference from other Cordelia Street boys; and he felt a good deal more manly, more honest, even, now that he had no need for boastful pretensions, now that he could, as his actor friends used to say, "dress the part." It was characteristic that remorse did not occur to him. His golden days went by without a shadow, and he made each as perfect as he could.

On the eighth day after his arrival in New York, he found the whole 57 affair exploited in the Pittsburgh papers, exploited with a wealth of detail which indicated that local news of a sensational nature was at a low ebb. The firm of Denny & Carson announced that the boy's father had refunded the full amount of his theft, and that they had no intention of prosecuting. The Cumberland minister had been interviewed, and expressed his hope of yet reclaiming the motherless lad, and Paul's Sabbath-school teacher declared that she would spare no effort to that end. The rumor had reached Pittsburgh that the boy had been seen in a New York hotel, and his father had gone East to find him and bring him home.

Paul had just come in to dress for dinner; he sank into a chair, weak in 58 the knees, and clasped his head in his hands. It was to be worse than jail, even; the tepid waters of Cordelia Street were to close over him finally and forever. The gray monotony stretched before him in hopeless, unrelieved years; Sabbath-school, Young People's Meeting, the yellow-papered room, the damp dish-towels; it all rushed back upon him with sickening vividness. He had the old feeling that the orchestra had suddenly stopped, the sinking sensation that the play was over. The sweat broke out on his face, and he sprang to his feet, looked about him with his white, conscious smile, and winked at himself in the mirror. With something of the childish belief in miracles with which he had so often gone to class, all his lessons unlearned, Paul dressed and dashed whistling down the corridor to the elevator.

He had no sooner entered the dining room and caught the measure of 59 the music, that his remembrance was lightened by his old elastic power of claiming the moment, mounting with it, and finding it all sufficient. The glare and glitter about him, the mere scenic accessories had again, and for the last time, their old potency. He would show himself that he was game, he would finish the thing splendidly. He doubted, more than ever, the existence of Cordelia Street, and for the first time he drank his wine recklessly. Was he not, after all, one of these fortunate beings? Was he not still himself, and in his own place? He drummed a nervous accompaniment to the music and looked about him, telling himself over and over that it had paid.

He reflected drowsily, to the swell of the violin and the chill sweetness   60
of his wine, that he might have done it more wisely. He might have caught
an outbound steamer and been well out of their clutches before now. But the
other side of the world had seemed too far away and too uncertain then; he
could not have waited for it; his need had been too sharp. If he had to choose
over again, he would do the same thing tomorrow. He looked affectionately
about the dining room, now glided with a soft mist. Ah, it had paid indeed!

Paul was awakened the next morning by a painful throbbing in his head   61
and feet. He had thrown himself across the bed without undressing, and had
slept with his shoes on. His limbs and hands were lead heavy, and his tongue
and throat were parched. There came upon him one of those fateful attacks
of clear-headedness that never occurred except when he was physically exhausted and his nerves hung loose. He lay still and closed his eyes and let the
tide of realities wash over him.

His father was in New York; "stopping at some joint or other," he told   62
himself. The memory of successive summers on the front stoop fell upon him
like a weight of black water. He had not a hundred dollars left, and he knew
now, more than ever, that money was everything, the wall that stood between all he loathed and all he wanted. The thing was winding itself up; he
had thought of that on his first glorious day in New York, and had even
provided a way to snap the thread. It lay on his dressing-table now; he had
got it out last night when he came blindly up from dinner—but the shiny
metal hurt his eyes, and he disliked the look of it, anyway.

He rose and moved about with a painful effort, succumbing now and   63
again to attacks of nausea. It was the old depression exaggerated; all the
world had become Cordelia Street. Yet somehow he was not afraid of anything, was absolutely calm; perhaps because he had looked into the dark
corner at last, and knew. It was bad enough, what he saw there; but somehow
not so bad as his long fear of it had been. He saw everything clearly now. He
had a feeling that he had made the best of it, that he had lived the sort of life
he was meant to live, and for half an hour sat staring at the revolver. But he
told himself that was not the way, so he went downstairs and took a cab to
the ferry.

When Paul arrived at Newark, he got off the train and took another   64
cab, directing the driver to follow the Pennsylvania tracks out of the town.
The snow lay heavy on the roadways and had drifted deep in the open fields.
Only here and there the dead grass or dried weed stalks projected, singularly
black, above it. Once well into the country, Paul dismissed the carriage and
walked, floundering along the tracks, his mind a medley of irrelevant things.
He seemed to hold in his brain an actual picture of everything he had seen
that morning. He remembered every feature of both his drivers, the toothless
old woman from whom he had bought the red flowers in his coat, the agent
from whom he had got his ticket, and all of his fellow-passengers on the
ferry. His mind, unable to cope with vital matters near at hand, worked

feverishly and deftly at sorting and grouping these images. They made for him a part of the ugliness of the world, of the ache in his head, and the bitter burning on his tongue. He stooped and put a handful of snow into his mouth as he walked, but that, too, seemed hot. When he reached a little hillside, where the tracks ran through a cut some twenty feet below him, he stopped and sat down.

The carnations in his coat were drooping with the cold, he noticed; all 65 their red glory over. It occurred to him that all the flowers he had seen in the show windows that first night must have gone the same way, long before this. It was only one splendid breath they had, in spite of their brave mockery at the winter outside the glass. It was a losing game in the end, it seemed, this revolt against the homilies by which the world is run. Paul took one of the blossoms carefully from his coat and scooped a little hole in the snow, where he covered it up. Then he dozed a while, from his weak condition, seeming insensible to the cold.

The sound of an approaching train woke him, and he started to his 66 feet, remembering only his resolution, and afraid lest he should be too late. He stood watching the approaching locomotive, his teeth chattering, his lips drawn away from them in a frightened smile; once or twice he glanceed nervously sidewise, as though he were being watched. When the right moment came, he jumped. As he fell, the folly of his haste occurred to him with merciless clearness, the vastness of what he had left undone. There flashed through his brain, clearer than ever before, the blue of Adriatic water, the yellow of Algerian sands.

He felt something strike his chest,—his body was being thrown swiftly 67 through the air, on and on, immeasurably far and fast, while his limbs gently relaxed. Then, because the picture-making mechanism was crushed, the disturbing visions flashed into black, and Paul dropped back into the immense design of things.

Questions for Study and Discussion

1. In the opening two paragraphs Cather provides us with a description of Paul. What can you tell about him from this description? Explain.

2. What complaints did Paul's teachers have about his behavior in school? Does Paul have particular character traits that tend to isolate him from others? In what ways is he different from his peers?

3. What are some of the major conflicts in this story? How does the confrontation between Paul and his teachers at the "inquisition" serve to prepare us for the conflicts that follow?

4. In paragraph 20 we learn that "Paul never went up Cordelia Street without a shudder of loathing." Why? What does his neighborhood represent for Paul, and why does he feel the need to escape it? In what ways do Paul's carnations contrast with Cordelia Street? Explain.

5. What is it that Paul wants in this world? What does the concert hall mean to him? Does he ever envision himself becoming an actor or musician? Does Paul believe that he will get what he wants?

6. What would change had Cather let Paul tell his own story instead of telling it in the third person as she does?

7. In paragraph 24 we are introduced to the young man "who was daily held up to Paul as a model" by his father. Why do you think Paul's father holds this young man up to his son? Why do you think Paul is unimpressed?

8. The members of the stock company, the faculty at Pittsburgh High School, and Paul's father all agree that "Paul's was a bad case." Do you agree? Why, or why not?

9. How do you feel about Paul in the end? What does he mean when he thinks that "all the world had become Cordelia Street"? Did Paul have any choices in the end, or was he driven to take his life? Why did he decide that the revolver "was not the way"?

Writing Topics

1. In a very real sense Paul is struggling to escape the deadening confines of conformity. Paul is different and wants to live a different life. Why is it so difficult for him to do so? In an essay, discuss the role of conformity—both its advantages and disadvantages—in our society. Do you think Paul would have found life as difficult today as at the time of the story (1905)?

2. Write an essay in which you discuss Paul's lying. Why did he believe he had to lie at home and at school? Why didn't he lie in New York? What was different about his New York experience? What conclusions can you draw about lying and the reasons people do it?

What Are Friends?

MARGARET MEAD and RHODA METRAUX

Margaret Mead (1901–1978) was a noted educator, anthropologist, and author.
Educated at Barnard College and Columbia University, she was for many years a
professor of anthropology at Columbia. She spent much of her life studying
foreign societies and became an expert in such fields as family structure, mental
health, drugs, environmental problems, and women's roles in society. Her best-
known books include *Coming of Age in Samoa* (1928), *Male and Female* (1949),
The Study of Culture at a Distance (1953), and *Childhood in Contemporary Cultures*
(1955). Rhoda Metraux was born in 1914 and is also an anthropologist. She was
educated at Vassar, Yale, and Columbia. Metraux first met Mead while working at
the American Museum of Natural History. A contributor to anthropological
journals, Metraux collaborated with Mead on *A Way of Seeing* (1970), from which
the following selection was taken. As you read this essay, notice the way the
authors use examples both to define friendship and to point out the way different
cultures regard friendship.

On Friendship

Few Americans stay put for a lifetime. We move from town to city to 1
suburb, from high school to college in a different state, from a job in one
region to a better job elsewhere, from the home where we raise our children
to the home where we plan to live in retirement. With each move we are
forever making new friends, who become part of our new life at that time.

For many of us the summer is a special time for forming new friend- 2
ships. Today millions of Americans vacation abroad, and they go not only to
see new sights but also—in those places where they do not feel too strange—
with the hope of meeting new people. No one really expects a vacation trip
to produce a close friend. But surely the beginning of a friendship is possible?
Surely in every country people value friendship?

They do. The difficulty when strangers from two countries meet is not 3
a lack of appreciation of friendship, but different expectations about what
constitutes friendship and how it comes into being. In those European countries that Americans are most likely to visit, friendship is quite sharply

distinguished from other, more casual relations, and is differently related to family life. For a Frenchman, a German or an Englishman friendship is usually more particularized and carries a heavier burden of commitment.

But as we use the word, "friend" can be applied to a wide range of 4 relationships—to someone one has known for a few weeks in a new place, to a close business associate, to a childhood playmate, to a man or woman, to a trusted confidant. There are real differences among these relations for Americans—a friendship may be superficial, casual, situational or deep and enduring. But to a European, who sees only our surface behavior, the differences are not clear.

As they see it, people known and accepted temporarily, casually, flow 5 in and out of Americans' homes with little ceremony and often with little personal commitment. They may be parents of the children's friends, house guests of neighbors, members of a committee, business associates from another town or even another country. Coming as a guest into an American home, the European visitor finds no visible landmarks. The atmosphere is relaxed. Most people, old and young, are called by first names.

Who, then, is a friend? 6

Even simple translation from one language to another is difficult. "You 7 see," a Frenchman explains, "if I were to say to you in French, 'This is my good friend,' that person would not be as close to me as someone about whom I say only, 'This is my friend.' Anyone about whom I have to say *more* is really less."

In France, as in many European countries, friends generally are of the 8 same sex, and friendship is seen as basically a relationship between men. Frenchwomen laugh at the idea that "women can't be friends," but they also admit sometimes that for women "it's a different thing." And many French people doubt the possibility of a friendship between a man and a woman. There is also a kind of relationship within a group—men and women who have worked together for a long time, who may be very close, sharing great loyalty and warmth of feeling. They may call one another *copains*—a word that in English becomes "friends" but has more the feeling of "pals" or "buddies." In French eyes this is not friendship, although two members of such a group may well be friends.

For the French, friendship is a one-to-one relationship that demands a 9 keen awareness of the other person's intellect, temperament and particular interests. A friend is someone who draws out your own best qualities, with whom you sparkle and become more of whatever the friendship draws upon. Your political philosophy assumes more depth, appreciation of a play becomes sharper, taste in food or wine is accentuated, enjoyment of a sport is intensified.

And French friendships are compartmentalized. A man may play chess 10 with a friend for thirty years without knowing his political opinions, or he may talk politics with him for as long a time without knowing about his personal life. Different friends fill different niches in each person's life. These friendships are not made part of family life. A friend is not expected to spend evenings being nice to children or courteous to a deaf grandmother. These duties, also serious and enjoined, are primarily for relatives. Men who are friends may meet in a café. Intellectual friends may meet in larger groups for evenings of conversation. Working people may meet at the little *bistro* where they drink and talk, far from the family. Marriage does not affect such friendships; wives do not have to be taken into account.

In the past in France, friendships of this kind seldom were open to any 11 but intellectual women. Since some women's lives centered on their homes, their warmest relations with other women often went back to their girlhood. The special relationship of friendship is based on what the French value most—on the mind, on compatibility of outlook, on vivid awareness of some chosen area of life.

Friendship heightens the sense of each person's individuality. Other 12 relationships commanding as great loyalty and devotion have a different meaning. In World War II the first resistance groups formed in Paris were built on the foundation of *les copains.* But significantly, as time went on these little groups, whose lives rested in one another's hands, called themselves "families." Where each had a total responsibility for all, it was kinship ties that provided the model. And even today such ties, crossing every line of class and personal interest, remain binding on the survivors of these small, secret bands.

In Germany, in contrast with France, friendship is much more articu- 13 lately a matter of feeling. Adolescents, boys and girls, form deeply sentimen- tal attachments, walk and talk together—not so much to polish their wits as to share their hopes and fears and dreams, to form a common front against the world of school and family and to join in a kind of mutual discovery of each other's and their own inner life. Within the family, the closest relation- ship over a lifetime is between brothers and sisters. Outside the family, men and women find in their closest friends of the same sex the devotion of a sister, the loyalty of a brother. Appropriately, in Germany friends usually are brought into the family. Children call their father's and their mother's friends "uncle" and "aunt." Between French friends, who have chosen each other for the congeniality of their point of view, lively disagreement and sharpness of argument are the breath of *life.* But for Germans, whose friend- ships are based on mutuality of feeling, deep disagreement on any subject that matters to both is regarded as a tragedy. Like ties of kinship, ties of friendship are meant to be irrevocably binding. Young Germans who come to the United States have great difficulty in establishing such friendships with Americans. We view friendship more tentatively, subject to changes in inten- sity as people move, change their jobs, marry, or discover new interests.

English friendships follow still a different pattern. Their basis is shared   14
activity. Activities at different stages of life may be of very different kinds—
discovering a common interest in school, serving together in the armed
forces, taking part in a foreign mission, staying in the same country house
during a crisis. In the midst of the activity, whatever it may be, people fall
into step—sometimes two men or two women, sometimes two couples,
sometimes three people—and find that they walk or play a game or tell
stories or serve on a tiresome and exacting committee with the same easy
anticipation of what each will do day by day or in some critical situation.
Americans who have made English friends comment that, even years later,
"you can take up just where you left off." Meeting after a long interval,
friends are like a couple who begin to dance again when the orchestra strikes
up after a pause. English friendships are formed outside the family circle, but
they are not, as in Germany, contrapuntal to the family nor are they, as in
France, separated from the family. And a break in an English friendship
comes not necessarily as a result of some irreconcilable difference of view-
point or feeling but instead as a result of misjudgment, where one friend
seriously misjudges how the other will think or feel or act, so that suddenly
they are out of step.

What, then, is friendship? Looking at these different styles, including   15
our own, each of which is related to a whole way of life, are there common
elements? There is the recognition that friendship, in contrast with kinship,
invokes freedom of choice. A friend is someone who chooses and is chosen.
Related to this is the sense each friend gives the other of being a special
individual, on whatever grounds this recognition is based. And between
friends there is inevitably a kind of equality of give-and-take. The similarities
make the bridge between societies possible, and the American's characteristic openness to different styles of relationship makes it possible for him to
find new friends abroad with whom he feels at home.

Questions for Study and Discussion

1. How, according to Mead and Metraux, do Americans use the term
friend? Do you agree with their sense of how the word is used? How does our use
of the word differ from that of Europeans?

2. What is the authors' purpose in this essay—to tell a story, to explain, to
persuade? How do you know?

3. What are the major differences between the way friends are viewed in
France, Germany, and England? Do any of these differences surprise you? Explain.

4. What do Mead and Metraux see as the differences between "friendship"
and "kinship"?

5. Why do Americans seem to be able to find new "friends" when traveling abroad?

Writing Topics

1. What are your expectations of a friendship? What does the term "best friend" mean to you? How has your conception of friendship changed as you've grown older? Present your responses to these three questions in an essay.

2. Is it possible for men and women to have friendships? What, if any, are the problems that could arise with such a relationship? Your essay may simply reflect on the issue, or it may take the form of an argument for or against the possibility of male-female friendships.

JENNIFER CRICHTON

Jennifer Crichton was born in New York City in 1957. She attended Brown University from 1974 to 1977 and graduated from Barnard College in 1979. It was in college that Crichton decided that she wanted to be a writer. Her articles have appeared in magazines such as *Vanity Fair*, *Cosmopolitan*, and *Ms.* In 1986 Crichton published her first book, *Delivery: A Nurse Midwife's Story*, which she describes as "faction"—a combination of fact and fiction. In order to show with passionate intensity how nurse-midwives work, Crichton did her homework; she followed them "on their hospital rounds and into delivery rooms and up to the postpartum wards, held the hands and fanned the faces of women in labor, and sat in on prenatal visits in inner-city clinics and private practices in nice breezy neighborhoods."

In "College Friends," which appeared in the "Campus Times" section of *Ms.* magazine, Crichton reflects on her college years and what it was like to form new friendships. In so many ways, "going away" to college offers each one of us a chance to make a fresh start in life, and that includes the friends we make and keep.

College Friends

As far as I'm concerned, the first semester away at college is possibly   1
the single worst time to make friends. You'll make them, but you'll probably get it all wrong, through no fault of your own, for these are desperate hours.

Here's desperation: standing in a stadium-like cafeteria, I became con-   2
vinced that a thousand students busy demolishing the contents of their trays were indifferent to me, and studying me with ill-disguised disdain at the same time. The ability to mentally grasp two opposing conceptions is often thought of as the hallmark of genius. But I credit my mind's crazed elasticity to panic. Sitting alone at a table, I see the girl I'd met that morning in the showers. I was thrilled to see her. The need for a friend had become violent. Back at the dorm, I told her more about my family's peculiarities and my cataclysmic summer fling than I'd ever let slip before. All the right sympathetic looks crossed her face at all the right moments, whereupon I deduced that through the good graces of the housing department, I'd stumbled upon a soulmate. But what seemed like two minds mixing and matching on a cosmic plane was actually two lonely freshmen under the influence of unprecedented amounts of caffeine and emotional upheaval. This wasn't a meeting of souls. This was a talking jag of monumental proportions.

By February, my first friend and I passed each other in the hall with   3 lame, bored smiles, and now I can't remember her name for the life of me. But that doesn't make me sad in the least.

Loneliness and the erosion of high school friendships through change   4 and distance leave yawning gaps that beg to be filled. Yet, I never made a real friend by directly applying for the position of confidante or soulmate. I made my best friendships by accident, with instant intimacy marking none of them—it wasn't mutual loneliness that drew us together.

I met my best friend Jean in a film class when she said Alfred Hitch-   5 cock was overrated. I disagreed and we argued out of the building and into a lifelong friendship where we argue still. We became friends without meaning to, and took our intimacy step by step. Deliberate choice, not desperate need, moved us closer. Our friendship is so much a part of us now that it seems unavoidable that we should have become friends. But there was nothing inevitable about it. It's easy to imagine Jean saying to me in that classroom, "Hitchcock's a hack, you're a fool, and that's all I have to say." But that was not all she had to say. Which is why we're friends today. We always have more to say.

Friendship's value wasn't always clear to me. In the back of my mind, I   6 believed that platonic friendships were a way of marking time until I struck the pay dirt of serious romance. I'd managed to digest many romantic notions by my first year of college, and chief among them was the idea that I'd meet the perfect lover who would be everything to me and make me complete. I saw plunging into a relationship as an advanced form of friendship, friendship plus sex. Lacking sex, platonic friendships seemed like a lower standard of living. As long as my boyfriend offered me so much in one convenient package, women friends were superfluous. I thought I was the girl who had everything.

But what made that relationship more—the sex—made it a bad re-   7 placement for friendship. Sexual tension charged the lines of communication between us. White noise crackled on the wire as desire and jealousy, fear of loss, and the need to be loved conspired to cloud and distort expression. Influenced by these powerful forces, I didn't always tell the truth. And on the most practical level, when my boyfriend and I broke up, I had lost more than my lover, I lost my best friend.

"You can't keep doing this," Suzanne told me later that same year.   8

"What?"   9

"Start up our friendship every time your relationship falls apart."   10

"I don't do that," I said. It was exactly what I did.   11

"Yes, you do, and I'm sick of it. I'm not second best. I'm something   12 entirely different."

Once you see that relationships and friendships are different beasts,   13 you'll never think of the two things as interchangeable again, with friendships as the inferior version. . . .

Friendships made in college set a standard for intimacy other friend-   14 ships are hard-pressed ever to approach. "I've become a narrow specialist in my friendships since graduation," says Pam. "With one friend I'll talk about work. With another, we're fitness fanatics together. But I don't really know much about them—how they live their lives, what they eat for breakfast, or if they eat breakfast at all, who their favorite uncle is, or when they got their contact lenses. I don't even know who they voted for for President. There will be a close connection in spots, but in general I feel as if I'm dealing with fractions of people. With my college friends, I feel I know them *whole*.

In college, there's time to reach that degree of intimacy. One night, my   15
best friend and I spent hours describing how our respective families celebrated Christmas. My family waited until everyone was awake and caf-
feinated before opening presents, hers charged out of bed to rip open the
boxes before they could wipe the sleep out of their eyes. We were as self-
righteous as religious fanatics, each convinced our own family was the only
one that did Christmas right. Did we really spend an entire night on a
subject like that? Did we really have that much time?

Operating on college time, my social life was unplanned and spontane-   16
ous. Keeping a light on in our rooms was a way of extending an invitation.
We had time to hang out, to learn to tell the difference between ordinary
crankiness and serious depressions in each other, and to follow the digressions that were at the heart of our friendships. But after college, we had to
change, and in scheduling our free-form friendships we felt, at first, self-
conscious and artificial.

When I had my first full-time job, I called my best friend to make a   17
dinner date a week in advance. She was still in graduate school, and thought
my planning was dire evidence that I'd tumbled into the pit of adult convention. "Why don't you have your girl call my girl and we'll set something up?"
she asked. Heavy sarcasm. While the terms of the friendship have shifted
from digressive, spontaneous socializing to a directed, scheduled style, and
we all feel a certain sense of loss, the value of friendship has, if anything,
increased.

If my college journals were ever published in the newspaper, the head-   18
line would most likely read, "FEM WRITER PENS GOO," but I did find something genuinely moving while reading through my hyper-perceptions the
other day. Freshman year I'd written: "I am interested in everything. Nothing bores me. I hope I don't die before I can read everything, visit every
place, and feel all there is to feel."

The sentiment would be a lot more poignant if I'd actually gone ahead   19
and died young, but I find it moving anyway because it exemplifies what's
good about being young: that you exist as the wide-eyed adventurer, fueled
by the belief that you might amount to something and anything, and that
your possibilities are endless. When I feel this way now, I'm usually half-
dreaming in bed on a breezy Saturday morning. Or I'm with a college

friend—someone with whom I'd pictured the future, back when the future was a dizzying haze viewed with the mind's eyes from the vantage point of a smoky dorm room. Together we carved out life with words and hopes. When I'm with her now, I remember that feeling and experience it all over again, because there's still a lot of hazy future to imagine and life to carve. With my friend, I can look to my future and through my past and remember who I am.

Questions for Study and Discussion

1. Why, according to Crichton, is the first semester at college the most difficult time to make friends? Was this the case for you? Explain.

2. Crichton recalls that she shared some personal information with her new dorm friend early in their relationship. Why do you suppose she did this? What eventually happened to their friendship?

3. How did Crichton meet her best friend, Jean? How did their friendship develop? In what ways was this relationship different from others that Crichton had in college?

4. According to Crichton, why do lovers make lousy best friends? Do you agree with her reasoning? Explain why, or why not.

5. In what ways do college friendships differ from friendships made after college, according to Crichton? What are some of the reasons for their differences?

6. What happens to Crichton when she visits with college friends? Have you ever had similar feelings? If so, when?

Writing Topics

1. Some people use the word *friend* very loosely, applying it to all the people they know or hang out with. Others feel that these sorts of people are mere acquaintances and that true friendship is something different. Write an essay in which you explain your idea of friendship. Illustrate your definition with examples from your experience or your reading.

2. Write a descriptive essay about a friend or relative whom you particularly admire or consider to be close. What first impressions of this person did you have? How have your impressions changed as you have gotten to know him or her better? Keep in mind that your reader will not know the person you are writing about, so you must make him or her come to life through anecdotes, quotations, or some other means. In preparing to write, consider what distinguishes that person from other people you know. How and why is he or she special to you?

3. Crichton believes that true friendships are not usually marked with "instant intimacy." Instead, lifelong friendships are built slowly, step by step. Write an essay in which you describe the process you followed in developing one of your lasting friendships.

MARC FEIGEN FASTEAU

Marc Feigen Fasteau is a practicing lawyer in New York City with a specialty in sex-discrimination litigation. While at Harvard Law School he was the editor of the *Harvard Law Review,* and later he worked in government service in Washington, D.C., his birthplace. Fasteau is a frequent lecturer on topics ranging from sex-discrimination legislation to sexual stereotypes, and is the author of *The Male Machine* (1974). His articles have appeared in scholarly journals as well as in such popular magazines as *Ms.*

In *The Male Machine* Fasteau analyzes the stereotype of the American male and concludes that the prevailing stereotype has, in part, dehumanized American men. The following selection is an excerpt from *The Male Machine* in which Fasteau explains why friendships among men are seemingly unfeeling.

Friendships among Men

There is a long-standing myth in our society that the great friendships   1
are between men. Forged through shared experience, male friendship is portrayed as the most unselfish, if not the highest form, of human relationship. The more traditionally masculine the shared experience from which it springs, the stronger and more profound the friendship is supposed to be. Going to war, weathering crises together at school or work, playing on the same athletic team, are some of the classic experiences out of which friendships between men are believed to grow.

By and large, men do prefer the company of other men, not only in   2
their structured time but in the time they fill with optional, nonobligatory activity. They prefer to play games, drink, and talk, as well as work and fight together. Yet something is missing. Despite the time men spend together, their contact rarely goes beyond the external, a limitation which tends to make their friendships shallow and unsatisfying.

My own childhood memories are of doing things with my friends—   3
playing games or sports, building walkie-talkies, going camping. Other people and my relationships to them were never legitimate subjects for attention. If someone liked me, it was an opaque, mysterious occurrence that bore no analysis. When I was slighted, I felt hurt. But relationships with people

"Friendships among Men" from *The Male Machine* by Marc Fasteau. © 1974. Reprinted by permission of Mc-Graw Hill Publishing Company.

just happened. I certainly had feelings about my friends, but I can't remember a single instance of trying consciously to sort them out until I was well into college.

For most men this kind of shying away from the personal continues   4
into adult life. In conversations with each other, we hardly ever use ourselves as reference points. We talk about almost everything except how we ourselves are affected by people and events. Everything is discussed as though it were taking place out there somewhere, as though we had no more felt response to it than to the weather. Topics that can be treated in this detached, objective way become conversational mainstays. The few subjects which are fundamentally personal are shaped into discussions of abstract general questions. Even in an exchange about their reactions to liberated women—a topic of intensely personal interest—the tendency will be to talk in general, theoretical terms. Work, at least its objective aspects, is always a safe subject. Men also spend an incredible amount of time rehashing the great public issues of the day. Until early 1973, Vietnam was the work-horse topic. Then came Watergate. It doesn't seem to matter that we've all had a hundred similar conversations. We plunge in for another round, trying to come up with a new angle as much as to impress the others with what we know as to keep from being bored stiff.

Games play a central role in situations organized by men. I remember a   5
weekend some years ago at the country house of a law-school classmate as a blur of softball, football, croquet, poker, and a dice-and-board game called Combat, with swimming thrown in on the side. As soon as one game ended, another began. Taken one at a time, these "activities" were fun, but the impression was inescapable that the host, and most of his guests, would do anything to stave off a lull in which they would be together without some impersonal focus for their attention. A snapshot of almost any men's club would show the same thing, 90 percent of the men engaged in some activity—ranging from backgammon to watching the tube—other than, or at least as an aid to, conversation.*

My composite memory of evenings spent with a friend at college and   6
later when we shared an apartment in Washington is of conversations punctuated by silences during which we would internally pass over any personal or emotional thoughts which had arisen and come back to the permitted track. When I couldn't get my mind off personal matters, I said very little. Talks with my father have always had the same tone. Respect for privacy was the rationale for our diffidence. His questions to me about how things were going at school or at work were asked as discreetly as he would have asked a friend about

---

*Women may use games as a reason for getting together—bridge clubs, for example. But the show is more for the rest of the world—to indicate that they are doing *something*— and the games themselves are not the only means of communication.

someone's commitment to a hospital for the criminally insane. Our conversations, when they touched these matters at all, to say nothing of more sensitive matters, would veer quickly back to safe topics of general interest.

In our popular literature, the archetypal hero embodying this personal muteness is the cowboy. The classic mold for the character was set in 1902 by Owen Wister's novel *The Virginian* where the author spelled out, with an explicitnesss that was never again necessary, the characteristics of his protagonist. Here's how it goes when two close friends the Virginian hasn't seen in some time take him out for a drink: 7

> All of them had seen rough days together, and they felt guilty with emotion.
> "It's hot weather," said Wiggin.
> "Hotter in Box Elder," said McLean. "My kid has started teething."
> Words ran dry again. They shifted their positions, looked in their glasses, read the labels on the bottles. They dropped a word now and then to the proprietor about his trade, and his ornaments.

One of the Virginian's duties is to assist at the hanging of an old friend as a horse thief. Afterward, for the first time in the book, he is visibly upset. The narrator puts his arm around the hero's shoulders and describes the Virginian's reaction:

> I had the sense to keep silent, and presently he shook my hand, not looking at me as he did so. He was always very shy of demonstration.

And, for explanation of such reticence, "As all men know, he also knew that many things should be done in this world in silence, and that talking about them is a mistake."

There are exceptions, but they only prove the rule. 8

One is the drunken confidence: "Bob, ole boy, I gotta tell ya—being 9 divorced isn't so hot. . . . [and see, I'm too drunk to be held responsible for blurting it out]." Here, drink becomes an excuse for exchanging confidences and a device for periodically loosening the restraint against expressing a need for sympathy and support from other men—which may explain its importance as a male ritual. Marijuana fills a similar need.

Another exception is talking to a stranger—who may be either some- 10 one the speaker doesn't know or someone who isn't in the same social or business world. (Several black friends told me that they have been on the receiving end of personal confidences from white acquaintances that they were sure had not been shared with white friends.) In either case, men are willing to talk about themselves only to other men with whom they do not have to compete or whom they will not have to confront socially later.

Finally, there is the way men depend on women to facilitate certain 11 conversations. The women in a mixed group are usually the ones who make the first personal reference, about themselves or others present. The men can then join in without having the onus of initiating a discussion of "person-alities." Collectively, the men can "blame" the conversation on the women. They can also feel in these conversations that since they are talking "to" the women instead of "to" the men, they can be excused for deviating from the masculine norm. When the women leave, the tone and subject invariably shift away from the personal.

The effect of these constraints is to make it extraordinarily difficult for   12
men to really get to know each other. A psychotherapist who has conducted a lengthy series of encounter groups for men summed it up:

> With saddening regularity [the members of these groups] described how much they wanted to have closer, more satisfying relationships with other men: "I'd settle for having one really close man friend. I supposedly have some close men friends now. We play golf or go for a drink. We complain about our jobs and our wives. I care about them and they care about me. We even have some physical contact—I mean we may even give a hug on a big occasion. But it's not enough."

The sources of this stifling ban on self-disclosure, the reasons why men hide from each other, lie in the taboos and imperatives of the masculine stereotype.

To begin with, men are supposed to be functional, to spend their time   13
working or otherwise solving or thinking about how to solve problems. Personal reaction, how one feels about something, is considered dysfunc-tional, at best an irrelevant distraction from the expected objectivity. Only weak men, and women, talk about—i.e., "give in," to their feelings. "I group my friends in two ways," said a business executive:

> those who have made it and don't complain and those who haven't made it. And only the latter spend time talking to their wives about their problems and how bad their boss is and all that. The ones who concentrate more on commu-nicating . . . are those who have realized that they aren't going to make it and therefore they have changed the focus of attention.

In a world which tells men they have to choose between expressiveness and manly strength, this characterization may be accurate. Most of the men who talk personally to other men *are* those whose problems have gotten the best of them, who simply can't help it. Men not driven to despair don't talk about themselves, so the idea that self-disclosure and expressiveness are associated with problems and weakness becomes a self-fulfilling prophecy.

Obsessive competitiveness also limits the range of communication in   14
male friendships. Competition is the principal mode by which men relate to each other—at one level because they don't know how else to make contact, but more basically because it is the way to demonstrate, to themselves and others, the key masculine qualities of unwavering toughness and the ability to dominate and control. The result is that they inject competition into situations which don't call for it.

In conversations, you must show that you know more about the subject   15
than the other man, or at least as much as he does. For example, I have often
engaged in a contest that could be called My Theory Tops Yours, disguised as
a serious exchange of ideas. The proof that it wasn't serious was that I was
willing to participate even when I was sure that the participants, including
myself, had nothing fresh to say. Convincing the other person—victory—is
the main objective, with control of the floor an important tactic. Men tend
to lecture each other, insist that the discussion follow their train of thought,
and are often unwilling to listen. As one member of a men's rap group said,

> When I was talking I used to feel that I had to be driving to a point, that it had
> to be rational and organized, that I had to persuade at all times, rather than
> exchange thoughts and ideas.

Even in casual conversation some men hold back unless they are absolutely
sure of what they are saying. They don't want to have to change a position
once they have taken it. It's "just like a woman" to change your mind, and,
more important, it is inconsistent with the approved masculine posture of
total independence.

Competition was at the heart of one of my closest friendships, now   16
defunct. There was a good deal of mutual liking and respect. We went out of
our way to spend time with each other and wanted to work together. We
both had "prospects" as "bright young men" and the same "liberal but tough"
point of view. We recognized this about each other, and this recognition was
the basis of our respect and of our sense of equality. That we saw each other
as equals was important—our friendship was confirmed by the reflection of
one in the other. But our constant and all-encompassing competition made
this equality precarious and fragile. One way or another, everything counted
in the measuring process. We fought out our tennis matches as though our
lives depended on it. At poker, the two of us would often play on for hours
after the others had left. These *mano a mano* poker marathons seem in
retrospect especially revealing of the competitiveness of the relationship:
playing for small stakes, the essence of the game is in outwitting, psychologi-
cally beating down the other player—the other skills involved are negligible.
Winning is the only pleasure, one that evaporates quickly, a truth that struck
me in inchoate form every time our game broke up at four A.M. and I walked
out the door with my five-dollar winnings, a headache, and a sense of time
wasted. Still, I did the same thing the next time. It was what we did
together, and somehow it counted. Losing at tennis could be balanced by
winning at poker; at another level, his moving up in the federal government
by my getting on the *Harvard Law Review*.

This competitiveness feeds the most basic obstacle to openness be-   17
tween men, the inability to admit to being vulnerable. Real men, we learn
early, are not supposed to have doubts, hopes and ambitions which may not
be realized, things they don't (or even especially do) like about themselves,

fears and disappointments. Such feelings and concerns, of course, are part of everyone's inner life, but a man must keep quiet about them. If others know how you really feel you can be hurt, and that in itself is incompatible with manhood. The inhibiting effect of this imperative is not limited to disclosures of major personal problems. Often men do not share even ordinary uncertainties and half-formulated plans of daily life with their friends. And when they do, they are careful to suggest that they already know how to proceed—that they are not really asking for help or understanding but simply for particular bits of information. Either way, any doubts they have are presented as external, carefully characterized as having to do with the issue as distinct from the speaker. They are especially guarded about expressing concern or asking a question that would invite personal comment. It is almost impossible for men to simply exchange thoughts about matters involving them personally in a comfortable, non-crisis atmosphere. If a friend tells you of his concern that he and a colleague are always disagreeing, for example, he is likely to quickly supply his own explanation—something like "different professional backgrounds." The effect is to rule out observations or suggestions that do not fit within this already reconnoitered protective structure. You don't suggest, even if you believe it is true, that in fact the disagreements arise because he presents his ideas in a way which tends to provoke a hostile reaction. It would catch him off guard; it would be something he hadn't already thought of and accepted about himself and, for that reason, no matter how constructive and well-intentioned you might be, it would put you in control for the moment. He doesn't want that; he is afraid of losing your respect. So, sensing he feels that way, because you would yourself, you say something else. There is no real give-and-take.

It is hard for men to get angry at each other honestly. Anger between 18 friends often means that one has hurt the other. Since the straightforward expression of anger in these situations involves an admission of vulnerability, it is safer to stew silently or find an "objective" excuse for retaliation. Either way, trust is not fully restored.

Men even try not to let it show when they feel good. We may report 19 the reasons for our happiness, if they have to do with concrete accomplishments, but we try to do it with a straight face, as if to say, "Here's what happened, but it hasn't affected my grown-up unemotional equilibrium, and I am not asking for any kind of response." Happiness is a precarious, "childish" feeling, easy to shoot down. Others may find the event that triggers it trivial or incomprehensible, or even threatening to their own self-esteem— in the sense that if one man is up, another man is down. So we tend not to take the risk of expressing it.

What is particularly difficult for men is seeking or accepting help from 20 friends. I, for one, learned early that dependence was unacceptable. When I was eight, I went to a summer camp I disliked. My parents visited me in the middle of the summer and, when it was time for them to leave, I wanted to go with them. They refused, and I yelled and screamed and was miserably unhappy for the rest of the day. That evening an older camper comforted me, sitting by my bed as I cried, patting me on the back soothingly and saying whatever it is that one says at times like that. He was in some way clumsy or funny-looking, and a few days later I joined a group of kids in cruelly making fun of him, an act which upset me, when I thought about it, for years. I can only explain it in terms of my feeling, as early as the age of eight, that by needing and accepting his help and comfort I had compromised myself, and took it out on him.

"You can't express dependence when you feel it," a corporate executive   21
said, "because it's a kind of absolute. If you are loyal 90 percent of the time and disloyal 10 percent, would you be considered loyal? Well, the same happens with independence: you are either dependent or independent; you can't be both." "Feelings of dependence," another explained, "are identified with weakness or 'untoughness' and our culture doesn't accept those things in men." The result is that we either go it alone or "act out certain games or rituals to provoke the desired reaction in the other and have our needs satisfied without having to ask for anything."

Somewhat less obviously, the expression of affection also runs into   22
emotional barriers growing out of the masculine stereotype. When I was in college, I was suddenly quite moved while attending a friend's wedding. The surge of feeling made me uncomfortable and self-conscious. There was noth-ing inherently difficult or, apart from the fact of being moved by a moment of tenderness, "unmasculine" about my reaction. I just did not know how to deal with or communicate what I felt. "I consider myself a sentimentalist," one man said, "and I think I am quite able to express my feelings. But the other day my wife described a friend of mine to some people as my best friend and I felt embarrassed when I heard her say it."

A major source of these inhibitions is the fear of being, of being   23
thought, homosexual. Nothing is more frightening to a heterosexual man in our society. It threatens, at one stroke, to take away every vestige of his claim to a masculine identity—something like knocking out the foundations of a building—and to expose him to the ostracism, ranging from polite tolerance to violent revulsion, of his friends and colleagues. A man can be labeled as homosexual not just because of an overt sexual act but because of almost any sign of behavior which does not fit the masculine stereotype. The touching of another man, other than shaking hands or, under emotional stress, an arm around the shoulder, is taboo. Women may kiss each other when they meet; men are uncomfortable when hugged even by close friends. Onlookers might misinterpret what they say, and more important, what would we think of ourselves if we felt a twinge of sensual pleasure from the embrace.

Direct verbal expressions of affection or tenderness are also something   24
that only homosexuals and women engage in. Between "real" men affection

has to be disguised in gruff, "you old son-of-a-bitch" style. Paradoxically, in some instances, terms of endearment between men can be used as a ritual badge of manhood, dangerous medicine safe only for the strong. The flirting with homosexuality that characterizes the initiation rites of many fraternities and men's clubs serves this purpose. Claude Brown wrote about black life in New York City in the 1950s:

> The term ["baby"] had a hip ring to it. . . . It was like saying, "Man, look at me. I've got masculinity to spare. . . . I can say 'baby' to another cat and he can say 'baby' to me, and we can say it with strength in our voices." If you could say it, this meant that you really had to be sure of yourself, sure of your masculinity.

Fear of homosexuality does more than inhibit the physical display of affection. One of the major recurring themes in the men's groups led by psychotherapist Don Clark was:

> A large segment of my feelings about other men are unknown or distorted because I am afraid they might have something to do with homosexuality. Now I'm lonely for other men and don't know how to find what I want with them.

As Clark observes, "The specter of homosexuality seems to be the dragon at the gateway to self-awareness, understanding, and acceptance of male-male needs. If a man tries to pretend the dragon is not there by turning a blind eye to erotic feelings for all other males, he also blinds himself to the rich variety of feelings that are related."

The few situations in which men do acknowledge strong feelings of   25
affection and dependence toward other men are exceptions which prove the rule. With "cop couples," for example, or combat soldier "buddies," intimacy and dependence are forced on the men by their work—they have to ride in the patrol car or be in the same foxhole with somebody—and the jobs themselves have such highly masculine images that the man can get away with behavior that would be suspect under any other conditions.

Furthermore, even these combat-buddy relationships, when looked at   26
closely, turn out not to be particularly intimate or personal. Margaret Mead has written:

> During the last war English observers were confused by the apparent contradiction between American soldiers' emphasis on the buddy, so grievously exemplified in the break-downs that followed a buddy's death, and the results of detailed inquiry which showed how transitory these buddy relationships were. It was found that men actually accepted their buddies as derivatives from their outfit, and from accidents of association, rather than because of any special personality characteristics capable of ripening into friendship.

One effect of the fear of appearing to be homosexual is to reinforce the   27
practice that two men rarely get together alone without a reason. I once

called up a friend to suggest that we have dinner together. "O.K.," he said. "What's up?" I felt uncomfortable telling him that I just wanted to talk, that there was no other reason for the invitation.

Men get together to conduct business, to drink, to play games and   28
sports, to re-establish contact after long absences, to participate in heterosexual social occasions—circumstances in which neither person is responsible for actually wanting to see the other. Men are particularly comfortable seeing each other in groups. The group situation defuses any possible assumptions about the intensity of feeling between particular men and provides the safety of numbers—"All the guys are here." It makes personal communication, which requires a level of trust and mutual understanding not generally shared by all members of a group, more difficult and offers an excuse for avoiding this dangerous territory. And it provides what is most sought after in men's friendships: mutual reassurance of masculinity.

Questions for Study and Discussion

1. Why does Fasteau think that the belief that the great friendships are between men is a long-standing myth?
2. Why does Fasteau find male friendships "shallow and unsatisfying"?
3. Why do men tend to shy away from anything that smacks of the personal? How do they rationalize this behavior?
4. Why do games play such an important role in men's lives? What role do they play in women's lives?
5. In what types of situations do men become personal?
6. According to Fasteau, what effect does competition have on male friendships? Do you agree with his analysis? Explain.
7. Fasteau concludes his essay by stating that the group situation "provides what is most sought after in men's friendships: mutual assurance of masculinity." Why do you suppose men need such reassurance? Do they seem to need it more today than in times past? Explain.

Writing Topics

1. Using your own experiences and observations write an essay in which you argue with Fasteau's position that "despite the time men spend together, their contact rarely goes beyond the external."
2. If you accept Fasteau's analysis of the "reasons why men hide from each other," what can be done to make more meaningful communication possible? Write an essay in which you propose some solutions.

E. B. WHITE

Of the seventeen books that E. B. White wrote, perhaps none is more fondly remembered than his children's novel *Charlotte's Web* (1952). It is the story of a runt pig named Wilbur who is born on Mr. Arable's farm. Wilbur appears destined to become ham and bacon but is saved from the ax by Fern, Arable's little daughter. The story soon turns to fantasy as Wilbur discovers he has the power of speech and begins to carry on conversations with other barnyard animals, especially the beautiful gray spider, Charlotte A. Cavatica. The poignancy of the tale, however, derives from White's insightful portrayal of the human emotions—love, faith, charity, and, through the memorable but self-centered rat, Templeton, even gluttony and nastiness—that these animal characters demonstrate. Charlotte becomes Wilbur's friend and confidante, teaching him and the reader many things, while wisely and imaginatively guiding him through life and protecting him from the slaughterer's knife.

The following selection is "Last Day," chapter 21 of the novel. Wilbur has won a medal at the county fair, and his future seems secure. He and his friend Charlotte are about ready to go home to the farm. Wilbur asks Charlotte why she has done all that she has for him, and she responds with her now classic explanation of friendship. In the end, Wilbur's own actions show how well he understands the concept.

Last Day (from *Charlotte's Web*)

Charlotte and Wilbur were alone. The families had gone to look for 1
Fern. Templeton was asleep. Wilbur lay resting after the excitement and strain of the ceremony. His medal still hung from his neck; by looking out of the corner of his eye he could see it.

"Charlotte," said Wilbur after a while, "why are you so quiet?" 2

"I like to sit still," she said. "I've always been rather quiet." 3

"Yes, but you seem specially so today. Do you feel all right?" 4

"A little tired, perhaps. But I feel peaceful. Your success in the ring this 5
morning was, to a small degree, *my* success. Your future is assured. You will live, secure and safe, Wilbur. Nothing can harm you now. These autumn days will shorten and grow cold. The leaves will shake loose from the trees and fall. Christmas will come, then the snows of winter. You will live to enjoy the beauty of the frozen world, for you mean a great deal to Zuckerman and he will not harm you, ever. Winter will pass, the days will lengthen, the ice will melt in the pasture pond. The song sparrow will return and sing, the frogs will awake, the warm wind will blow again. All these sights and sounds and smells will be yours to enjoy, Wilbur—this lovely world, these precious days . . ."

Charlotte stopped. A moment later a tear came to Wilbur's eye. "Oh,   6
Charlotte," he said. "To think that when I first met you I thought you were
cruel and bloodthirsty!"

When he recovered from his emotion, he spoke again.   7

"Why did you do all this for me?" he asked. "I don't deserve it. I've   8
never done anything for you."

"You have been my friend," replied Charlotte. "That in itself is a   9
tremendous thing. I wove my webs for you because I liked you. After all,
what's a life, anyway? We're born, we live a little while, we die. A spider's
life can't help being something of a mess, with all this trapping and eating
flies. By helping you, perhaps I was trying to lift up my life a trifle. Heaven
knows anyone's life can stand a little of that."

"Well," said Wilbur. "I'm no good at making speeches. I haven't got   10
your gift for words. But you have saved me, Charlotte, and I would gladly
give my life for you—I really would."

"I'm sure you would. And I thank you for your generous sentiments."   11

"Charlotte," said Wilbur. "We're all going home today. The Fair is   12
almost over. Won't it be wonderful to be back home in the barn cellar again
with the sheep and the geese? Aren't you anxious to get home?"

For a moment Charlotte said nothing. Then she spoke in a voice so low   13
Wilbur could hardly hear the words.

"I will not be going back to the barn," she said.   14

Wilbur leapt to his feet. "Not going back?" he cried. "Charlotte, what   15
are you talking about?"

"I'm done for," she replied. "In a day or two I'll be dead. I haven't even   16
strength enough to climb down into the crate. I doubt if I have enough silk
in my spinnerets to lower me to the ground."

Hearing this, Wilbur threw himself down in an agony of pain and   17
sorrow. Great sobs racked his body. He heaved and grunted with desolation.
"Charlotte," he moaned. "Charlotte! My true friend!"

"Come now, let's not make a scene," said the spider. "Be quiet, Wilbur.   18
Stop thrashing about!"

"But I can't *stand* it," shouted Wilbur. "I won't leave you here alone to   19
die. If you're going to stay here I shall stay, too."

"Don't be ridiculous," said Charlotte. "You can't stay here. Zuckerman   20
and Lurvy and John Arable and the others will be back any minute now, and
they'll shove you into that crate and away you'll go. Besides, it wouldn't
make any sense for you to stay. There would be no one to feed you. The Fair
Grounds will soon be empty and deserted."

Wilbur was in a panic. He raced round and round the pen. Suddenly he   21
had an idea—he thought of the egg sac and the five hundred and fourteen
little spiders that would hatch in the spring. If Charlotte herself was unable
to go home to the barn, at least he must take her children along.

Wilbur rushed to the front of his pen. He put his front feet up on the   22 top board and gazed around. In the distance he saw the Arables and the Zuckermans approaching. He knew he would have to act quickly.

"Where's Templeton?" he demanded. 23

"He's in that corner, under the straw, asleep," said Charlotte. 24

Wilbur rushed over, pushed his strong snout under the rat, and tossed 25
him into the air.

"Templeton!" screamed Wilbur. "Pay attention!" 26

The rat, surprised out of a sound sleep, looked first dazed then disgusted. 27

"What kind of monkeyshine is this?" he growled. "Can't a rat catch a 28
wink of sleep without being rudely popped into the air?"

"Listen to me!" cried Wilbur. "Charlotte is very ill. She has only a 29
short time to live. She cannot accompany us home, because of her condition. Therefore, it is absolutely necessary that I take her egg sac with me. I can't reach it, and I can't climb. You are the only one that can get it. There's not a second to be lost. The people are coming—they'll be here in no time. Please, please, *please*, Templeton, climb up and get the egg sac."

The rat yawned. He straightened his whiskers. Then he looked up at 30
the egg sac.

"So!" he said, in disgust. "So it's old Templeton to the rescue again, is 31
it? Templeton do this, Templeton do that, Templeton please run down to the dump and get me a magazine clipping, Templeton please lend me a piece of string so I can spin a web."

"Oh, hurry!" said Wilbur. "Hurry up, Templeton!" 32

But the rat was in no hurry. He began imitating Wilbur's voice. 33

"So it's 'Hurry up, Templeton,' is it?" he said. "Ho, ho. And what 34
thanks do I ever get for these services, I would like to know? Never a kind word for old Templeton, only abuse and wisecracks and side remarks. Never a kind word for a rat."

"Templeton," said Wilbur in desperation, "if you don't stop talking and 35
get busy, all will be lost, and I will die of a broken heart. Please climb up!"

Templeton lay back in the straw. Lazily he placed his forepaws behind 36
his head and crossed his knees, in an attitude of complete relaxation.

"Die of a broken heart," he mimicked. "How touching! My, my! I 37
notice that it's always me you come to when in trouble. But I've never heard of anyone's heart breaking on *my* account. Oh, no. Who cares anything about old Templeton?"

"Get up!" screamed Wilbur. "Stop acting like a spoiled child!" 38

Templeton grinned and lay still. "Who made trip after trip to the 39
dump?" he asked. "Why, it was old Templeton! Who saved Charlotte's life by scaring that Arable boy away with a rotten goose egg? Bless my soul, I believe it was old Templeton. Who bit your tail and got you back on your feet this morning after you had fainted in front of the crowd? Old Templeton. Has it ever occurred to you that I'm sick of running errands and doing favors? What do you think I am, anyway, a rat-of-all-work?"

Wilbur was desperate. The people were coming. And the rat was   40
failing him. Suddenly he remembered Templeton's fondness for food.

"Templeton," he said, "I will make you a solemn promise. Get Char-   41
lotte's egg sac for me, and from now on I will let you eat first, when Lurvy
slops me. I will let you have your choice of everything in the trough and I
won't touch a thing until you're through."

The rat sat up. "You mean that?" he said.   42

"I promise. I cross my heart."   43

"All right, it's a deal," said the rat. He walked to the wall and started to   44
climb. His stomach was still swollen from last night's gorge. Groaning and
complaining, he pulled himself slowly to the ceiling. He crept along till he
reached the egg sac. Charlotte moved aside for him. She was dying, but she
still had strength enough to move a little. Then Templeton bared his long
ugly teeth and began snipping the threads that fastened the sac to the
ceiling. Wilbur watched from below.

"Use extreme care!" he said. "I don't want a single one of those eggs   45
harmed."

"Thith thtuff thticks in my mouth," complained the rat. "It'th worth   46
than caramel candy."

But Templeton worked away at the job, and managed to cut the sac   47
adrift and carry it to the ground, where he dropped it in front of Wilbur.
Wilbur heaved a great sign of relief.

"Thank you, Templeton," he said. "I will never forget this as long as I   48
live."

"Neither will I," said the rat, picking his teeth. "I feel as though I'd   49
eaten a spool of thread. Well, home we go!"

Templeton crept into the crate and buried himself in the straw. He got   50
out of sight just in time. Lurvy and John Arable and Mr. Zuckerman came
along at that moment, followed by Mrs. Arable and Mrs. Zuckerman and
Avery and Fern. Wilbur had already decided how he would carry the egg
sac—there was only one way possible. He carefully took the little bundle in
his mouth and held it there on top of his tongue. He remembered what
Charlotte had told him—that the sac was waterproof and strong. It felt
funny on his tongue and made him drool a bit. And of course he couldn't say
anything. But as he was being shoved into the crate, he looked up at
Charlotte and gave her a wink. She knew he was saying good-bye in the only
way he could. And she knew her children were safe.

"Good-bye!" she whispered. Then she summoned all her strength and   51
waved one of her front legs at him.

She never moved again. Next day, as the Ferris wheel was being taken   52
apart and the race horses were being loaded into vans and the entertainers
were packing up their belongings and driving away in their trailers, Charlotte died. The Fair Grounds were soon deserted. The sheds and buildings
were empty and forlorn. The infield was littered with bottles and trash.

Nobody, of the hundreds of people that had visited the Fair, knew that a grey spider had played the most important part of all. No one was with her when she died.

Questions for Study and Discussion

1. Wilbur asks Charlotte, "Why did you do all this for me?" What is implied in his question?

2. How does Charlotte answer Wilbur's question? What does she mean when she says, "That in itself is a tremendous thing"?

3. What demands or advantages does White bring upon himself as a writer in presenting the nature of friendship and the inevitability of loss through the example of two animals who are able to converse?

4. How does Wilbur repay Charlotte's friendship? What motivates him?

5. Has Templeton been a friend to Wilbur and Charlotte? Why is he the object of so much abuse? What does White's portrayal of him teach us about people who act as he does? Can such individuals simply be ignored?

Writing Topics

1. Using examples from your own experience, write an essay explaining how a particular friendship has lifted your life "a trifle," as Charlotte puts it.

2. Try your hand at a short tale, aimed at children, that conveys your sense of what friendship is all about. You may want to model your writing on White's in having your characters be animals who can talk. Or, after reading some of Aesop's fables, you may want to try to fashion a modern fable about friendship.

III

Men and Women

Masculinity and Femininity may stand on either side of a mile-high wall, yet women and men share beds and homes, histories and children. So while racial and ethnographic stereotypes are fueled by segregation and prohibit familiarity . . . sexual stereotypes are formed in intimacy. This is what makes them unique, and uniquely troubling.
—JUDITH LEVINE

Marriage must be a relation either of sympathy or of conquest.
—GEORGE ELIOT

Gender Roles

SUSAN JACOBY

When Susan Jacoby became a newspaper reporter in 1963 at the age of seventeen, she had no intention of writing about "women's subjects." "To write about women was to write about trivia: charity balls, cake sales, and the like," she recalls. "I would have laughed at anyone who tried to tell me that one day I would believe the members of my own sex were important enough to write about." But times have changed. Although the old female stereotypes have not completely disappeared, many people have come to regard them as unfair and unacceptable. And Jacoby has, in fact, written extensively about women's subjects, often in the *New York Times* and *McCall's*. Many of these pieces have been collected in her book *The Possible She* (1979). In the following essay, originally published in the "Hers" column of the *Times* in 1978, Jacoby tells of two experiences when she felt mistreated because she was a woman and describes how she dealt with each situation.

Unfair Game

My friend and I, two women obviously engrossed in conversation, are 1 sitting at a corner table in the crowded Oak Room of the Plaza at ten o'clock on a Tuesday night. A man materializes and interrupts us with the snappy opening line, "A good woman is hard to find."

We say nothing, hoping he will disappear back into his bottle. But he 2 fancies himself as our genie and asks, "Are you visiting?" Still we say nothing. Finally my friend looks up and says, "We live here." She and I look at each other, the thread of our conversation snapped, our thoughts focused on how to get rid of this intruder. In a minute, if something isn't done, he will scrunch down next to me on the banquette and start offering to buy us drinks.

"Would you leave us alone, please," I say in a loud but reasonably polite 3 voice. He looks slightly offended but goes on with his bright social patter. I become more explicit. "We don't want to talk to you, we didn't ask you over here, and we want to be alone. Go away." This time he directs his full attention to me—and he is mad. "All right, all right, *excuse me.*" He pushes up the corners of his mouth in a Howdy Doody smile. "You ought to try smiling. You might even be pretty if you smiled once in a while."

At last the man leaves. He goes back to his buddy at the bar. I watch them out of the corner of my eye, and he gestures angrily at me for at least fifteen minutes. When he passes our table on the way out of the room, this well-dressed, obviously affluent man mutters, "Good-bye, bitch," under his breath.   4

Why is this man calling me names? Because I have asserted my right to sit at a table in a public place without being drawn into a sexual flirtation. Because he has been told, in no uncertain terms, that two attractive women prefer each other's company to his.   5

This sort of experience is an old story to any woman who travels, eats, or drinks—for business or pleasure—without a male escort. In Holiday Inns and at the Plaza, on buses and airplanes, in tourist and first class, a woman is always thought to be looking for a man in addition to whatever else she may be doing. The man who barged in on us at the bar would never have broken into the conversation of two men, and it goes without saying that he wouldn't have imposed himself on a man and a woman who were having a drink. But two women at a table are an entirely different matter. Fair game.   6

This might be viewed as a relatively small flaw in the order of the universe—something in a class with an airline losing luggage or a computer fouling up a bank statement. Except a computer doesn't foul up your bank account every month and an airline doesn't lose your suitcase every time you fly. But if you are an independent woman, you have to spend a certain amount of energy, day in and day out, in order to go about your business without being bothered by strange men.   7

On airplanes, I am a close-mouthed traveler. As soon as the "No Smoking" sign is turned off, I usually pull some papers out of my briefcase and start working. Work helps me forget that I am scared of flying. When I am sitting next to a woman, she quickly realizes from my monosyllabic replies that I don't want to chat during the flight. Most men, though, are not content to be ignored.   8

Once I was flying from New York to San Antonio on a plane that was scheduled to stop in Dallas. My seatmate was an advertising executive who kept questioning me about what I was doing and who remained undiscouraged by my terse replies until I ostentatiously covered myself with a blanket and shut my eyes. When the plane started its descent in Dallas, he made his move.   9

"You don't really have to get to San Antonio today, do you?"   10
"Yes."   11
"Come on, change your ticket. Spend the evening with me here. I'm staying at a wonderful hotel, with a pool, we could go dancing . . ."   12
"No."   13

"Well, you can't blame a man for trying." 14

I do blame a man for trying in this situation—for suggesting that a 15 woman change her work and travel plans to spend a night with a perfect stranger in whom she had displayed no personal interest. The "no personal interest" is crucial; I wouldn't have blamed the man for trying if I had been stroking his cheek and complaining about my dull social life.

There is a nice postscript to this story. Several months later, I was 16 walking my dog in Carl Schurz Park when I ran into my erstwhile seatmate, who was taking a stroll with his wife and children. He recognized me, all right, and was trying to avoid me when I went over and courteously reintroduced myself. I reminded him that we had been on the same flight to Dallas. "Oh yes," he said. "As I recall you were going on to somewhere else." "San Antonio," I said. "I was in a hurry that day."

The code of feminine politeness, instilled in girlhood, is no help in 17 dealing with the unwanted approaches of strange men. Our mothers didn't teach us to tell a man to get lost; they told us to smile and hint that we'd be just delighted to spend time with the gentleman if we didn't have other commitments. The man in the Oak Room bar would not be put off by a demure lowering of eyelids; he had to be told, roughly and loudly, that his presence was a nuisance.

Not that I am necessarily against men and women picking each other 18 up in public places. In most instances, a modicum of sensitivity will tell a woman or a man whether someone is open to approaches.

Mistakes can easily be corrected by the kind of courtesy so many people 19 have abandoned since the "sexual revolution." One summer evening, I was whiling away a half hour in the outdoor bar of the Stanhope Hotel. I was alone, dressed up, having a drink before going on to meet someone in a restaurant. A man at the next table asked, "If you're not busy, would you like to have a drink with me?" I told him I was sorry but I would be leaving shortly. "Excuse me for disturbing you," he said, turning back to his own drink. Simple courtesy. No insults and no hurt feelings.

One friend suggested that I might have avoided the incident in the 20 Oak Room by going to the Palm Court instead. It's true that the Palm Court is a traditional meeting place for unescorted ladies. But I don't like violins when I want to talk. And I wanted to sit in a large, comfortable leather chair. Why should I have to hide among the potted palms to avoid men who think I'm looking for something else?

Questions for Study and Discussion

1. What is the main point of Jacoby's essay? Where is it stated most directly? What was her purpose in writing this piece?

2. What solutions, if any, does Jacoby suggest for dealing with the problem she describes?

3. Jacoby complains about the code of feminine politeness. What exactly is this "code"? Does she seem constrained by it?

4. In paragraph 16, why does Jacoby say as her parting shot, "I was in a hurry that day"?

5. What is Jacoby's tone in this essay? How does she achieve this tone? Give several examples from the essay.

Writing Topics

1. Jacoby has written that this article drew a larger response than anything she has ever published. What kinds of responses do you imagine it drew from women? From men? How do you respond to this article? Compose a response as if you were going to send it to the *New York Times* or to Jacoby herself.

2. In one respect, the situations Jacoby describes have mainly to do with courtesy, with good and bad manners. Write an essay in which you define *courtesy*. What purpose does it serve? Should people be expected always to show consideration for others, or should they be free to say and do whatever they please? Why?

3. Write an essay on some aspect of dating. Why do people go on dates? What do people gain from dining together, or going to a movie together? How has dating changed since you started dating? How should one arrange a date with a stranger?

DEBORAH TANNEN

Born in 1945, Deborah Tannen is a professor of linguistics at Georgetown University, specializing in the study of the ways people talk to each other. Her first book, *That's Not What I Meant* (1986), catapulted her into the public spotlight, and she appeared on talk shows discussing the differences between male and female conversational patterns. In 1990 she published the best-selling book *You Just Don't Understand: Women and Men in Conversation.*

The following selection from *You Just Don't Understand* examines the differing ways that women and men use language in conversation with one another: Men, by lecturing, reinforce their independence and establish or test their status; women, by listening, establish rapport and closeness through self-revelation. The result, however, is that men tend to take over conversations by providing information and women become easily bored because the interaction they seek does not come about. Rather than place blame or suggest any drastic remedies to improve communication between the sexes, Tannen believes that "women and men both can gain by understanding the other gender's style, and by learning to use it on occasion."

"I'll Explain It to You": Lecturing and Listening

At a reception following the publication of one of my books, I noticed   1
a publicist listening attentively to the producer of a popular radio show. He was telling her how the studio had come to be built where it was, and why he would have preferred another site. What caught my attention was the length of time he was speaking while she was listening. He was delivering a monologue that could only be called a lecture, giving her detailed information about the radio reception at the two sites, the architecture of the station, and so on. I later asked the publicist if she had been interested in the information the producer had given her. "Oh, yes," she answered. But then she thought a moment and said, "Well, maybe he did go on a bit." The next day she told me, "I was thinking about what you asked. I couldn't have cared less about what he was saying. It's just that I'm so used to listening to men go on about things I don't care about, I didn't even realize how bored I was until you made me think about it."

I was chatting with a man I had just met at a party. In our conversa-   2
tion, it emerged that he had been posted in Greece with the RAF during 1944 and 1945. Since I had lived in Greece for several years, I asked him about his experiences: What had Greece been like then? How had the Greek villagers treated the British soldiers? What had it been *like* to be a

British soldier in wartime Greece? I also offered information about how Greece had changed, what it is like now. He did not pick up on my remarks about contemporary Greece, and his replies to my questions quickly changed from accounts of his own experiences, which I found riveting, to facts about Greek history, which interested me in principle but in the actual telling left me profoundly bored. The more impersonal his talk became, the more I felt oppressed by it, pinned involuntarily in the listener position.

At a showing of Judy Chicago's jointly created art work *The Dinner Party*, I was struck by a couple standing in front of one of the displays: The man was earnestly explaining to the woman the meaning of symbols in the tapestry before them, pointing as he spoke. I might not have noticed this unremarkable scene, except that *The Dinner Party* was radically feminist in conception, intended to reflect women's experiences and sensibilities.   3

While taking a walk in my neighborhood on an early summer evening at twilight, I stopped to chat with a neighbor who was walking his dogs. As we stood, I noticed that the large expanse of yard in front of which we were standing was aglitter with the intermittent flickering of fireflies. I called attention to the sight, remarking on how magical it looked. "It's like the Fourth of July," I said. He agreed, and then told me he had read that the lights of fireflies are mating signals. He then explained to me details of how these signals work—for example, groups of fireflies fly at different elevations and could be seen to cluster in different parts of the yard.   4

In all these examples, the men had information to impart and they were imparting it. On the surface, there is nothing surprising or strange about that. What is strange is that there are so many situations in which men have factual information requiring lengthy explanations to impart to women, and so few in which women have comparable information to impart to men.   5

The changing times have altered many aspects of relations between women and men. Now it is unlikely, at least in many circles, for a man to say, "I am better than you because I am a man and you are a woman." But women who do not find men making such statements are nonetheless often frustrated in their dealings with them. One situation that frustrates many women is a conversation that has mysteriously turned into a lecture, with the man delivering the lecture to the woman, who has become an appreciative audience.   6

Once again, the alignment in which women and men find themselves arrayed is asymmetrical. The lecturer is framed as superior in status and expertise, cast in the role of teacher, and the listener is cast in the role of student. If women and men took turns giving and receiving lectures, there would be nothing disturbing about it. What is disturbing is the imbalance.   7

Women and men fall into this unequal pattern so often because of the differences in their interactional habits. Since women seek to build rapport, they are inclined to play down their expertise rather than display it. Since men value the position of center stage and the feeling of knowing more, they seek opportunities to gather and disseminate factual information.

If men often seem to hold forth because they have the expertise, 8 women are often frustrated and surprised to find that when they have the expertise, they don't necessarily get the floor.

First Me, Then Me

I was at a dinner with faculty members from other departments in my 9 university. To my right was a woman. As the dinner began, we introduced ourselves. After we told each other what departments we were in and what subjects we taught, she asked what my research was about. We talked about my research for a little while. Then I asked her about her research and she told me about it. Finally, we discussed the ways that our research overlapped. Later, as tends to happen at dinners, we branched out to others at the table. I asked a man across the table from me what department he was in and what he did. During the next half hour, I learned a lot about his job, his research, and his background. Shortly before the dinner ended there was a lull, and he asked me what I did. When I said I was a linguist, he became excited and told me about a research project he had conducted that was related to neurolinguistics. He was still telling me about his research when we all got up to leave the table.

This man and woman were my colleagues in academia. What happens 10 when I talk to people at parties and social events, not fellow researchers? My experience is that if I mention the kind of work I do to women, they usually ask me about it. When I tell them about conversational style or gender differences, they offer their own experiences to support the patterns I describe. This is very pleasant for me. It puts me at center stage without my having to grab the spotlight myself, and I frequently gather anecdotes I can use in the future. But when I announce my line of work to men, many give me a lecture on language—for example, about how people, especially teenagers, misuse language nowadays. Others challenge me, for example questioning me about my research methods. Many others change the subject to something they know more about.

Of course not all men respond in this way, but over the years I have 11 encountered many men, and very few women, who do. It is not that speaking in this way is *the* male way of doing things, but that it is *a* male way. There are women who adopt such styles, but they are perceived as speaking like men.

If You've Got it, Flaunt it—or Hide it

I have been observing this constellation in interaction for more than a   12
dozen years. I did not, however, have any understanding of *why* this happens
until fairly recently, when I developed the framework of status and connection. An experimental study that was pivotal in my thinking shows that
expertise does not ensure women a place at center stage in conversation with
men.

Psychologist H. M. Leet-Pellegrini set out to discover whether gender   13
or expertise determined who would behave in what she terms a "dominant"
way—for example, by talking more, interrupting, and controlling the topic.
She set up pairs of women, pairs of men, and mixed pairs, and asked them to
discuss the effects of television violence on children. In some cases, she
made one of the partners an expert by providing relevant factual information
and time to read and assimilate it before the videotaped discussion. One
might expect that the conversationalist who was the expert would talk more,
interrupt more, and spend less time supporting the conversational partner
who knew less about the subject. But it wasn't so simple. On the average,
those who had expertise did talk more, but men experts talked more than
women experts.

Expertise also had a different effect on women and men with regard to   14
supportive behavior. Leet-Pellegrini expected that the one who did not have
expertise would spend more time offering agreement and support to the one
who did. This turned out to be true—*except* in cases where a woman was the
expert and her nonexpert partner was a man. In this situation, the women
experts showed support—saying things like "Yeah" and "That's right"—far
more than the nonexpert men they were talking to. Observers often rated the
male nonexpert as more dominant than the female expert. In other words,
the women in this experiment not only didn't wield their expertise as power,
but tried to play it down and make up for it through extra assenting behavior.
They acted as if their expertise were something to hide.

And perhaps it was. When the word *expert* was spoken in these experi-   15
mental conversations, in all cases but one it was the man in the conversation
who used it, saying something like "So, you're the expert." Evidence of the
woman's superior knowledge sparked resentment, not respect.

Furthermore, when an expert man talked to an uninformed woman, he   16
took a controlling role in structuring the conversation in the beginning *and*
the end. But when an expert man talked to an uninformed man, he dominated in the beginning but not always in the end. In other words, having
expertise was enough to keep a man in the controlling position if he was
talking to a woman, but not if he was talking to a man. Apparently, when a
woman surmised that the man she was talking to had more information on
the subject than she did, she simply accepted the reactive role. But another

man, despite a lack of information, might still give the expert a run for his money and possibly gain the upper hand by the end.

Reading these results, I suddenly understood what happens to me when   17
I talk to women and men about language. I am assuming that my acknowl-
edged expertise will mean I am automatically accorded authority in the conversation, and with women that is generally the case. But when I talk to men, revealing that I have acknowledged expertise in this area often invites challenges. I *might* maintain my position if I defend myself successfully against the challenges, but if I don't, I may lose ground.

One interpretation of the Leet-Pellegrini study is that women are get-   18
ting a bum deal. They don't get credit when it's due. And in a way, this is true. But the reason is not—as it seems to many women—that men are bums who seek to deny women authority. The Leet-Pellegrini study shows that many men are inclined to jockey for status, and challenge the authority of others, when they are talking to men too. If this is so, then challenging a woman's authority as they would challenge a man's could be a sign of respect and equal treatment, rather than lack of respect and discrimination. In cases where this is so, the inequality of the treatment results not simply from the men's behavior alone but from the differences in men's and women's styles: Most women lack experience in defending themselves against challenges, which they misrepresent as personal attacks on their credibility.

Even when talking to men who are happy to see them in positions of   19
status, women may have a hard time getting their due because of differences in men's and women's interactional goals. Just as boys in high school are not inclined to repeat information about popular girls because it doesn't get them what they want, women in conversation are not inclined to display their knowledge because it doesn't get them what they are after. Leet-Pellegrini suggests that the men in this study were playing a game of "Have I won?" while the women were playing a game of "Have I been sufficiently helpful?" I am inclined to put this another way: The game women play is "Do you like me?" whereas the men play "Do you respect me?" If men, in seeking respect, are less liked by women, this is an unsought side effect, as is the effect that women, in seeking to be liked, may lose respect. When a woman has a conversation with a man, her efforts to emphasize their similarities and avoid showing off can easily be interpreted, through the lens of status, as relegating her to a one-down position, making her appear either incompetent or insecure.

A Subtle Deference

Elizabeth Aries, a professor of psychology at Amherst College, set out   20
to show that highly intelligent, highly educated young women are no longer submissive in conversations with male peers. And indeed she found that the

college women did talk more than the college men in small groups she set up. But what they said was different. The men tended to set the agenda by offering opinions, suggestions, and information. The women tended to react, offering agreement or disagreement. Furthermore, she found that body language was as different as ever: the men sat with their legs stretched out, while the women gathered themselves in. Noting that research has found that speakers using the open-bodied position are more likely to persuade their listeners, Aries points out that talking more may not ensure that women will be heard.

In another study, Aries found that men in all-male discussion groups 21
spent a lot of time at the beginning finding out "who was best informed about movies, books, current events, politics, and travel" as a means of "sizing up the competition" and negotiating "where they stood in relation to each other." This glimpse of how men talk when there are no women present gives an inkling of why displaying knowledge and expertise is something that men find more worth doing than women. What the women in Aries's study spent time doing was "gaining a closeness through more intimate self-revelation."

It is crucial to bear in mind that both the women and the men in these 22
studies were establishing camaraderie, and both were concerned with their relationships to each other. But different aspects of their relationships were of primary concern: their place in a hierarchical order for the men, and their place in a network of intimate connections for the women. The consequence of these disparate concerns was very different ways of speaking.

Thomas Fox is an English professor who was intrigued by the differ- 23
ences between women and men in his freshman writing classes. What he observed corresponds almost precisely to the experimental findings of Aries and Leet-Pellegrini. Fox's method of teaching writing included having all the students read their essays to each other in class and talk to each other in small groups. He also had them write papers reflecting on the essays and the discussion groups. He alone, as the teacher, read these analytical papers.

To exemplify the two styles he found typical of women and men, Fox 24
chose a woman, Ms. M, and a man, Mr. H. In her speaking as well as her writing, Ms. M held back what she knew, appearing uninformed and uninterested, because she feared offending her classmates. Mr. H spoke and wrote with authority and apparent confidence because he was eager to persuade his peers. She did not worry about persuading; he did not worry about offending.

In his analytical paper, the young man described his own behavior in 25
the mixed-gender group discussions as if he were describing the young men in Leet-Pellegrini's and Aries's studies:

> In my sub-group I am the leader. I begin every discussion by stating my opinions as facts. The other two members of the sub-group tend to sit back and agree with me. . . . I need people to agree with me.

Fox comments that Mr. H reveals "a sense of self, one that acts to change himself and other people, that seems entirely distinct from Ms. M's sense of self, dependent on and related to others."

Calling Ms. M's sense of self "dependent" suggests a negative view of her way of being in the world—and, I think, a view more typical of men. This view reflects the assumption that the alternative to independence is dependence. If this is indeed a male view, it may explain why so many men are cautious about becoming intimately involved with others: It makes sense to avoid humiliating dependence by insisting on independence. But there is another alternative: *inter*dependence.   26

The main difference between these alternatives is symmetry. Dependence is an asymmetrical involvement: One person needs the other, but not vice versa, so the needy person is one-down. Interdependence is symmetrical: Both parties rely on each other, so neither is one-up or one-down. Moreover, Mr. H's sense of self is also dependent on others. He requires others to listen, agree, and allow him to take the lead by stating his opinions first.   27

Looked at this way, the woman and man in this group are both dependent on each other. Their differing goals are complementary, although neither understands the reasons for the other's behavior. This would be a fine arrangement, except that their differing goals result in alignments that enhance his authority and undercut hers.   28

Different Interpretations—and Misinterpretations

Fox also describes differences in the way male and female students in his classes interpreted a story they read. These differences also reflect assumptions about the interdependence or independence of individuals. Fox's students wrote their responses to "The Birthmark" by Nathaniel Hawthorne. In the story, a woman's husband becomes obsessed with a birthmark on her face. Suffering from her husband's revulsion at the sight of her, the wife becomes obsessed with it too and, in a reversal of her initial impulse, agrees to undergo a treatment he has devised to remove the birthmark—a treatment that succeeds in removing the mark, but kills her in the process.   29

Ms. M interpreted the wife's complicity as a natural response to the demand of a loved one: The woman went along with her husband's lethal schemes to remove the birthmark because she wanted to please and be appealing to him. Mr. H blamed the woman's insecurity and vanity for her fate, and he blamed her for voluntarily submitting to her husband's authority. Fox points out that he saw her as individually responsible for her actions, just as he saw himself as individually responsible for his own actions. To him, the issue was independence: The weak wife voluntarily took a submissive   30 role. To Ms. M, the issue was interdependence: The woman was inextricably bound up with her husband, so her behavior could not be separated from his.

Fox observes that Mr. H saw the writing of the women in the class as 31 spontaneous—they wrote whatever popped into their heads. Nothing would be farther from Ms. M's experience as she described it: When she knew her peers would see her writing, she censored everything that popped into her head. In contrast, when she was writing something that only her professor would read, she expressed firm and articulate opinions.

There is a striking but paradoxical complementarity to Ms. M's and 32 Mr. H's styles, when they are taken together. He needs someone to listen and agree. She listens and agrees. But in another sense, their dovetailing purposes are at cross-purposes. He misinterprets her agreement, intended in a spirit of connection, as a reflection of status and power: He thinks she is "indecisive" and "insecure." Her reasons for refraining from behaving as he does—firmly stating opinions as facts—have nothing to do with her attitudes toward her knowledge, as he thinks they do, but rather result from her attitudes toward her relationships with her peers.

These experimental studies by Leet-Pellegrini and Aries, and the obser- 33 vations by Fox, all indicate that, typically, men are more comfortable than women in giving information and opinions and speaking in an authoritative way to a group, whereas women are more comfortable than men in supporting others. . . .

Listener as Underling

Clearly men are not always talking and women are not always listen- 34 ing. I have asked men whether they ever find themselves in the position of listening to another man giving them a lecture, and how they feel about it. They tell me that this does happen. They may find themselves talking to someone who presses information on them so insistently that they give in and listen. They say they don't mind too much, however, if the information is interesting. They can store it away for future use, like remembering a joke to tell others later. Factual information is of less interest to women because it is of less use to them. They are unlikely to try to pass on the gift of information, more likely to give the gift of being a good audience.

Men as well as women sometimes find themselves on the receiving end 35 of a lecture they would as soon not hear. But men tell me that it is most likely to happen if the other man is in a position of higher status. They know they have to listen to lectures from fathers and bosses.

That men can find themselves in the position of unwilling listener is 36 attested to by a short opinion piece in which A. R. Gurney bemoans being frequently "cornered by some self-styled expert who harangues me with his considered opinion on an interminable agenda of topics." He claims that this tendency bespeaks a peculiarly American inability to "converse"—that is, engage in a balanced give-and-take—and cites as support the French observer of American customs Alexis de Tocqueville, who wrote, "An American . . . speaks to you as if he was addressing a meeting." Gurney credits his own appreciation of conversing to his father, who "was a master at eliciting and responding enthusiastically to the views of others, though this resiliency didn't always extend to his children. Indeed, now I think about it, he spoke to us many times as if he were addressing a meeting."

It is not surprising that Gurney's father lectured his children. The act of giving information by definition frames one in a position of higher status, while the act of listening frames one as lower. Children instinctively sense this—as do most men. But when women listen to men, they are not thinking in terms of status. Unfortunately, their attempts to reinforce connections and establish rapport, when interpreted through the lens of status, can be misinterpreted as casting them in a subordinate position—and are likely to be taken that way by many men.
37

What's so Funny?

The economy of exchanging jokes for laughter is a parallel one. In her study of college students' discussion groups, Aries found that the students in all-male groups spent a lot of time telling about times they had played jokes on others, and laughing about it. She refers to a study in which Barbara Miller Newman found that high school boys who were not "quick and clever" became the targets of jokes. Practical joking—playing a joke *on* someone—is clearly a matter of being one-up: in the know and in control. It is less obvious, but no less true, that *telling* jokes can also be a way of negotiating status.
38

Many women (certainly not all) laugh at jokes but do not later remember them. Since they are not driven to seek and hold center stage in a group, they do not need a store of jokes to whip out for this purpose. A woman I will call Bernice prided herself on her sense of humor. At a cocktail party, she met a man to whom she was drawn because he seemed at first to share this trait. He made many funny remarks, which she spontaneously laughed at. But when she made funny remarks, he seemed not to hear. What had happened to his sense of humor? Though telling jokes and laughing at them are both reflections of a sense of humor, they are very different social activities. Making others laugh gives you a fleeting power over them: As linguist Wallace Chafe points out, at the moment of laughter, a person is temporarily disabled. The man Bernice met was comfortable only when he was making her laugh, not the other way around. When Bernice laughed at his jokes, she thought she was engaging in a symmetrical activity. But he was engaging in an asymmetrical one.
39

A man told me that sometime around tenth grade he realized that he   40
preferred the company of women to the company of men. He found that his
female friends were more supportive and less competitive, whereas his male
friends seemed to spend all their time joking. Considering joking an asymmetrical activity makes it clearer why it would fit in with a style he perceived
as competitive. . . .

Mutual Accusations

Considering these dynamics, it is not surprising that many women   41
complain that their partners don't listen to them. But men make the same
complaint about women, although less frequently. The accusation "You're
not listening" often really means "You don't understand what I said in the
way that I meant it," or "I'm not getting the response I wanted." Being
listened to can become a metaphor for being understood and being valued.

In my earlier work I emphasized that women may get the impression   42
men aren't listening to them even when the men really are. This happens
because men have different habitual ways of showing they're listening. As
anthropologists Maltz and Borker explain, women are more inclined to ask
questions. They also give more listening responses—little words like *mhm*,
uh-uh, and *yeah*—sprinkled throughout someone else's talk, providing a
running feedback loop. And they respond more positively and enthusiastically, for example by agreeing and laughing.

All this behavior is doing the work of listening. It also creates rapport-   43
talk by emphasizing connection and encouraging more talk. The corresponding strategies of men—giving fewer listener responses, making statements
rather than asking questions, and challenging rather than agreeing—can be
understood as moves in a contest by incipient speakers rather than audience
members.

Not only do women give more listening signals, according to Maltz and   44
Borker, but the signals they give have different meanings for men and
women, consistent with the speaker/audience alignment. Women use "yeah"
to mean "I'm with you, I follow," whereas men tend to say "yeah" only when
they agree. The opportunity for misunderstanding is clear. When a man is
confronted with a woman who has been saying "yeah," "yeah," "yeah," and
then turns out not to agree, he may conclude that she has been insincere, or
that she was agreeing without really listening. When a woman is confronted
with a man who does *not* say "yeah"—or much of anything else—she may
conclude that *he* hasn't been listening. The men's style is more literally
focused on the message level of talk, while the women's is focused on the
relationship or meta-message level.

To a man who expects a listener to be quietly attentive, a woman   45
giving a stream of feedback and support will seem to be talking too much for

a listener. To a woman who expects a listener to be active and enthusiastic in showing interest, attention, and support, a man who listens silently will seem not to be listening at all, but rather to have checked out of the conversation, taken his listening marbles, and gone mentally home.

Because of these patterns, women may get the impression that men   46
aren't listening when they really are. But I have come to understand, more recently, that it is also true that men listen to women less frequently than women listen to men, because the act of listening has different meanings for them. Some men really *don't* want to listen at length because they feel it frames them as subordinate. Many women do want to listen, but they expect it to be reciprocal—I listen to you now; you listen to me later. They become frustrated when they do the listening now and now and now, and later never comes.

Mutual Dissatisfaction

If women are dissatisfied with always being in the listening position,   47
the dissatisfaction may be mutual. That a woman feels she has been assigned the role of silently listening audience does not mean that a man feels he has consigned her to that role—or that he necessarily likes the rigid alignment either.

During the time I was working on this book, I found myself at a book   48
party filled with people I hardly knew. I struck up a conversation with a charming young man who turned out to be a painter. I asked him about his work and, in response to his answer, asked whether there has been a return in contemporary art to figurative painting. In response to my question, he told me a lot about the history of art—so much that when he finished and said, "That was a long answer to your question," I had long since forgotten that I had asked a question, let alone what it was. I had not minded this monologue—I had been interested in it—but I realized, with something of a jolt, that I had just experienced the dynamic that I had been writing about.

I decided to risk offending my congenial new acquaintance in order to   49
learn something about his point of view. This was, after all, a book party, so I might rely on his indulgence if I broke the rules of decorum in the interest of writing a book. I asked whether he often found himself talking at length while someone else listened. He thought for a moment and said yes, he did, because he liked to explore ideas in detail. I asked if it happened equally with women and men. He thought again and said, "No, I have more trouble with men." I asked what he meant by trouble. He said, "Men interrupt. *They* want to explain to *me*."

Finally, having found this young man disarmingly willing to talk about   50
the conversation we had just had and his own style, I asked which he preferred: that a woman listen silently and supportively, or that she offer

opinions and ideas of her own. He said he thought he liked it better if she volunteered information, making the interchange more interesting.

When men begin to lecture other men, the listeners are experienced at 51 trying to sidetrack the lecture, or match it, or derail it. In this system, making authoritative pronouncements may be a way to begin an *exchange* of information. But women are not used to responding in that way. They see little choice but to listen attentively and wait for their turn to be alloted to them rather than seizing it for themselves. If this is the case, the man may be as bored and frustrated as the woman when his attempt to begin an exchange of information ends in his giving a lecture. From his point of view, she is passively soaking up information, so she must not have any to speak of. One of the reasons men's talk to women frequently turns into lecturing is *because* women listen attentively and do not interrupt with challenges, sidetracks, or matching information.

In the conversations with male and female colleagues that I recounted 52 at the outset of this chapter, this difference may have been crucial. When I talked to the woman, we each told about our own research in response to the other's encouragement. When I talked to the man, I encouraged him to talk about his work, and he obliged, but he did not encourage me to talk about mine. This may mean that he did not want to hear about it—but it also may not. In her study of college students' discussion groups, Aries found that women who did a lot of talking began to feel uncomfortable; they backed off and frequently drew out quieter members of the group. This is perfectly in keeping with women's desire to keep things balanced, so everyone is on an equal footing. Women expect their conversational partners to encourage them to hold forth. Men, who do not typically encourage quieter members to speak up, assume that anyone who has something to say will volunteer it. The men may be equally disappointed in a conversational partner who turns out to have nothing to say.

Similarly, men can be as bored by women's topics as women can be by 53 men's. While I was wishing the former RAFer would tell me about his personal experiences in Greece, he was probably wondering why I was boring him with mine and marveling at my ignorance of the history of a country I had lived in. Perhaps he would have considered our conversation a success if I had challenged or topped his interpretation of Greek history rather than listening dumbly to it. When men, upon hearing the kind of work I do challenge me about my research methods, they are inviting me to give them information and show them my expertise—something I don't like to do outside of the classroom or lecture hall, but something they themselves would likely be pleased to be provoked to do.

The publicist who listened attentively to information about a radio 54 station explained to me that she wanted to be nice to the manager, to smooth the way for placing her clients on his station. But men who want to ingratiate themselves with women are more likely to try to charm them by offering interesting information than by listening attentively to whatever information the women have to impart. I recall a luncheon preceding a talk I delivered to a college alumni association. My gracious host kept me entertained before my speech by regaling me with information about computers, which I politely showed interest in, while inwardly screaming from boredom and a sense of being weighed down by irrelevant information that I knew I would never remember. Yet I am sure he thought he was being interesting, and it is likely that at least some male guests would have thought that he was. I do not wish to imply that all women hosts have entertained me in the perfect way. I recall a speaking engagement before which I was taken to lunch by a group of women. They were so attentive to my expertise that they plied me with questions, prompting me to exhaust myself by giving my lecture over lunch before the formal lecture began. In comparison to this, perhaps the man who lectured to me about computers was trying to give me a rest.

The imbalance by which men often find themselves in the role of lecturer, and women often find themselves in the role of audience, is not the creation of only one member of an interaction. It is not something that men do to women. Neither is it something that women culpably "allow" or "ask for." The imbalance is created by the difference between women's and men's habitual styles. . . .　55

Hope for the Future

What is the hope for the future? Must we play out our assigned parts to the closing act? Although we tend to fall back on habitual ways of talking, repeating old refrains and familiar lines, habits can be broken. Women and men both can gain by understanding the other gender's style, and by learning to use it on occasion.　56

Women who find themselves unwillingly cast as the listener should practice propelling themselves out of that position rather than waiting patiently for the lecture to end. Perhaps they need to give up the belief that they must wait for the floor to be handed to them. If they have something to say on a subject, they might push themselves to volunteer it. If they are bored with a subject, they can exercise some influence on the conversation and change the topic to something they would rather discuss.　57

If women are relieved to learn that they don't always have to listen, there may be some relief for men in learning that they don't always have to have interesting information on the tips of their tongues if they want to impress a woman or entertain her. A journalist once interviewed me for an article about how to strike up conversations. She told me that another expert she had interviewed, a man, had suggested that one should come up with an interesting piece of information. I found this amusing, as it seemed　58 to typify a man's idea of a good conversationalist, but not a woman's. How much easier men might find the task of conversation if they realized that all they have to do is listen. As a woman who wrote a letter to the editor of *Psychology Today* put it, "When I find a guy who asks, 'How was your day?' and really wants to know, I'm in heaven."

Questions for Study and Discussion

1. Tannen begins her essay with four anecdotes or stories. What is particularly disturbing for Tannen about what happens in each of the four anecdotes? How effective do you find these stories as a beginning for her essay? Explain.

2. Tannen writes that the Leet-Pellegrini study was "pivotal" in her thinking. What in particular about that study made it so important?

3. Tannen says of Fox's observations that "what he observed corresponds almost precisely to the experimental findings of Aries and Leet-Pellegrini." If this is so, why does Tannen choose to include his findings? Are Fox's observations simply more support for her beliefs? Are there more profound implications in what he found?

4. Tannen has gathered information from several sources for her writing. What are those sources? She seems to like to draw information and conclusions for her experiences. Did you find her experiences more or less helpful or no different from the information and conclusions she drew from published research? Explain.

5. Would you agree that Tannen appears at times to bend over backward to be evenhanded and fair, especially toward men? If you agree, why do you think she does this? Does she fear offending her male readers? Does she think there is a possibility she might be incorrect in her analysis?

6. As far as your own observations are concerned, does what Tannen writes about telling jokes seem correct to you? Why, or why not?

7. What conversational strategies do men use when their attempts to lecture other men meet with opposition? Would these same strategies work for women in similar situations? Explain.

8. Tannen supplies titles for each of the sections of her essay. Did you find them helpful to your reading of the essay? Were they distracting? Are they a superficial structural device that seems to give more organization to the essay than it actually has? Did you think that any of the sections could have been omitted? If so, which, and why?

9. Having read Tannen's observations and the conclusions she reaches, are you thinking about changing your conversational habits? If so, how? If not, why not?

Writing Topics

1. Write an essay in which you analyze and critique your conversational style. You may first want to record a brief conversation so as to be better able to

analyze it and have it available for reference in your paper. Consider in your analysis whether what Tannen says applies to you.

2. Write an essay in which you provide your own analysis of what goes on in a conversation between a woman and a man, or in a group of women and men. Do you perceive conversational strategies and counterstrategies that Tannen does not examine in her essay? Are there aspects of conversational dynamics that you think need more attention than Tannen gives them? For example, does it make any difference how long people have known each other? Does it make any difference what the context or setting of a conversation is? Do the ages of the participants make any difference?

NOEL PERRIN

Noel Perrin is a New Yorker by birth and has spent much of his life in the academic world, yet he is most widely known as an essayist on the demands and rewards of country life. He was born in 1927, attended Williams College, Duke University, and Cambridge University, England, and is now a professor of English at Dartmouth College in New Hampshire. He lives in neighboring Vermont and wrote about his home state in *Vermont in All Weathers* (1973). His country pieces, which he calls "essays of a sometime farmer," have been collected in *First Person Rural* (1978), *Second Person Rural* (1980), and *Third Person Rural* (1982). In 1992 he wrote *Solo: Life with an Electric Car.*

In "The Androgynous Man," first published in the *New York Times* in 1984, Perrin addresses the restrictive roles that sexual stereotyping casts us into and the effects that these roles have on our personality and behavior. In keeping with the independent spirit of his other writings, he argues for freedom from such restrictive sex roles.

The Androgynous Man

The summer I was 16, I took a train from New York to Steamboat   1
Springs, Colo., where I was going to be assistant wrangler at a camp. The trip took three days, and since I was much too shy to talk to strangers, I had quite a lot of time for reading. I read all of *Gone With the Wind*. I read all of the interesting articles in a couple of magazines I had, and then I went back and read all the dull stuff. I also took all the quizzes, a thing of which magazines were fuller then than now.

The one that held my undivided attention was called "How Masculine/   2
Feminine Are You?" It consisted of a large number of inkblots. The reader was supposed to decide which of four objects each blot most resembled. The choices might be a cloud, a steam-engine, a caterpillar and a sofa.

When I finished the test, I was shocked to find that I was barely   3
masculine at all. On a scale of 1 to 10, I was about 1.2. Me, the horse wrangler? (And not just wrangler, either. That summer, I had to skin a couple of horses that died—the camp owner wanted the hides.)

The results of that test were so terrifying to me that for the first time in   4
my life I did a piece of original analysis. Having unlimited time on the train, I looked at the "masculine" answers over and over, trying to find what it was that distinguished real men from people like me—and eventually I discov-

ered two very simple patterns. It was "masculine" to think the blots looked like man-made objects, and "feminine" to think they looked like natural objects. It was masculine to think they looked like things capable of causing harm, and feminine to think of innocent things.

Even at 16, I had the sense to see that the compilers of the test were using rather limited criteria—maleness and femaleness are both more complicated than that—and I breathed a hugh sigh of relief. I wasn't necessarily a wimp, after all. 5

That the test did reveal something other than the superficiality of its makers I realized only many years later. What it revealed was that there is a large class of men and women both, to which I belong, who are essentially androgynous. That doesn't mean we're gay, or low in the appropriate hormones, or uncomfortable performing the jobs traditionally assigned our sexes. (A few years after that summer, I was leading troops in combat and, unfashionable as it now is to admit this, having a very good time. War is exciting. What a pity the 20th century went and spoiled it with high-tech weapons.) 6

What it does mean to be spiritually androgynous is a kind of freedom. Men who are all-male, or he-man, or 100% red-blooded Americans, have a little biological set that causes them to be attracted to physical power, and probably also to dominance. Maybe even to watching football. I don't say this to criticize them. Completely masculine men are quite often wonderful people: good husbands, good (though sometimes overwhelming) fathers, good members of society. Furthermore, they are often so unself-consciously at ease in the world that other men seem to imitate them. They just aren't as free as androgynes. They pretty nearly have to be what they are; we have a range of choices open. 7

The sad part is that many of us never discover that. Men who are not 100% red-blooded Americans—say those who are only 75% red-blooded—often fail to notice their freedom. They are too busy trying to copy the he-men ever to realize that men, like women, come in a wide variety of acceptable types. Why this frantic imitation? My answer is mere speculation, but not casual. I have speculated on this for a long time. 8

Partly they're just envious of the he-man's unconscious ease. Mostly they're terrified of finding that there may be something wrong with them deep down, some weakness at the heart. To avoid discovering that, they spend their lives acting out the role that the he-man naturally lives. Sad. 9

One thing that men owe to the women's movement is that this kind of failure is less common than it used to be. In releasing themselves from the single ideal of the dependent woman, women have more or less incidentally released a lot of men from the single ideal of the dominant male. The one mistake the feminists have made, I think, is in supposing that all men need this release, or that the world would be a better place if all men achieved it. It wouldn't. It would just be duller. 10

So far I have been pretty vague about just what the freedom of the   11
androgynous man is. Obviously it varies with the case. In the case I know
best, my own, I can be quite specific. It has freed me most as a parent. I am,
among other things, a fairly good natural mother. I like the nurturing role. It
makes me feel good to see a child eat—and it turns me to mush to see a 4-
year-old holding a glass with both small hands, in order to drink. I even
enjoyed sewing patches on the knees of my daughter Amy's Dr. Dentons
when she was at the crawling stage. All that pleasure I would have lost if I
had made myself stick to the notion of the paternal role that I started with.

Or take a smaller and rather ridiculous example. I feel free to kiss cats.   12
Until recently it never occurred to me that I would want to, though my
daughters have been doing it all their lives. But my elder daughter is now 22,
and in London. Of course, I get to look after her cat while she is gone. He's a
big, handsome farm cat named Petrushka, very unsentimental though used
from kittenhood to being kissed on the top of the head by Elizabeth. I've
gotten very fond of him (he's the adventurous kind of cat who likes to climb
hills with you), and one night I simply felt like kissing him on the top of the
head, and did. Why did no one tell me sooner how silky cat fur is?

Then there's my relation to cars. I am completely unembarrassed by my   13
inability to diagnose even minor problems in whatever object I happen to be
driving, and don't have to make some insider's remark to mechanics to try to
establish that I, too, am a "Man With His Machine."

The same ease extends to household maintenance. I do it, of course.   14
Service people are expensive. But for the last decade my house has func-
tioned better than it used to because I have had the aid of a volume called
"Home Repairs Any Woman Can Do," which is pitched just right for people
at my technical level. As a youth, I'd as soon have touched such a book as I
would have become a transvestite. Even though common sense says there is
really nothing sexual whatsoever about fixing sinks.

Or take public emotion. All my life I have easily been moved by certain   15
kinds of voices. The actress Siobhan McKenna's, to take a notable case. Give
her an emotional scene in a play, and within ten words my eyes are full of tears.
In boyhood, my great dread was that someone might notice. I struggled man-
fully, you might say, to suppress this weakness. Now, of course, I don't see it as
a weakness at all, but as a kind of fulfillment. I even suspect that the true he-
men feel the same way, or one kind of them does, at least, and it's only the poor
imitators who have to struggle to repress themselves.

Let me come back to the inkblots, with their assumption that mascu-   16
line equates with machinery and science, and feminine with art and nature.
I have no idea whether the right pronoun for God is He, She, or It. But this
I'm pretty sure of. If God could somehow be induced to take that test, God
would not come out macho and not feminismo, either, but right in the
middle. Fellow androgynes, it's a nice thought.

Questions for Study and Discussion

1. What does Perrin mean by *androgyny*? Where does he present his definition? Why does he present it at that point? Is he using the term in the strict dictionary sense?

2. State Perrin's thesis in your own words. What do you think his purpose is in writing the essay?

3. What does Perrin believe are the benefits of androgyny? Are all his examples equally convincing to you? Explain.

4. Perrin's essay first appeared in a weekly column called "About Men." Do you think Perrin intended his essay primarily for male readers or readers of both sexes?

5. Explain the meaning of Perrin's last paragraph. How effective is it as a conclusion? Explain.

Writing Topics

1. Write an essay in which you establish your own definition of masculinity or femininity. What are its identifying characteristics? How does your definition differ, if at all, from prevailing stereotypes?

2. Using Perrin's essay as a model, recount experiences you have had in growing up in which gender roles have been a significant factor. For example, were there ever summer jobs you felt you could not apply for? Or, were you ever made to feel inadequate in certain athletic or social situations? How were you able to resolve the problem?

KATHERINE ANNE PORTER

Born in 1890 in Texas, and a resident of Mexico for several years, Katherine Anne Porter knew firsthand the sunburnt, wide-open land in which her short story "Rope" is set. She also knew firsthand the tensions of marriage, which the story depicts in convincing detail. Educated in convent schools, she eloped from one of them at sixteen and between 1933 and 1942 was twice married and twice divorced. As she put it, her problem was that writing came before everything else. Even so, her collected short fiction consists of only twenty-seven stories and novellas, and she wrote only one full-length novel, *Ship of Fools* (1962). Her last book, reflecting her continuing concern with politics and social issues, is a remembrance of the Sacco-Vanzetti trial of the 1920s (*The Never Ending Wrong*, 1977). Porter died in 1980.

"Rope" comes from Porter's first collection of stories, *Flowering Judas* (1930). Without making grand statements, she uses a short, sharp quarrel between a husband and wife to reveal something of the risks and rewards of marriage.

Rope

On the third day after they moved to the country he came walking 1 back from the village carrying a basket of groceries and a twenty-four-yard coil of rope. She came out to meet him, wiping her hands on her green smock. Her hair was tumbled, her nose was scarlet with sunburn; he told her that already she looked like a born country woman. His gray flannel shirt stuck to him, his heavy shoes were dusty. She assured him he looked like a rural character in a play.

Had he brought the coffee? She had been waiting all day long for 2 coffee. They had forgot it when they ordered at the store the first day.

Gosh, no, he hadn't. Lord, now he'd have to go back. Yes, he would if 3 it killed him. He thought, though, he had everything else. She reminded him it was only because he didn't drink coffee himself. If he did he would remember it quick enough. Suppose they ran out of cigarettes? Then she saw the rope. What was that for? Well, he thought it might do to hang clothes on, or something. Naturally she asked him if he thought they were going to run a laundry? They already had a fifty-foot line hanging right before his eyes? Why, hadn't he noticed it, really? It was a blot on the landscape to her.

He thought there were a lot of things a rope might come in handy for. 4 She wanted to know what, for instance. He thought a few seconds, but nothing occurred. They could wait and see, couldn't they? You need all sorts of strange odds and ends around a place in the country. She said, yes, that was so; but she thought just at that time when every penny counted, it seemed funny to buy more rope. That was all. She hadn't meant anything else. She hadn't just seen, not at first, why he felt it was necessary.

Well, thunder, he had bought it because he wanted to, and that was all   5
there was to it. She thought that was reason enough, and couldn't under-stand why he hadn't said so, at first. Undoubtedly it would be useful, twenty-four yards of rope, there were hundreds of things, she couldn't think of any at the moment, but it would come in. Of course. As he had said, things always did in the country.

But she was a little disappointed about the coffee, and oh, look, look,   6
look at the eggs! Oh, my, they're all running! What had he put on top of them? Hadn't he known eggs mustn't be squeezed? Squeezed, who had squeezed them he wanted to know. What a silly thing to say. He had simply brought them along in the basket with the other things. If they got broke it was the grocer's fault. He should know better than to put heavy things on top of eggs.

She believed it was the rope. That was the heaviest thing in the pack,   7
she saw him plainly when he came in from the road, the rope was a big package on top of everything. He desired the whole wide world to witness that this was not a fact. He had carried the rope in one hand and the basket in the other, and what was the use of her having eyes if that was the best they could do for her?

Well, anyhow, she could see one thing plain: no eggs for breakfast.   8
They'd have to scramble them now, for supper. It was too damned bad. She had planned to have steak for supper. No ice, meat wouldn't keep. He wanted to know why she couldn't finish breaking the eggs in a bowl and set them in a cool place.

Cool place! if he could find one for her, she'd be glad to set them there.   9
Well, then, it seemed to him they might very well cook the meat at the same time they cooked the eggs and then warm up the meat for tomorrow. The idea simply choked her. Warmed-over meat, when they might as well have had it fresh. Second best and scraps and makeshifts, even to the meat! He rubbed her shoulder a little. It doesn't really matter so much, does it, dar-ling? Sometimes when they were playful, he would rub her shoulder and she would arch and purr. This time she hissed and almost clawed. He was getting ready to say that they could surely manage somehow when she turned on him and said, if he told her they could manage somehow she would certainly slap his face.

He swallowed the words red hot, his face burned. He picked up the   10
rope and started to put it on the top shelf. She would not have it on the top shelf, the jars and tins belonged there; positively she would not have the top shelf cluttered up with a lot of rope. She had borne all the clutter she meant

to bear in the flat in town, there was space here at least and she meant to keep things in order.

Well, in that case, he wanted to know what the hammer and nails were doing up there? And why had she put them there when she knew very well he needed that hammer and those nails upstairs to fix the window sashes? She simply slowed down everything and made double work on the place with her insane habit of changing things around and hiding them.

She was sure she begged his pardon, and if she had had any reason to believe he was going to fix the sashes this summer she would have left the hammer and nails right where he put them; in the middle of the bedroom floor where they could step on them in the dark. And now if he didn't clear the whole mess out of there she would throw them down the well.

Oh, all right, all right—could he put them in the closet? Naturally not, there were brooms and mops and dustpans in the closet, and why couldn't he find a place for his rope outside her kitchen? Had he stopped to consider there were seven God-forsaken rooms in the house, and only one kitchen?

He wanted to know what of it? And did she realize she was making a complete fool of herself? And what did she take him for, a three-year-old idiot? The whole trouble with her was she needed something weaker than she was to heckle and tyrannize over. He wished to God now they had a couple of children she could take it out on. Maybe he'd get some rest.

Her face changed at this, she reminded him he had forgot the coffee and had bought a worthless piece of rope. And when she thought of all the things they actually needed to make the place even decently fit to live in, well, she could cry, that was all. She looked so forlorn, so lost and despairing he couldn't believe it was only a piece of rope that was causing all the racket. What *was* the matter, for God's sake?

Oh, would he please hush and go away, and *stay* away, if he could, for five minutes? By all means, yes, he would. He'd stay away indefinitely if she wished. Lord, yes, there was nothing he'd like better than to clear out and never come back. She couldn't for the life of her see what was holding him, then. It was a swell time. Here she was, stuck, miles from a railroad, with a half-empty house on her hands, and not a penny in her pocket, and everything on earth to do; it seemed the God-sent moment for him to get out from under. She was surprised he hadn't stayed in town as it was until she had come out and done the work and got things straightened out. It was his usual trick.

It appeared to him that this was going a little far. Just a touch out of bounds, if she didn't mind his saying so. Why the hell had he stayed in town the summer before? To do a half-dozen extra jobs to get the money he had sent her. That was it. She new perfectly well they couldn't have done it otherwise. She had agreed with him at the time. And that was the only time so help him he had ever left her to do anything by herself.

Oh, he could tell that to his great-grandmother. She had her notion of   18
what had kept him in town. Considerably more than a notion, if he wanted
to know. So, she was going to bring all that up again, was she? Well, she
could just think what she pleased. He was tired of explaining. It may have
looked funny but he had simply got hooked in, and what could he do? It was
impossible to believe that she was going to take it seriously. Yes, yes, she
knew how it was with a man: if he was left by himself a minute, some woman
was certain to kidnap him. And naturally he couldn't hurt her feelings by
refusing!

Well, what was she raving about? Did she forget she had told him those   19
two weeks alone in the country were the happiest she had known for four
years? And how long had they been married when she said that? All right,
shut up! If she thought that hadn't stuck in his craw.

She hadn't meant she was happy because she was away from him. She   20
meant she was happy getting the devilish house nice and ready for him. That
was what she had meant, and now look! Bringing up something she had said
a year ago simply to justify himself for forgetting her coffee and breaking the
eggs and buying a wretched piece of rope they couldn't afford. She really
thought it was time to drop the subject, and now she wanted only two things
in the world. She wanted him to get that rope from underfoot, and go back
to the village and get her coffee, and if he could remember it, he might bring
a metal mitt for the skillets, and two more curtain rods, and if there were any
rubber gloves in the village, her hands were simply raw, and a bottle of milk
of magnesia from the drugstore.

He looked out at the dark blue afternoon sweltering on the slopes, and   21
mopped his forehead and sighed heavily and said, if only she could wait a
minute for *anything,* he was going back. He had said so, hadn't he, the very
instant they found he had overlooked it?

Oh, yes, well . . . run along. She was going to wash windows. The   22
country was so beautiful! She doubted they'd have a moment to enjoy it. He
meant to go, but he could not until he had said that if she wasn't such a
hopeless melancholiac she might see that this was only for a few days.
Couldn't she remember anything pleasant about the other summers? Hadn't
they ever had any fun? She hadn't time to talk about it, and now would he
please not leave that rope lying around for her to trip on? He picked it up,
somehow it had toppled off the table, and walked out with it under his arm.

Was he going this minute? He certainly was. She thought so. Some-   23
times it seemed to her he had second sight about the precisely perfect
moment to leave her ditched. She had meant to put the mattresses out to
sun, if they put them out this minute they would get at least three hours, he
must have heard her say that morning she meant to put them out. So of
course he would walk off and leave her to it. She supposed he thought the
exercise would do her good.

Well, he was merely going to get her coffee. A four-mile walk for two   24 pounds of coffee was ridiculous, but he was perfectly willing to do it. The habit was making a wreck of her, but if she wanted to wreck herself there was nothing he could do about it. If he thought it was coffee that was making a wreck of her, she congratulated him: he must have a damned easy conscience.

Conscience or no conscience, he didn't see why the mattresses couldn't   25 very well wait until tomorrow. And anyhow, for God's sake, were they living *in* the house, or were they going to let the house ride them to death? She paled at this, her face grew livid about the mouth, she looked quite danger-ous, and reminded him that housekeeping was no more her work than it was his: she had other work to do as well, and when did he think she was going to find time to do it at this rate?

Was she going to start on that again? She knew as well as he did that   26 his work brought in the regular money, hers was only occasional, if they depended on what *she* made—and she might as well get straight on this question once for all!

That was positively not the point. The question was, when both of   27 them were working on their own time, was there going to be a division of the housework, or wasn't there? She merely wanted to know, she had to make her plans. Why, he thought that was all arranged. It was understood that he was to help. Hadn't he always, in summers?

Hadn't he, though? Oh, just hadn't he? And when, and where, and   28 doing what? Lord, what an uproarious joke!

It was such a very uproarious joke that her face turned slightly purple,   29 and she screamed with laughter. She laughed so hard she had to sit down, and finally a rush of tears spurted from her eyes and poured down into the lifted corners of her mouth. He dashed towards her and dragged her up to her feet and tried to pour water on her head. The dipper hung by a string on a nail and he broke it loose. Then he tried to pump water with one hand while she struggled in the other. So he gave it up and shook her instead.

She wrenched away, crying for him to take his rope and go to hell, she   30 had simply given him up: and ran. He heard her high-heeled bedroom slippers clattering and stumbling on the stairs.

He went out around the house into the lane; he suddenly realized he   31 had a blister on his heel and his shirt felt as if it were on fire. Things broke so suddenly you didn't know where you were. She could work herself into a fury about simply nothing. She was terrible, damn it: not an ounce of reason. You might as well talk to a sieve as that woman when she got going. Damned if he'd spend his life humoring her! Well, what to do now? He would take back the rope and exchange it for something else. Things accumulated, things were mountainous, you couldn't move them or sort them out or get rid of them. They just lay and rotted around. He'd take it back. Hell, why should he? He wanted it. What was it anyhow? A piece of rope. Imagine anybody caring more about a piece of rope than about a man's feelings. What earthly right had she to say a word about it? He remembered all the useless, meaningless things she bought for herself. Why? because I wanted it; that's why! He stopped and selected a large stone by the road. He would put the rope behind it. He would put it in the tool-box when he got back. He'd heard enough about it to last him a life-time.

When he came back she was leaning against the post box beside the road waiting. It was pretty late, the smell of broiled steak floated nose high in the cooling air. Her face was young and smooth and fresh-looking. Her unmanageable funny black hair was all on end. She waved to him from a distance, and he speeded up. She called out that supper was ready and waiting, was he starved?   32

You bet he was starved. Here was the coffee. He waved it at her. She looked at his other hand. What was that he had there?   33

Well, it was the rope again. He stopped short. He had meant to exchange it but forgot. She wanted to know why he should exchange it, if it was something he really wanted. Wasn't the air sweet now, and wasn't it fine to be here?   34

She walked beside him with one hand hooked into his leather belt. She pulled and jostled him a little as he walked, and leaned against him. He put his arm clear around her and patted her stomach. They exchanged wary smiles. Coffee, coffee for the Ootsum-Wootsums! He felt as if he were bringing her a beautiful present.   35

He was a love, she firmly believed, and if she had had her coffee in the morning, she wouldn't have behaved so funny . . . There was a whippoor-will still coming back, imagine, clear out of season, sitting in the crab-apple tree calling all by himself. Maybe his girl stood him up. Maybe she did. She hoped to hear him once more, she loved whippoorwills . . . He knew how she was, didn't he?   36

Sure, he knew how she was.   37

Questions for Study and Discussion

1. Discuss the circumstances of the couple's move to the country. Why are they so disorganized?

2. How would you characterize the man and the woman in this story? What exactly do they seem to be quarreling about? What do you think is the underlying cause of their disagreement? Why does the man offer to go back to town?

3. The story is told by an impersonal third-person narrator. How would it be different if told from the wife's point of view? From the husband's point of view?

4. Though most of the story consists of conversation, Porter has chosen not to use any dialogue. What is the advantage of presenting the quarrel indirectly, instead of making the characters speak directly for themselves? How do you account for the large numbers of questions in the story?

5. At several points in the story the tone changes. Locate the places where this occurs. How do these changes in tone affect the development of the story?

6. Why do you think Porter introduces the whippoorwill in the concluding scene?

7. What is the significance of the story's title?

Writing Topics

1. Couples often get into quarrels over seemingly trivial matters, as in Porter's story. From your own experience and observation, what can such quarrels do to a relationship? What can they signify? When are they destructive, and when constructive? Write an essay in which you present your views of "lovers' " quarrels.

2. Like the man in the story, do you sometimes buy things without any particular reason? Or are you a person who buys things wisely and purposefully? Write an essay in which you analyze your buying habits.

Men and Women in the Workplace

GLORIA STEINEM

Gloria Steinem is a political activist, editor, lecturer, writer, and one of this country's leading feminists. She was born in Toledo, Ohio, in 1934 and graduated from Smith College in 1956. After college she traveled to India to study and then returned to New York, where she later helped to found two important magazines, *New York* and *Ms.* Steinem has published many articles and five books: *The Thousand Indias* (1957), *The Beach Book* (1963), *Outrageous Acts and Everyday Rebellions* (1983)—from which the following essay is taken—*Marilyn* (1987), and *Revolution from Within: A Book of Self-Esteem* (1992).

In "The Importance of Work" Steinem argues that the standard answer that women give to the question of why they work, "Womenworkbecausewehaveto," is inadequate and a self-deception. Women should be able, she claims, to admit openly that they work because it is a human right and because it is an activity that is both natural and pleasurable.

The Importance of Work

Toward the end of the 1970s, the *Wall Street Journal* devoted an eight-page, front-page series to "the working woman"—that is, the influx of women into the paid-labor force—as the greatest change in American life since the Industrial Revolution. 1

Many women readers greeted both the news and the definition with cynicism. After all, women have always worked. If all the productive work of human maintenance that women do in the home were valued at its replacement cost, the gross national product of the United States would go up by 26 percent. It's just that we are now more likely than ever before to leave our poorly rewarded, low-security, high-risk job of homemaking (though we're still trying to explain that it's a perfectly good one and that the problem is male society's refusal both to do it and to give it an economic value) for more secure, independent, and better-paid jobs outside the home. 2

Obviously, the real work revolution won't come until all productive   3
work is rewarded—including child rearing and other jobs done in the
home—and men are integrated into so-called women's work as well as vice
versa. But the radical change being touted by the *Journal* and other media is
one part of that long integration process: the unprecedented flood of women
into salaried jobs, that is, into the labor force as it has been male-defined and
previously occupied by men. We are already more than 41 percent of it—the
highest proportion in history. Given the fact that women also make up a
whopping 69 percent of the "discouraged labor force" (that is, people, who
need jobs but don't get counted in the unemployment statistics because
they've given up looking), plus an official female unemployment rate that is
substantially higher than men's, it's clear that we could expand to become
fully half of the national work force by 1990.

Faced with this determination of women to find a little independence   4
and to be paid and honored for our work, experts have rushed to ask: "Why?"
It's a question rarely directed at male workers. Their basic motivations of
survival and personal satisfaction are taken for granted. Indeed, men are
regarded as "odd" and therefore subjects for sociological study and journalistic reports only when they *don't* have work, even if they are rich and don't
need jobs or are poor and can't find them. Nonetheless, pollsters and sociolo-
gists have gone to great expense to prove that women work outside the home
because of dire financial need, or if we persist despite the presence of a wage-
earning male, out of some desire to buy "little extras" for our families, or
even out of good old-fashioned "penis envy."

Job interviewers and even our own families may still ask salaried   5
women the big "Why?" If we have small children at home or are in some job
regarded as "men's work," the incidence of such questions increases. Condescending or accusatory versions of "What's a nice girl like you doing in a
place like this?" have not disappeared from the workplace.

How do we answer these assumptions that we are "working" out of   6
some pressing or peculiar need? Do we feel okay about arguing that it's as
natural for us to have salaried jobs as for our husbands—whether or not we
have young children at home? Can we enjoy strong career ambitions without
worrying about being thought "unfeminine"? When we confront men's growing resentment to women competing in the work force (often in the form of
such guilt-producing accusations as "You're taking men's jobs away" or
"You're damaging your children"), do we simply state that a decent job is a
basic human right for everybody?

I'm afraid the answer is often no. As individuals and as a movement,   7
we tend to retreat into some version of a tactically questionable defense:
"Womenworkbecausewehaveto." The phrase has become one word, one key
on the typewriter—an economic form of the socially "feminine" stance of
passivity and self-sacrifice. Under attack, we still tend to present ourselves as

creatures of economic necessity and familial devotion. "Womenworkbe-causewehaveto" has become the easiest thing to say.

Like most truisms, this one is easy to prove with statistics. Economic 8 need *is* the most consistent work motive—for women as well as men. In 1976, for instance, 43 percent of all women in the paid-labor force were single, widowed, separated, or divorced, and working to support themselves and their dependents. An additional 21 percent were married to men who had earned less than ten thousand dollars in the previous year, the minimum then required to support a family of four. In fact, if you take men's pensions, stocks, real estate, and various forms of accumulated wealth into account, a good statistical case can be made that there are more women who "have" to work (that is, who have neither the accumulated wealth, nor husbands whose work or wealth can support them for the rest of their lives) than there are men with the same need. If we were going to ask one group "Do you really need this job?" we should ask men.

But the first weakness of the whole "have to work" defense is its 9 deceptiveness. Anyone who has ever experienced dehumanized life on wel-fare or any other confidence-shaking dependency knows that a paid job may be preferable to the dole, even when the handout is coming from a family member. Yet the will and self-confidence to work on one's own can diminish as dependency and fear increase. That may explain why—contrary to the "have to" rationale—wives of men who earn less than three thousand dollars a year are actually *less* likely to be employed than wives whose husbands make ten thousand dollars a year or more.

Furthermore, the greatest proportion of employed wives is found 10 among families with a total household income of twenty-five to fifty thou-sand dollars a year. This is the statistical underpinning used by some sociolo-gists to prove that women's work is mainly important for boosting families into the middle or upper middle class. Thus, women's incomes are largely used for buying "luxuries" and "little extras": a neat double-whammy that renders us secondary within our families, and makes our jobs expendable in hard times. We may even go along with this interpretation (at least, up to the point of getting fired so a male can have our job). It preserves a hus-bandly ego-need to be seen as the primary breadwinner, and still allows us a safe "feminine" excuse for working.

But there are often rewards that we're not confessing. As noted in *The* 11 *Two-Career Couple,* by Francine and Douglas Hall: "Women who hold jobs by choice, even blue-collar routine jobs, are more satisfied with their lives than are the full-time housewives."

In addition to personal satisfaction, there is also society's need for all its 12 members' talents. Suppose that jobs were given out on only a "have to work" basis to both women and men—one job per household. It would be unthink-able to lose the unique abilities of, for instance, Eleanor Holmes Norton, the distinguished chair of the Equal Employment Opportunity Commission. But would we then be forced to question the important work of her husband, Edward Norton, who is also a distinguished lawyer? Since men earn more than twice as much as women on the average, the wife in most households would be more likely to give up her job. Does that mean the nation could do as well without millions of its nurses, teachers, and secretaries? Or that the rare man who earns less than his wife should give up his job?

It was this kind of waste of human talents on a society-wide scale that 13 traumatized millions of unemployed or underemployed Americans during the Depression. Then, a one-job-per-household rule seemed somewhat justified, yet the concept was used to displace women workers only, create intolerable dependencies, and waste female talent that the country needed. That Depression experience, plus the energy and example of women who were finally allowed to work during the manpower shortage created by World War II, led Congress to reinterpret the meaning of the country's full-employment goal in its Economic Recovery Act of 1946. Full employment was officially defined as "the employment of those who want to work, without regard to whether their employment is, by some definition, necessary. This goal applies equally to men and to women." Since bad economic times are again creating a resentment of employed women—as well as creating more need for women to be employed—we need such a goal more than ever. Women are again being caught in a tragic double bind: We are required to be strong and then punished for our strength.

Clearly, anything less than government and popular commitment to 14 this 1946 definition of full employment will leave the less powerful groups, whoever they may be, in danger. Almost as important as the financial penalty paid by the powerless is the suffering that comes from being shut out of paid and recognized work. Without it, we lose much of our self-respect and our ability to prove that we are alive by making some difference in the world. That's just as true for the suburban woman as it is for the unemployed steel worker.

But it won't be easy to give up the passive defense of "wework- 15 becausewehaveto."

When a woman who is struggling to support her children and grandchil- 16 dren on welfare sees her neighbor working as a waitress, even though that neighbor's husband has a job, she may feel resentful; and the waitress (of course, not the waitress's husband) may feel guilty. Yet unless we establish the obligation to provide a job for everyone who is willing and able to work, that welfare woman may herself be penalized by policies that give out only one public-service job per household. She and her daughter will have to make a painful and divisive decision about which of them gets that precious job, and the whole household will have to survive on only one salary.

A job as a human right is a principle that applies to men as well as 17 women. But women have more cause to fight for it. The phenomenon of the "working woman" has been held responsible for everything from an increase in male impotence (which turned out, incidentally, to be attributable to medication for high blood pressure) to the rising cost of steak (which was due to high energy costs and beef import restrictions, not women's refusal to prepare the cheaper, slower-cooking cuts). Unless we see a job as part of every citizen's right to autonomy and personal fulfillment, we will continue to be vulnerable to someone else's idea of what "need" is, and whose "need" counts the most.

In many ways, women who do not have to work for simple survival, but   18
who choose to do so nonetheless, are on the frontier of asserting this right for all women. Those with well-to-do husbands are dangerously easy for us to resent and put down. It's easier still to resent women from families of inherited wealth, even though men generally control and benefit from that wealth. (There is no Rockefeller Sisters Fund, no J. P. Morgan & Daughters, and sons-in-law may be the ones who really sleep their way to power.) But to prevent a woman whose husband or father is wealthy from earning her own living, and from gaining the self-confidence that comes with that ability, is to keep her needful of that unearned power and less willing to disperse it. Moreover, it is to lose forever her unique talents.

Perhaps modern feminists have been guilty of a kind of reverse   19
snobbism that keeps us from reaching out to the wives and daughters of wealthy men; yet it was exactly such women who refused the restrictions of class and financed the first wave of feminist revolution.

For most of us, however, "womenworkbecausewehaveto" is just true   20
enough to be seductive as a personal defense.

If we use it without also staking out the larger human right to a job,   21
however, we will never achieve that right. And we will always be subject to the false argument that independence for women is a luxury affordable only in good economic times. Alternatives to layoffs will not be explored, acceptable unemployment will always be used to frighten those with jobs into accepting low wages, and we will never remedy the real cost, both to families and to the country, of dependent women and a massive loss of talent.

Worst of all, we may never learn to find productive, honored work as a   22
natural part of ourselves and as one of life's basic pleasures.

Questions for Study and Discussion

1. In your own words, what is Gloria Steinem's thesis in this essay?
2. Why did many women readers greet the *Wall Street Journal*'s definition of "the working woman" with cynicism? What was Steinem's response?
3. Steinem states that many women use the "Womenworkbecausewe-

haveto" defense when asked why they work. Why does Steinem believe they use this defense? Why does she object to it? And what does she gain from turning the sentence "Women work because we have to" into a single word? Explain.

4. How does Steinem dismiss the claim that women who enter the workplace are robbing men of their jobs and damaging their children?

5. What is Steinem's attitude toward women who work even though they don't need to financially? Does she believe they should be applauded or resented?

6. How is "full employment" defined in the Economic Recovery Act of 1946? Is it a definition that Steinem supports? How, according to Steinem, do attitudes toward working women change during bad economic times?

7. How does society benefit from the full employment of men and women? How do individuals benefit?

8. On the basis of Steinem's tone, diction, and the quality of her evidence in the essay, would you characterize her as a persuasive writer?

9. For what audience do you believe Steinem intended her article? What assumptions does she make about her audience? Would this audience find her argument convincing? Would a different audience be persuaded as well? Explain.

Writing Topics

1. Steinem believes that "a decent job is a basic human right for everybody." Is such a position realistic? Does America have an obligation to provide such a job for every citizen? Write an essay in which you argue your position.

2. In preparation for an essay on working parents, analyze your own family situation. Did only one or both of your parents work outside the home? What was the effect on the fabric of your family life? Would you have preferred the alternative situation?

MARY MEBANE

Mary Mebane was born in 1933 in Durham, North Carolina. After earning her B.A. at North Carolina State College, she went on to receive her M.A. and Ph.D. from the University of North Carolina and to teach, most recently at the University of Wisconsin at Milwaukee. Her writing has appeared in A Galaxy of Black Writers and The Eloquence of Protest; her play Take a Sad Song was produced in 1975. She has published two widely acclaimed autobiographical books, Mary (1981) and Mary, Wayfarer (1983). About her own work Mebane has said, "My writings center on the black folk of the South, post-1960. It is my belief that the black folk are the most creative, viable people that America has produced. They just don't know it."

In "Summer Job," taken from Mary, Mebane describes the process of getting a job in a Southern tobacco factory. And in so doing, she also introduces us to the plight of African-American women workers in the years preceding the Civil Rights Act of 1964.

Summer Job

It was summer 1949, and I needed a job. Everybody tries to "get on" at   1
the tobacco factory during "green season" when lots of extra workers were
hired to "work up" new tobacco—that is, process it for cigarettes. Some
people made their chief money of the year during the ten-to-twelve-week
green season. The factory paid more money than days work, so lots of women
gladly left their housekeeping jobs and went to the factories. In Durham
there were two major factories and several smaller ones. The major factories
worked up tobacco, but they also made cigarettes and had a shipping department and research laboratories. The smaller factories mainly worked up
tobacco for the larger ones, in Durham and in other cities. Of the two major
factories in Durham, Liggett and Myers did relatively little hiring in green
season; it had a stable year-round force and gave preference to its former
workers during the season. My mother worked there. The American Tobacco Company, the other factory, hired a great many temporary workers.

I was told that my best bet was the American. I wasn't eighteen, but I   2
was tall and stocky and could pass for older, and besides, they never asked to
see your birth certificate; so, a few months short of my sixteenth birthday, I
went to get work at the American, makers of Lucky Strike cigarettes and
other brands. From the start, I knew that I wouldn't get a job on the

"cigarette side." That was easy work, and I was told that mostly whites worked over there. I would get a chance on the belt on the "tobacco side." Several women in the neighborhood who had worked at the American during the green season instructed me about how to get on. I was told to get there early and stand on the sidewalk in front of the employment office and just as close as possible to it, so that when they came out to select workers I would be easily seen. Also I was told to say, if they asked me, that I had worked there before. Nobody ever checked the records. So, on the morning that hiring began for green season, I went to Durham.

I accompanied neighbors who had received postcards informing them   3
they could come to work. They left me outside while they went in. I was dismayed, for the whole street in front of the employment office was filled with black women. They crowded around the brick porch leading to the employment office; they were on the sidewalk; they overflowed the street and covered the sidewalk behind. They were directly in front of the office, spreading out fanwise in both directions from it. Nobody was allowed on the porch except those who already had cards.

A pudgy white man with a cigar in his mouth came and stood on the   4
porch and said, "All those who have cards, come forward." Those who had cards held them up over their heads and started pushing through the crowd. Sometimes they had to remonstrate with some stubborn woman who refused to give way: "Let me pass, please! Move out of my way!" Slowly the one blocking her path would grudgingly give ground. Others quickly surged forward, trying to fill the space that was left, taking advantage of the confusion to try to push even nearer the office. When the favored ones got in, there began the long wait for the man to come back and start selecting more "hands" from the crowd of women left standing there. The crowd continued to grow bigger by the minute as new arrivals came.

You could tell the veterans from the rookies by the way they were   5
dressed. The knowledgeable ones had their heads covered by kerchiefs, so that if they were hired, tobacco dust wouldn't get in their hair; they had on clean dresses that by now were faded and shapeless, so that if they were hired they wouldn't get tobacco dust and grime on their best clothes. Those who were trying for the first time had their hair freshly done and wore attractive dresses; they wanted to make a good impression. But the dresses couldn't be seen at the distance that many were standing from the employment office, and they were crumpled in the crush.

Some women looked as if they had large families; they looked tired and   6
anxious, but determined. Some looked single; they had on lipstick and eyebrow pencil, and some even wore black patent-leather pumps with stockings.

The morning passed and the sun got hotter; there was no shade on the   7
sidewalks or in the street. The street stayed full, except when trucks edged their way in and the crowd gave way slowly.

After a while, the pudgy white man with the big cigar came to the door   8 and stood and looked. Instantly the whole mass surged forward. The shorter ones tried to stand on tiptoe to be seen over the heads of their taller sisters. Hands shot up in the air, trying to make them notice them. Those at the front who'd gotten shoved against the brick porch shouted, "Stop pushing, stop pushing, ya'll! You're hurting me!"

Finally the pudgy man spoke, standing on the porch with his cigar in his mouth. "Until ya'll stop pushing and shoving I'm not gonna hire none of ya'll." Then he stood for a moment to see what effect his words were having on the crowd. Sensing that they were having no discernible effect, the man went back inside, and the surge forward stopped for the time being. 9

The women stood and stood; the sun grew hotter. Some grew tired of waiting: "I left my baby with a neighbor. I told her that if I didn't get on I'd be back before twelve. I gotta go." Others left saying that they were "tired of this mess." One woman said, "All ya'll might as well go home. He's got his number for today. Come back tomorrow when they'll know how many more they'll need." At that, even more women faded away. The mass shrunk, but it was still a mass. 10

Finally, shortly before noon, the pudgy man came quietly to the porch and pointed quickly to two women standing close by. Before the crowd knew people were getting on, the two women were on the porch and in the hall, following him. The crowd surged forward but the man was gone. "What time is it?" someone said. "High noon" was the answer and everyone seemed to agree that there would be no more hiring until one or two o'clock, after lunch. 11

Some sat right down on the sidewalk up against the building and took out their sandwiches. Others drifted away from the crowd and down to a nearby luncheonette for cold drinks and sandwiches. I had a tomato sandwich that had become soggy in the press and the heat. I went with some other women far down the street to sit on the grass and eat my sandwich. They talked in front of me as if I were grown, so I knew that I would have no trouble if I got hired. What they said was so interesting that the crowd was re-forming in front of the employment office in the hot, boiling sun before I knew it. 12

Word came over the grapevine that they needed some more helpers and would hire some more today. This gave everybody courage, so the crowd grew calm. Then the pudgy man came again. He made an announcement. "Any shoving, any pushing, and there'll be no more hiring today." The women grew quiet. Those who had been impatient hadn't come back from lunch, leaving those who were determined to get on. 13

The man selected two more women; the crowd gave a little surge forward, but nothing like the shoving and pushing of the morning. In another hour he came back for one more, and soon the word came over the grapevine that we might as well go home. The crowd started fading away, but not the diehards. They didn't believe the grapevine and were determined to stay to see what was going to happen. I had no choice; I was staying until the 14 people I rode with got off from work. It was now three o'clock and we all had been standing in the sun since eight o'clock in the morning. When the neighbors I was waiting for came, they said, "Don't worry. You'll get on tomorrow." Besides, they would go in earlier now that they were on.

I lay in bed that night, too tired to do anything else, and thought about 15
the day. Hundreds of women had stood in the hot sun for seven or eight hours under really bad conditions. There was no bathroom, no drinking fountain, no place to sit down. Those who had to leave lost their place in line and, thus, their chance for a job. Why was this? Because they needed work and the factory didn't need them. The factory had more hands available than it could use. That is why they could treat the surplus as they chose, and there was nothing that the women could do about it.

The next day I was there early and standing in place by the steps before 16
the employment office opened. I recognized some of the faces from the day before, and there were some that looked new to me. The crowd stretched out as far as it had the previous day. The sun was already hot when the pudgy man came to the platform with his cigar in his mouth. "Anyone here with a card?" he called. A few women who hadn't come in yesterday came forward. He went back inside.

I was close enough to see into the hall inside and the glass-faced side of 17
the employment office. It was shut off from the hall by glass because it was air-conditioned. There was a man, so slim and shapely that he looked like a girl, who came to the door and watched as the pudgy man came back and stood over the crowd. He watched the crowd surge forward, and he stepped back a little as if all the energy would wash over him. It seemed to give him great satisfaction to see the sea of black women struggling forward, trying to get a job in his factory; he'd stand and watch for a while, then turn and go into the air-conditioned office. At first the women thought that he was going to do some of the hiring and they pressed close to him and looked up. But once they'd determined that he had nothing to do with the hiring, he ceased to exist for them and they paid him no more attention.

More and more women were hired; the pudgy man would point here 18
and there, then take them off. In an hour or so, he'd come back and hire one or two more. Lunch came and the crowd scattered. I'd brought a meat sandwich, hoping that it wouldn't get crumpled and soggy like my tomato sandwich the day before. I knew enough not to leave my good place near the porch, so I ate standing in the hot sun, along with the rest of the women who had good places. I had been listening to the crowd for two days, so now I knew the words and phrases that would make me sound like a veteran, and I employed them. Evidently nothing was wrong with what I said, for no one looked at me "funny."

Around two o'clock the pudgy man came back and his eye fell on me and 19
the woman standing beside me. He motioned us in. I was now a factory hand.

The air-conditioning in the office chilled me after the heat of the street 20 as I gave the necessary information. I made up a birthday and nobody questioned it. Then I was taken to a "line" on the first floor.

It was a cavernous room, long and tall. The man who led me there called to the boss, who came over to tell me what to do, but the machinery was so loud that I couldn't hear him and I was so startled by my new surroundings that I really didn't concentrate on what he said. I was afraid to take a deep breath, for the room was so cloudy with tobacco dust that brown particles hung in the air. I held my breath as long as I could and then took a deep breath. I started to cough and my eyes watered. I saw lots of women and some men, each doing a task seemingly unrelated to the others', but I knew that there must be a plan.

My job had something to do with a conveyor belt. It was shaped like a child's sliding board, only it had a deep trough and it moved. Shredded tobacco was on this belt—I think that it came from upstairs—and my job was to sit by the belt and pick out the pieces whose stem was too large. I tried to determine what kind of stem was too large, for the belt was constantly moving, and obviously I couldn't pick out every single stem on the belt. I looked at the others, but I couldn't see what method they were using. I was in misery, for this was my first "public" job and I didn't want to do badly on it. I did the best that I could, but soon the boss came and told me he was going to put me on the belt upstairs. I was glad, for my back hurt from bending over, trying to pick out stems. Maybe I could do better upstairs.

The air was full of tobacco dust there, too, but not as much as it had been downstairs; also, it was quieter. This belt moved horizontally, from right to left; women stood parallel to it, two women facing each other on the same side of the belt, with a barrel of tied tobacco leaves in front of them. They worked in pairs, taking the tobacco from the barrel, the hogshead, and putting it on the belt. The important thing, as my partner explained to me, was to make sure that the tied ends faced me, for the belt was on its way to the cutter and the machine would cut off the hard tied end—which would not go into the making of cigarettes—while the leaves went another way.

The job seemed easy enough as I picked up bundle after bundle of tobacco and put it on the belt, careful to turn the knot end toward me so that it would be placed right to go under the cutting machine. Gradually, as we worked up our tobacco, I had to bend more, for as we emptied the hogshead we had to stoop over to pick up the tobacco, then straighten up and put it on the belt just right. Then I discovered the hard part of the job: the belt kept moving at the same speed all the time and if the leaves were not placed on the belt at the same tempo there would be a big gap where your bundle should have been. So that meant that when you got down lower, you had to bend down, get the tobacco, straighten up fast, make sure it was placed knot end toward you, place it on the belt, and bend down again. Soon you were bending down, up; down, up; down, up. All along the line, heads were bobbing—down, up; down, up—until you finished the barrel. Then you could rest until the men brought you another one.

To make sure that you kept the belt filled, there was a line boss, a little 25 blond man who looked scared most of the time. He'd walk up and down behind you, saying, "Put the tobacco on the belt, girls. Put the tobacco on the belt. Too many empty spaces, girls. Too many empty spaces." You'd be working away, when suddenly behind you'd hear this voice: "Put the tobacco on the belt, girls. Put the tobacco on the belt. No empty spaces, girls. No empty spaces." I noticed that no one paid him any mind. He could be standing right by the belt talking, and it was as if he were invisible. The line kept moving, and the women kept bending and putting tobacco on the belt.

Over him was the floor boss. He had charge of all the operations on the 26 floor. He was the line boss's boss, and the line boss was clearly afraid of him. Over the floor boss was the big boss, who seldom came on the floor unless there was real trouble. Most of the women had never seem him, but some had and said that he was mean as the devil.

I bent and straightened and bent and straightened and thought that my 27 back would break. Once in the afternoon I got a ten-minute break in the "house" (toilet). I went there and collapsed into a chair.

That evening on the way home I tried to talk cheerfully to my neigh- 28 bors about the new job. They were quite pleased that I had gotten on. That was the one thing that kept me from quitting. I didn't want to let them down by telling them that I found the work killing. So I made up my mind to stay, no matter what, for I knew it was a short season.

Questions for Study and Discussion

1. What expectations did Mebane have of work at the American Tobacco Company? How did she come to have these expectations? Mebane devotes the first two-thirds of her essay to the "hiring process." What would have been gained or lost had she shortened this drastically?

2. What jobs did Mebane perform once she was hired? What did she think about the work she performed?

3. Why did everybody seek work at the tobacco factories during the green season? Why do you think the work force was made up mostly of women?

4. Mebane's narrative is built upon a series of contrasts. What contrasts did you notice? Explain how they help her convey her experiences.

5. After only one day, Mebane found the work in the factory "killing." Why did she decide not to quit?

6. Mebane uses a great number of details in her writing to give the reader an accurate sense of where she is and what's going on. Cite several instances of her use of details that impressed you and attempt to explain the effect they had on your understanding of her situation.

7. How does Mebane's narrative help her establish the time, place, and circumstances of her narrative? Cite several examples to document your points.

Writing Topics

1. Write an essay in which you describe the process of seeking summer employment. What steps are generally involved? Offer some tips or suggestions that would enhance a person's chances of getting a summer job.

2. Using your own experiences or observations of summer jobs, write an essay in which you discuss the major differences and similarities between summer work and full-time employment. Is a summer job a fair and accurate introduction to what full-time work is really like? Explain. Write an essay in which you talk about your first summer job. What impressed you the most? The least? What did you think of your fellow workers? Of the working conditions? the pay? Did the job in any way affect your attitude toward education? Did it, for example, make you want to stay in school, or give you a greater appreciation of what school was doing for you?

BARBARA LAZEAR ASCHER

Barbara Lazear Ascher was born in 1946 and graduated from Bennington College in 1968. After earning her law degree from the Cardozo School of Law in 1979, she practiced law for two years. Having always considered herself a writer, she left the practice of law and began contributing articles to such publications as the *New York Times, Yale Review, Vogue, McCall's, Newsday,* and *Saturday Review.* Thus far she has published three books. *Playing After Dark,* published in 1988, and *The Habit of Loving,* published in 1989, are both collections of her articles. In 1992 she published *Landscape Without Gravity: A Memoir of Grief,* about the death of her brother from AIDS. In most of her writing Ascher is concerned with how women hang on to their feminist ideals in the home and the office and with their mates, relatives, and friends. In the following essay, taken from *The Habit of Loving,* Ascher examines the nature of power, particularly in the workplace, and the special problems women face in dealing with it.

On Power

When I graduated from law school, I was hired by what is known in the   1
business as a Prestigious New York Law Firm. I felt privileged to be associated with talent and money and respectability, to be in a place that promised me four weeks vacation, my own secretary, an office with a window, and, above all, a shot at power. I would not have preferred working for a single practitioner who struggled to pay rent on his windowless, one-room office in the Bronx.

There's a lot to be said for the accouterments of power. Those who   2
asked where I worked immediately assumed, upon being told the name of the firm, that I must have been at the top of my class, an editor of the Law Review and a clerk for a federal judge. I was none of these, but being where the power is frees you from having to explain yourself.

The "outsider's" version of the "insider" is always distorted by the   3
mental glass through which they observe. The outsider tends to think that once inside the power structure the voyage is over, destination reached. No more struggle or strain. But in fact, once you have "arrived," you discover that there are power structures within the power. You may share office space and a central switchboard, but that doesn't mean you are at the controls.

In my firm, the partners (male) took the young associates (also male),   4
resplendent in their red suspenders and newly sported cigars, to lunch, to

Dallas, Los Angeles, and Atlanta to meet the clients. The "girl" associates were sent to the library to do research. Actually, they were sent to the library to stay out of trouble.

Soon the clients with whom the associates dined were calling them for advice. These associates were learning how to practice law. Those of us hidden away in the stacks were learning how to be invisible.

A friend at a similar Prestigious New York Law Firm told me that she had tried and failed to enlist the cooperation of the one woman partner. "I suggested that we, the women associates and she, have monthly luncheons to discuss some of the problems we faced. After all, she'd been one of us." But she was no longer "one of us" and feared that if her partners perceived her as an ally of women associates, they might forget that she was, first and foremost, one of "them." She knew that hanging out with weak sisters was no way to safeguard her tentative grasp of success.

Eight years later, when my friend became a partner, she learned that the woman she had approached for help was powerless within the partnership. She was, in the eyes of the men, their token "girl" partner, and power, like beauty, is in the eye of the beholder. She was a lady and that's how she was perceived. How could her mother have known as she trained her daughter for power in the drawing room that what she would want was power in the boardroom?

However, even if hers was a token acceptance, she had entered that heady realm, she was feted around town as "the first woman partner" and she proceeded to follow a pattern not unusual for women who achieve some semblance of power. She refused to reach behind to pull other women along. It was too risky. She might fall backwards. I blush to recall that when, in fourth grade, I was the only girl on the boys' baseball team, I joined in their systematic "girl trashing." I enthusiastically participated in disparaging conversations about people who were "just girls." Who threw like girls. Who giggled like girls. Who couldn't whistle through their fingers, burp on command or slide into home plate. Then, all I knew was that my power depended on keeping other girls out. Now, I know about identification with the aggressor.

Not that it makes much difference. There are uncanny similarities between being the only girl on a fourth grade baseball team and the only woman in bigger boys' games. Take, for instance, the response of Harvard Business School's tenured, female professors when their former colleague, Barbara Bund Jackson, filed suit against the school for its refusal to grant her tenure. Nonsense, these women replied to Jackson's charge of a sexist "institutional bias." Not so, they said of her contention that the school sets "impossible standards for female faculty members." Why shouldn't they? Why should Harvard deviate from the accepted wisdom that a man can occasionally goof off and still be perceived as powerful? It's kind of cute, we say. Oh, look, he's got nice human touches, an ability to have fun. How boyish. How charming. Not so for a woman. She who goofs off is a goof-off.

Tenured Harvard professor Regina E. Herzlinger's response to Jackson's   10
claim of discrimination was, "I don't feel there is . . . friction caused by the
fact that there are few women on the faculty . . . I don't think there is
discrimination on the basis of sex." Of course there isn't friction for those
"few women." And Regina'd better keep quiet if she thinks otherwise. Boys
don't like girls who turn around and say, "But what about the other girls?" I
certainly never invited my friend Linda to play baseball with us, even though
she ran like the wind and threw overhand.

But power, who has it and who doesn't, is not limited to the realm of   11
male/female strife. My husband, a physician in practice for many years,
volunteers his time, one day a week at a hospital often described with the
same breathless reverence as my law firm. This is the place to which ailing
shahs and wealthy dowagers come to be healed. The full time attendings
(those with the power) don't like the voluntary attendings (those without
the power), and occasionally rise up to divest them of responsibility. How,
you might ask, when wise and seasoned physicians are willing to give their
time, free of charge, to teach students and treat patients, could there be a
complaint? The volunteers are not part of the power structure. And power's
particular drive is to grab more for itself, an act which invariably involves
stripping others of any.

Recently, some of the voluntary attendings went to the head of their   12
department and informed him, "You make us feel like second-class citizens."
He listened, nodded, and assured: "You are second-class citizens."

Irrational, you say? Of course. But whoever thought that the power   13
drive made sense?

In fifth grade, secret clubs were the order of the day. The purpose was,   14
first of all, the secret. A secret name. Secret rules. Secret members. Secret
meeting places. The purpose was to exclude, which is the first step in
establishing a power base. The second is to create fear in those excluded.
Those of us who assembled the group of meanest and most popular children
had the run of the playground. We were a force to contend with.

Recently, when I went to choose a puppy from a litter, I was told,   15
"Don't get the Alpha dog, whatever you do!" It seems that, like their
ancestors the wolves, each litter has a leader. He or she is the power in the
pack, and once the Alpha dog comes to live with your family, you become
the pack.

What does the Alpha dog get for his trouble? A certain haughtiness. A   16
certain swagger. What did the Alpha attorneys in my firm get for their
power? A certain haughtiness. A certain swagger. And an occasional invitation to the Piping Rock Country Club.

So who cares? We all did. We who sat in the library working on Blue   17
Sky Memos, something my twelve-year-old daughter could have done, given
the careful and patronizing instructions we received. We were enraged at
being excluded from Making It Big. What we didn't know at the time is that

the ones who Make It Big are always watching their backs, but then girls rarely have the opportunity to learn these finer points.

Power sanctions self-centeredness. (It could be argued that that's why   18 girls don't have it—"They're so giving.") It returns you, full circle, to the delicious years of being an infant and toddler when, it seemed, you were the center of the universe. But what is missing at thirty-five, forty, or fifty years of age is the innocence of the infant, the two- or three-year-old. It is a dangerous absence. Self-interest plus muscle power and experience combine to create a being more pervasively harmful than the sandbox bully.

Take, for instance, Manhattan real estate developers. They are cur-   19 rently a favorite target of the less powerful, and are, in some instances, a legitimate target. There are those who use their amassed fortunes to gain political sway by contributing to the campaign funds of elected officials. The elected officials then turn deaf ears to the complaints of less powerful con- stituents dispossessed from low rent buildings razed to make room for luxury high rises complete with Jacuzzis in every bath.

Donald Trump's song of himself is on the best-seller lists. *Vanity Fair*   20 featured a breathlessly infatuated profile of his wife. Why? Because if you can't be powerful, the next best thing is to fancy yourself on intimate terms with those who are. There is a hunger to know how they make their deals, shop for their children's Christmas presents, stay fresh and alert from five A.M. until Peter Duchin's orchestra plays its last charity ball waltz at mid- night. All this, and not a wrinkle in the brow to show for it.

People read about power for the same reason that little girls read   21 *Cinderella*, they want to believe that someday a prince will come to deliver a subject into sovereignty.

One might ask whether adulation of those who are flagrantly self-   22 involved makes any sense when there are thousands of dispossessed sleeping in Grand Central and Pennsylvania Station. It certainly doesn't make ma- ture sense.

But then power is not necessarily in mature hands. It is most often   23 achieved, and clung to, by those whose passion for it is fueled by childlike greed and self-interest. What they find, once they have it, is that being the proud possessor of power bears an uncanny similarity to being the two-year- old with the biggest plastic pail and shovel on the beach. It's a life of nervous guardianship.

I left the law because I wasn't motivated to engage in the struggle   24 required to move myself from library to the light of day and lunches with clients. The struggle would have required molding myself in the partners' images, a hard concept for them to visualize since I was female and they were male. It would have been necessary to remember when to speak and when to keep my mouth shut. I would have had to create an asexual aura. I would have had to work very, very hard.

I left the law because that wasn't the power that interested me. Which   25 is not to say that power itself doesn't interest me. I remember the full glory of being the only girl on the boy's baseball team. I remember the total sense of worthlessness that resulted when I grew breasts and the guys banished me from the pitcher's mound to the powerless world of hopscotch. Power is as tantalizing as a hypnotist's swinging pendulum. Power promises that you will never again be stuck with "the girls." Ask Regina Herzlinger. She knows.

Questions for Study and Discussion

1. How does Ascher define power in the legal profession? Do you think that her definition of power would be substantially different if she had entered some other profession? Is her definition of power limited to male/female situations?

2. What, according to Ascher, happens to women who achieve some measure of power in the professional world? How does she explain their behavior?

3. What did Ascher's experience on her fourth-grade baseball team teach her? What did she learn in fifth grade?

4. In paragraph 18, Ascher writes that "power sanctions self-centeredness." What does she mean? What is so dangerous about such sanctioning in the case of adults?

5. Despite her criticisms of power, Ascher has a healthy respect for it. What complexities of power is she referring to when she writes in paragraph 25, "Power is as tantalizing as a hypnotist's swinging pendulum. Power promises that you will never again be stuck with 'the girls' "?

6. What do you think about Ascher's decision to leave the legal profession? Was she simply unable to "make the cut"?

7. Ascher left the law to write. In making the change, was she more or less interested in gaining power, in your opinion?

Writing Topics

1. Write an essay in which you discuss the idea of power in the home and in the workplace. If you are a woman, what examples from your own experience in coming up against a male power structure can you relate? If you are a man, how much do you empathize with Ascher's arguments? Is it true, as she writes, that "power sanctions self-centeredness"?

2. In several major corporations, as well as small companies, professional-level women have fought for and won the right to work "flex-time" so they can spend more hours at home with their children. They argue that they can do as good a job in thirty hours a week as in forty if they are not worried about being away from their children for eight hours a day. Some feminists say that it will harm the movement to suggest that women with children are unable or unwilling to give full attention to executive-level responsibility. How do you respond to this debate? Write an essay in which you argue for or against a shortened work week for working mothers.

PATRICK FENTON

Patrick Fenton was born in Brooklyn in 1941, and at sixteen dropped out of school to go to work in a local factory before entering the army. After a two-year hitch in Germany, he went to work as an airport cargo handler at John F. Kennedy Airport in New York. At the same time he started to write articles for local publications. Eight years as a cargo handler proved to be too much. Fenton took a civil-service job and continued to work as a freelance writer. He is now a freelance writer and is working toward a college degree he began some years ago.

While working as a cargo handler for Seaboard World Airlines, Fenton wrote "Confessions of a Working Stiff," in which he tells us how he makes his living and how physically and spiritually debilitating such a job is. The essay was first published in the April 1973 issue of *New York* magazine.

Confessions of a Working Stiff

The Big Ben is hammering out its 5:45 alarm in the half-dark of   1
another Tuesday morning. If I'm lucky, my car down the street will kick over for me. I don't want to think about that now; all I want to do is roll over into the warm covers that hug my wife. I can hear the wind as it whistles up and down the sides of the building. Tuesday is always the worst day—it's the day the drudgery, boredom, and fatigue start all over again. I'm off from work on Sunday and Monday, so Tuesday is my blue Monday.

I make my living humping cargo for Seaboard World Airlines, one of   2
the big international airlines at Kennedy Airport. They handle strictly all cargo. I was once told that one of the Rockefellers is the major stockholder for the airline, but I don't really think about that too much. I don't get paid to think. The big thing is to beat that race with the time clock every morning of your life so the airline will be happy. The worst thing a man could ever do is to make suggestions about building a better airline. They pay people $40,000 a year to come up with better ideas. It doesn't matter that these ideas never work; it's just that they get nervous when a guy from South Brooklyn or Ozone Park acts like he actually has a brain.

I throw a Myadec high-potency vitamin into my mouth to ward off one   3
of the ten colds I get every year from humping mailbags out in the cold rain

255

at Kennedy. A huge DC-8 stretch jet waits impatiently for the 8,000 pounds of mail that I will soon feed its empty belly. I wash the Myadec down with some orange juice and grab a brown bag filled with bologna and cheese. Inside the lunch bag there is sometimes a silly note from my wife that says, "I Love You—Guess Who?" It is all that keeps me going to a job that I hate.

I've been going there for seven years now and my job is still the same.   4 It's weary work that makes a man feel used up and worn out. You push and you pull all day long with your back. You tie down pallets loaded with thousands of pounds of freight. You fill igloo-shaped containers with hundreds of boxes that look the same. If you're assigned to work the warehouse, it's really your hard luck. This is the job all the men hate most. You stack box upon box until the pallet resembles the exact shape of the inside of the plane. You get the same monotonous feeling an adult gets when he plays with a child's blocks. When you finish one pallet, you find another and start the whole dull process over again.

The airline pays me $192 a week for this. After they take out taxes and   5 $5.81 for the pension, I go home with $142. Once a month they take out $10 for term life insurance, and $5.50 for union dues. The week they take out the life insurance is always the worst: I go home with $132. My job will never change. I will fill up the same igloos with the same boxes for the next 34 years of my life, I will hump the same mailbags into the belly of the plane, and push the same 8,000-pound pallets with my back. I will have to do this until I'm 65 years old. Then I'll be free, if I don't die of a heart attack before that, and the airline will let me retire.

In winter the warehouse is cold and damp. There is no heat. The large   6 steel doors that line the warehouse walls stay open most of the day. In the cold months, wind, rain and snow blow across the floor. In the summer the warehouse becomes an oven. Dust and sand from the runways mix with the toxic fumes of fork lifts, leaving a dry, stale taste in your mouth. The high windows above the doors are covered with a thick, black dirt that kills the sun. The men work in shadows with the constant roar of jet engines blowing dangerously in their ears.

Working the warehouse is a tedious job that leaves a man's mind empty.   7 If he's smart he will spend his days wool-gathering. He will think about pretty girls that he once knew, or some other daydream of warm, dry places where you never had a chill. The worst thing he can do is to think about his problems. If he starts to think about how he is going to pay the mortgage on the $30,000 home that he can't afford, it will bring him down. He will wonder why he comes to the cargo airline every morning of his life, and even on Christmas Day. He will start to wonder why he has to listen to the deafening sound of the jets as they rev up their engines. He will wonder why he crawls on his hands and knees, breaking his back a little more every day.

To keep kids in that great place in the country in the summer, that   8 great place far away from Brooklyn and the South Bronx, he must work every hour of overtime that the airline offers him. If he never turns down an hour, if he works some 600 hours over, he can make about $15,000. To do this he must turn against himself, he must pray that the phone rings in the middle of the night, even though it's snowing out and he doesn't feel like working. He must hump cargo late into the night, eat meatball heroes for supper, drink coffee that starts to taste like oil, and then hope that his car starts when it's time to go home. If he gets sick—well, he better not think about that.

All over Long Island, Ozone Park, Brooklyn, and as far away as the   9
Bronx, men stir in the early morning hours as a new day begins. Every morning is the same as the last. Some of the men drink beer for breakfast instead of coffee. Way out in Bay Shore a cargoman snaps open a can of Budweiser. It's 6 A.M., and he covers the top of the can with his thumb in order to keep down the loud hiss as the beer escapes. He doesn't want to awaken his children as they dream away the morning in the next room. Soon he will swing his Pinto wagon up onto the crowded Long Island Expressway and start the long ride to the job. As he slips the car out of the driveway he tucks another can of beer between his legs.

All the men have something in common: they hate the work they are   10
doing and they drink a little too much. They come to work only to punch a timecard that has their last name on it. At the end of the week they will pick up a paycheck with their last name on it. They will never receive a bonus for a job well done, or even a party. At Christmastime a card from the president of the airline will arrive at each one of their houses. It will say Merry Christmas and have the president's name printed at the bottom of it. They know that the airline will be there long after they are dead. Nothing stops it. It runs non-stop, without sleep, through Christmas Day, New Year's Eve, Martin Luther King's birthday, even the deaths of Presidents.

It's seven in the morning and the day shift is starting to drift in. Huge   11
tractors are backing up to the big-mouth doors of the warehouse. Cattle trucks bring in tons of beef to feed its insatiable appetite for cargo. Smoke-covered trailers with refrigerated units packed deep with green peppers sit with their diesel engines idling. Names like White, Mack, and Kenworth are welded to the front of their radiators, which hiss and moan from the overload. The men walk through the factory-type gates of the parking lot with their heads bowed, oblivious of the shuddering diesels that await them.

Once inside the warehouse they gather in groups of threes and fours   12
like prisoners in an exercise yard. They stand in front of the two time clocks that hang below a window in the manager's office. They smoke and cough in the early morning hour as they await their work assignments. The manager, a nervous-looking man with a stomach that is starting to push out at his belt, walks out with the pink work sheets in his hand.

Eddie, a young Irishman with a mustache, has just bolted in through   13
the door. The manager has his timecard in his hand, holding it so no one else can hit Eddie in. Eddie is four minutes late by the time clock. His name will

now go down in the timekeeper's ledger. The manager hands the card to him with a "you'll be up in the office if you don't straighten out" look. Eddie takes the card, hits it in, and slowly takes his place with the rest of the men. He has been out till four in the morning drinking beer in the bars of Ozone Park; the time clock and the manager could blow up, for all he cares. "Jesus," he says to no one in particular, "I hope to Christ they don't put me in the warehouse this morning."

Over in another group, Kelly, a tall man wearing a navy knit hat, talks   14
to the men. "You know, I almost didn't make it in this morning. I passed this green VW on the Belt Parkway. The girl driving it was singing. Jesus, I thought to myself, it must be great going somewhere at 6:30 in the morning that makes you want to sing." Kelly is smiling as he talks. "I often think, why the hell don't you keep on going, Kelly? Don't get off at the cargo exit, stay on. Go anywhere, even if it's only Brooklyn. Christ, if I was a single man I think I would do just that. Some morning I'd pass this damn place by and drive as far away as Riverhead. I don't know what I'd do when I got there— maybe I'd pick up a pound of beefsteak tomatoes from one of those roadside stands or something."

The men laugh at Kelly but they know he is serious. "I feel the same way   15
sometimes," the man next to him says. "I find myself daydreaming a lot lately; this place drives you to do that. I get up in the morning and I just don't want to come to work. I get sick when I hit that parking lot. If it wasn't for the kids and the house I'd quit." The men then talk about how hard it is to get work on "the outside." They mention "outside" as if they were in a prison.

Each morning there is an Army-type roll call from the leads. The leads   16
are foremen who must keep the men moving; if they don't, it could mean their jobs. At one time they had power over the men but as time went by the company took away their little bit of authority. They also lost the deep interest, even enjoyment, for the hard work they once did. As the cargo airline grew, it beat this out of them, leaving only apathy. The ramp area is located in the backyard of the warehouse. This is where the huge jets park to unload their 70,000-pound payloads. A crew of men fall in behind the ramp lead as he mopes out of the warehouse. His long face shows the hopelessness of another day.

A brutal rain has started to beat down on the oil-covered concrete of   17
the ramp as the 306 screeches in off the runway. Its engines scream as they spit off sheets of rain and oil. Two of the men cover their ears as they run to put up a ladder to the front of the plane. The airline will give them ear covers only if they pay for half of them. A lot of the men never buy them. If they want, the airline will give them two little plugs free. The plugs don't work and hurt the inside of the ears.

The men will spend the rest of the day in the rain. Some of them will   18
set up conveyor belts and trucks to unload the thousands of pounds of cargo that sit in the deep belly of the plane. Then they will feed the awkward bird

until it is full and ready to fly again. They will crawl on their hands and knees in its belly, counting and humping hundreds of mailbags. The rest of the men will work up topside on the plane, pushing 8,000-pound pallets with their backs. Like Egyptians building a pyramid, they will pull and push until the pallet finally gives in and moves like a massive stone sliding through sand. They don't complain too much; they know that when the airline comes up with a better system some of them will go.

The old-timers at the airline can't understand why the younger men   19 stay on. They know what the cargo airline can do to a man. It can work him hard but make him lazy at the same time. The work comes in spurts. Sometimes a man will be pushed for three hours of sweat, other times he will just stand around bored. It's not the hard work that breaks a man at the airline, it's the boredom of doing the same job over and over again.

At the end of the day the men start to move in off the ramp. The rain is   20 still beating down at their backs but they move slowly. Their faces are red and raw from the rain-soaked wind that has been snapping at them for eight hours. The harsh wind moves in from the direction of the city. From the ramp you can see the Manhattan skyline, gray- and blue-looking, as it peeks up from the west wall of the warehouse. There is nothing to block the winter weather as it rolls in like a storm across a prairie. They head down to the locker room, heads bowed, like a football team that never wins.

With the workday almost over, the men move between the narrow, gray   21 rows of lockers. Up on the dirty walls that surround the lockers someone has written a couple of four-letter words. There is no wit to the words; they just say the usual. As they strip off their wet gear the men seem to come alive.

"Hey, Arnie! You want to stay four hours? They're asking for overtime   22 down in Export," one of the men yells over the lockers.

Arnie is sitting about four rows over, taking off his heavy winter cloth-   23 ing. He thinks about this for a second and yells back, "What will we be doing?"

"Working the meat trailer." This means that Arnie will be humping   24 huge sides of beef off rows of hooks for four hours. Blood will drip down onto his clothes as he struggles to the front of the trailer. Like most of the men, he needs the extra money, and knows that he should stay. He has Master Charge, Korvettes, Times Square Stores, and Abraham & Straus to pay.

"Nah, I'm not staying tonight. Not if it's working the meat trailer. Don   25 wanted to stop for a few beers at The Owl; maybe I'll stay tomorrow night."

It's four o'clock in the afternoon now—the men have twelve minutes   26 to go before they punch out. The airline has stopped for a few seconds as the men change shifts. Supervisors move frantically across the floor pushing the fresh lot of new men who have just started to come in. They hand out work sheets and yell orders: "Jack, get your men into their rain gear. Put three men in the bellies to finish off the 300 flight. Get someone on the pepper trailers, they've been here all morning."

The morning shift stands around the time clock with three minutes to 27
go. Someone says that Kevin Delahunty has just been appointed to the Fire
Department. Kevin, a young Irishman from Ozone Park, has been working
the cargo airline for six years. Like most of the men, he has hated every
minute of it. The men are openly proud of him as they reach out to shake his
hand. Kevin has found a job on "the outside." "Ah, you'll be leaving soon,"
he tells Pat. "I never thought I'd get out of here either, but you'll see, you're
going to make it."

The manager moves through the crowd handing out timecards and 28
stops when he comes to Kevin. Someone told him Kevin is leaving. "Is that
right, Delahunty? Well I guess we won't expect you in tomorrow, will we?
Going to become a fireman, eh? That means you'll be jumping out of
windows like a crazy man. Don't act like you did around here," he adds as he
walks back to his office.

The time clock hits 4:12 and the men pour out of the warehouse. 29
Kevin will never be back, but the rest of them will return in the morning to
grind out another eight hours. Some of them will head straight home to the
bills, screaming children, and a wife who tries to understand them. They'll
have a Schaefer or two, then they'll settle down to a night of television.

Some of them will start to fill up the cargo bars that surround Kennedy 30
Airport. They will head to places like Gaylor's on Rockaway Boulevard or
The Dew Drop Inn down near Farmers Boulevard. They will drink deep
glasses of whiskey and cold mugs of Budweiser. The Dew Drop has a honky-
tonk mood of the Old West to it. The barmaid moves around like a modern-
day Katie Elder. Like Brandy, she's a fine girl, but she can outcurse any
cargoman. She wears a low-cut blouse that reveals most of her breasts. The
jukebox will beat out some Country & Western as she says, "Ah, hell, you
played my song." The cargomen will hoot and holler as she substitutes some
of her own obscene lyrics.

They will drink late into the night, forgetting time clocks, Master 31
Charge, First National City, Korvettes, mortgages, cars that don't start, and
jet engines that hurt their ears. They will forget about damp, cold ware-
houses, winters that get longer and colder every year, minutes that drift by
like hours, supervisors that harass, and the thought of growing old on a job
they hate. At midnight they will fall dangerously into their cars and make
their way up onto the Southern State Parkway. As they ride into the dark
night of Long Island they will forget it all until 5:45 the next morning—
when the Big Ben will start up the whole grind all over again.

Questions for Study and Discussion

1. What is Fenton's attitude toward the airline company he works for?
What in particular does Fenton dislike about his job? What are the immediate

causes for his dissatisfaction? Why does he continue to work for the airline company?

2. Why, in your opinion, does the airline not do something to improve working conditions for its employees? Why does the airline company "get nervous when a guy from South Brooklyn or Ozone Park acts like he actually has a brain"?

3. What are "leads," and why does Fenton feel it is important to define and to discuss them?

4. For Fenton and his co-workers, working for the airline is a regimented, prison-like existence. How do Fenton's diction and imagery help to establish this motif?

5. Fenton uses concrete details and specific incidents to show rather than merely tell us how awful a job with the airline is. Identify several paragraphs that rely on concrete detail and two or three revealing incidents that dramatize the plight of the workers. Explain how these passages make the cause-and-effect relationship that Fenton sees real for the reader.

6. Comment on the appropriateness of the following similes, which Fenton uses to describe the workers:

    a. "like prisoners in an exercise yard" (12)

    b. "like Egyptians building a pyramid" (18)

    c. "like a football team that never wins" (20)

7. In the title of his essay Fenton refers to himself as a "working stiff." What does he mean?

8. What is it, according to Fenton, that breaks a man at the airline?

Writing Topics

1. In "Confessions of a Working Stiff," Patrick Fenton discusses the reasons why he hates his job. Not all people, of course, dislike their work. In fact, many people derive considerable satisfaction from the work they do. In an essay, discuss the reasons why some jobs are more satisfying than others. Why is it possible for a job to be satisfying for one person and not for another?

2. You are a manager who supervises a crew of Patrick Fentons. What do you think you could do as a manager to address the problems he raises in his essay? Write an essay in which you make proposals for such changes, explain how they would work, and argue for their acceptance.

3. Argue for or against the proposition that men are better suited than women for work in such jobs as cargo handling, warehousing, and road construction.

GARY SOTO

Born in Fresno, California, in 1952 to working-class Mexican-American parents, Gary Soto currently teaches English and Chicano studies at the University of California at Berkeley. After laboring as a migrant farm worker in the San Joaquin Valley during the 1960s, he studied geography at California State University at Fresno and the University of California at Irvine before turning his hand to poetry. In his first two collections of poetry—*The Elements of San Joaquin* (1977) and *The Tale of Sunlight* (1978)—Soto draws heavily on his childhood experiences as a Mexican-American growing up in southern California. As critics have noted, "his poems depict the violence of urban life, the exhausting labor of rural life, and the futility of trying to recapture the innocence of childhood." To date he has published four other volumes of poetry, a collection of short stories, and four works of nonfiction. His autobiographical collection of essays, *Living Up the Street: Narrative Recollections*, won Soto the American Book Award from the Before Columbus Foundation in 1985. His latest collection of essays, *A Summer Life*, appeared in 1991.

In "One Last Time," an essay taken from *Living Up the Street*, Soto reflects on his summers spent as a migrant worker picking grapes for the Sun-Maid raisin company and harvesting cotton in the San Joaquin Valley to earn money for school clothes.

One Last Time

Yesterday I saw the movie *Gandhi* and recognized a few of the people— not in the theater but in the film. I saw my relatives, dusty and thin as sparrows, returning from the fields with hoes balanced on their shoulders. The workers were squinting, eyes small and veined, and were using their hands to say what there was to say to those in the audience with popcorn and Cokes. I didn't have anything, though. I sat thinking of my family and their years in the fields, beginning with Grandmother who came to the United States after the Mexican revolution to settle in Fresno where she met her husband and bore children, many of them. She worked in the fields around Fresno, picking grapes, oranges, plums, peaches, and cotton, dragging a large white sack like a sled. She worked in the packing houses, Bonner and Sun-Maid Raisin, where she stood at a conveyor belt passing her hand over streams of raisins to pluck out leaves and pebbles. For over twenty years she worked at a machine that boxed raisins until she retired at sixty-five.

Grandfather worked in the fields, as did his children. Mother also found herself out there when she separated from Father for three weeks. I remember her coming home, dusty and so tired that she had to rest on the porch before she trudged inside to wash and start dinner. I didn't understand the complaints about her ankles or the small of her back, even though I had been in the grape fields watching her work. With my brother and sister I ran in and out of the rows; we enjoyed ourselves and pretended not to hear Mother scolding us to sit down and behave ourselves. A few years later, however, I caught on when I went to pick grapes rather than play in the rows.

Mother and I got up before dawn and ate quick bowls of cereal. She   3 drove in silence while I rambled on how everything was now solved, how I was going to make enough money to end our misery and even buy her a beautiful copper tea pot, the one I had shown her in Long's Drugs. When we arrived I was frisky and ready to go, self-consciously aware of my grape knife dangling at my wrist. I almost ran to the row the foreman had pointed out, but I returned to help Mother with the grape pans and jug of water. She told me to settle down and reminded me not to lose my knife. I walked at her side and listened to her explain how to cut grapes; bent down, hands on knees, I watched her demonstrate by cutting a few bunches into my pan. She stood over me as I tried it myself, tugging at a bunch of grapes that pulled loose like beads from a necklace. "Cut the stem all the way," she told me as last advice before she walked away, her shoes sinking in the loose dirt, to begin work on her own row.

I cut another bunch, then another, fighting the snap and whip of   4 vines. After ten minutes of groping for grapes, my first pan brimmed with bunches. I poured them on the paper tray, which was bordered by a wooden frame that kept the grapes from rolling off, and they spilled like jewels from a pirate's chest. The tray was only half filled, so I hurried to jump under the vines and begin groping, cutting, and tugging at the grapes again. I emptied the pan, raked the grapes with my hands to make them look like they filled the tray, and jumped back under the vine on my knees. I tried to cut faster because Mother, in the next row, was slowly moving ahead. I peeked into her row and saw trays gleaming in the early morning. I cut, pulled hard, and stopped to gather the grapes that missed the pan; already bored, I spat on a few to wash them before tossing them like popcorn into my mouth.

So it went. Two pans equaled one tray—or six cents. By lunchtime I   5 had a trail of thirty-seven trays behind me while mother had sixty or more. We met about halfway from our last trays, and I sat down with a grunt, knees wet from kneeling on dropped grapes. I washed my hands with the water from the jug, drying them on the inside of my shirt sleeve before I opened the paper bag for the first sandwich, which I gave to Mother. I dipped my hand in again to unwrap a sandwich without looking at it. I took a first bite and chewed it slowly for the tang of mustard. Eating in silence I looked straight ahead at the vines, and only when we were finished with cookies did we talk.

"Are you tired?" she asked.   6

"No, but I got a sliver from the frame," I told her. I showed her the web   7 of skin between my thumb and index finger. She wrinkled her forehead but said it was nothing.

"How many trays did you do?" 8

I looked straight ahead, not answering at first. I recounted in my mind 9 the whole morning of bend, cut, pour again and again, before answering a feeble "thirty-seven." No elaboration, no detail. Without looking at me she told me how she had done field work in Texas and Michigan as a child. But I had a difficult time listening to her stories. I played with my grape knife, stabbing it into the ground, but stopped when Mother reminded me that I had better not lose it. I left the knife sticking up like a small, leafless plant. She then talked about school, the junior high I would be going to that fall, and then about Rick and Debra, how sorry they would be that they hadn't come out to pick grapes because they'd have no new clothes for the school year. She stopped talking when she peeked at her watch, a bandless one she kept in her pocket. She got up with an "Ay, *Dios*," and told me that we'd work until three, leaving me cutting figures in the sand with my knife and dreading the return to work.

Finally I rose and walked slowly back to where I had left off, again 10 kneeling under the vine and fixing the pan under bunches of grapes. By that time, 11:30, the sun was over my shoulder and made me squint and think of the pool at the Y.M.C.A. where I was a summer member. I saw myself diving face first into the water and loving it. I saw myself gleaming like something new, at the edge of the pool. I had to daydream and keep my mind busy because boredom was a terror almost as awful as the work itself. My mind went dumb with stupid things, and I had to keep it moving with dreams of baseball and would-be girlfriends. I even sang, however softly, to keep my mind moving, my hands moving.

I worked less hurriedly and with less vision. I no longer saw that copper 11 pot sitting squat on our stove or Mother waiting for it to whistle. The wardrobe that I imagined, crisp and bright in the closet, numbered only one pair of jeans and two shirts because, in half a day, six cents times thirty-seven trays was two dollars and twenty-two cents. It became clear to me. If I worked eight hours, I might make four dollars. I'd take this, even gladly, and walk downtown to look into store windows on the mall and long for the bright madras shirts from Walter Smith or Coffee's, but settling for two imitation ones from Penney's.

That first day I laid down seventy-three trays while Mother had a 12 hundred and twenty behind her. On the back of an old envelope, she wrote out our numbers and hours. We washed at the pump behind the farm house and walked slowly to our car for the drive back to town in the afternoon heat. That evening after dinner I sat in a lawn chair listening to music from a transistor radio while Rick and David King played catch. I joined them in a game of pickle, but there was little joy in trying to avoid their tags because I couldn't get the fields out of my mind: I saw myself dropping on my knees under a vine to tug at a branch that wouldn't come off. In bed, when I closed my eyes, I saw the fields, yellow with kicked up dust, and a crooked trail of trays rotting behind me.

The next day I woke tired and started picking tired. The grapes rained into the pan, slowly filling like a belly, until I had my first tray and started my second. So it went all day, and the next, and all through the following week, so that by the end of thirteen days the foreman counted out, in tens mostly, my pay of fifty-three dollars. Mother earned one hundred and forty-eight dollars. She wrote this on her envelope, with a message I didn't bother to ask her about. 13

The next day I walked with my friend Scott to the downtown mall where we drooled over the clothes behind fancy windows, bought popcorn, and sat at a tier of outdoor fountains to talk about girls. Finally we went into Penney's for more popcorn, which we ate walking around, before we returned home without buying anything. It wasn't until a few days before school that I let my fifty-three dollars slip quietly from my hands, buying a pair of pants, two shirts, and a maroon T-shirt, the kind that was in style. At home I tried them on while Rick looked on enviously; later, the day before school started, I tried them on again wondering not so much if they were worth it as who would see me first in those clothes. 14

Along with my brother and sister I picked grapes until I was fifteen, before giving up and saying that I'd rather wear old clothes than stoop like a Mexican. Mother thought I was being stuck-up, even stupid, because there would be no clothes for me in the fall. I told her I didn't care, but when Rick and Debra rose at five in the morning, I lay awake in bed feeling that perhaps I had made a mistake but unwilling to change my mind. That fall Mother bought me two pairs of socks, a packet of colored T-shirts, and underwear. The T-shirts would help, I thought, but who would see that I had new underwear and socks? I wore a new T-shirt on the first day of school, then an old shirt on Tuesday, then another T-shirt on Wednesday, and on Thursday an old Nehru shirt that was embarrassingly out of style. On Friday I changed into the corduroy pants my brother had handed down to me and slipped into my last new T-shirt. I worked like a magician, blinding my classmates, who were all clothes conscious and small-time social climbers, by arranging my wardrobe to make it seem larger than it really was. But by spring I had to do something—my blue jeans were almost silver and my shoes had lost their form, puddling like black ice around my feet. That spring of my sixteenth year, Rick and I decided to take a labor bus to chop cotton. In his old Volkswagen, which was more noise than power, we drove on a Saturday morning to West Fresno—or Chinatown as some call it—parked, walked slowly toward a bus, and stood gawking at the winos, toothy blacks, Okies, *Tejanos* with gold teeth, whores, Mexican families, and labor contractors shouting "Cotton" or "Beets," the work of spring. 15

We boarded the "Cotton" bus without looking at the contractor who 16 stood almost blocking the entrance because he didn't want winos. We boarded scared and then were more scared because two blacks in the rear were drunk and arguing loudly about what was better, a two-barrel or four-barrel Ford carburetor. We sat far from them, looking straight ahead, and only glanced briefly at the others who boarded, almost all of them broken and poorly dressed in loudly mismatched clothes. Finally when the contractor banged his palm against the side of the bus, the young man at the wheel, smiling and talking in Spanish, started the engine, idled it for a moment while he adjusted the mirrors, and started off in slow chugs. Except for the windshield there was no glass in the windows, so as soon as we were on the rural roads outside Fresno, the dust and sand began to be sucked into the bus, whipping about like irate wasps as the gravel ticked about us. We closed our eyes, clotted up our mouths that wanted to open with embarrassed laughter because we couldn't believe we were on that bus with those people and the dust attacking us for no reason.

When we arrived at a field we followed the others to a pickup where we   17
each took a hoe and marched to stand before a row. Rick and I, self-conscious and unsure, looked around at the others who leaned on their hoes or squatted in front of the rows, almost all talking in Spanish, joking, lighting cigarettes—all waiting for the foreman's whistle to begin work. Mother had explained how to chop cotton by showing us with a broom in the backyard.

"Like this," she said, her broom swishing down weeds. "Leave one   18
plant and cut four—and cut them! Don't leave them standing or the foreman will get mad."

The foreman whistled and we started up the row stealing glances at   19
other workers to see if we were doing it right. But after awhile we worked like we knew what we were doing, neither of us hurrying or falling behind. But slowly the clot of men, women, and kids began to spread and loosen. Even Rick pulled away. I didn't hurry, though. I cut smoothly and cleanly as I walked at a slow pace, in a sort of funeral march. My eyes measured each space of cotton plants before I cut. If I missed the plants, I swished again. I worked intently, seldom looking up, so when I did I was amazed to see the sun, like a broken orange coin, in the east. It looked blurry, unbelievable, like something not of this world. I looked around in amazement, scanning the eastern horizon that was a taut line jutted with an occasional mountain. The horizon was beautiful, like a snapshot of the moon, in the early light of morning, in the quiet of no cars and few people.

The foreman trudged in boots in my direction, stepping awkwardly   20
over the plants, to inspect the work. No one around me looked up. We all worked steadily while we waited for him to leave. When he did leave, with a feeble complaint addressed to no one in particular, we looked up smiling under straw hats and bandanas.

By 11:00, our lunch time, my ankles were hurting from walking on   21
clods the size of hardballs. My arms ached and my face was dusted by a wind
that was perpetual, always busy whipping about. But the work was not bad, I
thought. It was better, so much better, than picking grapes, especially with
the hourly wage of a dollar twenty-five instead of piece work. Rick and I
walked sorely toward the bus where we washed and drank water. Instead of
eating in the bus or in the shade of the bus, we kept to ourselves by walking
down to the irrigation canal that ran the length of the field, to open our
lunch of sandwiches and crackers. We laughed at the crackers, which seemed
like a cruel joke from our Mother, because we were working under the sun
and the last thing we wanted was a salty dessert. We ate them anyway and
drank more water before we returned to the field, both of us limping in
exaggeration. Working side by side, we talked and laughed at our predicament because our Mother had warned us year after year that if we didn't get
on track in school we'd have to work in the fields and then we would see. We
mimicked Mother's whining voice and smirked at her smoky view of the
future in which we'd be trapped by marriage and screaming kids. We'd eat
beans and then we'd see.

Rick pulled slowly away to the rhythm of his hoe falling faster and   22
smoother. It was better that way, to work alone. I could hum made-up songs
or songs from the radio and think to myself about school and friends. At the
time I was doing badly in my classes, mainly because of a difficult stepfather,
but also because I didn't care anymore. All through junior high and into my
first year of high school there were those who said I would never do anything, be anyone. They said I'd work like a donkey and marry the first
Mexican girl that came along. I was reminded so often, verbally and in the
way I was treated at home, that I began to believe that chopping cotton
might be a lifetime job for me. If not chopping cotton, then I might get lucky
and find myself in a car wash or restaurant or junkyard. But it was clear; I'd
work, and work hard.

I cleared my mind by humming and looking about. The sun was di-   23
rectly above with a few soft blades of clouds against a sky that seemed bluer
and more beautiful than our sky in the city. Occasionally the breeze flurried
and picked up dust so that I had to cover my eyes and screw up my face. The
workers were hunched, brown as the clods under our feet, and spread across
the field that ran without end—fields that were owned by corporations, not
families.

I hoed trying to keep my mind busy with scenes from school and   24
pretend girlfriends until finally my brain turned off and my thinking went
fuzzy with boredom. I looked about, no longer mesmerized by the beauty of
the landscape, no longer wondering if the winos in the fields could hold out
for eight hours, no longer dreaming of the clothes I'd buy with my pay. My
eyes followed my chopping as the plants, thin as their shadows, fell with

each strike. I worked slowly with ankles and arms hurting, neck stiff, and eyes stinging from the dust and the sun that glanced off the field like a mirror.

By quitting time, 3:00, there was such an excruciating pain in my ankles that I walked as if I were wearing snowshoes. Rick laughed at me and I laughed too, embarrassed that most of the men were walking normally and I was among the first timers who had to get used to this work. "And what about you, wino," I came back at Rick. His eyes were meshed red and his long hippie hair was flecked with dust and gnats and bits of leaves. We placed our hoes in the back of a pickup and stood in line for our pay, which was twelve fifty. I was amazed at the pay, which was the most I had ever earned in one day, and thought that I'd come back the next day, Sunday. This was too good.   25

Instead of joining the others in the labor bus, we jumped in the back of a pickup when the driver said we'd get to town sooner and were welcome to join him. We scrambled into the truck bed to be joined by a heavy-set and laughing *Tejano* whose head was shaped like an egg, particularly so because the bandana he wore ended in a point on the top of his head. He laughed almost demonically as the pickup roared up the dirt path, a gray cape of dust rising behind us. On the highway, with the wind in our faces, we squinted at the fields as if we were looking for someone. The *Tejano* had quit laughing but was smiling broadly, occasionally chortling tunes he never finished. I was scared of him, though Rick, two years older and five inches taller, wasn't. If the *Tejano* looked at him, Rick stared back for a second or two before he looked away to the fields.   26

I felt like a soldier coming home from war when we rattled into China-town. People leaning against car hoods stared, their necks following us, owl-like; prostitutes chewed gum more ferociously and showed us their teeth; Chinese grocers stopped brooming their storefronts to raise their cadaverous faces at us. We stopped in front of the Chi Chi Club where Mexican music blared from the juke box and cue balls cracked like dull ice. The *Tejano*, who was dirty as we were, stepped awkwardly over the side rail, dusted himself off with his bandana, and sauntered into the club.   27

Rick and I jumped from the back, thanked the driver who said *de nada* and popped his clutch, so that the pickup jerked and coughed blue smoke. We returned smiling to our car, happy with the money we had made and pleased that we had, in a small way, proved ourselves to be tough; that we worked as well as other men and earned the same pay.   28

We returned the next day and the next week until the season was over and there was nothing to do. I told myself that I wouldn't pick grapes that summer, saying all through June and July that it was for Mexicans, not me. When August came around and I still had not found a summer job, I ate my words, sharpened my knife, and joined Mother, Rick, and Debra for one last time.   29

Questions for Study and Discussion

1. What does Soto mean when he says that he recognized a few of the people in the film *Gandhi*?

2. After returning from the fields, Soto's mother would complain about "her ankles or the small of her back." How did Soto come to understand what his mother was talking about?

3. Before he had finished picking his second tray of grapes, Soto confesses that he was "already bored." What was particularly boring about the job? What does Soto do to relieve his boredom?

4. What were Soto's expectations about the job at the beginning of the first day? How had they changed by the middle of the day?

5. In paragraphs 3 through 12, Soto describes his first day picking grapes in great detail. He then describes the next twelve days in a single paragraph. How does this contrast strike the reader? What does it say about the nature of the job?

6. Why didn't Soto want to continue picking grapes during his summers? How was he creative with his wardrobe "to make it seem larger than it really was"?

7. According to Soto, what was better than picking cotton? What career aspirations did Soto have as a teenager? Why?

8. If Soto hated picking grapes so much, why did he return to the vine-yards with his family? What is it about migrant work that makes laborers feel anxious, insecure, or powerless?

Writing Topics

1. What type of work do you see yourself doing ten years from now? Why? In an essay explain the reasons for your career choice.

2. Do you find that some types of work are satisfying while others are not? Write an essay in which you classify the various types of work that you do on a regular basis. What is it about some jobs that makes them rewarding? What is it about others that makes you want to avoid them?

3. Write an essay in which you compare and contrast Soto's thoughts about work with those of Patrick Fenton in "Confessions of a Working Stiff" (pp. 255–60). What conclusions can you draw about jobs that require little or no thinking?

4. Explore the problems that a person encounters when he or she enters a profession dominated by the opposite sex—for example, men who choose to be elementary school teachers, nurses, or secretaries, or women who choose to go into the clergy, engineering, or police work. Your essay should consider not only your ideas about the problems associated with the job, but also the problems associated with education, training, and even family and friends and their reactions.

4

Campus Life

Shall I teach you what knowledge is? When you know a thing, to recognize that you know it, and when you do not know a thing, to recognize that you do not know it. That is knowledge.
—Confucius

What I wish for all students is some release from the clammy grip of the future. I wish them a chance to savor each segment of their education as an experience in itself and not as a grim preparation for the next step. I wish them the right to experiment, to trip and fall, to learn that defeat is as instructive as victory and is not the end of the world.
—William Zinsser

Teaching and Learning

ALEXANDER CALANDRA

Tests in school and college are usually designed so that each question has only one correct answer, especially in such disciplines as the natural sciences. Yet many important discoveries have been made by individuals who have reached beyond the obvious and "known" answers—take Galileo, Columbus, and Einstein, for example. Alexander Calandra, a professor of physics at Washington University in St. Louis, once came across a college student who insisted on giving every answer but the expected one to a physics exam question. In this essay, originally published in *Saturday Review*, he tells what happened.

Angels on a Pin

Some time ago, I received a call from a colleague who asked if I would 1 be the referee on the grading of an examination question. He was about to give a student a zero for his answer to a physics question, while the student claimed he should receive a perfect score and would if the system were not set up against the student. The instructor and the student agreed to submit this to an impartial arbiter, and I was selected.

I went to my colleague's office and read the examination question: 2 "Show how it is possible to determine the height of a tall building with the aid of a barometer."

The student had answered: "Take the barometer to the top of the 3 building, attach a long rope to it, lower the barometer to the street, and then bring it up, measuring the length of the rope. The length of the rope is the height of the building."

I pointed out that the student really had a strong case for full credit, 4 since he had answered the question completely and correctly. On the other hand, if full credit were given, it could well contribute to a high grade for the student in his physics course. A high grade is supposed to certify competence in physics, but the answer did not confirm this. I suggested that the student have another try at answering the question. I was not surprised that my colleague agreed, but I was surprised that the student did.

I gave the student six minutes to answer the question, with the warn- 5
ing that his answer should show some knowledge of physics. At the end of five minutes, he had not written anything. I asked if he wished to give up, but he said no. He had many answers to this problem; he was just thinking of the best one. I excused myself for interrupting him, and asked him to please go on. In the next minute, he dashed off his answer, which read:

"Take the barometer to the top of the building and lean over the edge 6
of the roof. Drop the barometer, timing its fall with a stopwatch. Then using the formula $S = \frac{1}{2}at^2$, calculate the height of the building."

At this point, I asked my colleague if *he* would give up. He conceded, 7
and I gave the student almost full credit.

In leaving my colleague's office, I recalled that the student had said he 8
had other answers to the problem, so I asked him what they were. "Oh, yes," said the student. "There are many ways of getting the height of a tall building with the aid of a barometer. For example, you could take the barometer out on a sunny day and measure the height of the barometer, the length of its shadow, and the length of the shadow of the building, and by the use of a simple proportion, determine the height of the building."

"Fine," I said. "And the others?" 9

"Yes," said the student. "There is a very basic measurement method 10
that you will like. In this method, you take the barometer and begin to walk up the stairs. As you climb the stairs, you mark off the length of the barometer along the wall. You then count the number of marks, and this will give you the height of the building in barometer units. A very direct method."

"Of course, if you want a more sophisticated method, you can tie the 11
barometer to the end of a string, swing it as a pendulum, and determine the value of 'g' at the street level and at the top of the building. From the difference between the two values of 'g', the height of the building can, in principle, be calculated."

Finally, he concluded, there are many ways of solving the problem. 12
"Probably the best," he said, "is to take the barometer to the basement and knock on the superintendent's door. When the superintendent answers, you speak to him as follows: "Mr. Superintendent, here I have a fine barometer. If you will tell me the height of this building, I will give you this barometer.' "

At this point, I asked the student if he really did not know the conven- 13
tional answer to this question. He admitted that he did, but said that he was fed up with high school and college instructors trying to teach him how to think, to use the "scientific method," and to explore the deep inner logic of the subject in a pedantic way, as is often done in the new mathematics, rather than teaching him the structure of the subject. With this in mind, he decided to revive scholasticism as an academic lark to challenge the Sputnik-panicked classrooms of America.

Questions for Study and Discussion

1. What is the point of this essay? What makes the narrative more than a humorous story about a student and his physics exam?

2. What was the exam question supposed to test? Why did the question fail? How might the actual wording have caused this failure? How would you rewrite the question so that it would do what it was meant to do?

3. Why do you think the student gave the answer in paragraph 6 as the best one? Do you agree? What motivated him to avoid the conventional answer?

4. Why do you think the teacher accepted the answer in paragraph 6 but did not give the student full credit? Was he right to do so? Explain.

5. What relevant information does Calandra leave out of the essay? Why do you think he does this?

6. The scholastic philosophers of the Middle Ages used to debate theological questions that seem pointless to us today, such as how many angels could dance on the head of a pin. In this context, what do you think is meant by the reference to scholasticism in the last sentence of the essay? What does the title contribute to the essay?

7. How would you characterize all of the student's answers? Granting their imaginativeness, what other quality do they all possess?

Writing Topics

1. History and everyday life are full of examples of what Edward de Bono calls "lateral thinking," going outside the conventional limits of a problem to find an unexpected but effective answer. The student in Calandra's essay is obviously an imaginative lateral thinker. What examples of lateral thinking can you find in your own experience, or from other sources? How can one set about thinking laterally? Write an essay in which you discuss the benefits of lateral thinking.

2. What are tests and exams normally used for? What should they be used for? How can you tell a good examination question from a bad one? Based on exams that you have taken, write an essay that examines the function of testing in the educational process.

FREDERICK DOUGLASS

Frederick Douglass (1817–1895), born a slave in Maryland, taught himself to read and write and escaped from his owners by disguising himself as a sailor. Later he wrote of his experiences as a slave in *Narrative of the Life of Frederick Douglass, An American Slave* (1845), a book he revised twice to include later events in his life. Douglass's *Narrative* is a prime example of the fugitive-slave stories popular in the North before the Civil War. After his escape in 1836, Douglass founded a newspaper, published first as *The North Star* and later as *Frederick Douglass' Weekly and Monthly*. A skilled orator, he was an articulate and militant defender of civil rights for women as well as African-Americans. Douglass was also a friend to the radical abolitionist John Brown, served as a United States marshal, and was appointed recorder of deeds for the District of Columbia. His rich and varied experience stands as a paradigm for courage and indomitable spirit in the face of oppression.

In the following excerpt from his autobiography, Douglass tells of his struggle to learn to read and write, using every means at his disposal. Despite his master's efforts to keep his slaves ignorant, and the pain of learning about the hopelessness of the abolitionists' struggle, Douglass knew he had to learn to read and write if he was ever to be free.

How I Learned to Read and Write

I lived in Master Hugh's family about seven years. During this time, I 1 succeeded in learning to read and write. In accomplishing this, I was compelled to resort to various stratagems. I had no regular teacher. My mistress, who had kindly commenced to instruct me, had, in compliance with the advice and direction of her husband, not only ceased to instruct, but had set her face against my being instructed by any one else. It is due, however, to my mistress to say of her, that she did not adopt this course of treatment immediately. She at first lacked the depravity indispensable to shutting me up in mental darkness. It was at least necessary for her to have some training in the exercise of irresponsible power, to make her equal to the task of treating me as though I were a brute.

My mistress was, as I have said, a kind and tender-hearted woman; and 2 in the simplicity of her soul she commenced, when I first went to live with her, to treat me as she supposed one human being ought to treat another. In entering upon the duties of a slaveholder, she did not seem to perceive that I sustained to her the relation of a mere chattel, and that for her to treat me as a human being was not only wrong, but dangerously so. Slavery proved as injurious to her as it did to me. When I went there, she was a pious, warm, and tender-hearted woman. There was no sorrow or suffering for which she had not a tear. She had bread for the hungry, clothes for the naked, and comfort for every mourner that came within her reach. Slavery soon proved its ability to divest her of these heavenly qualities. Under its influence, the tender heart became stone, and the lamblike disposition gave way to one of tigerlike fierceness. The first step in her downward course was in her ceasing to instruct me. She now commenced to practice her husband's precepts. She finally became even more violent in her opposition than her husband himself. She was not satisfied with simply doing as well as he had commanded; she seemed anxious to do better. Nothing seemed to make her more angry than to see me with a newspaper. She seemed to think that here lay the danger. I have had her rush at me with a face made all up of fury, and snatch from me a newspaper, in a manner that fully revealed her apprehension. She was an apt woman; and a little experience soon demonstrated, to her satisfaction, that education and slavery were incompatible with each other.

From this time I was most narrowly watched. If I was in a separate room   3
any considerable length of time, I was sure to be suspected of having a book, and was at once called to give an account of myself. All this, however, was too late. The first step had been taken. Mistress, in teaching me the alphabet, had given me the *inch,* and no precaution could prevent me from taking the *ell.*

The plan which I adopted, and the one by which I was most successful,   4
was that of making friends of all the little white boys whom I met in the street. As many of these as I could, I converted into teachers. With their kindly aid, obtained at different times and in different places, I finally succeeded in learning to read. When I was sent on errands, I always took my book with me, and by going on one part of my errand quickly, I found time to get a lesson before my return. I used also to carry bread with me, enough of which was always in the house, and to which I was always welcome; for I was much better off in this regard than many of the poor white children in our neighborhood. This bread is used to bestow upon the hungry little urchins, who, in return, would give me that more valuable bread of knowledge. I am strongly tempted to give the names of two or three of those little boys, as a testimonial of the gratitude and affection I bear them; but prudence forbids;—not that it would injure me, but it might embarrass them; for it is almost an unpardonable offence to teach slaves to read in this Christian country. It is enough to say of the dear little fellows, that they lived on Philpot Street, very near Durgin and Bailey's shipyard. I used to talk this matter of slavery over with them. I would sometimes say to them, I wished I could be as free as they would be when they got to be men. "You will be free as soon as you are twenty-one, *but I am a slave for life!* Have not I as good a right to be free as you have?" These words used to trouble them; they would express for me the liveliest sympathy, and console me with the hope that something would occur by which I might be free.

I was now about twelve years old, and the thought of being *a slave for*   5
life began to bear heavily upon my heart. Just about this time, I got hold of a

book entitled "The Columbian Orator." Every opportunity I got, I used to read this book. Among much of other interesting matter, I found in it a dialogue between a master and his slave. The slave was represented as having run away from his master three times. The dialogue represented the conversation which took place between them, when the slave was retaken the third time. In this dialogue, the whole argument in behalf of slavery was brought forward by the master, all of which was disposed of by the slave. The slave was made to say some very smart as well as impressive things in reply to his master—things which had the desired though unexpected effect; for the conversation resulted in the voluntary emancipation of the slave on the part of the master.

In the same book, I met with one of Sheridan's mighty speeches on and in behalf of Catholic emancipation. These were choice documents to me. I read them over and over again with unabated interest. They gave tongue to interesting thoughts of my own soul, which had frequently flashed through my mind, and died away for want of utterance. The moral which I gained from the dialogue was the power of truth over the conscience of even a slaveholder. What I got from Sheridan was a bold denunciation of slavery, and a powerful vindication of human rights. The reading of these documents enabled me to utter my thoughts, and to meet the arguments brought forward to sustain slavery; but while they relieved me of one difficulty, they brought on another even more painful than the one of which I was relieved. The more I read, the more I was led to abhor and detest my enslavers. I could regard them in no other light than a band of successful robbers, who had left their homes, and gone to Africa, and stolen us from our homes, and in a strange land reduced us to slavery. I loathed them as being the meanest as well as the most wicked of men. As I read and contemplated the subject, behold! that very discontentment which Master Hugh had predicted would follow my learning to read had already come, to torment and sting my soul to unutterable anguish. As I writhed under it, I would at times feel that learning to read had been a curse rather than a blessing. It had given me a view of my wretched condition, without the remedy. It opened my eyes to the horrible pit, but to no ladder upon which to get out. In moments of agony, I envied my fellow-slaves for their stupidity. I have often wished myself a beast. I preferred the condition of the meanest reptile to my own. Any thing, no matter what, to get rid of thinking! It was this everlasting thinking of my condition that tormented me. There was no getting rid of it. It was pressed upon me by every object within sight or hearing, animate or inanimate. The silver trump of freedom had roused my soul to eternal wakefulness. Freedom now appeared, to disappear no more forever. It was heard in every sound, and seen in every thing. It was ever present to torment me with a sense of my wretched condition. I saw nothing without seeing it, I heard nothing without hearing it, and felt nothing without feeling it. It looked from every star, it smiled in every calm, breathed in every wind, and moved in every storm.

6

I often found myself regretting my own existence, and wishing myself   7
dead; and but for the hope of being free, I have no doubt but that I should
have killed myself, or done something for which I should have been killed.
While in this state of mind, I was eager to hear any one speak of slavery. I
was a ready listener. Every little while, I could hear something about the
abolitionists. It was some time before I found what the word meant. It was
always used in such connections as to make it an interesting word for me. If a
slave ran away and succeeded in getting clear, or if a slave killed his master,
set fire to a barn, or did any thing very wrong in the mind of a slaveholder, it
was spoken of as the fruit of *abolition*. Hearing the word in this connection
very often, I set about learning what it meant. The dictionary afforded me
little or no help. I found it was "the act of abolishing"; but then I did not
know what was to be abolished. Here I was perplexed. I did not dare to ask
any one about its meaning, for I was satisfied that it was something they
wanted me to know very little about. After a patient waiting, I got one of our
city papers, containing an accouunt of the number of petitions from the
north, praying for the abolition of slavery in the District of Columbia, and of
the slave trade between the States. From this time I understood the words
abolition and *abolitionist,* and always drew near when that word was spoken,
expecting to hear something of importance to myself and fellow-slaves. The
light broke in upon me by degrees. I went one day down on the wharf of Mr.
Waters; and seeing two Irishmen unloading a scow of stone, I went, unasked
and helped them. When we had finished, one of them came to me and asked
me if I were a slave. I told him I was. He asked, "Are ye a slave for life?" I
told him that I was. The good Irishman seemed to be deeply affected by the
statement. He said to the other that it was a pity so fine a little fellow as
myself should be a slave for life. He said it was a shame to hold me. They
both advised me to run away to the north; that I should find friends there,
and that I should be free. I pretended not to be interested in what they said,
and treated them as if I did not understand them; for I feared they might be
treacherous. White men have been known to encourage slaves to escape,
and then, to get the reward, catch them and return them to their masters. I
was afraid that these seemingly good men might use me so; but I nevertheless
remembered their advice, and from that time I resolved to run away. I looked
forward to a time at which it would be safe for me to escape. I was too young
to think of doing so immediately; besides, I wished to learn how to write, as I
might have occasion to write my own pass. I consoled myself with the hope
that I should one day find a good chance. Meanwhile, I would learn to write.

The idea as to how I might learn to write was suggested to me by being   8
in Durgin and Bailey's ship-yard, and frequently seeing the ship carpenters,
after hewing, and getting a piece of timber ready for use, write on the timber
the name of that part of the ship for which it was intended. When a piece of
timber was intended for the larboard side, it would be marked—"L." When a
piece was for the starboard side, it would be marked thus—"S." A piece for

the larboard side forward, would be marked thus—"L. F." When a piece was for starboard side forward, it would be marked thus—"S. F." For larboard aft, it would be marked thus—"L. A." For starboard aft, it would be marked thus—"S. A." I soon learned the name of these letters, and for what they were intended when placed upon a piece of timber in the ship-yard. I immediately commenced copying them, and in a short time was able to make the four letters named. After that, when I met with any boy who I knew could write, I would tell him I could write as well as he. The next word would be, "I don't believe you. Let me see you try it." I would then make the letters which I had been so fortunate as to learn, and ask him to beat that. In this way I got a good many lessons in writing, which it is quite possible I should never have gotten in any other way. During this time, my copy-book was the board fence, brick wall, and pavement; my pen and ink was a lump of chalk. With these, I learned mainly how to write. I then commenced and continued copying the Italics in Webster's Spelling Book, until I could make them all without looking on the book. By this time, my little Master Thomas had gone to school, and learned how to write, and had written over a number of copy-books. These had been brought home, and shown to some of our near neighbors, and then laid aside. My mistress used to go to class meeting at the Wilk Street meetinghouse every Monday afternoon, and leave me to take care of the house. When left thus, I used to spend the time in writing in the spaces left in Master Thomas's copy-book, copying what he had written. I continued to do this until I could write a hand very similar to that of Master Thomas. Thus, after a long, tedious effort for years, I finally succeeded in learning how to write.

Questions for Study and Discussion

1. How did Douglass's "mistress's" attitude toward him change? How was this change reflected in her treatment of him? In your own words, what are the dangers of bigotry to the bigot?

2. Clearly Douglass was passionate in his desire to learn to read and write. What were his reasons for wishing to read and write?

3. Master Hugh had warned Douglass that learning to read would lead to discontentedness. Was he right? What were the emotions Douglass felt after he learned to read? What kept him from destroying himself?

4. What "moral" did Douglass gain from reading *The Columbian Orator*? In your own words, explain the meaning of the moral Douglass learned.

5. How long did it take Douglass to learn to read and write? Do you think most people would have gone through what he did to gain these skills? How would you describe Douglass's character? Give examples from the text to support your answer.

6. How did Douglass organize his narrative?

7. Is this story the work of an uneducated or educated man? Review the

examples the author gives of the ways he learned to read and write. Do they help you draw a conclusion? Explain. What other elements of the story point to the author's education or lack of it?

8. Is the author's tone angry, ironic, or resigned? Is his tone different at different points in the story? Point to passages in the text to support your conclusion.

9. Douglass uses several figures of speech in his narrative. Identify some of them and explain how each one works to make the story effective.

Writing Topics

1. Write a story about an event in your life that is significant for its hardship and the emotional impact it has had on you. Be sure to include descriptions, as Douglass did, of the people and attitudes that made the ordeal especially bearable or unbearable. What lessons did you take away from the experience?

2. Douglass felt his life was changed forever after he read *The Columbian Orator*. Not only did it express powerful ideas, but it also "gave tongue to interesting thoughts of my own soul, which had frequently flashed through my mind, and died away for want of utterance." Think of all the books you have read and choose one or two that in some important way changed your outlook on life or expressed ideas for which you did not have words. In an essay, describe these books and explain why they had such an impact on you.

EUDORA WELTY

The following selection is taken from *One Writer's Beginnings*, Eudora Welty's account of her life and preparation as a writer, which has published in 1984. In this excerpt, Welty gives us a picture of her grade-school principal and the influence the principal had on her, as well as on the community and the state of Mississippi. For biographical information on Welty, see p. 129.

Miss Duling

From the first I was clamorous to learn—I wanted to know and begged 1
to be told not so much what, or how, or why, or where, as when. How soon?

Pear tree by the garden gate,
How much longer must I wait?

This rhyme from one of my nursery books was the one that spoke for me. But I lived not at all unhappily in this craving, for my wild curiosity was in large part suspense, which carries its own secret pleasure. And so one of the godmothers of fiction was already bending over me.

When I was five years old, I knew the alphabet, I'd been vaccinated 2
(for smallpox), and I could read. So my mother walked across the street to Jefferson Davis Grammar School and asked the principal if she would allow me to enter the first grade after Christmas.

"Oh, all right," said Miss Duling. "Probably the best thing you could do 3
with her."

Miss Duling, a lifelong subscriber to perfection, was a figure of author- 4
ity, the most whole-souled I have ever come to know. She was a dedicated schoolteacher who denied herself all she might have done or whatever other way she might have lived (this possibility was the last that could have

occurred to us, her subjects in school). I believe she came of well-off people, well-educated, in Kentucky, and certainly old photographs show she was a beautiful, high-spirited-looking young lady—and came down to Jackson to its new grammar school that was going begging for a principal. She must have earned next to nothing; Mississippi then as now was the nation's lowest-ranking state economically, and our legislature has always shown a painfully loud reluctance to give money to public education. That challenge *brought* her.

In the long run she came into touch, as teacher or principal, with three　5 generations of Jacksonians. My parents had not, but everybody else's parents had gone to school to her. She'd taught most of our leaders somewhere along the line. When she wanted something done—some civic oversight corrected, some injustice made right overnight, or even a tree spared that the fool telephone people were about to cut down—she telephoned the mayor, or the chief of police, or the president of the power company, or the head doctor at the hospital, or the judge in charge of a case, or whoever, and calling them by their first names, *told* them. It is impossible to imagine her meeting with anything less than compliance. The ringing of her brass bell from their days at Davis School would still be in their ears. She also proposed a spelling match between the fourth grade at Davis School and the Mississippi Legislature, who went through with it; and that told the Legislature.

Her standards were very high and of course inflexible, her authority　6 was total; why *wouldn't* this carry with it a brass bell that could be heard ringing for a block in directions? That bell belonged to the figure of Miss Duling as though it grew directly out of her right arm, as wings grew out of an angel or a tail out of the devil. When we entered, marching, into her school, by strictest teaching, surveillance, and order we learned grammar, arithmetic, spelling, reading, writing, and geography; and she, not the teachers, I believe, wrote out the examinations: need I tell you, they were "hard."

She's not the only teacher who has influenced me, but Miss Duling in　7 some fictional shape or form, has stridden into a larger part of my work than I'd realized until now. She emerges in my perhaps inordinate number of schoolteacher characters. I loved those characters in the writing. But I did not, in life, love Miss Duling. I was afraid of her high-arched bony nose, her eyebrows lifted in half-circles above her hooded, brilliant eyes, and of the Kentucky R's in her speech, and the long steps she took in her hightop shoes. I did nothing but fear her bearing-down authority, and did not connect this (as of course we were meant to) with our own need or desire to learn, perhaps because I already had this wish, and did not need to be driven.

She was impervious to lies or foolish excuses or the insufferable plea　8 of not knowing any better. She wasn't going to have any frills, either, at Davis School. When a new governor moved into the mansion, he sent his daughter to Davis School; her name was Lady Rachel Conner. Miss Duling at once called the governor to the telephone and told him, "She'll be plain Rachel here."

Miss Duling dressed as plainly as a Pilgrim on a Thanksgiving poster we made in the schoolroom, in a longish black-and-white checked gingham dress, a bright thick wool sweater the red of a railroad lantern—she'd knitted it herself—black stockings and her narrow elegant feet in black hightop shoes with heels you could hear coming, rhythmical as a parade drum down the hall. Her silky black curly hair was drawn back out of curl, fastened by high combs, and knotted behind. She carried her spectacles on a gold chain hung around her neck. Her gaze was in general sweeping, then suddenly at the point of concentration upon you. With a swing of her bell that took her whole right arm and shoulder, she rang it, militant and impartial, from the head of the front steps of Davis School when it was time for us all to line up, girls on one side, boys on the other. We were to march past her into the school building, while the fourth-grader she nabbed played time on the piano, mostly to a tune we could have skipped to, but we didn't skip into Davis School.

Little recess (open-air exercises) and big recess (lunch-boxes from home opened and eaten on the grass, on the girls' side and the boys' side of the yard) and dismissal were also regulated by Miss Duling's bell. The bell was also used to catch us off guard with fire drill.

It was examinations that drove my wits away, as all emergencies do. Being expected to measure up was paralysing. I failed to make 100 on my spelling exam because I missed one word and that word was "uncle." Mother, as I knew she would, took it personally. "You couldn't spell *uncle*? When you've got those five perfectly splendid uncles in West Virginia? What would *they* say to that?"

It was never that Mother wanted me to beat my classmates in grades; what she wanted was for me to have my answers right. It was unclouded perfection I was up against.

My father was much more tolerant of possible error. He only said, as he steeply and impeccably sharpened my pencils on examination morning, "Now just keep remembering: the examinations were made out for the *average* student to pass. That's the majority. And if the majority can pass, think how much better *you* can do."

I looked to my mother, who had her own opinions about the majority. My father wished to treat it with respect, she didn't. I'd been born left-handed, but the habit was broken when I entered the first grade in Davis School. My father had insisted. He pointed out that everything in life had been made for the convenience of right-handed people, because they were the majority, and he often used "what the majority wants" as a criterion for what was the best. My mother said she could not promise him, could not promise him at all, that I wouldn't stutter as a consequence. Mother had been born left-handed too; her family consisted of five left-handed brothers, a left-handed mother, and a father who could write with both hands at the same time, also backwards and forwards and upside down, different words with each hand. She had been broken of it when she was young, and said she used to stutter.

"But you still stutter," I'd remind her, only to hear her say loftily, "You should have heard me when I was your age." 15

In my childhood days, a great deal of stock was put, in general, in the value of doing well in school. Both daily newspapers in Jackson saw the honor roll as news and published the lists, and the grades, of all the honor students. The city fathers gave the children who made the honor roll free season tickets to the baseball games down at the grandstand. We all attended and all worshiped some player on the Jackson Senators: I offered up my 100's in arithmetic and spelling, reading and writing, attendance and, yes, deportment—I must have been a prig!—to Red McDermott, the third baseman. And our happiness matched that of knowing Miss Duling was on her summer vacation, far, far away in Kentucky. 16

Questions for Study and Discussion

1. What overriding characteristics did Miss Duling possess? How does Welty inform us of those qualities? Did Welty fear or love her as a child, or have yet another emotional response to her?

2. What functions did Miss Duling's bell serve? What did the bell come to symbolize?

3. How did Welty's parents differ in their attitudes toward her performance in school?

4. What message did Miss Duling send to the legislators when she proposed the spelling match between them and her students?

5. Why does Welty think that Miss Duling's authoritarian approach was superfluous in her case?

Writing Topics

1. In paragraph 7, Welty discusses Miss Duling, and others like her, as "schoolteacher characters," those you might like in writing but not in life. What does Welty mean? Think about the teachers you have had. Were any of them "schoolteacher characters"? What made them so? Write an essay in which you reflect on the teachers you have had, the ones you have always liked or disliked and the ones you liked when you had them but later thought less well of, as well as those you initially hated but later grew to appreciate. If your attitude toward your teachers has changed, what are the reasons for the change? What do you realize now that you did not then? What lessons do you see in your remembrances of your teachers?

2. In an essay, describe the qualities that would make an ideal teacher for you. Is the role of a teacher to act as an authority figure, source of encouragement, coach, taskmaster, or model? Should a teacher combine all these roles and more? Are there conflicting qualities in a good teacher? In your opinion, what is the relative importance of a teacher's personality and his or her grasp of the subject matter? Why might you like to be a teacher? Why would you not like to be a teacher?

LANGSTON HUGHES

Born in Joplin, Missouri, Langston Hughes (1902–1967) wrote poetry, fiction, and drama and regularly contributed a column to the *New York Post*. An important figure in the Harlem Renaissance, he is best known for *The Weary Blues* (1926), *Shakespeare in Harlem* (1942), and *Ask Your Mama* (1961), volumes of poetry that reflect his racial pride, his familiarity with the traditions of African-Americans, and his knowledge of jazz rhythms. The speaker of "Theme for English B" is a student at Columbia University, where Hughes had enrolled for a year in 1921. The poem, although quite short, embodies the two great themes of Hughes's work and indeed of the Harlem Renaissance: the celebration of African-American culture and the demand for equal treatment and respect.

Theme for English B

The instructor said,

    Go home and write
    a page tonight:
    And let that page come out of you—
    Then, it will be true.   5

I wonder if it's that simple?
I am twenty-two, colored, born in Winston-Salem.
I went to school there, then Durham, then here
to this college on the hill above Harlem.[1]
I am the only colored student in my class.   10

The steps from the hill lead down into Harlem,
through a park, then I cross St. Nicholas,
Eighth Avenue, Seventh, and I come to the Y,
the Harlem Branch Y, wherre I take the elevator
up to my room, sit down, and write this page: 15

---

[1]Refers to Columbia University, which is located next to Harlem.

It's not easy to know what is true for you or me
at twenty-two, my age. But I guess I'm what
I feel and see and hear, Harlem, I hear you:
hear you, hear me—we two—you, me, talk on this page.
(I hear New York, too.) Me—who?   20

Well, I like to eat, sleep, drink, and be in love.
I like to work, read, learn, and understand life.
I like a pipe for a Christmas present,
or records—Bessie,² bop, or Bach.
I guess being colored doesn't make me *not* like   25
the same things other folks like who are other races.
So will my page be colored that I write?
Being me, it will not be white.
But it will be
a part of you, instructor.   30
You are white—
yet a part of me, as I am a part of you.
That's American.
Sometimes perhaps you don't want to be a part of me.
Nor do I often want to be a part of you.   35
But we are, that's true!
As I learn from you,
I guess you learn from me—
although you're older—and white—
and somewhat more free.   40

This is my page for English B.

Questions for Study and Discussion

1. What does the instructor mean when he tells the student that the writing should "come out of you"? Why would it then be "true"?
2. Is the student in the poem Hughes himself? What in the poem led you to your conclusion?
3. What is the significance of the student's speaking of Columbia as "on the hill above Harlem"?
4. The student says that he is a part of his instructor and that his instructor is a part of him. What does he mean? Are we all part of each other? If so, in what way? If not, why not?

---

²Bessie Smith (1898?–1937), American blues singer, considered by many critics to be the greatest jazz singer of her time.

5. The student ends by saying, "This is my page for English B." Is the "page" what the instructor asked for or wanted? Why, or why not?

Writing Topics

1. The poem says, "As I learn from you, / I guess you learn from me." What do you think teachers learn from their students, if anything? What should they learn? Write an essay in which you describe what for you is the ideal student–teacher relationship.

2. What constitutes a good writing assignment? Compose one or two essay assignments for your class, keeping in mind the purpose of the course and other students' backgrounds and interests.

JOYCE CAROL OATES

Born in 1938 to a Roman Catholic family in Lockport, New York, Joyce Carol Oates earned a bachelor's degree from Syracuse University and a master of arts degree in English from the University of Wisconsin. She has taught English, first at the University of Detroit and then at the University of Windsor in Ontario, Canada. Since 1978 Oates has been teaching at Princeton University. A prodigious and versatile writer, Oates has published twenty-two novels, including *them* (a National Book Award winner in 1969), *Bellefleur* (1980), *Solstice* (1985), and *I Lock My Door Upon Myself* (1990); eighteen collections of short stories; eight books of poems; a collection of plays; and five volumes of nonfiction. "In the Region of Ice" is from her third collection of stories, *The Wheel of Love* (1970). In it, Sister Irene, a nun and a professor of literature at a Jesuit university, struggles to be true to her vocation when she is confronted by a searching and troubled student.

In the Region of Ice

Sister Irene was a tall, deft woman in her early thirties. What one could see of her face made a striking impression—serious, hard gray eyes, a long slender nose, a face waxen with thought. Seen at the right time, from the right angle, she was almost handsome. In her past teaching positions she had drawn a little upon the fact of her being young and brilliant and also a nun, but she was beginning to grow out of that.

This was a new university and an entirely new world. She had heard—of course it was true—that the Jesuit administration of this school had hired her at the last moment to save money and to head off the appointment of a man of dubious religious commitment. She had prayed for the necessary energy to get her through this first semester. She had no trouble with teaching itself; once she stood before a classroom she felt herself capable of anything. It was the world immediately outside the classroom that confused and alarmed her, though she let none of this show—the cynicism of her colleagues, the indifference of many of the students, and, above all, the looks she got that told her nothing much would be expected of her because she was a nun. This took energy, strength. At times she had the idea that she was on trial and that the excuses she made to herself about her discomfort were only the common

excuses made by guilty people. But in front of a class she had no time to
worry about herself or the conflicts in her mind. She became, once and for
all, a figure existing only for the benefit of others, an instrument by which
facts were communicated.

About two weeks after the semester began, Sister Irene noticed a new 3
student in her class. He was slight and fair-haired, and his face was blank,
but not blank by accident, blank on purpose, suppressed and restricted into a
dumbness that looked hysterical. She was prepared for him before he raised
his hand, and when she saw his arm jerk, as if he had at last lost control of it,
she nodded to him without hesitation.

"Sister, how can this be reconciled with Shakespeare's vision in *Ham-* 4
let? How can these opposing views be in the same mind?"

Students glanced at him, mildly surprised. He did not belong in the 5
class, and this was mysterious, but his manner was urgent and blind.

"There is no need to reconcile opposing views," Sister Irene said, 6
leaning forward against the podium. "In one play Shakespeare suggests one
vision, in another play another; the plays are not simultaneous creations,
and even if they were, we never demand a logical—"

"We must demand a logical consistency," the young man said. "The 7
idea of education is itself predicated upon consistency, order, sanity—"

He had interrupted her, and she hardened her face against him—for 8
his sake, not her own, since she did not really care. But he noticed nothing.
"Please see me after class," she said.

After class the young man hurried up to her. 9

"Sister Irene, I hope you didn't mind my visiting today. I'd heard some 10
things, interesting things," he said. He stared at her, and something in her
face allowed him to smile. "I . . . could we we talk in your office? Do you
have time?"

They walked down to her office. Sister Irene sat at her desk, and the 11
young man sat facing her; for a moment they were self-conscious and silent.

"Well, I suppose you know—I'm a Jew," he said. 12

Sister Irene stared at him. "Yes?" she said. 13

"What am I doing at a Catholic university, huh?" He grinned. "That's 14
what you want to know."

She made a vague movement of her hand to show that she had no 15
thoughts on this, nothing at all, but he seemed not to catch it. He was
sitting on the edge of the straight-backed chair. She saw that he was young
but did not really look young. There were harsh lines on either side of his
mouth, as if he had misused that youthful mouth somehow. His skin was
almost as pale as hers, his eyes were dark and not quite in focus. He looked at
her and through her and around her, as his voice surrounded them both. His
voice was a little shrill at times.

"Listen, I did the right thing today—visiting your class! God, what a 16
lucky accident it was; some jerk mentioned you, said you were a good

teacher—I thought, what a laugh! These people know about good teachers here? But yes, listen, yes, I'm not kidding—you are good. I mean that."

Sister Irene frowned. "I don't quite understand what all this means." 17

He smiled and waved aside her formality, as if he knew better. "Listen, 18 I got my B.A. at Columbia, then I came back here to this crappy city. I mean, I did it on purpose, I wanted to come back. I wanted to. I have my reasons for doing things. I'm on a three-thousand-dollar fellowship," he said, and waited for that to impress her. "You know, I could have gone almost anywhere with that fellowship, and I came back home here—my home's in the city—and enrolled here. This was last year. This is my second year. I'm working on a thesis, I mean I was, my master's thesis—but the hell with that. What I want to ask you is this: Can I enroll in your class, is it too late? We have to get special permission if we're late."

Sister Irene felt something nudging her, some uneasiness in him that was 19 pleading with her not to be offended by his abrupt, familiar manner. He seemed to be promising another self, a better self, as if his fair, childish, almost cherubic face were doing tricks to distract her from what his words said.

"Are you in English studies?" she asked. 20

"I was in history. Listen," he said, and his mouth did something odd, 21 drawing itself down into a smile that made the lines about it deepen like knives, "listen, they kicked me out."

He sat back, watching her. He crossed his legs. He took out a package 22 of cigarettes and offered her one. Sister Irene shook her head, staring at his hands. They were small and stubby and might have belonged to a ten-year-old, and the nails were a strange near-violet color. It took him awhile to extract a cigarette.

"Yeah, kicked me out. What do you think of that?" 23

"I don't understand." 24

"My master's thesis was coming along beautifully, and then this 25 bastard—I mean, excuse me, this professor, I won't pollute your office with his name—he started making criticisms, he said some things were unacceptable, he—" The boy leaned forward and hunched his narrow shoulders in a parody of secrecy. "We had an argument. I told him some frank things, things only a broad-minded person could hear about himself. That takes courage, right? He didn't have it! He kicked me out of the master's program, so now I'm coming into English. Literature is greater than history; European history is one big pile of garbage. Sky-high. Filth and rotting corpses, right? Aristotle says that poetry is higher than history; he's right; in your class today I suddenly realized that this is my field, Shakespeare, only Shakespeare is—"

Sister Irene guessed that he was going to say that only Shakespeare was 26 equal to him, and she caught the moment of recognition and hesitation, the half-raised arm, the keen, frowning forehead, the narrowed eyes; then he thought better of it and did not end the sentence. "The students in your class are mainly negligible, I can tell you that. You're new here, and I've been here a year—I would have finished my studies last year but my father got sick, he was hospitalized, I couldn't take exams and it was a mess—but I'll make it through English in one year or drop dead. I can do it, I can do anything. I'll take six courses at once—" He broke off, breathless. Sister Irene tried to smile. "All right then, it's settled? You'll let me in? Have I missed anything so far?"

He had no idea of the rudeness of his question. Sister Irene, feeling suddenly exhausted, said, "I'll give you a syllabus of the course."   27

"Fine! Wonderful!"   28

He got to his feet eagerly. He looked through the schedule, muttering to himself, making favorable noises. It struck Sister Irene that she was making a mistake to let him in. There were these moments when one had to make an intelligent decision. . . . But she was sympathetic with him, yes. She was sympathetic with something about him.   29

She found out his name the next day: Allen Weinstein.   30

After this she came to her Shakespeare class with a sense of excite- ment. It became clear to her at once that Weinstein was the most intelligent student in the class. Until he had enrolled, she had not understood what was lacking, a mind that could appreciate her own. Within a week his jagged, protean mind had alienated the other students, and though he sat in the center of the class, he seemed totally alone, encased by a miniature world of his own. When he spoke of the "frenetic humanism of the High Renais- sance," Sister Irene dreaded the raised eyebrows and mocking smiles of the other students, who no longer bothered to look at Weinstein. She wanted to defend him, but she never did, because there was something rude and dismal about his knowledge; he used it like a weapon, talking passionately of Nietzsche and Goethe and Freud until Sister Irene would be forced to close discussion.   31

In meditation, alone, she often thought of him. When she tried to talk about him to a young nun, Sister Carlotta, everything sounded gross. "But no, he's an excellent student," she insisted. "I'm very grateful to have him in class. It's just that . . . he thinks ideas are real." Sister Carlotta, who loved literature also, had been forced to teach grade-school arithmetic for the last four years. That might have been why she said, a little sharply, "You don't think ideas are real?"   32

Sister Irene acquiesced with a smile, but of course she did not think so: only reality is real.   33

When Weinstein did not show up for class on the day the first paper was due, Sister Irene's heart sank, and the sensation was somehow a familiar one. She began to lecture and kept waiting for the door to open and for him to hurry noisily back to his seat, grinning an apology toward her—but nothing happened.   34

If she had been deceived by him, she made herself think angrily, it was as a teacher and not as a woman. He had promised her nothing.   35

Weinstein appeared the next day near the steps of the liberal arts   36
building. She heard someone running behind her, a breathless exclamation:
"Sister Irene!" She turned and saw him, panting and grinning in embarrassment. He wore a dark-blue suit with a necktie, and he looked, despite his
childish face, like a little old man; there was something oddly precarious and
fragile about him. "Sister Irene, I owe you an apology, right?" He raised his
eyebrows and smiled a sad, forlorn, yet irritatingly conspiratorial smile. "The
first paper—not in on time, and I know what your rules are. . . . You won't
accept late papers, I know—that's good discipline, I'll do that when I teach
too. But, unavoidably, I was unable to come to school yesterday. There are
many—many—" He gulped for breath, and Sister Irene had the startling
sense of seeing the real Weinstein stare out at her, a terrified prisoner behind
the confident voice. "There are many complications in family life. Perhaps
you are unaware—I mean—"

She did not like him, but she felt this sympathy, something tugging and   37
nagging at her the way her parents had competed for her love so many years
before. They had been whining, weak people, and out of their wet need for
affection, the girl she had been (her name was Yvonne) had emerged
stronger than either of them, contemptuous of tears because she had seen so
many. But Weinstein was different; he was not simply weak—perhaps he was
not weak at all—but his strength was confused and hysterical. She felt her
customary rigidity as a teacher begin to falter. "You may turn your paper in
today if you have it," she said, frowning.

Weinstein's mouth jerked into an incredulous grin. "Wonderful! Marve-   38
lous!" he said. "You are very understanding, Sister Irene, I must say. I must
say . . . I didn't expect, really . . ." He was fumbling in a shabby old briefcase for the paper. Sister Irene waited. She was prepared for another of his
excuses, certain that he did not have the paper, when he suddenly straightened up and handed her something. "Here! I took the liberty of writing
thirty pages instead of just fifteen," he said. He was obviously quite excited;
his cheeks were mottled pink and white. "You may disagree violently with
my interpretation—I expect you to, in fact I'm counting on it—but let me
warn you, I have the exact proof, right here in the play itself!" He was
thumping at a book, his voice growing louder and shriller. Sister Irene,
startled, wanted to put her hand over his mouth and soothe him.

"Look," he said breathlessly, "may I talk with you? I have a class now I   39
hate, I loathe, I can't bear to sit through! Can I talk with you instead?"

Because she was nervous, she stared at the title page of the paper: 40
" 'Erotic Melodies in *Romeo and Juliet*' by Allen Weinstein, Jr."

"All right?" he said. "Can we walk around here? Is it all right? I've been   41
anxious to talk with you about some things you said in class."

She was reluctant, but he seemed not to notice. They walked slowly   42
along the shaped campus paths. Weinstein did all the talking, of course, and
Sister Irene recognized nothing in his cascade of words that she had men-

tioned in class. "The humanist must be committed to the totality of life," he said passionately. "This is the failing one finds everywhere in the academic world! I found it in New York and I found it here and I'm no ingénue, I don't go around with my mouth hanging open—I'm experienced, look, I've been to Europe, I've lived in Rome! I went everywhere in Europe except Germany, I don't talk about Germany . . . Sister Irene, think of the significant men in the last century, the men who've changed the world! Jews, right? Marx, Freud, Einstein! Not that I believe Marx, Marx is a madman . . . and Freud, no, my sympathies are with spiritual humanism. I believe that the Jewish race is the exclusive . . . the exclusive, what's the word, the exclusive means by which humanism will be extended . . . Humanism begins by excluding the Jew, and now," he said with a high, surprised laugh, "the Jew will perfect it. After the Nazis, only the Jew is authorized to understand humanism, its limitations and its possibilities. So, I say that the humanist is committed to life in its totality and not just to his profession! The religious person is totally religious, he is his religion! What else? I recognize in you a humanist and a religious person—"

But he did not seem to be talking to her or even looking at her.   43

"Here, read this," he said. "I wrote it last night." It was a long free-   44
verse poem, typed on a typewriter whose ribbon was worn out.

"There's this trouble with my father, a wonderful man, a lovely man,   45
but his health—his strength is fading, do you see? What must it be to him to see his son growing up? I mean, I'm a man now, he's getting old, weak, his health is bad—it's hell, right? I sympathize with him. I'd do anything for him, I'd cut open my veins, anything for a father—right? That's why I wasn't in school yesterday," he said, and his voice dropped for the last sentence, as if he had been dragged back to earth by a fact.

Sister Irene tried to read the poem, then pretended to read it. A jumble   46
of words dealing with "life" and "death" and "darkness" and "love." "What do you think?" Weinstein said nervously, trying to read it over her shoulder and crowding against her.

"It's very . . . passionate," Sister Irene said.   47

This was the right comment; he took the poem back from her in   48
silence, his face flushed with excitement. "Here, at this school, I have few people to talk with. I haven't shown anyone else that poem." He looked at her with his dark, intense eyes, and Sister Irene felt them focus upon her. She was terrified at what he was trying to do—he was trying to force her into a human relationship.

"Thank you for your paper," she said, turning away.   49

When he came the next day, ten minutes late, he was haughty and   50
disdainful. He had nothing to say and sat with his arms folded. Sister Irene took back with her to the convent a feeling of betrayal and confusion. She had been hurt. It was absurd, and yet—She spent too much time thinking about him, as if he were somehow a kind of crystallization of her own

loneliness; but she had no right to think so much of him. She did not want to think of him or of her loneliness. But Weinstein did so much more than think of his predicament: he embodied it, he acted it out, and that was perhaps why he fascinated her. It was as if he were doing a dance for her, a dance of shame and agony and delight, and so long as he did it, she was safe. She felt embarrassment for him, but also anxiety; she wanted to protect him. When the dean of the graduate school questioned her about Weinstein's work, she insisted that he was an "excellent" student, though she knew the dean had not wanted to hear that.

She prayed for guidance, she spent hours on her devotions, she was 51 closer to her vocation than she had been for some years. Life at the convent became tinged with unreality, a misty distortion that took its tone from the glowering skies of the city at night, identical smokestacks ranged against the clouds and giving to the sky the excrement of the populated and successful earth. This city was not her city, this world was not her world. She felt no pride in knowing this, it was a fact. The little convent was not like an island in the center of this noisy world, but rather a kind of hole or crevice the world did not bother with, something of no interest. The convent's rhythm of life had nothing to do with the world's rhythm, it did not violate or alarm it in any way. Sister Irene tried to draw together the fragments of her life and synthesize them somehow in her vocation as a nun: she was a nun, she was recognized as a nun and had given herself happily to that life, she had a name, a place, she had dedicated her superior intelligence to the Church, she worked without pay and without expecting gratitude, she had given up pride, she did not think of herself but only of her work and her vocation, she did not think of anything external to these, she saturated herself daily in the knowledge that she was involved in the mystery of Christianity.

A daily terror attended this knowledge, however, for she sensed herself 52 being drawn by that student, that Jewish boy, into a relationship she was not ready for. She wanted to cry out in fear that she was being forced into the role of a Christian, and what did that mean? What could her studies tell her? What could the other nuns tell her? She was alone, no one could help; he was making her into a Christian, and to her that was a mystery, a thing of terror, something others slipped on the way they slipped on their clothes, casually and thoughtlessly, but to her a magnificent and terrifying wonder.

For days she carried Weinstein's paper, marked A, around with her; he 53 did not come to class. One day she checked with the graduate office and was told that Weinstein had called in to say his father was ill and that he would not be able to attend class for a while. "He's strange, I remember him," the secretary said. "He missed all his exams last spring and made a lot of trouble. He was in and out of here every day."

So there was no more of Weinstein for a while, and Sister Irene stopped 54 expecting him to hurry into class. Then, one morning, she found a letter from him in her mailbox.

He had printed it in black ink, very carefully, as if he had not trusted   55
handwriting. The return address was in bold letters that, like his voice, tried to
grab onto her: Birchcrest Manor. Somewhere north of the city. "Dear Sister
Irene," the block letters said, "I am doing well here and have time for reading
and relaxing. The Manor is delightful. My doctor here is an excellent, intelligent man who has time for me, unlike my former doctor. If you have time, you
might drop in on my father, who worries about me too much I think, and
explain to him what my condition is. He doesn't seem to understand. I feel
about this new life the way that boy, what's his name, in *Measure for Measure*,
feels about the prospects of a different life; you remember what he says to his
sister when she visits him in prison, how he is looking forward to an escape
into another world. Perhaps you could *explain* this to my father and he would
stop worrying." The letter ended with his father's name and address, in letters
that were just a little too big. Sister Irene, walking slowly down the corridor as
she read the letter, felt her eyes cloud over with tears. She was cold with fear, it
was something she had never experienced before. She knew what Weinstein
was trying to tell her, and the desperation of his attempt made it all the more
pathetic; he did not deserve this, why did God allow him to suffer so?

She read through Claudio's speech to his sister, in *Measure for Measure*:   56

Ay, but to die, and go we know not where;
To lie in cold obstruction and to rot;
This sensible warm motion to become
A kneaded clod; and the delighted spirit
To bathe in fiery floods, or to reside
In thrilling region of thick-ribbed ice,
To be imprison'd in the viewless winds
And blown with restless violence round about
The pendent world; or to be worse than worst
Of those that lawless and incertain thought
Imagines howling! 'Tis too horrible!
The weariest and most loathed worldly life
That age, ache, penury, and imprisonment
Can lay on nature is a paradise
To what we fear of death.

Sister Irene called the father's number that day. "Allen Weinstein   57
residence, who may I say is calling?" a woman said, bored. "May I speak to
Mr. Weinstein? It's urgent—about his son," Sister Irene said. There was a
pause at the other end. "You want to talk to his mother, maybe?" the woman
said. "His mother? Yes, his mother, then. Please. It's very important."

She talked with this strange, unsuspected woman, a disembodied voice   58
that suggested absolutely no face, and insisted upon going over that afternoon. The woman was nervous, but Sister Irene, who was a university
professor, after all, knew enough to hide her own nervousness. She kept

waiting for the woman to say, "Yes, Allen has mentioned you . . ." but nothing happened.

She persuaded Sister Carlotta to ride over with her. This urgency of 59
hers was something they were all amazed by. They hadn't suspected that the set of her gray eyes could change to this blurred, distracted alarm, this sense of mission that seemed to have come to her from nowhere. Sister Irene drove across the city in the late afternoon traffic, with the high whining noises from residential streets where trees were being sawed down in pieces. She understood now the secret, sweet wildness that Christ must have felt, giving himself for man, dying for the billions of men who would never know of him and never understand the sacrifice. For the first time she approached the realization of that great act. In her troubled mind the city traffic was jumbled and yet oddly coherent, an image of the world that was always out of joint with what was happening in it, its inner history struggling with its external spectacle. This sacrifice of Christ's, so mysterious and legendary now, almost lost in time—it was that by which Christ transcended both God and man at one moment, more than man because of his fate to do what no other man could do, and more than God because no god could suffer as he did. She felt a flicker of something close to madness.

She drove nervously, uncertainly, afraid of missing the street and afraid 60
of finding it too, for while one part of her rushed forward to confront these people who had betrayed their son, another part of her would have liked nothing so much as to be waiting as usual for the summons to dinner, safe in her room. . . . When she found the street and turned onto it, she was in a state of breathless excitement. Here lawns were bright green and marred with only a few leaves, magically clean, and the houses were enormous and pomp- ous, a mixture of styles: ranch houses, colonial houses, French country houses, white-bricked wonders with curving glass and clumps of birch trees somehow encircled by white concrete. Sister Irene stared as if she had blundered into another world. This was a kind of heaven, and she was too shabby for it.

The Weinsteins' house was the strangest one of all: it looked like a 61
small Alpine lodge, with an inverted-V-shaped front entrance. Sister Irene drove up the black-topped driveway and let the car slow to a stop; she told Sister Carlotta she would not be long.

At the door she was met by Weinstein's mother, a small, nervous 62
woman with hands like her son's. "Come in, come in," the woman said. She had once been beautiful, that was clear, but now in missing beauty she was not handsome or even attractive but looked ruined and perplexed, the misshapen swelling of her white-blond professionally set hair like a cap lifting up from her surprised face. "He'll be right in. Allen?" she called, "our visitor is here." They went into the living room. There was a grand piano at one end and an organ at the other. In between were scatterings of brilliant modern furniture in conversational groups, and several puffed-up white rugs on the polished floor. Sister Irene could not stop shivering.

"Professor, it's so strange, but let me say when the phone rang I had a 63
feeling—I had a feeling," the woman said, with damp eyes. Sister Irene sat,
and the woman hovered about her. "Should I call you Professor? We
don't . . . you know . . . we don't understand the technicalities that go
with—Allen, my son, wanted to go here to the Catholic school; I told my
husband why not? Why fight? It's the thing these days, they do anything
they want for knowledge. And he had to come home, you know. He couldn't
take care of himself in New York, that was the beginning of the trouble. . . .
Should I call you Professor?"

"You can call me Sister Irene." 64

"Sister Irene?" the woman said, touching her throat in awe, as if 65
something intimate and unexpected had happened.

Then Weinstein's father appeared, hurrying. He took long, impatient 66
strides. Sister Irene stared at him and in that instant doubted everything—
he was in his fifties, a tall, sharply handsome man, heavy but not fat, holding
his shoulders back with what looked like an effort, but holding them back
just the same. He wore a dark suit and his face was flushed, as if he had run a
long distance.

"Now," he said, coming to Sister Irene and with a precise wave of his 67
hand motioning his wife off, "now, let's straighten this out. A lot of confusion over that kid, eh?" He pulled a chair over, scraping it across a rug and
pulling one corner over, so that its brown underside was exposed. "I came
home early just for this, Libby phoned me. Sister, you got a letter from him,
right?"

The wife looked at Sister Irene over her husband's head as if trying 68
somehow to coach her, knowing that this man was so loud and impatient
that no one could remember anything in his presence.

"A letter—yes—today—" 69

"He says what in it? You got the letter, eh? Can I see it?" 70

She gave it to him and wanted to explain, but he silenced her with a 71
flick of his hand. He read through the letter so quickly that Sister Irene
thought perhaps he was trying to impress her with his skill at reading. "So?"
he said, raising his eyes, smiling, "so what is this? He's happy out there, he
says. He doesn't communicate with us any more, but he writes to you and
says he's happy—what's that? I mean, what the hell is that?"

"But he isn't happy. He wants to come home," Sister Irene said. It was 72
so important that she make him understand that she could not trust her
voice; goaded by this man, it might suddenly turn shrill, as his son's did.
"Someone must read their letters before they're mailed, so he tried to tell me
something by making an allusion to—"

"What?" 73

"—an allusion to a play, so that I would know. He may be thinking 74
suicide, he must be very unhappy—"

She ran out of breath. Weinstein's mother had begun to cry, but the 75 father was shaking his head jerkily back and forth. "Forgive me, Sister, but it's a lot of crap, he needs the hospital, he needs help—right? It costs me fifty a day out there, and they've got the best place in the state, I figure it's worth it. He needs help, that kid, what do I care if he's unhappy? He's unbalanced!" he said angrily. "You want us to get him out again? We argued with the judge for two hours to get him in, an acquaintance of mine. Look, he can't control himself—he was smashing things here, he was hysterical. They need help, lady, and you do something about it fast! You do something! We made up our minds to do something and we did it! This letter—what the hell is this letter? He never talked like that to us!"

"But he means the opposite of what he says—"   76

"Then he's crazy! I'm the first to admit it." He was perspiring and his   77
face had darkened. "I've got no pride left this late. He's a little bastard, you want to know? He calls me names, he's filthy, got a filthy mouth—that's being smart, huh? They give him a big scholarship for his filthy mouth? I went to college too, and I got out and knew something, and I for Christ's sake did something with it; my wife is an intelligent woman, a learned woman, would you guess she does book reviews for the little newspaper out here? Intelligent isn't crazy—crazy isn't intelligent. Maybe for you at the school he writes nice papers and gets an A, but out here, around the house, he can't control himself, and we got him committed!"

"But—"   78

"We're fixing him up, don't worry about it!" He turned to his wife.   79
"Libby, get out of here, I mean it. I'm sorry, but get out of here, you're making a fool of yourself, go stand in the kitchen or something, you and the goddamn maid can cry on each other's shoulders. That one in the kitchen is nuts too, they're all nuts. Sister," he said, his voice lowering, "I thank you immensely for coming out here. This is wonderful, your interest in my son. And I see he admires you—that letter there. But what about that letter? If he did want to get out, which I don't admit—he was willing to be committed, in the end he said okay himself—if he wanted out I wouldn't do it. Why? So what if he wants to come back? The next day he wants something else, what then? He's a sick kid, and I'm the first to admit it."

Sister Irene felt that sickness spread to her. She stood. The room was so   80
big it seemed it must be a public place; there had been nothing personal or private about their conversation. Weinstein's mother was standing by the fireplace, sobbing. The father jumped to his feet and wiped his forehead in a gesture that was meant to help Sister Irene on her way out. "God, what a day," he said, his eyes snatching at hers for understanding, "you know—one of those days all day long? Sister, I thank you a lot. There should be more people in the world who care about others, like you. I mean that."

On the way back to the convent, the man's words returned to her, and   81
she could not get control of them; she could not even feel anger. She had

been pressed down, forced back, what could she do? Weinstein might have been watching her somehow from a barred window, and he surely would have understood. The strange idea she had had on the way over, something about understanding Christ, came back to her now and sickened her. But the sickness was small. It could be contained.

About a month after her visit to his father, Weinstein himself showed 82
up. He was dressed in a suit as before, even the necktie was the same. He came right into her office as if he had been pushed and could not stop.

"Sister," he said, and shook her hand. He must have seen fear in her 83
because he smiled ironically. "Look, I'm released. I'm let out of the nut house. Can I sit down?"

He sat. Sister Irene was breathing quickly, as if in the presence of an 84
enemy who does not know he is an enemy.

"So, they finally let me out. I heard what you did. You talked with him, 85
that was all I wanted. You're the only one who gave a damn. Because you're a humanist and a religious person, you respect . . . the individual. Listen," he said, whispering, "it was hell out there! Hell Birchcrest Manor! All fixed up with fancy chairs and *Life* magazines lying around—and what do they do to you? They locked me up, they gave me shock treatments! Shock treatments, how do you like that, it's discredited by everybody now—they're crazy out there themselves, sadists. They locked me up, they gave me hypodermic shots, they didn't treat me like a human being! Do you know what that is," Weinstein demanded savagely, "not to be treated like a human being? They made me an animal—for fifty dollars a day! Dirty filthy swine! Now I'm an outpatient because I stopped swearing at them. I found somebody's bobby pin, and when I wanted to scream I pressed it under my fingernail and it stopped me—the screaming went inside and not out—so they gave me good reports, those sick bastards. Now I'm an outpatient and I can walk along the street and breathe in the same filthy exhaust from the buses like all you normal people! Christ," he said, and threw himself back against the chair.

Sister Irene stared at him. She wanted to take his hand, to make some 86
gesture that would close the aching distance between them. "Mr. Weinstein—"

"Call me Allen!" he said sharply. 87
"I'm very sorry—I'm terribly sorry—" 88
"My own parents committed me, but of course they didn't know what it 89
was like. It was hell," he said thickly, "and there isn't any hell except what other people do to you. The psychiatrist out there, the main shrink, he hates Jews too, some of us were positive of that, and he's got a bigger nose than I do, a real beak." He made a noise of disgust. "A dirty bastard, a sick, dirty, pathetic bastard—all of them. Anyway, I'm getting out of here, and I came to ask you a favor."

"What do you mean?" 90

"I'm getting out. I'm leaving. I'm going up to Canada and lose myself.   91
I'll get a job, I'll forget everything, I'll kill myself maybe—what's the difference? Look, can you lend me some money?"

"Money?"   92

"Just a little! I have to get to the border, I'm going to take a bus."   93

"But I don't have any money—"   94

"No money?" He stared at her. "You mean—you don't have any? Sure   95
you have some!"

She stared at him as if he had asked her to do something obscene.   96
Everything was splotched and uncertain before her eyes.

"You must . . . you must go back," she said, "you're making a—"   97

"I'll pay it back. Look, I'll pay it back, can you go to where you live or   98
something and get it? I'm in a hurry. My friends are sons of bitches: one of
them pretended he didn't see me yesterday—I stood right in the middle of
the sidewalk and yelled at him, I called him some appropriate names! So he
didn't see me, huh? You're the only one who understands me, you understand me like a poet, you—"

"I can't help you, I'm sorry—I . . ."   99

He looked to one side of her and flashed his gaze back, as if he could   100
control it. He seemed to be trying to clear his vision.

"You have the soul of a poet," he whispered, "you're the only one.   101
Everybody else is rotten! Can't you lend me some money, ten dollars maybe?
I have three thousand in the bank, and I can't touch it! They take everything away from me, they make me into an animal. . . . You know I'm not
an animal, don't you? Don't you?"

"Of course," Sister Irene whispered.   102

"You could get money. Help me. Give me your hand or something,   103
touch me, help me—please. . . ." He reached for her hand and she drew
back. He stared at her and his face seemed about to crumble, like a child's. "I
want something from you, but I don't know what—I want something!" he
cried. "Something real! I want you to look at me like I was a human being, is
that too much to ask? I have a brain, I'm alive, I'm suffering—what does
that mean? Does that mean nothing? I want something real and not this
phony Christian love garbage—it's all in the books, it isn't personal—I want
something real—look. . . ."

He tried to take her hand again, and this time she jerked away. She got   104
to her feet. "Mr. Weinstein," she said, "please—"

"You! You nun!" he said scornfully, his mouth twisted into a mock grin.   105
"You nun! There's nothing under that ugly outfit, right? And you're not
particularly smart even though you think you are; my father has more brains
in his foot than you—"

He got to his feet and kicked the chair.   106

"You bitch!" he cried.   107

She shrank back against her desk as if she thought he might hit her, but   108
he only ran out of the office.

Weinstein: the name was to become disembodied from the figure, as   109
time went on. The semester passed, the autumn drizzle turned into snow,
Sister Irene rode to school in the morning and left in the afternoon, four days
a week, anonymous in her black winter cloak, quiet and stunned. University
teaching was an anonymous task, each day dissociated from the rest, with no
necessary sense of unity among the teachers: they came and went separately
and might for a year just miss a colleague who left his office five minutes
before they arrived, and it did not matter.

She heard of Weinstein's death, his suicide by drowning, from the   110
English Department secretary, a handsome white-haired woman who kept a
transistor radio on her desk. Sister Irene was not surprised; she had been
thinking of him as dead for months. "They identified him by some special
television way they have now," the secretary said. "They're shipping the
body back. It was up in Quebec. . . ."

Sister Irene could feel a part of herself drifting off, lured by the plains of   111
white snow to the north, the quiet, the emptiness, the sweep of the Great
Lakes up to the silence of Canada. But she called that part of herself back.
She could only be one person in her lifetime. That was the ugly truth, she
thought, that she could not really regret Weinstein's suffering and death; she
had only one life and had already given it to someone else. He had come too
late to her. Fifteen years ago, perhaps, but not now.

She was only one person, she thought, walking down the corridor in a   112
dream. Was she safe in this single person, or was she trapped? She had only
one identity. She could make only one choice. What she had done or hadn't
done was the result of that choice, and how was she guilty? If she could have
felt guilt, she thought, she might at least have been able to feel something.

Questions for Study and Discussion

 1. How does Sister Irene view her responsibilities as a teacher? as a nun?
In paragraph 51, she refers to her vocation; what exactly is that vocation?

 2. What profession is Allen preparing for? What does he say that suggests
why he might be attracted to that profession? In your opinion, does he seem
suited for it? Why, or why not?

 3. Does Oates make it clear whether Allen is really insane? If so, where?
How does this knowledge affect your reading of the story?

 4. What do you learn about Allen and the source of his disturbance from
Sister Irene's visit to his family? How does what we know of Sister Irene's own
upbringing help to explain her attitudes and behavior?

5. Why does Sister Irene think that Allen is "making her into a Christian"? Why is it a "terrifying wonder" for her to assume the role of a Christian?

6. Sister Irene says of Allen that he thinks ideas are real, but she thinks that only reality is real. What is the issue here? For example, what does it mean to speak of *ideas* that change the world?

7. Where does Oates draw the title of the story from? What does the title contribute to your understanding of the story?

8. What is the meaning of the last paragraph of the story?

Writing Topics

1. Sister Irene believes that teachers exist "only for the benefit of others" and that she is "an instrument by which facts [are] communicated." Allen, on the other hand, claims that humanists, including academics, must be "committed to life in its totality and not just to [their] profession." What can you say in support of each view? Can the two views be reconciled? Write an essay in which you present your conclusions.

2. Write an essay in which you explain how your attitudes toward school and your classmates relate to your ambitions and your view of life.

3. Read Willa Cather's story "Paul's Case" (pp. 164–79). What similarities do you see between Paul and Allen? What differences? What do the respective stories have to say about the nature and purpose of education? Write an essay in which you compare and contrast the students in these two stories.

Campus Issues
of the 1990s

BRUCE WEBER

Born in 1953, Bruce Weber is an editor of *The New York Times Magazine* and is the author of many magazine and newspaper articles on writers, sports personalities, and contemporary social life. In 1986 he edited *Look Who's Talking: An Anthology of Modern American Short Stories.*

In "The Unromantic Generation," which appeared in the April 5, 1987, issue of *The New York Times Magazine,* Weber discusses the ways in which logic has triumphed over passion in modern times.

The Unromantic Generation

Here is a contemporary love story.   1

Twenty-four-year-old Clark Wolfsberger, a native of St. Louis, and Kim   2
Wright, twenty-five, who is from Chicago, live in Dallas. They've been
going together since they met as students at Southern Methodist University
three years ago. They are an attractive pair, trim and athletic, she dark and
lissome, he broad-shouldered and square-jawed. They have jobs they took
immediately after graduating—Clark works at Talent Sports International, a
sports marketing and management company; Kim is an assistant account
executive at Tracy-Locke, a large advertising agency—and they are in love.

"We're very compatible," she says.   3

"We don't need much time together to confirm our relationship," he says.   4

When they speak about the future, they hit the two-career family notes   5
that are conventional now in the generations ahead of them. "At thirty, I'll
probably be married and planning a family," says Kim. "I'll stay in advertising. I'll be a late parent."

"By thirty, I'll definitely be married; either that or water-skiing naked   6
in Monaco," Clark says and laughs. "No. I'll be married. Well-established in
my line of work. Have the home, have the dog. Maybe not a kid yet, but
eventually. I'm definitely in favor of kids."

In the month I spent last winter visiting several cities around the 7
country, interviewing recent college graduates about marriage, relationships, modern romance I heard a lot of this, life equations already written,
doubt banished. I undertook the trip because of the impression so many of
us have; that in one wavelike rush to business school and Wall Street,
young Americans have succumbed to a culture of immediate gratification
and gone deep-down elitist on us. I set out to test the image with an
informal survey meant to take the emotional temperature of a generation,
not far behind my own, that *seems* so cynical, so full of such "material" girls
and boys.

The sixty or so people I interviewed, between the ages of twenty-two 8
and twenty-six, were a diverse group. They spoke in distinct voices, testify-
ing to a range of political and social views. Graduate students, lawyers,
teachers, entertainers, business people, they are pursuing a variety of interests. What they have in common is that they graduated from college, are
living in or around an urban center, and are heterosexual, mirrors of myself
when I graduated from college in 1975. And yet as I moved from place to
place, beginning with acquaintances of my friends and then randomly pursuing an expanding network of names and phone numbers, another quality
emerged to the degree that I'd call it characteristic: they are planners. It was
the one thing that surprised me, this looking ahead with certainty. They
have priorities. I'd ask about love, they'd give me a graph.

This isn't how I remember it. Twelve years ago, who knew? I was three 9
years away from my first full-time paycheck, six from anything resembling
the job I have now. It was all sort of desultory and hopeful, a time of dabbling
and waiting around for some event that would sprout a future. Frankly, I had
it in mind that meeting a woman would do it.

My cultural prototype was Benjamin Braddock, the character played by 10
Dustin Hoffman in Mike Nichols' 1967 film *The Graduate*, who, returning
home after his college triumphs, finds the prospect of life after campus
daunting in the extreme, and so plunges into inertia. His refrain "I'm just a
little worried about my future," served me nicely as a sort of wryly under-
stated mantra.

What hauls Benjamin from his torpor is love. Wisely or not, he re- 11
sponds to a force beyond logic and turns the world upside down for Elaine
Robinson. And though in the end their future together is undetermined, the
message of the movie is that love is meant to triumph, that its passion and
promise, however naïve, are its strength, and that if we are lucky it will seize
us and transform our lives.

Today I'm still single and, chastened by that, I suppose, a little more 12
rational about what to expect from love. Setting out on my trip, I felt as if I'd
be plumbing a little of my past. But the people I spoke with reminded me
more of the way I am now than the way I was then. I returned thinking that
young people are older than they used to be, *The Graduate* is out of date, and

for young people just out of college today, the belief that love is all you need no longer obtains.

"Kim's a great girl; I love her," Clark Wolfsberger says. "But she's very 13 career-oriented. I am, too, and with our schedules the way they are, we haven't put any restrictions on each other. I think that's healthy."

"He might want to go back to St. Louis," Kim Wright says. "I want to 14 go back to Chicago. If it works out, great. If not, that's fine, too. I can handle it either way."

They are not heartless, soulless, cold, or unimaginative. They *are* self- 15 preoccupied, but that's a quality, it seems to me, for which youthful generations have always been known. What distinguishes this generation from mine, I think, is that they're aware of it. News-conscious, media-smart, they are sophisticated in a way I was not.

They have come of age, of course, at a time when American social 16 traditions barely survive. Since 1975, there have been more than a million divorces annually, and it is well publicized that nearly half of all marriages now end in divorce. Yet the era of condoned casual promiscuity and sexual experimentation—itself once an undermining of the nation's social fabric— now seems to be drawing to a close with the ever-spreading plague of sexually transmitted disease.

The achievements of feminist activism—particularly the infusion of 17 women into the work force—have altered the expectations that the sexes have for each other and themselves.

And finally, the new college graduates have been weaned on scarifying 18 forecasts of economic gloom. They feel housing problems already; according to *American Demographics* magazine, the proportion of young people living at home with their parents was higher in 1985 than in the last three censuses. They're aware, too, of predictions that however affluent they are themselves, they're probably better off than their children will be.

With all this in mind, today's graduates seem keenly aware that the 19 future is bereft of conventional expectations, that what's ahead is more chaotic than mysterious. I've come to think it ironic that in a youth-minded culture such as ours, one that ostensibly grants greater freedom of choice to young people than it ever has before, those I spoke with seem largely re- strained. Concerned with, if not consumed by, narrowing the options down, getting on track, they are aiming already at a distant comfort and security. I spoke, on my travels, with several college counselors and administrators, and they concur that the immediate concerns of today's graduates are more practical than those of their predecessors. "I talk to them about sex," says Gail Short Hanson, dean of students at George Washington University. "I talk about careers. And marriage, with women, because of the balancing act they have to perform these days. But love? I can't remember the last conver- sation I had about love."

Career-minded, fiercely self-reliant, they responded to me, a single   20
man with a good job, with an odd combination of comradeliness and respect.
When the interviews were over, I fielded a lot of questions about what it's
like to work at *The New York Times*. How did I get my job? Occasionally,
someone would ask about my love life. Considering the subject of our discussions, I was surprised it happened so rarely. When it did, I told them I'd come
reasonably close to marriage once, but it didn't work out. Nobody asked me
why. Nobody asked if I was lonely.

Micah Materre, twenty-five, recently completed an internship at CBS   21
News in Chicago and is looking for a job in broadcast journalism. Like many
of the young people I talked to, she is farsighted in her romantic outlook: "I
went out with a guy last fall. He had a good job as a stockbroker. He was nice
to me. But then he started telling me about his family. And there were
problems. I thought, 'What happens if I fall in love and we get married?
What then?' "

It may be a memory lapse, but I don't recall thinking about marriage   22
much at all until I fell in love. I was twenty-nine; late, that's agreed. But the
point is that for me (and for my generation as a whole, I believe, though you
hate to make a statement like that), marriage loomed only as an outgrowth
of happenstance; you met a person. Today's graduates, however, seem uneasy
with that kind of serendipity. All of the married couples I spoke with are
delighted to be married, but they do say their friends questioned their judgment. "I heard a lot of reasons why I shouldn't do it," one recent bride told
me. "Finally, I just said to myself, 'I feel happier than I've ever felt. Why
should I give this up just because I'm young?' "

Most of them too young to remember the assassination of *either* Ken-   23
nedy, they are old enough to have romantic pasts, to have experienced the
trauma of failure in love. What surprised me was how easily so many of them
accepted it; it seems a little early to be resigned to the idea that things fall
apart. In each interview, I asked about past involvements. Were you ever
serious about anyone? Any marital close calls? And virtually everyone had a
story. But I heard very little about heartbreak or lingering grief. Instead, with
an almost uniform equanimity, they spoke of maturity gained, lessons
learned. It isn't disillusionment exactly, and they *are* too young to be weary;
rather, it sounds like determination.

Twenty-five-year-old Peter Mundy of San Francisco, for example, says   24
that until six months ago he'd had a series of steady girlfriends. "I'm down on
romance," he says. "There's too much pain, too much pressure. There are so
many variables, and you can't tell until you're in the middle of it whether it'll
be positive. It's only in retrospect that you can see how things went wrong.
In the meantime, you end up neglecting other things."

The prevalent notion is that chemistry is untrustworthy; partners need   25 to be up to snuff according to pretty rigorous standards. Ellen Lubin, twenty-six, of Los Angeles, for example, has just gotten engaged to the man she has been living with for two years. When she met him, she says: "I wasn't that attracted to him right away. But there were things about him that made me say, 'That is what I want in a man.' He's bright. He's a go-getter. He was making tons of money at the age of twenty-five. He's well-connected. He was like my mentor in coming to deal with life in the city."

At the end of *The Graduate*, Benjamin Braddock kidnaps his lady love   26
at the altar, an instant after she has sealed her vows to someone else, and they manage to make their escape because Benjamin bolts the church door from the outside with a cross. That was the 1960s, vehement times. When I graduated, we were less obstreperous. Sacraments you could take or leave. And marriage wasn't much of an issue. If we put it off, it wasn't for the sake of symbolism so much as that it didn't seem necessary. In the last few years, I have been to a number of weddings among my contemporaries, people in their thirties, and that impression of us is still with me. What we did was drift toward marriage, arriving at it eventually, and with some surprise. Some of us are still drifting.

Today's graduates have forged a new attitude entirely. In spite of the   27
high divorce rate, many of those I spoke with have marriage in mind. Overwhelmingly, they see it as not only desirable, but inevitable. Because of the odds, they approach it with wariness and pragmatism. More cautious than their parents (for American men in 1985, the median age at the time of their first marriage was 25.5, the highest since the turn of the century; it was 23.3 for women, a record), they are methodical in comparison with me.

Perhaps that explains why I find the way they speak about marriage so   28
unromantic. Men and women tend to couch their views in different terms, but they seem to share the perception that marriage is necessarily restricting. Nonetheless they trust in its rewards, whatever they are. Overall, it doesn't represent the kind of commitment that seems viable without adequate preparation.

"I've been dating someone for a year and a half," says Tom Grossman, a   29
twenty-four-year-old graduate of the University of Texas. "We don't talk about marriage, and frankly I don't think it'll occur." Currently area sales manager in San Antonio for the John H. Harland Company, a check-printing concern, Grossman says he has professional success in mind first. "I want to be really well-off financially, and I don't want that struggle to interfere with the marriage. There are too many other stress factors involved. I want to be able to enjoy myself right away. And I never want to look back and think that if I hadn't gotten married, I could have accomplished more."

Many young women say they responded with some alarm to last year's   30
Newsweek report on the controversial demographic study conducted at Harvard, which concluded that once past thirty, a woman faces rapidly dwin-

dling chances of marrying. At a time when women graduates often feel it incumbent on them to pursue careers, they worry that the possibility of "having it all" is, in fact, remote.

Janie Russell, twenty-five, graduated from the University of North 31 Carolina in 1983, left a serious boyfriend behind, and moved to Los Angeles to pursue a career in the film industry. Working now as a director of production services of New Visions Inc., like many other young women she believes the independence fostered by a career is necessary, not only for her own self-esteem but as a foundation for a future partnership. "I look forward to marriage," she says. "But this is a very selfish time for me. I have to have my career. I have to say to myself, 'I did this on my own.' It makes me feel more interesting than I would otherwise. Of course, what may happen is that I'll look up one day and say, 'O.K., husband, where are you?' and he won't be there."

About halfway through my trip I stopped interviewing married couples 32 because they tended to say similar things. They consider themselves the lucky ones. As twenty-four-year-old Adam Cooper put it, at dinner with his wife, Melanee, also twenty-four, in their Chicago apartment: "The grass is not greener on the other side."

I came away thinking it is as true as ever: all happy families are the 33 same. But the couples I spoke with seemed to me part of a generation other than their own, older even than mine. Calling the Coopers to arrange an interview, I was invited for "a good, home-cooked meal."

The next day, I met Micah Materre, who expressed the prevailing 34 contemporary stance as well as anyone. Outgoing and self-possessed, she gave me a long list of qualities she's looking for in a man: good looks, sense of humor, old-fashioned values, but also professional success, financial promise, and a solid family background. "Why not?" she said. "I deserve the best." But as I was folding up my notebook, she added a plaintive note: "I'll get married, won't I? It's the American way, right?"

Very early on in my sexual experience I was flattered by a woman who 35 told me she ordinarily wouldn't go to bed with men who were under twenty-six. "Until then," she said, "all they're doing when they're with you is congratulating themselves." For whatever reason, she never returned my calls after that night. Not an untypical encounter, all in all. Congratulations to both of us.

We were a lusty, if callow, bunch, not least because we thought we 36 could afford to be. Encouraged by the expansive social mores spawned by the sexual revolution, fortified by the advent of a widespread availability of birth control and fundamentally unaware of germs, we interpreted sex, for our convenience, as pure pleasure shared by "consenting parties." If it feels good, do it. Remember that?

It is an attitude that the current generation inherited and put into 37 practice at any early age. Asked about her circle of friends in Los Angeles, Lesley Bracker, twenty-three, puts it nonchalantly: "Oh, yeah, we were all sexually active as teen-agers. When we were younger, it was considered O.K. to sleep around."

Now, however, they are reconsidering. In general, on this topic, I found them shy. They hesitate to speak openly about their sex lives, are prone to euphemism ("I'm not exactly out there, you know, mingling"), and say they worry about promiscuity only because they have friends who still practice it. According to Laura Kavesh and Cheryl Lavin, who write a column about single life, "Tales from the Front," for the *Chicago Tribune* that is syndicated in some sixty other papers around the country, a letter from a reader about the virtues of virginity generated more supportive mail than anything that has appeared in the column in its two years of existence. I'm not about to say there's a new celibacy among the young, but my impression is that even if they're having twice as much sex as they say they're having, it's not as much as you would think. 38

The AIDS scare, of course, is of primary relevance. "I talk about AIDS on first dates," says Jill Rotenberg, twenty-five, publishing manager of a rare-book company in San Francisco. "I talk about it all the time. I've spoken with the guy I'm dating about taking an AIDS test. Neither one of us is thrilled about condoms. But we use them. The first time we had sex, I was the one who had one in my wallet." 39

Not everyone is so vehement. But seriously or jokingly, in earnest tête-à-tête or idly at dinner parties, they all talk about it. To some, the new concern is merely a source of disappointment. Several of the young people I spoke with express the sense of having been robbed. It's tough to find sex when you want it, tougher than it used to be, is the lament of many, mostly men. As it was put to me at one point, "I wish I'd been born ten years earlier." 40

Jill Rotenberg says she feels betrayed: "I've had one long relationship in my life. He was my first lover, and for a long time my only one. So I feel I've had an untainted past. Now I feel I'm being punished anyway, even though I've been a good girl." 41

"I feel like I'm over the hurdle," says Douglas Ertman, twenty-two, of San Francisco, who got engaged last summer. "I'm really lucky to know that I'll have one sexual partner forever." 42

Most agree that the solution is monogamy, at least on a temporary basis. "It's a coupled-up society," says Alan Forman, twenty-six, a law student of George Washington University who, for the last several months, has been in a monogamous relationship. "Now more than ever. A lot of people I know are feeling the pressure to get hooked up with somebody." 43

I ask Forman and his girlfriend, twenty-four-year-old Debra Golden, about their future together. They say they don't know ("I'm too insecure to make a decision like that," she says), and I get the sense they never talk 44 about it. Then she turns to him, genuinely curious. "Say you break up with me and go to New York next year," she says.

"I don't know," he says. "If I met someone and I like her, what do I 45
have to do, ask her to take a blood test?"

A decade ago, one of the privileges that my contemporaries and I 46
inferred from our sexual freedom was more or less to deny that there might be, in the sexual act, any innately implied emotional exchange. It's no longer feasible, however, to explain away sex as frivolity, inconsequential gratification. And that has complicated things for all of us, of course, whatever age, single or not.

But for young people, it's an issue, like marriage, that has been raised 47
early: what does sex mean, if it doesn't mean nothing?

It's clearly a struggle for them. In one of my first interviews, twenty- 48
five-year-old Karl Wright of Chicago told me: "Maybe there's a silver lining in all this. Maybe AIDS will bring back romance." The more I think about that, the more chilling it gets.

Beverly Caro, a twenty-five-year-old associate in the Dallas law firm of 49
Gardere & Wynne, graduated from Drake University, in Des Moines, in 1983, and attended law school there as well. Her office high above the street looks out on the city's jungle of futuristic skyscrapers. She had offers from firms in Denver and her hometown of Kansas City, Mo., she says, but chose to come to Dallas because, "I see upward mobility here; that's what I was looking for."

Ms. Caro has an attractive, thoughtful manner and a soft voice, but 50
like many of her contemporaries, given the chance to discuss her personal goals, she speaks with a certitude that borders on defiance. Currently, she sees two men "somewhat regularly," she says. "I'd like to have a companion. A friend, I guess. But finding a man is not a top priority. I want to travel. I want to establish myself in the community. I don't see any drastic changes in my life by the time I turn thirty. Except that I'll be a property owner."

During my interviews, the theme of getting on track and staying there 51
surfaced again and again. I came to think of it as the currency of self-definition. As a generation, they are not a particularly well-polled group, but certain figures bear out my impression.

According to annual surveys of 300,000 college freshmen conducted by 52
the Higher Education Research Institute at the Graduate School of Education of the University of California at Los Angeles, young people today, by the time they *enter* college, are more inclined to express concrete life objectives than they've been for many years. Of those surveyed last fall, 73.2 percent cited being "very well off financially" as an essential or very important objective. That's up from 63.3 percent in 1980, 49.5 percent in 1975. Other objectives that the survey shows have risen in importance include "obtain recognition from colleagues for contributions to my special field";

"have administrative responsibility for the work of others"; "be successful in my own business"; and "raise a family." At the same time, the percentage of freshmen who consider it important to "develop a meaningful philosophy of life" has declined from 64.2 percent in 1975 to 40.6 percent last year.

Many of the people I spoke to feel the pressure of peer scrutiny. A status thing has evolved, to which many seem to have regretfully succumbed. Several expressed a weariness with meeting someone new and having to present themselves by their credentials. Yet, overwhelmingly, asked what they're looking for in a romantic partner, they responded first with phrases such as "an educated professional" and "someone with direction." They've conceded, more or less consciously, that unenlightened and exclusionary as it is, it's very uncool not to know what you want and not to be already chasing it. 53

"Seems like everyone in our generation has to be out there achieving," says Scott Birnbaum, twenty-five, who is the chief accountant for TIC United Corp., a holding company in Dallas. 54

Birnbaum graduated from the University of Texas in 1984, where, he says, "For me, the whole career-oriented thing kicked in." A native Texan with a broad drawl, he lives in the Greenville section of the city, an area populated largely by young singles. His apartment is comfortably roomy, not terribly well appointed. He shakes his head amiably as he points to the television set propped on a beer cooler. "What do I need furniture for?" he says. "Most of my time is taken up going to work." 55

Confident in himself professionally, Birnbaum was one of very few interviewees who spoke frankly about the personal cost of career success. Many speculated that they'll be worried if, in their thirties, they haven't begun to settle their love lives; this was more true of women than men. But Birnbaum confesses a desire to marry now. "It's kind of lonely being single," he says. "I'd hate to find myself successful at thirty without a family. Maybe once I'm married and have children, that might make being successful career-wise less important." 56

The problem, he goes on, is the collective outlook he's part and parcel of. "Here's how we think," he says. "Get to this point, move on. Get to that point, move on. Acquire, acquire. Career, career. We're all afraid to slow down for fear of missing out on something. That extends to your social life as well. You go out on a date and you're thinking, 'Hell, is there someone better for me?' I know how terrible that sounds but it seems to be my problem. Most of my peers are in the same position. Men and women. I tell you, it's tough out there right now." 57

When I returned to New York, I called Alex de Gramont, whom I'd been saving to interview last. I've known Alex for a long time, since he was a gawky and curious high school student and I was his teacher. Handsome now, gentle-looking, he's a literary sort, prone to attractive gloom and a 58 certain lack of perspective. He once told me that his paradigm of a romantic, his role model, was Heathcliff, the mad, doomed passion-monger from Emily Brontë's *Wuthering Heights*.[1]

A year out of Wesleyan University in Middletown, Conn., Alex has   59
reasons to be hopeful. His book-length senior thesis about Albert Camus[2]
has been accepted for publication, and on the strength of it, he has applied
to four graduate programs in comparative literature. But he's unenthusiastic,
and he has applied to law schools, too. In the meantime, he is living with his
parents in New Jersey.

He tells me that last summer he went to West Germany in pursuit of a   60
woman he'd met when he was in college. He expected to live there with her,
but he was back in this country in a couple of weeks. "Camus has a line,"
Alex says, " 'Love can burn or love can last. It can't do both.' " Like
Benjamin Braddock, Alex is a little worried about his future.

Dustin Hoffman is forty-nine. I'm thirty-three. Both of us are doing   61
pretty well. Alex, at twenty-three, confesses to considerable unease. "Every
minute I'm not accomplishing something, I feel is wasted," he says, sort of
miserably. "I feel a lot of pressure to decide what to do with my life. I'm a
romantic, but these are very unromantic times."

Questions for Study and Discussion

1. Why did Weber conduct his survey? What did he expect to find? What
did he find that surprised him?
2. How would you characterize Weber's attitude toward contemporary
young adults? Is it neutral, angry, supportive, or something else? Cite examples
of his diction and phrasing to support your answer.
3. What kinds of people comprised Weber's survey group? How were they
different? What did they have in common? Do you think they were representative enough? Why or why not?
4. What qualities do modern young people look for in a relationship?
What qualities inherent in old-fashioned romance make it unattractive to the
modern generation? Where are these objections best stated?
5. What are some of the reasons Weber offers for the shift in romantic
priorities? Can you think of any others?
6. In paragraphs 9 through 11, Weber explains the nature of romance in
his day. Does he ever conclude that his way might have been better than the

---

[1]Emily Brontë (1818–1848) wrote *Wuthering Heights*, one of the most famous English
novels, in 1847.
[2]French philosopher, dramatist, and novelist (1913–1960), who won the Nobel Prize for
literature in 1957.

modern way? What are the advantages and disadvantages of the new way and the old way?

7. Weber waits until paragraph 28 to mention romance. How does he define it? Why do you think he waits so long to use the word?

8. In paragraph 48, Weber responds to the idea that the fear of AIDS may "bring back romance" by saying, "The more I think about that, the more chilling it gets." What does he mean by this remark? Do you agree or disagree?

Writing Topics

1. According to Weber, young people have become less romantic as material goals have taken precedence in their lives. Yet Weber quotes a source who predicts that the AIDS epidemic will bring back romance. Among your contemporaries, which factors in Weber's article seem to have the most influence on romantic style? How has the fear of AIDS and other sexually transmitted diseases affected relationships? What role does ambition play in modern romance? Do you and your friends "plan" your future to the extent that Weber suggests? What factors, other than the ones Weber discusses, do you see working to make relationships either more or less romantic?

2. The notion of "romantic love" is relatively new in Western culture. Do some research to find out when it first became the standard. How were love and marriage viewed before that time? What kinds of relationships can you envision for the future? Can you imagine a relationship unlike either the "romantic" love Weber remembers or the "planned" relationship he finds in the present?

SARAH CRICHTON

Sarah Crichton is one of seven assistant managing editors at *Newsweek* and, at the magazine, staffers refer to Crichton and her colleagues as "The Wallendas" in recognition of the balancing acts they perform on a weekly basis. At *Newsweek* Crichton has overseen such cover projects as "A World Without Fathers: The Struggle to Save the Black Family" (August 30, 1993), "AIDS and the Arts: A Lost Generation" (January 18, 1993), and "The Twisted Truth of JFK" (December 23, 1991), which offered a critique of Oliver Stone's controversial movie and the many conspiracy theories surrounding the assassination of President John F. Kennedy. In addition to her work at *Newsweek*, Crichton has taught magazine writing at New York University and the Columbia University Graduate School of Journalism and has written articles for the *New York Times*, *Esquire*, *Village Voice*, *Harper's*, *New England Monthly*, and many other publications.

"Sexual Correctness: Has It Gone Too Far?" was the cover story for the October 25, 1993, issue of *Newsweek*.

Sexual Correctness: Has It Gone Too Far?

The women at Brown University play hardball. Three years ago, fed up 1 with an administration that wasn't hopping into action, they scrawled the names of alleged rapists on the bathroom stalls. Brown woke up, revamped its disciplinary system and instituted mandatory sexual-assault education for freshmen. But that really hasn't calmed the siege mentality. This fall, Alan S., class of '94, returned to Brown after a one-year suspension for "non-consensual physical contact of a sexual nature," the first student to come back after such disciplinary action. And two weeks ago, all over Brown—on the doors of dorms, on bulletin boards, by the mailroom in Faunce House—posters cropped up. Under a mug shot cut from a class book, it read, "These are the facts: [Alan S.] was convicted of 'sexual misconduct' by the UDC, was sentenced to a one-year suspension; he has served his term and is back on campus." It was signed "rosemary and time." As these posters go, it was low-key. But that doesn't matter. Alan S. had been publicly branded as an "assaulter."

No big deal, said senior Jennifer Rothblatt, hanging out in the Blue 2 Room, a campus snack bar. "As a protest against the system, it's valid and necessary," she said, brushing her long, golden-brown hair off her face. Besides, she added, the posters simply state the facts.

Well, wait. What are the facts? Who is the victimizer here and who is 3
the victim? In the ever-morphing world of Thou Shalt Not Abuse Women
it's getting mighty confusing. Crimes that hurt women are bad; we know
that. But just as opportunities keep expanding for women, the list of what
hurts them seems to grow, too. A Penn State professor claims Goya's luscious
"The Naked Maja," a print of which hangs in her classroom, hurts her ability
to teach; it sexually harasses her. A Northwestern University law professor is
trying to make street remarks—your basic "hey baby" stuff—legally punish-
able as assaultive behavior that limits a woman's liberty. Verbal coercion can
now constitute rape. But what is verbal coercion—"Do me or die"? Or,
"C'mon, Tiffany, if you won't, I'm gonna go off with Heather." If the woman
didn't want it, it's sexual assault. And thanks to nature, he's got the deadly
weapon.

Feminist politics have now homed in like missiles on the twin issues 4
of date rape and sexual harassment, and the once broad-based women's
movement is splintering over the new sexual correctness. "The Morning
After: Sex, Fear and Feminism on Campus," a controversial new book by
Katie Roiphe, argues that issues like date rape reduce women to helpless
victims in need of protective codes of behavior. The much-publicized rules
governing sexual intimacy at Antioch College seem to stultify relations
between men and women on the cusp of adulthood. Like political correctness on campuses, there's pitifully little room for debate or diverse points of
view. For expressing her ideas, Roiphe has received threats. A *Newsweek*
photographer at Antioch—a woman who had permission to photograph—
was attacked by a mob of students and, yes, sexually harassed by several
who exposed themselves.

The workplace, the campuses and the courts are the new testing grounds 5
of sexual correctness. Complaints of harassment on the job have ballooned in
the last three years as men and women try to sort out when they can and
cannot flirt, flatter, offer a friendly pat. Too many rules? Maybe. The obsession
with correct codes of behavior seems to portray women not as thriving on their
hard-won independence but as victims who can't take care of themselves. Will
the new rules set women free? Or will they set them back?

Young men and women used to be sent off to college with a clear sense 6
of how it would be. Back in the dark ages, when guys still wielded mighty
swords and girls still protected their virtue (which is to say, the mid-1960s),
in a military school overlooking the Tennessee River, a colonel gathered his
graduating cadets for the everything-you-need-to-know-about-sex lecture.

"Gentlemen," he drawled, "soon you'll go off and get married and 7
before you do, you need to understand the differences between men and
women."

He began to draw a chart on the blackboard. At the top of one column 8
he wrote MEN, at the top of another, WOMEN. It looked like this:

MEN WOMEN
love LOVE
SEX sex

"That's what men and women believe in," he said, and then went on 9
to describe a typical wedding night. When the bride finally climbs into bed
and sees the groom, he warned, "chances are she'll scream and probably
throw up. Don't worry: this is perfectly natural."

Bette Midler had a name for a night like that. Back in the early '70s, 10
she sang of romantic disappointment in a little ditty called "Bad Sex."
Everyone had bad sex back then and, to hear them tell, survived just fine.
Now feminists on campus quote Andrea Dworkin: "The hurting of women
is . . . basic to the sexual pleasure of men."

Rape and sexual harassment are real. But between crime and sexual bliss 11
are some cloudy waters. To maneuver past the shoals, corporations and universities try a two-pronged approach: re-education and regulations. Some rules
make sense: "It is unacceptable to have sex with a person if he/she is unconscious." Others seem silly. After attending mandatory sexual-harassment seminars at Geffen Records where she works, Bryn Bridenthal is rethinking every
move she makes. "Everybody is looking for anything to be misinterpreted."
Bridenthal used to quite innocently stroke the arm of a man who had a
penchant for wearing luxuriously soft cashmere sweaters. "I never thought
anything about it, but through the seminars I realized that I shouldn't do that,"
she says. "It's not worth doing anything that might be construed by anyone as
sexual harassment."

If it's chilly in the workplace, it's down-right freezing on campus. No 12
school has concocted guidelines quite as specific as Antioch College's. Deep
among the cornfields and pig farms of central Ohio in the town of Yellow
Springs, Antioch prides itself on being "A Laboratory for Democracy." The
dress code is grunge and black; multiple nose rings are *de rigueur,* and green
and blue hair are preferred (if you have hair). Seventy percent of the student
body are womyn (for the uninitiated, that's women—without the dreaded
m-e-n). And the purpose of the Sexual Offense Policy is to empower these
students to become equal partners when it comes time to mate with males.
The goal is 100 percent consensual sex, and it works like this: it isn't enough
to ask someone if she'd like to have sex, as an Antioch women's center
advocate told a group of incoming freshmen this fall. You must obtain consent every step of the way. "If you want to take her blouse off, you have to
ask. If you want to touch her breast, you have to ask. . . ."

How silly this all seems; how sad. It criminalizes the delicious unexpect- 13
edness of sex—a hand suddenly moves to here, a mouth to there. What is
the purpose of sex if not to lose control? (To be unconscious, no.) The
advocates of sexual correctness are trying to take the danger out of sex, but
sex is inherently dangerous. It leaves one exposed to everything from eupho-

ria to crashing disappointment. That's its great unpredictability. But of course, that's sort of what we said when we were all made to wear seat belts.

What is implicit in the new sex guidelines is that it's the male who does   14
the initiating and the woman who at any moment may bolt. Some young women rankle at that. "I think it encourages wimpy behavior by women and [the idea] that women need to be handled with kid gloves," says Hope Segal, 22, a fourth-year Antioch student. Beware those boys with their swords, made deaf by testosterone and, usually, blinded by drink.

Drink—the abuse of it, the abuses that occur because of it—is key. In   15
up to 70 percent of acquaintance rapes, alcohol plays a role, says Manhattan sex-crimes prosecutor Linda Fairstein, author of "Sexual Violence: Our War Against Rape." And because alcohol poses such a powerful problem, it is the rule at almost every school (and the law in most states) that "consent is not meaningful" if given while under the influence of alcohol, drugs or prescription medication. If she's drunk, she's not mentally there, and her consent counts for zip. If the man is just as drunk as the woman, that's no excuse. Mary P. Koss is a professor of psychology at the University of Arizona and the author of a highly regarded, if controversial, survey of rape and college-age students. "The Scope of Rape" indicates that one in four college-age students has been the victim of a rape or an attempted rape. In those numbers Koss includes women who have been coerced into having sex while intoxicated. "The law punishes the drunk driver who kills a pedestrian," she argues. "And likewise, the law needs to be there to protect the drunk woman from the driver of the penis."

"Men and women just think differently," Antioch president Alan   16
Guskin says, "and we've got to help the students understand the differences." It's a policy, he says, designed to create a "safe" campus environment. But for all the attempts to make them feel secure, a lot of young college women just feel like sitting ducks. "As a potential survivor . . ." a Barnard student said to a visiting reporter. As a *what?* Potential survivor equals an inevitable victim. Every Wednesday night at Dartmouth, a group of undergraduate women gather to warn one another about potential date rapists. At the University of Michigan, and several other schools as well, when sorority women attend frat parties, a designated "sober" monitor stands guard over her friends. "Whenever people start going upstairs, you go up to them right away," says Marcy Myers. "You ask, 'Do you know this guy? You're drunk, do you want to go home? You can call him tomorrow'." "My friends won't go to parties at Dartmouth without other women," says Abby Ross, and before they leave the dorm, they check each other's outfits, too. No one wears short skirts. "You should be able to wear whatever you want. But the reality is that you're not dealing with people who have the same set of values," says Ross.

This defensive mind-set is at the heart of the escalating battle over date   17
rape. Critics charge feminists with hyping the statistics and so broadening the definition of rape that sex roles are becoming positively Victorian.

Women are passive vessels with no responsibility for what happens; men are domineering brutes with just one thing on their minds. "People have asked me if I have ever been date-raped," writes Katie Roiphe in "The Morning After." "And thinking back on complicated nights, on too many glasses of wine, on strange and familiar beds, I would have to say yes. With such a sweeping definition of rape, I wonder how many people there are, male or female, who haven't been date-raped at one point or another . . . If verbal coercion constitutes rape, then the word 'rape' itself expands to include any kind of sex a woman experiences as negative."

Roiphe, 25, a Harvard graduate and now a doctoral candidate at Prince- 18 ton, argues that a hysteria has gripped college campuses, fomented by "rape-crisis feminists." "The image that emerges from feminist preoccupations with rape and sexual harassment is that of women as victims, offended by a professor's dirty joke, verbally pressured into sex by peers. This image of a delicate woman bears a striking resemblance to that '50s ideal my mother and the other women of her generation fought so hard to get away from. They didn't like her passivity . . . her excessive need for protection . . . But here she is again, with her pure intentions and her wide eyes. Only this time it is the feminists themselves who are breathing new life into her."

Roiphe is getting whomped for her provocative, though too-loosely 19 documented, book. A "traitor," says Gail Dines, a professor of sociology and women's studies at Wheelock College, who lectures about rape and pornography. She calls Roiphe the "Clarence Thomas of women," just trying to suck up to the "white-male patriarchy." She thinks Roiphe will get her comeuppance. Warns Dines, in a most unsisterly fashion: "[When] she walks down the street, she's one more woman."

So how much of a threat is rape? What are women facing on dates with 20 acquaintances or on the streets with strangers? Throughout her book, Roiphe wrestles with Koss's one-in-four statistic. "If I was really standing in the middle of an epidemic, a crisis," she asks, "if 25 percent of my female friends were really being raped, wouldn't I know about it?"

Heresy! Denial! Backlash! In an essay in The New Yorker, Katha 21 Pollitt fired back: "As an experiment, I applied Roiphe's anecdotal method myself, and wrote down what I knew about my own circle of acquaintance: eight rapes by strangers (including one on a college campus), two sexual assaults (one Central Park, one Prospect Park), one abduction (woman walking down street forced into car full of men), one date rape involving a Mickey Finn, which resulted in pregnancy and abortion, and two stalkings (one ex-lover, one deranged fan); plus one brutal beating by a boyfriend, three incidents of childhood incest (none involving therapist-aided "recovered memories"), and one bizarre incident in which a friend went to a man's apartment after meeting him at a party and was forced by him to spend the night under the shower, naked, while he debated whether to kill her, rape her, or let her go."

Holy moly. Pollitt is one of the wisest essayists around; a fine poet, too. 22
And far be it for us to question her list. So what does the list prove? Well,
that even wise feminists fall precisely into the same trap as Roiphe: you can't
extrapolate from your circle of acquaintance; friends don't constitute a statistical average. What's more, Pollitt is almost 20 years older than Roiphe; her
friends presumably have lived more years, too. Still, Pollitt's litany is shocking. It's punch-my-victim-card time: How full's yours?

"When one woman is raped on campus, all women are afraid to go to 23
the library and finish their chemistry homework." Pat Reuss, a senior policy
analyst with the NOW Legal Defense Fund, told a workshop at the NOW
National Convention this summer. Today, college students are handed, as
part of their orientation programs, pamphlets that spell out the threat and,
over and over, the same dire figures appear: As Penn State's Sexual Assault
Awareness pamphlet reads, in can't-miss-it type: "FBI statistics indicate that
one in three women in our society will be raped during her lifetime."

Except there are no such FBI figures. The figures the FBI does have to 24
offer are both out-of-date and so conservative that most people dismiss them.
The FBI recognizes rape only as involving forcible penetration of the vagina
with a penis. Oral sex, anal sex, penetration with an object—these do not
officially constitute rape. It doesn't matter to the FBI if a woman was made
incapacitated by alcohol or drugs, and the agency certainly isn't interested in
verbal coercion. Rape is as narrowly defined by the FBI as could be imagined.

So, in the rape-crisis mentality, the numbers keep being bloated. Which 25
is crazy, considering the fact that even the most conservative numbers are
horrifying. College students are a high-risk group. The No. 1 group to be
sexually assaulted in this country are 16- to 19-year-olds. The second largest
group hit are the 20- to 24-year-old age bracket. Women are four times more
likely to be assaulted during these years than at any other time in their lives.
Forty-five percent of all rapists arrested are under 25. And as for the most
conservative, yet trustworthy, numbers: according to the National Victim
Center survey last year—a survey that did not include intoxication—13
percent of adult women are victims of forcible rape. That's one in seven.

That's a lot, but it doesn't mean all women are victims—or survivors, 26
as we are supposed to call them. And it sure doesn't mean all "suffering"
warrants attention or retribution—or even much sympathy. When New York
state Assemblyman Harvey Weisenberg misspoke during a speech and said
"sex" instead of "six," he covered up his error by looking at Assemblywoman
Earlene Hill (Democrat of Hempstead) and joked, "Whenever I think of
Earlene, I think of sex." Another brutish colleague wouldn't move his legs so
she could get to her seat and made her climb over him. Sexual harassment,
she cried, saying: "If I don't speak up, then they won't realize it's wrong and
there will be a new victim." Oh, please. A student at the University of
Virginia told The New York Times that she favored a ban on all student/

faculty dating because "One of my professors asked me out and it made me really uncomfortable." So tell him to bug off. Artist Sue Williams plopped a six-feet-in-diameter piece of plastic vomit on the floor of the Whitney Museum as her protest against the male-dominated beauty-obsessed culture that makes women stick fingers down their throats. Tell them to get some therapy and cut it out. You want to talk victimization? Talk to the mothers all over America whose children have been slaughtered in urban cross-fire.

"I'm sick of women wallowing in the victim state," says Betty Friedan.   27
"We have empowered ourselves. We are able to blow the whistle on rape. I am not as concerned with that as I am with violence in our whole society."

It does seem ironic that the very movement created to encourage   28
women to stand up and fight their own battles has taken this strange detour, and instead is making them feel vulnerable and in need of protection. From the grade schools to the workplace, women are asking that everything be codified: How to act; what to say. Who to date; how to date; when to mate. They're huddling in packs, insisting on a plethora of rules on which to rely, and turning to authority figures to complain when anything goes wrong. We're not creating a society of Angry Young Women. These are Scared Little Girls.

For all the major advances in the status of women in the last 25 years,   29
the shifts in attitudes don't seem to have percolated down to our kids. Parents still raise girls to become wives, and sons to be sons. "I think to some extent we're dealing with a cultural lag," says Janet Hansche, a clinical psychologist and director of the Counseling and Testing Center at Tulane University. "Society still trains women to be pliant, to be nice, to try to avoid saying no, and my guess is that that's most everywhere."

And we're not doing any better raising boys. Obviously something's   30
still screwy in this society. Boys are still being brought up to believe it's the height of cool to score—as if ejaculation were a notable achievement for an adolescent male. Young men still "get tremendous status from aggressiveness," says Debra Haffner, executive director of SECUS (the Sex Information and Education Council of the U.S.). "But no one teaches them how to live in the real world." It is a weird real world when "nice" boys in a "nice" community, good students, good athletes, good family, rape a mentally handicapped girl with a broomstick handle and a plastic baseball bat, and try to claim it was consensual. "Aren't they virile specimens?" Don Belman boasted to a New York Times reporter about his three Spur Posse sons, one of whom was awaiting trial for allegedly trying to run over several girls with a pickup truck while another had been arrested on sexual charges.

All right. Not all boys turn into Glen Ridge, Spur Posse, Tailhook-   31
grabbing beings. But when it comes to human sexuality, the messages that are being sent to kids—male and female—remain cloaked in myth. In 1993, girls who want sex are still sluts, those who don't are still teases. And those who finally make it to college are completely befuddled.

Which is why it's time for everyone who doesn't have a serious problem to pipe down. What is happening on the campuses is scary, because it is polarizing men and women. Rather than encouraging them to work together, to trust one another, to understand one another, it is intensifying suspicion. Brown sophomore David Danon complains, "Women have all the power here on sexual conduct . . . It's very dangerous for us." If women are so profoundly distrustful of men, how will they raise boys? And if men are so defensive about women, how will they raise little girls? The most pressing problem the majority of American women face isn't rape or sexual harassment. It's the fact that, in addition to holding down full-time work, they still are burdened with the lion's share of parenting and housework responsibility. Add it up, says sociologist Arlie Hochschild, and it comes to a full month's worth of 24-hour days. Line up the 100 most involved fathers you know and ask one question: what size shoes do your children wear?

Real life is messy, rife with misunderstandings and contradictions. There's no eight-page guide on how to handle it. There are no panels of mediators out there to turn to unless it gets truly bad. Those who are growing up in environments where they don't have to figure out what the rules should be, but need only follow what's been prescribed, are being robbed of the most important lesson there is to learn. And that's how to live.

Questions for Study and Discussion

1. Into what two camps does Crichton believe that feminist politics has broken with regard to the "sexual correctness" movement? How would you describe their opposing viewpoints?

2. Who is Katie Roiphe and why has she created such a stir? Do you agree with her views? Why or why not?

3. Crichton says in paragraph 11, "between crime and sexual bliss are some cloudy waters." To what is she referring? In your opinion, what should be done, if anything, to help make those waters less cloudy?

4. What is the Sexual Offense Policy of Antioch College? What is Crichton's attitude toward it?

5. How does Crichton incorporate Katha Pollitt's *New Yorker* essay and its differing set of statistics with regard to rape in response to Roiphe's argument?

6. What is Crichton's attitude toward the cries of victimization that she describes in paragraph 26?

7. What is regrettable about the polarization of the sexes that is occurring on college campuses, according to Crichton? What needs to take place instead?

8. Crichton assumes a chatty, at times very expressive, tone in her essay. What examples can you find of her colloquial tone? Why do you suppose she assumes that voice? Do you think it is an effective voice given the nature of her subject? Explain.

Writing Topics

1. In referring to today's college women in paragraph 28, Crichton writes, "We're not creating a society of Angry Young Women. These are Scared Little Girls." Write an essay in which you argue for or against her assessment. Or perhaps there is yet another view of today's college women for which you'd like to argue.

2. After reading Crichton's article, especially her opinions on parental roles in child rearing, write an essay in which you reflect on your own upbringing with regard to the kinds of issues Crichton raises. Are you able to deal with a "real life" that is, as Crichton puts it, "messy, rife with misunderstandings and contradictions"?

3. Read Katie Roiphe's *The Morning After: Sex, Fear and Feminism on Campus* and write an assessment of the book.

CAROLINE BIRD

Caroline Bird was born in New York City, attended Vassar College for three years, and received her B.A. from the University of Toledo and her M.A. from the University of Wisconsin. A feminist writer throughout most of her career, Bird has focused her attention on women's roles in the business world. She has published such influential and well-reviewed books as *The Invisible Scar: The Great Depression and What It Did to American Life, from Then Until Now* (1966) with Sarah Welles Briller, *Born Female: The High Cost of Keeping Women Down* (1968), *Everything a Woman Needs to Know to Get Paid What She's Worth* (1973), *Enterprising Women: Their Contribution to the American Economy, 1776–1976* (1976), *What Women Want* (1978), *The Two-Paycheck Marriage: How Women at Work Are Changing Life in America* (1979), and *The Good Years: Your Life in the Twenty-first Century* (1983).

In the following selection Bird turns her attention away from feminist issues and asks whether a college education is a worthwhile financial investment. What would be the result, for example, if you were to take the money that you will spend on your college education and invest it and become gainfully employed instead of attending school?

College Is a Waste of Time and Money

A great majority of our nine million college students are not in school   1
because they want to be or because they want to learn. They are there because it has become the thing to do or because college is a pleasant place to be; because it's the only way they can get parents or taxpayers to support them without working at a job they don't like; because Mother wanted them to go, or some other reason entirely irrelevant to the course of studies for which college is supposedly organized.

As I crisscross the United States lecturing on college campuses, I am   2
dismayed to find that professors and administrators, when pressed for a candid opinion, estimate that no more than 25 percent of their students are turned on by classwork. For the rest, college is at best a social center or aging vat, and at worst a young folks' home or even a prison that keeps them out of the mainstream of economic life for a few more years.

The premise—which I no longer accept—that college is the best place   3
for all high-school graduates grew out of a noble American ideal. Just as the United States was the first nation to aspire to teach every small child to read and write, so, during the 1950s, we became the first and only great nation to aspire to higher education for all. During the '60s, we damned the expense and built great state university systems as fast as we could. And adults—

parents, employers, high-school counselors—began to push, shove, and cajole youngsters to "get an education."

It became a mammoth industry, with taxpayers footing more than half   4
the bill. By 1970, colleges and universities were spending more than 30 billion dollars annually. But still only half of our high-school graduates were going on. According to estimates made by the economist Fritz Machlup, if we had been educating every young person until age 22 in that year of 1970, the bill for higher education would have reached 47.5 billion dollars, 12.5 billion more than the total corporate profits for the year.

Figures such as these have begun to make higher education for all look   5
financially prohibitive, particularly now when colleges are squeezed by the pressures of inflation and a drop-off in the growth of their traditional market.

Predictable demography has caught up with the university empire build-   6
ers. Now that the record crop of postwar babies has graduated from college, the rate of growth of the student population has begun to decline. To keep their mammoth plants financially solvent, many institutions have begun to use hard-sell, Madison-Avenue techniques to attract students. They sell college like soap, promoting features they think students want: innovative programs, an environment conducive to meaningful personal relationships, and a curriculum so free that it doesn't sound like college at all.

Pleasing the customers is something new for college administrators.   7
Colleges have always known that most students don't like to study, and that at least part of the time they are ambivalent about college, but before the student riots of the 1960s educators never thought it either right or necessary to pay any attention to student feelings. But when students rebelling against the Vietnam war and the draft discovered they could disrupt a campus completely, administrators had to act on some student complaints. Few understood that the protests tapped the basic discontent with college itself, a discontent that did not go away when the riots subsided.

Today students protest individually rather than in concert. They turn   8
inward and withdraw from active participation. They drop out to travel to India or to feed themselves on subsistence farms. Some refuse to go to college at all. Most, of course, have neither the funds nor the self-confidence for constructive articulation of their discontent. They simply hang around college unhappily and reluctantly.

All across the country, I have been overwhelmed by the prevailing   9
sadness on American campuses. Too many young people speak little, and then only in drowned voices. Sometimes the mood surfaces as diffidence, weariness, or coolness, but whatever its form, it looks like a defense mechanism, and that rings a bell. This is the way it used to be with women, and just as society had systematically damaged women by insisting that their proper place was in the home, so we may be systematically damaging 18-year-olds by insisting that their proper place is in college.

Campus watchers everywhere know what I mean when I say students   10 are sad, but they don't agree on the reason for it. During the Vietnam war some ascribed the sadness to the draft; now others blame affluence or say it has something to do with permissive upbringing.

Not satisfied with any of these explanations, I looked for some answers   11
with the journalistic tools of my trade—scholarly studies, economic analyses, the historical record, the opinions of the especially knowledgeable, conversations with parents, professors, college administrators, and employers, all of whom spoke as alumni, too. Mostly I learned from my interviews with hundreds of young people on and off campuses all over the country.

My unnerving conclusion is that students are sad because they are not   12
needed. Somewhere between the nursery and the employment office, they become unwanted adults. No one has anything in particular against them. But no one knows what to do with them either. We already have too many people in the world of the 1970s, and there is no room for so many newly minted 18-year-olds. So we temporarily get them out of the way by sending them to college where in fact only a few belong.

To make it more palatable, we fool ourselves into believing that we are   13
sending them there for their own best interests, and that it's good for them, like spinach. Some, of course, learn to like it, but most wind up preferring green peas.

Educators admit as much. Nevitt Sanford, distinguished student of   14
higher education, says students feel they are "capitulating to a kind of voluntary servitude." Some of them talk about their time in college as if it were a sentence to be served. I listened to a 1970 Mount Holyoke graduate: "For two years I was really interested in science, but in my junior and senior years I just kept saying, 'I've done two years; I'm going to finish.' When I got out I made up my mind that I wasn't going to school anymore because so many of my courses had been bullshit."

But bad as it is, college is often preferable to a far worse fate. It is better   15
than the drudgery of an uninspiring nine-to-five job, and better than doing nothing when no jobs are available. For some young people, it is a graceful way to get away from home and become independent without losing the financial support of their parents. And sometimes it is the only alternative to an intolerable home situation.

It is difficult to assess how many students are in college reluctantly. The   16
conservative Carnegie Commission estimates from 5 to 30 percent. Sol Linowitz, who was once chairman of a special committee on campus tension of the American Council on Education, found that "a significant number were not happy with their college experience because they felt they were there only in order to get the 'ticket to the big show' rather than to spend the years as productively as they otherwise could."

Older alumni will identify with Richard Baloga, a policeman's son,   17
who stayed in school even though he "hated it" because he thought it would do him some good. But fewer students each year feel this way. Daniel

Yankelovich has surveyed undergraduate attitudes for a number of years, and reported in 1971 that 74 percent thought education was "very important." But just two years earlier, 80 percent thought so.

The doubters don't mind speaking up. Leon Lefkowitz, chairman of the   18 department of social studies at Central High School in Valley Stream, New York, interviewed 300 college students at random, and reports that 200 of them didn't think that the education they were getting was worth the effort. "In two years I'll pick up a diploma," said one student, "and I can honestly say it was a waste of my father's bread."

Nowadays, says one sociologist, you don't have to have a reason for   19 going to college; it's an institution. His definition of an institution is an arrangement everyone accepts without question; the burden of proof is not on why you go, but why anyone thinks there might be a reason for not going. The implication is that an 18-year-old is too young and confused to know what he wants to do, and that he should listen to those who know best and go to college.

I don't agree. I believe that college has to be judged not on what other   20 people think is good for students, but on how good it feels to the students themselves.

I believe that people have an inside view of what's good for them. If a   21 child doesn't want to go to school some morning, better let him stay at home, at least until you find out why. Maybe he knows something you don't. It's the same with college. If high-school graduates don't want to go, or if they don't want to go right away, they may perceive more clearly than their elders that college is not for them. It is no longer obvious that adolescents are best off studying a core curriculum that was constructed when all educated men could agree on what made them educated, or that professors, advisors, or parents can be of any particular help to young people in choosing a major or a career. High-school graduates see college graduates driving cabs and decide it's not worth going. College students find no intellectual stimulation in their studies and drop out.

If students believe that college isn't necessarily good for them, you   22 can't expect them to stay on for the general good of mankind. They don't go to school to beat the Russians to Jupiter, improve the national defense, increase the GNP, or create a new market for the arts—to mention some of the benefits taxpayers are supposed to get for supporting higher eduation.

Nor should we expect to bring about social equality by putting all   23 young people through four years of academic rigor. At best, it's a roundabout and expensive way to narrow the gap between the highest and lowest in our society anyway. At worst, it is unconsciously elitist. Equalizing opportunity through universal higher education subjects the whole population to the intellectual mode natural only to a few. It violates the fundamental egalitarian principle of respect for the differences between people.

Of course, most parents aren't thinking of the "higher" good at all.   24

They send their children to college because they are convinced young people benefit financially from those four years of higher education. But if money is the only goal, college is the dumbest investment you can make. I say this because a young banker in Poughkeepsie, New York, Stephen G. Necel, used a computer to compare college as an investment with other investments available in 1974, and college did not come out on top.

For the sake of argument, the two of us invented a young man whose   25
rich uncle gave him, in cold cash, the cost of a four-year education at any college he chose, but the young man didn't have to spend the money on college. After bales of computer paper, we had our mythical student write to his uncle: "Since you said I could spend the money foolishly if I wished, I am going to blow it all on Princeton."

The much respected financial columnist Sylvia Porter echoed the com-   26
mon assumption when she said last year, "A college education is among the very best investments you can make in your entire life." But the truth is not quite so rosy, even if we assume that the Census Bureau is correct when it says that as of 1972, a man who completed four years of college would expect to earn $199,000 more between the ages of 22 and 64 than a man who had only a high-school diploma.

If a 1972 Princeton-bound high-school graduate had put the $34,181   27
that his four years of college would have cost him into a savings bank at 7.5 percent interest compounded daily, he would have had at age 64 a total of $1,129,200, or $528,200 more than the earnings of a male college graduate, and more than five times as much as the $199,000 extra the more educated man could expect to earn between 22 and 64.

The big advantage of getting your college money in cash now is that   28
you can invest it in something that has a higher return than a diploma. For instance, a Princeton-bound high-school graduate of 1972 who liked fooling around with cars could have banked his $34,181, and gone to work at the local garage at close to $1,000 more per year than the average high-school graduate. Meanwhile, as he was learning to be an expert auto mechanic, his money would be ticking away in the bank. When he became 28, he would have earned $7,199 less on his job from age 22 to 28 than his college-educated friend, but he would have had $73,113 in his passbook—enough to buy out his boss, go into the used-car business, or acquire his own new car dealership. If successful in business, he could expect to make more than the average college graduate. And if he had the brains to get into Princeton, he would be just as likely to make money without the four years spent on campus. Unfortunately, few college-bound high-school graduates get the opportunity to bank such a large sum of money and then wait for it to make them rich. And few parents are sophisticated enough to understand that in financial returns alone, their children would be better off with the money than with the education.

Rates of return and dollar signs on education are fascinating brain   29 teasers, but obviously there is a certain unreality to the game. Quite aside from the noneconomic benefits of college, and these should loom larger once the dollars are cleared away, there are grave difficulties in assigning a dollar value to college at all.

In fact there is no real evidence that the higher income of college   30 graduates is due to college. College may simply attract people who are slated to earn more money anyway; those with higher IQs, better family backgrounds, a more enterprising temperament. No one who has wrestled with the problem is prepared to attribute all of the higher income to the impact of college itself.

Christopher Jencks, author of *Inequality,* a book that assesses the effect   31 of family and schooling in America, believes that education in general accounts for less than half of the difference in income in the American population. "The biggest single source of income differences," writes Jencks, "seems to be the fact that men from high-status families have higher incomes than men from low-status families even when they enter the same occupations, have the same amount of education, and have the same test scores."

Jacob Mincer of the National Bureau of Economic Research and Colum-   32 bia University states flatly that of "20 to 30 percent of students at any level, the additional schooling has been a waste, at least in terms of earnings." College fails to work its income-raising magic for almost a third of those who go. More than half of those people in 1972 who earned $15,000 or more reached that comfortable bracket without the benefit of a college diploma. Jencks says that financial success inn the U.S. depends a good deal on luck, and the most sophisticated regression analyses have yet to demonstrate otherwise.

But most of today's students don't go to college to earn more money   33 anyway. In 1968, when jobs were easy to get, Daniel Yankelovich made his first nationwide survey of students. Sixty-five percent of them said they "would welcome less emphasis on money." By 1973, when jobs were scarce, that figure jumped to 80 percent.

The young are not alone. Americans today are all looking less to the   34 pay of a job than to the work itself. They want "interesting" work that permits then "to make a contribution," "express themselves" and "use their special abilities," and they think college will help them find it.

Jerry Darring of Indianapolis knows what it is to make a dollar. He   35 worked with his father in the family plumbing business, on the line at Chevrolet, and in the Chrysler foundry. He quit these jobs to enter Wright State University in Dayton, Ohio, because "in a job like that a person only has time to work, and after that he's so tired that he can't do anything else but come home and go to sleep."

Jerry came to college to find work "helping people." And he is perfectly   36 willing spend the dollars he earns at dull, well-paid work to prepare for lower-paid work that offers the reward of service to others.

Jerry's case is not unusual. No one works for money alone. In order to 37 deal with the nonmonetary rewards of work, economists have coined the concept of "psychic income," which according to one economic dictionary means "income that is reckoned in terms of pleasure, satisfaction of general feeling of euphoria."

Psychic income is primarily what college students mean when they talk 38 about getting a good job. During the most affluent years of the late 1960s and early 1970s college students told their placement officers that they wanted to be researchers, college professors, artists, city planners, social workers, poets, book publishers, archaeologists, ballet dancers, or authors.

The psychic income of these and other occupations popular with stu- 39 dents is so high that these jobs can be filled without offering high salaries. According to one study, 93 percent of urban university professors would choose the same vocation again if they had the chance, compared with only 16 percent of unskilled auto workers. Even though the monetary gap be- tween college professor and auto worker is now surprisingly small, the differ- ence in psychic income is enormous.

But colleges fail to warn students that jobs of these kinds are hard to 40 come by, even for qualified applicants, and they rarely accept the responsibil- ity of helping students choose a career that will lead to a job. When a young person says he is interested in helping people, his counselor tells him to become a psychologist. But jobs in psychology are scarce. The Department of Labor, for instance, estimates there will be 4,300 new jobs for psychologists in 1975 while colleges are expected to turn out 58,430 B.A.s in psychology that year.

Of thirty psych majors who reported back to Vassar what they were 41 doing a year after graduation in 1973, only five had jobs in which they could possibly use their courses in psychology, and two of these were working for Vassar.

The outlook isn't much better for students majoring in other psychic- 42 pay disciplines: sociology, English, journalism, anthropology, forestry, educa- tion. Whatever college graduates want to do, most of them are going to wind up doing what there is to do.

John Shingleton, director of placement at Michigan State University, 43 accuses the academic community of outright hypocrisy. "Educators have never said, 'Go to college and get a good job,' but this has been implied, and now students expect it. . . . If we care what happens to students after col- lege, then let's get involved with what should be one of the basic purposes of education: career preparation."

In the 1970s, some of the more practical professors began to see that 44 jobs for graduates meant jobs for professors too. Meanwhile, students them- selves reacted to the shrinking job market, and a "new vocationalism" ex- ploded on campus. The press welcomed the change as a return to the ethic of achievement and service. Students were still idealistic, the reporters wrote, but they now saw that they could best make the world better by healing the sick as physicians or righting individual wrongs as lawyers.

But there are no guarantees in these professions either. The American   45
Enterprise Institute estimated in 1971 that there would be more than the target ratio of 100 doctors for every 100,000 people in the population by 1980. And the odds are little better for would-be lawyers. Law schools are already graduating twice as many new lawyers every year as the Department of Labor thinks will be needed, and the oversupply is growing every year.

And it's not at all apparent that what is actually learned in a "profes-   46
sional" education is necessary for success. Teachers, engineers, and others I talked to said they find that on the job they rarely use what they learned in school. In order to see how well college prepared engineers and scientists for actual paid work in their fields, The Carnegie Commission queried all the employees with degrees in these fields in two large firms. Only one in five said the work they were doing bore a "very close relationship" to their college studies, while almost a third saw "very little relationship at all." An overwhelming majority could think of many people who were doing their same work, but had majored in different fields.

Majors in nontechnical fields report even less relationship between   47
their studies and their jobs. Charles Lawrence, a communications major in college and now the producer of "Kennedy & Co.," the Chicago morning television show, says, "You have to learn all that stuff and you never use it again. I learned my job doing it." Others employed as architects, nurses, teachers, and other members of the so-called learned professions report the same thing.

Most college administrators admit that they don't prepare their gradu-   48
ates for the job market. "I just wish I had the guts to tell parents that when you get out of this place you aren't prepared to do anything," the academic head of a famous liberal-arts college told us. Fortunately, for him, most people believe that you don't have to defend a liberal-arts education on those grounds. A liberal-arts education is supposed to provide you with a value system, a standard, a set of ideas, not a job. "Like Christianity, the liberal arts are seldom practiced and would probably be hated by the majority of the populace if they were," said one defender.

The analogy is apt. The fact is, of course, that the liberal arts are a   49
religion in every sense of that term. When people talk about them, their language becomes elevated, metaphorical, extravagant, theoretical and reverent. And faith in personal salvation by the liberal arts is professed in a creed intoned on ceremonial occasions such as commencements.

If the liberal arts are a religious faith, the professors are its priests. But   50
disseminating ideas in a four-year college curriculum is slow and most expensive. If you want to learn about Milton, Camus, or even Margaret Mead you can find them in paperback books, the public library, and even on television.

And when most people talk about the value of a college education, 51
they are not talking about great books. When at Harvard commencement,
the president welcomes the new graduates into "the fellowship of educated
men and women," what he could be saying is, "Here is a piece of paper that is
a passport to jobs, power, and instant prestige." As Glenn Bassett, a person-
nel specialist at G.E., says, "In some parts of G.E., a college degree appears
completely irrelevant to selection to, say, a manager's job. In most, however,
it is a ticket of admission."

But now that we have doubled the number of young people attending 52
college, a diploma cannot guarantee even that. The most charitable conclusion we can reach is that college probably has very little, if any, effect on
people and things at all. Today, the false premises are easy to see:

First, college doesn't make people intelligent, ambitious, happy, or 53
liberal. It's the other way around. Intelligent, ambitious, happy, liberal
people are attracted to higher education in the first place.

Second, college can't claim much credit for the learning experiences 54
that really change students while they are there. Jobs, friends, history, and
most of all the sheer passage of time, have as big an impact as anything even
indirectly related to the campus.

Third, colleges have changed so radically that a freshman entering in 55
the fall of 1974 can't be sure to gain even the limited value research studies
assigned to colleges in the '60s. The sheer size of undergraduate campuses of
the 1970s makes college even less stimulating now than it was 10 years ago.
Today even motivated students are disappointed with their college courses
and professors.

Finally, a college diploma no longer opens as many vocational doors. 56
Employers are beginning to realize that when they pay extra for someone
with a diploma, they are paying only for an empty credential. The fact is that
most of the work for which employers now expect college training is now or
has been capably done in the past by people without higher educations.

College, then, may be a good place for those few young people who are 57
really drawn to academic work, who would rather read than eat, but it has
become too expensive, in money, time, and intellectual effort, to serve as a
holding pen for large numbers of our young. We ought to make it possible for
those reluctant, unhappy students to find alternative ways of growing up and
more realistic preparation for the years ahead.

Questions for Study and Discussion

1. What reasons does Bird give for believing that college is a waste of time
and money? Which reasons, if any, do you find most compelling? Explain why.
2. Why, according to Bird, do people go to college? Do you agree with her
assessment? Why or why not?

3. In the 1960s and early 1970s students protested en masse on campuses across the country. How, according to Bird, do students protest today? Is this true of students on your campus? Explain.

4. In traveling to college campuses across the country Bird was struck by the "prevailing sadness." Why does she believe students are sad? Do you think she's right? Why or why not?

5. Why, after going through the exercises of showing the economic advantages of investing money instead of spending it on a college education, does Bird admit that "there is a certain unreality to the game"? Do you agree with her when she says, "Few parents are sophisticated enough to understand that in financial returns alone, their children would be better off with the money than with the education"?

6. What, according to Bird, is psychic income? How can a person estimate the value of psychic income? How important is such income to you and your peers?

7. What is the "new vocationalism" of the 1970s that Bird refers to? Is this still a campus reality in the 1990s? Explain.

8. What types of sources does Bird use to substantiate her argument? In what ways do these sources help her to avoid the charges of being opinionated, cynical, or sensational?

9. How are paragraphs 52 through 57 related to what comes before? Does this block of paragraphs function as an appropriate conclusion? Explain.

Writing Topics

1. Bird says that college is "at best a social center or aging vat, and at worst a young folks' home or even a prison that keeps them out of the mainstream of economic life for a few more years." She concludes her essay by saying, "We ought to make it possible for those reluctant, unhappy students to find alternative ways of growing up and more realistic preparation for the years ahead." Write an essay in which you explore new learning experiences and opportunities for personal growth designed to prepare our youth for the years ahead.

2. College is, or at least should be, something more than a place to get the credentials necessary to earn more money in your chosen career. Write an essay in which you explain what you hope to gain intellectually, morally, and socially from your college education.

SHELBY STEELE

Award-winning essayist and nonfiction writer Shelby Steele was born in Chicago in 1946 and graduated from Coe College in Iowa. He earned his master's degree at Southern Illinois University and his doctorate at the University of Utah. Currently he teaches English at San Jose State University. Steele established a reputation in the 1980s with searching examinations of race relations in America. In 1989 he received a National Magazine Award for his articles in *Harper's*, *The American Scholar*, *Black World*, the *Washington Post*, *The New Republic*, and *The New York Times Magazine*. His 1988 article "On Being Black and Middle Class" was selected for inclusion in the 1989 edition of *The Best American Essays*, and in 1991, Steele's first book, *The Content of Our Character: A New Vision of Race in America* (1990), won a National Book Critics Circle Award.

In the following essay, first published in *Harper's* and later reprinted in *The Content of Our Character*, Steele examines the virtual explosion of racial incidents on college campuses. At a time when people are calling for greater diversity, Steele wants universities to stress commonality and values of integration.

The Recoloring of Campus Life

In the past few years, we have witnessed what the National Institute   1
Against Prejudice and Violence calls a "proliferation" of racial incidents on college campuses around the country. Incidents of on-campus, "intergroup conflict" have occurred at more than 160 colleges in the last three years, according to the institute. The nature of these incidents has ranged from open racial violence—most notoriously, the October 1986 beating of a black student at the University of Massachusetts at Amherst after an argument about the World Series turned into a racial bashing, with a crowd of up to 3,000 whites chasing twenty blacks—to the harassment of minority students, to acts of racial or ethnic insensitivity, with by far the greatest number falling in the last two categories. At Dartmouth College, three editors of the *Dartmouth Review*, the off-campus right-wing student weekly, were suspended last winter for harassing a black professor in his lecture hall. At Yale University last year a swastika and the words "white power" were painted on the school's Afro-American cultural center. Racist jokes were aired not long ago on a campus radio station at the University of Michigan. And at the University of Wisconsin at Madison, members of the Zeta Beta Tau fraternity held a mock slave auction in which pledges painted their faces black and wore Afro wigs. Two weeks after the president of Stanford University informed the

incoming freshman class last fall that "bigotry is out, and I mean it," two freshmen defaced a poster of Beethoven—gave the image thick lips—and hung it on a black student's door.

In response, black students around the country have rediscovered the militant protest strategies of the Sixties. At the University of Massachusetts at Amherst, Williams College, Penn State University, UC Berkeley, UCLA, Stanford, and countless other campuses, black students have sat in, marched, and rallied. But much of what they were marching and rallying about seemed less a response to specific racial incidents than a call for broader action on the part of the colleges and universities they were attending. Black students have demanded everything from more black faculty members and new courses on racism to the addition of "ethnic" foods in the cafeteria. There is the sense in these demands that racism runs deep.

Of course, universities are not where racial problems tend to arise. When I went to college in the mid-Sixties, colleges were oases of calm and understanding in a racially tense society; campus life—with its traditions of tolerance and fairness, its very distance from the "real" world—imposed a degree of broad-mindedness on even the most provincial students. If I met whites who were not anxious to be friends with blacks, most were at least vaguely friendly to the cause of our freedom. In any case, there was no guerrilla activity against our presence, no "mine field of racism" (as one black student at Berkeley recently put it) to negotiate. I wouldn't say that the phrase "campus racism" is a contradiction in terms, but until recently it certainly seemed an incongruence.

But a greater incongruence is the generational timing of this new problem on the campuses. Today's undergraduates were born after the passage of the 1964 Civil Rights Act. They grew up in an age when racial equality was for the first time enforceable by law. This too was a time when blacks suddenly appeared on television, as mayors of big cities, as icons of popular culture, as teachers, and in some cases even as neighbors. Today's black and white college students, veterans of *Sesame Street* and often of integrated grammar and high schools, have had more opportunities to know each other—whites and blacks—than any previous generation in American history. Not enough opportunities, perhaps, but enough to make the notion of racial tension on campus something of a mystery, at least to me.

To try to unravel this mystery I left my own campus, where there have been few signs of racial tension, and talked with black and white students at California schools where racial incidents had occurred: Stanford, UCLA, Berkeley. I spoke with black and white students—and not with Asians and Hispanics—because, as always, blacks and whites represent the deepest lines of division, and because I hesitate to wander onto the complex territory of other minority groups. A phrase by William H. Gass—"the hidden internality of things"—describes with maybe a little too much grandeur what I hoped to find. But it *is* what I wanted to find, for this is the kind of problem that makes a black person nervous, which is not to say that it doesn't unnerve whites as well. Once every six months or so someone yells "nigger" at me from a passing car. I don't like to think that these solo artists might soon make up a chorus or, worse, that this chorus might one day soon sing to me from the paths of my own campus.

I have long believed that trouble between the races is seldom what it 6 appears to be.[1] It was not hard to see after my first talk with students that racial tension on campus is a problem that misrepresents itself. It has the same look, the archetypal pattern, of America's timeless racial conflict—white racism and black protest. And I think part of our concern over it comes from the fact that it has the feel of a relapse, illness gone and come again. But if we are seeing the same symptoms, I don't believe we are dealing with the same illness. For one thing, I think racial tension on campus is the result more of racial equality than inequality.

How to live with racial difference has been America's profound social 7 problem. For the first 100 years or so following emancipation it was controlled by a legally sanctioned inequality that acted as a buffer between the races. No longer is this the case. On campuses today, as throughout society, blacks enjoy equality under the law—a profound social advancement. No student may be kept out of a class or a dormitory or an extracurricular activity because of his or her race. But there is a paradox here: On a campus where members of all races are gathered, mixed together in the classroom as well as socially, differences are more exposed than ever. And this is where the trouble starts. For members of each race—young adults coming into their own, often away from home for the first time—bring to this site of freedom, exploration, and now, today, equality very deep fears and anxieties, inchoate feelings of racial shame, anger, and guilt. These feelings could lie dormant in the home, in familiar neighborhoods, in simpler days of childhood. But the college campus, with its structures of interaction and adult-level competition—the big exam, the dorm, the "mixer"—is another matter. I think campus racism is born of the rub between racial difference and a setting, the campus itself, devoted to interaction and equality. On our campuses, such concentrated micro-societies, all that remains unresolved between blacks and whites, all the old wounds and shames that have never been addressed, present themselves for attention—and present our youth with pressures they cannot always handle.

I have mentioned one paradox: racial fears and anxieties among blacks 8 and whites bubbling up in an era of racial equality under the law, in settings that are among the freest and fairest in society. And there is another, related paradox, stemming from the notion of—and practice of—affirmative action.

---

[1]See my essay, "I'm Black, You're White, Who's Innocent? Race and Power in an Era of Blame," *Harper's Magazine*, June 1988.

Under the provisions of the Equal Employment Opportunity Act of 1972, all state governments and institutions (including universities) were forced to initiate plans to increase the proportion of minority and women employees—in the case of universities, of students too. Affirmative action plans that establish racial quotas were ruled unconstitutional more than ten years ago in *University of California Regents v. Bakke.* But quotas are only the most controversial aspect of affirmative action; the principle of affirmative action is reflected in various university programs aimed at redressing and overcoming past patterns of discrimination. Of course, to be conscious of patterns of discrimination—the fact, say, that public schools in the black inner cities are more crowded and employ fewer top-notch teachers than white suburban public schools, and that this is a factor in student performance—is only reasonable. However, in doing this we also call attention quite obviously to difference: in the case of blacks and whites, racial difference. What has emerged on campus in recent years—as a result of the new equality and affirmative action, in a sense, as a result of progress—is a *politics of difference,* a troubling, volatile politics in which each group justifies itself, its sense of worth and its pursuit of power, through difference alone.

In this context, racial, ethnic, and gender differences become forms of 9 sovereignty, campuses become balkanized, and each group fights with whatever means are available. No doubt there are many factors that have contributed to the rise of racial tension on campus: What has been the role of fraternities, which have returned to campus with their inclusions and exclusions? What role has the heightened notion of college as some first step to personal, financial success played in increasing competition, and thus tension? Mostly what I sense, though, is that in interactive settings, while fighting the fights of "difference," old ghosts are stirred, and haunt again. Black and white Americans simply have the power to make each other feel shame and guilt. In the "real" world, we may be able to deny these feelings, keep them at bay. But these feelings are likely to surface on college campuses, where young people are groping for identity and power, and where difference is made to matter so greatly. In a way, racial tension on campus in the Eighties might have been inevitable.

I would like, first, to discuss black students, their anxieties and 10 vulnerabilities. The accusation that black Americans have always lived with is that they are inferior—inferior simply because they are black. And this accusation has been too uniform, too ingrained in cultural imagery, too enforced by law, custom, and every form of power not to have left a mark. Black inferiority was a precept accepted by the founders of this nation; it was a principle of social organization that relegated blacks to the sidelines of American life. So when today's young black students find themselves on white campuses, surrounded by those who historically have claimed superiority, they are also surrounded by the myth of their inferiority.

Of course it is true that many young people come to college with some   11
anxiety about not being good enough. But only blacks come wearing a color
that is still, in the minds of some, a sign of inferiority. Poles, Jews, Hispanics,
and other groups also endure degrading stereotypes. But two things make the
myth of black inferiority a far heavier burden—the broadness of its scope and
its incarnation in color. There are not only more stereotypes of blacks than
of other groups, but these stereotypes are also more dehumanizing, more
focused on the most despised of human traits—stupidity, laziness, sexual
immorality, dirtiness, and so on. In America's racial and ethnic hierarchy,
blacks have clearly been relegated to the lowest level—have been burdened
with an ambiguous, animalistic humanity. Moreover, this is made unavoidable for blacks by the sheer visibility of black skin, a skin that evokes the
myth of inferiority on sight. And today this myth is sadly reinforced for many
black students by affirmative action programs, under which blacks may often
enter college with lower test scores and high-school grade point averages
than whites. "They see me as an affirmative action case," one black student
told me at UCLA.

So when a black student enters college, the myth of inferiority com-   12
pounds the normal anxiousness over whether he or she will be good enough.
This anxiety is not only personal but also racial. The families of these
students will have pounded into them the fact that blacks are not inferior.
And probably more than anything, it is this pounding that finally leaves a
mark. If I am not inferior, why the need to say so?

This myth of inferiority constitutes a very sharp and ongoing anxiety   13
for young blacks, the nature of which is very precise: It is the terror that
somehow, through one's actions or by virtue of some "proof" (a poor grade, a
flubbed response in class), one's fear of inferiority—inculcated in ways large
and small by society—will be confirmed as real. On a university campus,
where intelligence itself is the ultimate measure, this anxiety is bound to be
triggered.

A black student I met at UCLA was disturbed a little when I asked him   14
if he ever felt vulnerable—anxious about "black inferiority"—as a black
student. But after a long pause, he finally said, "I think I do." The example
he gave was of a large lecture class he'd taken with more than 300 students.
Fifty or so black students sat in the back of the lecture hall and "acted out
every stereotype in the book." They were loud, ate food, came in late—and
generally got lower grades than the whites in the class. "I knew I would be
seen like them, and I didn't like it. I never sat by them." Seen like what? I
asked, though we both knew the answer. "As lazy, ignorant, and stupid," he
said sadly.

Had the group at the back been white fraternity brothers, they would not   15
have been seen as dumb *whites*, of course. And a frat brother who worried
about his grades would not worry that he would be seen "like them." The terror
in this situation for the student I spoke with was that his own deeply buried

anxiety would be given credence, that the myth would be verified, and that he would feel shame and humiliation not because of who he was but simply because he was black. In this lecture hall his race, quite apart from his performance, might subject him to four unendurable feelings—diminishment, accountability to the preconceptions of whites, a powerlessness to change those preconceptions, and, finally, shame. These are the feelings that make up his racial anxiety, and that of all blacks on any campus. On a white campus a black is never far from these feelings, and even his unconscious knowledge that he is subject to them can undermine his self-esteem. There are blacks on every campus who are not up to doing good college-level work. Certain black students may not be happy or motivated or in the appropriate field of study— *just like whites*. (Let us not forget that many white students get poor grades, fail, drop out.) Moreover, many more blacks than whites are not quite prepared for college, may have to catch up, owing to factors beyond their control: poor previous schooling, for example. But the white who has to catch up will not be anxious that his being behind is a matter of his whiteness, of his being *racially* inferior. The black student may well have such a fear.

This, I believe, is one reason why black colleges in America turn out 16 34 percent of all black college graduates, though they enroll only 17 percent of black college students. Without whites around on campus the myth of inferiority is in abeyance and, along with it, a great reservoir of culturally imposed self-doubt. On black campuses feelings of inferiority are personal; on campuses with a white majority, a black's problems have a way of becoming a "black" problem.

But this feeling of vulnerability a black may feel in itself is not as 17 serious a problem as what he or she does with it. To admit that one is made anxious in integrated situations about the myth of racial inferiority is difficult for young blacks. It seems like admitting that one *is* racially inferior. And so, most often, the student will deny harboring those feelings. This is where some of the pangs of racial tension begin, because denial always involves distortion.

In order to deny a problem we must tell ourselves that the problem is 18 something different than what it really is. A black student at Berkeley told me that he felt defensive every time he walked into a class and saw mostly white faces. When I asked why, he said, "Because I know they're all racists. They think blacks are stupid." Of course it may be true that some whites feel this way, but the singular focus on white racism allows this student to obscure his own underlying racial anxiety. He can now say that his problem—facing a class full of white faces, *fearing* that they think he is dumb—is entirely the result of certifiable white racism and has nothing to do with his own anxieties, or even that this particular academic subject may not be his best. Now all the terror of his anxiety, its powerful energy, is devoted to simply *seeing* racism. Whatever evidence of racism he finds—and looking this hard, he will no doubt find some—can be brought in to buttress his distorted view of the problem, while his actual deep-seated anxiety goes unseen.

Denial, and the distortion that results, places the problem *outside* the self and in the world. It is not that I have any inferiority anxiety because of my race; it is that I am going to school with people who don't like blacks. This is the shift in thinking that allows black students to reenact the protest pattern of the Sixties. Denied racial anxiety-distortion-reenactment is the process by which feelings of inferiority are transformed into an exaggerated white menace—which is then protested against with the techniques of the past. Under the sway of this process, black students believe that history is repeating itself, that it's just like the Sixties, or Fifties. In fact, it is the not yet healed wounds from the past, rather than the inequality that created the wounds, that is the real problem.

This process generates an unconscious need to exaggerate the level of racism on campus—to make it a matter of the system, not just a handful of students. Racism is the avenue away from the true inner anxiety. How many students demonstrating for a black "theme house"—demonstrating in the style of the Sixties, when the battle was to win for blacks a place on campus—might be better off spending their time reading and studying? Black students have the highest dropout rate and lowest grade point average of any group in American universities. This need not be so. And it is not the result of not having black theme houses.

It was my very good fortune to go to college in 1964, when the question of black "inferiority" was openly talked about among blacks. The summer before I left for college I heard Martin Luther King Jr. speak in Chicago, and he laid it on the line for black students everywhere. "When you are behind in a footrace, the only way to get ahead is to run faster than the man in front of you. So when your white roommate says he's tired and goes to sleep, you stay up and burn the midnight oil." His statement that we were "behind in a footrace" acknowledged that because of history, of few opportunities, of racism, we were, in a sense, "inferior." But this had to do with what had been done to our parents and their parents, not with inherent inferiority. And because it was acknowledged, it was presented to us as a challenge rather than a mark of shame.

Of the eighteen black students (in a student body of 1,000) who were on campus in my freshman year, all graduated, though a number of us were not from the middle class. At the university where I currently teach, the dropout rate for black students is 72 percent, despite the presence of several academic-support programs; a counseling center with black counselors; an Afro-American studies department; black faculty, administrators, and staff; a general education curriculum that emphasizes "cultural pluralism"; an Educational Opportunities Program; a mentor program; a black faculty and staff association; and an administration and faculty that often announce the need to do more for black students.

It may be unfair to compare my generation with the current one. Parents do this compulsively and to little end but self-congratulation. But I don't congratulate my generation. I think we were advantaged. We came along at a time when racial integration was held in high esteem. And integration was a very challenging social concept for both blacks and whites. We were remaking ourselves—that's what one did at college—and making history. We had something to prove. This was a profound advantage; it gave us clarity and a challenge. Achievement in the American mainstream was the goal of integration, and the best thing about this challenge was its secondary message—that we *could* achieve. 23

There is much irony in the fact that black power would come along in the late Sixties and change all this. Black power was a movement of uplift and pride, and yet it also delivered the weight of pride—a weight that would burden black students from then on. Black power "nationalized" the black identity, made blackness itself an object of celebration and allegiance. But if it transformed a mark of shame into a mark of pride, it also, in the name of pride, required the denial of racial anxiety. Without a frank account of one's anxieties, there is no clear direction, no concrete challenge. Black students today do not get as clear a message from their racial identity as my generation got. They are not filled with the same urgency to prove themselves, because black pride has said, You're already proven, already equal, as good as anybody. 24

The "black identity" shaped by black power most powerfully contributes to racial tensions on campuses by basing entitlement more on race than on constitutional rights and standards of merit. With integration, black entitlement was derived from constitutional principles of fairness. Black power changed this by skewing the formula from rights to color—if you were black, you were entitled. Thus, the United Coalition Against Racism (UCAR) at the University of Michigan could "demand" two years ago that all black professors be given immediate tenure, that there be special pay incentives for black professors, and that money be provided for an all-black student union. In this formula, black becomes the very color of entitlement, an extra right in itself, and a very dangerous grandiosity is promoted in which blackness amounts to specialness. 25

Race is, by any standard, an unprincipled source of power. And on campuses the use of racial power by one group makes racial or ethnic or gender *difference* a currency of power for all groups. When I make my difference into power, other groups must seize upon their difference to contain my power and maintain their position relative to me. Very quickly a kind of politics of difference emerges in which racial, ethnic, and gender groups are forced to assert their entitlement and vie for power based on the single quality that makes them different from one another. 26

On many campuses today academic departments and programs are   27
established on the basis of difference—black studies, women's studies, Asian
studies, and so on—despite the fact that there is nothing in these "difference" departments that cannot be studied within traditional academic disciplines. If their rationale truly is past exclusion from the mainstream curriculum, shouldn't the goal now be complete inclusion rather than separateness?
I think this logic is overlooked because these groups are too interested in the
power their difference can bring, and they insist on separate departments and
programs as a tribute to that power.

This politics of difference makes everyone on campus a member of a   28
minority group. It also makes racial tensions inevitable. To highlight one's
difference as a source of advantage is also, indirectly, to inspire the enemies
of that difference. When blackness (and femaleness) becomes power, then
white maleness is also sanctioned as power. A white male student at Stanford
told me, "One of my friends said the other day that we should get together
and start up a white student union and come up with a list of demands."

It is certainly true that white maleness has long been an unfair source of   29
power. But the sin of white male power is precisely its use of race and gender
as a source of entitlement. When minorities and women use their race,
ethnicity, and gender in the same way, they not only commit the same sin
but also, indirectly, sanction the very form of power that oppressed them in
the first place. The politics of difference is based on a tit-for-tat sort of logic
in which every victory only calls one's enemies to arms.

This elevation of difference undermines the communal impulse by   30
making each group foreign and inaccessible to others. When difference is
celebrated rather than remarked, people must think in terms of difference,
they must find meaning in difference, and this meaning comes from an
endless process of contrasting one's group with other groups. Blacks use
whites to define themselves as different, women use men. Hispanics use
whites and blacks, and on it goes. And in the process each group mytholo-
gizes and mystifies its difference, puts it beyond the full comprehension of
outsiders. Difference becomes an inaccessible preciousness toward which
outsiders are expected to be simply and uncomprehendingly reverential. But
beware: In this world, even the insulated world of the college campus,
preciousness is a balloon asking for a needle. At Smith College, graffiti
appears: "Niggers, Spics, and Chinks quit complaining or get out."

Most of the white students I talked with spoke as if from under a faint   31
cloud of accusation. There was always a ring of defensiveness in their complaints about blacks. A white student I spoke with at UCLA told me: "Most
white students on this campus think the black student leadership here is
made up of oversensitive crybabies who spend all their time looking for
things to kick up a ruckus about." A white student at Stanford said: "Blacks

do nothing but complain and ask for sympathy when everyone really knows they don't do well because they don't try. If they worked harder, they could do as well as everyone else."

That these students felt accused was most obvious in their compulsion   32
to assure me that they were not racists. Oblique versions of some-of-my-best-friends-are stories came ritualistically before or after critiques of black students. Some said flatly, "I am not a racist, but . . ." Of course, we all deny being racists, but we only do this compulsively, I think, when we are working against an accusation of bias. I think it was the color of my skin, itself, that accused them.

This was the meta-message that surrounded these conversations like an   33
aura, and in it, I believe, is the core of white American racial anxiety. My skin not only accused them, it judged them. And this judgment was a sad gift of history that brought them to account whether they deserved such an accounting or not. It said that wherever and whenever blacks were concerned, they had reason to feel guilt. And whether it was earned or unearned, I think it was guilt that set off the compulsion in these students to disclaim. I believe it is true that in America black people make white people feel guilty.

Guilt is the essence of white anxiety, just as inferiority is the essence of   34
black anxiety. And the terror that it carries for whites is the terror of discovering that one has reason to feel guilt where blacks are concerned— not so much because of what blacks might think but because of what guilt can say about oneself. If the darkest fear of blacks is inferiority, the darkest fear of whites is that their better lot in life is at least partially the result of their capacity for evil—their capacity to dehumanize an entire people for their own benefit, and then to be indifferent to the devastation their dehumanization has wrought on successive generations of their victims. This is the terror that whites are vulnerable to regarding blacks. And the mere fact of being white is sufficient to feel it, since even whites with hearts clean of racism benefit from being white—benefit at the expense of blacks. This is a conditional guilt having nothing to do with individual intentions or actions. And it makes for a very powerful anxiety because it threatens whites with a view of themselves as inhuman, just as inferiority threatens blacks with a similar view of themselves. At the dark core of both anxieties is a suspicion of incomplete humanity.

So the white students I met were not just meeting me; they were also   35
meeting the possibility of their own inhumanity. And this, I think, is what explains how some young white college students in the late Eighties can so frankly take part in racially insensitive and outright racist acts. They were expected to be cleaner of racism than any previous generation—they were born into the Great Society. But this expectation overlooks the fact that, for them, color is still an accusation and judgment. In black faces there is a discomforting reflection of white collective shame. Blacks remind them that

their racial innocence is questionable, that they are the beneficiaries of past and present racism, and that the sins of the father may well have been visited on the children.

And yet young whites tell themselves that they had nothing to do with the oppression of black people. They have a stronger belief in their racial innocence than any previous generation of whites, and a natural hostility toward anyone who would challenge that innocence. So (with a great deal of individual variation) they can end up in the paradoxical position of being hostile to blacks as a way of defending their own racial innocence. 36

I think this is what the young white editors of the *Dartmouth Review* were doing when they shamelessly harassed William Cole, a black music professor. Weren't they saying, in effect, I am so free of racial guilt that I can afford to ruthlessly attack blacks and still be racially innocent? The ruthlessness of that attack was a form of denial, a badge of innocence. The more they were charged with racism, the more ugly and confrontational their harassment became. Racism became a means of rejecting racial guilt, a way of showing that they were not ultimately racists. 37

The politics of difference sets up a struggle for innocence among all groups. When difference is the currency of power, each group must fight for the innocence that entitles it to power. Blacks sting whites with guilt, remind them of their racist past, accuse them of new and more subtle forms of racism. One way whites retrieve their innocence is to discredit blacks and deny their difficulties, for in this denial is the denial of their own guilt. To blacks this denial looks like racism, a racism that feeds black innocence and encourages them to throw more guilt at whites. And so the cycle continues. The politics of difference leads each group to pick at the sore spots of the other. 38

Men and women who run universities—whites, mostly—also participate in the politics of difference, although they handle their guilt differently than many of their students. They don't deny it, but still they don't want to *feel* it. And to avoid this *feeling* of guilt they have tended to go along with whatever blacks put on the table rather than work with them to assess their real needs. University administrators have too often been afraid of their own guilt and have relied on negotiation and capitulation more to appease that guilt than to help blacks and other minorities. Administrators would never give white students a racial theme house where they could be "more comfortable with people of their own kind," yet more and more universities are doing this for black students, thus fostering a kind of voluntary segregation. To avoid the anxieties of integrated situations, blacks ask for theme houses; to avoid guilt, white administrators give them theme houses. 39

When everyone is on the run from his anxieties about race, race relations on campus can be reduced to the negotiation of avoidances. A pattern of demand and concession develops in which each side uses the other 40 to escape itself. Black studies department, black deans of student affairs, black counseling programs, Afro houses, black theme houses, black home-coming dances and graduation ceremonies—black students and white admin-istrators have slowly engineered a machinery of separatism that, in the name of sacred difference, redraws the ugly lines of segregation.

Black students have not sufficiently helped themselves, and universi- 41 ties, despite all their concessions, have not really done much for blacks. If both faced their anxieties, I think they would see the same thing: Academic parity with all other groups should be the overriding mission of black stu-dents, and it should also be the first goal that universities have for their black students. Blacks can only *know* they are as good as others when they are, in fact, as good—when their grades are higher and their dropout rate lower. Nothing under the sun will substitute for this and no amount of concessions will bring it about.

Universities and colleges can never be free of guilt until they truly help 42 black students, which means leading and challenging them rather than negotiating and capitulating. It means inspiring them to achieve academic parity, nothing less, and helping them see their own weaknesses as their greatest challenge. It also means dismantling the machinery of separatism, breaking the link between difference and power, and skewing the formula for entitlement away from race and gender and back to constitutional rights.

As for the young white students who have rediscovered swastikas and 43 the word "nigger," I think they suffer from an exaggerated sense of their own innocence, as if they were incapable of evil and beyond the reach of guilt. But it is also true that the politics of difference creates an environment which threatens their innocence and makes them defensive. White students are not invited to the negotiating table from which they see blacks and others walk away with concessions. The presumption is that they do not deserve to be there because they are white. So they can only be defensive, and the less mature among them will be aggressive. Guerrilla activity will ensue. Of course this is wrong, but it is also a reflection of an environment where difference carries power and where whites have the wrong "difference."

I think universities should emphasize commonality as a higher value 44 than "diversity" and "pluralism"—buzzwords for the politics of difference. Difference that does not rest on a clearly delineated foundation of commonal-ity not only is inaccessible to those who are not part of the ethnic or racial group but is antagonistic to them. Difference can enrich only the common ground.

Integration has become an abstract term today, having to do with little 45 more than numbers and racial balances. But it once stood for a high and admirable set of values. It made difference second to commonality, and it asked members of all races to face whatever fears they inspired in each other. I doubt the word will have a new vogue, but the values, under whatever name, are worth working for.

Questions for Study and Discussion

1. Why does Steele find racial tension on our college campuses difficult to understand? In what ways are colleges different today than they were when Steele was a student in the 1960s?

2. How did Steele go about informing himself about racial tension on today's campuses? Are there any advantages to his method over, say, a carefully prepared questionnaire? Explain.

3. Steele believes that "racial tension on campus is a problem that misrepresents itself." What does he mean?

4. What are the "politics of difference"? According to Steele, how did this politics of difference emerge, and why does it make racial tensions inevitable? What happens when difference is perceived as power?

5. What is the myth of black inferiority? How does Steele use this concept to help explain racial tension on campuses?

6. According to Steele, what is wrong with groups claiming race and gender as a basis for entitlement?

7. What does Steele mean when he says, "Difference becomes an inaccessible preciousness toward which outsiders are expected to be simply and uncomprehendingly reverential"? Is Steele against all differences? Explain.

8. What, according to Steele, is the "essense of white anxiety"? What is the "darkest fear" of whites?

9. What is the relationship between integration and anxiety for both blacks and whites? What does Steele believe needs to be done to reduce racial tensions on campuses? Does he believe that the politics of difference offers any solutions? Why, or why not? What does Steele mean when he says, "Difference can enrich only the common ground"?

10. What is it that Steele believes black students really need? How can colleges and universities help them get it?

Writing Topics

1. Write an essay in which you describe the racial situation on your campus. Like Steele, you may want to interview a group of students to hear what they are thinking. How closely does the racial situation on your campus fit Steele's description of college campuses in the late 1980s? What, if anything, has changed?

2. What are your own feelings about race, about racial differences? Is race an issue that causes you any anxiety? If so, do you think that Steele has correctly diagnosed your feelings? Present your thinking on the issue of race in a well-organized essay.

JI-YEON MARY YUHFILL

Ji-Yeon Mary Yuhfill was born Yuh Ji-Yeon in 1965 in Seoul, Korea, and immigrated to the United States in 1970. A 1987 graduate of Stanford University, Yuhfill worked as a reporter for the *Omaha World-Reporter* and *Newsday* before entering the University of Pennsylvania doctoral program in history. Her scholarly interest is in immigration and multicultural studies. She currently lives with her husband in Korea.

In the following essay, which first appeared in the *Philadelphia Inquirer*, Yuhfill uses her own educational experiences in this country as a springboard for her argument that "downplaying ethnicity will not bolster national unity." Yuhfill believes that we should stress to our young people the diversity that lies at the very foundation of the United States.

Let's Tell the Story of All America's Cultures

I grew up hearing, seeing and almost believing that America was white— 1
albeit with a little black tinged here and there—and that white was best.

The white people were everywhere in my 1970s Chicago childhood: 2
Founding Fathers, Lewis and Clark, Lincoln, Daniel Boone, Carnegie, presidents, explorers and industrialists galore. The only black people were slaves. The only Indians were scalpers.

I never heard one word about how Benjamin Franklin was so impressed 3
by the Iroquois Federation of nations that he adapted that model into our system of state and federal government. Or that the Indian tribes were systematically betrayed and massacred by a greedy young nation that stole their land and called it the United States.

I never heard one word about how Asian immigrants were among the 4
first to turn California's desert into fields of plenty. Or about Chinese immigrant Ah Bing, who bred the cherry now on sale in groceries across the nation. Or that plantation owners in Hawaii imported labor from China, Japan, Korea and the Philippines to work the sugar cane fields. I never learned that Asian immigrants were the only immigrants denied U.S. citizenship, even though they served honorably in World War I. All the immigrants in my textbook were white.

I never learned about Frederick Douglass, the runaway slave who be-   5
came a leading abolitionist and statesman, or about black scholar W.E.B. Du
Bois. I never learned that black people rose up in arms against slavery. Nat
Turner wasn't one of the heroes in my childhood history class.

I never learned that the American Southwest and California were   6
already settled by Mexicans when they were annexed after the Mexican-
American War. I never learned that Mexico once had a problem keeping
land-hungry white men on the U.S. side of the border.

So when other children called me a slant-eyed chink and told me to go   7
back where I came from, I was ready to believe that I wasn't really an
American because I wasn't white.

America's bittersweet legacy of struggling and failing and getting an-   8
other step closer to democratic ideals of liberty and equality and justice for all
wasn't for the likes of me, an immigrant child from Korea. The history books
said so.

Well, the history books were wrong.   9

Educators around the country are finally realizing what I realized as a   10
teenager in the library, looking up the history I wasn't getting in school.
America is a multicultural nation, composed of many people with varying
histories and varying traditions who have little in common except their
humanity, a belief in democracy and a desire for freedom.

America changed them, but they changed America too.   11

A committee of scholars and teachers gathered by the New York State   12
Department of Education recognizes this in their recent report, "One Nation, Many Peoples: A Declaration of Cultural Interdependence."

They recommend that public schools provide a "multicultural educa-   13
tion, anchored to the shared principles of a liberal democracy."

What that means, according to the report, is recognizing that America   14
was shaped and continues to be shaped by people of diverse backgrounds. It
calls for students to be taught that history is an ongoing process of discovery
and interpretation of the past, and that there is more than one way of
viewing the world.

Thus, the westward migration of white Americans is not just a heroic   15
settling of an untamed wild, but also the conquest of indigenous peoples.
Immigrants were not just white, but Asian as well. Blacks were not merely
passive slaves freed by northern whites, but active fighters for their own
liberation.

In particular, according to the report, the curriculum should help chil-   16
dren "to assess critically the reasons for the inconsistencies between the
ideals of the U.S. and social realities. It should provide information and
intellectual tools that can permit them to contribute to bringing reality
closer to the ideals."

In other words, show children the good with the bad, and give them   17
the skills to help improve their country. What could be more patriotic?

Several dissenting members of the New York committee publicly worry 18 that America will splinter into the ethnic fragments if this multicultural curriculum is adopted. They argue that the committee's report puts the focus on ethnicity at the expense of national unity.

But downplaying ethnicity will not bolster national unity. The history 19 of America is the story of how and why people from all over the world came to the United States, and how in struggling to make a better life for themselves, they changed each other, they changed the country and they all came to call themselves Americans.

E pluribus unum. Out of many, one. 20

This is why I, with my Korean background, and my childhood tormentors, with their lost-in-the-mist-of-time European backgrounds, are all Americans. 21

It is the unique beauty of this country. It is high time we let all our children gaze upon it. 22

Questions for Study and Discussion

1. What is Yuhfill's thesis in this essay?
2. In paragraph 10, Yuhfill writes, "Educators around the country are finally realizing what I realized as a teenager in the library, looking up the history I wasn't getting in school." What exactly wasn't she getting?
3. What is the importance for the author of the New York State Department of Education report "One Nation, Many Peoples: A Declaration of Cultural Interdependence"?
4. In your own words, state the argument that exists between those who think multiculturalism is the true story of America and those who think multiculturalism will destroy the nation's unity. What assumptions are made by those on each side of the argument?
5. What is Yuhfill's tone in this essay? Cite examples of the diction she uses that help to establish that tone.

Writing Topics

1. With respect to multiculturalism, what principles would guide you in writing a curriculum for the public schools? State your ideas in an introduction to that hypothetical curriculum.
2. In an essay, describe your own educational experiences learning about the diversity of people and customs that make up America. Do you feel that you were given an accurate picture in the textbooks you read and in the lessons you were taught? Try to provide a number of illustrative examples to substantiate your description and the points you make.

5

Language in America

Language is not merely a more or less systematic inventory of the various items of experience . . . but actually defines experience for us because of our unconscious projection of its expectations onto the field of experience. . . . The "real world"" is to a large extent built up on the language habits of the group.
—Edward A. Sapir

Our speech has its weaknesses and defects, like all the rest. Most of the occasions for the troubles of the world are grammatical. Our lawsuits spring only from debate about the interpretation of the laws, and most of our wars from the inability to express clearly the conventions and agreements of princes.
—Michel de Montaigne

Language, Prejudice, and Sexism

GORDON ALLPORT

When Gordon Allport was writing *The Nature of Prejudice*, the influential book from which the following essay is taken, much of the United States was still racially segregated and Senator Joseph McCarthy was at the height of his sensational career, chasing suspected Communists and subversives from the national government. Allport's book appeared in 1954, the year in which things began to change. McCarthy's influence was finally ended by Senate censure. That same year the Supreme Court ruled against racial segregation in public schools, and in 1955 Martin Luther King, Jr., led the boycott against Montgomery's segregated bus system that began the modern civil rights movement.

Allport himself was not one to join the picket lines. He was born in 1897 in Montezuma, Indiana, attended Harvard University, and ultimately returned there as a professor of psychology; he retired in 1962 and died five years later. His articles and books on personality established him as a leading authority in his field. *The Nature of Prejudice* remains his most widely read book, however, as readable and relevant today as it was when first published. In this selection, Allport identifies and discusses some of the ways in which language itself, often very subtly, can express prejudice and even cause it.

The Language of Prejudice

Without words we should scarcely be able to form categories at all. A   1
dog perhaps forms rudimentary generalizations, such as small-boys-are-to-be-avoided—but this concept runs its course on the conditioned reflex level, and does not become the object of thought as such. In order to hold a generalization in mind for reflection and recall, for identification and for action, we need to fix it in words. Without words our world would be, as William James said, an "empirical sand-heap."

Nouns That Cut Slices

In the empirical world of human beings there are some [four] billion   2
grains of sand corresponding to our category "the human race." We cannot

possibly deal with so many separate entities in our thought, nor can we individualize even among the hundreds whom we encounter in our daily round. We must group them, form clusters. We welcome, therefore, the names that help us to perform the clustering.

The most important property of a noun is that it brings many grains of sand into a single pail, disregarding that fact that the same grains might have fitted just as appropriately into another pail. To state the matter technically, a noun *abstracts* from a concrete reality some one feature and assembles different concrete realities only with respect to this one feature. The very act of classifying forces us to overlook all other features, many of which might offer a sounder basis than the rubric we select. Irving Lee gives the following example: 3

> I knew a man who lost the use of both eyes. He was called a "blind man." He could also be called an expert typist, a conscientious worker, a good student, a careful listener, a man who wanted a job. But he couldn't get a job in the department store order room where employees sat and typed orders which came over the telephone. The personnel man was impatient to get the interview over. "But you're a blind man," he kept saying, and one could almost feel his silent assumption that somehow the incapacity in one aspect made the man incapable in every other. So blinded by the label was the interviewer that he could not be persuaded to look beyond it.

Some labels, such as "blind man," are exceedingly salient and powerful. They tend to prevent alternative classification, or even cross-classification. Ethnic labels are often of this type, particularly if they refer to some highly visible feature, e.g., Negro, Oriental. They resemble the labels that point to some outstanding incapacity—*feeble-minded, cripple, blind man*. Let us call such symbols "labels of primary potency." These symbols act like shrieking sirens, deafening us to all finer discriminations that we might otherwise perceive. Even though the blindness of one man and the darkness of pigmentation of another may be defining attributes for some purposes they are irrelevant and "noisy" for others. 4

Most people are unaware of this basic law of language—that every label applied to a given person refers properly only to one aspect of his nature. You may correctly say that a certain man is *human, a philanthropist, a Chinese, a physician, an athlete*. A given person may be all of these; but the chances are 5

that *Chinese* stands out in your mind as the symbol of primary potency. Yet neither this nor any other classificatory label can refer to the whole of a man's nature. (Only his proper name can do so.)

Thus each label we use, especially those of primary potency, distracts our attention from concrete reality. The living, breathing, complex individual—the ultimate unit of human nature—is lost to sight. As in Figure 1 the label magnifies one attribute out of all proportion to its true significance, and masks other important attributes of the individual. . . .   6

A category, once formed with the aid of a symbol of primary potency, tends to attract more attributes than it should. The category labeled *Chinese* comes to signify not only ethnic membership but also reticence, impassivity, poverty, treachery. To be sure . . . there may be genuine ethnic-linked traits, making for a certain *probability* that the member of an ethnic stock may have these attributes. But our cognitive process is not cautious. The labeled category, as we have seen, includes indiscriminately the defining attribute, probable attributes, and wholly fanciful, nonexistent attributes.   7

Even proper names—which ought to invite us to look at the individual person—may act like symbols of primary potency, especially if they arouse ethnic associations. Mr. Greenberg is a person, but since his name is Jewish, it activates in the hearer his entire category of Jews-as-a-whole. An ingenious experiment performed by Razran shows this point clearly, and at the same time demonstrates how a proper name, acting like an ethnic symbol, may bring with it an avalanche of stereotypes.   8

> Thirty photographs of college girls were shown on a screen to 150 students. The subjects rated the girls on a scale from one to five for *beauty, intelligence, character, ambition, general likability.* Two months later the same subjects were asked to rate the same photographs (and fifteen additional ones introduced to complicate the memory factor). This time five of the original photographs were given Jewish surnames (Cohen, Kantor, etc.), five Italian (Valenti, etc.), five Irish (O'Brien, etc.); and the remaining girls were given names chosen from the signers of the Declaration of Independence and from the Social Register (Davis, Adams, Clark, etc.).
>
> When Jewish names were attached to photographs there occurred the following changes in ratings:
> decrease in liking
> decrease in character
> decrease in beauty
> increase in intelligence
> increase in ambition
> For those photographs given Italian names there occurred:
> decrease in liking
> decrease in character
> decrease in beauty
> decrease in intelligence

Thus a mere proper name leads to prejudgments of personal attributes. The individual is fitted to the prejudice ethnic category, and not judged in his own right.

While the Irish names also brought about depreciated judgment, the depreciation was not as great as in the case of the Jews and Italians. The falling of likability of the "Jewish girls" was twice as great as for "Italians" and five times as great as for "Irish." We note, however, that the "Jewish" photographs caused higher ratings in *intelligence* and in *ambition*. Not all stereotypes of out-groups are unfavorable.

The anthropologist, Margaret Mead, has suggested that labels of pri-   9
mary potency lose some of their force when they are changed from nouns into adjectives. To speak of a Negro soldier, a Catholic teacher, or a Jewish artist calls attention to the fact that some other group classifications are just as legitimate as the racial or religious. If George Johnson is spoken of not only as a Negro but also as a *soldier*, we have at least two attributes to know him by, and two are more accurate than one. To depict him truly as an individual, of course, we should have to name many more attributes. It is a useful suggestion that we designate ethnic and religious membership where possible with *adjectives* rather than with *nouns*.

Emotionally Toned Labels

Many categories have two kinds of labels—one less emotional and one   10
more emotional. Ask yourself how you feel, and what thoughts you have, when you read the words *school teacher*, and then *school marm*. Certainly the second phrase calls up something more strict, more ridiculous, more disagreeable than the former. Here are four innocent letters: m-a-r-m. But they make us shudder a bit, laugh a bit, and scorn a bit. They call up an image of a spare, humorless, irritable old maid. They do not tell us that she is an individual human being with sorrows and troubles of her own. They force her instantly into a rejective category.

In the ethnic sphere even plain labels such as Negro, Italian, Jew,   11
Catholic, Irish-American, French-Canadian may have emotional tone for a reason that we shall soon explain. But they all have their higher key equivalents: nigger, wop, kike, papist, harp, canuck. When these labels are employed we can be almost certain that the speaker *intends* not only to characterize the person's membership, but also to disparage and reject him.

Quite apart from the insulting intent that lies behind the use of certain   12
labels, there is also an inherent ("physiognomic") handicap in many terms designating ethnic membership. For example, the proper names characteristic of certain ethic memberships strike us as absurd. (We compare them, of course, with what is familiar and therefore "right.") Chinese names are short and silly; Polish names intrinsically difficult and outlandish. Unfamiliar dia-

lects strike us as ludicrous. Foreign dress (which, of course, is a visual ethnic symbol) seems unnecessarily queer.

But of all these "physiognomic" handicaps the reference to color, clearly 13 implied in certain symbols, is the greatest. The word Negro comes from the Latin *niger* meaning black. In point of fact, no Negro has a black complexion, but by comparison with other blonder stocks, he has come to be known as a "black man." Unfortunately *black* in the English language is a word having a preponderance of sinister connotations: the outlook is black, blackball, black-guard, blackhearted, black death, blacklist, blackmail, Black Hand. In his novel *Moby Dick,* Herman Melville considers at length the remarkably in morbid connotations of black and the remarkably virtuous connotations of white.

Nor is the ominous flavor of black confined to the English language. A 14 cross-cultural study reveals that the semantic significance of black is more or less universally the same. Among certain Siberian tribes, members of a privileged clan call themselves "white bones," and refer to all others as "black bones." Even among Uganda Negroes there is some evidence for a white god at the apex of the theocratic hierarchy; certain it is that a white cloth, signifying purity, is used to ward off evil spirit and disease.

There is thus an implied value-judgment in the very concept of *white race* 15 and *black race.* One might also study the numerous unpleasant connotations of *yellow,* and their possible bearing on our conception of the people of the Orient.

Such reasoning should not be carried too far, since there are undoubtedly, 16 in various contexts, pleasant associations with both black and yellow. Black velvet is agreeable; so too are chocolate and coffee. Yellow tulips are well liked; the sun and moon are radiantly yellow. Yet it is true that "color" words are used with chauvinistic overtones more than most people realize. There is certainly condescension indicated in many familiar phrases: dark as a nigger's pocket, darktown strutters, white hope (a term originated when a white contender was sought against the Negro heavyweight champion, Jack Johnson), the white man's burden, the yellow peril, black boy. Scores of everyday phrases are stamped with the flavor of prejudice, whether the user knows it or not.

We spoke of the fact that even the most proper and sedate labels for 17 minority groups sometimes seem to exude a negative flavor. In many contexts and situations the very terms *French-Canadian, Mexican,* or *Jew,* correct and nonmalicious though they are, sound a bit opprobrious. The reason is that they are labels of social deviants. Especially in a culture where uniformity is prized, the name of *any* deviant carries with it *ipso facto* a negative value-judgment. Words like *insane, alcoholic, pervert* are presumably neutral designations of a human condition, but they are more: they are finger-pointings at deviance. Minority groups are deviants, and for this reason, from the very outset, the most innocent labels in many situations imply a shading of disrepute. When we wish to highlight the deviance and denigrate it still further we use words of a higher emotional key: crackpot, soak, pansy, greaser, Okie, nigger, harp, kike.

Members of minority groups are often understandably sensitive to names   18
given them. Not only do they object to deliberately insulting epithets, but
sometimes see evil intent where none exists. Often the word Negro is spelled
with a small *n*, occasionally as a studied insult, more often from ignorance.
(The term is not cognate with white, which is not capitalized, but rather with
Caucasian, which is.) Terms like "mulatto" or "octoroon" cause hard feeling
because of the condescension with which they have often been used in the
past. Sex differentiations are objectionable, since they seem doubly to emphasize ethnic difference: why speak of Jewess and not of Protestantess, or of
Negress and not of whitess? Similar overemphasis is implied in the terms like
Chinaman or Scotchman; why not American man? Grounds for misunderstanding lie in the fact that minority group members are sensitive to such
shadings, while majority members may employ them unthinkingly.

The Communist Label

Until we label an out-group it does not clearly exist in our minds. Take   19
the curiously vague situation that we often meet when a person wishes to
locate responsibility on the shoulders of some out-group whose nature he
cannot specify. In such a case he usually employs the pronoun "they" without
an antecedent. "Why don't they make these sidewalks wider?" "I hear they
are going to build a factory in this town and hire a lot of foreigners." "I won't
pay this tax bill; they can just whistle for their money." If asked "who?" the
speaker is likely to grow confused and embarrassed. The common use of the
orphaned pronoun *they* teaches us that people often want and need to designate out-groups (usually for the purpose of venting hostility) even when they
have no clear conception of the out-group in question. And so long as the
target of wrath remains vague and ill-defined specific prejudice cannot crys-
tallize around it. To have enemies we need labels.

Until relatively recently—strange as it may seem—there was no agreed-   20
upon symbol for *communist*. The word, of course, existed but it had no special
emotional connotation, and did not designate a public enemy. Even when,
after World War I, there was a growing feeling of economic and social menace
in this country, there was no agreement as to the actual source of the menace.

A content analysis of the *Boston Herald* for the year 1920 turned up the   21
following list of labels. Each was used in a context implying some threat.
Hysteria had overspread the country, as it did after World War II. Someone
must be responsible for the postwar malaise, rising prices, uncertainty. There
must be a villain. But in 1920 the villain was impartially designated by
reporters and editorial writers with the following symbols:

alien, agitator, anarchist, apostle of bomb and torch, Bolshevik, communist, communist laborite, conspirator, emissary of false promise, extremist,

foreigner, hyphenated-American, incendiary, IWW, parlor anarchist, parlor pink, parlor socialist, plotter, radical, red, revolutionary, Russian agitator, socialist, Soviet, syndicalist, traitor, undesirable.[1]

From this excited array we note that the *need* for an enemy (someone to serve as a focus for discontent and jitters) was considerably more apparent than the precise *identity* of the enemy. At any rate, there was no clearly agreed upon label. Perhaps partly for this reason the hysteria abated. Since no clear category of "communism" existed there was no true focus for the hostility.   22

But following World War II this collection of vaguely interchangeable labels became fewer in number and more commonly agreed upon. The outgroup menace came to be designated almost always as *communist* or *red*. In 1920 the threat, lacking a clear label, was vague; after 1945 both symbol and thing became more definite. Not that people knew precisely what they meant when they said "communist," but with the aid of the term they were at least able to point consistently to *something* that inspired fear. The term developed the power of signifying menace and led to various repressive measures against anyone to whom the label was rightly or wrongly attached.   23

Logically, the label should apply to specifiable defining attributes, such as members of the Communist Party, or people whose allegiance is with the Russian system, or followers, historically, or Karl Marx. But the label came in for more extensive use.   24

What seems to have happened is approximately as follows. Having suffered through a period of war and being acutely aware of devastating revolutions abroad, it is natural that most people should be upset, dreading to lose their possessions, annoyed by high taxes, seeing customary moral and religious values threatened, and dreading worse disasters to come. Seeking an explanation for this unrest, a single identifiable enemy is wanted. It is not enough to designate "Russia" or some other distant land. Nor is it satisfactory to fix blame on "changing social conditions." What is needed is a human agent near at hand: someone in Washington, someone in our schools, in our factories, in our neighborhood. If we *feel* an immediate threat, we reason, there must be a near-lying danger. It is, we conclude, communism, not only in Russia but also in America, at our doorstep, in our government, in our churches, in our colleges, in our neighborhood.   25

Are we saying that hostility toward communism is prejudice? Not necessarily. There are certainly phases of the dispute wherein realistic social conflict is involved. American values (e.g., respect for the person) and totalitarian values as represented in Soviet practice are intrinsically at odds. A realistic opposition in some form will occur. Prejudice enters only when   26

---

[1] The IWW, or Industrial Workers of the World, was a radical labor organization that advocated violence. Syndicalism advocated that labor unions take over the government and industry.

the defining attributes of "communist" grow imprecise, when anyone who favors any form of social change is called a communist. People who fear social change are the ones most likely to affix the label to any persons or practices that seem to them threatening.

For them the category is undifferentiated. It includes books, movies, preachers, teachers who utter what for them are uncongenial thoughts. If evil befalls—perhaps forest fires or a factory explosion—it is due to communist saboteurs. The category becomes monopolistic, covering almost anything that is uncongenial. On the floor of the House of Representatives in 1946, Representative Rankin called James Roosevelt a communist. Congressman Outland replied with psychological acumen, "Apparently everyone who disagrees with Mr. Rankin is a communist."

When differentiated thinking is at a low ebb—as it is in times of social crises—there is a magnification of two-valued logic. Things are perceived as either inside or outside a moral order. What is outside is likely to be called "communist." Correspondingly—and here is where damage is done—whatever is called communist (however erroneously) is immediately cast outside the moral order.

This associative mechanism places enormous power in the hands of a demagogue. For several years Senator McCarthy managed to discredit many citizens who thought differently from himself by the simple device of calling them a communist. Few people were able to see through this trick and many reputations were ruined. But the famous senator has no monopoly on the device. As reported in the *Boston Herald* on November 1, 1946, Representative Joseph Martin, Republican leader in the House, ended his election campaign against his Democratic opponent by saying, "The people will vote tomorrow between chaos, confusion, bankruptcy, state socialism or communism, and the preservation of our American life, with all its freedom and its opportunities." Such an array of emotional labels placed his opponent outside the accepted moral order. Martin was re-elected. . . .

Not everyone, or course, is taken in. Demagogy, when it goes too far, meets with ridicule. Elizabeth Dilling's book, *The Red Network*, was so exaggerated in its two-valued logic that it was shrugged off by many people with a smile. One reader remarked, "Apparently if you step off the sidewalk with your left foot you're a communist." But it is not easy in times of social strain and hysteria to keep one's balance, and to resist the tendency of a verbal symbol to manufacture large and fanciful categories of prejudiced thinking.

Verbal Realism and Symbol Phobia

Most individuals rebel at being labeled, especially if the label is uncomplimentary. Very few are willing to be called *fascistic, socialistic,* or *anti-Semitic.* Unsavory labels may apply to others, but not to us.

An illustration of the craving that people have to attach favorable 32
symbols to themselves is seen in the community where white people banded
together to force out a Negro family that had moved in. They called themselves "Neighborly Endeavor" and chose as their motto the Golden Rule.[2]
One of the first acts of this symbol-sanctified band was to sue the man who
sold property to Negroes. They then flooded the house which another Negro
couple planned to occupy. Such were the acts performed under the banner of
the Golden Rule.

Studies made by Stagner and Hartmann show that a person's political 33
attitudes may in fact entitle him to be called a fascist or a socialist, and yet he
will emphatically repudiate the unsavory label, and fail to endorse any movement or candidate that overtly accepts them. In short, there is a *symbol phobia*
that corresponds to *verbal realism.* We are more inclined to the former when we
ourselves are concerned, though we are much less critical when epithets of
"fascist," "communist," "blind man," "school marm" are applied to others.

When symbols provoke strong emotions they are sometimes regarded 34
no longer as symbols, but as actual things. The expressions "son of a bitch"
and "liar" are in our culture frequently regarded as "fighting words." Softer
and more subtle expressions of contempt may be accepted. But in these
particular cases, the epithet itself must be "taken back." We certainly do not
change our opponent's attitude by making him take back a word, but it seems
somehow important that the word itself be eradicated.

Such verbal realism may reach extreme length. 35

The City Council of Cambridge, Massachusetts, unanimously passed a
resolution (December, 1939) making it illegal "to possess, harbor, seques-
ter, introduce or transport, within the city limits, any book, map, magazine, newspaper, pamphlet, handbill or circular containing the words
Lenin or Leningrad."

Such naiveté in confusing language with reality is hard to comprehend
unless we recall that word-magic plays an appreciable part in human thinking. The following examples, like the one preceding are taken from
Hayakawa.[3]

The Malagasy soldier must eschew kidneys, because in the Malagasy language the word for kidney is the same as that for "shot"; so shot he would
certainly be if he ate a kidney.

In May, 1937, a state senator of New York bitterly opposed a bill for the
control of syphilis because "the innocence of children might be corrupted

[2]"Do unto others are you would have others do unto you."
[3]S. I. Hayakawa, author of *Language in Thought and Action.*

by a widespread use of the term. . . . This particular word creates a shudder in every decent woman and decent man."

This tendency to reify words underscores the close cohesion that   3(
exists between category and symbol. Just the mention of "communist," "Negro," "Jew," "England," "Democrats," will send some people into a panic of fear or a frenzy of anger. Who can say whether it is the word or the thing that annoys them? The label is an intrinsic part of any monopolistic category. Hence to liberate a person from ethnic or political prejudice it is necessary at the same time to liberate him from *word fetishism*. This fact is well known to students of general semantics who tell us that prejudice is due in large part to verbal realism and to symbol phobia. Therefore any program for the reduction of prejudice must include a large measure of semantic therapy.

Questions for Study and Discussion

1. Where does Allport state his main point? How does he support and develop that point in this essay?
2. Names and nouns are essential if we are to make sense of the world, as Allport suggests in his opening paragraph, yet he goes on to say that nouns are inherently unfair. Why is this so?
3. Why are "labels of primary potency" so important? Should we always avoid the use of such labels? Does Allport suggest any ways in which the force of these labels can be diminished? If so, what are they?
4. In paragraphs 10 through 18, Allport observes that different words with approximately the same literal meaning often express different attitudes. What about this passage had the greatest impact on you? Did any of it seem no longer valid? Why? What does the passage, and your response to it, suggest about the relation between language and prejudice?
5. Paragraphs 19 through 30 deal with an attitude that was widespread in the early 1950s but is much rarer now. Is Allport's point nonetheless still relevant? Why? If so, what present-day examples would you give to make its relevance plain?
6. What does Allport mean by "symbol phobia" and "verbal realism"? Give your own examples of each.

Writing Topics

1. Everyone can be placed in various categories according to sex, race, religion, cultural background, and even appearance. How would you categorize yourself? What is your own image of the categories to which you belong? How do outsiders view these categories? In what ways has language been used to stigmatize you or the categories to which you belong? How do you feel about it?

2. In recent years, members of various groups have sought to have new labels applied to themselves, labels that express their own views rather than those of outsiders. Two prominent examples are women and the African-Americans. Choose a group and trace how it has named itself and how this has influenced the labels others use. What conclusions can you draw from that history?

GLORIA NAYLOR

Novelist and essayist Gloria Naylor was born in New York City in 1950. She worked first as a missionary for the Jehovah's Witnesses from 1967 to 1975, then as a telephone operator until 1981. That year she graduated from Brooklyn College and started her master's degree in Afro-American studies at Yale University. In her fiction Naylor explores the lives of African-American women, drawing freely from her own experiences and those of women in her extended family. She received the American Book Award for First Fiction for *The Women of Brewster Place* (1982), a novel that was later adapted for television. This success was followed by *Linden Hills* in 1985 and *Mama Day* in 1988. Her stories and essays have appeared widely.

More than any other form of prejudiced language, racial slurs are intended to wound and shame. In the following essay, which first appeared in the *New York Times* in 1986, Naylor remembers a time when a third-grade classmate called her "nigger." By examining the ways in which words can take on meaning depending on who uses them and to what purpose, Naylor concludes that "words themselves are innocuous; it is the consensus that gives them true power."

The Meanings of a Word

Language is the subject. It is the written form with which I've managed   1
to keep the wolf away from the door and, in diaries, to keep my sanity. In spite of this, I consider the written word inferior to the spoken, and much of the frustration experienced by novelists is the awareness that whatever we manage to capture in even the most transcendent passages falls far short of the richness of life. Dialogue achieves its power in the dynamics of a fleeting moment of sight, sound, smell, and touch.

I'm not going to enter the debate here about whether it is language that   2
shapes reality or vice versa. That battle is doomed to be waged whenever we seek intermittent reprieve from the chicken and egg dispute. I will simply take the position that the spoken word, like the written word, amounts to a nonsensical arrangement of sounds or letters without a consensus that assigns "meaning." And building from the meanings of what we hear, we order reality. Words themselves are innocuous; it is the consensus that gives them true power.

I remember the first time I heard the word *nigger*. In my third-grade   3
class, our math tests were being passed down the rows, and as I handed the papers to a little boy in back of me, I remarked that once again he had received a much lower mark than I did. He snatched his test from me and spit out that word. Had he called me a nymphomaniac or a necrophiliac, I

couldn't have been more puzzled. I didn't know what a nigger was, but I knew that whatever it meant, it was something he shouldn't have called me. This was verified when I raised my hand, and in a loud voice repeated what he had said and watched the teacher scold him for using a "bad" word. I was later to go home and ask the inevitable question that every black parent must face—"Mommy, what does *nigger* mean?"

And what exactly did it mean? Thinking back, I realize that this could   4
not have been the first time the word was used in my presence. I was part of a large extended family that had migrated from the rural South after World War II and formed a close-knit network that gravitated around my maternal grandparents. Their ground-floor apartment in one of the buildings they owned in Harlem was a weekend mecca for my immediate family, along with countless aunts, uncles, and cousins who brought along assorted friends. It was a bustling and open house with assorted neighbors and tenants popping in and out to exchange bits of gossip, pick up an old quarrel, or referee the ongoing checkers game in which my grandmother cheated shamelessly. They were all there to let down their hair and put up their feet after a week of labor in factories, laundries, and shipyards of New York.

Amid the clamor, which could reach deafening proportions—two or   5
three conversations going on simultaneously, punctuated by the sound of a baby's crying somewhere in the back rooms or out on the street—there was still a rigid set of rules about what was said and how. Older children were sent out of the living room when it was time to get into the juicy details about "you-know-who" up on the third floor who had gone and gotten herself "p-r-e-g-n-a-n-t!" But my parents, knowing that I could spell well beyond my years, always demanded that I follow the others out to play. Beyond sexual misconduct and death, everything else was considered harmless for our young ears. And so among the anecdotes of the triumphs and disappointments in the various workings of their lives, the word *nigger* was used in my presence, but it was set within contexts and inflections that caused it to register in my mind as something else.

In the singular, the word was always applied to a man who had distin-   6
guished himself in some situation that brought their approval for his strength, intelligence, or drive:

"Did Johnny *really* do that?"   7

"I'm telling you, that nigger pulled in $6,000 of overtime last year. Said   8
he got enough for a down payment on a house."

When used with a possessive adjective by a woman—"my nigger"—it   9
became a term of endearment for her husband or boyfriend. But it could be more than just a term applied to a man. In their mouths it became the pure essence of manhood—a disembodied force that channeled their past history of struggle and present survival against the odds into a victorious statement of being: "Yeah, that old foreman found out quick enough—you don't mess with a nigger."

In the plural, it became a description of some group within the community that had overstepped the bounds of decency as my family defined it. Parents who neglected their children, a drunken couple who fought in public, people who simply refused to look for work, those with excessively dirty mouths or unkempt households were all "trifling niggers." This particular circle could forgive hard times, unemployment, the occasional bout of depression—they had gone through all of that themselves—but the unforgivable sin was lack of self-respect. 10

A woman could never be a "nigger"in the singular, with its connotation of confirming worth. The noun *girl* was its closest equivalent in that sense, but only when used in direct address and regardless of the gender doing the addressing. *Girl* was a token of respect for a woman. The one-syllable word was drawn out to sound like three in recognition of the extra ounce of wit, nerve, or daring that the woman had shown in the situation under discussion. 11

"G-i-r-l, stop. You mean you said that to his face?" 12

But if the word was used in a third-person reference or shortened so that it almost snapped out of the mouth, it always involved some element of communal disapproval. And age became an important factor in these exchanges. It was only between individuals of the same generation, or from any older person to a younger (but never the other way around), that *girl* would be considered a compliment. 13

I don't agree with the argument that use of the word *nigger* at this social stratum of the black community was an internalization of racism. The dynamics were the exact opposite: the people in my grandmother's living room took a word that whites used to signify worthlessness or degradation and rendered it impotent. Gathering there together, they transformed *nigger* to signify the varied and complex human beings they knew themselves to be. If the word was to disappear totally from the mouths of even the most liberal of white society, no one in that room was naive enough to believe it would disappear from white minds. Meeting the word head-on, they proved it had absolutely nothing to do with the way they were determined to live their lives. 14

So there must have been dozens of times that *nigger* was spoken in front of me before I reached the third grade. But I didn't "hear" it until it was said by a small pair of lips that had already learned it could be a way to humiliate me. That was the word I went home and asked my mother about. And since she knew that I had to grow up in America, she took me in her lap and explained. 15

Questions for Study and Discussion

1. According to Naylor, how do words acquire meanings?
2. How does Naylor explain her preference for the spoken word over the written word? What does she mean by "context"?

3. Naylor says she must have heard the word *nigger* many times while growing up, yet she "heard" it for the first time when she was in third grade. How does she explain this seeming contradiction?

4. In the context of her family, what does the word *nigger* mean to Naylor? Why do you suppose she offers so little in the way of a definition of her classmate's use of the word? What is the effect on you as a reader? Explain.

5. Naylor gives a detailed description of her family and its lifestyle in paragraphs 4 and 5. What kinds of details does she include in her brief story? How do these paragraphs contribute to your understanding of the word *nigger* as used by her family?

6. In what context is *girl* "a token of respect for a woman"? How do you think women in general would—or should—react to being called "girls"? Explain.

7. Would you characterize Naylor's tone in this essay as angry, objective, cynical, or something else? Cite examples of her diction to support your answer.

8. What is the meaning of Naylor's last sentence? How well does it work as an ending for her essay? Explain.

9. Naylor disagrees with the notion that the use of the word *nigger* in the African-American community can be taken as an "internalization of racism." Reexamine her essay and discuss how her definition of *nigger* affirms or denies her position.

Writing Topics

1. Since the early 1960s, African-Americans have sought a self-identifying label for themselves. After suffering for years under the labels "nigger," "colored," and "Negro," imposed by the dominant white society, they have experimented with such labels as "Afro-American" and "black." Currently, "African-American" and "people of color" are used. Write an essay in which you analyze the connotative differences among the various labels that have been used in the past thirty years.

2. Write an essay in which you discuss and explore a word that has more than one meaning depending on the point of view. For example, consider *chick, gay, lesbian, liberal, macho, radical,* or *wife.*

HAIG A. BOSMAJIAN

Haig Bosmajian was born in 1928 in Fresno, California, and was educated at the University of California, the University of the Pacific, and Stanford University. A professor of speech at the University of Washington, he has built a considerable reputation as an expert in freedom of speech and the language of suppression. Whether reporting on the treatment of women, African-Americans, gays, Jews, or war protesters, Bosmajian has sought to show a now familiar pattern in which language is used to "de-civilize," dehumanize, isolate, and legally redefine those people that a dominant power structure deems unworthy. In the following essay, Bosmajian focuses his attention on American Indians and the way language has been used against them by their oppressors.

Defining the "American Indian": A Case Study in the Language of Suppression

One of the first important acts of an oppressor is to redefine the op-   1
pressed victims he intends to jail or eradicate so that they will be looked
upon as creatures warranting suppression and in some cases separation and
annihilation. I say "creatures" because the redefinition usually implies a
dehumanization of the individual. The Nazis redefined the Jews as "bacilli,"
"parasites," "disease," and "demon."[1] The language of white racism has for
centuries attempted to "keep the nigger in his place."[2] Our sexist language
has allowed men to define who and what a woman is.[3] The labels "traitors,"

[1]See Haig A. Bosmajian, "The Magic Word in Nazi Persuasion," ETC., 23 (March 1966), 9–23; Werner Betz, "The National-Socialist Vocabulary," The Third Reich (London: Weidenfeld and Nicolson, 1955); Heniz Paechter, Nazi-Deutsch (New York: Frederick Ungar, 1944).

[2]See Simon Podair, "Language and Prejudice," Phylon Review, 17 (1956), 390–394; Haig A. Bosmajian, "The Language of White Racism," College English, 31 (December 1969), 263–272.

[3]See Haig A. Bosmajian, "The Language of Sexism," ETC., 29 (September 1972), 305–313.

"queers," "pinkos," "saboteurs," and "obscene degenerates" have all been used to attack students protesting the war in Vietnam and the economic and political injustices in this country.[4] One obviously does not listen to, much less talk to, traitors and outlaws, sensualists and queers. One only punishes them or, as Spiro Agnew suggested in one of his 1970 campaign speeches, indicates that there are some dissenters who should be separated "from our society with no more regret than we should feel over discarding rotten apples from a barrel."[5]

Through the use of the language of suppression the human animal can   2
seemingly justify the unjustifiable, make palatable the unpalatable, and make decent the indecent. Just as our thoughts affect our language, so does our language affect our thoughts and eventually our action and behavior. As George Orwell observed in his famous essay "Politics and the English Language," our language becomes ugly and inaccurate because our thoughts are foolish and then "the slovenliness of our language makes it easier for us to have foolish thoughts." Orwell maintained that "the decadence of our language is probably curable" and that "silly words and expressions have often disappeared, not through any evolutionary process but owing to the conscious action of a minority."[6] This then is our task: to identify the decadence in our language, the silly words and expressions which have been used to justify oppression of varying degrees. . . .

A case study of this inhumane use of language and of the linguistic   3
dehumanization process is provided in the manner in which the European invaders of the New World redefined the occupants of what is now called North America and the manner in which white Americans have perpetuated through language the suppression of the "Indians" into the twentieth century. This essay will focus on and examine (1) the natural-religious redefinition of the "Indians"; (2) the political-cultural redefinition of the "Indians"; and (3) the legal redefinition of the "Indians."

The Natural-Religious Redefinition

The "de-civilization," the dehumanization and redefinition of the In-   4
dian, began with the arrival of Columbus in the New World. The various peoples in the New World, even though the differences between them were as great as between Italians and Irish or Finns and Portuguese, were all

---

[4]See Haig A. Bosmajian, "The Protest Generation and Its Critics," *Discourse: A Review of the Liberal Arts*, 9 (Autumn 1966), 464–469.

[5]*The New York Times*, October 31, 1969, p. 25.

[6]"Politics and the English Language," in C. Muscatine and M. Griffith, *The Borzoi College Reader*, 2nd ed. (New York: Alfred A. Knopf, 1971), p. 88.

dubbed "Indians," and then "American Indians."[7] Having renamed the inhabitants, the invaders then proceeded to enslave, torture, and kill them, justifying this inhumanity by defining these inhabitants as "savages" and "barbarians." The Europeans' plundering and killing of the Indians in the West Indies outraged a Spanish Dominican missionary, Bartolome de las Casas, who provided the following account of the conquest of the Arawaks and Caribs in his *Brief Relation of the Destruction of the Indies:*

> They [the Spaniards] came with their Horsemen well armed with Sword and Launce, making most cruel havocks and slaughters. . . . Overrunning Cities and Villages, where they spared no sex nor age; neither would their cruelty pity Women with childe, whose bellies they would rip up, taking out the Infant to hew it in pieces. . . . The children they would take by the feet and dash their innocent heads against the rocks, and when they were fallen into the water, with a strange and cruel derision they would call on them to swim. . . . They erected certain Gallowses. . . . upon every one of which they would hang thirteen persons, blasphemously affirming that they did it in honor of our Redeemer and his Apostles, and then putting fire under them, they burnt the poor wretches alive. Those whom their pity did think to spare, they would send away with their hands cut off, and so hanging by the skin.[8]

After the arrival of the Spaniards, "whole Arawak villages disappeared through slavery, disease, and warfare, as well as by flight into the mountains. As a result, the native population of Haiti, for example, declined from an estimated 200,000 in 1492 to a mere 29,000 only twenty-two years later."[9]

The Spaniards were followed by the English who brought with them   5
their ideas of their white supremacy. In his *The Indian Heritage in America*, Alvin M. Josephy, Jr., observes that "in the early years of the sixteenth century educated whites, steeped in the ideological teaching of Europe, argued learnedly about whether or not Indians were humans with souls, whether they, too, derived from Adam and Eve (and were therefore sinful like the rest of mankind), or whether they were a previously subhuman species."[10] Uncivilized and satanic as the Indian may have been, according to the European invaders, he could be saved; but if he could not be saved then he would be destroyed. As Roy H. Pearce has put it, "Convinced thus of his divine right to

---

[7]Peter Farb, *Man's Rise to Civilization as Shown by the Indians of North America from Primeval Times to the Coming of the Industrial State* (New York: E. P. Dutton and Company, 1968), p. xx.

[8]Alvin M. Josephy, Jr., *The Indian Heritage of America* (New York: Bantam Books, Inc., 1969), p. 286.

[9]Farb, p. 243.

[10] Josephy, p. 4.

Indian lands, the Puritan discovered in the Indians themselves evidence of a Satanic opposition to the very principle of divinity."[11] However, continues Pearce, the Indian "also was a man who had to be brought to the civilized responsibilities of Christian manhood, a wild man to be improved along with wild lands, a creature who had to be made into a Puritan if he was to be saved. Save him, and you saved one of Satan's victims. Destroy him, and you destroy one of Satan's partisans."[12] Indians who resisted Puritan invasions of their lands were dubbed "heathens," the "heathen" definition and status in turn justifying the mass killing of Indians who refused to give up their lands to the white invaders: "when the Pequots resisted the migration of settlers into the Connecticut Valley in 1637, a party of Puritans surrounded the Pequot village and set fire to it. . . . Cotton Mather was grateful to the Lord that 'on this day we have sent six hundred heathen souls to hell.' "[13]

The European invaders, having defined themselves as culturally supe-   6
rior to the inhabitants they found in the New World, proceeded to their "manifest destiny" and subsequently to the massive killing of the "savages." "This sense of superiority over the Indians," write L. L. Knowles and K. Prewitt in *Institutional Racism in America*, "which was fostered by the religious ideology they carried to the new land, found its expression in the self-proclaimed mission to civilize and Christianize—a mission which was to find its ultimate expression in ideas of a 'manifest destiny' and a 'white man's burden.' "[14] But the Christianizing and "civilizing" process did not succeed and "thus began an extended process of genocide, giving rise to such aphorisms as 'The only good Indian is a dead Indian'. . . . Since Indians were capable of reaching only the state of 'savage,' they should not be allowed to impede the forward (westward, to be exact) progress of white civilization. The Church quickly acquiesced in this redefinition of the situation."[15]

The Political-Cultural Redefinition

If the Indians were not defined as outright "savages" or "barbarians,"   7
they were labeled "natives," and as Arnold Toynbee has observed in Volume One of *A Study of History*, "when we Westerners call people 'Natives' we

---

[11]Roy H. Pearce, *The Savages of America* (Baltimore: The Johns Hopkins Press, 1965), p. 21.

[12]Pearce, pp. 21–22.

[13]Farb, p. 247.

[14]Louis L. Knowles and Kenneth Prewitt, eds., *Institutional Racism in America* (Englewood Cliffs, N.J.: Prentice-Hall, Inc., 1969), p. 7.

[15]Knowles and Prewitt, p. 8.

implicitly take the cultural colour out of our perceptions of them. We see them as trees walking, or as wild animals infesting the country in which we happen to come across them. In fact, we see them as part of the local flora and fauna, and not as men of like passions with ourselves; and, seeing them thus as something infrahuman, we feel entitled to treat them as though they did not possess ordinary human rights."[16] Once the Indian was labeled "native" by the white invaders, the latter had in effect established the basis for domesticating or exterminating the former.

In 1787, at the Constitutional Convention, it had to be decided what 8
inhabitants of the total population in the newly formed United States should be counted in determining how many representatives each state would have in Congress. The Founding Fathers decided: "Representatives and direct taxes shall be apportioned among the several states . . . according to their respective numbers, which shall be determined by adding to the whole number of free persons, including those bound to service for a terms of years, and excluding Indians not taxed, three fifths of all other persons." The enslaved black came out three fifths of a person and the Indian came out a nonentity.

When the Indians had been defined as "savages" with no future, the 9
final result, as Pearce states, "was an image of the Indian out of society and out of history."[17] Once the Indians were successfully defined as governmental nonentities, no more justification was needed to drive them off their lands and to force them into migration and eventual death. In the nineteenth century, even the "civilized Indians" found themselves being systematically deprived of life and property. . . .

While the state and the church as institutions have defined the Indians 10
into subjugation, there has been in operation the use of a suppressive language by society at large which has perpetuated the dehumanization of the Indian. Our language includes various phrases and words which relegate the Indian to an inferior status: "The only good Indian is a dead Indian"; "Give it back to the Indians"; "drunken Indians," "dumb Indians," and "Redskins." Writings and speeches include references to the "Indian problem" in the same manner that references have been made by white Americans to the "Negro problem" and by the Nazis to the "Jewish problem." There was no "Jewish problem" in Germany until the Nazis created the myth; there was no "Negro problem" until white Americans created the myth; similarly, the "Indian problem" has been created in such a way that the oppressed, not the oppressor, evolve as "the problem."

---

[16]*A Study of History* (London: Oxford University Press, 1935), I, p. 152. For further discussion of the connotation of "natives," see Volume II of *A Study of History*, pp. 574–580.
[17]Pearce, p. 135.

The Legal Redefinition

As the list of negative "racial characteristics" of the "Indian race" grew   11
longer and longer over the years, the redefinition of the individual Indian
became easier and easier. He was trapped by the racial definitions, stereotypes, and myths. No matter how intelligent, how "civilized" the Indian
became, he or she was still an Indian. Even the one who managed to become
a citizen (prior to 1924) could not discard his or her "Indian-ness" sufficiently to participate in white society. The language of the law was used to
reinforce the redefinition of the oppressed into non-persons and this language of suppression, as law, became governmentally institutionalized, and
in effect legitimatized. One of the most blatant examples of the use of the
racial characteristic argument appears in an 1897 Minnesota Supreme Court
decision dealing with the indictment of one Edward Wise for selling intoxi-
cating liquors to an Indian who had severed all his relations with his tribe
and had through the provision of the "Land in Severality Act" of February 8,
1887, become a citizen of the United States.[18] Wise was indicted for violating a statute which provided that "whoseover sells . . . any spiritous liquors
or wines to any Indian in this state shall on conviction thereof be punished. . . ." In finding against Wise, the Minnesota Supreme Court emphasized the weaknesses of the "Indian race" and the fact that as a race Indians
were not as "civilized" as the whites:

> . . . in view of the nature and manifest purpose of this statute and the
> well-known conditions which induce its enactment, there is no warrant
> for limiting it by excluding from its operation sales of intoxicating liquors
> to any person of Indian blood, even although he may have become a
> citizen of the United States, by compliance with the act of congress. The
> statute is a police regulation. It was enacted in view of the well-known
> social condition, habits, and tendencies of Indians as a race. While there
> are doubtless notable individual exceptions to the rule, yet it is a well-
> known fact that Indians as a race are not as highly civilized as the whites;
> that they are less subject to moral restraint, more liable to acquire an
> inordinate appetite for intoxicating liquors, and also more liable to be
> dangerous to themselves and others when intoxicated.[19]

The Minnesota statute, said the Court, applied to and included "all Indians
as a race, without reference to their political status. . . . The difference in
condition between Indians as a race and the white race constituted a sufficient basis of classification."[20] Under the Court's reasoning, the individual

---

[18]*State v. Wise*, 72 N.W. 843 (1897).

[19]*In re Liquor Election in Beltrami County*, 989.

[20]*In re Liquor Election in Beltrami County*, 989.

Indian could not control his or her identity. Like it or not, the individual Indian was defined by the Court's language, by the "well-known fact" that "Indians as a race are not as highly civilized as whites," that Indians are "less subject to moral restraint." Like it or not, the individual Indian was identified in terms of the "characteristics" of the "Indians as a race," whether he or she had those characteristics or not, whether he or she was a citizen of the United States or not.

Twenty years later, Minnesota denied voting rights to Indians on the　12
basis of their not being "civilized." . . .[21]

The state of Arizona, the state with the largest Indian population,　13
until 1948 did not allow Indians the right to vote. Article 7 of Arizona's Constitution concerning the qualifications of voters placed the Indians in that state in the same category as traitors and felons, the same category as persons not of sound mind and the insane; Article 7 provided, in part: "No person under guardianship, *non compos mentis* or insane shall be qualified to vote in any election nor shall any person convicted of treason or felony, be qualified to vote at any election unless restored to civil rights." In 1928, the Arizona Supreme Court decided in *Porter v. Hall* that Arizona Indians did not have the right to vote since they were within the specific provisions of Article 7 denying suffrage to "persons under guardianship";[22] the Arizona Supreme Court said that ". . . so long as the federal government insists that, not-withstanding their citizenship, their responsibility under our law differs from that of the ordinary citizen, and that they are, or may be, regulated by that government, by virtue of its guardianship, in any manner different from that which may be used in regulation of white citizens, they are, within the meaning of our constitutional provision, 'persons under guardianship,' and not entitled to vote."[23] In defining the Indians of Arizona as it did in the above decision, the Arizona Supreme Court denied suffrage rights to the Indians even though four years earlier, on June 2, 1924, all non-citizen Indians born within the territorial limits of the United States were made citizens thereof by an Act of Congress. After devoting a paragraph to defining "insanity" and "*non compos mentis,*" the Arizona Supreme Court followed with a definition and discussion of "persons under guardianship," the category into which the Indians were placed:

> Broadly speaking, persons under guardianship may be defined as those who
> because of some peculiarity of status, defect of age, understanding or self-

[21]*In re Liquor Election in Beltrami County,* 990.

[22]*Porter v. Hall,* 271 P. 411 (1928).

[23]*Porter v. Hall,* 419.

control, are considered incapable of managing their own affairs, and who therefore have some other person lawfully invested with the power and charged with the duty of taking care of their persons or managing their property, or both. It will be seen from the foregoing definitions that there is one common quality found in each: The person falling within any one of the classes is to some extent and for some reason considered by the law as incapable of managing his own affairs as a normal person, and needing some special care from the state.[24]

In 1948, however, the Porter decision was overruled in the case of   14
Harrison v. Laveen,[25] thus allowing Indians in Arizona the right to vote. In the 1948 decision, the Supreme Court of Arizona stated that the designation of "persons under guardianship" as it appeared in Article 7 did not apply to Indians. As to the argument that the Indians generally fell into that group of people "incapable of managing their own affairs," the Court said in 1948 that "to ascribe to all Indians residing on reservations the quality of being 'incapable of handling their own affairs in an ordinary manner' would be a grave injustice, for amongst them are educated persons as fully capable of handling their affairs as their white neighbors."[26] Finally, four and a half centuries after Columbus "discovered" "America," almost all the descendants of the original occupants of this land were allowed by the descendants of the invaders to participate, through the vote, in effecting some control (however small) over their destiny in their own land. Almost all of the "red natives" of the land finally were recognized legally as being as fully capable of handling their affairs as "their white neighbors." . . .

Questions for Study and Discussion

1. What is the relationship between language and action that Bosmajian points to in paragraph 2?
2. In your own words, explain the concept of natural-religious redefinition.
3. How did the Indians become defined as "governmental nonentities"? How specifically did the courts "help" in this effort?
4. Bosmajian writes that it took four and a half centuries for Indians to "participate, through the vote, in effecting some control (however small) over their destiny in their own land." What might Bosmajian be referring to by the words "however small"?

---

[24]*Porter v. Hall,* 416.

[25]*Harrison v. Laveen,* 196 P. 2d 456 (1948).

[26]*Harrison v. Laveen,* 463.

Writing Topics

1. American Indians as a group have a very high rate of alcoholism. With what other social problems are they struggling? In what ways are their problems a product of the historical linguistic oppression that Bosmajian discusses in his esssay? Write an essay in which you apply your understanding of Bosmajian's arguments by examining the oppression that Indians continue to endure.

2. What individuals or groups of people with which you are familiar are being "de-civilized" and dehumanized? Write an essay in which you try to come to an understanding of the plight of one of these groups or individuals, using the principles that Bosmajian has explained.

ALLEEN PACE NILSEN

Alleen Pace Nilsen is a teacher and writer who specializes in children's literature and the study of sexist language. Born in 1936 in Phoenix, Arizona, she is a graduate of Brigham Young Univeristy and the University of Iowa. She has been a professor and administrator at Arizona State University. Her books on language study include *Pronunciation Contrasts in English* (1971), *Language Play: An Introduction to Linguistics* (1978), and *The Language of Humor/The Humor of Language* (1983).

In the beginning of her essay, Nilsen explains why and how she undertook her study of the words in the dictionary for what they could reveal about the antifemale bias in our culture. As she explains later, the "chicken metaphor" tells the whole story. A young girl is a *chick*, then she marries and begins feeling *cooped up*, so she goes to *hen parties* where she *cackles* with her friends. Then she has her *brood*. And when *they leave the nest*, she begins to *henpeck* her husband, finally turning into an *old biddy*.

Sexism in English: A 1990s Update

Twenty years ago I embarked on a study of the sexism inherent in American English. I had just returned to Ann Arbor, Michigan, after living for two years (1967–1969) in Kabul, Afghanistan, where I had begun to look critically at the role society assigned to women. The Afghan version of the *chaderi* prescribed for Moslem women was particularly confining. Afghan jokes and folklore were blatantly sexist, such as this proverb: "If you see an old man, sit down and take a lesson; if you see an old woman, throw a stone." 1

But it wasn't only the native culture that made me question women's roles, it was also the American community. 2

Most of the American women were like myself—wives and mothers whose husbands were either career diplomats, employees of USAID, or college professors who had been recruited to work on various contract teams. We were suddenly bereft of our traditional roles: some of us became alcoholics, others got very good at bridge, while still others searched desperately for ways to contribute either to our families or to the Afghans. The local economy provided few jobs for women and certainly none for foreigners; we were isolated from former friends and the social goals we had grown up with. 3

When I returned in the fall of 1969 to the University of Michigan in 4

Ann Arbor, I was surprised to find that many other women were also questioning the expectations they had grown up with. In the spring of 1970, a women's conference was announced. I hired a babysitter and attended, but I returned home more troubled than ever. The militancy of these women frightened me. Since I wasn't ready for a revolution, I decided I would have my own feminist movement. I would study the English language and see what it could tell me about sexism. I started reading a desk dictionary and making notecards on every entry that seemed to tell something about male and female. I soon had a dog-eared dictionary, along with a collection of notecards filling two shoe boxes.

Ironically, I started reading the dictionary because I wanted to avoid   5
getting involved in social issues, but what happened was that my notecards brought me right back to looking at society. Language and society are as intertwined as a chicken and an egg. The language a culture uses is telltale evidence of the values and beliefs of that culture. And because there is a lag in how fast a language changes—new words can easily be introduced, but it takes a long time for old words and usages to disappear—a careful look at English will reveal the attitudes that our ancestors held and that we as a culture are therefore predisposed to hold. My notecards revealed three main points. Friends have offered the opinion that I didn't need to read the dictionary to learn such obvious facts. Nevertheless, it was interesting to have linguistic evidence of sociological observations.

Women Are Sexy; Men Are Successful

First, in American culture a woman is valued for the attractiveness and   6
sexiness of her body, while a man is valued for his physical strength and accomplishments. A woman is sexy. A man is successful.

A persuasive piece of evidence supporting this view are the eponyms—   7
words that have come from someone's name—found in English. I had a two-and-a-half-inch stack of cards taken from men's names but less than a half-inch stack from women's names, and most of those came from Greek mythology. In the words that came into American English since we separated from Britain, there are many eponyms based on the names of famous American men: *Bartlett pear*, *boysenberry*, *diesel engine*, *Franklin stove*, *Ferris wheel*, *Gatling gun*, *mason jar*, *sideburns*, *sousaphone*, *Schick test*, and *Winchester rifle*. The only common eponyms taken from American women's names are *Alice blue* (after Alice Roosevelt Longworth), *bloomers* (after Amelia Jenks Bloomer), and *Mae West jacket* (after the buxom actress). Two out of three feminine eponyms relate closely to a woman's physical anatomy, while the masculine eponyms (except for *sideburns* after General Burnsides) have nothing to do with the namesake's body but, instead, honor the man for an accomplishment of some kind.

Although in Greek mythology women played a bigger role than they   8
did in the biblical stories of Judeo-Christian cultures and so the names of
goddesses are accepted parts of the language in such place names as Pomona
from the goddess of fruit and Athens from Athena and in such common
words as *cereal* from Ceres, *psychology* from Psyche, and *arachnoid* from
Arachne, the same tendency to think of women in relation to sexuality is
seen in the eponyms *aphrodisiac* from Aphrodite, the Greek name for the
goddess of love and beauty, and *venereal disease* from Venus, the Roman
name for Aphrodite.

Another interesting word from Greek mythology is *Amazon.* Accord-   9
ing to Greek folk etymology, the *a* means "without" as in *atypical* or *amoral,*
while *mazon* comes from *mazos* meaning "breast" as still seen in *mastectomy.*
In the Greek legend, Amazon women cut off their right breasts so that they
could better shoot their bows. Apparently, the storytellers had a feeling that
for women to play the active, "masculine" role the Amazons adopted for
themselves they had to trade in part of their femininity.

This preoccupation with women's breasts is not limited to ancient   10
stories. As a volunteer for the University of Wisconsin's *Dictionary of American Regional English (DARE)*, I read a western trapper's diary from the 1930s.
I was to make notes of any unusual usages or language patterns. My most
interesting finding was that the trapper referred to a range of mountains as
The Teats, a metaphor based on the similarity between the shapes of the
mountains and women's breasts. Because today we use the French wording,
The Grand Tetons, the metaphor isn't as obvious, but I wrote to mapmakers
and found the following listings: *Nippletop* and *Little Nipple Top* near Mount
Marcy in the Adirondacks; *Nipple Mountain* in Archuleta County, Colorado;
Nipple Peak in Coke County, Texas; *Nipple Butte* in Pennington, South
Dakota; *Squaw Peak* in Placer County, California (and many other loca-
tions); *Maiden's Peak* and *Squaw Tit* (they're the same mountain) in the
Cascade Range in Oregon; *Mary's Nipple* near Salt Lake City, Utah; and *Jane
Russell Peaks* near Stark, New Hampshire.

Except for the movie star Jane Russell, the women being referred to are   11
anonymous—it's only a sexual part of their body that is mentioned. When
topographical features are named after men, it's probably not going to draw
attention to a sexual part of their bodies but instead to honor individuals for an
accomplishment. For example, no one thinks of a part of the male body when
hearing a reference to Pike's Peak, Colorado, or Jackson Hole, Wyoming.

Going back to what I learned from my dictionary cards, I was surprised   12
to realize how many pairs of words we have in which the feminine word has
acquired sexual connotations while the masculine word retains a serious
businesslike aura. For example, a *callboy* is the person who calls actors when
it is time for them to go on stage, but a *callgirl* is a prostitute. Compare *sir* and
madam. Sir is a term of respect, while *madam* has acquired the specialized
meaning of a brothel manager. Something similar has happened to *master*

and *mistress*. Would you rather have a painting by an *old master* or an *old mistress?*

It's because the word *woman* had sexual connotations, as in "She's his 13 woman," that people began avoiding its use, hence such terminology as *ladies' room*, *lady of the house*, and *girls' school* or *school for young ladies*. Feminists, who ask that people use the term *woman* rather than *girl* or *lady*, are rejecting the idea that *woman* is primarily a sexual term. They have been at least partially successful in that today *woman* is commonly used to communicate gender without intending implications about sexuality.

I found two hundred pairs of words with masculine and feminine forms, 14 e.g., *heir-heiress*, *hero-heroine*, *steward-stewardess*, *usher-usherette*. In nearly all such pairs, the masculine word is considered the base, with some kind of feminine suffix being added. The masculine form is the one from which compounds are made, e.g., from *king-queen* comes *kingdom* but not *queendom*, from *sportsman-sportslady* comes *sportsmanship* but not *sportsladyship*. There is one—and only one—semantic area in which the masculine word is not the base or more powerful word. This is in the area dealing with sex and marriage. When someone refers to a *virgin*, a listener will probably think of a female, unless the speaker specifies *male* or uses a masculine pronoun. The same is true for *prostitute*.

In relation to marriage, there is much linguistic evidence showing that 15 weddings are more important to women than to men. A woman cherishes the wedding and is considered a bride for a whole year, but a man is referred to as a groom only on the day of the wedding. The word *bride* appears in *bridal attendant*, *bridal gown*, *bridesmaid*, *bridal shower*, and even *bridegroom*. *Groom* comes from the Middle English *grom*, meaning "man," and in the sense is seldom used outside the wedding. With most pairs of male/female words, people habitually put the masculine word first, *Mr. and Mrs.*, *his and hers*, *boys and girls*, *men and women*, *kings and queens*, *brothers and sisters*, *guys and dolls*, and *host and hostess*, but it is the *bride and groom* who are talked about, not the *groom and bride*.

The importance of marriage to a woman is also shown by the fact that 16 when a marriage ends in death, the woman gets the title of *widow*. A man gets the derived title of *widower*. This term is not used in other phrases or contexts, but *widow* is seen in *widowhood*, *widow's peak*, and *widow's walk*. A *widow* in a card game is an extra hand of cards, while in typesetting it is an extra line of type.

How changing cultural ideas bring changes to language is clearly visible 17 in this semantic area. The feminist movement has caused the differences between the sexes to be downplayed, and since I did my dictionary study two decades ago, the word *singles* has largely replaced such sex specific and value-laden terms as *bachelor*, *old maid*, *spinster*, *divorcee*, *widow*, and *widower*. And in 1970 I wrote that when a man is called *a professional* he is thought to be a doctor or a lawyer, but when people hear a woman referred to as *a professional* they are likely to think of a prostitute. That's not as true today because so many women have become doctors and lawyers and it's no longer incongruous to think of women in these professional roles.

Another change that has taken place is in wedding announcements. 18 They used to be sent out from the bride's parents and did not even give the name of the groom's parents. Today, most couples choose to list either all or none of the parents' names. Also it is now much more likely that both the bride and groom's picture will be in the newspaper, while a decade ago only the bride's picture was published on the "Women's" or the "Society" page. Even the traditional wording of the wedding ceremony is being changed. Many officials now pronounce the couple "husband and wife" instead of "man and wife," and they ask the bride if she promises "to love, honor, and cherish," instead of "to love, honor and obey."

Women Are Passive; Men Are Active

The wording of the wedding ceremony also relates to the second point 19 that my cards showed, which is that women are expected to play a passive or weak role while men play an active or strong role. In the traditional ceremony, the official asks, "Who gives the bride away?" and the father answers, "I do." Some fathers answer, "Her mother and I do," but that doesn't solve the problem inherent in the question. The idea that a bride is something to be handed over from one man to another bothers people because it goes back to the days when a man's servants, his children, and his wife were all considered to be his property. They were known by his name because they belonged to him, and he was responsible for their actions and their debts.

The grammar used in talking or writing about weddings as well as other 20 sexual relationships shows the expectation of men playing the active role. Men *wed* women while women *become* brides of men. A man *possesses* a woman; he *deflowers* her; he *performs*; he *scores*; he *takes away* her virginity. Although a woman can *seduce* a man, she cannot offer him her virginity. When talking about virginity, the only way to make the woman the actor in the sentence is to say that "She lost her virginity," but people lose things by accident rather than by purposeful actions, and so she's only the grammatical, not the real-life, actor.

The reason that women tried to bring the term Ms. into the language to 21 replace Miss and Mrs. relates to this point. Married women resent being identified only under their husband's names. For example, when Susan Glascoe did something newsworthy, she would be identified in the newspaper only as Mrs. John Glascoe. The dictionary cards showed what appeared to be an attitude on the part of the editors that it was almost indecent to let a respectable woman's name march unaccompanied across the pages of a dictionary. Women were listed with male names whether or not the male contributed to the woman's reason for being in the dictionary or in his own right was as famous as the woman. For example, Charlotte Brontë was identified as Mrs. Arthur B. Nicholls, Amelia Earhart as Mrs. George Palmer Putnam, Helen Hayes as Mrs. Charles MacArthur, Jenny Lind as Mme. Otto Goldschmit, Cornelia Otis Skinner as the daughter of Otis, Harriet Beecher Stowe as the sister of Henry Ward Beecher, and Edith Sitwell as the sister of Osbert and Sacheverell. A very small number of women got into the dictionary without the benefit of a masculine escort. They were rebels and crusaders: temperance leaders Frances Elizabeth Caroline Willard and Carry Nation, women's rights leaders Carrie Chapman Catt and Elizabeth Cady Stanton, birth control educator Margaret Sanger, religious leader Mary Baker Eddy, and slaves Harriet Tubman and Phillis Wheatley.

Etiquette books used to teach that if a woman had *Mrs.* in front of her   22
name, then the husband's name should follow because *Mrs.* is an abbreviated form of *Mistress* and a woman couldn't be a mistress of herself. As with many arguments about "correct" language usage, this isn't very logical because *Miss* is also an abbreviation of *Mistress*. Feminists hoped to simplify matters by introducing *Ms.* as an alternative to both *Mrs.* and *Miss,* but what happened is that *Ms.* largely replaced *Miss,* to became a catch-all business title for women. Many married women still prefer the title *Mrs.*, and some resent being addressed with the term *Ms.* As one frustrated newspaper reporter complained, "Before I can write about a woman, I have to know not only her marital status but also her political philosophy." The result of such complications may contribute to the demise of titles, which are already being ignored by many computer programmers who find it more efficient to simply use names, for example in a business letter: "Dear Joan Garcia," instead of "Dear Mrs. Joan Garcia," "Dear Ms. Garcia," or "Dear Mrs. Louis Garcia."

The titles given to royalty provide an example of how males can be   23
disadvantaged by the assumption that they are always to play the more powerful role. In British royalty, when a male holds a title, his wife is automatically given the feminine equivalent. But the reverse is not true. For example, a *count* is a high political officer with a *countess* being his wife. The same is true for a *duke* and a *duchess* and a *king* and a *queen.* But when a female holds the royal title, the man she marries does not automatically acquire the matching title. For example, Queen Elizabeth's husband has the title of *prince* rather than *king,* but if Prince Charles should become king while he is still married to Lady or Princess Diana, she will be known as queen. The reasoning appears to be that since masculine words are stronger, they are reserved for true heirs and withheld from males coming into the royal family by marriage. If Prince Phillip were called *King Phillip,* it would be much easier for British subjects to forget where the true power lies.

The names that people give their children show the hopes and dreams   24
they have for them, and when we look at the differences between male and female names in a culture, we can see the cumulative expectations of that

culture. In our culture girls often have names taken from small, aesthetically pleasing items, e.g., *Ruby, Jewel,* and *Pearl. Esther* and *Stella* mean "star," *Ada* means "ornament," and *Vanessa* means "butterfly." Boys are more likely to be given names with meanings of power and strength, e.g., *Neil* means "champion," *Martin* is from Mars, the God of War, *Raymond* means "wise protection," *Harold* means "chief of the army," *Ira* means "vigilant," *Rex* means "king," and *Richard* means "strong king."

We see similar differences in food metaphors. Food is a passive sub- 25
stance just sitting there waiting to be eaten. Many people have recognized this and so no longer feel comfortable describing women as "delectable morsels." However, when I was a teenager, it was considered a compliment to refer to a girl (we didn't call anyone a *woman* until she was middle-aged) as a *cute tomato,* a *peach,* a *dish,* a *cookie, honey, sugar,* or *sweetie-pie.* When being affectionate, women will occasionally call a man *honey* or *sweetie,* but in general, food metaphors are used much less often with men than with women. If a man is called a *fruit,* his masculinity is being questioned. But it's perfectly acceptable to use a food metaphor if the food is heavier and more substantive than that used for women. For example pin-up pictures of women have long been known as *cheesecake,* but when Burt Reynolds posed for a nude centerfold the picture was immediately dubbed *beefcake,* c.f., *a hunk of meat.* That such sexual references to men have come into the language is another reflection of how society is beginning to lessen the differences between their attitudes toward men and women.

Something similar to the *fruit* metaphor happens with references to 26
plants. We insult a man by calling him a *pansy,* but it wasn't considered particularly insulting to talk about a girl being a *wallflower,* a *clinging vine,* or a *shrinking violet,* or to give girls such names as *Ivy, Rose, Lily, Iris, Daisy, Camellia, Heather,* and *Flora.* A plant metaphor can be used with a man if the plant is big and strong, for example, Andrew Jackson's nickname of *Old Hickory.* Also, the phrases *blooming idiots* and *budding geniuses* can be used with either sex, but notice how they are based on the most active thing a plant can do which is to bloom or bud.

Animal metaphors also illustrate the different expectations for males 27
and females. Men are referred to as *studs, bucks,* and *wolves* while women are referred to with such metaphors as *kitten, bunny, beaver, bird, chick,* and *lamb.* In the 1950s we said that boys went *tomcatting,* but today it's *catting around* and both boys and girls do it. When the term *foxy,* meaning that someone was sexy, first became popular it was used only for girls, but now someone of either sex can be described as a *fox.* Some animal metaphors that are used predominantly with men have negative connotations based on the size and/or strength of the animals, e.g., *beast, bull-headed, jackass, rat, loanshark,* and *vulture.* Negative metaphors used with women are based on smaller animals, e.g., *social butterfly, mousy, catty,* and *vixen.* The feminine terms connote action, but not the same kind of large scale action as with the masculine terms.

Women Are Connected with Negative Connotations; Men with Positive Connotations

The final point that my notecards illustrated was how many positive   28
connotations are associated with the concept of masculine, while there are
either trivial or negative connotations connected with the corresponding
feminine concept. An example from the animal metaphors makes a good
illustration. The word *shrew* taken from the name of a small but especially
vicious animal was defined in my dictionary as "an ill-tempered scolding
woman," but the word *shrewd* taken from the same root was defined as
"marked by clever, discerning awareness" and was illustrated with the phrase
"a shrewd businessman."

Early in life, children are conditioned to the superiority of the mascu-   29
line roles. As child psychologists point out, little girls have much more
freedom to experiment with sex roles than do little boys. If a little girl acts
like a *tomboy*, most parents have mixed feelings, being at least partially
proud. But if their little boy acts like a *sissy* (derived from *sister*), they call a
psychologist. It's perfectly acceptable for a little girl to sleep in the crib that
was purchased for her brother, to wear his hand-me down jeans and shirts,
and to ride the bicycle that he has outgrown. But few parents would put a
boy baby in a white and gold crib decorated with frills and lace, and virtually
no parents woul have their little boy wear his sister's hand-me-down dresses,
nor would they have their son ride a girl's pink bicycle with a flower-
bedecked basket. The proper names given to girls and boys show this same
attitude. Girls can have "boy" names—*Cris, Craig, Jo, Kelly, Shawn, Teri,
Toni,* and *Sam*—but it doesn't work the other way around. A couple of
generations ago, *Beverley, Frances, Hazel, Marion,* and *Shirley* were common
boys' names. As parents gave these names to more and more girls, they fell
into disuse for males, and some older men who have these names prefer to go
by their initials or by such abbreviated form as *Haze* or *Shirl*.

When a little girl is told to *be a lady*, she is being told to sit with her   30
knees together and to be quiet and dainty. But when a little boy is told to *be a
man* he is being told to be noble, strong, and virtuous—to have all the
qualities that the speaker looks on as desirable. The concept of manliness has
such positive connotations that it used to be a compliment to call someone a
he-man, to say that he was doubly a man. Today many people are more
ambivalent about this term and respond to it much as they do to the word
macho. But calling someone a *manly man* or a *virile man* is nearly always
meant as a compliment. *Virile* comes from the Indo-European *vir* meaning
"man," which is also the basis of *virtuous*. Contrast the positive connotations
of both *virile* and *virtuous* with the negative connotations of both *virile* and
virtuous with the negative connotations of *hysterical*. The Greeks took this
latter word from their name for *uterus* (as still seen in *hysterectomy*). They

thought that women were the only ones who experienced uncontrolled emotional outbursts, and so the condition must have something to do with a part of the body that only women have.

Differences in the connotations between positive male and negative   31
female connotations can be seen in several pairs of words that differ denotatively only in the matter of sex. *Bachelor* as compared to *spinster* or *old maid* has such positive connotations that women try to adopt them by using the term *bachelor-girl* or *bachelorette*. *Old maid* is so negative that it's the basis for metaphors: pretentious and fussy old men are called *old maids,* as the left-over kernels of unpopped popcorn, and the last card in a popular children's game.

Patron and *matron* (Middle English for *father* and *mother*) have such   32
different levels of prestige that women try to borrow the more positive masculine connotations with the word *patroness,* literally "female father." Such a peculiar term came about because of the high prestige attached to *patron* in such phrases as *a patron of the arts* or *a patron saint. Matron* is more apt to be used in talking about a woman in charge of a jail or a public restroom.

When men are doing jobs that women often do, we apparently try to   33
pay the men extra by giving them fancy titles, for example, a male cook is more likely to be called a *chef* while a male seamstress will get the title of *tailor.* The armed forces have a special problem in that they recruit under such slogans as "The Marine Corps builds men!" and "Join the Army! Become a Man." Once the recruits are enlisted, they find themselves doing much of the work that has been traditionally thought of as a "women's work." The solution to getting the work done and not insulting anyone's masculinity was to change the title as shown below:

waitress	orderly
nurse	medic or corpsman
secretary	clerk-typist
assistant	adjutant
dishwasher or kitchen helper	KP (kitchen police)

Compare *brave* and *squaw.* Early settlers in America truly admired   34
Indian men and hence named them with a word that carried connotations of youth, vigor, and courage. But they used the Algonquin's name for "woman" and over the years it developed almost opposite connotations to those of *brave. Wizard* and *witch* contrast almost as much. The masculine *wizard* implies skill and wisdom combined with magic, while the feminine *witch* implies evil intentions combined with magic. Part of the unattractiveness of both *witch* and *squaw* is that they have been used so often to refer to old women, something with which our culture is particularly uncomfortable, just as the Afghans were. Imagine my surprise when I ran across the phrases

grandfatherly advice and *old wives' tales* and realized that the underlying implication is the same as the Afghan proverb about old men being worth listening to while old women talk only foolishness.

Other terms that show how negatively we view old women as compared   35
to young women are *old nag* as compared to *filly*, *old crow* or *old bat* as compared to *bird*, and of being *catty* as compared to being *kittenish*. There is no matching set of metaphors for men. The chicken metaphor tells the whole story of a woman's life. In her youth she is a *chick*. The she marries and begins *feathering her nest*. Soon she begins feeling *cooped up*, so she goes to *hen parties* where she *cackles* with her friends. The she has her *brood*, begins to *henpeck* her husband, and finally turns into an *old biddy*.

I embarked on my study of the dictionary not with the intention of   36
prescribing language change but simply to see what the language would tell me about sexism. Nevertheless I have been both surprised and pleased as I've watched the changes that have occurred over the past two decades. I'm one of those linguists who believes that new language customs will cause a new generation of speakers to grow up with different expectations. This is why I'm happy about people's efforts to use inclusive language, to say *he or she* or *they* when speaking about individuals whose names they do not know. I'm glad that leading publishers have developed guidelines to help writers use language that is fair to both sexes, and I'm glad that most newspapers and magazines list women by their own names instead of only by their husbands' names and that educated and thoughtful people no longer begin their business letters with "Dear Sir" or "Gentlemen," but instead use a memo form or begin with such salutations as "Dear Colleagues," "Dear Reader," or "Dear Committee Members." I'm also glad that such words as *poetess, authoress, conductress,* and *aviatrix* now sound quaint and old-fashioned and that *chairman* is giving way to *chair* or *head, mailman* to *mail carrier, clergyman* to *clergy,* and *stewardess* to *flight attendant.* I was also pleased when the National Oceanic and Atmospheric Administration bowed to feminist complaints and in the late 1970s began to alternate men's and women's names for hurricanes. However, I wasn't so pleased to discover that the change did not immediately erase sexist thoughts from everyone's mind, as shown by a headline about Hurricane David in a 1979 New York tabloid, "David Rapes Virgin Islands." More recently a similar metaphor appeared in a headline in the *Arizona Republic* about Hurricane Charlie, "Charlie Quits Carolinas, Flirts with Virginia."

What these incidents show is that sexism is not something existing   37
independently in American English or in the particular dictionary that I happened to read. Rather, it exists in people's minds. Language is like an X ray in providing visible evidence of invisible thoughts. The best thing about people being interested in and discussing sexist language is that as they make conscious decisions about what pronouns they will use, what jokes they will tell or laugh at, how they will write their names, or how they will begin their

letters, they are forced to think about the underlying issue of sexism. This is good because as a problem that begins in people's assumptions and expectations, it's a problem that will be solved only when a great many people have given it a great deal of thought.

Questions for Study and Discussion

1. What inspired Nilsen's investigation of sexism in the English language? How did her private "feminist movement" differ from the feminist movement of others? Why was she unable to avoid facing social issues head on?

2. What points does Nilsen make about each of the following?
   a. English words derived from the name of a person
   b. geographical names
   c. pairs of words, one masculine and the other feminine
   d. the use of words referring to foods, plants, and animals in connection with women
   e. the first names given to male and female infants
   f. the use of Ms.
   g. dictionary entries concerning famous women
   h. positive and negative connotations connected with the concepts "masculine" and "feminine."

3. Most dictionary makers try to describe accurately the ways in which speakers of English use the language. Can we, therefore, reasonably fault them for reflecting cultural attitudes in word definitions?

4. According to Nilsen, in what two areas does the English language reveal the importance of women?

5. Nilsen states she has seen many changes in the language since she began her study more than twenty years ago. List these changes and discuss what Nilsen says they reveal to her about the nature of sexist language. In what ways, for example, has the pronoun Ms. proven unsatisfactory?

Writing Topics

1. Nilsen provides us with an extensive catalog of words that reveal a disparaging attitude toward women. It is not her purpose, however, to offer any solutions to the problem of bias in the language. Write an essay in which you discuss the possible improvements that you as a user of the language, lexicographers as makers of dictionaries, and women and men committed to sexual equality can bring about.

2. Like any attempt to change the status quo, women's attempts to change language have aroused a great deal of opposition. Who is the opposition? To what does it seem to be reacting? Does the opposition seem justified in any of its objections? What techniques does the opposition employ?

SHARON OLDS

Poet Sharon Olds was born in San Francisco in 1942. A graduate of Stanford University, she earned her doctorate at Columbia University in 1972. Olds has taught poetry at a number of schools including Sarah Lawrence College and Columbia University. Since 1992 she has been professor of English at New York University. In her first collection of poems *Satan Says* (1980), reviewers recognized her "raw power." Olds received a National Book Critics Circle Award for her second volume *The Dead and the Living* (1984). Since then, four other collections have appeared, most recently *The Father* (1992). Olds's poems have been published in a variety of literary journals and magazines including *The New Yorker, Atlantic Monthly, Paris Review, Ms., Kenyon Review,* and *Yale Review.* Readers have praised Olds's poetry for its graphic depiction of family life and its accurate observations of people. The critic Elizabeth Gaffney believes that "out of private revelations she makes poems of universal truth, of sex, death, fear, love. Her poems are sometimes jarring, unexpected, bold, but always loving and deeply rewarding."

In the following poem from her collection *The Gold Cell* (1987), Olds recounts a chance meeting on a subway that made her confront her fears and prejudices surrounding race. As you read "On the Subway," note the sharp, powerful images that Olds uses to capture the emotional intensity of this racial encounter.

On the Subway

The boy and I face each other.
His feet are huge, in black sneakers
laced with white in a complex pattern like a
set of intentional scars. We are stuck on
opposite sides of the car, a couple of   5
molecules stuck in a rod of light
rapidly moving through darkness. He has the
casual cold look of a mugger,
alert under hooded lids. He is wearing
red, like the inside of the body   10
exposed, I am wearing dark fur, the
whole skin of an animal taken and
used. I look at his raw face,
he looks at my fur coat, and I don't
know if I am in his power—   15
he could take my coat so easily, my
briefcase, my life—

or if he is in my power, the way I am
living off his life, eating the steak
he does not eat, as if I am taking   20
the food from his mouth. And he is black
and I am white, and without meaning or
trying to I must profit from his darkness,
the way he absorbs the murderous beams of the
nation's heart, as black cotton   25
absorbs the heat of the sun and holds it. There is
no way to know how easy this
white skin makes my life, this
life he could take so easily and
break across his knee like a stick the way his   30
own back is being broken, the
rod of his soul that at birth was dark and
fluid and rich as the heart of a seedling
ready to thrust up into any available light.

Questions for Study and Discussion

1. The speaker encounters a young black boy on the subway. What are her first impressions of him? Does the speaker's attitude toward the boy change as the poem proceeds? Explain.

2. In lines 2 through 4 the speaker says that the white laces on the boy's black sneakers are "like a / set of intentional scars." How does this simile work, and what does it contribute to the speaker's description and impression of the boy?

3. Identify several other figures of speech and explain how each functions in the context of the poem.

4. In what sense can the boy's face be considered "raw"?

5. What does the speaker mean when she says "without meaning or / trying to I must profit from his darkness"? In what sense is the boy in the speaker's power? Explain.

6. How well does Olds capture the racial stereotyping and racial tensions of America today for you? Point to particular images that affected you strongly.

Writing Topics

1. Members of a group often have different perceptions of the characteristics of that group than those held by outsiders. What is your image of the racial, national, religious, and social groups to which you belong? How do non-members view these groups? How many of the images that non-members have are based on stereotypes? Just how powerful are such stereotypes? Explain. Write

an essay in which you compare the two images and attempt to account for the differences.

2. Look up the words *black* and *white* in your dictionary. What are the connotations of most phrases and metaphors that include the word *black*? The word *white*? Why do you suppose the word *black* has more negative connotations? Is it for racist reasons? Discuss your opinion and your reasons for having it in an essay.

CHARLOTTE PERKINS GILMAN

Charlotte Perkins Gilman (1860–1935) was a reformer and feminist who was born in Hartford, Connecticut. In addition to her distinguished career as a writer of stories, poetry, and nonfiction, and a lecturer on the labor movement and feminism, she edited the *Forerunner*, a liberal journal. Suffering from an incurable disease, Perkins Gilman died by her own hand. *Women and Economics* (1898) is considered to be her most important work. However, the reemergence of the feminist movement brought "The Yellow Wallpaper" into a prominence it hardly enjoyed when it was written.

Referred to by one critic as a "literary masterpiece" and by another as a story to "freeze our . . . blood," "The Yellow Wallpaper" is drawn from Perkins Gilman's own life. In it she makes the reader witness a woman's mental breakdown with vivid and frightening detail.

The Yellow Wallpaper

It is very seldom that mere ordinary people like John and myself secure ancestral halls for the summer. 1

A colonial mansion, a hereditary estate, I would say a haunted house, and reach the height of romantic felicity—but that would be asking too much of fate! 2

Still I will proudly declare that there is something queer about it. 3

Else, why should it be let so cheaply? And why have stood so long untenanted? 4

John laughs at me, of course, but one expects that in marriage. 5

John is practical in the extreme. He has no patience with faith, an intense horror of superstition, and he scoffs openly at any talk of things not to be felt and seen and put down in figures. 6

John is a physician, and *perhaps*—(I would not say it to a living soul, of course, but this is dead paper and a great relief to my mind)—*perhaps* that is one reason I do not get well faster. 7

You see he does not believe I am sick! 8

And what can one do? 9

If a physician of high standing, and one's own husband, assures friends and relatives that there is really nothing the matter with one but 10 temporary nervous depression—a slight hysterical tendency—what is one to do?

My brother is also a physician, and also of high standing, and he says   11
the same thing.

So I take phosphates or phosphites—whichever it is, and tonics, and   12
journeys, and air, and exercise, and am absolutely forbidden to "work" until I
am well again.

Personally, I disagree with their ideas.   13

Personally, I believe that congenial work, with excitement and change,   14
would do me good.

But what is one to do?   15

I did write for a while in spite of them; but it *does* exhaust me a good   16
deal—having to be so sly about it, or else meet with heavy opposition.

I sometimes fancy that in my condition if I had less opposition and   17
more society and stimulus—but John says the very worst thing I can do is to
think about my condition, and I confess it always makes me feel bad.

So I will let it alone and talk about the house.   18

The most beautiful place! It is quite alone, standing well back from the   19
road, quite three miles from the village. It makes me think of English places
that you read about, for there are hedges and walls and gates that lock, and
lots of separate little houses for the gardeners and people.

There is a *delicious* garden! I never saw such a garden—large and shady,   20
full of box-bordered paths, and lined with long grape-covered arbors with
seats under them.

There were greenhouses, too, but they are all broken now.   21

There was some legal trouble, I believe, something about the heirs and   22
coheirs; anyhow, the place has been empty for years.

That spoils my ghostliness, I am afraid, but I don't care—there is   23
something strange about the house—I can feel it.

I even said so to John one moonlight evening, but he said what I felt   24
was a *draught,* and shut the window.

I get unreasonably angry with John sometimes. I'm sure I never used to   25
be so sensitive. I think it is due to this nervous condition.

But John says if I feel so, I shall neglect proper self-control; so I take   26
pains to control myself—before him, at least, and that makes me very tired.

I don't like our room a bit. I wanted one downstairs that opened on the   27
piazza and had roses all over the window, and such pretty old-fashioned
chintz hangings! But John would not hear of it.

He said there was only one window and not room for two beds, and no   28
near room for him if he took another.

He is very careful and loving, and hardly lets me stir without special   29
direction.

I have a schedule prescription for each hour in the day; he takes all care   30
from me, and so I feel basely ungrateful not to value it more.

He said we came here solely on my account, that I was to have perfect 31
rest and all the air I could get. "Your exercise depends on your strength, my
dear," said he, "and your food somewhat on your appetite; but air you can
absorb all the time." So we took the nursery at the top of the house.

It is a big, airy room, the whole floor nearly, with windows that look all 32
ways, and air and sunshine galore. It was nursery first and then play-room
and gymnasium, I should judge; for the windows are barred for little children, and there are rings and things in the walls.

The paint and paper look as if a boys' school had used it. It is stripped 33
off—the paper—in great patches all around the head of my bed, about as far
as I can reach, and in a great place on the other side of the room low down. I
never saw a worse paper in my life.

One of those sprawling flamboyant patterns committing every artistic 34
sin.

It is dull enough to confuse the eye in following, pronounced enough 35
to constantly irritate and provoke study, and when you follow the lame
uncertain curves for a little distance they suddenly commit suicide—plunge
off at outrageous angles, destroy themselves in unheard of contradictions.

The color is repellent, almost revolting; a smouldering unclean yellow, 36
strangely faded by the slow-turning sunlight.

It is a dull yet lurid orange in some places, a sickly sulphur tint in 37
others.

No wonder the children hated it! I should hate it myself if I had to live 38
in this room long.

There comes John, and I must put this away,—he hates to have me 39
write a word.

We have been here two weeks, and I haven't felt like writing before, 40
since that first day.

I am sitting by the window now, up in this atrocious nursery, and there 41
is nothing to hinder my writing as much as I please, save lack of strength.

John is away all day, and even some nights when his cases are serious. 42
I am glad my case is not serious! 43
But these nervous troubles are dreadfully depressing. 44
John does not know how much I really suffer. He knows there is no 45
reason to suffer, and that satisfies him.

Of course it is only nervousness. It does weigh on me so not to do my 46
duty in any way!

I meant to be such a help to John, such a real rest and comfort, and 47
here I am a comparative burden already!

Nobody would believe what an effort it is to do what little I am able,— 48
to dress and entertain, and order things.

It is fortunate Mary is so good with the baby. Such a dear baby! 49
And yet I *cannot* be with him, it makes me so nervous. 50

I suppose John never was nervous in his life. He laughs at me so about 51 this wall-paper!

At first he meant to repaper the room, but afterwards he said I was 52 letting it get the better of me, and that nothing was worse for a nervous patient than to give way to such fancies.

He said that after the wall-paper was changed it would be the heavy 53 bedstead, and then the barred windows, and then that gate at the head of the stairs, and so on.

"You know the place is doing you good," he said, "and really, dear, I 54 don't care to renovate the house just for a three months' rental."

"Then do let us go downstairs," I said, "there are such pretty rooms 55 there."

Then he took me in his arms and called me a blessed little goose, and 56 said he would go down to the cellar, if I wished, and have it whitewashed into the bargain.

But he is right enough about the beds and windows and things. 57

It is an airy and comfortable room as any one need wish, and, of 58 course, I could not be so silly as to make him uncomfortable just for a whim.

I'm really getting quite fond of the big room, all but that horrid paper. 59

Out of one window I can see the garden, those mysterious deepshaded 60 arbors, the riotous old-fashioned flowers, and bushes and gnarly trees.

Out of another I get a lovely view of the bay and a little private wharf 61 belonging to the estate. There is a beautiful shaded lane that runs down there from the house. I always fancy I see people walking in these numerous paths and arbors, but John has cautioned me not to give way to fancy in the least. He says that with my imaginative power and habit of story-making, a nervous weakness like mine is sure to lead to all manner of excited fancies, and that I ought to use my will and good sense to check the tendency. So I try.

I think sometimes that if I were only well enough to write a little it 62 would relieve the press of ideas and rest me.

But I find I get pretty tired when I try. 63

It is so discouraging not to have any advice and companionship about 64 my work. When I get really well, John says we will ask Cousin Henry and Julia down for a long visit; but he says he would as soon put fireworks in my pillow-case as to let me have those stimulating people about now.

I wish I could get well faster. 65

But I must not think about that. This paper looks to me as if it *knew* 66 what a vicious influence it had!

There is a recurrent spot where the pattern lolls like a broken neck and 67 two bulbous eyes stare at you upside down.

I get positively angry with the impertinence of it and the everlasting- 68 ness. Up and down and sideways they crawl, and those absurd, unblinking eyes are everywhere. There is one place where two breaths didn't match, and the eyes go all up and down the line, one a little higher than the other.

I never saw so much expression in an inanimate thing before, and we   69
all know how much expression they have! I used to lie awake as a child and
get more entertainment and terror out of blank walls and plain furniture than
most children could find in a toy-store.

I remember what a kindly wink the knobs of our big, old bureau used to   70
have, and there was one chair that always seemed like a strong friend.

I used to feel that if any of the other things looked too fierce I could   71
always hop into that chair and be safe.

The furniture in this room is no worse than inharmonious, however,   72
for we had to bring it all from downstairs. I suppose when this was used as a
playroom they had to take the nursery things out, and no wonder! I never
saw such ravages as the children have made here.

The wall-paper, as I said before, is torn off in spots, and it sticketh   73
closer than a brother—they must have had perseverance as well as hatred.

Then the floor is scratched and gouged and splintered, the plaster itself   74
is dug out here and there, and this great heavy bed which is all we found in
the room, looks as if it had been through the wars.

But I don't mind it a bit—only the paper.   75

There comes John's sister. Such a dear girl as she is, and so careful of   76
me! I must not let her find me writing.

She is a perfect and enthusiastic housekeeper, and hopes for no better   77
profession. I verily believe she thinks it is the writing which made me sick!

But I can write when she is out, and see her a long way off from these   78
windows.

There is one that commands the road, a lovely shaded winding road,   79
and one that just looks off over the country. A lovely country, too, full of
great elms and velvet meadows.

This wall-paper has a kind of sub-pattern in a different shade, a particu-   80
larly irritating one, for you can only see it in certain lights, and not clearly
then.

But in the places where it isn't faded and where the sun is just so—I   81
can see a strange, provoking, formless sort of figure, that seems to skulk
about behind that silly and conspicuous front design.

There's sister on the stairs!   82

Well, the Fourth of July is over! The people are all gone and I am tired   83
out. John thought it might do me good to see a little company, so we just had
mother and Nellie and the children down for a week.

Of course I didn't do a thing. Jennie sees to everything now.   84

But it tired me all the same.   85

John says if I don't pick up faster he shall send me to Weir Mitchell in   86
the fall.

But I don't want to go there at all. I had a friend who was in his hands   87
once, and she says he is just like John and my brother, only more so!

Besides, it is such an undertaking to go so far.   88

I don't feel as if it was worth while to turn my hand over for anything,   89
and I'm getting dreadfully fretful and querulous.

I cry at nothing, and cry most of the time.   90

Of course I don't when John is here, or anybody else, but when I am   91
alone.

And I am alone a good deal just now. John is kept in town very often by   92
serious cases, and Jennie is good and lets me alone when I want her to.

So I walk a little in the garden or down that lovely lane, sit on the   93
porch under the roses, and lie down up here a good deal.

I'm getting really fond of the room in spite of the wall-paper. Perhaps   94
because of the wall-paper.

It dwells in my mind so!   95

I lie here on this great immovable bed—it is nailed down, I believe—   96
and follow that pattern about by the hour. It is as good as gymnastics, I assure
you. I start, we'll say, at the bottom, down in the corner over there where it
has not been touched, and I determine for the thousandth time that I *will*
follow that pointless pattern to some sort of conclusion.

I know a little of the principle of design, and I know this thing was not   97
arranged on any laws of radiation, or alternation, or repetition, or symmetry,
or anything else that I ever heard of.

It is repeated, of course, by the breadths, but not otherwise.   98

Looked at in one way each breadth stands alone, the bloated curves   99
and flourishes—a kind of "debased Romanesque" with *delirium tremens*—go
waddling up and down in isolated columns of fatuity.

But, on the other hand, they connect diagonally, and the sprawling   100
outlines run off in great slanting waves of optic horror, like a lot of wallowing
seaweeds in full chase.

The whole thing goes horizontally, too, at least it seems so, and I   101
exhaust myself in trying to distinguish the order of its going in that direction.

They have used a horizontal breadth for a frieze, and that adds wonder-   102
fully to the confusion.

There is one end of the room where it is almost intact, and there, when   103
the crosslights fade and the low sun shines directly upon it, I can almost
fancy radiation after all,—the interminable grotesques seem to form around
a common center and rush off in headlong plunges of equal distraction.

It makes me tired to follow it. I will take a nap I guess.   104

I don't know why I should write this.   105

I don't want to.   106

I don't feel able.   107

And I know John would think it absurd. But I *must* say what I feel and   108
think in some way—it is such a relief!

But the effort is getting to be greater than the relief.   109

Half the time now I am awfully lazy, and lie down ever so much.   110

John says I mustn't lose my strength, and has me take cod liver oil and   111
lots of tonics and things, to say nothing of ale and wine and rare meat.

Dear John! He loves me very dearly, and hates to have me sick. I   112
tried to have a real earnest reasonable talk with him the other day, and tell
him how I wish he would let me go and make a visit to Cousin Henry and
Julia.

But he said I wasn't able to go, nor able to stand it after I got there; and   113
I did not make out a very good case for myself, for I was crying before I had
finished.

It is getting to be a great effort for me to think straight. Just this   114
nervous weakness I suppose.

And dear John gathered me up in his arms, and just carried me upstairs   115
and laid me on the bed, and sat by me and read to me till it tired my head.

He said I was his darling and his comfort and all he had, and that I   116
must take care of myself for his sake, and keep well.

He says no one but myself can help me out of it, that I must use my will   117
and self-control and not let any silly fancies run away with me.

There's one comfort, the baby is well and happy, and does not have to   118
occupy this nursery with the horrid wall-paper.

If we had not used it, that blessed child would have! What a fortunate   119
escape! Why, I couldn't have a child of mine, an impressionable little thing,
live in such a room for worlds.

I never thought of it before, but it is lucky that John kept me here after   120
all, I can stand it so much easier than a baby, you see.

Of course I never mention it to them any more—I am too wise,—but I   121
keep watch of it all the same.

There are things in that paper that nobody knows but me, or ever will.   122

Behind that outside pattern the dim shapes get clearer every day.   123

It is always the same shape, only very numerous.   124

And it is like a woman stooping down and creeping about behind that   125
pattern. I don't like it a bit. I wonder—I begin to think—I wish John would
take me away from here!

It is so hard to talk with John about my case, because he is so wise, and   126
because he loves me so.

But I tried it last night.   127

It was moonlight. The moon shines in all around just as the sun does.   128

I hate to see it sometimes, it creeps so slowly, and always comes in by   129
one window or another.

John was asleep and I hated to waken him, so I kept still and watched   130
the moonlight on that undulating wall-paper till I felt creepy.

The faint figure behind seemed to shake the pattern, just as if she   131
wanted to get out.

I got up softly and went to feel and see if the paper *did* move, and when   132
I came back John was awake.

"What is it, little girl?" he said. "Don't go walking about like that— you'll get cold."

I thought it was a good time to talk, so I told him that I really was not gaining here, and that I wished he would take me away.

"Why darling!" said he, "our lease will be up in three weeks, and I can't see how to leave before."

"The repairs are not done at home, and I cannot possibly leave town just now. Of course if you were in any danger, I could and would, but you really are better, dear, whether you can see it or not. I am a doctor, dear, and I know. You are gaining flesh and color, your appetite is better, I feel really much easier about you."

"I don't weigh a bit more," said I, "nor as much; and my appetite may better in the evening when you are here, but it is worse in the morning when you are away!"

"Bless her little heart!" said he with a big hug, "she shall be as sick as she pleases! But now let's improve the shining hours by going to sleep, and talk about it in the morning!"

"And you won't go away?" I asked gloomily.

"Why, how can I, dear? It is only three weeks more and then we will take a nice little trip of a few days while Jennie is getting the house ready. Really dear you are better!"

"Better in body perhaps—" I began, and stopped short, for he sat up straight and looked at me with such a stern, reproachful look that I could not say another word.

"My darling," said he, "I beg of you, for my sake and for our child's sake, as well as for your own, that you will never for one instant let that idea enter your mind! There is nothing so dangerous, so fascinating, to a temperament like yours. It is a false and foolish fancy. Can you not trust me as a physician when I tell you so?"

So of course I said no more on that score, and we went to sleep before long. He thought I was asleep first, but I wasn't, and lay there for hours trying to decide whether that front pattern and the back pattern really did move together or separately.

On a pattern like this, by daylight, there is a lack of sequence, a defiance of law, that is a constant irritant to a normal mind.

The color is hideous enough, and unreliable enough, and infuriating enough, but the pattern is torturing.

You think you have mastered it, but just as you get well underway in following, it turns a back-somersault and there you are. It slaps you in the face, knocks you down, and tramples upon you. It is like a bad dream.

The outside pattern is a florid arabesque, reminding one of a fungus. If you can imagine a toadstool in joints, an interminable string of toadstools, budding and sprouting in endless convolutions—why, that is something like it.

That is, sometimes! 148

There is one marked peculiarity about this paper, a thing nobody seems 149
to notice but myself, and that is that it changes as the light changes.

When the sun shoots in through the east window—I always watch for 150
the first long, straight ray—it changes so quickly that I never can quite
believe it.

That is why I watch it always. 151

By moonlight—the moon shines in all night when there is a moon—I 152
wouldn't know it was the same paper.

At night in any kind of light, in twilight, candle light, lamplight, and 153
worst of all by moonlight, it becomes bars! The outside pattern I mean, and
the woman behind it as plain as can be.

I didn't realize for a long time what the thing was that showed behind, 154
that dim sub-pattern, but now I am quite sure it is a woman.

By daylight she is subdued, quiet. I fancy it is the pattern that keeps her 155
so still. It is so puzzling. It keeps me quiet by the hour.

I lie down ever so much now. John says it is good for me, and to sleep 156
all I can.

Indeed he started the habit by making me lie down for an hour after 157
each meal.

It is a very bad habit I am convinced, for you see I don't sleep. 158

And that cultivates deceit, for I don't tell them I'm awake—O no! 159

The fact is I am getting a little afraid of John. 160

He seems very queer sometimes, and even Jennie has an inexplicable 161
look.

It strikes me occasionally, just as a scientific hypothesis,—that perhaps 162
it is the paper!

I have watched John when he did not know I was looking, and come 163
into the room suddenly on the most innocent excuses, and I've caught him
several times *looking at the paper!* And Jennie too. I caught Jennie with her
hand on it once.

She didn't know I was in the room, and when I asked her in a quiet, a 164
very quiet voice, with the most restrained manner possible, what she was
doing with the paper—she turned around as if she had been caught stealing,
and looked quite angry—asked me why I should frighten her so!

The she said that the paper stained everything it touched, that she had 165
found yellow smooches on all my clothes and John's, and she wished we
would be more careful!

Did not that sound innocent? But I know she was studying that pat- 166
tern, and I am determined that nobody shall find it out but myself!

Life is very much more exciting now than it used to be. You see I have 167
something more to expect, to look forward to, to watch. I really do eat
better, and am more quiet than I was.

John is so pleased to see me improve! He laughed a little the other day, 168
and said I seemed to be flourishing in spite of my wall-paper.

I turned it off with a laugh. I had no intention of telling him it was 169
because of the wall-paper—he would make fun of me. He might even want to
take me away.

I don't want to leave now until I have found it out. There is a week 170
more, and I think that will be enough.

I'm feeling ever so much better! I don't sleep much at night, for it is 171
so interesting to watch developments; but I sleep a good deal in the
daytime.

In the daytime it is tiresome and perplexing. 172

There are always new shoots on the fungus, and new shades of yellow 173
all over it. I cannot keep count of them, though I have tried conscientiously.

It is the strangest yellow, that wall-paper! It makes me think of all the 174
yellow things I ever saw—not beautiful ones like buttercups, but old foul,
bad yellow things.

But there is something else about that paper—the smell! I noticed it 175
the moment we came into the room, but with so much air and sun it was not
bad. Now we have had a week of fog and rain, and whether the windows are
open or not, the smell is here.

It creeps all over the house. 176

I find it hovering in the dining-room, skulking in the parlor, hiding in 177
the hall, lying in wait for me on the stairs.

It gets into my hair. 178

Even when I go to ride, if I turn my head suddenly and surprise it— 179
there is that smell!

Such a peculiar odor, too! I have spent hours in trying to analyze it, to 180
find what it smelled like.

It is not bad—at first, and very gentle, but quite the subtlest, most 181
enduring odor I ever met.

In this damp weather it is awful, I wake up in the night and find it 182
hanging over me.

It used to disturb me at first. I thought seriously of burning the house— 183
to reach the smell.

But now I am used to it. The only thing I can think of that it is like is 184
the *color* of the paper! A yellow smell.

There is a very funny mark on this wall, low down, near the mopboard. 185
A streak that runs round the room. It goes behind every piece of furniture,
except the bed, a long, straight, even *smooch,* as if it had been rubbed over
and over.

I wonder how it was done and who did it, and what they did it for. 186
Round and round and round—round and round and round—it makes me
dizzy!

I really have discovered something at last. 187

Through watching so much at night, when it changes so, I have finally 188
found out.

The front pattern *does* move—and no wonder! The woman behind 189
shakes it!

Sometimes I think there are a great many women behind, and some- 190
times only one, and she crawls around fast, and her crawling shakes it all over.

Then in the very bright spots she keeps still, and in the very shady 191
spots she just takes hold of the bars and shakes them hard.

And she is all the time trying to climb through. But nobody could climb 192
through that pattern—it strangles so; I think that is why it has so many heads.

They get through, and then the pattern strangles them off and turns 193
them upside down, and makes their eyes white!

If those heads were covered or taken off it would not be half so bad. 194

I think that woman gets out in the daytime! 195

And I'll tell you why—privately—I've seen her! 196

I can see her out of every one of my windows! 197

It is the same woman, I know, for she is always creeping, and most 198
women do not creep by daylight.

I see her on that long road under the trees, creeping along, and when a 199
carriage comes she hides under the blackberry vines.

I don't blame her a bit. It must be very humiliating to be caught 200
creeping by daylight!

I always lock the door when I creep by daylight. I can't do it at night, 201
for I know John would suspect something at once.

And John is so queer now, that I don't want to irritate him. I wish he 202
would take another room! Besides, I don't want anybody to get that woman
out at night but myself.

I often wonder if I could see her out of all windows at once. 203

But, turn as fast as I can, I can only see out of one at one time. 204

And though I always see her, she *may* be able to creep faster than I 205
can turn!

I have watched her sometimes away off in the open country, creeping 206
as fast as a cloud shadow in a high wind.

If only that top pattern could be gotten off from the under one! I mean 207
to try it, little by little.

I have found out another funny thing, but I shan't tell it this time! It 208
does not do to trust people too much.

There are only two more days to get this paper off, and I believe John is 209
beginning to notice. I don't like the look in his eyes.

And I heard him ask Jennie a lot of professional questions about me. 210
She had a very good report to give.

She said I slept a good deal in the daytime. 211

John knows I don't sleep very well at night, for all I'm so quiet! 212

He asked me all sorts of questions, too, and pretended to be very loving 213
and kind.

As if I couldn't see through him! 214

Still, I don't wonder he acts so, sleeping under this paper for three 215
months.

It only interests me, but I feel sure John and Jennie are secretly affected 216
by it.

Hurrah! This is the last day, but it is enough. John to stay in town over 217
night, and won't be out until this evening.

Jennie wanted to sleep with me—the sly thing! But I told her I should 218
undoubtedly rest better for a night all alone.

That was clever, for really I wasn't alone a bit! As soon as it was 219
moonlight and that poor thing began to crawl and shake the pattern, I got up
and ran to help her.

I pulled and she shook, I shook and she pulled, and before morning we 220
had peeled off yards of that paper.

A strip about as high as my head and half around the room. 221

And then when the sun came and that awful pattern began to laugh at 222
me, I declared I would finish it to-day!

We go away to-morrow, and they are moving all my furniture down 223
again to leave things as they were before.

Jennie looked at the wall in amazement, but I told her merrily that I 224
did it out of pure spite at the vicious thing.

She laughed and said she wouldn't mind doing it herself, but I must not 225
get tired.

How she betrayed herself that time! 226

But I am here, and no person touches this paper but me,—not *alive!* 227

She tried to get me out of the room—it was too patent! But I said it was so 228
quiet and empty and clean now that I believed I would lie down again and sleep
all I could; and not to wake me even for dinner—I would call when I woke.

So now she is gone, and the servants are gone, and the things are gone, 229
and there is nothing left but that great bedstead nailed down, with the
canvas mattress we found on it.

We shall sleep downstairs to-night, and take the boat home to-morrow. 230

I quite enjoy the room, now it is bare again. 231

How those children did tear about here! 232

This bedstead is fairly gnawed! 233

But I must get to work. 234

I have locked the door and thrown the key down into the front path. 235

I don't want to go out, and I don't want to have anybody come in, till 236
John comes.

I want to astonish him. 237

I've got a rope up here that even Jennie did not find. If that woman 238
does get out, and tries to get away, I can tie her!

But I forgot I could not reach far without anything to stand on! 239

This bed will *not* move! 240

I tried to lift and push it until I was lame, and then I got so angry I bit 241
off a little piece at one corner—but it hurt my teeth.

Then I peeled off all the paper I could reach standing on the floor. It 242
sticks horribly and the pattern just enjoys it! All those strangled heads and
bulbous eyes and waddling fungus growths just shriek with derision!

I am getting angry enough to do something desperate. To jump out of 243
the window would be admirable exercise, but the bars are too strong even
to try.

Besides I wouldn't do it. Of course not. I know well enough that a step 244
like that is improper and might be misconstrued.

I don't like to *look* out of the windows even—there are so many of 245
those creeping women, and they creep so fast.

I wonder if they all come out of that wall-paper as I did! 246

But I am securely fastened now by my well-hidden rope—you don't get 247
me out in the road there!

I suppose I shall have to get back behind the pattern when it comes 248
night, and that is hard!

It is so pleasant to be out in this great room and creep around as I 249
please!

I don't want to go outside. I won't, even if Jennie asks me to. 250

For outside you have to creep on the ground, and everything is green 251
instead of yellow.

But here I can creep smoothly on the floor, and my shoulder just fits in 252
that long smooch around the wall, so I cannot lose my way.

Why there's John at the door! 253

It is no use, young man, you can't open it! 254

How he does call and pound! 255

Now he's crying for an axe. 256

It would be a shame to break down that beautiful door! 257

"John dear!" said I in the gentlest voice, "the key is down by the front 258
steps, under a plantain leaf!"

That silenced him for a few moments. 259

Then he said—very quietly indeed. "Open the door, my darling!" 260

"I can't," said I. "The key is down by the front door under a plan- 261
tain leaf!"

And then I said it again, several times, very gently and slowly, and said 262
it so often that he had to go and see, and he got it of course, and came in. He
stopped short by the door.

"What is the matter?" he cried. "For God's sake, what are you doing!" 263

I kept on creeping just the same, but I looked at him over my shoulder. 26

"I've got out at last," said I, "in spite of you and Jane. And I've pulled 26
off most of the paper, so you can't put me back!"

Now why should that man have fainted? But he did, and right across 26
my path by the wall, so that I had to creep over him every time!

Questions for Study and Discussion

1. What sorts of activities make the heroine tired?

2. How is the paper a metaphor for the woman's life? For the life of all
women of her time? What is the significance of the paper's having a "front
pattern" and a "back pattern"?

3. How does the wife's attitude toward her husband change during the
story? What words does she use to describe him early and then later?

4. The husband "knows there is no *reason* to suffer." Is he right? What is
really wrong with his wife?

5. Based on clues from the story, how would you contrast the husband's
image of his wife with what you learn about her?

6. What are some of the ways the author makes the wife's illness real for
us? Cite examples of figures of speech, diction, and pace.

7. Why do the women in the wallpaper "creep"?

8. What are the similarities between the wife's attitudes toward her writing and toward the wallpaper?

9. How does her attitude toward the room change? What does this change
signify? Why is she so afraid to go out of the house in the end? Does she achieve
any kind of victory?

Writing Topics

1. In the story we learn that the wife has recently had a baby. Today her
"condition" might be diagnosed as postpartum depression. However, the author
wishes to make the point that the wife is also the victim of misunderstanding and
the unrealistic expectations of an insensitive husband. Look up "postpartum
depression" in your encyclopedia. How well does it explain the wife's symptoms?
How are you inclined to explain the wife's illness? Does a hormonal explanation
strengthen or weaken the point of Perkins Gilman's story or does it have no
effect at all?

2. Charlotte Perkins Gilman was born before married women in this country could own their own property, and she died only shortly after they won the
legal right to vote. Read more about the life of the author and her other works of
fiction. Are all her heroines similarly doomed? What role model did she provide
to women of her time? What other role models does she offer through her
fiction?

Language and Persuasion

GEORGE ORWELL

In the totalitarian state of George Orwell's novel *1984* (1949), the government has imposed on its subjects a simplified language, Newspeak, which is continually revised to give them fewer words with which to express themselves. Words like *terrible, abhorrent,* and *evil,* for example, have all been replaced by the single expression *double-plus-ungood.* The way people use language, Orwell maintained, is a result of the way they think as well as an important influence on their thought. This is also the point of his classic essay "Politics and the English Language." Though published in 1946, the essay is as accurate and relevant now as it was then. Indeed, during the war in Vietnam various American officials were still using euphemisms such as "pacification" and "transfer of population," as if Orwell hadn't long since exposed those phrases as doubletalk. But Orwell goes beyond exposé. He not only holds up to public view and ridicule some choice examples of political language at its worst, but also offers a few short, simple, and effective rules for writers who want to do better. (For biographical information about Orwell, see p. 50–56)

Politics and the English Language

Most people who bother with the matter at all would admit that the English language is in a bad way, but it is generally assumed that we cannot by conscious action do anything about it. Our civilization is decadent and our language—so the argument runs—must inevitably share in the general collapse. It follows that any struggle against the abuse of language is a sentimental archaism, like preferring candles to electric light or hansom cabs to aeroplanes. Underneath this lies the half-conscious belief that language is a natural growth and not an instrument which we shape for our own purposes.

Now, it is clear that the decline of a language must ultimately have political and economic causes: it is not due simply to the bad influence of this or that individual writer. But an effect can become a cause, reinforcing the original cause and producing the same effect in an intensified form, and so on indefinitely. A man may take to drink because he feels himself to be a failure, and then fail all the more completely because he drinks. It is rather the same thing that is happening to the English language. It becomes ugly and inaccurate because our thoughts are foolish, but the slovenliness of our language makes it easier for us to have foolish thoughts. The point is that the process is reversible. Modern English, especially written English, is full of bad habits which spread by imitation and which can be avoided if one is willing to take the necessary trouble. If one gets rid of these habits one can think more clearly, and to think clearly is a necessary first step toward political regeneration: so that the fight against bad English is not frivolous and is not the exclusive concern of professional writers. I will come back to this presently, and I hope that by that time the meaning of what I have said here will have become clearer. Meanwhile, here are five specimens of the English language as it is now habitually written.

These five passages have not been picked out because they are espe-   3 cially bad—I could have quoted far worse if I had chosen—but because they illustrate various of the mental vices from which we now suffer. They are a little below the average, but are fairly representative samples. I number them so that I can refer back to them when necessary:

> (1) I am not, indeed, sure whether it is not true to say that the Milton who once seemed not unlike a seventeenth-century Shelley had not become, out of an experience even more bitter in each year, more alien [sic] to the founder of that Jesuit sect which nothing could induce him to tolerate.
>
> Professor Harold Laski (Essay in *Freedom of Expression*)

> (2) Above all, we cannot play ducks and drakes with[1] a native battery of idioms which prescribes such egregious collections of vocables as the Basic *put up with* for *tolerate* or *put at a loss* for *bewilder*.
>
> Professor Lancelot Hogben (*Interglossa*)

> (3) On the one side we have the free personality: by definition it is not neurotic, for it has neither conflict nor dream. Its desires, such as they are, are transparent, for they are just what institutional approval keeps in the forefront of consciousness; another institutional pattern would alter their number and intensity; there is little in them that is natural, irreducible, or culturally dangerous. But *on the other side*, the social bond itself is nothing but the mutual reflection of these self-secure integrities. Recall the definition of love. Is not this the very picture of a small academic? Where is there a place in this hall of mirrors for either personality or fraternity?
>
> Essay on psychology on *Politics* (New York)

> (4) All the "best people" from the gentlemen's clubs, and all the frantic fascist captains, united in common hatred of Socialism and bestial

---

[1]Squander.

horror of the rising tide of the mass revolutionary movement, have turned to acts of provocation, to foul incendiarism, to medieval legends of poisoned wells, to legalize their own destruction of proletarian organizations, and rouse the agitated petty-bourgeoisie to chauvinistic fervor on behalf of the fight against the revolutionary way out of the crisis.

Communist pamphlet

(5) If a new spirit *is* to be infused into this old country, there is one thorny and contentious reform which must be tackled, and that is the humanization and galvanization of the B.B.C.[2] Timidity here will bespeak canker and atrophy of the soul. The heart of Britain may be sound and of strong beat, for instance, but the British Lion's roar at present is like that of Bottom in Shakespeare's *Midsummer Night's Dream*—as gentle as any sucking dove. A virile new Britain cannot continue indefinitely to be traduced in the eyes or rather ears, of the world by the effete languors of Langham Place, brazenly masquerading as "standard English." When the Voice of Britain is heard at nine o'clock, better far and infinitely less ludicrous to hear aitches honestly dropped than the present priggish, inflated, inhibited, school-ma'amish arch braying of blameless bashful mewing maidens!

Letter in *Tribune*

Each of these passages has faults of its own, but, quite apart from avoidable ugliness, two qualities are common to all of them. The first is staleness of imagery; the other is lack of precision. The writer either has a meaning and cannot express it, or he inadvertently says something else, or he is almost indifferent as to whether his words mean anything or not. This mixture of vagueness and sheer incompetence is the most marked characteristic of modern English prose, and especially of any kind of political writing. As soon as certain topics are raised, the concrete melts into the abstract and no one seems able to think of turns of speech that are not hackneyed: prose consists less and less of *words* chosen for the sake of their meaning, and more and more of *phrases* tacked together like the sections of a prefabricated henhouse. I list below, with notes and examples, various of the tricks by means of which the work of prose-construction is habitually dodged:

Dying Metaphors

A newly invented metaphor assists thought by evoking a visual image, while on the other hand a metaphor which is technically "dead" (e.g., *iron resolution*) has in effect reverted to being an ordinary word and can generally be used without loss of vividness. But in between these two classes there is a huge dump of worn-out metaphors which have lost all evocative power and

---

[2]British Broadcasting Corporation, the government-run radio and television network. "B.B.C. English" is meant to reflect standard pronunciation in England.

are merely used because they save people the trouble of inventing phrases for themselves. Examples are: *Ring the changes on, take up the cudgels for, toe the line, ride roughshod over, stand shoulder to shoulder with, play into the hands of, no axe to grind, grist to the mill, fishing in troubled waters, on the order of the day, Achilles' heel, swan song, hotbed.* Many of these are used without knowledge of their meaning (what is a "rift," for instance?), and incompatible metaphors are frequently mixed, a sure sign that the writer is not interested in what he is saying. Some metaphors now current have been twisted out of their original meaning without those who use them even being aware of the fact. For example, *toe the line* is sometimes written *tow the line.* Another example is *the hammer and the anvil,* now always used with the implication that the anvil gets the worst of it. In real life it is always the anvil that breaks the hammer, never the other way about: a writer who stopped to think what he was saying would be aware of this, and would avoid perverting the original phrase.

Operators or Verbal False Limbs

These save the trouble of picking out appropriate verbs and nouns, and   6
at the same time pad each sentence with extra syllables which give it an appearance of symmetry. Characteristic phrases are *render inoperative, militate against, make contact with, be subjected to, give rise to, give grounds for, have the effect of, play a leading part (role) in, make itself felt, take effect, exhibit a tendency to, serve the purpose of,* etc., etc. The keynote is the elimination of simple verbs. Instead of being a single word, such as *break, stop, spoil, mend, kill,* a verb becomes a *phrase,* made up of a noun or adjective tacked on to some general-purpose verb such as *prove, serve, form, play, render.* In addition, the passive voice is wherever possible used in preference to the active, and noun constructions are used instead of gerunds (*by examination of* instead of *by examining*). The range of verbs is further cut down by means of the *-ize* and *de-* formations, and the banal statements are given an appearance of profundity by means of the *not un-* formation. Simple conjunctions and prepositions are replaced by such phrases as *with respect to, having regard to, the fact that, by dint of, in view of, in the interests of, on the hypothesis that;* and the ends of sentences are saved from anticlimax by such resounding commonplaces as *greatly to be desired, cannot be left out of account, a development to be expected in the near future, deserving of serious consideration, brought to a satisfactory conclusion,* and so on and so forth.

Pretentious Diction

Words like *phenomenon, element, individual* (as noun), *objective, categori-*   7
cal, effective, virtual, basic, primary, promote, constitute, exhibit, exploit, utilize,

eliminate, liquidate, are used to dress up simple statements and give an air of scientific impartiality to biased judgments. Adjectives like *epoch-making, epic, historic, unforgettable, triumphant, age-old, inevitable, inexorable, veritable*, are used to dignify the sordid process of international politics, while writing that aims at glorifying war usually takes on an archaic color, its characteristic words being: *realm, throne, chariot, mailed fist, trident, sword, shield, buckler, jackboot, clarion.* Foreign words and expressions such as *cul de sac, ancien régime, deus ex machina, mutatis mutandis, status quo, gleichschaltung, weltanschauung*, are used to give an air of culture and elegance. Except for the useful abbreviations *i.e., e.g.,* and *etc.,* there is no real need for any of the hundreds of foreign phrases now current in English. Bad writers, and especially scientific, political, and sociological writers, are nearly always haunted by the notion that Latin or Greek words are grander than Saxon ones, and unnecessary words like *expedite, ameliorate, predict, extraneous, deracinated, clandestine, subaqueous*, and hundreds of others constantly gain ground from their Anglo-Saxon opposite numbers.[3] The jargon peculiar to Marxist writing (*hyena, hangman, cannibal, petty bourgeois, these gentry, lackey, flunkey, mad dog, White Guard*, etc.) consists largely of words and phrases translated from Russian, German, or French; but the normal way of coining a new word is to use a Latin or Greek root with the appropriate affix and, where necessary, the size formation. It is often easier to make up words of this kind (*deregionalize, impermissible, extramarital, nonfragmentary* and so forth) than to think up the English words that will cover one's meaning. The result, in general, is an increase in slovenliness and vagueness.

Meaningless Words

In certain kinds of writing, particularly in art criticism and literary   8
criticism, it is normal to come across long passages which are almost completely lacking in meaning.[4] Words like *romantic, plastic, values, human, dead, sentimental, natural, vitality*, as used in art criticism, are strictly meaningless,

---

[3]An interesting illustration of this is the way in which the English flower names which were in use till very recently are being ousted by Greek ones, *snapdragon* becoming *antirrhinum, forget-me-not* becoming *myosotis*, etc. It is hard to see any practical reason for this change of fashion: it is probably due to an instinctive turning away from the more homely word and a vague feeling that the Greek word is scientific. [Orwell's note]

[4]Example: "[Alex] Comfort's catholicity of perception and image, strangely Whitmanesque in range, almost the exact opposite in aesthetic compulsion, continues to evoke that trembling atmospheric accumulative hinting at a cruel, an inexorably serene timelessness. . . . Wrey Gardiner scores by aiming at simple bull's-eyes with precision. Only they are not so simple, and through this contented sadness runs more than the surface bittersweet or resignation." (*Poetry Quarterly.*) [Orwell's note]

in the sense that they not only do not point to any discoverable object, but are hardly ever expected to do so by the reader. When one critic writes, "The outstanding feature of Mr. X's work is its living quality," while another writes, "The immediately striking thing about Mr. X's work is its peculiar deadness," the reader accepts this as a simple difference of opinion. If words like *black* and *white* were involved, instead of the jargon words *dead* and *living,* he would see at once that language was being used in an improper way. Many political words are similarly abused. The word *Fascism* has now no meaning except in so far as it signifies "something not desirable." The words *democracy, socialism, freedom, patriotic, realistic, justice,* have each of them several different meanings which cannot be reconciled with one another. In the case of a word like *democracy,* not only is there no agreed definition, but the attempt to make one is resisted from all sides. It is almost universally felt that when we call a country democratic we are praising it: consequently the defenders of every kind of régime claim that it is a democracy, and fear that they might have to stop using the word if it were tied down to any one meaning. Words of this kind are often used in a consciously dishonest way. That is, the person who uses them has his own private definition, but allows his hearer to think he means something quite different. Statements like *Marshal Pétain was a true patriot,*[5] *The Soviet press is the freest in the world, The Catholic Church is opposed to persecution,* are almost always made with intent to deceive. Other words used in variable meanings, in most cases more or less dishonestly, are: *class, totalitarian, science, progressive, reactionary, bourgeois, equality.*

Now that I have made this catalogue of swindles and perversions, let   9
me give another example of the kind of writing that they lead to. This time it must of its nature be an imaginary one. I am going to translate a passage of good English into Modern English of the worst sort. Here is a well-known verse from *Ecclesiastes:*

> I returned and saw under the sun, that the race is not to the swift, nor the battle to the strong, neither yet bread to the wise, nor yet riches to men of understanding, nor yet favour to men of skill; but time and chance happeneth to them all.

Here it is in modern English:

> Objective consideration of contemporary phenomena compels the conclusion that success or failure in competitive activities exhibits no tendency to be commensurate with innate capacity, but that a considerable element of the unpredictable must invariably be taken into account.

---

[5]In fact, Pétain was the Nazi-supported ruler of much of France from 1940 to 1944, and was convicted of treason in 1945.

This is a parody, but not a very gross one. Exhibit (3), above, for   10
instance, contains several patches of the same kind of English. It will be seen
that I have not made a full translation. The beginning and ending of the
sentence follow the original meaning fairly closely, but in the middle the
concrete illustrations—race, battle, bread—dissolve into the vague phrase
"success or failure in competitive activities." This had to be so, because no
modern writer of the kind I am discussing—no one capable of using phrases
like "objective consideration of contemporary phenomena"—would ever
tabulate his thoughts in that precise and detailed way. The whole tendency
of modern prose is away from concreteness. Now analyze these two sentences
a little more closely. The first contains forty-nine words but only sixty
syllables, and all its words are those of everyday life. The second contains
thirty-eight words of ninety syllables: eighteen of its words are from Latin
roots, and one from Greek. The first sentence contains six vivid images, and
only one phrase ("time and chance") that could be called vague. The second
contains not a single fresh, arresting phrase, and in spite of its ninety syllables it gives only a shortened version of the meaning contained in the first.
Yet without a doubt it is the second kind of sentence that is gaining ground
in modern English. I do not want to exaggerate. This kind of writing is not
yet universal, and outcrops of simplicity will occur here and there in the
worst-written page. Still, if you or I were told to write a few lines on the
uncertainty of human fortunes, we should probably come much nearer to my
imaginary sentence than to the one from *Ecclesiastes*.

As I have tried to show, modern writing at its worst does not consist in   11
picking out words for the sake of their meaning and inventing images in order
to make the meaning clearer. It consists in gumming together long strips of
words which have already been set in order by someone else, and making the
result presentable by sheer humbug. The attraction of this way of writing is
that it is easy. It is easier—even quicker, once you have the habit—to say *In
my opinion it is not an unjustifiable assumption that* than to say *I think.* If you use
ready-made phrases, you not only don't have to hunt about for words, you also
don't have to bother with the rhythms of your sentences, since these phrases
are generally so arranged as to be more or less euphonious. When you are
composing in a hurry—when you are dictating to a stenographer, for instance,
or making a public speech—it is natural to fall into a pretentious, Latinized
style. Tags like *a consideration which we should do well to bear in mind* or *a
conclusion to which all of us would readily assent* will save many a sentence from
coming down with a bump. By using stale metaphors, similes, and idioms, you
save much mental effort, at the cost of leaving your meaning vague, not only
for your reader but for yourself. This is the significance of mixed metaphors.
The sole aim of a metaphor is to call up a visual image. When these images
clash—as in *The Fascist octopus has sung its swan song, the jackboot is thrown into
the melting pot*—it can be taken as certain that the writer is not seeing a mental
image of the objects he is naming; in other words he is not really thinking.

Look again at the examples I gave at the beginning of this essay. Professor Laski (1) uses five negatives in fifty-three words. One of these is superfluous, making nonsense of the whole passage, and in addition there is the slip—*alien* for akin—making further nonsense, and several avoidable pieces of clumsiness which increase the general vagueness. Professor Hogben (2) plays ducks and drakes with a battery which is able to write prescriptions, and, while disapproving of the everyday phrase *put up with*, is unwilling to look *egregious* up in the dictionary and see what it means; (3), if one takes an uncharitable attitude towards it, is simply meaningless; probably one could work out its intended meaning by reading the whole of the article in which it occurs. In (4), the writer knows more or less what he wants to say, but an accumulation of stale phrases chokes him like tea leaves blocking a sink. In (5), words and meaning have almost parted company. People who write in this manner usually have a general emotional meaning—they dislike one thing and want to express solidarity with another—but they are not interested in the detail of what they are saying. A scrupulous writer, in every sentence that he writes, will ask himself at least four questions, thus: What am I trying to say? What words will express it? What image or idiom will make it clearer? Is this image fresh enough to have an effect? And he will probably ask himself two more: Could I put it more shortly? Have I said anything that is avoidably ugly? But you are not obliged to go to all this trouble. You can shirk it by simply throwing your mind open and letting the ready-made phrases come crowding in. They will construct your sentences for you—even think your thoughts for you, to a certain extent—and at need they will perform the important service of partially concealing your meaning even from yourself. It is at this point that the special connection between politics and the debasement of language becomes clear.

In our time it is broadly true that political writing is bad writing. 12 Where it is not true, it will generally be found that the writer is some kind of rebel, expressing his private opinions and not a "party line." Orthodoxy, of whatever color, seems to demand a lifeless, imitative style. The political dialects to be found in pamphlets, leading articles, manifestoes, White Papers and the speeches of undersecretaries do, of course, vary from party to party, but they are all alike in that one almost never finds in them a fresh, vivid, homemade turn of speech. When one watches some tired hack on the platform mechanically repeating the familiar phrases—*bestial atrocities, iron heel, bloodstained tyranny, free peoples of the world, stand shoulder to shoulder*—one often has a curious feeling that one is not watching a live human being but some kind of dummy: a feeling which suddenly becomes stronger at moments when the light catches the speaker's spectacles and turns them into blank discs which seem to have no eyes behind them. And this is not altogether fanciful. A speaker who uses that kind of phraseology has gone some distance toward turning himself into a machine. The appropriate noises are coming out of his larynx, but his brain is not involved as it would be if he were choosing his words for himself. If the speech he is making is one that he is accustomed to make over and over again, he may be almost unconscious of what he is saying, as one is when one utters the responses in church. And this reduced state of consciousness, if not indispensable, is at any rate favorable to political conformity.

In our time, political speech and writing are largely the defense of the 13 indefensible. Things like the continuance of British rule in India, the Russian purges and deportations, the dropping of the atom bombs on Japan, can indeed be defended, but only by arguments which are too brutal for most people to face, and which do not square with the professed aims of political parties. Thus political language has to consist largely of euphemism, question-begging and sheer cloudy vagueness. Defenseless villages are bombarded from the air, the inhabitants driven out into the countryside, the cattle machine-gunned, the huts set on fire with incendiary bullets: this is called *pacification*. Millions of peasants are robbed of their farms and sent trudging along the roads with no more than they can carry: this is called *transfer of population* or *rectification of frontiers*. People are imprisoned for years without trial, or shot in the back of the neck or sent to die of scurvy in Arctic lumber camps: this is called *elimination of unreliable elements*. Such phraseology is needed if one wants to name things without calling up mental pictures of them. Consider for instance some comfortable English professor defending Russian totalitarianism. He cannot say outright, "I believe in killing your opponents when you get good results by doing so." Probably, therefore, he will say something like this:

"While freely conceding that the Soviet régime exhibits certain fea- 14 tures which the humanitarian may be inclined to deplore, we must, I think, agree that a certain curtailment of the right to political opposition is an unavoidable concomitant of transitional periods, and that the rigors which the Russian people have been called upon to undergo have been amply justified in the sphere of concrete achievement."

The inflated style is itself a kind of euphemism. A mass of Latin words 15 falls upon the facts like soft snow, blurring the outlines and covering up all the details. The great enemy of clear language is insincerity. When there is a gap between one's real and one's declared aims, one turns as it were instinctively to long words and exhausted idioms, like a cuttlefish squirting out ink. In our age there is no such thing as "keeping out of politics." All issues are political issues, and politics itself is a mass of lies, evasions, folly, hatred, schizophrenia. When the general atmosphere is bad, language must suffer. I should expect to find—this is a guess which I have not sufficient knowledge to verify—that the German, Russian and Italian languages have all deteriorated in the last ten or fifteen years, as a result of dictatorship.

But if thought corrupts language, language can also corrupt thought. A 16 bad usage can spread by tradition and imitation, even among people who should and do know better. The debased language that I have been discussing is in some ways very convenient. Phrases like *a not unjustifiable assumption, leaves much to be desired, would serve no good purpose, a consideration which we should do well to bear in mind,* are a continuous temptation, a packet of aspirins always at one's elbow. Look back through this essay, and for certain you will find that I have again and again committed the very faults I am protesting against. By this morning's post I have received a pamphlet dealing with conditions in Germany. The author tells me that he "felt impelled" to write it. I open it at random, and here is almost the first sentence that I see: "[The Allies] have an opportunity not only of achieving a radical transformation of Germany's social and political structure in such a way as to avoid a nationalistic reaction in Germany itself, but at the same time of laying the foundations of a co-operative and unified Europe." You see, he "feels impelled" to write—feels, presumably, that he has something new to say—and yet his words, like cavalry horses answering the bugle, group themselves automatically into the familiar dreary pattern. This invasion of one's mind by ready-made phrases (*lay the foundations, achieve a radical transformation*) can only be prevented if one is constantly on guard against them, and every such phrase anaesthetizes a portion of one's brain.

I said earlier that the decadence of our language is probably curable.   17 Those who deny this would argue, if they produced an argument at all, that language merely reflects existing social conditions, and that we cannot influence its development by any direct tinkering with words and constructions. So far as the general tone or spirit of a language goes, this may be true, but it is not true in detail. Silly words and expressions have often disappeared, not through any evolutionary process but owing to the conscious action of a minority. Two recent examples were *explore every avenue* and *leave no stone unturned,* which were killed by the jeers of a few journalists. There is a long list of flyblown metaphors which could similarly be got rid of if enough people would interest themselves in the job; and it should also be possible to laugh the *not un-* formation out of existence,[6] to reduce the amount of Latin and Greek in the average sentence, to drive out foreign phrases and strayed scientific words, and, in general, to make pretentiousness unfashionable. But all these are minor points. The defense of the English language implies more than this, and perhaps it is best to start by saying what it does *not* imply.

To begin with it has nothing to do with archaism, with the salvaging of   18 obsolete words and turns of speech, or with the setting up of a "standard English" which must never be departed from. On the contrary, it is especially concerned with the scrapping of every word or idiom which has outworn its usefulness. It has nothing to do with correct grammar and syntax, which are of no importance so long as one makes one's meaning clear, or with the

---

[6]One can cure oneself of the *not un-* formation by memorizing this sentence: *A not unblack dog was chasing a not unsmall rabbit across a not ungreen field.*

avoidance of Americanisms, or with having what is called a "good prose style." On the other hand it is not concerned with fake simplicity and the attempt to make written English colloquial. Nor does it even imply in every case preferring the Saxon word to the Latin one, though it does imply using the fewest and shortest words that will cover one's meaning. What is above all needed is to let the meaning choose the word, and not the other way about. In prose, the worst thing one can do with words is to surrender to them. When you think of a concrete object, you think wordlessly, and then, if you want to describe the thing you have been visualizing you probably hunt about till you find the exact words that seem to fit it. When you think of something abstract you are more inclined to use words from the start, and unless you make a conscious effort to prevent it, the existing dialect will come rushing in and do the job for you, at the expense of blurring or even changing your meaning. Probably it is better to put off using words as long as possible and get one's meaning as clear as one can through pictures or sensations. Afterward one can choose—not simply *accept*—the phrases that will best cover the meaning, and then switch round and decide what impression one's words are likely to make on another person. This last effort of the mind cuts out all stale or mixed images, all prefabricated phrases, needless repetitions, and humbug and vagueness generally. But one can often be in doubt about the effect of a word or a phrase, and one needs rules that one can rely on when instinct fails. I think the following rules will cover most cases:

(i) Never use a metaphor, simile, or other figure of speech which you are used to seeing in print.

(ii) Never use a long word where a short one will do.

(iii) If it is possible to cut a word out, always cut it out.

(iv) Never use the passive where you can use the active.

(v) Never use a foreign phrase, a scientific word, or a jargon word if you can think of an everyday English equivalent.

(vi) Break any of these rules sooner than say anything outright barbarous.

These rules sound elementary, and so they are, but they demand a deep change of attitude in anyone who has grown used to writing in the style now fashionable. One could keep all of them and still write bad English, but one could not write the kind of stuff that I quoted in those five specimens at the beginning of this article.

I have not here been considering the literary use of language, but merely language as an instrument of expressing and not for concealing or preventing thought. Stuart Chase and others have come near to claiming that all abstract words are meaningless, and have used this as a pretext for advocating a kind of political quietism. Since you don't know what Fascism is, how can you struggle against Fascism? One need not swallow such absurdities as this, but one ought to recognize that the present political chaos is

19

connected with the decay of language, and that one can probably bring about some improvement by starting at the verbal end. If you simplify your English, you are freed from the worst follies of orthodoxy. You cannot speak any of the necessary dialects, and when you make a stupid remark its stupidity will be obvious, even to yourself. Political language—and with variations this is true of all political parties, from Conservatives to Anarchists—is designed to make lies sound truthful and murder respectable, and to give an appearance of solidity to pure wind. One cannot change this all in a moment, but one can at least change one's own habits, and from time to time one can even, if one jeers loudly enough, send some worn-out and useless phrase—some *jackboot, Achilles' heel, hotbed, melting pot, acid test, veritable inferno,* or other lump of verbal refuse—into the dustbin where it belongs.

Questions for Study and Discussion

1. In your own words, explain the relationship Orwell sees between politics and the English language. Do you agree with him? Why or why not?

2. What terms and concepts does Orwell define in his essay? What is his purpose in defining them? How does he go about it?

3. Our world is becoming increasingly prefabricated. In what way does the concept of prefabrication relate to Orwell's observations about the prevalence of habitual and trite phrases?

4. Orwell uses the following comparisons in his essay. How does each of them reinforce or clarify his meaning?
    a. "But in between these two classes there is a huge dump of worn-out metaphors which have lost all evocative power . . ." (paragraph 5)
    b. "The writer knows more or less what he wants to say, but an accumulation of stale phrases chokes him like tea leaves blocking a sink." (paragraph 11)
    c. "A mass of Latin words falls upon the facts like soft snow, blurring the outlines and covering up all the details." (paragraph 15)
    d. "When there is a gap between one's real and one's declared aims, one turns as it were instinctively to long words and exhausted idioms, like a cuttlefish squirting out ink." (paragraph 15)
    e. "He 'feels impelled' to write—feels, presumably, that he has something new to say—and yet his words, like cavalry horses answering the bugle, group themselves automatically into the familiar dreary pattern." (paragraph 16)

5. Orwell confesses that he himself is guilty, in this essay, of some of the errors he is pointing out. Can you detect any of them? What is the effect on you of these "errors" and of Orwell's confession?

6. The last of Orwell's six rules for better English reads, "Break any of these rules sooner than say anything outright barbarous." What do you think he means by this?

Writing Topics

1. As some of Orwell's examples suggest, language is sometimes used not to express our meanings but to conceal them. Is this true only of politics? Can you think of any situations in which you, or others you know, have been under pressure to say something yet had nothing you were ready or willing to say? What happened? How can one handle such situations honestly?

2. Gather five examples of recent American political English that you consider, in Orwell's words, "ugly and inaccurate." Can you analyze them using Orwell's terms? If not, what new terms would you invent to classify them?

3. Read Orwell's discussion of Newspeak in 1984. What is the relation between politics and language in Oceania? How does it connect with Orwell's views in "Politics and the English Language"?

DONNA WOOLFOLK CROSS

Most people are opposed to propaganda in principle, but few know exactly what it is and how it works. Donna Woolfolk Cross has looked closely at the subject, and her observations have been published in *Word Abuse: How the Words We Use, Use Us* (1979). She was born in New York City in 1947, and graduated from the University of Pennsylvania and UCLA. She now teaches at Onondaga Community College in New York State. For several years prior to teaching she worked in publishing and advertising, practicing as well as observing some of the techniques she writes about in her book *Mediaspeak* (1983).

Propaganda is a Latin term meaning "that which is to be made known" and is basically a means of persuasion. As such, it can be used "for good causes as well as bad." In the following essay, adapted by the author from *Speaking of Words* (1986), Cross discusses thirteen fallacies that propagandists can use to trick and mislead us and offers advice on how we can avoid being manipulated by the propaganda that is part of our everyday lives.

Propaganda: How Not to Be Bamboozled

Propaganda. If an opinion poll were taken tomorrow, we can be sure that nearly everyone would be against it because it *sounds* so bad. When we say, "Oh, that's just propaganda," it means, to most people, "That's a pack of lies." But really, propaganda is simply a means of persuasion and so it can be put to work for good causes as well as bad—to persuade people to give to charity, for example, or to love their neighbors, or to stop polluting the environment. 1

For good or evil, propaganda pervades our daily lives, helping to shape our attitudes on a thousand subjects. Propaganda probably determines the brand of toothpaste you use, the movies you see, the candidates you elect when you get to the polls. Propaganda works by tricking us, by momentarily distracting the eye while the rabbit pops out from beneath the cloth. Propaganda works best with an uncritical audience. Joseph Goebbels, Propaganda Minister in Nazi Germany, once defined his work as "the conquest of the masses." The masses would not have been conquered, however, if they had known how to challenge and to question, how to make distinctions between propaganda and reasonable argument. 2

People are bamboozled mainly because they don't recognize propaganda when they see it. They need to be informed about the various devices 3 that can be used to mislead and deceive—about the propagandist's overflowing bag of tricks. The following, then, are some common pitfalls for the unwary.

1. Name-Calling

As its title suggests, this device consists of labeling people or ideas with   4
words of bad connotation, literally, "calling them names." Here the propagandist tries to arouse our contempt so we will dismiss the "bad name" person or idea without examining its merits.

Bad names have played a tremendously important role in the history of   5
the world. They have ruined reputations and ended lives, sent people to prison and to war, and just generally made us mad at each other for centuries.

Name-calling can be used against policies, practices, beliefs and ideals,   6
as well as against individuals, groups, races, nations. Name-calling is at work when we hear a candidate for office described as a "foolish idealist" or a "two-faced liar" or when an incumbent's policies are denounced as "reckless," "reactionary," or just plain "stupid." Some of the most effective names a public figure can be called are ones that may not denote anything specific: "Congresswoman Jane Doe is a *bleeding heart!*" (Did she vote for funds to help paraplegics?) or "The Senator is a *tool of Washington!*" (Did he happen to agree with the President?) Senator Yakalot uses name-calling when he denounces his opponent's "radical policies" and calls them (and him) "socialist," "pinko," and part of a "heartless plot." He also uses it when he calls small cars "puddle-jumpers," "canopeners," and "motorized baby buggies."

The point here is that when the propagandist uses name-calling, he   7
doesn't want us to think—merely to react, blindly, unquestioningly. So the best defense against being taken in by name-calling is to stop and ask, "Forgetting the bad name attached to it, what are the merits of the idea itself? What does this name really mean, anyway?"

2. Glittering Generalities

Glittering generalities are really name-calling in reverse. Name-calling   8
uses words with bad connotations; glittering generalities are words with good connotations—"virtue words," as the Institute for Propaganda Analysis has called them. The Institute explains that while name-calling tries to get us to *reject* and *condemn* someone or something without examining the evidence, glittering generalities try to get us to *accept* and *agree* without examining the evidence.

We believe in, fight for, live by "virtue words" which we feel deeply   9
about: "justice," "motherhood," "the American way," "our Constitutional

rights," "our Christian heritage." These sound good, but when we examine them closely, they turn out to have no specific, definable meaning. They just make us feel good. Senator Yakalot uses glittering generalities when he says, "I stand for all that is good in America, for our American way and our American birthright." But what exactly *is* "good for America"? How can we define our "American birthright"? Just what parts of the American society and culture does "our American way" refer to?

We often make the mistake of assuming we are personally unaffected by glittering generalities. The next time you find yourself assuming that, listen to a political candidate's speech on TV and see how often the use of glittering generalities elicits cheers and applause. That's the danger of propaganda; it *works*. Once again, our defense against it is to ask questions: Forgetting the virtue words attached to it, what are the merits of the idea itself? What does "Americanism" (or "freedom" or "truth") really *mean* here? . . .

Both name-calling and glittering generalities work by stirring our emotions in the hope that this will cloud our thinking. Another approach that propaganda uses is to create a distraction, a "red herring," that will make people forget or ignore the real issues. There are several different kinds of "red herrings" that can be used to distract attention.

3. Plain Folks Appeal

"Plain folks" is the device by which a speaker tries to win our confidence and support by appearing to be a person like ourselves—"just one of the plain folks." The plain-folks appeal is at work when candidates go around shaking hands with factory workers, kissing babies in supermarkets, and sampling pasta with Italians, fried chicken with Southerners, bagels and blintzes with Jews. "Now I'm a businessman like yourselves" is a plain-folks appeal, as is "I've been a farm boy all my life." Senator Yakalot tries the plain-folks appeal when he says, "I'm just a small-town boy like you fine people." The use of such expressions once prompted Lyndon Johnson to quip, "Whenever I hear someone say, 'I'm just an old country lawyer,' the first thing I reach for is my wallet to make sure it's still there."

The irrelevancy of the plain-folks appeal is obvious: even if the man *is* "one of us" (which may not be true at all), that doesn't mean his ideas and programs are sound—or even that he honestly has our best interests at heart. As with glittering generalities, the danger here is that we may mistakenly assume we are immune to this appeal. But propagandists wouldn't use it unless it had been proved to work. You can protect yourself by asking, "Aside from his 'nice guy next door' image, what does this man stand for? Are his ideas and his past record really supportive of my best interests?"

4. Argumentum ad Populum (Stroking)

Argumentum ad populum means "argument to the people" or "telling the 14
people what they want to hear." The colloquial term from the Watergate era
is "stroking," which conjures up pictures of small animals or children being
stroked or soothed with compliments until they come to like the person
doing the complimenting—and, by extension, his or her ideas.

We all like to hear nice things about ourselves and the group we belong 15
to—we like to be liked—so it stands to reason that we will respond warmly
to a person who tells us we are "hard-working taxpayers" or "the most
generous, free-spirited nation in the world." Politicians tell farmers they are
the "backbone of the American economy" and college students that they are
the "leaders and policy makers of tomorrow." Commercial advertisers use
stroking more insidiously by asking a question which invites a flattering
answer: "What kind of a man reads *Playboy?*" (Does he really drive a Porsche
and own $10,000 worth of sound equipment?) Senator Yakalot is stroking his
audience when he calls them the "decent law-abiding citizens that are the
great pulsing heart and the life blood of this, our beloved country," and when
he repeatedly refers to them as "you fine people," "you wonderful folks."

Obviously, the intent here is to sidetrack us from thinking critically 16
about the man and his ideas. Our own good qualities have nothing to do
with the issue at hand. Ask yourself, "Apart from the nice things he has to
say about me (and my church, my nation, my ethnic group, my neighbors),
what does the candidate stand for? Are his or her ideas in my best interests?

5. Argumentum ad Hominem

Argumentum ad hominem means "argument to the man," and that's 17
exactly what it is. When a propagandist uses *argumentum ad hominem*, he
wants to distract our attention from the issue under consideration with
personal attacks on the people involved. For example, when Lincoln issued
the Emancipation Proclamation, some people responded by calling him the
"baboon." But Lincoln's long arms and awkward carriage had nothing to do
with the merits of the Proclamation or the question of whether or not slavery
should be abolished.

Today *argumentum ad hominem* is still widely used and very effective. 18
You may or may not support the Equal Rights Amendment, but you should
be sure your judgment is based on the merits of the idea itself, and not the
result of someone's denunciation of the people who support the ERA as
"fanatics" or "lesbians" or "frustrated old maids." Senator Yakalot is using
argumentum ad hominen when he dismisses the idea of using smaller automobiles with a reference to the personal appearance of one of its supporters,
Congresswoman Doris Schlepp. Refuse to be waylaid by *argumentum ad*

hominem and ask, "Do the personal qualities of the person being discussed have anything to do with the issues at hand? Leaving him or her aside, how good is the idea itself?"

6. *Transfer (Guilt or Glory by Association)*

In *argumentum ad hominem,* an attempt is made to associate negative   19
aspects of a person's character or personal appearance with an issue or idea he supports. The transfer device uses this same process of association to make us accept or condemn a given person or idea.

A better name for the transfer device is guilt (or glory) by association.   20
In glory by association, the propagandist tries to transfer the positive feelings of something we love and respect to the group or idea he wants us to accept. "This bill for a new dam is in the best tradition of this country, the land of Lincoln, Jefferson, and Washington," is glory by association at work. Lincoln, Jefferson, and Washington were great leaders that most of us revere and respect, but they have no logical connection to the proposal under consideration—the bill to build a new dam. Senator Yakalot uses glory by association when he says full-sized cars "have always been as American as Mom's apple pie or a Sunday drive in the country."

The process works equally well in reverse, when guilt by association is   21
used to transfer our dislike or disapproval of one idea or group to some other idea or group that the propagandist wants us to reject and condemn. "John Doe says we need to make some changes in the way our government operates; well, that's exactly what the Ku Klux Klan has said, so there's a meeting of great minds!" That's guilt by association for you; there's no logical connection between John Doe and the Ku Klux Klan apart from the one the propagandist is trying to create in our minds. He wants to distract our attention from John Doe and get us thinking (and worrying) about the Ku Klux Klan and its politics of violence. (Of course, there are sometimes legitimate associations between the two things; if John Doe had been a *member* of the Ku Klux Klan, it would be reasonable and fair to draw a connection between the man and his group.) Senator Yakalot tries to trick his audience with guilt by association when he remarks that "the words 'Community' and 'Communism' look an awful lot alike!" He does it again when he mentions that Mr. Stu Pott "sports a Fidel Castro beard."

How can we learn to spot the transfer device and distinguish between   22
fair and unfair associations? We can teach ourselves to *suspend judgment* until we have answered these questions: "Is there any legitimate connection between the idea under discussion and the thing it is associated with? Leaving the transfer device out of the picture, what are the merits of the idea by itself?"

7. Bandwagon

Ever hear of the small, ratlike animal called the lemming? Lemmings 23 are arctic rodents with a very odd habit: periodically, for reasons no one entirely knows, they mass together in a large herd and commit suicide by rushing into deep water and drowning themselves. They all run in together, blindly, and not one of them ever seems to stop and ask, "*Why* am I doing this? Is this really what I want to do?" and thus save itself from destruction. Obviously, lemmings are driven to perform their strange mass suicide rites by common instinct. People choose to "follow the herd" for more complex reasons, yet we are still all too often the unwitting victims of the bandwagon appeal.

Essentially, the bandwagon urges us to support an action or an opinion 24 because it is popular—because "everyone else is doing it." This call to "get on the bandwagon" appeals to the strong desire in most of us to be one of the crowd, not to be left out or alone. Advertising makes extensive use of the bandwagon appeal ("Join the Pepsi people"), but so do politicians ("Let us join together in this great cause"). Senator Yakalot uses the bandwagon appeal when he says that "More and more citizens are rallying to my cause every day," and asks his audience to "join them—and me—in our fight for America."

One of the ways we can see the bandwagon appeal at work is in the 25 overwhelming success of various fashions and trends which capture the interest (and the money) of thousands of people for a short time, then disappear suddenly and completely. For a year or two in the fifties, every child in North America wanted a coonskin cap so they could be like Davy Crockett; no one wanted to be left out. After that there was the hulahoop craze that helped to dislocate the hips of thousands of Americans. More recently, what made millions of people rush out to buy their very own "pet rocks"?

The problem here is obvious: just because everyone's doing it doesn't 26 mean that *we* should too. Group approval does not prove that something is true or is worth doing. Large numbers of people have supported actions we now condemn. Just a generation ago, Hitler and Mussolini rose to absolute and catastrophically repressive rule in two of the most sophisticated and cultured countries of Europe. When they came into power they were welled up by massive popular support from millions of people who didn't want to be "left out" at a great historical moment.

Once the mass begins to move—on the bandwagon—it becomes 27 harder and harder to perceive the leader *riding* the bandwagon. So don't be a lemming, rushing blindly on to destruction because "everyone else is doing it." Stop and ask, "Where is this bandwagon headed? Never mind about everybody else, is this what is best for *me*?" . . .

As we have seen, propaganda can appeal to us by arousing our emo- 28 tions or distracting our attention from the real issues at hand. But there's a third way that propaganda can be put to work against us—by the use of faulty logic. This approach is really more insidious than the other two because it gives the appearance of reasonable, fair argument. It is only when we look more closely that the holes in the logic fiber show up. The following are some of the devices that make use of faulty logic to distort and mislead.

8. Faulty Cause and Effect

As the name suggests, this device sets up a cause-and-effect relation- 29
ship that may not be true. The Latin name for this logical fallacy is *post hoc ergo propter hoc*, which means "after this, therefore because of this." But just because one thing happened after another doesn't mean that one *caused* the other.

An example of false cause-and-effect reasoning is offered by the story 30
(probably invented) of the woman aboard the ship *Titanic*. She woke up from a nap and, feeling seasick, looked around for a call button to summon the steward to bring her some medication. She finally located a small button on one of the walls of her cabin and pushed it. A split second later, the *Titanic* grazed an iceberg in the terrible crash that was to send the entire ship to its destruction. The woman screamed and said, "Oh, God, what have I done? What have I done?" The humor of that anecdote comes from the absurdity of the woman's assumption that pushing the small red button resulted in the destruction of a ship weighing several hundred tons: "It happened after I pushed it, therefore it must be *because* I pushed it"—*post hoc ergo propter hoc* reasoning. There is, of course, no cause-and-effect relationship there.

The false cause-and-effect fallacy is used very often by political candi- 31
dates. "After I came to office, the rate of inflation dropped to 6 percent." But did the person do anything to cause the lower rate of inflation or was it the result of other conditions? Would the rate of inflation have dropped anyway, even if he hadn't come to office? Senator Yakalot uses false cause and effect when he says "our forefathers who made this country great never had free hot meal handouts! And look what they did for our country!" He does it again when he concludes that "driving full-sized cars means a better car safety record on our American roads today."

False cause-and-effect reasoning is terribly persuasive because it seems 32
so logical. Its appeal is apparently to experience. We swallowed X product— and the headache went away. We elected Y official and unemployment went down. Many people think, "There *must* be a connection." But causality is an immensely complex phenomenon; you need a good deal of evidence to prove that an event that follows another in time was "therefore" caused by the first event.

Don't be taken in by false cause and effect; be sure to ask, "Is there 33 enough evidence to prove that this cause led to that effect? Could there have been any *other* causes?"

9. False Analogy

An analogy is a comparison between two ideas, events, or things. But 34 comparisons can be fairly made only when the things being compared are alike in significant ways. When they are not, false analogy is the result.

A famous example of this is the old proverb "Don't change horses in 35 the middle of a stream," often used as analogy to convince voters not to change administrations in the middle of a war or other crisis. But the analogy is misleading because there are so many differences between the things compared. In what ways is a war or a political crisis like a stream? Is the President or head of state really very much like a horse? And is a nation of millions of people comparable to a man trying to get across a stream? Analogy is false and unfair when it compares two things that have little in common and assumes that they are identical. Senator Yakalot tries to hoodwink his listeners with false analogy when he says, "Trying to take Americans out of the kind of cars they love is as undemocratic as trying to deprive them of the right to vote."

Of course, analogies can be drawn that are reasonable and fair. It would 36 be reasonable, for example, to compare the results of busing in one small Southern city with the possible results in another, *if* the towns have the same kind of history, population, and school policy. We can decide for ourselves whether an analogy is false or fair by asking, "Are the things being compared truly alike in significant ways? Do the differences between them affect the comparison?"

10. Begging the Question

Actually, the name of this device is rather misleading, because it does 37 not appear in the form of a question. Begging the question occurs when, in discussing a questionable or debatable point, a person assumes as already established the very point that he is trying to prove. For example, "No thinking citizen could approve such a completely unacceptable policy as this one." But isn't the question of whether or not the policy *is* acceptable the very point to be established? Senator Yakalot begs the question when he announces that his opponent's plan won't work "because it is unworkable."

We can protect ourselves against this kind of faulty logic by asking, 38 "What is assumed in this statement? Is the assumption reasonable, or does it need more proof?"

11. The Two-Extremes Fallacy (False Dilemma)

Linguists have long noted that the English language tends to view   39
reality in sets of two extremes or polar opposites. In English, things are either
black or white, tall or short, up or down, front or back, left or right, good or
bad, guilty or not guilty. We can ask for a "straightforward yes-or-no answer"
to a question, the understanding being that we will not accept or consider
anything in between. In fact, reality cannot always be dissected along such
strict lines. There may be (usually are) *more* than just two possibilities or
extremes to consider. We are often told to "listen to both sides of the
argument." But who's to say that every argument has only two sides? Can't
there be a third—even a fourth or fifth—point of view?

The two-extremes fallacy is at work in this statement by Lenin, the   40
great Marxist leader: "You cannot eliminate *one* basic assumption, one substantial part of this philosophy of Marxism (it is as if it were a block of steel),
without abandoning truth, without falling into the arms of bourgeois-
reactionary falsehood." In other words, if we don't agree 100 percent with
every premise of Marxism, we must be placed at the opposite end of the
political-economic spectrum—for Lenin, "bourgeois-reactionary falsehood."
If we are not entirely *with* him, we must be against him; those are the only
two possibilities open to us. Of course, this is a logical fallacy; in real life
there are any number of political positions one can maintain *between* the two
extremes of Marxism and capitalism. Senator Yakalot uses the two-extremes
fallacy in the same way as Lenin when he tells his audience that "in this
world a man's either for private enterprise or he's for socialism."

One of the most famous examples of the two-extremes fallacy in recent   41
history is the slogan, "America, Love it or leave it," with its implicit suggestion that we either accept everything just as it is in America today without
complaint—or get out. Again, it should be obvious that there is a whole
range of action and belief between the two extremes.

Don't be duped; stop and ask, "Are those really the only two options I   42
can choose from? Are there other alternatives not mentioned that deserve
consideration?"

12. Card Stacking

Some questions are so multifaceted and complex that no one can make   43
an intelligent decision about them without considering a wide variety of
evidence. One selection of facts could make us feel one way or another
selection could make us feel just the opposite. Card stacking is a device of
propaganda which selects only the facts that support the propagandist's point
of view, and ignores all the others. For example, a candidate could be made
to look like a legislative dynamo if you say, "Representative McNerd intro-

duced more new bills than any other member of the Congress," and neglect to mention that most of them were so preposterous that they were laughed off the floor.

Senator Yakalot engages in card stacking when he talks about the proposal to use smaller cars. He talks only about jobs without mentioning the cost to the taxpayers or the very real—though still denied—threat of depletion of resources. He says he wants to help his countrymen keep their jobs, but doesn't mention that the corporations that offer the jobs will also make large profits. He praises the "American chrome industry," overlooking the fact that most chrome is imported. And so on.   44

The best protection against card stacking is to take the "Yes, but . . ." attitude. This device of propaganda is not untrue, but then again it is not the *whole* truth. So ask yourself, "Is this person leaving something out that I should know about? Is there some other information that should be brought to bear on this question?" . . .   45

So far, we have considered three approaches that the propagandist can use to influence our thinking: appealing to our emotions, distracting our attention, and misleading us with logic that may appear to be reasonable but is in fact faulty and deceiving. But there is a fourth approach that is probably the most common propaganda trick of them all.   46

13. Testimonial

The testimonial device consists in having some loved or respected person give a statement of support (testimonial) for a given product or idea. The problem is that the person being quoted may *not* be an expert in the field; in fact, he may know nothing at all about it. Using the name of a man who is skilled and famous in one field to give a testimonial for something in another field is unfair and unreasonable.   47

Senator Yakalot tries to mislead his audience with testimonial when he tells them that "full-sized cars have been praised by great Americans like John Wayne and Jack Jones, as well as by leading experts on car safety and comfort."   48

Testimonial is used extensively in TV ads, where it often appears in such bizarre forms as Joe Namath's endorsement of a pantyhose brand. Here, of course, the "authority" giving the testimonial not only is no expert about pantyhose, but obviously stands to gain something (money!) by making the testimonial.   49

When celebrities endorse a political candidate, they may not be making money by doing so, but we should still question whether they are in any better position to judge than we ourselves. Too often we are willing to let others we like or respect make our decisions *for us*, while we follow along acquiescently. And this is the purpose of testimonial—to get us to agree and   50 accept *without* stopping to think. Be sure to ask, "Is there any reason to believe that this person (or organization or publication or whatever) has any more knowledge or information than I do on this subject? What does the idea amount to on its own merits, without the benefit of testimonial?"

The cornerstone of democratic society is reliance upon an informed and educated electorate. To be fully effective citizens we need to be able to challenge and to question wisely. A dangerous feeling of indifference toward our political processes exists today. We often abandon our right, our duty, to criticize and evaluate by dismissing *all* politicans as "crooked," *all* new bills and proposals as "just more government bureaucracy." But there are important distinctions to be made, and this kind of apathy can be fatal to democracy. 51

If we are to be led, let us not be led blindly, but critically, intelligently, with our eyes open. If we are to continue to be a government "by the people," let us become informed about the methods and purposes of propaganda, so we can be the masters, not the slaves of our destiny. 52

Questions for Study and Discussion

1. What are the four general types of propaganda devices that Cross discusses?

2. What, according to Cross, is the most common propaganda trick of them all? Give some examples from your experience.

3. What organization does Cross use for each of her discussions of a propaganda device? Do you see any purpose for the order in which she presents the thirteen devices?

4. Who is Senator Yakalot? What is his significance in Cross's essay?

5. Cross uses an analogy in her discussion of bandwagon appeal. How does this analogy work? Is it a true or a false analogy, according to Cross's own definitions? Explain.

Writing Topics

1. As Cross says in the beginning of her essay, propaganda "can be put to work for good causes as well as bad." Using materials from the Red Cross, United Way, or some other public service organization, write an essay in which you discuss the propaganda used by such organizations. How would you characterize their appeals? Do you ever find such propaganda objectionable? Does the end always justify the means?

2. In an effort to better understand the thought processes involved in propaganda, try writing a piece yourself. Using the devices described by Cross, try to persuade your classmates to (a) join a particular campus organization, (b) support, either spiritually or financially, a controversial movement or issue on campus, or (c) vote for one candidate and not another in a campus election.

JIB FOWLES

An expert in the analysis of industrial culture, Jib Fowles was born in Hartford, Connecticut, in 1940, and graduated from Wesleyan University. After completing his graduate studies at Columbia University and New York University, he accepted a teaching post at the University of Houston, where he is currently a professor of studies of the future. Fowles has written *Mass Advertising as Social Forecast* (1976) and is the editor of the *Handbook of Futures Research* (1978). More recently, Fowles has turned his attention to television and the reasons why people watch. He has written two books on this subject, *Television Viewers vs. Media Snobs: What TV Does for People* (1982) and *Why Viewers Watch: A Reappraisal of Television's Effects* (1992).

In the following article, published in *ETC.: A Review of General Semantics*, Fowles discusses the basic emotions to which advertisers appeal to. Not coincidentally, the appeals parallel a "hierarchy of needs" described by leading psychologists.

Advertising's Fifteen Basic Appeals

Emotional Appeals

The nature of effective advertisements was recognized full well by the late media philosopher Marshall McLuhan. In his *Understanding Media*, the first sentence of the section on advertising reads, "The continuous pressure is to create ads more and more in the image of audience motives and desires." 1

By giving form to people's deep-lying desires, and picturing states of being that individuals privately yearn for, advertisers have the best chance of arresting attention and affecting communication. And that is the immediate goal of advertising: to tug at our psychological shirt sleeves and slow us down long enough for a word or two about whatever is being sold. We glance at a picture of a solitary rancher at work, and "Marlboro" slips into our minds. 2

Advertisers (I'm using the term as a shorthand for both the products' manufacturers, who bring the ambition and money to the process, and the advertising agencies, who supply the know-how) are ever more compelled to invoke consumers' drives and longings; this is the "continuous pressure" McLuhan refers to. Over the past century, the American marketplace has grown increasingly congested as more and more products have entered into the frenzied competition after the public's dollars. The economics of other nations are quieter than ours since the volume of goods being hawked does not so greatly exceed demand. In some economies, consumer wares are 3 scarce enough that no advertising at all is necessary. But in the United States, we go to the other extreme. In order to stay in business, an advertiser must strive to cut through the considerable commercial hub-bub by any means available—including the emotional appeals that some observers have held to be abhorrent and underhanded.

The use of subconscious appeals is a comment not only on conditions   4
among sellers. As time has gone by, buyers have become stoutly resistant to advertisements. We live in a blizzard of these messages and have learned to turn up our collars and ward off most of them. A study done a few years ago at Harvard University's Graduate School of Business Administration ventured that the average American is exposed to some 500 ads daily from television, newspapers, magazines, radio, billboards, direct mail, and so on. If for no other reason than to preserve one's sanity, a filter must be developed in every mind to lower the number of ads a person is actually aware of—a number this particular study estimated at about seventy-five ads per day. (Of these, only twelve typically produce a reaction—nine positive and three negative, on the average.) To be among the few messages that do manage to gain access to minds, advertisers must be strategic, perhaps even a little underhanded at times.

There are assumptions about personality underlying advertisers' efforts   5
to communicate via emotional appeals, and while these assumptions have stood the test of time, they still deserve to be aired. Human beings, it is presumed, walk around with a variety of unfulfilled urges and motives swirling in the bottom half of their minds. Lusts, ambitions, tenderness, vulnerabilities—they are constantly bubbling up, seeking resolution. These mental forces energize people, but they are too crude and irregular to be given excessive play in the real world. They must be capped with the competent, sensible behavior that permits individuals to get along well in society. However, this upper layer of mental activity, shot through with caution and rationality, is not receptive to advertising's pitches. Advertisers want to circumvent this shell of conscious if they can, and latch on to one of the lurching, subconcious drives.

In effect, advertisers over the years have blindly felt their way around   6
the underside of the American psyche, and by trial and error have discovered the softest points of entree, the places where their messages have the greatest likelihood of getting by consumers' defenses. As McLuhan says elsewhere, "Gouging away at the surface of public sales resistance, the ad men are constantly breaking through into the *Alice in Wonderland* territory behind the looking glass, which is the world of subrational impulses and appetites."

An advertisement communicates by making use of a specifically se-   7
lected image (of a supine female, say, or a curly-headed child, or a celebrity) which is designed to stimulate "subrational impulses and desires" even when they are at ebb, even if they are unacknowledged by their possessor. Some few ads have their emotional appeal in the text, but for the greater number

by far the appeal is contained in the artwork. This makes sense, since visual communication better suits more primal levels of the brain. If the viewer of an advertisement actually has the importuned motive, and if the appeal is sufficiently well-fashioned to call it up, then the person can be hooked. The product in the ad may then appear to take on the semblance of gratification for the summoned motive. Many ads seem to be saying, "If you have this need, then this product will help satisfy it." It is a primitive equation, but not an ineffective one for selling.

Thus, most advertisements appearing in national media can be under- 8
stood as having two orders of content. The first is the appeal to deep-running drives in the minds of consumers. The second is information regarding the good or service being sold: its name, its manufacturer, its picture, its packaging, its objective attributes, its functions. For example, the reader of a brassiere advertisement sees a partially undraped but blandly unperturbed woman standing in an otherwise commonplace public setting, and may experience certain sensations; the reader also sees the name "Maidenform," a particular brassiere style, and, in tiny print, words about the material, colors, price. Or, the viewer of a television commercial sees a demonstration with four small boxes labelled 650, 650, 650, and 800; something in the viewer's mind catches hold of this, as trivial as thoughtful consideration might reveal it to be. The viewer is also exposed to the name "Anacin," its bottle, and its purpose.

Sometimes there is an apparently logical link between an ad's emo- 9
tional appeal and its product information. It does not violate common sense that Cadillac automobiles be photographed at country clubs, or that Japan Air Lines be associated with Orientalia. But there is no real need for the linkage to have a bit of reason behind it. Is there anything inherent to the connection between Salem cigarettes and mountains, Coke and a smile, Miller Beer and comradeship? The link being forged in minds between product and appeal is a pre-logical one.

People involved in the advertising industry do not necessarily talk in 10
the terms being used here. They are stationed at the sending end of this communications channel, and may think they are up to any number of things—Unique Selling Propositions, explosive copywriting, the optimal use of demographics or psychographics, ideal media buys, high recall ratings, or whatever. But when attention shifts to the receiving end of the channel, and focuses on the instant of reception, then commentary becomes much more elemental: an advertising message contains something primary and primitive, an emotional appeal, that in effect is the thin end of the wedge, trying to find its way into a mind. Should this occur, the product information comes along behind.

When enough advertisements are examined in this light, it becomes 11
clear that the emotional appeals fall into several distinguishable categories, and that every ad is a variation on one of a limited number of basic appeals.

While there may be several ways of classifying these appeals, one particular list of fifteen has proven to be especially valuable.

Advertisements can appeal to: 12

1. The need for sex
2. The need for affiliation
3. The need to nurture
4. The need for guidance
5. The need to aggress
6. The need to achieve
7. The need to dominate
8. The need for prominence
9. The need for attention
10. The need for autonomy
11. The need to escape
12. The need to feel safe
13. The need for aesthetic sensations
14. The need to satisfy curiosity
15. Physiological needs: food, drink, sleep, etc.

Murray's List

Where does this list of advertising's fifteen basic appeals come from? 13
Several years ago, I was involved in a research project which was to have as one segment an objective analysis of the changing appeals made in post–World War II American advertising. A sample of magazine ads would have their appeals coded into the categories of psychological needs they seemed aimed at. For this content analysis to happen, a complete roster of human motives would have to be found.

The first thing that came to mind was Abraham Maslow's famous four- 14
part hierarchy of needs. But the briefest look at the range of appeals made in advertising was enough to reveal that they are more varied, and more pro-fane, than Maslow had cared to account for. The search led on to the work of psychologist Henry A. Murray, who together with his colleagues at Harvard Psychological Clinic had constructed a full taxonomy of needs. As described in *Explorations in Personality*, Murray's team had conducted a lengthy series of depth interviews with a number of subjects in order to derive from scratch what they felt to be the essential variables of personality. Forty-four variables were distinguished by the Harvard group, of which twenty were motives. The need for achievement ("to overcome obstacles and obtain a high stan-dard") was one, for instance; the need to defer was another; the need to aggress was a third; and so forth.

Murray's list had served as the groundwork for a number of subsequent 15
projects. Perhaps the best-known of these was David C. McClelland's exten-

sive study of the need for achievement, reported in his *The Achieving Society*. In the process of demonstrating that a people's high need for achievement is predictive of later economic growth, McClelland coded achievement imagery and references out of a nation's folklore, songs, legends, and children's tales.

Following McClelland, I too wanted to cull the motivational appeals 16 from a culture's imaginative product—in this case, advertising. To develop categories expressly for this purpose, I took Murray's twenty motives and added to them others he had mentioned in passing in *Explorations in Personality* but not included on the final list. The extended list was tried out on a sample of advertisements, and motives which never seemed to be invoked were dropped. I ended up with eighteen of Murray's motives, into which 770 print ads were coded. The resulting distribution is included in the 1976 book *Mass Advertising as Social Forecast*.

Since that time, the list of appeals has undergone refinements as a 17 result of using it to analyze television commercials. A few more adjustments have stemmed from the efforts of students in my advertising classes to decode appeals; tens of term papers surveying thousands of advertisements have caused some inconsistencies in the list to be hammered out. Fundamentally, though, the list remains the creation of Henry Murray. In developing a comprehensive, parsimonious inventory of human motives, he pinpointed the subsurface mental forces that are the least quiescent and the most susceptible to advertising's entreaties.

Fifteen Appeals

1. *Need for sex.* Let's start with sex, because this is the appeal which 18 seems to pop up first whenever the topic of advertising is raised. Whole books have been written about this one alone, to find a large audience of mildly titillated readers. Lately, due to campaigns to sell blue jeans, concern with sex in ads has redoubled.

The fascinating thing is not how much sex there is in advertising, but 19 how little. Contrary to impressions, unambiguous sex is rare in these messages. Some of this surprising observation may be a matter of definition: the Jordache ads with the lithe, blouse-less female astride a similarly clad male is clearly an appeal to the audience's sexual drives, but the same cannot be said about Brooke Shields in the Calvin Klein commercials. Directed at young women and their credit-card-carrying mothers, the image of Miss Shields instead invokes the need to be looked at. Buy Calvins and you'll be the center of much attention, just as Brooke is, the ads imply; they do not primarily inveigle their target audience's need for sexual intercourse.

In the content analysis reported in *Mass Advertising as Social Forecast*, 20 only two percent of ads were found to pander to this motive. Even *Playboy* ads shy away from sexual appeals: a recent issue contained eighty-three full-page ads, and just four of them (or less than five percent) could be said to have sex on their minds.

The reason this appeal is so little used is that it is too blaring and tends 21 to obliterate the product information. Nudity in advertising has the effect of reducing brand recall. The people who do remember the product may do so because they have been made indignant by the ad; this is not the response most advertisers seek.

To the extent that sexual imagery is used, it conventionally works 22 better on men than women; typically a female figure is offered up to the male reader. A Black Velvet liquor advertisement displays an attractive woman wearing a tight black outfit, recumbent under the legend, "Feel the Velvet." The figure does not have to be horizontal, however, for the appeal to be present, as National Airlines revealed in its "Fly me" campaign. Indeed, there does not even have to be a female in the ad: "Flick my Bic" was sufficient to convey the idea to many.

As a rule, though, advertisers have found sex to be a tricky appeal, to 23 be used sparingly. Less controversial and equally fetching are the appeals to our need for affectionate human contact.

2. *Need for affiliation.* American mythology upholds autonomous indi- 24 viduals, and social statistics suggest that people are ever more going it alone in their lives, yet the high frequency of affiliative appeals in ads belies this. Or maybe it does not: maybe all the images of companionship are compensation for what Americans privately lack. In any case, the need to associate with others is widely invoked in advertising and is probably the most prevalent appeal. All sorts of goods and services are sold by linking them to our unfulfilled desires to be in good company.

According to Henry Murray, the need for affiliation consists of desires 25 "to draw near and enjoyably cooperate or reciprocate with another; to please and win affection of another; to adhere and remain loyal to a friend." The manifestations of this motive can be segmented into several different types of affiliation, beginning with romance.

Courtship may be swifter nowadays, but the desire for pair-bonding is far 26 from satiated. Ads reaching for this need commonly depict a youngish male and female engrossed in each other. The head of the male is usually higher than the female's, even at this late date; she may be sitting or leaning while he is standing. They are not touching in the Smirnoff vodka ads, but obviously there is an intimacy, sometimes frolicsome, between them. The couple does touch for Martell Cognac when "The moment was Martell." For Wind Song perfume they have touched, and "Your Wind Song stays on his mind."

Depending on the audience, the pair does not absolutely have to be 27 young—just together. He gives her a DeBeers diamond, and there is a tear in her laugh lines. She takes Geritol and preserves herself for him. And numbers of consumers, wanting affection too, follow suit.

Warm family feelings are fanned in ads when another generation is   28
added to the pair. Hallmark Cards bring grandparents into the picture, and
Johnson and Johnson Baby Powder has Dad, Mom, and baby, all fresh from
the bath, encircled in arms and emblazoned with "Share the Feeling." A talc
has been fused to familial love.

Friendship is yet another form of affiliation pursued by advertisers. Two   29
women confide and drink Maxwell House coffee together; two men walk
through the woods smoking Salem cigarettes. Miller Beer promises that
afternoon "Miller Time" will be staffed with three or four good buddies.
Drink Dr. Pepper, as Mickey Rooney is coaxed to do, and join in with all the
other Peppers. Coca-Cola does not even need to portray the friendliness; it
has reduced this appeal to "a Coke and a smile."

The warmth can be toned down and disguised, but it is the same   30
affiliative need that is being fished for. The blonde has a direct gaze and her
friends are firm businessmen in appearance, but with a glass of Old Bushmill
you can sit down and fit right in. Or, for something more upbeat, sing along
with the Pontiac choirboys.

As well as presenting positive images, advertisers can play to the need   31
for affiliation in negative ways, by invoking the fear of rejection. If we don't
use Scope, we'll have the "Ugh! Morning Breath" that causes the male and
female models to avert their faces. Unless we apply Ultra-Brite or Close-Up
to our teeth, it's goodbye romance. Our family will be cursed with "House-a-
tosis" if we don't take care. Without Dr. Scholl's anti-perspirant foot spray,
the bowling team will keel over. There go all the guests when the supply of
Dorito's nacho cheese chips is exhausted. Still more rejection if our shirts
have ring-around-the-collar, if our car needs to be Midasized. But make a few
purchases, and we are back in the bosom of human contact.

As self-directed as Americans pretend to be, in the last analysis we   32
remain social animals, hungering for the positive, endorsing feelings that
only those around us can supply. Advertisers respond, urging us to "Reach
out and touch someone," in the hopes our monthly bills will rise.

3. *Need to nurture.* Akin to affiliative needs is the need to take care of   33
small, defenseless creatures—children and pets, largely. Reciprocity is of less
consequence here, though; it is the giving that counts. Murray uses syn-
onyms like "to feed, help, support, console, protect, comfort, nurse, heal."
A strong need it is, woven deep into our genetic fabric, for if it did not exist
we could not successfully raise up our replacements. When advertisers put
forth the image of something diminutive and furry, something that elicits the
word "cute" or "precious," then they are trying to trigger this motive. We
listen to the childish voice singing the Oscar Mayer wiener song, and our
next hot-dog purchase is prescribed. Aren't those darling kittens something,
and how did this Meow Mix get into our shopping cart?

This pitch is often directed at women, as Mother Nature's chief   34
nurturers. "Make me some Kraft macaroni and cheese, please," says the

elfin preschooler just in from the snowstorm, and mothers' hearts go out, and Kraft's sales go up. "We're cold, wet, and hungry," whine the husband and kids, and the little woman gets the Manwiches ready. A fascimile of this need can be hit without children or pets; the husband is ill and sleepless in the television commercial, and the wife grudgingly fetches the NyQuil.

But it is not women alone who can be touched by this appeal. The father nurses his son Eddie through adolescence while the John Deere lawn tractor survives the years. Another father counts pennies with his young son as the subject of New York Life Insurance comes up. And all over America are businessmen who don't know why they dial Quantas Airlines when they have to take a trans-Pacific trip; the koala bear knows.   35

4. *Need for guidance.* The opposite of the need to nurture is the need to be nurtured: to be protected, shielded, guided. We may be loath to admit it, but the child lingers on inside every adult—and a good thing it does, or we would not be instructable in our advancing years. Who wants a nation of nothing but flinty personalities?   36

Parent-like figures can successfully call up this need. Robert Young recommends Sanka coffee, and since we have experienced him for twenty-five years as television father and doctor, we take his word for it. Florence Henderson as the expert mom knows a lot about the advantages of Wesson oil.   37

The parent-ness of the spokesperson need not be so salient; sometimes pure authoritativeness is better. When Orson Welles scowls and intones, "Paul Masson will sell no wine before its time," we may not know exactly what he means, but we still take direction from him. There is little material about Brenda Vaccaro when she speaks up for Tampax, but there is a certainty to her that many accept.   38

A celebrity is not a necessity in making a pitch to the need for guidance, since a fantasy figure can serve just as well. People accede to the Green Giant, or Betty Crocker, or Mr. Goodwrench. Some advertisers can get by with no figure at all: "When E. F. Hutton talks, people listen."   39

Often it is tradition or custom that advertisers point to and consumers take guidance from. Bits and pieces of American history are used to sell whiskeys like Old Crow, Southern Comfort, Jack Daniels. We conform to traditional male/female roles and age-old social norms when we purchase Barclay cigarettes, which informs us "The pleasure is back."   40

The product itself, if it has been around for a long time, can constitute a tradition. All those old labels in the ad for Morton salt convince us that we should continue to buy it. Kool-Aid says, "You loved it as a kid. You trust it as a mother," hoping to get more consumers to go along.   41

Even when the product has no history at all, our need to conform to tradition and to be guided are strong enough that they can be invoked through bogus nostalgia and older actors. Country-Time lemonade sells because consumers want to believe it has a past they can defer to.   42

So far the needs and the ways they can be invoked which have been looked at are largely warm and affiliative; they stand in contrast to the next set of needs, which are much more egoistic and assertive.   43

5. *Need to aggress.* The pressures of the real world create strong retaliatory feelings in every functioning human being. Since these impulses can come forth as bursts of anger and violence, their display is normally tabooed. Existing as harbored energy, aggressive drives present a large, tempting target for advertisers. It is not a target to be aimed at thoughtlessly, though, for few manufacturers want their products associated with destructive motives. There is always the danger that, as in the case of sex, if the appeal is too blatant, public opinion will turn against what is being sold.   44

Jack-in-the-Box sought to abruptly alter its marketing by going after older customers and forgetting the younger ones. Their television commercials had a seventy-ish lady command, "Waste him," and the Jack-in-the-Box clown exploded before our eyes. So did public reaction, until the commercials were toned down. Print ads for Club cocktails carried the faces of octogenarians under the headline, "Hit me with a Club"; response was contrary enough to bring the campaign to a stop.   45

Better disguised aggressive appeals are less likely to backfire: Triumph cigarettes has models making a lewd gesture with their uplifted cigarettes, but the individuals are often laughing and usually in the close company of others. When Exxon said, "There's a Tiger in your tank," the implausibility of it concealed the invocation of aggressive feelings.   46

Depicted arguments are a common way for advertisers to tap the audience's needs to aggress. Don Rickles and Linda Carter trade gibes, and consumers take sides as the name of Seven-Up is stitched on minds. The Parkay tub has a difference of opinion with the user; who can forget it, or who (or what) got the last word in?   47

6. *Need to achieve.* This is the drive that energizes people, causing them to strive in their lives and careers. According to Murray, the need for achievement is signalled by the desires "to accomplish something difficult. To overcome obstacles and attain a high standard. To excel one's self. To rival and surpass others." A prominent American trait, it is one that advertisers like to hook on to because it identifies their product with winning and success.   48

The Cutty Sark ad does not disclose that Ted Turner failed at his latest attempt at yachting's America Cup; here he is represented as a champion on the water as well as off in his television enterprises. If we drink this whiskey, we will be victorious alongside Turner. We can also succeed with O. J. Simpson by renting Hertz cars, or with Reggie Jackson by bringing home some Panasonic equipment. Cathy Rigby and Stayfree Maxipads will put people out front.   49

Sports heroes are the most convenient means to snare consumers' needs to achieve, but they are not the only one. Role models can be estab-   50 lished, ones which invite emulation, as with the profiles put forth by Dewar's scotch. Successful, tweedy individuals relate they have "graduated to the flavor of Myer's rum." Or the advertiser can establish a prize: two neighbors play one-on-one basketball for a Michelob beer in a television commercial, while in a print ad a bottle of Johnnie Walker Black Label has been gilded like a trophy.

Any product that advertises itself in superlatives—the best, the first, 51 the finest—is trying to make contact with our needs to succeed. For many consumers, sales and bargains belong to this category of appeals, too; the person who manages to buy something at fifty percent off is seizing an opportunity and coming out ahead of others.

7. *Need to dominate.* This fundamental need is the craving to be 52 powerful—perhaps omnipotent, as in the Xerox ad where Brother Dominic exhibits heavenly powers and creates miraculous copies. Most of us will settle for being just a regular potentate, though. We drink Budweiser because it is the King of Beers, and here come the powerful Clydesdales to prove it. A taste of Wolfschmidt vodka and "The spirit of the Czar lives on."

The need to dominate and control one's environment is often thought 53 of as being masculine; [but, as close students of human nature, advertisers know it is not so circumscribed.] Women's aspirations for control are suggested in the campaign theme, "I like my men in English Leather, or nothing at all." The females in the Chanel No. 19 ads are "outspoken" and wrestle their men around.

Male and female, what we long for is clout; what we get in its place is 54 Mastercard.

8. *Need for prominence.* Here comes the need to be admired and re- 55 spected, to enjoy prestige and high social status. These times, it appears, are not so egalitarian after all. Many ads picture the trappings of high position; the Oldsmobile stands before a manorial doorway, the Volvo is parked beside a steeplechase. A book-lined study is the setting for Dewar's 12, and Lenox China is displayed in a dining room chock full of antiques.

Beefeater gin represents itself as "The Crown Jewel of England" and 56 uses no illustrations of jewels or things British, for the words are sufficient indicators of distinction. Buy that gin and you will rise up the prestige hierarchy, or achieve the same effect on yourself with Seagram's 7 Crown, which unambiguously describes itself as "classy."

Being respected does not have to entail the usual accoutrements of 57 wealth: "Do you know who I am?" the commercials ask, and we learn that the prominent person is not so prominent without his American Express card.

9. *Need for attention.* The previous need involved being *looked up to,* 58 while this is the need to be *looked at.* The desire to exhibit ourselves in such a way as to make others look at us is a primitive, insuppressible instinct. The clothing and cosmetic industries exist just to serve this need, and this is the

way they pitch their wares. Some of this effort is aimed at males, as the ads for Hathaway shirts and Jockey underclothes. But the greater bulk of such appeals is targeted singlemindedly at women.

To come back to Brooke Shields: this is where she fits into American 59 marketing. If I buy Calvin Klein jeans, consumers infer, I'll be the object of fascination. The desire for exhibition has been most strikingly played to in a print campaign of many years duration, that of Maidenform lingerie. The woman exposes herself, and sales surge. "Gentlemen prefer Hanes" the ads dissemble, and women who want eyes upon them know what they should do. Peggy Fleming flutters her legs for L'eggs, encouraging females who want to be the star in their own lives to purchase this product.

The same appeal works for cosmetics and lotions. For years, the little 60 girl with the exposed backside sold gobs of Coppertone, but now the company has picked up the pace a little: as a female, you are supposed to "Flash 'em a Coppertone tan." Food can be sold the same way, especially to the diet-conscious; Angie Dickinson poses for California avocadoes and says, "Would this body lie to you?" Our eyes are too fixed on her for us to think to ask if she got that way by eating mounds of guacamole.

10. *Need for autonomy.* There are several ways to sell credit card ser- 61 vices, as has been noted: Mastercard appeals to the need to dominate, and American Express to the need for prominence. When Visa claims, "You can have it the way you want it," yet another primary motive is being beckoned forward—the need to endorse the self. The focus here is upon the independence and integrity of the individual; this need is the antithesis of the need for guidance and is unlike any of the social needs. "If running with the herd isn't your style, try ours," says Rotan-Mosle, and many Americans feel they have finally found the right brokerage firm.

The photo is of a red-coated Mountie on his horse, posed on a snow- 62 covered ledge; the copy reads, "Windsor—one Canadian stands alone." This epitome of the solitary and proud individual may work best with male customers, as may Winston's man in the red cap. But one-figure advertisements also strike the strong need for autonomy among American women. As Shelly Hack strides for Charlie perfume, females respond to her obvious pride and flair; she is her own person. The Virginia Slims' tale is of people who have come a long way from subservience to independence. Cachet perfume feels it does not need a solo figure to work this appeal, and uses three different faces in its ads; it insists, though, "It's different on every woman who wears it."

Like many psychological needs, this one can also be appealed to in a 63 negative fashion, by invoking the loss of independence or self-regard. Guilt and regrets can be stimulated: "Gee, I could have had a V-8." Next time, get one and be good to yourself.

11. *Need to escape.* An appeal to the need for autonomy often co- 64 occurs with one for the need to escape, since the desire to duck out of our

social obligations, to seek rest or adventure, frequently takes the form of one-person flight. The dashing image of a pilot, in fact, is a standard way of quickening this need to get away from it all.

Freedom is the pitch here, the freedom that every individual yearns for whenever life becomes too oppressive. Many advertisers like appealing to the need for escape because the sensation of pleasure often accompanies escape, and what nicer emotional nimbus could there be for a product? "You deserve a break today," says McDonalds, and Stouffer's frozen foods chime in, "Set yourself free." 65

For decades men have imaginatively bonded themselves to the Marlboro cowboy who dwells untarnished and unencumbered in Marlboro Country some distance from modern life; smokers' aching needs for autonomy and escape are personified by that cowpoke. Many women can identify with the lady ambling through the woods behind the words, "Benson and Hedges and mornings and me." 66

But escape does not have to be solitary. Other Benson and Hedges ads, part of the same campaign, contain two strolling figures. In Salem cigarette advertisements, it can be several people who escape together into the mountaintops. A commercial for Levi's pictured a cloudbank above a city through which ran a whole chain of young people. 67

There are varieties of escape, some wistful like the Boeing "Someday" campaign of dream vacations, some kinetic like the play and parties in soft drink ads. But in every instance, the consumer exposed to the advertisement is invited to momentarily depart his everyday life for a more carefree experience, preferably with the product in hand. 68

12. *Need to feel safe.* Nobody in their right mind wants to be intimidated, menaced, battered, poisoned. We naturally want to do whatever it takes to stave off threats to our well-being, and to our families'. It is the instinct for self-preservation that makes us responsive to the ad of the St. Bernard with the keg of Chivas Regal. We pay attention to the stern talk of Karl Malden and the plight of the vacationing couples who have lost all their funds in the American Express travelers cheques commercials. We want the omnipresent stag from Hartford Insurance to watch over us too. 69

In the interest of keeping failure and calamity from our lives, we like to see the durability of products demonstrated. Can we ever forget that Timex takes a licking and keeps on ticking? When the American Tourister suitcase bounces all over the highway and the egg inside doesn't break, the need to feel safe has been adroitly plucked. 70

We take precautions to diminish future threats. We buy Volkswagen Rabbits for the extraordinary mileage, and MONY insurance policies to avoid the tragedies depicted in their black-and-white ads of widows and orphans. 71

We are careful about our health. We consume Mazola margarine because it has "corn goodness" backed by the natural food traditions of the 72

American Indians. In the medicine cabinet is Alka-Seltzer, the "home rem-edy"; having it, we are snug in our little cottage.

We want to be safe and secure; buy these products, advertisers are   73
saying, and you'll be safer than you are without them.

13. *Need for aesthetic sensations.* There is an undeniable aesthetic com-   74
ponent to virtually every ad run in the national media: the photography or
filming or drawing is near-perfect, the type style is well chosen, the layout
could scarcely be improved upon. Advertisers know there is little chance of
good communication occurring if an ad is not visually pleasing. Consumers
may not be aware of the extent of their own sensitivity to artwork, but it is
undeniably large.

Sometimes the aesthetic element is expanded and made into an ad's   75
primary appeal. Charles Jourdan shoes may or may not appear in the accompanying avant-garde photographs; Kohler plumbing fixtures catch attention
through the high style of their desert settings. Beneath the slightly out of
focus photograph, languid and sensuous in tone, General Electric feels called
upon to explain, "This is an ad for the hair dryer."

This appeal is not limited to female consumers: J and B scotch says "It   76
whispers" and shows a bucolic scene of lake and castle.

14. *Need to satisfy curiosity.* It may seem odd to list a need for informa-   77
tion among basic motives, but this need can be as primal and compelling as
any of the others. Human beings are curious by nature, interested in the
world around them, and intrigued by tidbits of knowledge and new developments. Trivia, percentages, observations counter to conventional wisdom—
these items all help sell products. Any advertisement in a question-and-
answer format is strumming this need.

A dog groomer has a question about long distance rates, and Bell   78
Telephone has a chart with all the figures. An ad for Porsche 911 is replete
with diagrams and schematics, numbers and arrows. Lo and behold, Anacin
pills have 150 more milligrams than its competitors; should we wonder if this
is better or worse for us?

15. *Physiological needs.* To the extent that sex is solely a biological   79
need, we are now coming around full circle, back towards the start of the list.
In this final category are clustered appeals to sleeping, eating, drinking. The
art of photographing food and drink is so advanced, sometimes these tempta-
tions are wondrously caught in the camera's lens: the crab meat in the Red
Lobster restaurant ads can start us salivating, the Quarterpounder can almost
be smelled, the liquor in the glass glows invitingly. Imbibe, these ads scream.

Styles

Some common ingredients of advertisements were not singled out for   80
separate mention in the list of fifteen because they are not appeals in and of

themselves. They are stylistic features, influencing the way a basic appeal is presented. The use of humor is one, and the use of celebrities is another. A third is time imagery, past and future, which goes to several purposes.

For all of its employment in advertising, humor can be treacherous, 81 because it can get out of hand and smother the product information. Supposedly, this is what Alka-Seltzer discovered with its comic commercials of the late sixties; "I can't believe I ate the whole thing," the sad-faced husband lamented, and the audience cackled so much it forgot the antacid. Or, did not take it seriously.

But used carefully, humor can punctuate some of the softer appeals and 82 soften some of the harsher ones. When Emma says to the Fruit-of-the-Loom fruits, "Hi, cuties. Whatcha doing in my laundry basket?" we smile as our curiosity is assuaged along with hers. Bill Cosby gets consumers tickled about the children in his Jell-O commercials, and strokes the need to nurture.

An insurance company wants to invoke the need to feel safe, but does 83 not want to leave readers with an unpleasant aftertaste; cartoonist Rowland Wilson creates an avalanche about to crush a gentleman who is saying to another, "My insurance company? New England Life, of course. Why?" The same tactic of humor undercutting threat is used in the cartoon commercials for Safeco when the Pink Panther wanders from one disaster to another. Often humor masks aggression: comedian Bob Hope in the outfit of a boxer promises to knock out the knock-knocks with Texaco; Rodney Dangerfield, who "can't get no respect," invites aggression as the comic relief in Miller Lite commercials.

Roughly fifteen percent of all advertisements incorporate a celebrity, 84 almost always from the fields of entertainment, for celebrities are human beings too, and fully capable of the most remarkable behavior; if anything distasteful about them emerges, it is likely to reflect on the product. The advertisers making use of Anita Bryant and Billy Jean King suffered several anxious moments. An untimely death can also reflect poorly on a product. But advertisers are willing to take these risks because celebrities can be such a good link between producers and consumers, performing the social role of introducer.

There are several psychological needs these middlemen can play upon. 85 Let's take the product class of cameras and see how different celebrities can hit different needs. The need for guidance can be invoked by Michael Landon, who plays such a wonderful dad on "Little House on the Prairie"; when he says to buy Kodak equipment, many people listen. James Garner for Polaroid cameras is put in a similar authoritative role, so defined by a mocking spouse. The need to achieve is summoned up by Tracy Austin and other tennis stars for Canon AE-1; the advertiser first makes sure we see these athletes playing to win. When Cheryl Tiegs speaks up for Olympus cameras, it is the need for attention that is being targeted.

The past and future, being outside our grasp, are exploited by advertis- 86 ers as locales for the projection of needs. History can offer up heroes (and call up the need to achieve) or traditions (need for guidance) as well as art objects (need for aesthetic sensations). Nostalgia is a kindly version of personal history and is developed by advertisers to rouse needs for affiliation and for guidance; the need to escape can come in here, too. The same need to escape is sometimes the point of futuristic appeals, but picturing the avant-garde can also be a way to get at the need to achieve.

Analyzing Advertisements

When analyzing ads yourself for their emotional appeals, it takes a bit   87
of practice to learn to ignore the product information (as well as one's own experience and feelings about the product). But that skill comes soon enough, as does the ability to quickly sort out from all the non-product aspects of an ad the chief element which is the most striking, the most likely to snag attention first and penetrate brains furthest. The key to the appeal, this element usually presents itself centrally and forwardly to the reader or viewer.

Another clue: the viewing angle which the audience has on the ad's   88
subjects is informative. If the subjects are photographed or filmed from below and thus are looking down at you much as the Green Giant does, then the need to be guided is a good candidate for the ad's emotional appeal. If, on the other hand, the subjects are shot from above and appear deferential, as is often the case with children or female models, then other needs are being appealed to.

To figure out an ad's emotional appeal, it is wise to know (or have a good   89
hunch about) who the targeted consumers are; this can often be inferred from the magazine or television show it appears in. This piece of information is a great help in determining the appeal and in deciding between two different interpretations. For example, if an ad features a partially undressed female, this would typically signal one appeal for readers of *Penthouse* (need for sex) and another for readers of *Cosmopolitan* (need for attention).

It would be convenient if every ad made just one appeal, were aimed at   90
just one need. Unfortunately, things are often not that simple. A cigarette ad with a couple at the edge of a polo field is trying to hit both the need for affiliation and the need for prominence; depending on the attitude of the male, dominance could also be an ingredient in this. An ad for Chimere perfume incorporates two photos: in the top one the lady is being commanding at a business luncheon (need to dominate), but in the lower one she is being bussed (need for affiliation). Better ads, however, seem to avoid being too diffused; in the study of post–World War II advertising described earlier, appeals grew more focused as the decades passed. As a rule of thumb, about sixty percent have two conspicuous appeals; the last twenty percent have

three or more. Rather than looking for the greatest number of appeals, decoding ads is most productive when the loudest one or two appeals are discerned, since those are the appeals with the best chance of grabbing people's attention.

Finally, analyzing ads does not have to be a solo activity and probably   91 should not be. The greater number of people there are involved, the better chance there is of transcending individual biases and discovering the essential emotional lure built into an advertisement.

Do They or Don't They?

Do the emotional appeals made in advertisements add up to the sinister   92 manipulation of consumers?

It is clear that these ads work. Attention is caught, communication   93 occurs between producers and consumers, and sales result. It turns out to be difficult to detail the exact relationship between a specific ad and a specific purchase, or even between a campaign and subsequent sales figures; because advertising is only one of a host of influences upon consumption. Yet no one is fooled by this lack of perfect proof; everyone knows that advertising sells. If this were not the case, then tight-fisted American businesses would not spend a total of fifty billion dollars annually on these messages.

But before anyone despairs that advertisers have our number to the   94 extent that they can marshall us at will and march us like automatons to the check-out counters, we should recall the resiliency and obduracy of the American consumer. Advertisers may have uncovered the softest spots in minds, but that does not mean they have found truly gaping apertures. There is no evidence that advertising can get people to do things contrary to their self-interests. Despite all the finesse of advertisements, and all the subtle emotional tugs, the public resists the vast majority of the petitions. According to the marketing division of the A. C. Nielsen Company, a whopping seventy-five percent of all new products die within a year in the marketplace, the victims of consumer disinterest which no amount of advertising could overcome. The appeals in advertising may be the most captivating there are to be had, but they are not enough to entrap the wiley consumer.

The key to understanding the discrepancy between, on the one hand,   95 the fact that advertising truly works, and, on the other, the fact that it hardly works, is to take into account the enormous numbers of people exposed to an ad. Modern-day communications permit an ad to be displayed to millions upon millions of individuals; if the smallest fraction of that audience can be moved to buy the product, then the ad has been successful. When one percent of the people exposed to a television advertising campaign reach for their wallets, that could be one million sales, which may be enough to keep the product and the advertisements coming.

In arriving at an evenhanded judgment about advertisements and their   96
emotional appeals, it is good to keep in mind that many of the purchases
which might be credited to these ads are experienced as genuinely gratifying
to the consumer. We sincerely like the good or service we have bought, and
we may even like some of the emotional drapery that an ad suggests comes
with it. It has sometimes been noted that the most avid students of advertisements are the people who have just brought the product; they want to steep
themselves in the associated imagery. This may be the reason that Americans, when polled, are not negative about advertising and do not disclose
any sense of being misused. The volume of advertising may be an irritant,
but the product information as well as the imaginative material in ads are
partial compensation.

A productive understanding is that advertising messages involve costs   97
and benefits at both ends of the communication channel. For those few ads
which do make contact, the consumer surrenders a moment of time, has the
lower brain curried, and receives notice of a product; the advertiser has given
up money and has increased the chance of sales. In this sort of communications activity, neither party can be said to be the loser.

Questions for Study and Discussion

1. In paragraph 4, Fowles states that buyers have become resistant to
advertisements and we turn up our collars at most of them. Do you agree with
this statement?
2. How would you define Fowles's tone? Use examples of diction to support your answer.
3. Fowles theorizes that in addition to using unsubstantiated or misleading
text, TV advertisers appeal to viewers' emotions. What kind of evidence does he
offer to support his argument? Is he convincing?
4. Where does Fowles feel the emotional appeal is contained in an ad?
5. How does Florence Henderson help sell Wesson Oil according to
Fowles? What does his explanation reveal about his attitude toward consumers?
What is your reaction to his attitude? Explain.
6. Fowles implies that viewer response brought a halt to Club Cocktails'
ad campaigns. Is his explanation realistic? What type of action do you think it
would take to halt an ad campaign?

Writing Topics

1. One topic Fowles did not discuss in relation to advertising and psychology is subliminal advertising. This tactic works by hiding a message in a commercial, for example, inserting one frame of "Buy Krunchy Kookie Cereal" in an ad
for this product. The eye never acknowledges it, but the mind picks up the

message. In an essay, discuss your feelings regarding the use of psychology and the subliminal in advertising.

2. *Adweek,* an advertising trade journal, annually accepts nominations for the year's worst advertisements. Contributors to the "BADvertising" feature selected ads that they dislike for one reason or another. Nominate five ads that irritate you and another five that you consider ineffective. In an essay explain how each qualifies for an award in its category.

BILL CLINTON

On January 20, 1993, William Jefferson Clinton, former governor of the state of Arkansas, took the oath of office as the forty-second president of the United States. The transition of power from George Bush to Bill Clinton marked a transition from one generation to another. Clinton is the first of the post–World War II generation—the so-called baby boomers—to hold the nation's highest office. In the opinion of many political analysts—both supporters and detractors—he is also one of the most verbally adept of our recent presidents. Moments after being sworn in by Chief Justice William Rehnquist, Clinton delivered the following inaugural address to an audience estimated at more than forty million people.

Inaugural Address, 1993

My fellow citizens, today we celebrate the mystery of American renewal. This ceremony is held in the depth of winter, but by the words we speak and the faces we show the world, we force the spring. A spring reborn in the world's oldest democracy that brings forth the vision and courage to reinvent America.

When our founders boldly declared America's independence to the world and our purposes to the Almighty, they knew that America to endure would have to change. Not change for change's sake but change to preserve America's ideals—life, liberty, the pursuit of happiness. Though we march to the music of our time, our mission is timeless. Each generation of Americans must define what it means to be an American.

On behalf of our nation, I salute my predecessor, President Bush, for his half-century of service to America.

And I thank the millions of men and women whose steadfastness and sacrifice triumphed over depression, fascism and communism. Today, a generation raised in the shadows of the cold war assumes new responsibilities in a world warmed by the sunshine of freedom but threatened still by ancient hatreds and new plagues.

Raised in unrivaled prosperity, we inherit an economy that is still the world's strongest but is weakened by business failures, stagnant wages, increasing inequality and deep divisions among our own people.

When George Washington first took the oath I have just sworn to   6
uphold, news traveled slowly across the land by horseback and across the ocean by boat. Now the sights and sounds of this ceremony are broadcast instantaneously to billions around the world. Communications and commerce are global, investment is mobile, technology is almost magical, and ambition for a better life is now universal. We earn our livelihood in America today in peaceful competition with people all across the earth. Profound and powerful forces are shaking and remaking our world. And the urgent question of our time is whether we can make change our friend and not our enemy.

This new world has already enriched the lives of millions of Americans   7
who are able to compete and win in it. But when most people are working harder for less, when others cannot work at all, when the cost of health care devastates families and threatens to bankrupt our enterprises great and small, when the fear of crime robs law-abiding citizens of their freedom, and when millions of poor children cannot even imagine the lives we are calling them to lead, we have not made change our friend. We know we have to face hard truths and take strong steps, but we have not done so. Instead, we have drifted, and that drifting has eroded our resources, fractured our economy and shaken our confidence.

Though our challenges are fearsome, so are our strengths. Americans   8
have ever been restless, questing, hopeful people, and we must bring to our task today the vision and will of those who came before us. From our Revolution to the Civil War, to the Great Depression, to the civil rights movement, our people have always mustered the determination to construct from these crises the pillars of our history.

Thomas Jefferson believed that to preserve the very foundations of our   9
nation we would need dramatic change from time to time. Well my fellow Americans, this is our time. Let us embrace it.

Our democracy must be not only the envy of the world but the engine   10
of our own renewal. There is nothing wrong with America that cannot be cured by what is right with America. And so today we pledge an end to the era of deadlock and drift, and a new season of American renewal has begun.

To renew America we must be bold. We must do what no generation   11
has had to do before. We must invest more in our own people—in their jobs and in their future—and at the same time cut our massive debt. And we must do so in a world in which we must compete for every opportunity. It will not be easy. It will require sacrifice. But it can be done and done fairly. Not choosing sacrifice for its own sake, but for our own sake. We must provide for our nation the way a family provides for its children.

Our founders saw themselves in the light of posterity. We can do no   12 less. Anyone who has ever watched a child's eyes wander into sleep knows what posterity is. Posterity is the world to come. The world for whom we hold our ideals, from whom we have borrowed our planet and to whom we bear sacred responsibility. We must do what America does best: offer more opportunity to all and demand more responsibility from all.

It is time to break the bad habit of expecting something for nothing   13
from our Government or from each other. Let us all take more responsibility not only for ourselves and our families but for our communities and our country.

To renew America we must revitalize our democracy. This beautiful   14
capital, like every capital since the dawn of civilization, is often a place of intrigue and calculation. Powerful people maneuver for position and worry endlessly about who is in and who is out, who is up and who is down, forgetting those people whose toil and sweat sends us here and pays our way.

Americans deserve better, and in this city today there are people who   15
want to do better. And so I say to all of you here, let us resolve to reform our politics so that power and privilege no longer shout down the voice of the people. Let us put aside personal advantage so that we can feel the pain and see the promise of America. Let us resolve to make our Government a place for what Franklin Roosevelt called bold, persistent experimentation, a Government for our tomorrows, not our yesterdays. Let us give this capital back to the people to whom it belongs.

To renew America, we must meet challenges abroad as well as at home.   16
There is no longer a clear division between what is foreign and what is domestic. The world economy, the world environment, the world AIDS crisis, the world arms race—they affect us all.

Today, as an old order passes, the new world is more free but less stable.   17
Communism's collapse has called forth old animosities and new dangers. Clearly, America must continue to lead the world we did so much to make.

While America rebuilds at home, we will not shrink from the chal-   18
lenges nor fail to seize the opportunities of this new world. Together with our friends and allies we will work to shape change lest it engulf us. When our vital interests are challenged or the will and conscience of the international community is defied, we will act, with peaceful diplomacy whenever possible, with force when necessary.

The brave Americans serving our nation today in the Persian Gulf and   19
Somalia, and wherever else they stand, are testament to our resolve.

But our greatest strength is the power of our ideas, which are still new   20
in many lands. Across the world we see them embraced and we rejoice. Our hopes, our hearts, our hands are with those on every continent who are building democracy and freedom. Their cause is America's cause.

The American people have summoned the change we celebrate today.   21
You have raised your voices in an unmistakable chorus, you have cast your

votes in historic numbers, and you have changed the face of Congress, the Presidency and the political process itself. Yes, you, my fellow Americans, have forced the spring.

Now we must do the work the season demands. To that work I now   22
turn with all the authority of my office. I ask the Congress to join with me. But no President, no Congress, no government can undertake this mission alone. My fellow Americans, you, too, must play your part in our renewal.

I challenge a new generation of young Americans to a season of ser-   23
vice; to act on your idealism by helping troubled children, keeping company with those in need, reconnecting our torn communities. There is so much to be done. Enough, indeed, for millions of others who are still young in spirit to give of themselves in service, too.

In serving, we recognize a simple but powerful truth: We need each   24
other and we must care for one another. Today we do more than celebrate America, we rededicate ourselves to the very idea of America: An idea born in revolution and renewed through two centuries of challenge; an idea tempered by the knowledge that but for fate we, the fortunate and the unfortunate, might have been each other; an idea ennobled by the faith that our nation can summon from its myriad diversity the deepest measure of unity; an idea infused with the conviction that America's long, heroic journey must go forever upward.

And so, my fellow Americans, as we stand at the edge of the 21st   25
century, let us begin anew with energy and hope, with faith and discipline. And let us work until our work is done. The Scripture says, "And let us not be weary in well-doing, for in due season we shall reap if we faint not."

From this joyful mountaintop of celebration we hear a call to service in   26
the valley. We have heard the trumpets, we have changed the guard. And now each in our own way, and with God's help, we must answer the call.

Thank you, and God bless you all.   27

Questions for Study and Discussion

1. What are the key points of Clinton's speech? What aspects of the speech are particularly important to you?

2. In what sense is the inauguration of the U.S. president a celebration of "the mystery of American renewal"? In this context, how does Clinton's image of spring work? Explain.

3. Clinton says that "each generation of Americans must define what it means to be an American." How does Clinton define what it means to be an American? Do you find yourself agreeing or disagreeing with his definition? Why, or why not?

4. Clinton believes that "there is nothing wrong with America that cannot be cured by what is right with America." What to Clinton is right with

America? What do you see as America's strengths? What needs to be done to renew America?

5. How would you characterize Clinton's tone in this speech? What in his diction led you to this conclusion?

Writing Topics

1. In an essay, reflect on the importance of Clinton's inaugural address. Is it simply a lot of high-blown rhetoric, filled with "meaningless words" as George Orwell said was true of all political speeches? Does it try to "bamboozle" its audience through any of the techniques Donna Woolfolk Cross describes (see pp. 418–28)? Or does the speech do something more by both symbolically and concretely setting a direction for the country's citizens?

2. Compare Clinton's inaugural speech to that of a previous president, for example, Lincoln, Kennedy, or Bush. What similarities and differences do you find? What conclusions can you draw about inaugural speeches?

3. Imagine that you have just been elected president of the United States. Although you do not need to be as detailed as Clinton was, attempt to tell the American people what you think they need to hear, what direction you think America should take in the next few years.

TONI MORRISON

The black American novelist Toni Morrison was born Chloe Anthony Wofford near Lake Erie in Lorain, Ohio. She published her first novel, *The Bluest Eye,* in 1969; it was followed by *Sula* in 1973, *Song of Solomon* in 1977, *Tar Baby* in 1981, *Beloved* in 1987, and *Jazz* in 1992. Her works have won her both popular and critical acclaim as a talented storyteller whose characters struggle for their identity and dignity in a society that seems all too ready to stand in their way. As a novelist she has risen to a preeminent position in American letters for her portrayals of the black experience in both myth and reality.

It came as no surprise to her critics and fans alike when, in accepting the 1993 Nobel Prize for literature, Morrison turned to language as her subject. As Caroline Morehead wrote in the *Spectator,* Morrison "writes energetically and richly, using words in a way very much her own. The effect is one of exoticism, and exciting curiousness in the language, a balanced sense of the possible that stops, always, short of the absurd." Other critics have called her style "elegant," "lyrical," "evocative," and "impressionistic." In "When Language Dies: 1993 Nobel Prize for Literature Lecture" Morrison speaks to us of our responsibility not to violate the power and beauty of our language, but to maximize its magical and generative properties.

When Language Dies: 1993 Nobel Prize for Literature Lecture

"Once upon a time there was an old woman. Blind but wise." Or was it 1
an old man? A guru, perhaps. Or a griot soothing restless children. I have
heard this story, or one exactly like it, in the lore of several cultures.

"Once upon a time there was an old woman. Blind. Wise." 2

In the version I know the woman is the daughter of slaves, black, 3
American, and lives alone in a small house outside of town. Her reputation for
wisdom is without peer and without question. Among her people she is both
the law and its transgression. The honor she is paid and the awe in which she is
held reach beyond her neighborhood to places far away; to the city where the
intelligence of rural prophets is the source of much amusement.

One day the woman is visited by some young people who seem to be 4
bent on disproving her clairvoyance and showing her up for the fraud they
believe she is. Their plan is simple: they enter her house and ask the one
question the answer to which rides solely on her difference from them, a
difference they regard as a profound disability: her blindness. They stand
before her, and one of them says, "Old woman, I hold in my hand a bird. Tell
me whether it is living or dead."

She does not answer, and the question is repeated. "Is the bird I am   5
holding living or dead?"

Still she doesn't answer. She is blind and cannot see her visitors, let   6
alone what is in their hands. She does not know their color, gender or
homeland. She only knows their motive.

The old woman's silence is so long, the young people have trouble   7
holding their laughter.

Finally she speaks and her voice is soft but stern. "I don't know," she   8
says. "I don't know whether the bird you are holding is dead or alive, but
what I do know is that it is in your hands. It is in your hands."

Her answer can be taken to mean: if it is dead, you have either found it   9
that way or you have killed it. If it is alive, you can still kill it. Whether it is
to stay alive, it is your decision. Whatever the case, it is your responsibility.

For parading their power and her helplessness, the young visitors are   10
reprimanded, told they are responsible not only for the act of mockery but
also for the small bundle of life sacrificed to achieve its aims. The blind
woman shifts attention away from assertions of power to the instrument
through which that power is exercised.

Speculation on what (other than its own frail body) that bird-in-the-   11
hand might signify has always been attractive to me, but especially so now,
thinking as I have been, about the work I do that has brought me to this
company. So I choose to read the bird as language and the woman as a
practice writer. She is worried about how the language she dreams in, given
to her at birth, is handled, put into service, even withheld from her for
certain nefarious purposes. Being a writer she thinks of language partly as a
system, partly as a living thing over which one has control, but mostly as
agency—as an act with consequences. So the question the children put to
her: "Is it living or dead?" is not unreal because she thinks of language as
susceptible to death, erasure; certainly imperiled and salvageable only by an
effort of the will. She believes that if the bird in the hands of her visitors is
dead the custodians are responsible for the corpse. For her a dead language is
not only one no longer spoken or written, it is unyielding language content
to admire its own paralysis. Like statist language, censored and censoring.
Ruthless in its policing duties, it has no desire or purpose other than maintaining the free range of its own narcotic narcissism, its own exclusivity and
dominance. However, moribund, it is not without effect for it actively
thwarts the intellect, stalls conscience, suppresses human potential. Unre-
ceptive to interrogation, it cannot form or tolerate new ideas, shape other
thoughts, tell another story, fill baffling silences. Official language smith-
ered to sanction ignorance and preserve privilege is a suit of armor, polished
to shocking glitter, a husk from which the knight departed long ago. Yet
there it is: dumb, predatory, sentimental. Exciting reverence in school-
children, providing shelter for despots, summoning false memories of stability, harmony among the public.

She is convinced that when language dies, out of carelessness, disuse,   12
and absence of esteem, indifference or killed by fiat, not only she herself, but
all users and makers are accountable for its demise. In her country children
have bitten their tongues off and use bullets instead to iterate the voice of
speechlessness, of disabled and disabling language, of language adults have
abandoned altogether as a device for grappling with meaning, providing
guidance, or expressing love. But she knows tongue-suicide is not only the
choice of children. It is common among the infantile heads of state and
power merchants whose evacuated language leaves them with no access to
what is left of their human instincts for they speak only to those who obey, or
in order to force obedience.

The systematic looting of language can be recognized by the tendency   13
of its users to forgo its nuanced, complex, mid-wifery properties for menace
and subjugation. Oppressive language does more than represent violence; it
is violence; does more than represent the limits of knowledge; it limits
knowledge. Whether it is obscuring state language or the faux-language of
mindless media; whether it is the proud but calcified language of the academy or the commodity driven language of science; whether it is the malign
language of law-without-ethics, or language designed for the estrangement of
minorities, hiding its racist plunder in its literary cheek—it must be rejected,
altered and exposed. It is the language that drinks blood, laps vulnerability,
tucks its fascist boots under crinolines of respectability and patriotism as it
moves relentlessly toward the bottom line and the bottomed-out mind.
Sexist language, racist language, theistic language—all are typical of the
policing languages of mastery, and cannot, do not permit new knowledge or
encourage the mutual exchange of ideas.

The old woman is keenly aware that no intellectual mercenary, nor   14
insatiable dictator, no paid-for politician or demagogue; no counterfeit journalist would be persuaded by her thoughts. There is and will be rousing language
to keep citizens armed and arming; slaughtered and slaughtering in the malls,
courthouses, post offices, playgrounds, bedrooms and boulevards; stirring,
memorializing language to mask the pity and waste of needless death. There
will be more diplomatic language to countenance rape, torture, assassination.
There is and will be more seductive, mutant language designed to throttle
women, to pack their throats like paté-producing geese with their own unsay-
able, transgressive words; there will be more of the language of surveillance
disguised as research; of politics and history calculated to render the suffering
of millions mute; language glamorized to thrill the dissatisfied and bereft into
assaulting their neighbors; arrogant pseudo-empirical language crafted to lock
creative people into cages of inferiority and hopelessness.

Underneath the eloquence, the glamour, the scholarly associations,   15
however, stirring or seductive, the heart of such language is languishing, or
perhaps not beating at all—if the bird is already dead.

She has thought about what could have been the intellectual history of   16 any discipline if it had not insisted upon, or been forced into, the waste of time and life that rationalizations for and representations of dominance required—lethal discourses of exclusion blocking access to cognition for both the excluder and the excluded.

The conventional wisdom of the Tower of Babel story is that the   17
collapse was a misfortune. That it was the distraction, or the weight of many languages that precipitated the tower's failed architecture. That one mono-lithic language would have expedited the building and heaven would have been reached. Whose heaven, she wonders? And what kind? Perhaps the achievement of Paradise was premature, a little hasty if no one could take the time to understand other languages, other views, other narratives. Had they, the heaven they imagined might have been found at their feet. Compli-cated, demanding yes, but a view of heaven as life; not heaven as post-life.

She would not want to leave her young visitors with the impression   18
that language should be forced to stay alive merely to be. The vitality of language lies in its ability to limn the actual, imagined and possible lives of its speakers, readers, writers. Although its poise is sometimes in displacing experience it is not a substitute for it. It arcs toward the place where meaning may lie. When a President of the United States thought about the graveyard his country had become, and said "The world will little note nor long remember what we say here. But it will never forget what they did here." His simple words are exhilarating in their life-sustaining properties because they refused to encapsulate the reality of 600,000 dead men in a cataclysmic race war. Refusing to monumentalize, disdaining the "final word", the precise "summing up", acknowledging their "poor power to add or detract", his words signal deference to the uncapturability of the life it mourns. It is the deference that moves her, that recognition that language can never live up to life once and for all. Nor should it. Language can never "pin down" slavery, genocide, war. Nor should it yearn for the arrogance to be able to do so. Its force, its felicity is in its reach toward the ineffable.

Be it grand or slender, burrowing, blasting, or refusing to sanctify;   19
whether it laughs out loud or is a cry without an alphabet, the choice word, the chosen silence, unmolested language surges toward knowledge, not its destruction. But who does not know of literature banned because it is inter-rogative; discredited because it is critical; erased because alternate? And how many are outraged by the thought of a self-ravaged tongue?

Word-work is sublime, she thinks, because it is generative; it makes   20
meaning that secures our difference, our human difference—the way in which we are like no other life.

We die. That may be the meaning of life. But we do language. That   21
may be the measure of our lives.

"Once upon a time, ..." visitors ask an old woman a question. Who   22
are they, these children? What did they make of that encounter? What did they hear in those final words: "The bird is in your hands"? A sentence that

gestures toward possibility or one that drops a latch? Perhaps what the children heard was "It's not my problem. I am old, female, black, blind. What wisdom I have now is in knowing I can not help you. The future of language is yours."

They stand there. Suppose nothing was in their hands? Suppose the visit was only a ruse, a trick to get to be spoken to, taken seriously as they have not been before? A chance to interrupt, to violate the adult world, its miasma of discourse about them, for them, but never to them? Urgent questions are at stake, including the one they have asked: "Is the bird we hold living or dead?" Perhaps the question meant: "Could someone tell us what is life? What is death?" No trick at all; no silliness. A straightforward question worthy of the attention of a wise one. An old one. And if the old and wise who have lived life and faced death cannot describe either, who can? 23

But she does not; she keeps her secret; her good opinion of herself; her gnomic pronouncements; her art without commitment. She keeps her distance, enforces it and retreats into the singularity of isolation, in sophisticated, privileged space. 24

Nothing, no word follows her declarations of transfer. That silence is deep, deeper than the meaning available in the words she has spoken. It shivers, this silence, and the children, annoyed, fill it with language invented on the spot. 25

"Is there no speech," they ask her, "no words you can give us that helps us break through your dossier of failures? Through the education you have just given us that is no education at all because we are paying close attention to what you have done as well as to what you have said? To the barrier you have erected between generosity and wisdom? 26

"We have no bird in our hands, living or dead. We have only you and our important question. Is the nothing in our hands something you could not bear to contemplate, to even guess? Don't you remember being young when language was magic without meaning? When what you could say, could not mean? When the invisible was what imagination strove to see? When questions and demands for answers burned so brightly you trembled with fury at not knowing? 27

"Do we have to begin consciousness with a battle heroines and heroes like you have already fought and lost leaving us with nothing in our hands except what you have imagined is there? Your answer is artful, but its artiness embarrasses us and ought to embarrass you. Your answer is indecent in its self-congratulation. A made-for-television script that makes no sense if there is nothing in our hands. 28

"Why didn't you reach out, touch us with your soft fingers, delay the sound bite, the lesson, until you knew who we were? Did you so despise our trick, our modus operandi you could not see that we were baffled about how to get your attention? We are young. Unripe. We have heard all our short lives that we have to be responsible. What could that possibly mean in the 29 catastrophe this word has become; where, as a poet said, "nothing needs to be exposed since it is already barefaced." Our inheritance is an affront. You want us to have your old, blank eyes and see only cruelty and mediocrity. Do you think we are stupid enough to perjure ourselves again and again with the fiction of nationhood? How dare you talk to us of duty when we stand waist deep in the toxin of your past?

"You trivialize us and trivialize the bird that is not in our hands. Is there   30
no context for our lives? No song, no literature, no poem full of vitamins, no history connected to experience that you can pass along to help us start strong? You are an adult. The old one, the wise one. Stop thinking about saving your face. Think of our lives and tell us your particularized world. Make up a story. Narrative is radical, creating us at the very moment it is being created. We will not blame you if your reach exceeds your grasp; if love so ignites your words they go down in flames and nothing is left but their scald. Or if, with the reticence of a surgeon's hands, your words suture only the places where blood might flow. We know you can never do it properly— once and for all. Passion is never enough; neither is skill. But try. For our sake and yours forget your name in the street; tell us what the world has been to you in the dark places and in the light. Don't tell us what to believe, what to fear. Show us belief's wide skirt and the stitch that unravels fear's caul. You, old woman, blessed with blindness, can speak the language that tells us what only language can: how to see without pictures. Language alone protects us from the scariness of things with no names. Language alone is meditation.

"Tell us what it is to be a woman so that we may know what it is to be a   31
man. What moves at the margin. What it is to have no home on this place. To be set adrift from the one you knew. What it is to live at the edge of towns that cannot bear your company.

"Tell us about ships turned away from shorelines at Easter, placenta in a   32
field. Tell us about a wagonload of slaves, how they sang so softly their breath was indistinguishable from the falling snow. How they knew from the hunch of the nearest shoulder that the next stop would be their last. How, with hands prayered in their sex they thought of heat, then suns. Lifting their faces, as though is was there for the taking. Turning as though there for the taking. They stop at an inn. The driver and his mate go in with the lamp leaving them humming in the dark. The horse's void steams into the snow beneath its hooves and its hiss and melt is the envy of the freezing slaves.

"The inn door opens: a girl and a boy step away from its light. They   33
climb into the wagon bed. The boy will have a gun in three years, but now he carries a lamp and a jug of warm cider. They pass it from mouth to mouth. The girl offers bread, pieces of meat and something more: a glance into the eyes of the one she serves. One helping for each man, two for each woman. And a look. They look back. The next stop will be their last. But not this one. This one is warmed."

It's quiet again when the children finish speaking, until the woman   34
breaks into the silence.

"Finally," she says, "I trust you now. I trust you with the bird that is not   35
in your hands because you have truly caught it. Look. How lovely it is, this
thing we have done—together."

Questions for Study and Discussion

1. What significance does Morrison give her story of the old blind woman
and the young people who visit her with the bird?

2. Why were the young people reprimanded?

3. In paragraph 11, Morrison refers to the deadening qualities of "statist
language." To what is she referring? Why is such language abhorrent to her?

4. Who is responsible for the "looting of language" to which she refers in
paragraph 13?

5. What is the story of the Tower of Babel? What significance does Morrison see in the story? Does she see the alternative of a single language as good or
bad? Explain.

6. Morrison claims that language should never be a substitute for life
itself. She writes, "Its force, its felicity is in its reach toward the ineffable." What
does she mean by this statement?

7. What questions by the young people for the old woman does Morrison
project? What is she driving at through these exhortations?

8. The questions that Morrison asks through the young people turn slowly
into a narrative about slaves in a wagon. What does the story signify for the old
blind woman? At the end, why does she feel she can trust the young people?
What have they "done—together"?

Writing Topics

1. The young people in Morrison's speech ask the old woman, "Don't you
remember being young when language was magic without meaning? When what
you could say, could not mean? When the invisible was what imagination strove
to see? When questions and demands for answers burned so brightly you trembled with fury at not knowing?" Does that description of the sense of language for
young people sound familiar to you? What was language like for you as you grew
older? What was lost as you grew? What was gained? Write an essay describing
your experiences with the different faces of language, with the magic of language. In preparation for writing, think of the nursery rhymes you knew, the
stories that you heard, that you read, or that were read to you. Think of the
songs you sang, the secret words you knew, the taunts and cheers you offered and
received. What special dialects did you hear people around you speaking? What
shaped and characterized the dialogue between people? How did your imagination find expression?

2. It has often been said that what separates humans from other creatures is our ability to express ourselves. Humans use language in a highly sophisticated manner to convey emotions and knowledge, feelings and ideas. Perhaps one of the greatest benefits of language, however, is the ability to imagine, to envision what might be, what could be achieved—in short, language gives us the power to imagine a different world. Write an essay in which you analyze further this extraordinary power and the special demands it places on us as humans.

KURT VONNEGUT, JR.

Our Declaration of Independence states as a "self-evident truth" that all men are created equal. But what does it mean to be "equal"? In the following story, Kurt Vonnegut, Jr., shows what it does *not* mean. Vonnegut was born in 1922 in Indianapolis, Indiana. While he was a student at Cornell University, he joined the army to serve in World War II and was sent to Europe. Taken prisoner by the German army, he witnessed the Allied firebombing of Dresden in 1945, a bloody and pointless incident that inspired his novel *Slaughterhouse-Five* (1969). After the war he completed his education at the University of Chicago, then from 1947 to 1950 worked in the public relations department of General Electric; since then, he has worked full time as a writer. Probably his best-known novels besides *Slaughterhouse-Five* are *Player Piano* (1952) and *Cat's Cradle* (1963). Some of his short stories have been collected in *Welcome to the Monkey House* (1968). More recently he has written *Deadeye Dick* (1983), *Galápagos* (1986), *Bluebird* (1987), and *Hocus Pocus* (1990). "Harrison Bergeron," from *Welcome to the Monkey House*, is set in 2081, but like much science fiction it offers a critique of the present as much as a prediction of the future.

Harrison Bergeron

The year was 2081, and everybody was finally equal. They weren't   1
only equal before God and the law. They were equal every which way. Nobody was smarter than anybody else. Nobody was better looking than anybody else. Nobody was stronger or quicker than anybody else. All this equality was due to the 211th, 212th, and 213th Amendments to the Constitution, and to the unceasing vigilance of agents of the United States Handicapper General.

Some things about living still weren't quite right, though. April, for   2
instance, still drove people crazy by not being springtime. And it was in that clammy month that the H-G men took George and Hazel Bergeron's fourteen-year-old son, Harrison, away.

It was tragic, all right, but George and Hazel couldn't think about it   3
very hard. Hazel had a perfectly average intelligence, which meant she couldn't think about anything except in short bursts. And George, while his intelligence was way above normal, had a little mental handicap radio in his ear. He was required by law to wear it at all times. It was tuned to a government transmitter. Every twenty seconds or so, the transmitter would send out some sharp noise to keep people like George from taking unfair advantage of their brains.

George and Hazel were watching television. There were tears on Hazel's cheeks, but she'd forgotten for the moment what they were about.   4

On the television screen were ballerinas.   5

A buzzer sounded in George's head. His thoughts fled in panic, like bandits from a burglar alarm.   6

"That was a real pretty dance, that dance they just did," said Hazel.   7

"Huh?" said George.   8

"That dance—it was nice," said Hazel.   9

"Yup," said George. He tried to think a little about the ballerinas. They weren't really very good—no better than anybody else would have been, anyway. They were burdened with sashweights and bags of birdshot, and their faces were masked, so that no one, seeing a free and graceful gesture or a pretty face, would feel like something the cat drug in. George was toying with the vague notion that maybe dancers shouldn't be handicapped. But he didn't get very far with it before another noise in his ear radio scattered his thoughts.   10

George winced. So did two out of the eight ballerinas.   11

Hazel saw him wince. Having no mental handicap herself, she had to ask George what the latest sound had been.   12

"Sounded like somebody hitting a milk bottle with a ball peen hammer," said George.   13

"I'd think it would be real interesting, hearing all the different sounds," said Hazel, a little envious. "All the things they think up."   14

"Um," said George.   15

"Only, if I was Handicapper General, you know what I would do?" said Hazel. Hazel, as a matter of fact, bore a strong resemblance to the Handicapper General, a woman named Diana Moon Glampers. "If I was Diana Moon Glampers," said Hazel, "I'd have chimes on Sunday—just chimes. Kind of in honor of religion."   16

"I could think, if it was just chimes," said George.   17

"Well—maybe make 'em real loud," said Hazel. "I think I'd make a good Handicapper General."   18

"Good as anybody else," said George.   19

"Who knows better'n I do what normal is?" said Hazel.   20

"Right," said George. He began to think glimmeringly about his abnormal son who was now in jail, about Harrison, but a twenty-one gun salute in his head stopped that.   21

"Boy!" said Hazel, "that was a doozy, wasn't it?"   22

It was such a doozy that George was white and trembling, and tears stood on the rims of his red eyes. Two of the eight ballerinas had collapsed to the studio floor, were holding their temples.   23

"All of a sudden you look so tired," said Hazel. "Why don't you stretch out on the sofa, so's you can rest your handicap bag on the pillows, honeybunch." She was referring to the forty-seven pounds of birdshot in a   24

canvas bag, which was padlocked around George's neck. "Go on and rest the
bag for a little while, she said. "I don't care if you're not equal to me for a
while."

George weighed the bag with his hands. "I don't mind it," he said. "I
don't notice it any more. It's just a part of me." 25

"You been so tired lately—kind of wore out," said Hazel. "If there was
just some way we could make a little hole in the bottom of the bag, and just
take out a few of them lead balls. Just a few." 26

"Two years in prison and two thousand dollars fine for every ball I took
out," said George. "I don't call that a bargain." 27

"If you could just take a few out when you came home from work," said
Hazel. "I mean—you don't compete with anybody around here. You just set
around." 28

"If I tried to get away with it," said George, "then other people'd get
away with it—and pretty soon we'd be right back to the dark ages again,
with everybody competing against everybody else. You wouldn't like that,
would you?" 29

"I'd hate it," said Hazel. 30

"There you are," said George. "The minute people start cheating on
laws, what do you think happens to society?" 31

If Hazel hadn't been able to come up with an answer to this question,
George couldn't have supplied one. A siren was going off in his head. 32

"Reckon it'd fall all apart," said Hazel. 33

"What would?" said George blankly. 34

"Society," said Hazel uncertainly. "Wasn't that what you just said?" 35

"Who knows?" said George. 36

The television program was suddenly interrupted for a news bulletin. It
wasn't clear at first as to what the bulletin was about, since the announcer,
like all announcers, had a serious speech impediment. For about half a
minute, and in a state of high excitement, the announcer tried to say,
"Ladies and gentlemen—" 37

He finally gave up, handed the bulletin to a ballerina to read. 38

"That's all right—" Hazel said to the announcer, "he tried. That's the
big thing. He tried to do the best he could with what God gave him. He
should get a nice raise for trying so hard." 39

"Ladies and gentlemen—" said the ballerina, reading the bulletin. She
must have been extraordinarily beautiful, because the mask she wore was
hideous. And it was easy to see that she was the strongest and most graceful
of all the dancers, for her handicap bags were as big as those worn by two-
hundred-pound men. 40

And she had to apologize at once for her voice, which was a very unfair
voice for a woman to use. Her voice was a warm, luminous, timeless, mel-
ody. "Excuse me—" she said, and she began again, making her voice absolutely uncompetitive. 41

"Harrison Bergeron, age fourteen," she said in a grackle squawk, "has   42
just escaped from jail, where he was held on suspicion of plotting to overthrow the government. He is a genius and an athlete, is underhandicapped,
and should be regarded as extremely dangerous."

A police photograph of Harrison Bergeron was flashed on the screen—   43
upside down, then sideways, upside down again, then right side up. The
picture showed the full length of Harrison against a background calibrated in
feet and inches. He was exactly seven feet tall.

The rest of Harrison's appearance was Halloween and hardware. No-   44
body had ever borne heavier handicaps. He had outgrown hindrances faster
than the H-G men could think them up. Instead of a little ear radio for a
mental handicap, he wore a tremendous pair of earphones and spectacles
with thick wavy lenses. The spectacles were intended to make him not only
half blind, but to give him whanging headaches besides.

Scrap metal was hung all over him. Ordinarily, there was a certain   45
symmetry, a military neatness to the handicaps issued to strong people, but
Harrison looked like a walking junkyard. In the race of life, Harrison carried
three hundred pounds.

And to offset his good looks, the H-G men required that he wear at all   46
times a red rubber ball for a nose, keep his eyebrows shaved off, and cover his
even white teeth with black caps at snaggle-tooth random.

"If you see this boy," said the ballerina, "do not—I repeat, do not—try   47
to reason with him."

There was the shriek of a door being torn from its hinges.   48

Screams and barking cries of consternation came from the television   49
set. The photograph of Harrison Bergeron on the screen jumped again and
again, as though dancing to the tune of an earthquake.

George Bergeron correctly identified the earthquake, and well he   50
might have—for many was the time his own home had danced to the same
crashing tune. "My God—" said George, "that must be Harrison!"

The realization was blasted from his mind instantly by the sound of an   51
automobile collision in his head.

When George could open his eyes again, the photograph of Harrison   52
was gone. A living, breathing Harrison filled the screen.

Clanking, clownish, and huge, Harrison stood in the center of the   53
studio. The knob of the uprooted studio door was still in his hand. Ballerinas, technicians, musicians, and announcers cowered on their knees before
him, expecting to die.

"I am the Emperor!" cried Harrison. "Do you hear? I am the Emperor!   54
Everybody must do what I say at once!" He stamped his foot and the studio
shook.

"Even as I stand here—" he bellowed, "crippled, hobbled, sickened—I   55
am a greater ruler than any man who ever lived! Now watch me become
what I *can* become!"

Harrison tore the straps of his handicap harness like wet tissue paper, tore straps guaranteed to support five thousand pounds. 56

Harrison's scrap-iron handicaps crashed to the floor. 57

Harrison thrust his thumbs under the bar of the padlock that secured his head harness. The bar snapped like celery. Harrison smashed his headphones and spectacles against the wall. 58

He flung away his rubber-ball nose, revealed a man that would have awed Thor, the god of thunder. 59

"I shall now select my Empress!" he said, looking down on the cowering people. "Let the first woman who dares rise to her feet claim her mate and her throne!" 60

A moment passed, and then a ballerina rose, swaying like a willow. 61

Harrison plucked the mental handicap from her ear, snapped off her physical handicaps with marvelous delicacy. Last of all, he removed her mask. 62

She was blindingly beautiful. 63

"Now—" said Harrison, taking her hand, "shall we show the people the meaning of the word dance? Music!" he commanded. 64

The musicians scrambled back into their chairs, and Harrison stripped them of their handicaps, too. "Play your best," he told them, "and I'll make you barons and dukes and earls." 65

The music began. It was normal at first—cheap, silly, false, but Harrison snatched two musicians from their chairs, waved them like batons as he sang the music as he wanted it played. He slammed them back into their chairs. 66

The music began again and was much improved. 67

Harrison and his Empress merely listened to the music for a while— listened gravely, as though synchronizing their heartbeats with it. 68

They shifted their weights to their toes. 69

Harrison placed his big hands on the girl's tiny waist, letting her sense the weightlessness that would soon be hers. 70

And then, in an explosion of joy and grace, into the air they sprang! 71

Not only were the laws of the land abandoned, but the law of gravity and the laws of motion as well. 72

They reeled, whirled, swiveled, flounced, capered, gamboled, and spun. 73

They leaped like deer on the moon. 74

The studio ceiling was thirty feet high, but each leap brought the dancers nearer to it. 75

It became their obvious intention to kiss the ceiling. 76

They kissed it. 77

And then, neutralizing gravity with love and pure will, they remained suspended in air inches below the ceiling, and they kissed each other for a long, long time. 78

It was then that Diana Moon Glampers, the Handicapper General 79
came into the studio with a double-barreled ten-gauge shotgun. She fired
twice, and the Emperor and Empress were dead before they hit the floor.

Diana Moon Glampers loaded the gun again. She aimed it at the musi- 80
cians and told them they had ten seconds to get their handicaps back on.

It was then that the Bergerons' television tube burned out. 81

Hazel turned to comment about the blackout to George. But George 82
had gone out into the kitchen for a can of beer.

George came back in with the beer, paused while a handicap signal 83
shook him up. And then he sat down again. "You've been crying?" he said to
Hazel.

"Yup," she said. 84
"What about?" he said. 85
"I forget," she said. "Something real sad on television." 86
"What was it?" he said. 87
"It's all kind of mixed up in my mind," said Hazel. 88
"Forget sad things," said George. 89
"I always do," said Hazel. 90
"That's my girl," said George. He winced. There was the sound of a 91
rivetting gun in his head.

"Gee—I could tell that one was a doozy," said Hazel. 92
"You can say that again," said George. 93
"Gee—" said Hazel, "I could tell that one was a doozy." 94

Questions for Study and Discussion

1. In what ways is Vonnegut's world of 2081 little changed from the
present? What is different? What can you infer from this about Vonnegut's
message in this story?

2. Why does George refer to the competitive past as the "dark ages"?
What solution does "handicapping" offer? In what ways does being underhandicapped make Harrison dangerous?

3. Consider the specific handicaps that above-average people have to
wear in the story. How do you respond to Vonnegut's descriptions? What do
those handicaps suggest about the collective mentality of 2081 society?

4. Why does Vonnegut make Harrison a fourteen-year-old child? What
qualities of a teenager does Harrison display?

5. Vonnegut's story is plausible up to the point where Harrison and the
ballerina defy "the law of gravity and the laws of motion." Why do you think
Vonnegut shifts to fantasy at this point? Would the story have been better or
worse if he had kept to the physically possible? Why do you think so?

6. What can you say about the Handicapper General, Diana Moon
Glampers? What does the story tell you, or allow you to infer, about her position
in 2081 society and her way of doing her job?

7. The words *equality* and *average* refer to similar but essentially different concepts. In what significant way do they differ? How does this difference relate to the theme of Vonnegut's story?

Writing Topics

1. Is there a typical American attitude toward people of exceptional talent or achievement? What is your attitude? Are there dangers in too much respect for such people—or too little? Write an essay in which you present your views on this important social issue. Use examples from your own experiences whenever appropriate.

2. Choose an area of contemporary society in which handicaps are imposed to achieve social ends, such as affirmative action in employment, open admissions in schools and colleges, or the progressive income tax. What social ends does the handicap serve? What are its benefits? What harm does it do? Write an essay in which you discuss the pros and/or cons of imposing handicaps to achieve equality in the area of contemporary society you have selected.

3. In an essay, compare and contrast "Harrison Bergeron" with W. H. Auden's "The Unknown Citizen" (pp. 659–60) as depictions of society.

6

Cultural Encounters

The United States, by its very nature, by its very development, is the essence of diversity. It is diverse in its geography, population, institutions, technology; its social, cultural, and intellectual modes. It is a society that at its best does not consider quality to be monolithic in form or finite in quantity, or to be inherent in class. Quality in our society proceeds in large measure out of the stimulus of diverse modes of thinking and acting; out of the creativity made possible by the different ways in which we approach things; out of diversion from paths or modes hallowed by tradition.
—Arturo Madrid

Red Jacket, who was given the name *Otetiani* when he was born and the name *Sagu-yu-what-hah* when he became chief of the Senecas, was well known for his strong personality, oratory skills, and political savvy. After being drawn into the Revolutionary War on the side of the British, he began wearing the famous red coat of its army, from which he got his colorful name. In the following selection, taken from *Indian Speeches, Delivered by Farmer's Brother and Red Jacket, Two Seneca Chiefs* (1809), the anonymous editor provides the context for the meeting in which Red Jacket gave his now famous reply to the Reverend Mr. Cram.

Chief Red Jacket Responds to the Reverend Mr. Cram

[In the summer of 1805, a number of the principal Chiefs and War- 1 riors of the Six Nations, principally Senecas, assembled at Buffalo Creek, in the state of New York, at the particular request of Rev. Mr. Cram, a Missionary from the state of Massachusetts. The Missionary being furnished with an Interpreter, and accompanied by the Agent of the United States for Indian affairs, met the Indians in Council, when the following talk took place.]

FIRST, BY THE AGENT. "*Brothers of the Six Nations;* I rejoice to meet you 2 at this time, and thank the Great Spirit, that he has preserved you in health, and given me another opportunity of taking you by the hand.

"*Brothers;* The person who sits by me, is a friend who has come a great 3 distance to hold a talk with you. He will inform you what his business is, and it is my request that you would listen with attention to his words."

MISSIONARY. "*My Friends;* I am thankful for the opportunity afforded us 4 of uniting together at this time. I had a great desire to see you, and inquire into your state and welfare; for this purpose I have travelled a great distance, being sent by your old friends, the Boston Missionary Society. You will recollect they formerly sent missionaries among you, to instruct you in religion, and labor for your good. Although they have not heard from you for a long time, yet they have not forgotten their brothers the Six Nations, and are still anxious to do you good.

"*Brothers;* I have not come to get your lands or your money, but to   5
enlighten your minds, and to instruct you how to worship the Great Spirit agreeably to his mind and will, and to preach to you the gospel of his son Jesus Christ. There is but one religion, and but one way to serve God, and if you do not embrace the right way, you cannot be happy hereafter. You have never worshipped the Great Spirit in a manner acceptable to him; but have, all your lives, been in great errors and darkness. To endeavor to remove these errors, and open your eyes, so that you might see clearly, is my business with you.

"*Brothers;* I wish to talk with you as one friend talks with another; and,   6
if you have any objections to receive the religion which I preach, I wish you to state them; and I will endeavor to satisfy your minds, and remove the objections.

"*Brothers;* I want you to speak your minds freely; for I wish to reason   7
with you on the subject, and, if possible, remove all doubts, if there be any on your minds. The subject is an important one, and it is of consequence that you give it an early attention while the offer is made you. Your friends, the Boston Missionary Society, will continue to send you good and faithful ministers, to instruct and strengthen you in religion, if, on your part, you are willing to receive them.

"*Brothers;* Since I have been in this part of the country, I have visited   8
some of your small villages, and talked with your people. They appear willing to receive instruction, but, as they look up to you as their older brothers in council, they want first to know your opinion on the subject.

"You have now heard what I have to propose at present. I hope you will   9
take it into consideration, and give me an answer before we part."

[After about two hours consultation among themselves, the Chief,   10
commonly called by the white people, Red Jacket (whose Indian name is Sagu-yu-what-hah, which interpreted is *Keeper awake*) rose and spoke as follows:]

"*Friend and Brother;* It was the will of the Great Spirit that we should   11
meet together this day. HE orders all things, and has given us a fine day for our Council. HE has taken his garment from before the sun, and caused it to shine with brightness upon us. Our eyes are opened, that we see clearly; our ears are unstopped, that we have been able to hear distinctly the words you have spoken. For all these favors we thank the Great Spirit; and HIM *only*.

"*Brother;* This council fire was kindled by you. It was at your request   12
that we came together at this time. We have listened with attention to what you have said. You requested us to speak our minds freely. This gives us great joy; for we now consider that we stand upright before you, and can speak what we think. All have heard your voice, and all speak to you now as one man. Our minds are agreed.

"*Brother;* You say you want an answer to your talk before you leave this   13
place. It is right you should have one, as you are a great distance from home,
and we do not wish to detain you. But we will first look back a little, and tell
you what our fathers have told us, and what we have heard from the white
people.

"*Brother;* Listen to what we say.   14

"There was a time when our forefathers owned this great island. Their   15
seats extended from the rising to the setting sun. The Great Spirit had made
it for the use of Indians. HE had created the buffalo, the deer, and other
animals for food. HE had made the bear and the beaver. Their skins served us
for clothing. HE had caused the earth to produce corn for bread. All this HE
had done for his red children, because HE loved them. If we had some
disputes about our hunting ground, they were generally settled without the
shedding of much blood. But an evil day came upon us. Your forefathers
crossed the great water, and landed on this island. Their numbers were small.
They found friends and not enemies. They told us they had fled from their
country for fear of wicked men, and had come here to enjoy their religion.
They asked for a small seat. We took pity on them, granted their request; and
they sat down amongst us. We gave them corn and meat, they gave us poison
[alluding, it is supposed, to ardent spirits] in return.

"The white people had now found our country. Tidings were carried   16
back, and more came amongst us. Yet we did not fear them. We took them to
be friends. They called us brothers. We believed them, and gave them a
larger seat. At length their numbers had greatly increased. They wanted
more land; they wanted our country. Our eyes were opened, and our minds
became uneasy. Wars took place. Indians were hired to fight against Indians,
and many of our people were destroyed. They also brought strong liquor
amongst us. It was strong and powerful, and has slain thousands.

"*Brother;* Our seats were once large and yours were small. You have now   17
become a great people, and we have scarcely a place left to spread our
blankets. You have got our country, but are not satisfied; you want to force
your religion upon us.

"*Brother;* Continue to listen.   18

"You say that you are sent to instruct us how to worship the Great   19
Spirit agreeably to his mind, and, if we do not take hold of the religion
which you white people teach, we shall be unhappy hereafter. You say that
you are right and we are lost. How do we know this to be true? We understand that your religion is written in a book. If it was intended for us as well
as you, why has not the Great Spirit given to us, and not only to us, but why
did he not give to our forefathers, the knowledge of that book, with the
means of understanding it rightly? We only know what you tell us about it.
How shall we know when to believe, being so often decieved by the white
people?

"*Brother;* You say there is but one way to worship and serve the Great   20

Spirit. If there is but one religion; why do you white people differ so much about it? Why not all agreed, as you can all read the book?

"*Brother;* We do not understand these things. 21

"We are told that your religion was given to your forefathers, and has 22 been handed down from father to son. We also have a religion, which was given to our forefathers, and has been handed down to us their children. We worship in that way. It teaches us to be thankful for all the favors we receive; to love each other, and to be united. We never quarrel about religion.

"*Brother;* The Great Spirit has made us all, but he has made a great 23 difference between his white and red children. HE has given us different complexions and different customs. To you HE has given the arts. To these HE has not opened our eyes. We know these things to be true. Since HE has made so great a difference between us in other things; why may we not conclude that HE HAS GIVEN US A DIFFERENT RELIGION ACCORDING TO OUR UNDERSTANDING? THE GREAT SPIRIT DOES RIGHT. HE knows what is best for his children; we are satisfied.

"*Brother;* We do not wish to destroy your religion, or take it from you. 24 We only want to enjoy our own.

"*Brother;* We are told that you have been preaching to the white people 25 in this place. These people are our neighbors. We are acquainted with them. We will wait a little while, and see what effect your preaching has upon them. If we find it does them good, makes them honest and less disposed to cheat Indians; we will then consider again of what you have said.

"*Brother;* You have now heard our answer to your talk, and this is all we 26 have to say at present.

"As we are going to part, we will come and take you by the hand, and 27 hope the Great Spirit will protect you on your journey, and return you safe to your friends."

[As the Indians began to approach the missionary, he rose hastily from 28 his seat and replied, that he could not take them by the hand; that there was no fellowship between the religion of God and the works of the devil.

This being interpreted to the Indians, they smiled, and retired in a 29 peaceable manner.

It being afterwards suggested to the missionary that his reply to the Indi- 30 ans was rather indiscreet; he observed, that he supposed the ceremony of shaking hands would be received by them as a token that he assented to what they had said. Being otherwise informed, he said he was sorry for the expressions.]

Questions for Study and Discussion

1. What assumptions does the missionary make in paragraph 5?
2. What reasons does Red Jacket give for rejecting the missionary's proposal? In your judgment, are they sound reasons? Explain.

3. The missionary repeats several times that he wishes to hear the Indians' objections to his proposal, in order to reason with them. But when he is given the reasons why they won't worship his God, he does not respond to their objections or attempt to persuade them. Why?

4. Red Jacket says that his people will in time reconsider the white man's religion. On what grounds does he say that the reconsideration will be made?

5. Why does the Reverend Mr. Cram refuse to shake hands with Red Jacket? What do the smiles of the Indians indicate?

6. Do you think that the missionary misunderstood the meaning of the handshakes offered him? In your opinion, was his apology for the slight sincere?

Writing Topics

1. How would you have replied to the Reverend Mr. Cram's request? Write a letter to him stating your views.

2. What do we learn about the ways cultures sometimes clash from the Red Jacket–Reverend Mr. Cram encounter? Should such meetings never take place? Would greater understanding be the result? Have similar encounters taken place more recently? With better results? Could the participants have prepared better for the meeting?

3. We will never know if Red Jacket was speaking for all his people, as he claimed. What if there were members of his tribe who wished to become Christians? Should they have been allowed to follow their own wishes? Write an essay in which you argue for a better way in which nations, ethnic groups, and people of different religions can come together for greater understanding.

SHANLON WU

Shanlon Wu was born in New York City in 1959 to Chinese parents. After completing his studies at Vassar College, Wu earned an M.F.A. in creative writing at Sarah Lawrence College and a law degree from Georgetown University. A practicing lawyer in the U.S. attorney's office in Washington, D.C., Wu is at work on a novel about the Chinese-American experience.

In the following essay Wu recounts his youthful "hunger for images of powerful Asian men" and how the scarcity of such heroes affected his self-image as a young Chinese boy growing up in America.

In Search of Bruce Lee's Grave

It's Saturday morning in Seattle, and I am driving to visit Bruce Lee's grave. I have been in the city for only a couple of weeks and so drive two blocks past the cemetery before realizing that I've passed it. I double back and turn through the large wrought-iron gate, past a sign that reads: "Open to 9 P.M. or dusk, whichever comes first."

It's a sprawling cemetery, with winding roads leading in all directions. I feel silly trying to find his grave with no guidance. I think that my search for his grave is similar to my search for Asian heroes in America.

I was born in 1959, an Asian-American in Westchester County, N.Y. During my childhood there were no Asian sports stars. On television, I can recall only that most pathetic of Asian characters, Hop Sing, the Cartwright family houseboy on "Bonanza." But in my adolescence there was Bruce.

I was 14 years old when I first saw "Enter the Dragon," the granddaddy of martial-arts movies. Bruce had died suddenly at the age of 32 of cerebral edema, an excess of fluid in the brain, just weeks before the release of the film. Between the ages of 14 and 17, I saw "Enter the Dragon" 22 times before I stopped counting. During those years I collected Bruce Lee posters, putting them up at all angles in my bedroom. I took up Chinese martial arts and spent hours comparing my physique with his.

I learned all I could about Bruce: that he had married a Caucasian, 5
Linda; that he had sparred with Kareem Abdul-Jabbar; that he was a buddy of
Steve McQueen and James Coburn, both of whom were his pallbearers.

My parents, who immigrated to America and had become professors at 6
Hunter College, tolerated my behavior, but seemed puzzled at my admiration
of an "entertainer." My father jokingly tried to compare my obsession with
Bruce to his boyhood worship of Chinese folk-tale heroes.

"I read them just like you read American comic books," he said. 7

But my father's heroes could not be mine; they came from an ancient 8
literary tradition, not comic books. He and my mother had grown up in a
land where they belonged to the majority. I could not adopt their childhood
and they were wise enough not to impose it upon me.

Although I never again experienced the kind of blind hero worship I 9
felt for Bruce, my need to find heroes remained strong.

In college, I discovered the men of the 442d Regimental Combat 10
Team, a United States Army all-Japanese unit in World War II. Allowed to
fight only against Europeans, they suffered heavy casualties while their families were put in internment camps. Their motto was "Go for Broke."

I saw them as Asians in a Homeric epic, the protagonists of a Shake- 11
spearean tragedy; I knew no Eastern myths to infuse them with. They embodied my own need to prove myself in the Caucasian world. I imagined how
their American-born flesh and muscle must have resembled mine: epicanthic
folds set in strong faces nourished on milk and beef. I thought how much
they had proved where there was so little to prove.

After college, I competed as an amateur boxer in an attempt to find my 12
self-image in the ring. It didn't work. My fighting was only an attempt to
copy Bruce's movies. What I needed was instruction on how to live. I quit
boxing after a year and went to law school.

I was an anomaly there: a would-be Asian litigator. I had always liked 13
to argue and found I liked doing it in front of people even more. When I won
the first-year moot court competition in law school, I asked an Asian classmate if he thought I was the first Asian to win. He laughed and told me I was
probably the only Asian to even compete.

The law-firm interviewers always seemed surprised that I wanted to 14
litigate.

"Aren't you interested in Pacific Rim trade?" they asked. 15

"My Chinese isn't good enough," I quipped. 16

My pat response seemed to please them. It certainly pleased me. I 17
thought I'd found a place of my own—a place where the law would insulate
me from the pressure of defining my Asian maleness. I sensed the possibility
of merely being myself.

But the pressure reasserted itself. One morning, the year after graduat- 18
ing from law school, I read the obituary of Gen. Minoru Genda—the man
who planned the Pearl Harbor attack. I'd never heard of him and had

assumed that whoever did that planning was long since dead. But the general had been alive all those years—rising at 4 every morning to do his exercises and retiring every night by 8. An advocate of animal rights, the obituary said.

I found myself drawn to the general's life despite his association with   19
the Axis powers. He seemed a forthright, graceful man who died unhumbled. The same paper carried a front-page story about Congress's failure to pay the Japanese-American internees their promised reparation money. The general, at least, had not died waiting for reparations.

I was surprised and frightened by my admiration for General Genda, by   20
my still-strong hunger for images of powerful Asian men. That hunger was my vulnerability manifested, a reminder of my lack of place.

The hunger is eased this gray morning in Seattle. After asking direc-   21
tions from a policeman—Japanese—I easily locate Bruce's grave. The headstone is red granite with a small picture etched into it. The picture is very Hollywood—Bruce wears dark glasses—and I think the calligraphy looks a bit sloppy. Two tourists stop but leave quickly after glancing at me.

I realize I am crying. Bruce's grave seems very small in comparison to   22
his place in my boyhood. So small in comparison to my need for heroes. Seeing his grave, I understand how large the hole in my life has been and how desperately I'd sought to fill it.

I had sought an Asian hero to emulate. But none of my choices quite fit   23
me. Their lives were defined through heroic tasks—they had villains to defeat and wars to fight—while my life seemed merely a struggle to define myself.

But now I see how that very struggle has defined me. I must be my own   24
hero even as I learn to treasure those who have gone before.

I have had my powerful Asian male images: Bruce, the men of the 442d   25
and General Genda; I may yet discover others. Their lives beckon like fireflies on a moonless night, and I know that they—like me—may have been flawed by foolhardiness and even cruelty. Still, their lives were real. They were not houseboys on "Bonanza."

Questions for Study and Discussion

1. Who was Bruce Lee? Why was Lee important to the teenage Wu?
2. Hop Sing is the only Asian character on television that Wu recalls from his childhood. Why was Hop Sing an unsatisfactory role model for Wu?
3. How did Wu's childhood and adolescence differ from those of his parents? Why, according to Wu, did they choose not to impose their childhood on him?
4. Why did Wu's stint as an amateur boxer fail to help him in his search for self-definition? What does he mean when he says, "What I needed was instruction on how to live"?

5. In addition to Bruce Lee, who were Wu's other Asian heroes? In what ways did they help Wu? In what ways were they not what he was looking for?

6. Why was Wu's visit to Bruce Lee's grave an emotional experience? In what ways is Wu's "search for [Lee's] grave . . . similar to [his] search for Asian heroes in America"?

7. What value does Wu see in his struggle to define his Asian maleness? Explain.

Writing Topics

1. Wu writes about the difficulties of establishing or defining his identity while growing up in white America. Even in law school, Wu felt that he was an anomaly. Have you ever found yourself in a situation in which you were in the minority? Write an essay in which you recount what it was like to be in conflict with the dominant culture.

2. Why do children and adolescents need heroes? Who are some of the dominant heroes in America today? Did you have any heroes when you were in high school, or like Wu, did you find heroes hard to come by while you were growing up? Write an essay in which you explore the importance of heroes for you.

Edite Cunha was born in Portugal and moved with her family to Peabody, Massachusetts, when she was seven years old. In 1991 Cunha graduated from Smith College where she was an Ada Comstock Scholar. Despite this success, her experiences in the United States were not always easy ones. Shortly after moving to Massachusetts, Edite's name was changed by her elementary-school teacher. Far from being a helpful gesture, allowing her to fit into a new culture, the name change left her feeling deprived of her personal identity. This situation only added to her difficulties in learning a new language. In addition, Cunha faced the challenges of a bilingual world. As her family's translator, she had to be her father's "voice," a responsibility she dreaded.

In the following essay, which first appeared in *New England Monthly* in August 1990, Cunha recounts the cultural shock she experienced upon her arrival in America.

Talking in the New Land

Before I started school in America I was Edite. Maria Edite dos Anjos 1
Cunha. Maria, in honor of the Virgin Mary. In Portugal it was customary to use Maria as a religious and legal prefix to every girl's name. Virtually every girl was so named. It had something to do with the apparition of the Virgin to three shepherd children at Fatima. In naming their daughters Maria, my people were expressing their love and reverence for their Lady of Fatima.

Edite came from my godmother, Dona Edite Baetas Ruivo. The parish 2
priest argued that I could not be named Edite because in Portugal the name was not considered Christian. But Dona Edite defended my right to bear her name. No one had argued with her family when they had christened her Edite. Her family had power and wealth. The priest considered privileges endangered by his stand, and I became Maria Edite.

The dos Anjos was for my mother's side of the family. Like her mother 3
before her, she had been named Maria dos Anjos. And Cunha was for my father's side. Carlos dos Santos Cunha, son of Abilio dos Santos Cunha, the tailor from Saíl.

I loved my name. "Maria Edite dos Anjos Cunha," I'd recite at the least 4
provocation. It was melodious and beautiful. And through it I knew exactly who I was.

478

At the age of seven I was taken from our little house in Sobreira, São   5
Martinho da Cortiċa, Portugal, and brought to Peabody, Massachusetts. We
moved into the house of Senhor João, who was our sponsor in the big land. I
was in America for about a week when someone took me to school one
morning and handed me over to the teacher, Mrs. Donahue.

Mrs. Donahue spoke Portuguese, a wondrous thing for a woman with a   6
funny, unpronounceable name.

"*Como é que te chamas?*" she asked as she led me to a desk by big   7
windows.

"Maria Edite dos Anjos Cunha," I recited, all the while scanning   8
Mrs. Donahue for clues. How could a woman with such a name speak my
language?

In fact, Mrs. Donahue was Portuguese. She was a Silva. But she had   9
married an Irishman and changed her name. She changed my name, too, on
the first day of school.

"Your name will be Mary Edith Cunha," she declared. "In America you   10
only need two or three names. Mary Edith is a lovely name. And it will be
easier to pronounce."

My name was Edite. Maria Edite. Maria Edite dos Anjos Cunha. I had   11
no trouble pronouncing it.

"Mary Edith, Edithhh, Mary Edithhh," Mrs. Donahue exaggerated it.   12
She wrinkled up her nose and raised her upper lip to show me the proper
positioning of the tongue for the *th* sound. She looked hideous. There was a
big pain in my head. I wanted to scream out my name. But you could never
argue with a teacher.

At home I cried and cried. Màe and *Pai* wanted to know about the day.   13
I couldn't pronounce the new name for them. Senhor João's red face wrinkled in laughter.

Day after day Mrs. Donahue made me practice pronouncing that name   14
that wasn't mine. Mary Edithhhhh. Mary Edithhh. Mary Edithhh. But
weeks later I still wouldn't respond when she called it out in class. Mrs.
Donahue became cross when I didn't answer. Later my other teachers shortened it to Mary. And I never knew quite who I was. . . .

Mrs. Donahue was a small woman, not much bigger than my seven-year-old   15
self. Her graying hair was cut into a neat, curly bob. There was a smile that
she wore almost every day. Not broad. Barely perceptible. But it was there,
in her eyes, and at the corners of her mouth. She often wore gray suits with
jackets neatly fitted about the waist. On her feet she wore matching black
leather shoes, tightly laced. Matching, but not identical. One of them had
an extra-thick sole, because like all of her pupils, Mrs. Donahue had an
oddity. We, the children, were odd because we were of different colors and
sizes, and did not speak in the accepted tongue. Mrs. Donahue was odd
because she had legs of different lengths.

I grew to love Mrs. Donahue. She danced with us. She was the only   16
teacher in all of Carroll School who thought it was important to dance.
Every day after recess she took us all to the big open space at the back of the
room. We stood in a cricle and joined hands. Mrs. Donahue would blow a
quivering note from the little round pitch pipe she kept in her pocket, and
we became a twirling, singing wheel. Mrs. Donahue hobbled on her short leg
and sang in a high trembly voice, "Here we go, loop-de-loop." We took three
steps, then a pause. Her last "loop" was always very high. It seemed to squeak
above our heads, bouncing on the ceiling. "Here we go, loop-de-lie." Three
more steps, another pause, and on we whirled. "Here we go, loop-de-loop."
Pause. "All on a Saturday night." To anyone looking in from the corridor we
were surely an irregular sight, a circle of children of odd sizes and colors
singing and twirling with our tiny hobbling teacher.

I'd been in Room Three with Mrs. Donahue for over a year when she   17
decided that I could join the children in the regular elementary classes at
Thomas Carroll School. I embraced the news with some ambivalence. By
then the oddity of Mrs. Donahue's classroom had draped itself over me like a
warm safe cloak. Now I was to join the second grade class of Mrs. Laitinen.
In preparation, Mrs. Donahue began a phase of relentless drilling. She
talked to me about what I could expect in second grade. Miss Laitinen's class
was well on its way with cursive writing, so we practiced that every day. We
intensified our efforts with multiplication. And we practiced pronouncing
the new teacher's name.

"Lay-te-nun." Mrs. Donahue spewed the *t* out with excessive force to   18
demonstrate its importance. I had a tendency to forget it.

"Lay-nun."   19

"Mary Edith, don't be lazy. Use that tongue. It's Lay-te"—she bared   20
her teeth for the *t* part—"nun."

One morning, with no warning, Mrs. Donahue walked me to the end   21
of the hall and knocked on the door to Room Six. Miss Laitinen opened the
door. She looked severe, carrying a long rubber-tipped pointer which she
held horizontally before her with both hands. Miss Laitinen was a big,
masculine woman. Her light, coarse hair was straight and cut short. She
wore dark cardigans and very long, pleated plaid kilts that looked big enough
to cover my bed.

"This is Mary Edith," Mrs. Donahue said. Meanwhile I looked at their   22
shoes. Miss Laitinen wore flat, brown leather shoes that laced up and
squeaked on the wooden floor when she walked. They matched each other
perfectly, but they were twice as big as Mrs. Donahue's.

"Mary Edith, say hello to Miss Laitinen." Mrs. Donahue stressed the   23
t—a last-minute reminder.

"Hello, Miss Lay-te-nun," I said, leaning my head back to see her face.   24
Miss Laitinen was tall. Mrs. Donahue's head came just to her chest. They
both nodded approvingly before I was led to my seat.

* * *

Peabody, Massachusetts. "The Leather City." It is stamped on the city seal,   25
along with the image of a tanned animal hide. And Peabody, an industrial
city of less than fifty thousand people, has the smokestacks to prove it. They
rise up all over town from sprawling, dilapidated factories. Ugly, leaning,
wooden buildings that often stretch over a city block. Strauss Tanning Co.
A. C. Lawrence Leather Co. Gnecco & Grilk Tanning Corp. In the early
sixties, the tanneries were in full swing. The jobs were arduous and health-
threatening, but it was the best-paying work around for unskilled laborers
who spoke no English. The huge, firetrap factories were filled with men and
women from Greece, Portugal, Ireland, and Poland.

In one of these factories, João Nunes, who lived on the floor above us,   26
fed animal skins into a ravenous metal monster all day, every day. The pace
was fast. One day the monster got his right arm and wouldn't let go. When
the machine was turned off João had a little bit of arm left below his elbow.
His daughter Teresa and I were friends. She didn't come out of her house for
many days. When she returned to school, she was very quiet and cried a lot.

"*Rosa Veludo's been hurt.*" News of such tragedies spread through the   27
community fast and often. People would tell what they had seen, or what
they had heard from those who had seen. "*She was taken to the hospital by
ambulance. Someone wrapped her fingers in a paper bag. The doctors may be able
to sew them back on.*"

A few days after our arrival in the United States, my father went to work   28
at the Gnecco & Grilk leather tannery, on the corner of Howley and Walnut
streets. Senhor João had worked there for many years. He helped *Pai* get the job.
Gnecco & Grilk was a long, rambling, four-story factory that stretched from the
corner halfway down the street to the railroad tracks. The roof was flat and
slouched in the middle like the back of an old workhorse. There were hundreds
of windows. The ones on the ground floor were covered with a thick wire mesh.

Pai worked there for many months. He was stationed on the ground   29
floor, where workers often had to stand ankle-deep in water laden with
chemicals. One day he had a disagreement with his foreman. He left his
machine and went home vowing never to return. . . .

Pai and I stood on a sidewalk in Salem facing a clear glass doorway. The   30
words on the door were big. DIVISION OF EMPLOYMENT SECURITY. There was
a growing coldness deep inside me. At Thomas Carroll School, Miss
Laitinen was probably standing at the side blackboard, writing perfect alphabet letters on straight chalk lines. My seat was empty. I was on a sidewalk
with *Pai* trying to understand a baffling string of words. DIVISION had something to do with math, which I didn't particularly like. EMPLOYMENT I had
never seen or heard before. SECURITY I knew. But not at that moment.

Pai reached for the door. It swung open into a little square of tiled floor.   31
We stepped in to be confronted by the highest, steepest staircase I had ever

seen. At the top, we emerged into a huge, fluorescently lit room. It was too bright and open after the dim, narrow stairs. *Pai* took off his hat. We stood together in a vast empty space. The light, polished tiles reflected the fluorescent glow. There were no windows.

Far across the room, a row of metal desks lined the wall. Each had a green vinyl-covered chair beside it. Off to our left, facing the empty space before us, was a very high green metal desk. It was easily twice as high as a normal-size desk. Its odd size and placement in the middle of the room gave it the appearance of a kind of altar that divided the room in half. There were many people working at desks or walking about, but the room was so big that it still seemed empty.   32

The head and shoulders of a white-haired woman appeared to rest on the big desk like a sculptured bust. She sat very still. Above her head the word CLAIMS dangled from two pieces of chain attached to the ceiling. As I watched the woman she beckoned to us. *Pai* and I walked toward her.   33

The desk was so high that *Pai*'s shoulders barely cleared the top. Even when I stood on tiptoe I couldn't see over it. I had to stretch and lean my head way back to see the woman's round face. I thought that she must have very long legs to need a desk that high. The coldness in me grew. My neck hurt.   34

"My father can't speak English. He has no work and we need money."   35

She reached for some papers from a wire basket. One of her fingers was encased in a piece of orange rubber.   36

"Come around over here so I can see you." She motioned to the side of the desk. I went reluctantly. Rounding the desk I saw with relief that she was a small woman perched on a stool so high it seemed she would need a ladder to get up there.   37

"How old are you?" She leaned down toward me.   38
"Eight."   39
"My, aren't you a brave girl. Only eight years old and helping daddy like that. And what lovely earrings you have."   40

She liked my earrings. I went a little closer to let her touch them. Maybe she would give us money.   41

"What language does your father speak?" She was straightening up, reaching for a pencil.   42

"Portuguese."   43
"What is she saying?" *Pai* wanted to know.   44
"Wait," I told him. The lady hadn't yet said anything about money.   45
"Why isn't your father working?"   46
"His factory burned down."   47
"What is she saying?" *Pai* repeated.   48
"She wants to know why you aren't working."   49
"Tell her the factory burned down."   50
"I know. I did." The lady was looking at me. I hoped she wouldn't ask me what my father had just said.   51

"What is your father's name?"   52

"Carlos S. Cunha. C-u-n-h-a." No one could ever spell *Cunha. Pai*   53
nodded at the woman when he heard his name.

"Where do you live?"   54

"Thirty-three Tracey Street, Peabody, Massachusetts." *Pai* nodded   55
again when he heard the address.

"When was your father born?"   56

"Quando é que tu naèstes?"   57

"When was the last day your father worked?"   58

"Qual foi o último dia que trabalhastes?"   59

"What was the name of the factory?"   60

"Qual éra o nome du fábrica?"   61

"How long did he work there?"   62

"Quanto tempo trabalhastes lá?"   63

"What is his Social Security number?"   64

I looked at her blankly, not knowing what to say. What was a Social   65
Security number?

"What did she say?" Pai prompted me out of silence.   66

"I don't know. She wants a kind of number." I was feeling very tired and   67
worried. But *Pai* took a small card from his wallet and gave it to the lady. She
copied something from it onto her papers and returned it to him. I felt a great
sense of relief. She wrote silently for a while as we stood and waited. Then
she handed some papers to *Pai* and looked at me.

"Tell your father that he must have these forms filled out by his em-   68
ployer before he can receive unemployment benefits."

I stared at her. What was she saying? Employer? Unemployment bene-   69
fits? I was afraid she was saying we couldn't have any money. Maybe not,
though. Maybe we could have money if I could understand her words.

"What did she say? Can we have some money?"   70

"I don't know. I can't understand the words."   71

"Ask her again if we can have money," Pai insisted. *"Tell her we have to pay*   72
the rent."

"We need money for the rent," I told the lady, trying to hold back   73
tears.

"You can't have money today. You must take the forms to your father's   74
employer and bring them back completed next week. Then your father must
sign another form which we will keep here to process his claim. When he
comes back in two weeks there may be a check for him." The cold in me was
so big now. I was trying not to shiver.

"Do you understand?" The lady was looking at me.   75

I wanted to say, "No, I don't," but I was afraid we would never get   76
money and *Pai* would be angry.

"Tell your father to take the papers to his boss and come back next   77
week."

Boss. I could understand boss.   78

"*She said you have to take these papers to your 'bossa' and come back next*   79
week."

"*We can't have money today?*"   80

"*No. She said maybe we can have money in two weeks.*"   81

"*Did you tell her we have to pay the rent?*"   82

"*Yes, but she said we can't have money yet.*"   83

The lady was saying good-bye and beckoning the next person from the   84
line that had formed behind us.

I was relieved to move on, but I think *Pai* wanted to stay and argue   85
with her. I knew that if he could speak English, he would have. I knew that
he thought it was my fault we couldn't have money. And I myself wasn't so
sure that wasn't true.

That night I sat at the kitchen table with a fat pencil and a piece of   86
paper. In my second-grade scrawl I wrote: Dear Miss Laitinen, Mary Edith
was sick.

I gave the paper to *Pai* and told him to sign his name.   87

"*What does it say?*"   88

"*It says that I was sick today. I need to give it to my teacher.*"   89

"*You weren't sick today.*"   90

"*Ya, but it would take too many words to tell her the truth.*"   91

Pai signed the paper. The next morning in school, Miss Laitinen read it   92
and said that she hoped I was feeling better.

When I was nine, *Pai* went to an auction and bought a big house on Tremont   93
Street. We moved in the spring. The yard at the side of the house dipped
downward in a gentle slope that was covered with a dense row of tall lilac
bushes. I soon discovered that I could crawl in among the twisted trunks to
hide from my brothers in the fragrant shade. It was paradise. . . .

I was mostly wild and joyful on Tremont Street. But there was a shadow that   94
fell across my days now and again.

"*Ó Ediiiite.*" *Pai* would call me, without the least bit of warning, to be   95
his voice. He expected me to drop whatever I was doing to attend him. Of
late, I'd had to struggle on the telephone with the voice of a woman who
wanted some old dishes. The dishes, along with lots of old furniture and
junk, had been in the house when we moved in. They were in the cellar,
stacked in cardboard boxes and covered with dust. The woman called many
times wanting to speak with *Pai*.

"My father can't speak English," I would say. "He says to tell you that   96
the dishes are in our house and they belong to us." But she did not seem to
understand. Every few days she would call.

"*Ó Ediiiite.*" *Pai's* voice echoed through the empty rooms. Hearing it   97
brought on a chill. It had that tone. As always my first impulse was to

pretend I had not heard, but there was no escape. I couldn't disappear into thin air as I wished to do at such calls. We were up in the third-floor apartment of our new house. *Pai* was working in the kitchen. Carlos and I had made a cavern of old cushions and were sitting together deep in its bowels when he called. It was so dark and comfortable there I decided not to answer until the third call, though that risked *Pai*'s wrath.

"*Ó Ediiite.*" Yes, that tone was certainly there. *Pai* was calling me to do 98 something only I could do. Something that always awakened a cold beast deep in my gut. He wanted me to be his bridge. What was it now? Did he have to talk to someone at City Hall again? Or was it the insurance company? They were always using words I couldn't understand: liability, and premium, and dividend. It made me frustrated and scared.

"You wait. My dotta come." *Pai* was talking to someone. Who could it 99 be? That was some relief. At least I didn't have to call someone on the phone. It was always harder to understand when I couldn't see people's mouths.

"*Ó Ediiiiite.*" I hated Carlos. *Pai* never called his name like that. He 100 never had to do anything but play.

"*Que ééé?*" 101

"*Come over here and talk to this lady.*" 102

Reluctantly I crawled out from the soft darkness and walked through 103 the empty rooms toward the kitchen. Through the kitchen door I could see a slim lady dressed in brown standing at the top of the stairs in the windowed perch. She had on very skinny high-heeled shoes and a brown purse to match. As soon as *Pai* saw me he said to the lady, "Dis my dotta." To me he said. "*See what she wants.*"

The lady had dark hair that was very smooth and puffed away from her 104 head. The ends of it flipped up in a way that I liked.

"Hello. I'm the lady who called about the dishes." 105

I stared at her without a word. My stomach lurched. 106

"*What did she say?*" *Pai* wanted to know. 107

"*She says she's the lady who wants the dishes.*" 108

Pai's face hardened some. 109

"*Tell her she's wasting her time. We're not giving them to her. Didn't you* 110 *already tell her that on the telephone?*"

I nodded, standing helplessly between them. 111

"*Well, tell her again.*" *Pai* was getting angry. I wanted to disappear. 112

"My father says he can't give you the dishes," I said 'the lady. She 113 clutched her purse and leaned a little forward.

"Yes, you told me that on the phone. But I wanted to come in person 114 and speak with your father because it's very important to me that—"

"My father can't speak English," I interrupted her. Why didn't she just 115 go away? She was still standing in the doorway with her back to the stairwell. I wanted to push her down.

"Yes, I understand that. But I wanted to see him." She looked at *Pai*, who was standing in the doorway to the kitchen holding his hammer. The kitchen was up one step from the porch. *Pai* was a small man, but he looked kind of scary staring down at us like that.

"*What is she saying?*"

"*She says she wanted to talk to you about getting her dishes.*"

"*Tell her the dishes are ours. They were in the house. We bought the house and everything in it. Tell her the lawyer said so.*"

The brown lady was looking at me expectantly.

"My father says the dishes are ours because we bought the house and the lawyers said everything in the house is ours now."

"Yes, I know that, but I was away when the house was being sold. I didn't know . . ."

"*Eeii.*" There were footsteps on the stairs behind her. It was *Mãe* coming up from the second floor to find out what was going on. The lady moved away from the door to let *Mãe* in.

"Dis my wife," *Pai* said the lady. The lady said hello to *Mãe*, who smiled and nodded her head. She looked at me, than at *Pai* in a questioning way.

"*It's the lady who wants our dishes,*" *Pai* explained.

"*Ó.*" *Mãe* looked at her again and smiled, but I could tell she was a little worried.

We stood there in kind of a funny circle; the lady looked at each of us in turn and took a deep breath.

"I didn't know," she continued, "that the dishes were in the house. I was away. They are very important to me. They belonged to my grand-mother. I'd really like to get them back." She spoke this while looking back and forth between *Mãe* and *Pai*. Then she looked down at me, leaning forward again. "Will you tell your parents, please?"

The cold beast inside me had begun to rise up toward my throat as the lady spoke. I knew that soon it would try to choke out my words. I spoke in a hurry to get them out.

"*She said she didn't know the dishes were in the house she was away they were her grandmother's dishes she wants them back.*" I felt a deep sadness at the thought of the lady returning home to find her grandmother's dishes sold.

"*We don't need all those dishes. Let's give them to her,*" *Mãe* said in her calm way. I felt relieved. We could give the lady the dishes and she would go away. But *Pai* got angry.

"*I already said what I had to say. The dishes are ours. That is all.*"

"*Pai, she said she didn't know. They were her grandmother's dishes. She needs to have them.*" I was speaking wildly and loud now. The lady looked at me questioningly, but I didn't want to speak to her again.

"*She's only saying that to trick us. If she wanted those dishes she should have*" taken them out before the house was sold. Tell her we are not fools. Tell her to forget it. She can go away. Tell her not to call or come here again."

"What is he saying?" The lady was looking at me again.   135

I ignored her. I felt sorry for *Pai* for always feeling that people were   136
trying to trick him. I wanted him to trust people. I wanted the lady to have
her grandmother's dishes. I closed my eyes and willed myself away.

"Tell her what I said!" Pai yelled.   137

"Pai, just give her the dishes! They were her grandmother's dishes!" My   138
voice cracked as I yelled back at him. Tears were rising.

I hated *Pai* for being so stubborn. I hated the lady for not taking the   139
dishes before the house was sold. I hated myself for having learned to speak
English.

Questions for Study and Discussion

1. Where did each part of Cunha's full name—Maria Edite dos Anjos
Cunha—come from? What, then, was the significance of her name?
2. Why did Mrs. Donahue change Cunha's name? Do you think that Mrs.
Donahue's own ethnic heritage may have motivated her in making the change?
Explain.
3. Did Cunha dislike Mrs. Donahue? How do you know? What irony do
you see in paragraph 6?
4. Why is it important for Cunha to describe Mrs. Donahue? What significant and ironic information do we get from the description?
5. Explain the irony in Mrs. Donahue's efforts to get Cunha to pronounce
Miss Laitinen's name correctly.
6. In her final sentence Cunha says, "I hated myself for having learned to
speak English." Why do you suppose she felt this way?
7. Why do you feel that Cunha needed to write this essay?
8. Why does Cunha recreate the scene in which she and her father visit
the Division of Employment Security and the one in which they try to respond
to the woman who wants the dishes? How do these two scenes help Cunha
achieve her purpose in writing the essay?

Writing Topics

1. Discuss your own experiences learning a second language. What were
the greatest stumbling blocks for you, and how did you overcome them? Were
your experiences at all like Cunha's? Write an essay about the difficulties of
learning another language.
2. How important is a person's name? Would you mind if someone wanted

to change your name? Write an essay in which you explain the origin, significance, and meaning of your name and its relation to your personal identity.

3. Think back to your early experiences with language. Did you have problems learning English? What were they? Do you now find that you have a greater facility with language? How do you account for any changes? You may find it helpful to talk with your parents or other family members about your memories of childhood experiences with language.

MARIANNA DE MARCO TORGOVNICK

Marianna De Marco Torgovnick was born in 1949 in Bensonhurst, a neighborhood in Brooklyn, New York, which she describes in her essay. Going to college and getting a doctorate in English was not what her family, relatives, or neighbors expected of her. As a young Italian-American woman, she was to go to secretarial school, get married to a man who could provide for her, have children, and, if possible, settle in the neighborhood. Now a professor of English at Duke University, Torgovnick was deeply affected by the racially motivated violence that rocked Bensonhurst in the summer of 1989, when three young black men were attacked and one was killed as they walked through the neighborhood. In this essay, the attack conjures memories of life in Bensonhurst for Torgovnick, of her earlier need for escape, and of the nature of the people and attitudes that made such an attack—regrettably—almost inevitable.*

On Being White, Female, and Born in Bensonhurst

The Mafia protects the neighborhood, our fathers say, with that peculiar   1
satisfied pride with which law-abiding Italian Americans refer to the Mafia:
the Mafia protects the neighborhood from "the coloreds." In the fifties and
sixties, I heard that information repeated, in whispers, in neighborhood parks
and in the yard at school in Bensonhurst. The same information probably
passes today in the parks (the word now "blacks," not "coloreds") but perhaps
no longer in the schoolyards. From buses each morning, from neighborhoods
outside Bensonhurst, spill children of all colors and backgrounds—American
black, West Indian black, Hispanic, and Asian. But the blacks are the only
ones especially marked for notice. Bensonhurst is no longer entirely protected
from "the coloreds." But in a deeper sense, at least for Italian Americans,
Bensonhurst never changes.

Italian-American life continues pretty much as I remember it. Families   2
with young children live side by side with older couples whose children are
long gone to the suburbs. Many of those families live "down the block" from
the last generation or, sometimes still, live together with parents or grandpar-

*In this memoir, some names and circumstances have been altered slightly.

ents. When a young family leaves, as sometimes happens, for Long Island or New Jersey or (very common now) for Staten Island, another arrives, without any special effort being required, from Italy or a poorer neighborhood in New York. They fill the neat but anonymous houses that make up the mostly tree-lined streets: two-, three-, or four-family houses for the most part (this is a working, lower to middle-middle class area, and people need rents to pay mortgages), with a few single family or small apartment houses tossed in at random. Tomato plants, fig trees, and plaster madonnas often decorate small but well-tended yards which face out onto the street; the grassy front lawn, like the grassy back yard, is relatively uncommon.

Crisscrossing the neighborhood and marking out ethnic zones— 3
Italian, Irish, and Jewish, for the most part, though there are some Asian Americans and some people (usually Protestants) called simply Americans— are the great shopping streets: Eighty-sixth Street, Kings Highway, Bay Parkway, Eighteenth Avenue, each with its own distinctive character. On Eighty-sixth Street, crowds bustle along sidewalks lined with ample, packed fruit stands. Women wheeling shopping carts or baby strollers check the fruit carefully, piece by piece, and often bargain with the dealer, cajoling for a better price or letting him know that the vegetables, this time, aren't up to snuff. A few blocks down, the fruit stands are gone and the streets are lined with clothing and record shops, mobbed by teenagers. Occasionally, the el rumbles overhead, a few stops out of Coney Island on its way to the city, a trip of around one hour.

On summer nights, neighbors congregate on stoops which during the 4
day serve as play yards for children. Air conditioning exists everywhere in Bensonhurst, but people still sit outside in the summer—to supervise children, to gossip, to stare at strangers. "*Buona sera,*" I say, or "*Buona notte,*" as I am ritually presented to Sal and Lily and Louie, the neighbors sitting on the stoop. "*Grazie,*" I say when they praise my children or my appearance. It's the only time I use Italian, which I learned at high school, although my parents (both second-generation Italian Americans, my father Sicilian, my mother Calabrian) speak it at home to each other but never to me or my brother. My accent is the Tuscan accent taught at school, not the southern Italian accents of my parents and the neighbors.

It's important to greet and please the neighbors; any break in this 5
decorum would seriously offend and aggrieve my parents. For the neighbors are the stern arbiters of conduct in Bensonhurst. Does Mary keep a clean house? Did Gina wear black long enough after her mother's death? Was the food good at Tony's wedding? The neighbors know and pass judgment. Any news of family scandal (my brother's divorce, for example) provokes from my mother the agonized words: "But what will I *tell* people?" I sometimes collaborate in devising a plausible script.

A large sign on the church I attended as a child sums up for me the 6
ethos of Bensonhurst. The sign urges contributions to the church building

fund with the message, in huge letters: "EACH YEAR ST. SIMON AND JUDE SAVES THIS NEIGHBORHOOD ONE MILLION DOLLARS IN TAXES." Passing the church on the way from largely Jewish and middle-class Sheepshead Bay (where my in-laws live) to Bensonhurst, year after year, my husband and I look for the sign and laugh at the crass level of its pitch, its utter lack of attention to things spiritual. But we also understand exactly the values it represents.

In the summer of 1989, my parents were visiting me at my house in Durham, North Carolina, from the apartment in Bensonhurst where they have lived since 1942: three small rooms, rent-controlled, floor clean enough to eat off, every corner and crevice known and organized. My parents' longevity in a single apartment is unusual even for Bensonhurst, but not that unusual; many people live for decades in the same place or move within a ten-block radius. When I lived in this apartment, there were four rooms; one has since been ceded to a demanding landlord, one of the various landlords who have haunted my parents' life and must always be appeased lest the ultimate threat—removal from the rent-controlled apartment—be brought into play. That summer, during their visit, on August 23 (my younger daughter's birthday) a shocking, disturbing, news report issued from the neighborhood: it had become another Howard Beach. 7

Three black men, walking casually through the streets at night, were attacked by a group of whites. One was shot dead, mistaken, as it turned out, for another black youth who was dating a white, although part-Hispanic, girl in the neighborhood. It all made sense: the crudely protective men, expecting to see a black arriving at the girl's house and overreacting; the rebellious girl dating the outsider boy; the black dead as a sacrifice to the feelings of the neighborhood. 8

I might have felt outrage, I might have felt guilt or shame, I might have despised the people among whom I grew up. In a way I felt all four emotions when I heard the news. I expect that there were many people in Bensonhurst who felt the same rush of emotions. But mostly I felt that, given the set-up, this was the only way things could have happened. I detested the racial killing, but I also understood it. Those streets, which should be public property available to all, belong to the neighborhood. All the people sitting on the stoops on August 23 knew that as well as they knew their own names. The black men walking through probably knew it too—though their casual walk sought to deny the fact that, for the neighbors, even the simple act of blacks walking through the neighborhood would be seen as invasion. 9

Italian Americans in Bensonhurst are notable for their cohesiveness and provinciality; the slightest pressure turns those qualities into prejudice and racism. Their cohesiveness is based on the stable economic and ethical level that links generation to generation, keeping Italian Americans in Bensonhurst and the Italian-American community alive as the Jewish-American community of my youth is no longer alive. (Its young people routinely moved to the suburbs or beyond and were never replaced, so that Jews in 10

Bensonhurst today are almost all very old people.) Their provinciality results from the Italian Americans' devotion to jealous distinctions and discriminations. Jews are suspect, but (the old Italian women admit) "they make good husbands." The Irish are okay, fellow Catholics, but not really "like us"; they make bad husbands because they drink and gamble. Even Italians come in varieties, by region (Sicilian, Calabrian, Neapolitan, very rarely any region further north) and by history in this country (the newly arrived and ridiculed "gaffoon" versus the second or third generation).

Bensonhurst is a neighborhood dedicated to believing that its values are 11 the only values; it tends toward certain forms of inertia. When my parents visit me in Durham, they routinely take chairs from the kitchen and sit out on the lawn in front of the house, not on the chairs on the back deck; then they complain that the streets are too quiet. When they walk around my neighborhood (these De Marcos who have friends named Travaglianti and Occhipinti), they look at the mailboxes and report that my neighbors have strange names. Prices at my local supermarket are compared, in unbelievable detail, with prices on Eighty-sixth Street. Any rearrangement of my kitchen since their last visits is registered and criticized. Difference is not only unwelcome, it is unacceptable. One of the most characteristic things my mother ever said was in response to my plans for renovating my house in Durham. When she heard my plans, she looked around, crossed her arms, and said, "If it was me, I wouldn't change nothing." My father once asked me to level with him about a Jewish boyfriend who lived in a different part of the neighborhood, reacting to his Jewishness, but even more to the fact that he often wore Bermuda shorts: "Tell me something, Marianna. Is he a Communist?" Such are the standards of normality and political thinking in Bensonhurst.

I often think that one important difference between Italian Americans 12 in New York neighborhoods like Bensonhurst and Italian Americans elsewhere is that the others moved on—to upstate New York, to Pennsylvania, to the Midwest. Though they frequently settled in communities of fellow Italians, they did move on. Bensonhurst Italian Americans seem to have felt that one large move, over the ocean, was enough. Future moves could be only local: from the Lower East Side, for example, to Brooklyn, or from one part of Brooklyn to another. Bensonhurst was for many of these people the summa of expectations. If their America were to be drawn as a *New Yorker* cover, Manhattan itself would be tiny in proportion to Bensonhurst and to its satellites, Staten Island, New Jersey, and Long Island.

"Oh, no," my father says when he hears the news about the shooting. 13 Though he still refers to blacks as "coloreds," he's not really a racist and is upset that this innocent youth was shot in his neighborhood. He has no trouble acknowledging the wrongness of the death. But then, like all the news accounts, he turns to the fact, repeated over and over, that the blacks had been on their way to look at a used car when they encountered the hostile mob of whites. The explanation is right before him but, "Yeah," he says, still shaking his head, "yeah, but what were they *doing* there? They didn't belong."

Over the next few days, the television news is even more disturbing.   14 Rows of screaming Italians lining the streets, most of them looking like my relatives. I focus especially on one woman who resembles almost completely my mother: stocky but not fat, mid-seventies but well preserved, full face showing only minimal wrinkles, ample steel-gray hair neatly if rigidly coiffed in a modified beehive hairdo left over from the sixties. She shakes her fist at the camera, protesting the arrest of the Italian-American youths in the neighborhood, protesting the shooting. I look a little nervously at my mother (the parent I resemble), but she has not even noticed the woman and stares impassively at the television.

What has Bensonhurst to do with what I teach today and write? Why did   15 I need to write about this killing in Bensonhurst, but not in the manner of a news account or a statistical sociological analysis? Within days of hearing the news, I began to plan this essay, to tell the world what I knew, even though I was aware that I could publish the piece only someplace my parents or their neighbors would never see or hear about it. I sometimes think that I looked around from my baby carriage and decided that someday, the sooner the better, I would get out of Bensonhurst. Now, much to my surprise, Bensonhurst—the antipode of the intellectual life I sought, the least interesting of places—had become a respectable intellectual topic. People would be willing to hear about Bensonhurst—and all by the dubious virtue of a racial killing in the streets.

The story as I would have to tell it would be to some extent a class   16 narrative: about the difference between working class and upper middle class, dependence and a profession, Bensonhurst and a posh suburb. But I need to make it clear that I do not imagine myself as writing from a position of enormous self-satisfaction, or even enormous distance. You can take the girl out of Bensonhurst (that much is clear), but you may not be able to take Bensonhurst out of the girl. And upward mobility is not the essence of the story, though it is an important marker and symbol.

In Durham today, I live in a twelve-room house surrounded by an acre   17 of trees. When I sit on my back deck on summer evenings, no houses are visible through the trees. I have a guaranteed income, teaching English at an excellent university, removed by my years of education from the fundamental economic and social conditions of Bensonhurst. The one time my mother ever expressed pleasure at my work was when I got tenure, what my father still calls, with no irony intended, "ten years." "What does that mean?" my mother asked when she heard the news. Then she reached back into her experience as a garment worker, subject to periodic layoffs. "Does it mean they can't fire you just for nothing and can't lay you off?" When I said that was exactly what it means, she said, "Very good. Congratulations. That's *wonderful.*" I was free from the *padrones*, from the network of petty anxieties that had formed, in large part, her very existence. Of course, I wasn't really free of petty anxieties: would my salary increase keep pace with my colleagues', how would my office compare, would this essay be accepted for publication, am I happy? The line between these workers and my mothers' is the line between the working class and the upper middle class.

But getting out of Bensonhurst never meant to me a big house, or nice   18
clothes, or a large income. And it never meant feeling good about looking down on what I left behind or hiding my background. Getting out of Bensonhurst meant freedom—to experiment, to grow, to change. It also meant knowledge in some grand, abstract way. All the material possessions I have acquired, I acquired simply along the way—and for the first twelve years after I left Bensonhurst, I chose to acquire almost nothing at all. Now, as I write about the neighborhood, I recognize that although I've come far in physical and material distance, the emotional distance is harder to gauge. Bensonhurst has everything to do with who I am and even with what I write. Occasionally I get reminded of my roots, of their simultaneously choking and nutritive power.

Scene one: It's after a lecture at Duke, given by a visiting professor   19
from a major university. The lecture was long and a little dull and—bad luck—I had agreed to be one of the people having dinner with the lecturer afterward. We settle into our table at the restaurant: this man, me, the head of the comparative literature program (also a professor of German), and a couple I like who teach French, the husband at my university, the wife at one nearby. The conversation is sluggish, as it often is when a stranger, like the visiting professor, has to be assimilated into a group, so I ask the visitor a question to personalize things a bit. "How did you get involved in what you do? What made you become a professor of German?" The man gets going and begins talking about how it was really unlikely that he, a nice Jewish boy from Bensonhurst, would have chosen, in the mid-fifties, to study German. Unlikely indeed.

I remember seeing *Judgment at Nuremberg* in a local movie theater and   20
having a woman in the row in back of me get hysterical when some clips of a concentration camp were shown. "My God," she screamed in a European accent, "look at what they did. Murderers, MURDERERS!"—and she had to be supported out by her family. I couldn't see, in the dark, whether her arm bore the neatly tattooed numbers that the arms of some of my classmates' parents did—and that always affected me with a thrill of horror. Ten years older than me, this man had lived more directly through those feelings, lived with and *among* those feelings. The first chance he got, he raced to study German. I myself have twice chosen not to visit Germany, but I understand his impulse.

At the dinner, the memory about the movie pops into my mind but I   21
pick up instead on the Bensonhurst—I'm also from there, but Italian American. Like a flash, he asks something I haven't been asked in years: Where did I go to high school and (a more common question) what was my maiden name? I went to Lafayette High School, I say, and my name was De Marco.

Everything changes: his facial expression, his posture, his accent, his voice. "Soo, Dee Maw-ko," he says, "dun anything wrong at school today—got enny pink slips? Wanna meet me later at the park or maybe bye the Baye?" When I laugh, recognizing the stereotype that Italians get pink slips for misconduct at school and the notorious chemistry between Italian women and Jewish men, he says, back in his elegant voice: "My God, for a minute I felt like I was turning into a werewolf."

It's odd that although I can remember almost nothing else about this   22
man—his face, his body type, even his name—I remember this lapse into his "real self" with enormous vividness. I am especially struck by how easily he was able to slip into the old, generic Brooklyn accent. I myself have no memory of ever speaking in that accent, though I also have no memory of trying not to speak it, except for teaching myself, carefully, to say "oil" rather than "earl."

But the surprises aren't over. The female French professor, whom I   23
have known for at least five years, reveals for the first time that she is also from the neighborhood, though she lived across the other side of Kings Highway, went to a different, more elite high school, and was Irish American. Three of six professors, sitting at an eclectic vegetarian restaurant in Durham, all from Bensonhurst—a neighborhood where (I swear) you couldn't get the *New York Times* at any of the local stores.

Scene two: I still live in Bensonhurst. I'm waiting for my parents to   24
return from a conference at my school, where they've been summoned to discuss my transition from elementary to junior high school. I am already a full year younger than any of my classmates, having skipped a grade, a not uncommon occurrence for "gifted" youngsters. Now the school is worried about putting me in an accelerated track through junior high, since that would make me two years younger. A compromise was reached: I would be put in a special program for gifted children, but one that took three, not two, years. It sounds okay.

Three years later, another wait. My parents have gone to school this   25
time to make another decision. Lafayette High School has three tracks: academic, for potentially college-bound kids; secretarial, mostly for Italian-American girls or girls with low aptitude-test scores (the high school is de facto segregated, so none of the tracks is as yet racially coded, though they are coded by ethnic group and gender); and vocational, mostly for boys with the same attributes, ethnic or intellectual. Although my scores are superb, the guidance counselor has recommended the secretarial track; when I protested, the conference with my parents was arranged. My mother's preference is clear: the secretarial track—college is for boys; I will need to make a "good living" until I marry and have children. My father also prefers the secretarial track, but he wavers, half proud of my aberrantly high scores, half worried. I press the attack, saying that if I were Jewish I would have been placed, without question, in the academic track. I tell him I have sneaked a

peak at my files and know that my IQ is at genius level. I am allowed to insist on the change into the academic track.

What I did, and I was ashamed of it even then, was to play upon my   26 father's competitive feelings with Jews: his daughter could and should be as good as theirs. In the bank where he was a messenger, and at the insurance company where he worked in the mailroom, my father worked with Jews, who were almost always his immediate supervisors. Several times, my father was offered the supervisory job but turned it down after long conversations with my mother about the dangers of making a change, the difficulty of giving orders to friends. After her work in a local garment shop, after cooking dinner and washing the floor each night, my mother often did piecework making bows; sometimes I would help her for fun, but it *wasn't* fun, and I was free to stop while she continued for long, tedious hours to increase the family income. Once a week, her part-time boss, Dave, would come by to pick up the boxes of bows. Short, round, with his shirttails sloppily tucked into his pants and a cigar almost always dangling from his lips, Dave was a stereotyped Jew but also, my parents always said, a nice guy, a decent man.

Years after, similar choices come up, and I show the same assertiveness I   27 showed with my father, the same ability to deal for survival, but tinged with Bensonhurst caution. Where will I go to college? Not to Brooklyn College, the flagship of the city system—I know that, but don't press the invitations I have received to apply to prestigious schools outside of New York. The choice comes down to two: Barnard, which gives me a full scholarship, minus five hundred dollars a year that all scholarship students are expected to contribute from summer earnings, or New York University, which offers me one thousand dollars above tuition as a bribe. I waver. My parents stand firm: they are already losing money by letting me go to college; I owe it to the family to contribute the extra thousand dollars plus my summer earnings. Besides, my mother adds, harping on a favorite theme, there are no boys at Barnard; at NYU I'm more likely to meet someone to marry. I go to NYU and do marry in my senior year, but he is someone I didn't meet at college. I was secretly relieved, I now think (though at the time I thought I was just placating my parents' conventionality), to be out of the marriage sweepstakes.

The first boy who ever asked me for a date was Robert Lubitz, in eighth   28 grade: tall and skinny to my average height and teenage chubbiness. I turned him down, thinking we would make a ridiculous couple. Day after day, I cast my eyes at stylish Juliano, the class cutup; day after day, I captivated Robert Lubitz. Occasionally, one of my brother's Italian-American friends would ask me out, and I would go, often to ROTC dances. My specialty was making political remarks so shocking that the guys rarely asked me again. After a while I recognized destiny: the Jewish man was a passport out of Bensonhurst. I of course did marry a Jewish man, who gave me my freedom and, very important, helped remove me from the expectations of Bensonhurst.

Though raised in a largely Jewish section of Brooklyn, he had gone to college in Ohio and knew how important it was, as he put it, "to get past the Brooklyn Bridge." We met on neutral ground, in Central Park, at a performance of Shakespeare. The Jewish-Italian marriage is a common enough catastrophe in Bensonhurst for my parents to have accepted, even welcomed, mine—though my parents continued to treat my husband like an outsider for the first twenty years ("Now Marianna. Here's what's going on with you brother. But don't tell-a you husband").

Along the way I make other choices, more fully marked by Ben-   29
sonhurst cautiousness. I am attracted to journalism or the arts as careers, but the prospects for income seem iffy. I choose instead to imagine myself as a teacher. Only the availability of NDEA fellowships when I graduate, with their generous terms, propels me from high school teaching (a thought I never much relished) to college teaching (which seems like a brave new world). Within the college teaching profession, I choose offbeat specializations: the novel, interdisciplinary approaches (not something clear and clubby like Milton or the eighteenth century). Eventually I write the book I like best about primitive others as they figure within Western obsessions: my identification with "the Other," my sense of being "Other," surfaces at last. I avoid all mentoring structures for a long time but accept aid when it comes to me on the basis of what I perceive to be merit. I'm still, deep down, Italian-American Bensonhurst, though by the time I'm a lot of other things as well.

Scene three: In the summer of 1988, a little more than a year before   30
the shooting in Bensonhurst, my father woke up trembling and in what appeared to be a fit. Hospitalization revealed that he had a pocket of blood on his brain, a frequent consequence of falls for older people. About a year earlier, I had stayed home, using my children as an excuse, when my aunt, my father's much loved sister, died, missing her funeral; only now does my mother tell me how much my father resented my taking his suggestion that I stay home. Now, confronted with what is described as brain surgery but turns out to be less dramatic than it sounds, I fly home immediately.

My brother drives three hours back and forth from New Jersey every   31
day to chauffeur me and my mother to the hospital: he is being a fine Italian-American son. For the first time in years, we have long conversations alone. He is two years older than I am, a chemical engineer who has also left the neighborhood but has remained closer to its values, with a suburban, Republican inflection. He talks a lot about New York, saying that (except for neighborhoods like Bensonhurst) it's a "third-world city now." It's the summer of the Tawana Brawley incident, when Brawley accused white men of abducting her and smearing racial slurs on her body with her own excrement. My brother is filled with dislike for Al Sharpton and Brawley's other vocal supporters in the black community—not because they're black, he says, but

because they're troublemakers, stirring things up. The city is drenched in racial hatred that makes itself felt in the halls of the hospital: Italians and Jews in the beds and as doctors; blacks as nurses and orderlies.

This is the first time since I left New York in 1975 that I have visited   32
Brooklyn without once getting into Manhattan. It's the first time I have spent several days alone with my mother, living in her apartment in Bensonhurst. My every move is scrutinized and commented on. I feel like I am going to go crazy.

Finally, it's clear that my father is going to be fine, and I can go home.   33
She insists on accompanying me to the travel agent to get my ticket for home, even though I really want to be alone. The agency (a Mafia front?) has no one who knows how to ticket me for the exotic destination of North Carolina and no computer for doing so. The one person who can perform this feat by hand is out. I have to kill time for an hour and suggest to my mother that she go home, to be there for my brother when he arrives from Jersey. We stop in a Pork Store, where I buy a stash of cheeses, sausages, and other delicacies unavailable in Durham. My mother walks home with the shopping bags, and I'm on my own.

More than anything I want a kind of *sorbetto* or ice I remember from my   34
childhood, a *cremolata*, almond-vanilla-flavored with large chunks of nuts. I pop into the local bakery (at the unlikely hour of 11 A.M.) and ask for a *cremolata*, usually eaten after dinner. The woman—a younger version of my mother—refuses: they haven't made a fresh ice yet, and what's left from the day before is too icy, no good. I explain that I'm about to get on a plane for North Carolina and want that ice, good or not. But she has her standards and holds her ground, even though North Carolina has about the same status in her mind as Timbuktoo and she knows I will be banished, perhaps forever, from the land of *cremolata*.

Then, while I'm taking a walk, enjoying my solitude, I have another   35
idea. On the block behind my parents' house, there's a club for men, for men from a particular town or region in Italy: six or seven tables, some on the sidewalk beneath a garish red, green, and white sign; no women allowed or welcome unless they're with men, and no women at all during the day when the real business of the club—a game of cards for old men—is in progress. Still, I know that inside the club would be coffee and a *cremolata* ice. I'm thirty-eight, well-dressed, very respectable looking; I know what I want. I also know I'm not supposed to enter that club. I enter anyway, asking the teenage boy behind the counter firmly, in my most professional tones, for a *cremolata* ice. Dazzled, he complies immediately. The old men at the card table have been staring at this scene, unable to place me exactly, though my facial type is familiar. Finally, a few old men's hisses pierce the air. "*Strega,*" I hear as I leave, "*mala strega*"—"witch," or "brazen whore." I have been in Bensonhurst less than a week, but I have managed to reproduce, on my final

day there for this visit, the conditions of my youth. Knowing the rules, I have broken them. I shake hands with my discreetly rebellious past, still an outsider walking through the neighborhood, marked and insulted—though unlikely to be shot.

Questions for Study and Discussion

1. At the end of her first paragraph, Torgovnick writes, "in a deeper sense, at least for Italian Americans, Bensonhurst never changes." How does she support that belief throughout her essay?

2. Torgovnick writes in paragraph 9, "I detested the racial killing, but I also understood it." What exactly does she understand about it?

3. Why was the need to escape from Bensonhurst so strong for Torgovnick when she was growing up? Was her escape a complete one? What does she mean when she writes, "You can take the girl out of Bensonhurst (that much is clear), but you may not be able to take Bensonhurst out of the girl"? Does she feel superior to her upbringing now that she lives and works in Durham, North Carolina?

4. What does Torgovnick mean when she writes at the end of paragraph 18, "Occasionally I get reminded of my roots, of their simultaneously choking and nutritive power"?

5. In paragraph 23, Torgovnick ends her discussion of a dinner party with colleagues, three of whom surprisingly grew up in Bensonhurst, by writing, "Bensonhurst—a neighborhood where (I swear) you couldn't get the *New York Times* at any of the local stores." What is the irony that she seems to be pointing to here? What is reassuring to Torgovnick as she discusses her old neighborhood with her colleagues?

6. In paragraph 35, Torgovnick tells of her visit to the men's club behind her parents' house. Why is this story a fitting conclusion to her essay?

Writing Topics

1. Think about a neighborhood or neighborhoods where you have lived. How were the various value systems and attitudes of the people who lived there played out in their relationships with one another? Write an essay in which you, like Torgovnick, compare your present value system with the one that was instilled in you or to which you were exposed as you grew up.

2. Throughout her essay, Torgovnick is very conscious of the dynamics of racial, ethnic, and gender interactions, of the deep-seated prejudices that flare when people of different origins and backgrounds come into contact with one another. Despite her background, she married outside her religion and ethnic heritage. She chooses, however, not to reflect at any length in this essay on the problems her mixed marriage may have created for her and her husband. That

subject is a related matter but not the focus of her essay; nevertheless, it may be an interesting one for you to pursue in an essay of your own. Would you marry outside your ethnic heritage, your race, your religion? Why, or why not? What special benefits or problems might arise from such a union? How would you deal with the problems? Do you think the special relationship you would have with another person would be enough to overcome the problems?

PAT MORA

Born in El Paso, Texas, in 1942, poet Pat Mora graduated from Texas Western College in 1963 and earned her Master's degree at the University of Texas at El Paso. Starting first as an English teacher in the public schools of El Paso, Mora later taught at El Paso Community College and the University of Texas at El Paso, where she is currently the director of the university museum. Mora writes about what she knows best: the deserts of the southwest and her Chicana heritage. She is a champion of ethnic diversity in the United States; she says, "I write, in part, because Hispanic perspectives need to be part of our literary heritage; I want to be part of that validation process. I also write because I am fascinated by the pleasure and power of words." Her two volumes of poetry—*Chants* (1984) and *Borders* (1986)—won Southwest Book Awards. In her poetry, Mora seeks to preserve her Mexican-American background and to explore the encounters that occur living on the border between two countries and two cultures.

In the following poem, taken from her collection *Borders*, Mora explores the public and private lives of immigrant families. She sympathizes with the anguish that immigrant parents feel as they try to ensure their children's acceptance in American society.

Immigrants

wrap their babies in the American flag,
feed them mashed hot dogs and apple pie,
name them Bill and Daisy,
buy them blonde dolls that blink blue
eyes or a football and tiny cleats   5
before the baby can even walk,
speak to them in thick English,
    hallo, babee, hallo,
whisper in Spanish or Polish
when the babies sleep, whisper   10
in a dark parent bed, that dark
parent fear, "Will they like
our boy, our girl, our fine american
boy, our fine american girl?"

Questions for Study and Discussion

1. According to the speaker in this poem, what makes an "American"? How did you react to the catalogue of characteristics that the speaker presents in lines 1 through 7? Would you add anything to this list? Explain.

2. Why do you suppose "American" is capitalized in line 1 and not in lines 13 and 14?

3. Why do you think that the immigrants "speak" in public, while they "whisper" in private? What differences are being suggested by the speaker? What does the speaker mean by "thick English"?

4. Explain the meanings of "dark" in line 11. What are the immigrant parents afraid of?

5. To whom does "they" refer in line 12?

6. Is the speaker of the poem for or against conformity and assimilation? How do you know? What in particular in the poem led you to your conclusion?

Writing Topics

1. After reading this poem, what feelings do you have about Americans' tolerance for difference? Do you think that Americans still think of the nation as a "melting pot" where differences are supposed to disappear, or are Americans now moving toward an acceptance of cultural diversity where individual differences are celebrated? Does assimilation into the dominant culture necessarily mean a loss of individuality? Present your thinking on the issue of assimilation versus diversity in an essay.

2. With the exception of Native Americans, most of us can trace our roots back to some other country—we are all in a sense immigrants. Write an essay in which you trace your family's coming to America. What were your ancestors' expectations about America? Were they fulfilled? You may find it helpful to talk with your parents or grandparents before you start writing.

7

Contemporary Issues

One of the great problems of mankind is that we suffer from a poverty of the spirit which stands in glaring contrast to our scientific and technological abundance. The richer we have become materially, the poorer we have become morally and spiritually.
—Martin Luther King, Jr.

More than any other time in history, mankind faces a crossroads. One path leads to despair and utter hopelessness. The other, to total extinction. Let us pray we have the wisdom to choose correctly.
—Woody Allen

JONATHAN KOZOL

Born in 1936, Jonathan Kozol received his B.A. from Harvard in 1958. He has taught at Yale University and the University of Massachusetts as well as in the Boston and Newton, Massachusetts, public schools and is considered to be in the forefront in the move for educational reform. Kozol has received fellowships from the Guggenheim, Ford, and Rockefeller foundations to support his writing and research, and the National Book Award for *Death at an Early Age: The Destruction of the Hearts and Minds of Negro Children in the Boston Public Schools* (1967). Kozol's other books include *The Night Is Dark and I Am Far Away from Home* (1975), *Children of the Revolution* (1978), *Prisoners of Silence: Breaking the Bonds of Adult Illiteracy in the United States* (1979), *On Being a Teacher* (1981), *Illiterate America* (1985), *Rachel and Her Children: Homeless Families in America* (1986), and *Savage Inequalities: Children in America's Schools* (1991).

The following selection is from *Illiterate America*, Kozol's magnum opus on illiteracy in which he advocates and outlines a grass-roots solution to the problem. In "The Human Cost of an Illiterate Society," Kozol attempts to convince readers of the seriousness of the homeless problem using an unexpected argument. Unlike other writers who advocate affordable housing as a solution to the problem of homelessness, Kozol suggests that illiteracy is the chief obstacle facing many people without homes.

The Human Cost of an Illiterate Society

PRECAUTIONS. READ BEFORE USING.
POISON: CONTAINS SODIUM HYDROXIDE (CAUSTIC SODA-LYE).
CORROSIVE: CAUSES SEVERE EYE AND SKIN DAMAGE, MAY CAUSE BLINDNESS.
HARMFUL OR FATAL IF SWALLOWED.
IF SWALLOWED, GIVE LARGE QUANTITIES OF MILK OR WATER.
DO NOT INDUCE VOMITING.
IMPORTANT: KEEP WATER OUT OF CAN AT ALL TIMES TO
PREVENT CONTENTS FROM VIOLENTLY ERUPTING. . .
                                            —*warning on a can of Drano*

We are speaking here no longer of the dangers faced by passengers on   1
Eastern Airlines or the dollar costs incurred by U.S. corporations and

Excerpt(s) from *Illiterate America* by Jonathan Kozol, copyright © 1985 by Jonathan Kozol. Used by permission of Doubleday, a division of Bantam, Doubleday, Dell Publishing Group, Inc.

It is a violation of the law to reproduce this selection by any means whatsoever without the written permission of the copyright holder.

taxpayers. We are speaking now of human suffering and of the ethical dilemmas that are faced by a society that looks upon such suffering with qualified concern but does not take those actions which its wealth and ingenuity would seemingly demand.

Questions of literacy, in Socrates' belief, must at length be judged as matters of morality. Socrates could not have had in mind the moral compromise peculiar to a nation like our own. Some of our Founding Fathers did, however, have this question in their minds. One of the wisest of those Founding Fathers (one who may not have been most compassionate but surely was more prescient than some of his peers) recognized the special dangers that illiteracy would pose to basic equity in the political construction that he helped to shape.

"A people who mean to be their own governors," James Madison wrote, "must arm themselves with the power knowledge gives. A popular government without popular information or the means of acquiring it, is but a prologue to a farce or a tragedy, or perhaps both."

Tragedy looms larger than farce in the United States today. Illiterate citizens seldom vote. Those who do are forced to cast a vote of questionable worth. They cannot make informed decisions based on serious print information. Sometimes they can be alerted to their interests by aggressive voter education. More frequently, they vote for a face, a smile, or a style, not for a mind or character or body of beliefs.

The number of illiterate adults exceeds by 16 million the entire vote cast for the winner in the 1980 presidential contest. If even one third of all illiterates could vote, and read enough and do sufficient math to vote in their self-interest, Ronald Reagan would not likely have been chosen president. There is, of course, no way to know for sure. We do know this: Democracy is a mendacious term when used by those who are prepared to countenance the forced exclusion of one third of our electorate. So long as 60 million people are denied significant participation, the government is neither of, nor for, nor by, the people. It is a government, at best, of those two thirds whose wealth, skin color, or parental privilege allows them opportunity to profit from the provocation and instruction of the written word.

The undermining of democracy in the United States is one "expense" that sensitive Americans can easily deplore because it represents a contradiction that endangers citizens of all political positions. The human price is not so obvious at first.

Since I first immersed myself within this work I have often had the following dream: I find that I am in a railroad station or a large department store within a city that is utterly unknown to me and where I cannot understand the printed words. None of the signs or symbols is familiar. Everything looks strange: like mirror writing of some kind. Gradually I understand that I am in the Soviet Union. All the letters on the walls around me are Cyrillic. I look for my pocket dictionary but I find that it has been mislaid. Where have I left it? Then I recall that I forgot to bring it with me when I packed my bags in Boston. I struggle to remember the name of my hotel. I try to ask somebody for directions. One person stops and looks at me in a peculiar way. I lose the nerve to ask. At last I reach into my wallet for an ID card. The card is missing. Have I lost it? Then I remember that my card was confiscated for some reason, many years before. Around this point, I wake up in a panic.

This panic is not so different from the misery that millions of adult 8
illiterates experience each day within the course of their routine existence in the U.S.A.

Illiterates cannot read the menu in a restaurant. 9

They cannot read the cost of items on the menu in the *window* of the 10
restaurant before they enter.

Illiterates cannot read the letters that their children bring home from 11
their teachers. They cannot study school department circulars that tell them of the courses that their children must be taking if they hope to pass the SAT exams. They cannot help with homework. They cannot write a letter to the teacher. They are afraid to visit in the classroom. They do not want to humiliate their child or themselves.

Illiterates cannot read instructions on a bottle of prescription medi- 12
cine. They cannot find out when a medicine is past the year of safe consumption; nor can they read of allergenic risks, warnings to diabetics, or the potential sedative effect of certain kinds of nonprescription pills. They cannot observe preventive health care admonitions. They cannot read about "the seven warning signs of cancer" or the indications of blood-sugar fluctuations or the risks of eating certain foods that aggravate the likelihood of cardiac arrest.

Illiterates live, in more than literal ways, an uninsured existence. They 13
cannot understand the written details on a health insurance form. They cannot read the waivers that they sign preceding surgical procedures. Several women I have known in Boston have entered a slum hospital with the intention of obtaining a tubal ligation and have emerged a few days later after having been subjected to a hysterectomy. Unaware of their rights, incognizant of jargon, intimidated by the unfamiliar air of fear and atmosphere of ether that so many of us find oppressive in the confines even of the most attractive and expensive medical facilities, they have signed their names to documents they could not read and which nobody, in the hectic situation that prevails so often in those overcrowded hospitals that serve the urban poor, had even bothered to explain.

Childbirth might seem to be the last inalienable right of any female 14
citizen within a civilized society. Illiterate mothers, as we shall see, already have been cheated of the power to protect their progeny against the likelihood of demolition in deficient public schools and, as a result, against the verbal servitude within which they themselves exist. Surgical denial of the

right to bear that child in the first place represents an ultimate denial, an unspeakable metaphor, a final darkness that denies even the twilight gleamings of our own humanity. What greater violation of our biological, our biblical, our spiritual humanity could possibly exist than that which takes place nightly, perhaps hourly these days, within such overburdened and benighted institutions as the Boston City Hospital? Illiteracy has many costs; few are so irreversible as this.

Even the roof above one's head, the gas or other fuel for heating that 15 protects the residents of northern city slums against the threat of illness in the winter months become uncertain guarantees. Illiterates cannot read the lease that they must sign to live in an apartment which, too often, they cannot afford. They cannot manage checking accounts and therefore seldom pay for anything by mail. Hours and entire days of difficult travel (and the cost of bus or other public transit) must be added to the real cost of whatever they consume. Loss of interest on the checking accounts they do not have, and could not manage if they did, must be regarded as another of the excess costs paid by the citizen who is excluded from the common instruments of commerce in a numerate society.

"I couldn't understand the bills," a woman in Washington, D.C., 16 reports, "and then I couldn't write the checks to pay them. We signed things. We didn't know what they were."

Illiterates cannot read the notices that they receive from welfare offices 17 or from the IRS. They must depend on word-of-mouth instruction from the welfare worker—or from other persons whom they have good reason to mistrust. They do not know what rights they have, what deadlines and requirements they face, what options they might choose to exercise. They are half-citizens. Their rights exist in print but not in fact.

Illiterates cannot look up numbers in a telephone directory. Even if 18 they can find the names of friends, few possess the sorting skills to make use of the yellow pages; categories are bewildering and trade names are beyond decoding capabilities for millions of nonreaders. Even the emergency numbers listed on the first page of the phone book—"Ambulance," "Police," and "Fire"—are too frequently beyond the recognition of nonreaders.

Many illiterates cannot read the admonition on a pack of cigarettes. 19 Neither the Surgeon General's warning nor its reproduction on the package can alert them to the risks. Although most people learn by word of mouth that smoking is related to a number of grave physical disorders, they do not get the chance to read the detailed stories which can document this danger with the vividness that turns concern into determination to resist. They can see the handsome cowboy or the slim Virginia lady lighting up a filter cigarette; they cannot heed the words that tell them that this product is (not "may be") dangerous to their health. Sixty million men and women are condemned to be the unalerted, high-risk candidates for cancer.

Illiterates do not buy "no-name" products in the supermarkets. They 20 must depend on photographs or the familiar logos that are printed on the packages of brand-name groceries. The poorest people, therefore, are denied the benefits of the least costly products.

Illiterates depend almost entirely upon label recognition. Many labels, however, are not easy to distinguish. Dozens of different kinds of Campbell's soup appear identical to the nonreader. The purchaser who cannot read and does not dare to ask for help, out of the fear of being stigmatized (a fear which is unfortunately realistic), frequently comes home with something which she never wanted and her family never tasted.   21

Illiterates cannot read instructions on a pack of frozen food. Packages sometimes provide an illustration to explain the cooking preparations; but illustrations are of little help to someone who must "boil water, drop the food—*within* its plastic wrapper—in the boiling water, wait for it to simmer, instantly remove."   22

Even when labels are seemingly clear, they may be easily mistaken. A woman in Detroit brought home a gallon of Crisco for her children's dinner. She thought that she had bought the chicken that was pictured on the label. She had enough Crisco now to last a year—but no more money to go back and buy the food for dinner.   23

Recipes provided on the package of certain staples sometimes tempt a semiliterate person to prepare a meal her children have not tasted. The longing to vary the uniform and often starchy content of low-budget meals provided to the family that relies on food stamps commonly leads to ruinous results. Scarce funds have been wasted and the food must be thrown out. The same applies to distribution of food-surplus produce in emergency conditions. Government inducements to poor people to "explore the ways" by which to make a tasty meal from tasteless noodles, surplus cheese, and powdered milk are useless to nonreaders. Intended as benevolent advice, such recommendations mock reality and foster deeper feelings of resentment and of inability to cope. (Those, on the other hand, who cautiously refrain from "innovative" recipes in preparation of their children's meals must suffer the opprobrium of "laziness," "lack of imagination . . .")   24

Illiterates cannot travel freely. When they attempt to do so, they encounter risks that few of us can dream of. They cannot read traffic signs and, while they often learn to recognize and to decipher symbols, they cannot manage street names which they haven't seen before. The same is true for bus and subway stops. While ingenuity can sometimes help a man or woman to discern directions from familiar landmarks, buildings, cemeteries, churches, and the like, most illiterates are virtually immobilized. They seldom wander past the streets and neighborhoods they know. Geographical paralysis becomes a bitter metaphor for their entire existence. They are immobilized in almost every sense we can imagine. They can't move up. They cannot see beyond. Illiterates may take an oral test for drivers' permits in most sections of America. It is a questionable concession. Where will they   25 go? How will they get there? How will they get home? Could it be that some of us might like it better if they stayed where they belong?

Travel is only one of many instances of circumscribed existence. 26 Choice, in almost all its facets, is diminished in the life of an illiterate adult. Even the printed TV schedule, which provides most people with the luxury of preselection, does not belong within the arsenal of options in illiterate existence. One consequence is that the viewer watches only what appears at moments when he happens to have time to turn the switch. Another conse- quence, a lot more common, is that the TV set remains in operation night and day. Whatever the program offered at the hour when he walks into the room will be the nutriment that he accepts and swallows. Thus, to passivity, is added frequency—indeed, almost uninterrupted continuity. Freedom to select is no more possible here than in the choice of home or surgery or food.

"You don't choose," said one illiterate woman. "You take your wishes 27 from somebody else." Whether in perusal of a menu, selection of highways, purchase of groceries, or determination of affordable enjoyment, illiterate Americans must trust somebody else: a friend, a relative, a stranger on the street, a grocery clerk, a TV copywriter.

"All of our mail we get, it's hard for her to read. Settin' down and 28 writing a letter, she can't do it. Like if we get a bill . . . we take it over to my sister-in-law . . . My sister-in-law reads it."

Billing agencies harass poor people for the payment of the bills for 29 purchases that might have taken place six months before. Utility companies offer an agreement for a staggered payment schedule on a bill past due. "You have to trust them," one man said. Precisely for this reason, you end up by trusting no one and suspecting everyone of possible deceit. A submerged sense of distrust becomes the corollary to a constant need to trust. "They are cheating me . . . I have been tricked . . . I do not know . . ."

Not knowing: This is a familiar theme. Not knowing the right word for 30 the right thing at the right time is one form of subjugation. Not knowing the world that lies concealed behind those words is a more terrifying feeling. The longitude and latitude of one's existence are beyond all easy apprehension. Even the hard, cold stars within the firmament above one's head begin to mock the possibilities for self-location. Where am I? Where did I come from? Where will I go?

"I've lost a lot of jobs," one man explains. "Today, even if you're a 31 janitor, there's still reading and writing . . . They leave a note saying, 'Go to room so-and-so . . .' You can't do it. You can't read it. You don't know."

"The hardest thing about it is that I've been places where I didn't know 32 where I was. You don't know where you are . . . You're lost."

"Like I said: I have two kids. What do I do if one of my kids starts 33 choking? I go running to the phone . . . I can't look up the hospital phone number. That's if we're at home. Out on the street, I can't read the sign. I get to a pay phone. 'Okay, tell us where you are. We'll send an ambulance.' I look at the street sign. Right there, I can't tell you what it says. I'd have to spell it out, letter for letter. By that time, one of my kids would be dead . . . These are the kinds of fears you go with, every single day . . ."

"Reading directions, I suffer with. I work with chemicals . . . That's   34
scary to begin with . . ."

"You sit down. They throw the menu in front of you. Where do you go   35
from there! Nine times out of ten you say, 'Go ahead. Pick out something for
the both of us.' I've eaten some weird things, let me tell you!"

Menus. Chemicals. A child choking while his mother searches for a   36
word she does not know to find assistance that will come too late. Another
mother speaks about the inability to help her kids to read: "I can't read to
them. Of course that's leaving them out of something they should have. Oh,
it matters. You *believe* it matters! I ordered all these books. The kids belong
to a book club. Donny wanted me to read a book to him. I told Donny: 'I
can't read.' He said: 'Mommy, you sit down. I'll read it to you.' I tried it one
day, reading from the pictures. Donny looked at me. He said, 'Mommy,
that's not right.' He's only five. He knew I couldn't read . . ."

A landlord tells a woman that her lease allows him to evict her if her   37
baby cries and causes inconvenience to her neighbors. The consequence of
challenging his words conveys a danger which appears, unlikely as it seems,
even more alarming than the danger of eviction. Once she admits that she
can't read, in the desire to maneuver for the time in which to call a friend,
she will have defined herself in terms of an explicit impotence that she
cannot endure. Capitulation in this case is preferable to self-humiliation.
Resisting the definition of oneself in terms of what one cannot do, what
others take for granted, represents a need so great that other imperatives
(even one so urgent as the need to keep one's home in winter's cold)
evaporate and fall away in face of fear. Even the loss of home and shelter, in
this case, is not so terrifying as the loss of self.

"I come out of school. I was sixteen. They had their meetings. The   38
directors meet. They said that I was wasting their school paper. I was wasting
pencils . . ."

Another illiterate, looking back, believes she was not worthy of her   39
teacher's time. She believes that it was wrong of her to take up space within
her school. She believes that it was right to leave in order that somebody
more deserving could receive her place.

Children choke. Their mother chokes another way: on more than   40
chicken bones.

People eat what others order, know what others tell them, struggle not   41
to see themselves as they believe the world perceives them. A man in
California speaks about his own loss of identity, of self-location, definition:

"I stood at the bottom of the ramp. My car had broke down on the   42
freeway. There was a phone. I asked for the police. They was nice. They said
to tell them where I was. I looked up at the signs. There was one that I had
seen before. I read it to them: ONE WAY STREET. They thought it was a joke. I
told them I couldn't read. There was other signs above the ramp. They told

me to try. I looked around for somebody to help. All the cars was going by real fast. I couldn't make them understand that I was lost. The cop was nice. He told me: 'Try once more.' I did my best. I couldn't read. I only knew the sign above my head. The cop was trying to be nice. He knew that I was trapped. 'I can't send out a car to you if you can't tell me where you are.' I felt afraid. I nearly cried. I'm forty-eight years old. I only said: 'I'm on a one-way street . . .' "

Perhaps we might slow down a moment here and look at the realities   43
described above. This is the nation that we live in. This is a society that most of us did not create but which our President and other leaders have been willing to sustain by virtue of malign neglect. Do we possess the character and courage to address a problem which so many nations, poorer than our own, have found it natural to correct?

The answers to these questions represent a reasonable test of our belief   44
in the democracy to which we have been asked in public school to swear allegiance.

Questions for Study and Discussion

1. Why has Kozol chosen to begin his essay with the warning label from a Drano can? How does it work to set the tone for the rest of his essay?

2. What kinds of evidence does Kozol use to support his argument? Which kinds of evidence did you find most convincing? Explain.

3. Reread paragraph 5. What does Kozol say is one consequence of illiteracy?

4. In your own words, exactly what is the cost to America of an illiterate society?

5. Does Kozol make a rational or emotional appeal to the reader by his use of examples? Support your answer by citing some of Kozol's examples from the text.

6. What does the essay imply about an illiterate's ability to verbalize and remember? How does Kozol characterize the illiterates he speaks of?

7. Was there anything in Kozol's essay to make readers appreciate their advantage in being able to read? Explain.

Writing Topics

1. Kozol offers no solutions for the illiteracy problem. In an essay, discuss what is currently being done and what steps need to be taken to reduce illiteracy.

2. Interview a professor on your campus who teaches first-year English or who is a faculty adviser to first-year students. How serious is the problem of illiteracy among first-year students on your campus? How do illiterate students graduate from high school and go on to college? What is being done about illiteracy at your school? What more can be done?

ANNA QUINDLEN

Following a career as a reporter for the *New York Times*, Anna Quindlen began in the early eighties to write the enormously popular column "Life in the Thirties," also for the *Times*. In a warm and witty style Quindlen shared her reflections on the pleasures and pitfalls of a "thirtysomething" career woman, wife, and mother, from dealing with a son's fear of the bogeyman to a woman's need for solitude. In 1989, just before the arrival of her third child, Quindlen informed readers that she was leaving her job to stay at home and work on her first novel. Less than a year later, Quindlen was back at her desk at the *Times* with a new column, "Public & Private." As its title suggests, Quindlen's column is about issues that arise farther from home, such as "women in battle" and "the plight of the homeless," and it describes the ways these issues are experienced in the everyday life of a woman. The best of her columns have been collected in two volumes, *Living Out Loud* (1988) and *Thinking Out Loud: On the Personal, the Political, the Public, and the Private* (1993). She has also written a novel, *Object Lessons* (1991).

In "Abortion Is Too Complex to Feel All One Way About," taken from one of her earlier columns, Quindlen shares her dilemma over whether abortion should be a matter of choice for women. Quindlen argues that for "thoughtful" people, those who have pondered the arguments on both sides of the issue, there are no easy answers.

Abortion Is Too Complex to Feel All One Way About

It was always the look on their faces that told me first. I was the 1
freshman dormitory counselor and they were the freshmen at a women's college where everyone was smart. One of them could come into my room, a golden girl, a valedictorian, an 800 verbal score on the SAT's, and her eyes would be empty, seeing only a busted future, the devastation of her life as she knew it. She had failed biology, messed up the math; she was pregnant.

That was when I became pro-choice. 2

It was the look in his eyes that I will always remember, too. They were 3
as black as the bottom of a well, and in them for a few minutes I thought I saw myself the way I had always wished to be—clear, simple, elemental, at peace. My child looked at me and I looked back at him in the delivery room, and I realized that out of a sea of infinite possibilities it had come down to this: a specific person born on the hottest day of the year, conceived on a Christmas Eve, made by his father and me miraculously from scratch.

Once I believed that there was a little blob of formless protoplasm in 4 there and a gynecologist went after it with a surgical instrument, and that was that. Then I got pregnant myself—eagerly, intentionally, by the right man, at the right time—and I began to doubt. My abdomen still flat, my stomach roiling with morning sickness. I felt not that I had protoplasm inside but instead a complete human being in miniature to whom I could talk, sing, make promises. Neither of these views was accurate; instead, I think, the reality is something in the middle. And that is where I find myself now, in the middle, hating the idea of abortions, hating the idea of having them outlawed.

For I know it is the right thing in some times and places. I remember   5
sitting in a shabby clinic far uptown with one of those freshmen, only three months after the Supreme Court had made what we were doing possible, and watching with wonder as the lovely first love she had had with a nice boy unraveled over the space of an hour as they waited for her to be called, degenerated into sniping and silences. I remember a year or two later seeing them pass on campus and not even acknowledge one another because their conjoining had caused them so much pain, and I shuddered to think of them married, with a small psyche in their unready and unwilling hands.

I've met 14-year-olds who were pregnant and said they could not have   6
abortions because of their religion, and I see in their eyes the shadows of 22-year-olds I've talked to who lost their kids to foster care because they hit them or used drugs or simply had no money for food and shelter. I read not long ago about a teen-ager who said she meant to have an abortion but she spent the money on clothes instead; now she has a baby who turns out to be a lot more trouble than a toy. The people who hand out those execrable little pictures of dismembered fetuses at abortion clinics seem to forget the extraordinary pain children may endure after they are born when they are unwanted, even hated or simply tolerated.

I believe that in a contest between the living and the almost living, the   7
latter must, if necessary, give way to the will of the former. That is what the fetus is to me, the almost living. Yet these questions began to plague me—and, I've discovered, a good many other women—after I became pregnant. But they became even more acute after I had my second child, mainly
because he is so different from his brother. On two random nights 18 months apart the same two people managed to conceive, and on one occasion the tumult within turned itself into a curly-haired brunet with merry black eyes who walked and talked late and loved the whole world, and on another it became a blond with hazel Asian eyes and a pug nose who tried to conquer the world almost as soon as he entered it.

If we were to have an abortion next time for some reason or another,   8
which infinite possibility becomes, not a reality, but a nullity? The girl with the blue eyes? The improbable redhead? The natural athlete? The thinker? My husband, ever at the heart of the matter, put it another way. Knowing that he is finding two children somewhat more overwhelming than he ex-

pected, I asked if he would want me to have an abortion if I accidentally became pregnant again right away. "And waste a perfectly good human being?" he said.

Coming to this quandary has been difficult for me. In fact, I believe the 9 issue of abortion is difficult for all thoughtful people. I don't know anyone who has had an abortion who has not been haunted by it. If there is one thing I find intolerable about most of the so-called right-to-lifers, it is that they try to portray abortion rights as something that feminists thought up on a slow Saturday over a light lunch. That is nonsense. I also know that some people who support abortion rights are most comfortable with a monolithic position because it seems the strongest front against the smug and sometimes violent opposition.

But I don't feel all one way about abortion anymore, and I don't think 10 it serves a just cause to pretend that many of us do. For years I believed that a woman's right to choose was absolute, but now I wonder. Do I, with a stable home and marriage and sufficient stamina and money, have the right to choose abortion because a pregnancy is inconvenient right now? Legally I do have that right; legally I want always to have that right. It is the morality of exercising it under those circumstances that makes me wonder.

Technology has foiled us. The second trimester has become a time of 11 resurrection; a fetus at six months can be one woman's late abortion, another's premature, viable child. Photographers now have film of embryos the size of a grape, oddly human, flexing their fingers, sucking their thumbs. Women have amniocentesis to find out whether they are carrying a child with birth defects that they may choose to abort. Before the procedure, they must have a sonogram, one of those fuzzy black-and-white photos like a love song heard through static on the radio, which shows someone is in there.

I have taped on my VCR a public-television program in which some- 12 how, inexplicably, a film is shown of a fetus in utero scratching its face, seemingly putting up a tiny hand to shield itself from the camera's eye. It would make a potent weapon in the arsenal of the antiabortionists. I grow sentimental about it as it floats in the salt water; part fish, part human being. It is almost living, but not quite. It has almost turned my heart around, but not quite turned my head.

Questions for Study and Discussion

1. Quindlen begins her essay with two stories. How effective is this beginning for her essay? Would another beginning have been better? Why or why not?
2. Make a list of the things Quindlen "believes" or "thinks" to be true. What do they have in common? Make another list of the things she is uncertain about. What do they have in common?

3. After reading Quindlen's essay, what precisely would you say is the "quandary" she faces?

4. Quindlen bases her questioning of abortion on feelings she experienced only after she had children of her own. In your opinion, is this a strength or a weakness in her argument? Explain.

5. Quindlen refers to the "pro-choicers," the "right-to-lifers," and the "thoughtful." What distinguishes them according to Quindlen? What seems to be her attitude toward the people in each group? In which group does she include herself?

6. Whom is Quindlen writing for? What risk did she take in writing this essay for that audience? Why do you suppose she took that risk?

Writing Topics

1. As you might expect, Quindlen's essay on abortion generated more mail than any other essay she had written for the *New York Times*. Write your own letter to the editor in response to her essay.

2. Write an essay in which you defend one side of a controversial issue—for example, abortion, euthanasia, or the distribution of condoms to college students. What kinds of examples will you use to argue your position? Who will your audience be? How easy or difficult is it for you to be "thoughtful" about an emotionally charged issue?

BRENT STAPLES

Brent Staples was born in 1951 in Chester, Pennsylvania, an industrial city southwest of Philadelphia. He studied at Widener University in Chester and the University of Chicago. Formerly a teacher, Staples began his newspaper career as a reporter for the *Chicago Sun-Times*. He later became an editor for the *New York Times Book Review* and now serves as Assistant Metropolitan Editor for the *New York Times*. The following essay first appeared in the *New York Times Magazine* on March 30, 1986.

A Brother's Murder

It has been more than two years since my telephone rang with the news   1
that my younger brother Blake—just twenty-two years old—had been murdered. The young man who killed him was only twenty-four. Wearing a ski
mask, he emerged from a car, fired six times at close range with a massive .44
Magnum, then fled. The two had once been inseparable friends. A senseless
rivalry—beginning, I think, with an argument over a girlfriend—escalated
from posturing, to threats, to violence, to murder. The way the two were
living, death could have come to either of them from anywhere. In fact, the
assailant had already survived multiple gunshot wounds from an accident
much like the one in which my brother lost his life.

As I wept for Blake I felt wrenched backward into events and circum-   2
stances that had seemed light-years gone. Though a decade apart, we both
were raised in Chester, Pennsylvania, an angry, heavily black, heavily poor,
industrial city southwest of Philadelphia. There, in the 1960s, I was introduced to mortality, not by the old and failing, but by beautiful young men
who lay wrecked after sudden explosions of violence. The first, I remembered from my fourteenth year—Johnny, brash lover of fast cars, stabbed to
death two doors from my house in a fight over a pool game. The next year,
my teenage cousin, Wesley, whom I loved very much, was shot dead. The

517

summers blur. Milton, an angry young neighbor, shot a crosstown rival, wounding him badly. William, another teenage neighbor, took a shotgun blast to the shoulder in some urban drama and displayed his bandages proudly. His brother, Leonard, severely beaten, lost an eye and donned a black patch. It went on.

I recall not long before I left for college, two local Vietnam veterans—   3
one from the Marines, one from the Army—arguing fiercely, nearly at blows about which outfit had done the most in the war. The most killing, they meant. Not much later, I read a magazine that set that dispute in a context. In the story, a noncommissioned officer—a sergeant, I believe—said he would pass up any number of affluent, suburban-born recruits to get hard-core soldiers from the inner city. They jumped into the rice paddies with "their manhood on their sleeves," I believe he said. These two items—the veterans arguing and the sergeant's words—still characterize for me the circumstances under which black men in their teens and twenties kill one another with such frequency. With a touchy paranoia born of living battered lives, they are desperate to be *real* men. Killing is only machismo taken to the extreme. Incursions to be punished by death were many and minor, and they remain so: they include stepping on the wrong toe, literally; cheating in a drug deal; simply saying "I dare you" to someone holding a gun; crossing territorial lines in a gang dispute. My brother grew up to wear his manhood on his sleeve. And when he died, he was in that group—black, male and in its teens and early twenties—that is far and away the most likely to murder or be murdered.

I left the East Coast after college, spent the mid- and late 1970s in   4
Chicago as a graduate student, taught for a time, then became a journalist. Within ten years of leaving my hometown, I was over-educated and "up-wardly mobile," ensconced on a quiet, tree-lined street where voices raised in anger were scarcely ever heard. The telephone, like some grim umbilical, kept me connected to the old world with news of deaths, imprisonings and misfortune. I felt emotionally beaten up. Perhaps to protect myself, I added a psychological dimension to the physical distance I had already achieved. I rarely visited my hometown. I shut it out.

As I fled the past, so Blake embraced it. On Christmas of 1983, I   5
traveled from Chicago to a black section of Roanoke, Virginia, where he then lived. The desolate public housing projects, the hopeless, idle young men crashing against one another—these reminded me of the embittered town we'd grown up in. It was a place where once I would have been comfortable, or at least sure of myself. Now, hearing of my brother's forays into crime, his scrapes with police and street thugs, I was scared, unsteady on foreign terrain.

I saw that Blake's romance with the street life and the hustler image   6
had flowered dangerously. One evening that late December, standing in some Roanoke dive among drug dealers and grim, hair-trigger losers, I told him I feared for his life. He had affected the image of the tough he wanted to

be. But behind the dark glasses and the swagger, I glimpsed the baby-faced toddler I'd once watched over. I nearly wept. I wanted desperately for him to live. The young think themselves immortal, and a dangerous light shone in his eyes as he spoke laughingly of making fools of the policemen who had raided his apartment looking for drugs. He cried out as I took his right hand. A line of stitches lay between the thumb and index finger. Kickback from a shotgun, he explained, nothing serious. Gunplay had become part of his life.

I lacked the language simply to say: Thousands have lived this for you and died. I fought the urge to lift him bodily and shake him. This place and the way you are living smells of death to me, I said. Take some time away, I said. Let's go downtown tomorrow and buy a plane ticket anywhere, take a bus trip, anything to get away and cool things off. He took my alarm casually. We arranged to meet the following night—an appointment he would not keep. We embraced as though through glass. I drove away. 7

As I stood in my apartment in Chicago holding the receiver that evening in February 1984, I felt as though part of my soul had been cut away. I questioned myself then, and I still do. Did I not reach back soon enough or earnestly enough for him? For weeks I awoke crying from a recurrent dream in which I chased him, urgently trying to get him to read a document I had, as though reading it would protect him from what had happened in waking life. His eyes shining like black diamonds, he smiled and danced just beyond my grasp. When I reached for him, I caught only the space where he had been. 8

Questions for Study and Discussion

1. Staples opens his essay with a jarring account of his brother's death. How effective is this opening? How does it set the tone for the rest of his essay?
2. When and how does Staples first encounter "mortality"? What is unusual about this encounter?
3. In paragraph 3, Staples relates the story of the Vietnam veterans and the sergeant. Why does he use these incidents to illustrate his point? What does Staples mean when he writes that "killing is only machismo taken to the extreme"?
4. Staples goes to great pains to contrast his life and that of his brother. What are some of the points of contrast? What do they reveal about his attitude toward his brother's fate?
5. What is the meaning of Staples's last line? Who or what does Staples blame for his brother's death?

Writing Topics

1. Staples suggests that getting out of the ghetto was his salvation. However, for many lower-income people living in the inner city, the solution is not

so simple. Taking your cues from circumstances Staples mentions in his essay and your own knowledge of the problems facing inner cities, write an essay in which you discuss what society and the law can do to help young men like Blake.

2. What is "machismo" and how much do you think it contributed to Blake's death? Was it harmful only when combined with the other conditions of life in the ghetto? Is it less harmful and perhaps even desirable in any situation you can think of? Write an essay in which you define "machismo" and discuss its effects within American society.

JEAN BETHKE ELSHTAIN

Born in Windsor, Colorado, in 1941, Jean Bethke Elshtain has distinguished herself as both a writer and a professor of political science. After graduating from Colorado State University in 1963, she earned her master's degree at the University of Colorado and her doctorate at Brandeis University. She has taught at a number of schools including Northeastern University and the University of Massachusetts at Amherst. Currently Elshtain is Centennial Professor of political science at Vanderbilt University. Her essays and articles have appeared in such political science journals and popular magazines as *Commonweal, Dissent, Quest, Nation, Newsday,* and *The Progressive.* Elshtain often writes about women's issues, always challenging what she herself calls the "received 'truths' from the history of political thought." Her moral and ethical concerns are clearly evidenced in her books, including *Public Man, Private Woman: Women in Social and Political Thought* (1981), *Women and War* (1987), and *Power Trips and Other Journeys: Essays in Feminism as Civic Discourse* (1990).

In the following essay, which first appeared in the March 1990 issue of *The Progressive,* Elshtain presents a historical overview of the efforts of animal-rights groups in the United States to eliminate, or at least limit, animal experimentation in the name of "progress." She clearly identifies the key controversies and explains the competing philosophical positions of the parties in what she calls our current "animal wars."

Why Worry about the Animals?

These things are happening or have happened recently: 1

- *The wings of seventy-four mallard ducks are snapped to see whether crippled birds can survive in the wild. (They can't.)*
- *Infant monkeys are deafened to study their social behavior, or turned into amphetamine addicts to see what happens to their stress level.*
- *Monkeys are separated from their mothers, kept in isolation, addicted to drugs, and induced to commit "aggressive" acts.*
- *Pigs are blowtorched and observed to see how they respond to third-degree burns. No painkillers are used.*
- *Monkeys are immersed in water and vibrated to cause brain damage.*
- *For thirteen years, baboons have their brains bashed at the University of Pennsylvania as research assistants laugh at signs of the animals' distress.*
- *Monkeys are dipped in boiling water; other animals are shot in the face with high-powered rifles.*

The list of cruelties committed in the name of "science" or "research"   2
could be expanded endlessly. "Fully 80 percent of the experiments involving rhesus monkeys are either unnecessary, represent useless duplication of previ-

ous work, or could utilize nonanimal alternatives," says John E. McArdle, a biologist and specialist in primates at Illinois Wesleyan University.

Growing awareness of animal abuse is helping to build an increasingly 3 militant animal-welfare movement in this country and abroad—a movement that is beginning to have an impact on public policy. Secretary of Health and Human Services Frederick Goodwin complained recently that complying with new federal regulations on the use—or abuse—of animals will drain off some 17 percent of the research funds appropriated to the National Institutes of Health. (It is cheaper to purchase, use, and destroy animals than to retool for alternative procedures.) One of the institutes, the National Institute of Mental Health, spends about thirty million dollars a year on research that involves pain and suffering for animals.

The new animal-welfare activists are drawing attention in part be- 4 cause of the tactics they espouse. Many preach and practice civil disobedience, violating laws against, say, breaking and entering. Some have been known to resort to violence against property and—on a few occasions— against humans.

Some individuals and groups have always fretted about human responsi- 5 bility toward nonhuman creatures. In the ancient world, the historian Plutarch and the philosopher Porphyry were among those who insisted that human excellence embodied a refusal to inflict unnecessary suffering on all other creatures, human and nonhuman.

But with the emergence of the Western rationalist tradition, animals 6 lost the philosophic struggle. Two of that tradition's great exponents, René Descartes and Immanuel Kant, dismissed out of hand the moral worth of animals. Descartes's view, which has brought comfort to every human who decides to confine, poison, cripple, infect, or dismember animals in the interest of human knowledge, was the more extreme: he held that animals are simply machines, devoid of consciousness or feeling. Kant, more sophisticated in his ethical reasoning, knew that animals could suffer but denied that they were self-conscious. Therefore, he argued, they could aptly serve as means to human ends.

To make sure that human sensibilities would not be troubled by the 7 groans, cries, and yelps of suffering animals—which might lead some to suspect that animals not only bleed but feel pain—researchers have for a century subjected dogs and other animals to an operation called a centriculocordectomy, which destroys their vocal cords.

Still, there have long been groups that placed the suffering of animals 8 within the bounds of human concern. In the nineteenth and early twentieth centuries, such reform movements as women's suffrage and abolitionism made common cause with societies for the prevention of cruelty to animals. On one occasion in 1907, British suffragettes, trade unionists, and their animal-welfare allies battled London University medical students in a riot triggered by the vivisection of a dog.

Traditionally, such concern has been charitable and, frequently, highly   9
sentimental. Those who perpetrated the worst abuses against animals were denounced for their "beastly" behavior—the farmer who beat or starved his horse; the householder who chained and kicked his dog; the aristocratic hunter who, with his guests, slew birds by the thousands in a single day on his private game preserve.

For the most part, however, animals have been viewed, even by those   10
with "humane" concerns, as means to human ends. The charitable impulse, therefore, had a rather condescending, patronizing air: alas, the poor creatures deserve our pity.

The new animal-welfare movement incorporates those historic con-   11
cerns but steers them in new directions. Philosophically, animal-rights activists seek to close the gap between "human" and "beast," challenging the entire Western rationalist tradition which holds that the ability to reason abstractly is *the* defining human attribute. (In that tradition, women were often located on a scale somewhere between "man" and "beast," being deemed human but not quite rational.)

Politically, the new abolitionists, as many animal-welfare activists call   12
themselves, eschew sentimentalism in favor of a tough-minded, insistent claim that animals, too, have rights, and that violating those rights constitutes oppression. It follows that animals must be liberated—and since they cannot liberate themselves in the face of overwhelming human hegemony, they require the help of liberators much as slaves did in the last century.

Thus, the rise of vocal movements for animal well-being has strong   13
historic antecedents. What is remarkable about the current proliferation of efforts is their scope and diversity. Some proclaim animal "rights." Others speak of animal "welfare" or "protection." Still others find the term "equality" most apt, arguing that we should have "equal concern" for the needs of all sentient creatures.

When so many issues clamor for our attention, when so many problems   14
demand our best attempts at fair-minded solution, why animals, why now? There is no simple explanation for the explosion of concern, but it is clearly linked to themes of peace and justice. Perhaps it can be summed up this way: those who are troubled by the question of who is or is not within the circle of moral concern; those who are made queasy by our use and abuse of living beings for our own ends; those whose dreams of a better world are animated by some notion of a peaceable kingdom, *should* consider our relationship with the creatures that inhabit our planet with us—the creatures that have helped sustain us and that may share a similar fate with us unless we find ways to deflect if not altogether end the destruction of our earthly habitat.

Dozens of organizations have sprung up, operating alongside—and   15 sometimes in conflict with—such older mainline outfits as the Humane Society, the Anti-Vivisection League, and the World Wildlife Fund. Among the new groups are People for the Ethical Treatment of Animals (PETA), Trans-Species Unlimited, In Defense of Animals, the Gorilla Foundation, Primarily Primates, Humane Farming Association, Farm Animal Reform, Alliance for Animals, Citizens to End Animal Suffering and Exploitation (CEASE), Whale Adoption Project, Digit Fund—the list goes on and on.

Some organizations focus on the plight of animals on factory farms, 16 especially the condition of anemic, imprisoned veal calves kept in darkness and unable to turn around until they are killed at fourteen weeks. Others are primarily concerned with conditions in the wild, where the habitat of the panda, among others, is being destroyed or where great and wonderful creatures like the black rhinoceros and the African elephant or magnificent cats like the snow leopard or the Siberian tiger are marching toward extinction, victims of greedy buyers of illegal tusks or pelts.

Another group of activists clusters around the use of animals in such 17 profitable pursuits as greyhound racing, where dogs by the hundreds are destroyed once they cease "earning their keep," or in tourist attractions where such wonderfully intelligent social beings as the orca and the dolphin are turned into circus freaks for profit. In the wild, orcas can live for up to one hundred years; in captivity, the average, sadly misnamed "killer whale" lasts about five.

Those wonderful chimpanzees that have been taught to speak to us 18 through sign-language also arouse concern. If the funding ends or a researcher loses interest, they are sometimes killed, sometimes turned over to the less-than-tender mercies of laboratory researchers to be addicted to cocaine, infected with a virus, or subjected to some other terrible fate. Eugene Linden describes, in his study *Silent Partners*, chimps desperately trying to convey their pain and fear and sadness to uncomprehending experimenters.

Use of animals in war research is an industry in itself, though one 19 usually shielded from public view. Monkeys are the most likely subjects of experiments designed to measure the effects of neutron-bomb radiation and the toxicity of chemical-warfare agents. Beginning in 1957, monkeys were placed at varying distances from ground zero during atomic testing; those that didn't die immediately were encaged so that the "progress" of their various cancers might be noted.

Radiation experiments on primates continue. Monkeys' eyes are irradi- 20 ated, and the animals are subjected to shocks of up to twelve hundred volts. Junior researchers are assigned the "death watch," and what they see are primates so distressed that they claw at themselves and even bite hunks from their own arms or legs in a futile attempt to stem the pain. At a government proving ground in Aberdeen, Maryland, monkeys are exposed to chemical-warfare agents.

Dolphins, animals of exquisite intelligence, have been trained by the   21
military in such scenarios as injecting carbon dioxide cartridges into Vietnam-
ese divers and planting and removing mines. The navy announced in April
1989 that it would continue its thirty-million-dollar clandestine program,
expanded in the Reagan years, to put dolphins to military use. The aim, the
New York Times reported, is to use dolphins captured in the Gulf of Mexico to
guard the Trident Nuclear Submarine Base at Bangor, Washington.

Several years ago, when I was writing a book on women and war, I   22
came across references to the use of dogs in Vietnam. When I called the
Pentagon and was put through to the chief of military history, Southeast Asia
Branch, he told me that no books existed on the subject, but he did send me
an excerpt from the *Vietnam War Almanac* that stated the U.S. military
"made extensive use of dogs for a variety of duties in Vietnam, including
scouting, mine detecting, tracking, sentry duty, flushing out tunnels, and
drug detecting." Evidently, many of these dogs were killed rather than returned home, since it was feared their military training ill-suited them for
civilian life.

Much better known, because of an increasingly successful animal-   23
rights campaign, is the use of animals to test such household products as
furniture polish and such cosmetics as shampoo and lipstick.

For years, industry has determined the toxicity of floor wax and deter-   24
gents by injecting various substances into the stomachs of beagles, rabbits,
and calves, producing vomiting, convulsions, respiratory illness, and paralysis. The so-called LD (lethal dose) 50 test ends only when half the animals in
a test group have died. No anesthesia or pain killers are administered.

Dr. Andrew Rowan, assistant dean of the Tufts University School of   25
Medicine, has offered persuasive evidence that such testing methods are
crude and inaccurate measures of a product's safety. For one thing, a number
of potentially significant variables, including the stress of laboratory living,
are not taken into account, thus tainting any comparison of the effect of a
given substance on human consumers.

The LD50 is notoriously unreproducible; the method for rating irrita-   26
tion is extremely subjective; and interspecies variations make test results
highly suspect when applied to the human organism.

Most notorious of the "tests" deployed by the multibillion-dollar cos-   27
metics industry is the Draize, which has been used since the 1940s to measure the potential irritative effects of products. Rabbits—used because their
eyes do not produce tears and, therefore, cannot cleanse themselves—are
placed into stocks and their eyes are filled with foreign substances. When a
rabbit's eyes ulcerate—again, no pain killers are used—the cosmetics testers
(who are usually not trained laboratory researchers) report a result. To call
this procedure "scientific" is to demean authentic science.

Curiously, neither the LD50 test nor the Draize is required by law. They   28
continue in use because manufacturers want to avoid alarming consumers by

placing warning labels on products. More accurate methods available include computer simulations to measure toxicity, cell-culture systems, and organ-culture tests that use chicken-egg membranes.

The disdainful response by corporate America to animal-protection concerns seems, at least in this area, to be undergoing a slow shift toward new laboratory techniques that abandon wasteful, crude, and cruel animal testing. Several large cosmetics manufacturers, including Revlon, have only recently announced that they will phase out animal testing, confirming the claim of animal-welfare groups that the tests are unnecessary.   29

Among the nastier issues in the forefront of the "animal wars" is the controversy over hunting and trapping.   30

It's estimated that about seventeen million fur-bearing animals (plus "trash" animals—including pets—the trapper doesn't want) are mangled each year in steel-jaw leg-hold traps that tear an animal's flesh and break its bones. Many die of shock or starvation before the trapper returns. Some animals chew off part of a limb in order to escape. More than sixty countries now ban the leg-hold trap, requiring the use of less painful and damaging devices.   31

Protests against the manufacture, sale, and wearing of fur coats have been aggressively—and successfully—mounted in Western Europe. In Holland, fur sales have dropped 80 percent in the last few years. Radical groups in Sweden have broken into fur farms to release minks and foxes. An effort to shame women who wear fur has had enormous impact in Great Britain.   32

Similar campaigns have been mounted in the United States, but the fur industry is waging a well-financed counterattack in this country. Curiously, the industry's efforts have been tacitly supported by some rights-absolutists within feminism who see wearing a fur coat as a woman's right. It's difficult to think of a greater reductio ad absurdum of the notion of "freedom of choice," but it seems to appeal to certain adherents of upwardly mobile, choice-obsessed political orthodoxy.   33

Hunting may be the final frontier for animal-welfare groups. Because hunting is tied to the right to bear arms, any criticism of hunting is construed as an attack on constitutional freedoms by hunting and gun organizations, including the powerful and effective National Rifle Association. A bumper sticker I saw on a pickup truck in Northampton, Massachusetts, may tell the tale: My wife, yes. My dog, maybe. But my gun, never.   34

For some animal protectionists, the case against hunting is open and shut. They argue that the vast majority of the estimated 170 million animals shot to death in any given year are killed for blood sport, not for food, and that the offspring of these slaughtered creatures are left to die of exposure or starvation. Defenders of blood sports see them as a skill and a tradition, a lingering relic of America's great frontier past. Others—from ninteenth-   35 century feminists to the Norman Mailer of *Why Are We in Vietnam?*—link the national mania for hunting with a deeper thirst for violence.

I am not convinced there is an inherent connection between animal 36 killing and a more general lust for violence, but some disquieting evidence is beginning to accumulate. Battered and abused women in rural areas often testify, for example, that their spouses also abused animals, especially cows, by stabbing them with pitchforks, twisting their ears, kicking them, or, in one reported incident, using a board with a nail in it to beat a cow to death.

But even people who recoil from hunting and other abuses of animals 37 often find it difficult to condemn such experiments as those cited at the beginning of this article, which are, after all, conducted to serve "science" and, perhaps, to alleviate human pain and suffering. Sorting out this issue is no easy task if one is neither an absolute prohibitionist nor a relentless defender of the scientific establishment. When gross abuses come to light, they are often reported in ways that allow and encourage us to distance ourselves from emotional and ethical involvement. Thus the case of the baboons whose brains were bashed in at the University of Pennsylvania prompted the *New York Times* to editorialize, on July 31, 1985, that the animals "seemed" to be suffering. They *were* suffering, and thousands of animals suffer every day.

Reasonable people should be able to agree on this: that alternatives to 38 research that involves animal suffering must be vigorously sought; that there is no excuse for such conditions as dogs lying with open incisions, their entrails exposed, or monkeys with untreated, protruding broken bones, exposed muscle tissue, and infected wounds, living in grossly unsanitary conditions amidst feces and rotting food; that quick euthanasia should be administered to a suffering animal after the conclusion of a pain-inducing procedure; that pre- and postsurgical care must be provided for animals; that research should not be needlessly duplicated, thereby wasting animal lives, desensitizing generations of researchers, and flushing tax dollars down the drain.

What stands in the way of change? Old habits, bad science, unreflec- 39 tive cruelty, profit, and, in some cases, a genuine fear that animal-welfare groups want to stop all research dead in its tracks. "Scientists fear shackles on research," intones one report. But why are scientists so reluctant to promote such research alternatives as modeling, in-vitro techniques, and the use of lower organisms? Because they fear that the public may gain wider knowledge of what goes on behind the laboratory door. Surely those using animals should be able to explain themselves and to justify their expenditure of the lives, bodies, and minds of other creatures.

There is, to be sure, no justification for the harassment and terror 40 tactics used by some animal-welfare groups. But the scientist who is offended when an animal-welfare proponent asks, "How would you feel if someone treated your child the way you treat laboratory animals?" should ponder one of the great ironies in the continuing debate: research on animals is justified on grounds that they are "so like us."

I *do* appreciate the ethical dilemma here. As a former victim of polio, I have thought long and hard for years about animal research and human welfare. This is where I come down, at least for now: 41

First, most human suffering in this world cannot be ameliorated in any way by animal experimentation. Laboratory infliction of suffering on animals will not keep people healthy in Asia, Africa, and Latin America. As philosopher Peter Singer has argued, we already know how to cure what ails people in desperate poverty; they need "adequate nutrition, sanitation, and health care. It has been estimated that 250,000 children die each week around the world, and that one-quarter of these deaths are by dehydration due to diarrhea. A simple treatment, already known and needing no animal experimentation, could prevent the deaths of these children." 42

Second, it is not clear that a cure for terrible and thus far incurable diseases such as AIDS is best promoted with animal experimentation. Some American experts on AIDS admit that French scientists are making more rapid progress toward a vaccine because they are working directly with human volunteers, a course of action Larry Kramer, a gay activist, has urged upon American scientists. Americans have been trying since 1984 to infect chimpanzees with AIDS, but after the expenditure of millions of dollars, AIDS has not been induced in any nonhuman animal. Why continue down this obviously flawed route? 43

Third, we could surely agree that a new lipstick color, or an even more dazzling floor wax, should never be promoted for profit over the wounded bodies of animals. The vast majority of creatures tortured and killed each year suffered for *nonmedical* reasons. Once this abuse is eliminated, the really hard cases having to do with human medical advance and welfare can be debated, item by item. 44

Finally, what is at stake is the exhaustion of the eighteenth-century model of humanity's relationship to nature, which had, in the words of philosopher Mary Midgley, "built into it a bold, contemptuous rejection of the nonhuman world." 45

Confronted as we are with genetic engineering and a new eugenics, with the transformation of farms where animals ranged freely into giant factories where animals are processed and produced like objects, with callous behavior on a scale never before imagined under the rubric of "science," we can and must do better than to dismiss those who care as irrational and emotional animal-lovers who are thinking with their hearts (not surprisingly, their ranks are heavily filled with women), and who are out to put a stop to the forward march of rationalism and science. 46

We humans do not deserve peace of mind on this issue. Our sleep should be troubled and our days riddled with ethical difficulties as we come 47 to realize the terrible toll one definition of "progress" has taken on our fellow creatures.

We must consider our meat-eating habits as well. Meat-eating is one of   48
the most volatile, because most personal, of all animal questions. Meat-eaters do not consider themselves immoral, though hard-core vegetarians find meat-eating repugnant—the consumption of corpses. Such feminist theorists as Carol Adams insist that there is a connection between the butchering of animals and the historic maltreatment of women. Certainly, there is a politics of meat that belongs on the agenda along with other animal-welfare issues.

I, for one, do not believe humans and animals have identical rights.   49
But I do believe that creatures who can reason in their own ways, who can suffer, who are mortal beings like ourselves, have a value and dignity we must take into account. Animals are not simply a means to our ends.

When I was sixteen years old, I journeyed on a yellow school bus from   50
LaPorte, Colorado, to Fairbanks, Iowa, on a 4-H Club "exchange trip." On the itinerary was a visit to a meat-packing plant in Des Moines. As vivid as the day I witnessed it is the scene I replay of men in blood-drenched coats "bleeding" pigs strung up by their heels on a slowly moving conveyer belt. The pigs—bright and sensitive creatures, as any person who has ever met one knows—were screaming in terror before the sharp, thin blade entered their jugular veins. They continued to struggle and squeal until they writhed and fell silent.

The men in the slaughter room wore boots. The floor was awash in   51
blood. I was horrified. But I told myself this was something I should remember. For a few months I refused to eat pork. But then I fell back into old habits—this was Colorado farm country in the late 1950s, after all.

But at one point, a few years ago, that scene and those cries of terror   52
returned. This time I decided I would not forget, even though I knew my peace of mind would forever be disturbed.

Questions for Study and Discussion

1. In her opening paragraph, Elshtain presents a list of seven "cruelties committed in the name of 'science' or 'research.' " What impact did this list have on you? How does it prepare you for the rest of her essay?

2. According to Elshtain, what differentiates the new animal-welfare movement from its forebears? How does she account for the current proliferation of animal-rights organizations?

3. What are the main areas of concern for animal-rights groups today? For each area, briefly discuss some of the abuses or cruelties pointed out by Elshtain.

4. What is the LD50 test? Why do most people including Elshtain find it objectionable?

5. Why do you suppose Elshtain cites the bumper sticker "My wife, yes. My dog, maybe. But my gun, never"? How effective was this example for you? Explain.

6. In paragraph 38, Elshtain lists statements that she believes "reasonable people" should agree on. Do you agree with this list? What does she gain by addressing her readers as "reasonable people"? Where else in her essay does Elshtain use similar language?

7. If animal experimentation is as "bad" as some groups claim that it is, why haven't researchers and scientists abandoned it or at least modified its crueller aspects?

8. Elshtain states that the claim "research on animals is justified on grounds that they are 'so like us' " is one of the great ironies of the animal-rights debate. What does she mean by this?

9. Where does Elshtain stand on the issue of animal research and human welfare? Is it important that she tells us that she was a victim of polio? Why, or why not?

10. Why do you suppose Elshtain chose to conclude her essay with her memory of visiting a meat-packing plant as a sixteen-year-old 4-H member? What impact did this story have on you? Was it an effective way to conclude her essay? Explain.

Writing Topics

1. In paragraphs 41 through 45, Elshtain presents her position on the animal experimentation issue. Write an essay in which you argue for or against the four main points in her position statement.

2. If you are for animal rights, does it follow that you must be a vegetarian? Argue for or against a philosophy of vegetarianism that is based on the refusal to take the life of animals for meat.

3. Using information from Elshtain's essay and other material that you find in your school library, argue not for more or fewer laboratory experiments using live animals, but for stricter monitoring of research proposals to prevent duplication, poor research design, ill-conceived objectives, and the unnecessary use of animals.

ROBERT JAMES BIDINOTTO

A staff writer for *Reader's Digest* and an award-winning freelance writer and lecturer who specializes in cultural and political issues, Robert James Bidinotto was born in New Castle, Pennsylvania, in 1949 and attended Grove City College in Pennsylvania. For a couple of years after school, Bidinotto was a contributing editor for *Oasis* magazine and *On Principle*, a political newsletter. His feature articles, essays, and book and film reviews have appeared in publications including *Success*, the *American Spectator*, the *Intellectual Activist*, and the *Boston Herald*. He is also a frequent speaker and talk-show guest.

In the late 1980s, Bidinotto became interested by the controversy over the supposed "greenhouse effect" on the planet Earth. In the following essay from the February 1990 issue of *Reader's Digest*, Bidinotto presents the results of his study of the latest information on global warming.

What Is the Truth about Global Warming?

In the summer of 1988, one of the century's worst heat waves gripped the East Coast and had Midwest farmers wondering if the Dust Bowl had returned. On June 23, at a Senate hearing on global climate change, James Hansen, a respected atmospheric scientist and director of NASA's Goddard Institute for Space Studies, gave alarming testimony. "The earth is warmer in 1988 than at any time in the history of instrumental measurements," he said. "The greenhouse effect is changing our climate now." 1

Hansen's remark touched off a firestorm of publicity. A major news magazine speculated that the Great Plains would be depopulated. On NBC's "Today" show, biologist Paul Ehrlich warned that melting polar ice could raise sea levels and inundate coastal cities, swamping much of Florida, Washington, D.C., and the Los Angeles basin. And in his recent book, *Global Warming*, Stephen Schneider of the National Center for Atmospheric Research imagined New York overcome by a killer heat wave, a baseball double-header in Chicago called because of a thick black haze created by huge forest fires in Canada, and Long Island devastated by a hurricane—all spawned by the "greenhouse effect." 2

In Paris last July, the leaders of seven industrial democracies, including President Bush and British Prime Minister Margaret Thatcher, called for 3 common effects to limit emissions of carbon dioxide and other "greenhouse gases." To accomplish this, many environmentalists have proposed draconian regulations—and huge new taxes—that could significantly affect the way we live. Warns Environmental Protection Agency head William Reilly: "To slow down the global heating process, the scale of economic and societal intervention will be enormous."

The stakes are high: the public could be asked to decide between   4
environmental catastrophe and enormous costs. But do we really have to make this choice? Many scientists believe the danger is real, but others are much less certain. What is the evidence? Here is what we know:

What is the greenhouse effect? When sunlight warms the earth, cer-   5
tain gases in the lower atmosphere, acting like the glass in a greenhouse, trap some of the heat as it radiates back into space. These greenhouse gases, primarily water vapor and including carbon dioxide, methane, and man-made chlorofluorocarbons, warm our planet, making life possible.

If they were more abundant, greenhouse gases might trap too much   6
heat. Venus, for example, has 60,000 times more carbon dioxide in its atmosphere than Earth, and its temperature averages above 800 degrees Fahrenheit. But if greenhouse gases were less plentiful or entirely absent, temperatures on Earth would average below freezing.

Because concentrations of greenhouse gases have been steadily rising,   7
many scientists are concerned about global warming. Researchers at the Goddard Institute and at the University of East Anglia in England foresee a doubling of greenhouse gas concentrations during the next century, which might raise average global temperatures as much as nine degrees Fahrenheit.

What is causing the buildup? Nature accounts for most of the green-   8
house gases in the atmosphere. For example, carbon dioxide (CO_2), the most plentiful trace gas, is released by volcanoes, oceans, decaying plants and even by our breathing. But much of the *buildup* is man-made.

CO_2 is given off when we burn wood or such fossil fuels as coal and oil.   9
In fact, the amount in the atmosphere has grown more than 25 percent since the Industrial Revolution began around 200 years ago—over 11 percent since 1958 alone.

Methane, the next most abundant greenhouse gas, is released when   10
organic matter decomposes in swamps, rice paddies, livestock yards—even in the guts of termites and cud-chewing animals. The amount is growing about one percent per year, partly because of increased cattle raising and use of natural gas.

Chlorofluorocarbons (CFCs), a third culprit, escape from refrigerators,   11
air conditioners, plastic foam, solvents and spray cans. The amount in the atmosphere is tiny compared with CO_2, but CFCs are thousands of times more potent in absorbing heat and have also been implicated in the "ozone hole."

What does the ozone hole have to do with the greenhouse effect? For   12
all practical reasons, nothing. Ozone, a naturally occurring form of oxygen,

is of concern for another reason. In the upper atmosphere it helps shield us from ultraviolet sunlight, which can cause skin cancer. In 1985, scientists confirmed a temporary thinning in the ozone layer over Antarctica, leading to a new concern: if ozone thinning spreads to populated areas, it could cause an increase in the disease.

The ozone hole appears only from September to November, and only over the Antarctic region, and then it repairs itself when atmospheric conditions change a few weeks later. It also fluctuates: in 1988, there was little ozone thinning. 13

Ozone is constantly created and destroyed by nature. Volcanoes, for example, can release immense quantities of chlorine, some of which may get into the stratosphere and destroy ozone molecules. 14

But the most popular theory to explain the appearance of the ozone hole is that man-made chlorofluorocarbons release chlorine atoms in the upper atmosphere. 15

Despite thinning of upper atmospheric ozone over Antarctica, no increase in surface ultraviolet radiation outside of that area is expected. John E. Frederick, and atmospheric scientist who chaired a United Nations Environment Program panel on trends in atmospheric ozone, has dismissed fears of a skin-cancer epidemic as science fiction. "You would experience a much greater increase in biologically damaging ultraviolet radiation if you moved from New York City to Atlanta than you would with the ozone depletion that we estimate will occur over the next 30 years," he says. 16

Will destruction of forests worsen the greenhouse effect? When trees and plants grow, they remove CO_2 from the air. When they are burned or decay, they release stored CO_2 back into the atmosphere. In nations such as Brazil, thousands of square miles of tropical rain forests are being cleared and burned, leading many to be concerned about further CO_2 buildup. 17

Worldwide, millions of acres are planted with seedling trees each years, however; and new studies reveal that there has been no reliable data about the impact of forest destruction on global warming. Research by Daniel Botkin and Lloyd Simpson at the University of California at Santa Barbara and by Sandra Brown at the University of Illinois at Urbana shows that the carbon content of forests had been vastly overestimated, suggesting that deforestation is not as great a source of CO_2 as was once thought. 18

Can we be certain that global warming will occur? Virtually all scientists agree that if greenhouse gases increase and all other factors remain the same, the earth will warm up. But "the crucial issue," explains Prof. S. Fred Singer, as atmospheric scientist at the Washington Institute for Values in Public Policy, "is to what extent other factors remain the same." Climatic forces interact in poorly understood ways, and some may counteract warming. 19

At any given time, for example, clouds cover 60 percent of the planet, trapping heat radiating from its surface, but also reflecting sunlight back into space. So, if the oceans heat up and produce more clouds through evapora- 20

534 Robert James Bidinotto

tion, the increased cover might act as a natural thermostat and keep the planet from heating up. After factoring more detailed cloud simulations into its computer models, the British Meteorologist Office recently showed that current global-warming projections could be cut in half.

Oceans have a major effect upon climate, but scientists have only 21 begun to understand how. Investigators at the National Center for Atmospheric Research attributed the North American drought in the summer of 1988 primarily to temperature changes in the tropical Pacific involving a current called El Niño—not to the greenhouse effect. And when ocean currents were included in recent computerized climate simulations, the Antarctic Ocean didn't warm—diminishing the likelihood that part of its ice sheet will break up and add to coastal flooding.

How heat travels through the atmosphere and back into space is an- 22 other big question mark for the global-warming theory. So is the sunspot cycle, as well as the effect of atmospheric pollution and volcanic particles that can reflect sunlight back into space. Such factors throw predictions about global warming into doubt.

So what is the bottom line? Has the earth begun to heat up? Two 23 widely reported statistics *seem* to present a powerful case for global warming. Some temperature records show about one degree Fahrenheit of warming over the past century, a period that has also seen a noticeable increase in greenhouse gases. And the six warmest years globally since record keeping began 100 years ago have all been in the 1980s.

As for the past decade, the increased warmth in three of its hottest 24 years—1983, 1987 and 1988—is almost certainly associated with El Niño events in the Pacific.

Paradoxically, the historical records of temperature change do not jibe 25 with the greenhouse theory. Between 1880 and 1940, temperatures appeared to rise. Yet between 1940 and 1965, a period of much heavier fossil-fuel use and deforestation, temperatures dropped, which seems inconsistent with the greenhouse effect. And a comprehensive study of past global ocean records by researchers from Britain and M.I.T. revealed no significant rising temperature trends between 1856 and 1986. Concludes Richard Lindzen of M.I.T.'s department of Earth, Atmospheric and Planetary Sciences, "The data as we have it does not support a warming."

Taking everything into account, few climatologists are willing to attri- 26 bute any seeming warming to the greenhouse effect. Last May, 61 scientists participating in a greenhouse workshop in Amherst, Mass., declared that "such an attribution cannot now be made with any degree of confidence."

Is there any other evidence of global warming? Atmospheric research- 27 ers use complex computer programs called General Circulation Models (GCMs) to plot climate change. But a computer is no more reliable than its input, and poorly understood oceanic, atmospheric and continental processes are only crudely represented even in the best GCMs.

Computer calculations do not even accurately predict the past: they 28
fail to match historical greenhouse-gas concentrations to expected temperatures. Because of these uncertainties, Stephen Schneider says in *Global
Warming,* it is "an even bet that the GCMs have overestimated future warming by a factor of two."

In time, the computer models will undoubtedly improve. For now, the 29
lack of evidence and reliable tools leaves proponents of global warming with
little but theory.

Should we do anything to offset the possible warming up of the globe? 30
Fossil fuels now provide 90 percent of the world's energy. Some environmentalists have advocated huge tax increases to discourage use of coal and other
fossil fuels. Some have suggested a gasoline tax. There are also proposals that
the government subsidize solar, windmill and geothermal power; that some
foreign debts be swapped for protecting forests; and that worldwide population growth be slowed.

The buildup of greenhouse gases is cause for scientific study, but not for 31
panic. Yet the facts sometimes get lost in the hysteria. Stephen Schneider
confesses to an ethical dilemma. He admits the many uncertainties about
global warming. Nevertheless, to gain public support through media cover-
age, he explains that sometimes scientists "have to offer up scary scenarios,
make simplified, dramatic statements, and make little mention of any doubts
we might have." Each scientist, he says, must decide the "right balance"
between "being effective and being honest. I hope that means being both."

The temptation to bend fears for political ends is also ever present. 32
"We've got to ride the global-warming issue," Sen. Timothy Wirth (D.,
Colo.) explained to a reporter, "Even if the theory is wrong, we will be doing
the right thing in terms of economic and environmental policy."

But many scientists are troubled when inconclusive evidence is used for 33
political advocacy. "The greenhouse warming has become a 'happening,' "
says Richard Lindzen. To call for action, he adds, "has become a litmus test
of morality."

We still know far too little to be stampeded into rash, expensive propos- 34
als. Before we take such steps, says Patrick J. Michaels, an associate professor
of environmental sciences at the University of Virginia, "the science should
be much less murky than it is now."

Further research and climatic monitoring are certainly warranted. If 35
the "greenhouse signal" then emerges from the data, we can decide on the
most prudent course of action.

Questions for Study and Discussion

1. According to Bidinotto, what is the greenhouse effect? By what process
is it brought about? Are scientists worried about it? Why, or why not?

2. According to scientists, what part do people play in the buildup of greenhouse gases?

3. John Frederick believes that the depletion of the ozone layer will not result in an increase of ultraviolet radiation. Has Bidinotto explained to your satisfaction why Frederick believes this is so? Why, or why not?

4. Why is the eventuality of a dangerous buildup of greenhouse gases still uncertain? Why are some scientists skeptical about it?

5. What is El Niño? What role do scientists believe it plays in the earth's atmospheric temperature?

6. According to Bidinotto, why are computer models of future global warming patterns problematic? How may the issue of cloud cover, especially if the oceans warm, affect the computer models?

7. How does politics enter into the global warming controversy? How has the issue of global warming affected political and governmental concerns?

8. Bidinotto poses a question in his title. To what extent does he answer this question in his essay? Explain.

Writing Topics

1. If instrument readings in the years ahead offer further support for the belief that the earth's atmosphere is warming, what should we do or what can we do about the situation? In an essay discuss the measures mentioned by Bidinotto in paragraph 30 that might be taken to relieve the problem. Are they realistic as far as we know? What else needs to be done? Is nuclear energy a possible solution for our power needs? What can ordinary citizens do about the depletion of the ozone layer? Should products containing chlorofluorocarbons be banned from manufacture and sale?

2. Discuss the importance of obtaining reliable information about global warming before jumping to conclusions or making hasty decisions. How do responsible citizens know what a healthy degree of concern or skepticism should be, especially when the subject is scientific or technical? What roles do education, the media, politics, and government policies play in response to an issue such as global warming?

3. In his essay, Bidinotto quotes scientist Stephen Schneider as saying that scientists sometimes "have to offer up scary scenarios, make simplified, dramatic statements, and make little mention of any doubts [they] might have." Write an essay in which you discuss the possible consequences of such a practice. Does it pose any dangers to public well-being? Can you envision any justifications for the practice?

DENNIS OVERBYE

The increasing danger to the environment resulting from our industrialized society was one of the major issues of the late 1980s and will probably continue to dominate political and social discussion throughout the nineties. On one side of the issue are the doomsayers who say it is too late to make the needed changes to save our planet. At the other end of the spectrum are the optimists who say we broke it but we can fix it.

Dennis Overbye, a contributing essayist to *Time* magazine, and the author of *Lonely Hearts of the Cosmos: The Scientific Quest for the Secret of the Universe* (1991), is one of the latter. In the following essay, which appeared in an October 1989 issue of *Time,* Overbye suggests a paradox—that we are fortunate to have the technology to aid us in charting and repairing the environmental damage created by the unwise use of technology.

Fear in a Handful of Numbers

Everybody talks about the weather, goes the saying (often wrongly attributed to Mark Twain), *but nobody does anything about it.* The word from scientists is that whoever said this was wrong. All of us, as we go about the mundane business of existence, are helping change the weather and every other aspect of life on this fair planet: Los Angelenos whipping their sunny basin into a brown blur on the way to work every morning; South Americans burning and cutting their way through the rain forest in search of a better life; a billion Chinese, their smokestacks belching black coal smoke, marching toward the 21st century and a rendezvous with modernization. 1

On the flanks of Mauna Loa in Hawaii, an instrument that records the concentration of carbon dioxide dumped into the atmosphere as a result of all this activity traces a wobbly rising line that gets steeper and steeper with time. Sometime in the next 50 years, say climatologists, all that carbon dioxide, trapping the sun's heat like a greenhouse, could begin to smother the planet, raising temperatures, turning farmland to desert, swelling oceans anywhere from four feet to 20 feet. Goodbye Venice, goodbye Bangladesh. Goodbye to millions of species of animals, insects and plants that haven't already succumbed to acid rain, ultraviolet radiation leaking through the damaged ozone layer, spreading toxic wastes or bulldozers. 2

A species that can change its planet's chemistry just by day-to-day 3
coming and going has, I suppose, achieved a kind of coming-of-age. We
could celebrate or tremble. What do we do when it is not war that is killing
us but progress? When it is not the actions of a deranged dictator threatening
the world but the ordinary business of ordinary people? When there are no
bombs dropping, nobody screaming, nothing to fear but a line on a graph or
a handful of numbers on a computer printout? Dare we change the world on
the basis of a wobbly line on a graph? We can change the world, and those
numbers, slowly, painfully—we can ration, recycle, carpool, tax and use the
World Bank to bend underdeveloped nations to our will. But the problem is
neither the world nor those numbers. The problem is ourselves.

In our relations with nature, we've been playing a deadly game of 4
cowboys and Indians. We all started as Indians. Many primitive cultures—
and the indigenous peoples still clinging today to their pockets of under-
development—regarded the earth and all its creatures as alive. Nature was
a whistling wind tunnel of spirits. With the rise of a scientific, clockwork
cosmos and of missionary Christianity, with its message of man's dominion
and relentless animus against paganism, nature was metaphorically transformed. It became dead meat.

The West was won, Los Angeles and the 20th century were built, by 5
the cowboy mind. To the cowboy, nature was a vast wilderness waiting to be
tamed. The land was a stage, a backdrop against which he could pursue his
individual destiny. The story of the world was the story of a man, usually a
white man, and its features took their meaning from their relationship to
him. A mountain was a place to test one's manhood; an Asian jungle with its
rich life and cultures was merely a setting for an ideological battle. The
natives are there to be "liberated." By these standards even Communists are
cowboys.

The cowboys won—everywhere nature is being tamed—but victory 6
over nature is a kind of suicide. The rules change when there is only one
political party allowed in a country or there is only one company selling oil
or shoes. So too when a species becomes numerous and powerful enough to
gain the illusion of mastery. What we have now is a sort of biological
equivalent to a black hole, wherein a star becomes so massive and dense that
it bends space and time totally around itself and then pays the ultimate price
of domination by disappearing.

Modern science, a cowboy achievement, paradoxically favors the In- 7
dian view of life. Nature is alive. The barest Antarctic rock is crawling with
microbes. Viruses float on the dust. Bacteria help digest our food for us.
According to modern evolutionary biology, our very cells are cities of formerly independent organisms. On the molecular level, the distinction between self and nonself disappears in a blur of semipermeable membranes.
Nature goes on within and without us. It wafts through us like a breeze
through a screened porch. On the biological level, the world is a seamless

continuum of energy and information passing back and forth, a vast complicated network of exchange. Speech, food, posture, infection, respiration, scent are but a few pathways of communication. Most of those circuits are still a mystery, a labyrinth we have barely begun to acknowledge or explore.

The great anthropologist and philosopher Gregory Bateson pointed out   8
20 years ago that this myriad of feedback circuits resemble the mathematical models of thinking being developed for the new science of artificial intelligence. A forest or a coral reef or a whole planet, then, with its checks and balances and feedback loops and delicate adjustments always striving for light and equilibrium, is like *a mind*. In this way of thinking, pollution is literal insanity (Bateson was also a psychologist). To dump toxic waste in a swamp, say, is like trying to repress a bad thought or like hitting your wife every night and assuming that because she doesn't fight back, you can abuse her with impunity—30 years later she sets your bed on fire.

Some of these circuits are long and slow, so that consequences may   9
take years or generations to manifest themselves. That helps sustain the cowboy myth that nature is a neutral, unchanging backdrop. Moreover, evolution seems to have wired our brains to respond to rapid changes, the snap of a twig or a movement in the alley, and to ignore slow ones. When these consequences do start to show up, we don't notice them. Anyone who has ever been amazed by an old photograph of himself or herself can attest to the merciful ignorance of slow change, that is, aging—*Where did those clothes and that strange haircut come from? Was I really that skinny?*

We weren't born with the ability to taste carbon dioxide or see the ozone   10
layer, but science and technology have evolved to fill the gap to help us measure what we cannot feel or taste or see. We have old numbers with which, like old photographs, we can gauge the ravages of time and our own folly. In that sense, the "technological fix" that is often wishfully fantasized—cold fusion, anyone?—has already appeared. The genius of technology has already saved us, as surely as the Ghost of Christmas Future saved Scrooge by rattling the miser's tight soul until it cracked. A satellite photograph is technology, and so are the differential equations spinning inside a Cray supercomputer. There is technology in the wobbly rising trace on a piece of graph paper. There is technology in a handful of numbers.

The trick is to become more like Indians without losing the best parts   11
of cowboy culture—rationalism and the spirit of inquiry. We need more science now, not less. How can we stretch our nerves around those numbers and make them as real and as ominous as our cholesterol readings? Repeat them each night on the evening news? We need feedback, as if we were the audience in a giant public radio fund-raising drive hitting the phones and making pledges. Like expert pilots navigating through a foggy night, we need the faith to fly the planet collectively by our instruments and not by the seat of our pants. In the West we need the faith and courage to admit the bitter truth, that our prosperity is based as much on cheap energy as on free

markets. A long-postponed part of the payment for that energy and prosperity is coming due if we want to have any hope of dissuading the Chinese and the rest of the Third World from emulating us and swaddling the planet with fumes and wastes.

What if the spirit doesn't hit? We can't afford to wait if we want to survive. While we are waiting for this sea change of attitude, we could pretend—a notion that sounds more whimsical than it is. Scientists have found that certain actions have a feedback effect on the actor. Smilers actually feel happier; debaters become enamored of their own arguments; a good salesman sells himself first. You become what you pretend to be. We can pretend to be unselfish and connected to the earth. We can pretend that 30-ft.-long, black-tinted glass, air-conditioned limos are unfashionable because we know that real men don't need air conditioning. We can pretend that we believe it is wrong to loot the earth for the benefit of a single generation of a single species. We can pretend to care about our children's world.   12

The air has been poisoned before, 3 billion years ago, when the blue-green algae began manufacturing oxygen. That was the first ecological crisis. Life survived then. Life will not vanish now, but this may be the last chance for humans to go along gracefully.   13

Questions for Study and Discussion

1. Irony is the use of words to suggest something other than their literal meaning. What is the irony in Overbye's use of the expression "Everybody talks about the weather, but nobody does anything about it"? How is the expression generally intended? What is its meaning in the context of Overbye's essay?

2. Overbye uses the analogy of cowboys and Indians to argue that progress is killing us. In what ways is this analogy particularly fitting for his argument? What does it reveal about whom he intends for his audience?

3. Throughout his essay, Overbye asks the reader several questions. How does he answer them? How would you respond?

4. In what ways is pollution a "kind of suicide"?

5. Overbye uses several metaphors in his essay. Identify a few of them and discuss how they work to help make his point.

6. In your own words, what is the paradox of science that Overbye mentions in paragraph 7?

7. Overbye says, "We need more science now, not less." How do numbers figure in his solution? In light of his point that progress is killing us, his emphasis on the "technological fix" can be seen as a contradiction. How well does he resolve it for the reader?

8. What is the "long-postponed" payment Overbye refers to in paragraph 11?

9. Overbye wrote his essay in October 1989 when readers were already

well aware of the dangers of the greenhouse effect. In what ways, if any, are the solutions he offers to the problem of pollution new and unexpected?

Writing Topics

1. Choose one of Overbye's solutions to the greenhouse effect and explain the ways in which it might be implemented. What would be the difficulties in implementing it? Whom would you approach first? What expectations for success would you have?

2. Compare "What Is the Truth about Global Warming?" (pp. 531–36) by Robert James Bidinotto with Overbye's essay. What differences do you find in the tone and approach of the two writers to the subject of pollution and global warming? How might you account for those differences? What is your own position on the subject? Explain.

Suppose that someone is dying and is experiencing great pain that no medicine can relieve. Is it better to keep that person alive as long as possible, despite the suffering, or to end the suffering quickly through euthanasia? Active euthanasia, or "mercy killing," is legally considered murder, but passive euthanasia—withholding treatment that would keep the patient alive—is not; indeed, it is even endorsed by the American Medical Association. James Rachels, a professor of philosophy who is particularly concerned with ethical issues, disputes this position. Born in 1941 in Columbus, Georgia, Rachels earned degrees at Mercer University and the University of California, and has taught at the University of Miami, Coral Gables, since 1972. He is the editor of *Moral Problems*, a reader in the ethical dimensions of contemporary social issues, and the author of *The Elements of Moral Philosophy* (1986), *The End of Life: Euthanasia and Mortality* (1986), and *Created from Animals: The Moral Implications of Darwinism* (1991).

"Active and Passive Euthanasia" was first published in the *New England Journal of Medicine* in 1975, and has since been often reprinted and widely discussed. Arguing that mercy killing is morally no worse than allowing people to die, Rachels challenges doctors—and indeed all of us—to reconsider some basic assumptions.

Active and Passive Euthanasia

The distinction between active and passive euthanasia is thought to be 1 crucial for medical ethics. The idea is that it is permissible, at least in some cases, to withhold treatment and allow a patient to die, but it is never permissible to take any direct action designed to kill the patient. This doctrine seems to be accepted by most doctors, and it is endorsed in a statement adopted by the House of Delegates of the American Medical Association on December 4, 1973:

> The intentional termination of the life of one human being by another— mercy killing—is contrary to that for which the medical profession stands and is contrary to the policy of the American Medical Association.
>
> The cessation of the employment of extraordinary means to prolong the life of the body when there is irrefutable evidence that biological death is imminent is the decision of the patient and/or his immediate family. The advice and judgment of the physician should be freely available to the patient and/or his immediate family.

However, a strong case can be made against this doctrine. In what follows I will set out some of the relevant arguments, and urge doctors to reconsider their views on this matter.

To begin with a familiar type of situation, a patient who is dying of   2
incurable cancer of the throat is in terrible pain, which can no longer be
satisfactorily alleviated. He is certain to die within a few days, even if present
treatment is continued, but he does not want to go on living for those days
since the pain is unbearable. So he asks the doctor for an end to it, and his
family joins in the request.

Suppose the doctor agrees to withhold treatment, as the conventional   3
doctrine says he may. The justification for his doing so is that the patient is
in terrible agony, and since he is going to die anyway, it would be wrong to
prolong his suffering needlessly. But now notice this. If one simply withholds
treatment, it may take the patient longer to die, and so he may suffer more
than he would if more direct action were taken and a lethal injection given.
This fact provides strong reason for thinking that, once the initial decision
not to prolong his agony has been made, active euthanasia is actually preferable to passive euthanasia, rather than the reverse. To say otherwise is to
endorse the option that leads to more suffering rather than less, and is
contrary to the humanitarian impulse that prompts the decision not to
prolong his life in the first place.

Part of my point is that the process of being "allowed to die" can be   4
relatively slow and painful, whereas being given a lethal injection is relatively quick and painless. Let me give a different sort of example. In the
United States about one in 600 babies is born with Down's syndrome. Most
of these babies are otherwise healthy—that is, with only the usual pediatric
care, they will proceed to an otherwise normal infancy. Some, however, are
born with congenital defects such as intestinal obstructions that require
operations if they are to live. Sometimes, the parents and the doctor will
decide not to operate, and let the infant die. Anthony Shaw describes what
happens then:

> . . . When surgery is denied [the doctor] must try to keep the infant
> from suffering while natural forces sap the baby's life away. As a surgeon whose
> natural inclination is to use the scalpel to fight off death, standing by and
> watching a salvageable baby die is the most emotionally exhausting experience
> I know. It is easy at a conference, in a theoretical discussion, to decide that
> such infants should be allowed to die. It is altogether different to stand by in
> the nursery and watch as dehydration and infection wither a tiny being over
> hours and days. This is a terrible ordeal for me and the hospital staff—much
> more so than for the parents who never set foot in the nursery.[1]

I can understand why some people are opposed to all euthanasia, and insist
that such infant must be allowed to live. I think I can also understand why

---

[1]A. Shaw, "Doctor, Do We Have a Choice?" *The New York Times Magazine*, January 30,
1972, p. 54. [Author's note.]

other people favor destroying these babies quickly and painlessly. But why should anyone favor letting "dehydration and infection wither a tiny being over hours and days?" The doctrine that says that a baby may be allowed to dehydrate and wither, but may not be given an injection that would end its life without suffering, seems so patently cruel as to require no further refutation. The strong langauge is not intended to offend, but only to put the point in the clearest possible way.

My second argument is that the conventional doctrine leads to deci-   5
sions concerning life and death made on irrelevant grounds.

Consider again the case of the infants with Down's syndrome who need   6
operations for congenital defects unrelated to the syndrome to live. Sometimes, there is no operation, and the baby dies, but when there is no such defect, the baby lives on. Now, an operation such as that to remove an intestinal obstruction is not prohibitively difficult. The reason why such operations are not performed in these cases is, clearly, that the child has Down's syndrome and the parents and doctor judge that because of that fact it is better for the child to die.

But notice that this situation is absurd, no matter what view one takes   7
of the lives and potentials of such babies. If the life of such an infant is worth preserving, what does it matter if it needs a simple operation? Or, if one thinks it better that such a baby should not live on, what difference does it make that it happens to have an unobstructed intestinal tract? In either case, the matter of life and death is being decided on irrelevant grounds. It is the Down's syndrome, and not the intestines, that is the issue. The matter should be decided, if at all, on that basis, and not be allowed to depend on the essentially irrelevant question of whether the intestinal tract is blocked.

What makes this situation possible, of course, is the idea that when there   8
is an intestinal blockage, one can "let the baby die," but when there is no such defect there is nothing that can be done, for one must not "kill" it. The fact that this idea leads to such results as deciding life or death on irrelevant grounds is another good reason why the doctrine should be rejected.

One reason why so many people think that there is an important moral   9
difference between active and passive euthanasia is that they think killing someone is morally worse than letting someone die. But is it? Is killing, in itself, worse than letting die? To investigate this issue, two cases may be considered that are exactly alike except that one involves killing whereas the other involves letting someone die. Then, it can be asked whether this difference makes any difference to the moral assessments. It is important that the cases be exactly alike, except for this one difference, since otherwise one cannot be confident that it is this difference and not some other that accounts for any variation in the assessments of the two cases. So, let us consider this pair of cases:

In the first, Smith stands to gain a large inheritance if anything should   10
happen to his six-year-old cousin. One evening while the child is taking his

bath, Smith sneaks into the bathroom and drowns the child, and then arranges things so that it will look like an accident.

In the second, Jones also stands to gain if anything should happen to his six-year-old cousin. Like Smith, Jones sneaks in planning to drown the child in his bath. However, just as he enters the bathroom Jones sees the child slip and hit his head, and fall face down in the water. Jones is delighted; he stands by, ready to push the child's head back under if it is necessary, but it is not necessary. With only a little thrashing about, the child drowns all by himself, "accidentally," as Jones watches and does nothing.

Now Smith killed the child, whereas Jones "merely" let the child die. That is the only difference between them. Did either man behave better, from a moral point of view? If the difference between killing and letting die were in itself a morally important matter, one should say that Jones's behavior was less reprehensible than Smith's. But does one really want to say that? I think not. In the first place, both men acted from the same motive, personal gain, and both had exactly the same end in view when they acted. It may be inferred from Smith's conduct that he is a bad man, although that judgment may be withdrawn or modified if certain further facts are learned about him—for example, that he is mentally deranged. But would not the very same thing be inferred about Jones from his conduct? And would not the same further considerations also be relevant to any modification of this judgment? Moreover, suppose Jones pleaded, in his own defense, "After all, I didn't do anything except just stand there and watch the child drown. I didn't kill him; I only let him die." Again, if letting die were in itself less bad than killing, this defense should have at least some weight. But it does not. Such a "defense" can only be regarded as a grotesque perversion of moral reasoning. Morally speaking, it is no defense at all.

Now, it may be pointed out, quite properly, that the cases of euthanasia with which doctors are concerned are not like this at all. They do not involve personal gain or the destruction of normal healthy children. Doctors are concerned only with cases in which the patient's life is of no further use to him, or in which the patient's life has become or will soon become a terrible burden. However, the point is the same in these cases: the bare difference between killing and letting die does not, in itself, make a moral difference. If a doctor lets a patient die, for humane reasons, he is in the same moral position as if he had given the patient a lethal injection for humane reasons. If his decision was wrong—if, for example, the patient's illness was in fact curable—the decision would be equally regrettable no matter which method was used to carry it out. And if the doctor's decision was the right one, the method used is not in itself important.

The AMA policy statement isolates the crucial issue very well; the crucial issue is "the intentional termination of the life of one human being by another." But after identifying this issue, and forbidding "mercy killing," the statement goes on to deny that the cessation of treatment is the intentional termination of a life. This is where the mistake comes in, for what is the cessation of treatment, in these circumstances, if it is not "the intentional termination of the life of one human being by another"? Of course it is exactly that, and if it were not, there would be no point to it.

Many people will find this judgment hard to accept. One reason, I think, is that it is very easy to conflate the question of whether killing is, in itself, worse than letting die, with the very different question of whether most actual cases of killing are more reprehensible than most actual cases of letting die. Most actual cases of killing are clearly terrible (think, for example, of all the murders reported in the newspapers), and one hears of such cases every day. On the other hand, one hardly ever hears of a case of letting die, except for the actions of doctors who are motivated by humanitarian reasons. So one learns to think of killing in a much worse light than of letting die. But this does not mean that there is something about killing that makes it in itself worse than letting die, for it is not the bare difference between killing and letting die that makes the difference in these cases. Rather, the other factors—the murderer's motive of personal gain, for example, contrasted with the doctor's humanitarian motivation—account for different reactions to the different cases. 15

I have argued that killing is not in itself any worse than letting die; if my contention is right, it follows that active euthanasia is not any worse than passive euthanasia. What arguments can be given on the other side? The most common, I believe, is the following: 16

"The most important difference between active and passive euthanasia is that, in passive euthanasia, the doctor does not do anything to bring about the patient's death. The doctor does nothing, and the patient dies of whatever ills already afflict him. In active euthanasia, however, the doctor does something to bring about the patient's death: he kills him. The doctor who gives the patient with cancer a lethal injection has himself caused his patient's death; whereas if he merely ceases treatment, the cancer is the cause of the death." 17

A number of points need to be made here. The first is that it is not exactly correct to say that in passive euthanasia the doctor does nothing, for he does do one thing that is very important: he lets the patient die. "Letting someone die" is certainly different, in some respects, from other types of actions—mainly in that it is a kind of action that one may perform by way of not performing certain other actions. For example, one may let a patient die by way of not giving medication, just as one may insult someone by way of not shaking his hand. But for any purpose of moral assessment, it is a type of action nonetheless. The decision to let a patient die is subject to moral appraisal in the same way that a decision to kill him would be subject to moral appraisal: it may be assessed as wise or unwise, compassionate or sadistic, right or wrong. If a doctor deliberately let a patient die who was suffering from a routinely curable illness, the doctor would certainly be to 18

blame for what he had done, just as he would be to blame if he had needlessly killed the patient. Charges against him would then be appropriate. If
so, it would be no defense at all for him to insist that he didn't "do anything." He would have done something very serious indeed, for he let his
patient die.

Fixing the cause of death may be very important from a legal point of   19
view, for it may determine whether criminal charges are brought against the
doctor. But I do not think that this notion can be used to show a moral
difference between active and passive euthanasia. The reason why it is
considered bad to be the cause of someone's death is that death is regarded as
a great evil—and so it is. However, if it had been decided that euthanasia—
even passive euthanasia—is desirable in a given case, it has also been decided that in this instance death is no greater an evil than the patient's
continued existence. And if this is true, the usual reason for not wanting to
be the cause of someone's death simply does not apply.

Finally, doctors may think that all of this is only of academic interest—   20
the sort of thing that philosophers may worry about but that has no practical
bearing on their own work. After all, doctors must be concerned about the
legal consequences of what they do, and active euthanasia is clearly forbidden by law. But even so, doctors should also be concerned with the fact that
the law is forcing upon them a moral doctrine that may well be indefensible,
and has a considerable effect on their practices. Of course, most doctors are
not now in the position of being coerced in this matter, for they do not
regard themselves as merely going along with what the law requires. Rather,
in statements such as the AMA policy statement that I have quoted, they are
endorsing this doctrine as a central point of medical ethics. In that statement, active euthanasia is condemned not merely as illegal but as "contrary
to that for which the medical profession stands," whereas passive euthanasia
is approved. However, the preceding considerations suggest that there is
really no moral difference between the two, considered in themselves (there
may be important moral differences in some cases in their *consequences*, but,
as I pointed out, these differences may make active euthanasia, and not
passive euthanasia, the morally preferable option). So, whereas doctors may
have to discriminate between active and passive euthanasia to satisfy the law,
they should not do any more than that. In particular, they should not give
the distinction any added authority and weight by writing it into official
statements of medical ethics.

Questions for Study and Discussion

1. What is Rachels's thesis? Is he in favor of euthanasia? Support your
answer.

2. According to Rachels, what is the difference between active and passive

euthanasia? Which is generally considered more ethical? Which is more humane in Rachels's view? What do you think?

3. Is the example in paragraph 4 and the following discussion relevant to Rachels's thesis? Why does he include it?

4. What is the purpose of the hypothetical case involving Smith and Jones? Why do you think Rachels invented an example instead of drawing it from real life? What are the example's advantages and its limitations?

5. What was Rachels's purpose in writing this article? Who are his expected readers? How can you tell? Why is the article relevant to other readers?

Writing Topics

1. Are there any circumstances in which you might wish for euthanasia? If so, what are the circumstances and what would be your reasons? If not, what are your objections to euthanasia? Write an essay in which you explain your position.

2. As doctors have discovered means of prolonging the lives of terminally ill people, the debate over euthanasia has intensified. Some terminally ill people have taken their lives and their deaths into their own hands. This of course amounts to suicide and is prohibited by law. It is defended, however, under the banner of "death and dignity." Research the issues involved and discuss the pros and cons of euthanasia, taking medical, legal, and moral considerations into account.

3. As Rachels's article shows, the law often intervenes in moral questions. Do you think this is a proper function of the law? When, if ever, should we seek to legislate morality? How effective is such legislation? How should we respond when the law compels us to act against our moral sense? Write an essay in which you address one or more of these questions.

MARY HOOD

The works of short story writer and essayist Mary Hood have been favorably compared to such notable Southern female writers as Carson McCullers, Eudora Welty, and Flannery O'Connor. Hood was born in Brunswick, Georgia, and graduated from Georgia State University in 1967. Her reputation rests on two books, *How Far She Went*, a collection of short stories published in 1984, and *And Venus Is Blue*, a novella and short stories published in 1986. *How Far She Went*, which won both the Flannery O'Connor Award and the *Southern Review* Short Fiction Award, consists of nine short stories set in rural Georgia that explore loneliness and isolation. In the following selection, the title story from that collection, a grandmother and her granddaughter who are having difficulty communicating reach a level of understanding only after finding themselves in a threatening situation.

How Far She Went

They had quarreled all morning, squalled all summer about the inciden-   1
tals: how tight the girl's cut-off jeans were, the "Every Inch a Woman" T-
shirt, her choice of music and how loud she played it, her practiced inatten-
tion, her sullen look. Her granny wrung out the last boiled dish-cloth,
pinched it to the line, giving the basin a sling and a slap, the water flying out
in a scalding arc onto the Queen Anne's lace by the path, never mind if it
bloomed, that didn't make it worth anything except to chiggers, but the girl
would cut it by the everlasting armload and cherish it in the old churn, going
to that much trouble for a weed but not bending once—unbegged—to pick
the nearest bean; she was sulking now. Bored. Displaced.

"And what do you think happens to a chigger if nobody ever walks by   2
his weed?" her granny asked, heading for the house with that sidelong
uneager unanswered glance, hoping for what? The surprise gift of a smile?
Nothing. The woman shook her head and said it. "Nothing." The door
slammed behind her. Let it.

"I hate it here!" the girl yelled then. She picked up a stick and broke it   3
and threw the pieces—one from each hand—at the laundry drying in the
noon. Missed. Missed.

Then she turned on her bare, haughty heel and set off high-shouldered   4

549

into the heat, quick but not far, not far enough—no road was *that* long— only as far as she dared. At the gate, a rusty chain swinging between two lichened posts, she stopped, then backed up the raw drive to make a run at the barrier, lofting, clearing it clean, her long hair wild in the sun. Trium- phant, she looked back at the house where she caught at the dark window her granny's face in its perpetual eclipse of disappointment, old at fifty. She stepped back, but the girl saw her.

"You don't know me!" the girl shouted, chin high, and ran till her ribs   5
ached.

As she rested in the rattling shade of the willows, the little dog found   6 her. He could be counted on. He barked all the way, and squealed when she pulled the burr from his ear. They started back to the house for lunch. By then the mailman had long come and gone in the old ruts, leaving the one letter folded now to fit the woman's apron pocket.

If bad news darkened her granny's face, the girl ignored it. Didn't talk   7 at all, another of her distancings, her defiances. So it was as they ate that the woman summarized, "Your daddy wants you to cash in the plane ticket and buy you something. School clothes. For here."

Pale, the girl stared, defenseless only an instant before blurting out,   8 "You're lying."

The woman had to stretch across the table to leave her handprint on   9 that blank cheek. She said, not caring if it stung or not, "He's been planning it since he sent you here."

"I could turn this whole house over, dump it! Leave you slobbering   10 over that stinking jealous dog in the dust!" The girl trembled with the vision, with the strength it gave her. It made her laugh. "Scatter the Holy Bible like confetti and ravel the crochet into miles of stupid string! I could! I will! I won't stay here!" But she didn't move, not until her tears rose to meet her color, and then to escape the shame of minding so much she fled. Just headed away, blind. It didn't matter, this time, how far she went.

The woman set her thoughts against fretting over their bickering, just   11 went on unalarmed with chores, clearing off after the uneaten meal, bring- ing in the laundry, scattering corn for the chickens, ladling manure tea onto the porch flowers. She listened though. She always had been a listener. It gave her a cocked look. She forgot why she had gone into the girl's empty room, that ungirlish, tenuous lodging place with its bleak order, its ready suitcases never unpacked, the narrow bed, the contested radio on the win- dowsill. The woman drew the cracked shade down between the radio and the August sun. There wasn't anything else to do.

It was after six when she tied on her rough oxfords and walked down   12 the drive and dropped the gate chain and headed back to the creosoted shed where she kept her tools. She took a hoe for snakes, a rake, shears to trim the grass where it grew, and seed in her pocket to scatter where it never had grown at all. She put the tools and her gloves and the bucket in the trunk of the old Chevy, its prime and rust like an Appaloosa's spots through the chalky white finish. She left the trunk open and the tool handles sticking out. She wasn't going far.

The heat of the day had broken, but the air was thick, sultry, weighted   13
with honeysuckle in second bloom and the Nu-Grape scent of kudzu. The maple and poplar leaves turned over, quaking, silver. There wouldn't be any rain. She told the dog to stay, but he knew a trick. He stowed away when she turned her back, leaped right into the trunk with the tools, then gave himself away with exultant barks. Hearing him, her court jester, she stopped the car and welcomed him into the front seat beside her. Then they went on. Not a mile from her gate she turned onto the blue gravel of the cemetery lane, hauled the gearshift into reverse to whoa them, and got out to take the idle walk down to her buried hopes, bending all along to rout out a handful of weeds from between the markers of old acquaintances. She stood there and read, slow. The dog whined at her hem; she picked him up and rested her chin on his head, then he wriggled and whined to run free, contrary and restless as a child.

The crows called strong and bold MOM! MOM! A trick of the ear to   14
hear it like that. She knew it was the crows, but still she looked around. No one called her that now. She was done with that. And what was it worth anyway? It all came to this: solitary weeding. The sinful fumble of flesh, the fear, the listening for a return that never came, the shamed waiting, the unanswered prayers, the perjury on the certificate—hadn't she lain there weary of the whole lie and it only beginning? and a voice telling her, "Here's your baby, here's your girl," and the swaddled package meaning no more to her than an extra anything, something store-bought, something she could take back for a refund.

"Tie her to the fence and give her a bale of hay," she had murmured,   15
drugged, and they teased her, excused her for such a welcoming, blaming the anesthesia, but it went deeper than that; *she* knew, and the *baby* knew: there was no love in the begetting. That was the secret, unforgivable, that not another good thing could ever make up for, where all the bad had come from, like a visitation, a punishment. She knew that was why Sylvie had been wild, had gone to earth so early, and before dying had made this child in sudden wedlock, a child who would be just like her, would carry the hurting on into another generation. A matter of time. No use raising her hand. But she *had* raised her hand. Still wore on its palm the memory of the sting of the collision with the girl's cheek; had she broken her jaw? Her heart? Of course not. She said it aloud: "Takes more than that."

She went to work then, doing what she could with her old tools. She   16
pecked the clay on Sylvie's grave, new-looking, unhealed after years. She tried again, scattering seeds from her pocket, every last possible one of them.

Off in the west she could hear the pulpwood cutters sawing through another acre across the lake. Nearer, there was the racket of motorcycles laboring cross-country, insect-like, distracting.

She took her bucket to the well and hung it on the pump. She had half filled it when the bikers roared up, right down the blue gravel, straight at her. She let the bucket overflow, staring. On the back of one of the machines was the girl. Sylvie's girl! Her bare arms wrapped around the shirtless man riding between her thighs. They were first. The second biker rode alone. She studied their strangers' faces as they circled her. They were the enemy, all of them. Laughing. The girl was laughing too, laughing like her mama did. Out in the middle of nowhere the girl had found these two men, some moth-musk about her drawing them (too soon!) to what? She shouted it: "What in God's—" They roared off without answering her, and the bucket of water tipped over, spilling its stain blood-dark on the red dust.

The dog went wild barking, leaping after them, snapping at the tires, and there was no calling him down. The bikers made a wide circuit of the churchyard, then roared straight across the graves, leaping the ditch and landing upright on the road again, heading off toward the reservoir.

Furious, she ran to her car, past the barking dog, this time leaving him behind, driving after them, horn blowing nonstop, to get back what was not theirs. She drove after them knowing what they did not know, that all the roads beyond that point dead-ended. She surprised them, swinging the Impala across their path, cutting them off; let them hit it! They stopped. She got out, breathing hard, and said, when she could, "She's underage." Just that. And put out her claiming hand with an authority that made the girl's arms drop from the man's insolent waist and her legs tremble.

"I was just riding," the girl said, not looking up.

Behind them the sun was heading on toward down. The long shadows of the pines drifted back and forth in the same breeze that puffed the distant sails on the lake. Dead limbs creaked and clashed overhead like the antlers of locked and furious beasts.

"Sheeeut," the lone rider said. "I told you." He braced with his muddy boot and leaned out from his machine to spit. The man the girl had been riding with had the invading sort of eyes the woman had spent her lifetime bolting doors against. She met him now, face to face.

"Right there, missy," her granny said, pointing behind her to the car.

The girl slid off the motorcycle and stood halfway between her choices. She started slightly at the poosh! as he popped another top and chugged the beer in one uptilting of his head. His eyes never left the woman's. When he was through, he tossed the can high, flipping it end over end. Before it hit the ground he had his pistol out and, firing once, winged it into the lake.

"Freaking lucky shot," the other one grudged.

"I don't need luck," he said. He sighted down the barrel of the gun at the woman's head. "POW!" he yelled, and when she recoiled, he laughed.

He swung around to the girl; he kept aiming the gun, here, there, high, low, all around. "Y'all settle it," he said, with a shrug.

The girl had to understand him then, had to know him, had to know 27 better. But still she hesitated. He kept looking at her, then away.

"She's fifteen," her granny said. "You can go to jail." 28

"You can go to hell," he said. 29

"Probably will," her granny told him. "I'll save you a seat by the fire." 30 She took the girl by the arm and drew her to the car; she backed up, swung around, and headed out the road toward the churchyard for her tools and dog. The whole way the girl said nothing, just hunched against the far door, staring hard-eyed out at the pines going past.

The woman finished watering the seed in, and collected her tools. As 31 she worked, she muttered, "It's your own kin buried here, you might have the decency to glance this way one time . . ." The girl was finger-tweezing her eyebrows in the side mirror. She didn't look around as the dog and the woman got in. Her granny shifted hard, sending the tools clattering in the trunk.

When they came to the main road, there were the men. Watching for 32 them. Waiting for them. They kicked their machines into life and followed, close, bumping them, slapping the old fenders, yelling. The girl gave a wild glance around at the one by her door and said, "Gran'ma?" and as he drew his pistol, "Gran'ma!" just as the gun nosed into the open window. She frantically cranked the glass up between her and the weapon, and her granny, seeing, spat, "Fool!" She never had been one to pray for peace or rain. She stamped the accelerator right to the floor.

The motorcycles caught up. Now she braked, hard, and swerved off the 33 road into an alley between the pines, not even wide enough for the school bus, just a fire scrape that came out a quarter mile from her own house, if she could get that far. She slewed on the pine straw, then righted, tearing along the dark tunnel through the woods. She had for the time being bested them; they were left behind. She was winning. Then she hit the wallow where the tadpoles were already five weeks old. The Chevy plowed in and stalled. When she got it cranked again, they were stuck. The tires spattered mud three feet up the near trunks as she tried to spin them out, to rock them out. Useless. "Get out and run!" she cried, but the trees were too close on the passenger side. The girl couldn't open her door. She wasted precious time having to crawl out under the steering wheel. The woman waited but the dog ran on.

They struggled through the dusky woods, their pace slowed by the 34 thick straw and vines. Overhead, in the last light, the martins were reeling free and sure after their prey.

"Why? Why?" the girl gasped, as they lunged down the old deer trail. 35 Behind them they could hear shots, and glass breaking as the men came to the bogged car. The woman kept on running, swatting their way clear through the shoulder-high weeds. They could see the Greer cottage, and made for it. But it was ivied-over, padlocked, the woodpile dry-rotting under its tarp, the electric meterbox empty on the pole. No help there.

The dog, excited, trotted on, yelping, his lips white-flecked. He scented the lake and headed that way, urging them on with thirsty yips. On the clay shore, treeless, deserted, at the utter limit of land, they stood defenseless, listening to the men coming on, between them and home. The woman pressed her hands to her mouth, stifling her cough. She was exhausted. She couldn't think.

"We can get under!" the girl cried suddenly, and pointed toward the Greers' dock, gap-planked, its walkway grounded on the mud. They splashed out to it, wading in, the woman grabbing up the telltale, tattletale dog in her arms. They waded out to the far end and ducked under. There was room between the foam floats for them to crouch neck-deep.

The dog wouldn't hush, even then; never had yet, and there wasn't time to teach him. When the woman realized that, she did what she had to do. She grabbed him whimpering; held him; held him under till the struggle ceased and the bubbles rose silver from his fur. They crouched there then, the two of them, submerged to the shoulders, feet unsteady on the slimed lake bed. They listened. The sky went from rose to ocher to violet in the cracks over their heads. The motorcycles had stopped now. In the silence there was the glissando of locusts, the dry crunch of boots on the flinty beach, their low man-talk drifting as they prowled back and forth. One of them struck a match.

"—they in these woods we could burn 'em out."

The wind carried their voices away into the pines. Some few words eddied back.

"—lippy old smartass do a little work on her knees besides praying—"

Laughter. It echoed off the deserted house. They were getting closer.

One of them strode directly out to the dock, walked on the planks over their heads. They could look up and see his boot soles. He was the one with the gun. He slapped a mosquito on his bare back and cursed. The carp, roused by the troubling of the waters, came nosing around the dock, guzzling and snorting. The girl and her granny held still, so still. The man fired his pistol into the shadows, and a wounded fish thrashed, dying. The man knelt and reached for it, chuffing out his beery breath. He belched. He pawed the lake for the dead fish, cursing as it floated out of reach. He shot it again, firing at it till it sank and the gun was empty. Cursed that too. He stood then and unzipped and relieved himself of some of the beer. They had to listen to that. To know that about him. To endure that, unprotesting.

Back and forth on shore the other one ranged, restless. He lit another cigarette. He coughed. He called, "Hey! They got away, man, that's all. Don't get your shorts in a wad. Let's go."

"Yeah." He finished. He zipped. He stumped back across the planks and leaped to shore, leaving the dock tilting amid widening ripples. Underneath, they waited.

The bike cranked. The other ratcheted, ratcheted, then coughed, 46 caught, roared. They circled, cut deep ruts, slung gravel, and went. Their roaring died away and away. Crickets resumed and a near frog bic-bic-bicked.

Under the dock, they waited a little longer to be sure. Then they 47 ducked below the water, scraped out from under the pontoon, and came up into free air, slogging toward shore. It had seemed warm enough in the water. Now they shivered. It was almost night. One streak of light still stood reflected on the darkening lake, drew itself thinner, narrowing into a final cancellation of day. A plane winked its way west.

The girl was trembling. She ran her hands down her arms and legs, 48 shedding water like a garment. She sighed, almost a sob. The woman held the dog in her arms; she dropped to her knees upon the random stones and murmured, private, haggard, "Oh, honey," three times, maybe all three times for the dog, maybe once for each of them. The girl waited, watching. Her granny rocked the dog like a baby, like a dead child, rocked slower and slower and was still.

"I'm sorry," the girl said then, avoiding the dog's inert, empty eye. 49

"It was him or you," her granny said, finally, looking up. Looking her 50 over. "Did they mess with you? With your britches? Did they?"

"No!" Then, quieter, "No, ma'am." 51

When the woman tried to stand up she staggered, lightheaded, clumsy 52 with the freight of the dog. "No, ma'am," she echoed, fending off the girl's "Let me." And she said again, "It was him or you. I know that. I'm not going to rub your face in it." They saw each other as well as they could in that failing light, in any light.

The woman started toward home, saying, "Around here, we bear our 53 own burdens." She led the way along the weedy shortcuts. The twilight bleached the dead limbs of the pines to bone. Insects sang in the thickets, silencing at their oncoming.

"We'll see about the car in the morning," the woman said. She bore her 54 armful toward her own moth-ridden dusk-to-dawn security light with that country grace she had always had when the earth was reliably progressing underfoot. The girl walked close behind her, exactly where *she* walked, matching her pace, matching her stride, close enough to put her hand forth (if the need arose) and touch her granny's back where the faded voile was clinging damp, the merest gauze between their wounds.

Questions for Study and Discussion

1. Describe the relationship between the grandmother and granddaughter. What problems are they experiencing? What is the source of those problems?

2. Where is the granddaughter's father? Her mother?

3. What was the relationship between the grandmother and her daughter, Sylvie, the girl's mother? Why is it important that we learn about that relationship?

4. What relationship does the grandmother have with her dog? Why is it important that Hood describe that relationship in some detail?

5. What does the grandmother know about the motorcyclists that the granddaughter does not suspect or care about?

6. What new relationship is established between the grandmother and granddaughter at the end of the story? What is your assessment of the appropriateness and effectiveness of the conclusion to the story? What significance is there in the fact that each of the main characters refers to the other as "ma'am" at the end of the story?

7. Why do you suppose that Hood did not give names to any of the characters except for the young girl's deceased mother?

8. What comments can you make about Hood's style in this story? About her skill as a storyteller?

Writing Topics

1. "How Far She Went" is, in part, a story about male aggressiveness, attempted violence, rape, and maybe even murder, certainly contemporary social issues. It is, as well, a story about love and protection. Indeed, in recommending Hood's writing to readers in the *West Coast Review of Books*, Randy S. Lavine said Hood "reaches to the core of human understanding." Use the story as a starting point for an essay in which you discuss the need for love, protection, and mutual concern in situations that are potentially threatening.

2. Write an essay in which you describe Hood's particular skills as a short story writer. You may find it helpful to review the material on the elements of the short story that appears in the introduction (pp. 1–35.)

8

The Individual and Society: Some Classic Statements

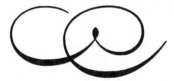

Talents are best nurtured in solitude; character is best formed in the stormy billows of the world.
—Johann Wolfgang von Goethe

Liberty lies in the hearts of men and women; when it dies there, no constitution, no law, no court can save it.
—Learned Hand

A social world does not become stable until its legal or customary rules can be understood as fragmentary and imperfect expressions of an imaginative scheme of human coexistence, rather than just as provisional truce lines in a brutal and amoral conflict.
—Roberto Mangabeira Unger

THOMAS JEFFERSON

In June 1776 the Continental Congress chose a committee of five to draft a justification for revolution. Benjamin Franklin, John Adams, and Thomas Jefferson were among its members. The committee in turn asked Jefferson to write a first draft. Born in 1743 in Albemarle County, Virginia, Jefferson was the youngest delegate to the Congress. He was, in time, to become a governor, secretary of state, and president before he died on July 4, 1826, but in 1776 he was known only as a talented lawyer out of William and Mary College with a gift for words. His draft was lightly revised by Adams and Franklin and amended during the Congress's debate, but it remains essentially the work not of a committee but of one man with the political insight, the vision, and the rhetorical skill to speak for his people.

The Declaration of Independence

When in the course of human events, it becomes necessary for one 1 people to dissolve the political bands which have connected them with another, and to assume among the Powers of the earth, the separate and equal station to which the Laws of Nature and of Nature's God entitle them, a decent respect to the opinions of mankind requires that they should declare the causes which impel them to the separation.

We hold these truths to be self-evident, that all men are created equal, 2 that they are endowed by their Creator with certain unalienable Rights, that among these are Life, Liberty and the pursuit of Happiness. That to secure these rights, Governments are instituted among Men deriving their just powers from the consent of the governed. That whenever any Form of Government becomes destructive of these ends, it is the Right of the People to alter or to abolish it, and to institute new Government, laying its foundation on such principles and organizing its powers in such form, as to them shall seem most likely to effect their Safety and Happiness. Prudence, indeed, will dictate that Governments long established should not be changed for light and transient causes; and accordingly all experience hath shown, that mankind are more disposed to suffer, while evils are sufferable, than to right themselves by abolishing the forms to which they are accustomed. But when a long train of abuses and usurpations pursuing invariably the same Object evinces a design to reduce them under absolute Despotism, it is their right, it is their duty, to throw off such government, and to provide new Guards for their future security. Such has been the patient sufferance of these Colonies; and such is now the necessity which constrains them to alter their former Systems of Government. The history of the present King of Great Britain is a history of repeated injuries and usurpations, all having in direct object the establishment of an absolute Tyranny over these States. To prove this, let Facts be submitted to a candid world.

He has refused his Assent to laws, the most wholesome and necessary   3
for the public good.

He has forbidden his Governors to pass Laws of immediate and pressing   4
importance, unless suspended in their operation till his Assent should be obtained; and when so suspended, he has utterly neglected to attend to them.

He has refused to pass other Laws for the accommodation of large   5
districts of people, unless those people would relinquish the right of Representation in the Legislature, a right inestimable to them and formidable to tyrants only.

He has called together legislative bodies at places unusual, uncomfort-   6
able, and distant from the depository of their Public Records, for the sole purpose of fatiguing them into compliance with his measures.

He has dissolved Representative Houses repeatedly, for opposing with   7
manly firmness his invasions on the rights of the people.

He has refused for a long time, after such dissolutions, to cause others   8
to be elected; whereby the Legislative Powers, incapable of Annihilation, have returned to the People at large for their exercise; the State remaining in the mean time exposed to all the dangers of invasion from without, and convulsions within.

He has endeavoured to prevent the population of these States; for that   9
purpose obstructing the Laws the Naturalization of Foreigners; refusing to pass others to encourage their migration hither, and raising the conditions of new Appropriations of Lands.

He has obstructed the Administration of Justice, by refusing his Assent   10
to Laws for establishing Judiciary Powers.

He has made Judges dependent on his Will alone, for the tenure of   11
their offices, and the amount and payment of their salaries.

He has erected a multitude of New Offices, and sent hither swarms of   12
Officers to harass our People, and eat out their substance.

He has kept among us, in time of peace, Standing Armies without the   13
Consent of our Legislature.

He has affected to render the Military independent of and superior to   14
the Civil Power.

He has combined with others to subject us to jurisdictions foreign to   15 our constitution, and unacknowledged by our laws; giving his Assent to their acts of pretended Legislation:

For quartering large bodies of armed troops among us: 16

For protecting them, by a mock Trial, from Punishment for any Murders which they should commit on the Inhabitants of these States: 17

For cutting off our Trade with all parts of the world: 18

For imposing Taxes on us without our Consent: 19

For depriving us in many cases, of the benefits of Trial by Jury: 20

For transporting us beyond Seas to be tried for pretended offenses: 21

For abolishing the free System of English Laws in a Neighbouring Province, establishing therein an Arbitrary government, and enlarging its boundaries so as to render it at once an example and fit instrument for introducing the same absolute rule into these Colonies: 22

For taking away our Charters, abolishing our most valuable Laws, and altering fundamentally the Forms of our Governments: 23

For suspending our own Legislatures, and declaring themselves invested with Power to legislate for us in all cases whatsoever. 24

He has abdicated Government here, by declaring us out of his Protection and waging War against us. 25

He has plundered our seas, ravaged our Coasts, burnt our towns and destroyed the Lives of our people. 26

He is at this time transporting large Armies of foreign Mercenaries to compleat works of death, desolation and tyranny, already begun with circumstances of Cruelty & perfidy scarcely paralleled in the most barbarous ages, and totally unworthy the Head of a civilized nation. 27

He has constrained our fellow Citizens taken Captive on the high Seas to bear Arms against their Country, to become the executioners of their friends and Brethren, or to fall themselves by their Hands. 28

He has excited domestic insurrections amongst us, and has endeavoured to bring on the inhabitants of our frontiers, the merciless Indian Savages, whose known rule of warfare, is an undistinguished destruction of all ages, sexes and conditions. 29

In every stage of these Oppressions We Have Petitioned for Redress in the most humble terms: Our repeated petitions have been answered only by repeated injury. A Prince, whose character is thus marked by every act which may define a Tyrant, is unfit to be the ruler of a free People. 30

Nor have We been wanting in attention to our British brethren. We have warned them from time to time of attempts by their legislature to extend an unwarrantable jurisdiction over us. We have reminded them of the circumstances of our emigration and settlement here. We have appealed to their native justice and magnanimity and we have conjured them by the ties of our common kindred to disavow these usurpations, which would inevitably interrupt our connections and correspondence. They too have been deaf to the voice of justice and of consanguinity. We must, therefore, acquiesce in 31 the necessity, which denounces our Separation, and hold them, as we hold the rest of mankind, Enemies in War, in Peace Friends.

We, therefore, the Representatives of the United States of America, in General Congress, Assembled, appealing to the Supreme Judge of the world for the rectitude of our intentions, do, in the Name, and by Authority of the good People of these Colonies, solemnly publish and declare, That these United Colonies are, and of Right ought to be Free and Independent States; that they are Absolved from all Allegiance to the British Crown, and that all political connection between them and the State of Great Britain, is and ought to be totally dissolved; and that as Free and Independent States, they have full power to levy War, conclude Peace, contract Alliances, establish Commerce, and to do all other Acts and Things which Independent States may of right do. And for the support of this Declaration, with a firm reliance on the protection of Divine Providence, we mutually pledge to each other our lives, our Fortunes and our sacred Honor.

Questions for Study and Discussion

1. According to the Declaration of Independence, what is the purpose of government? Are there other legitimate purposes that governments serve? If so, what are they?

2. What is the chief argument offered by the Declaration for "abolishing" English rule over the American colonies? How is that argument supported?

3. What argument does the Declaration make for overthrowing any unacceptable government? What assumptions underlie this argument? Where does sovereignty lie, according to the Declaration?

4. According to the Declaration, how did the colonists try to persuade the English king to rule more justly?

5. Is the language of the Declaration of Independence coolly reasonable or emotional, or does it change from one to the other? Give examples to support your answer.

Writing Topics

1. To some people the Declaration of Independence still accurately reflects America's political philosophy and way of life; to others it does not. What is your position? Discuss your analysis of the Declaration's contemporary relevance.

2. The adoption of the Declaration of Independence was, among other things, a matter of practical politics. Using library sources, research the deliberations of the Continental Congress and explain how and why the final version of the Declaration differs from Jefferson's first draft.

In 1845, at the age of twenty-eight, Henry David Thoreau built a cabin in the woods near Walden Pond and moved in. He wanted to live alone with nature and hoped to free his life from materialistic concerns. He stayed there for more than two years, an experience he later described in his greatest literary work, *Walden, or Life in the Woods* (1854).

Thoreau was born in 1817 in Concord, Massachusetts. After graduating from Harvard College, he worked as a schoolteacher, a house-painter, and a handyman—the latter for his mentor and friend, Ralph Waldo Emerson. Thoreau was always an activist, once going to jail rather than paying a poll tax to a government that made war with Mexico and supported slavery. This act of civil disobedience in protest of actions that he considered unjust is the subject of his essay "Civil Disobedience" (1849), which later inspired both Gandhi and Martin Luther King, Jr., in their nonviolent protests. Thoreau died in 1862.

Civil Disobedience

I heartily accept the motto, "That government is best which governs least;" and I should like to see it acted up to more rapidly and systematically. Carried out, it finally amounts to this, which also I believe—"That government is best which governs not at all;" and when men are prepared for it, that will be the kind of government which they will have. Government is at best but an expedient; but most governments are usually, and all governments are sometimes, inexpedient. The objections which have been brought against a standing army, and they are many and weighty, and deserve to prevail, may also at last be brought against a standing government. The standing army is only an arm of the standing government. The government itself, which is only the mode which the people have chosen to execute their will, is equally liable to be abused and perverted before the people can act through it. Witness the present Mexican war, the work of comparatively a few individuals using the standing government as their tool; for, in the outset, the people would not have consented to this measure.

This American government—what is it but a tradition, though a recent one, endeavoring to transmit itself unimpaired to posterity, but each instant losing some of its integrity? It has not the vitality and force of a single living man; for a single man can bend it to his will. It is a sort of wooden gun to the people themselves. But it is not the less necessary for this; for the people must have some complicated machinery or other, and hear its din, to satisfy that idea of government which they have. Governments show thus how successfully men can be imposed on, even impose on themselves, for their own advantage. It is excellent, we must all allow. Yet this government never of itself furthered any enterprise, but by the alacrity with which it got out of its way. *It* does not keep the country free. *It* does not settle the West. *It* does not educate. The character inherent in the American people has done all that has been accomplished; and it would have done somewhat more, if the government had not sometimes got in its way. For government is an expedient by which men would fain succeed in letting one another alone; and, as has been said, when it is most expedient, the governed are most let alone by it. Trade and commerce, if they were not made of india-rubber, would never manage to bounce over the obstacles which legislators are continually putting in their way; and, if one were to judge these men wholly by the effects of their actions and not partly by their intentions, they would deserve to be classed and punished with those mischievous persons who put obstructions on the railroads.

But, to speak practically and as a citizen, unlike those who call them- 3
selves no-government men, I ask for, not at once no government, but *at once* a better government. Let every man make known what kind of government would command his respect, and that will be one step toward obtaining it.

After all, the practical reason why, when the power is once in the 4
hands of the people, a majority are permitted, and for a long period con-tinue, to rule is not because they are most likely to be in the right, nor because this seems fairest to the minority, but because they are physically the strongest. But a government in which the majority rule in all cases cannot be based on justice, even as far as men understand it. Can there not be a government in which majorities do not virtually decide right and wrong, but conscience?—in which majorities decide only those questions to which the rule of expediency is applicable? Must the citizen ever for a moment, or in the last degree, resign his conscience to the legislator? Why has every man a conscience, then? I think that we should be men first, and subjects after-wards. It is not desirable to cultivate a respect for the law, so much as for the right. The only obligation which I have a right to assume is to do at any time what I think right. It is truly enough said that a corporation has no con-science; but a corporation of conscientious men is a corporation *with* a conscience. Law never made men a whit more just; and, by means of their respect for it, even the well-disposed are daily made the agents of injustice. A common and natural result of an undue respect for law is, that you may see a file of soldiers, colonel, captain, corporal, privates, powder-monkeys, and all, marching in admirable order over hill and dale to the wars, against their wills, ay, against their common sense and consciences, which makes it very steep marching indeed, and produces a palpitation of the heart. They have

no doubt that it is a damnable business in which they are concerned; they are all peaceably inclined. Now, what are they? Men at all? or small movable forts and magazines, at the service of some unscrupulous man in power? Visit the Navy-Yard, and behold a marine, such a man as an American government can make, or such as it can make a man with its black arts—a mere shadow and reminiscence of humanity, a man laid out alive and standing, and already, as one may say, buried under arms with funeral accompaniments, though it may be,—

Not a drum was heard, not a funeral note,
  As his corse to the rampart we hurried;
Not a soldier discharged his farewell shot
  O'er the grave where our hero was buried.[1]

    The mass of men serve the state thus, not as men mainly, but as   5 machines, with their bodies. They are the standing army, and the militia, jailers, constables, *posse comitatus*, etc. In most cases there is no free exercise whatever of the judgment or of the moral sense; but they put themselves on a level with wood and earth and stones; and wooden men can perhaps be manufactured that will serve the purpose as well. Such command no more respect than men of straw or a lump of dirt. They have the same sort of worth only as horses and dogs. Yet such as these even are commonly esteemed good citizens. Others—as most legislators, politicians, lawyers, ministers, and office-holders—serve the state chiefly with their heads; and, as they rarely make any moral distinctions, they are as likely to serve the devil, without *intending* it, as God. A very few—as heroes, patriots, martyrs, reformers in the great sense, and *men*—serve the state with their consciences also, and so necessarily resist it for the most part; and they are commonly treated as enemies by it. A wise man will only be useful as a man, and will not submit to be "clay," and "stop a hole to keep the wind away,"[2] but leave that office to his dust at least:—

I am too high-born to be propertied,
To be a secondary at control,
Or useful serving-man and instrument
To any sovereign state throughout the world.[3]

    He who gives himself entirely to his fellow-men appears to them useless   6 and selfish; but he who gives himself partially to them is pronounced a benefactor and philanthropist.

---

[1] Charles Wolfe, "The Burial of Sir John Moore at Corunna" (1817).

[2] *Hamlet*, V, i, ll. 236–37.

[3] *King John*, V, ii, ll. 79–82.

How does it become a man to behave toward this American govern-   7
ment today? I answer, that he cannot without disgrace be associated with it.
I cannot for an instant recognize that political organization as *my* government which is the *slave's* government also.

All men recognize the right of revolution; that is, the right to refuse   8
allegiance to, and to resist, the government, when its tyranny or its ineffi-
ciency are great and unendurable. But almost all say that such is not the case
now. But such was the case, they think, in the Revolution of '75. If one were
to tell me that this was a bad government because it taxed certain foreign
commodities brought to its ports, it is most probable that I should not make
an ado about it, for I can do without them. All machines have their friction;
and possibly this does enough good to counterbalance the evil. At any rate,
it is a great evil to make a stir about it. But when the friction comes to have
its machine, and oppression and robbery are organized, I say, let us not have
such a machine any longer. In other words, when a sixth of the population of
a nation which has undertaken to be the refuge of liberty are slaves, and a
whole country is unjustly overrun and conquered by a foreign army, and
subjected to military law, I think that it is not too soon for honest men to
rebel and revolutionize. What makes this duty the more urgent is the fact
that the country so overrun is not our own, but ours is the invading army.

Paley,[4] a common authority with many on moral questions, in his   9
chapter on the "Duty of Submission to Civil Government," resolves all civil
obligation into expediency; and he proceeds to say that "so long as the
interest of the whole society requires it, that is, so long as the established
government cannot be resisted or changed without public inconveniency, it
is the will of God . . . that the established government be obeyed—and no
longer. The principle being admitted, the justice of every particular case of
resistance is reduced to a computation of the quantity of the danger and
grievance on the one side, and of the probability and expense of redressing it
on the other." Of this, he says, every man shall judge for himself. But Paley
appears never to have contemplated those cases to which the rule of expediency does not apply, in which a people, as well as an individual, must do
justice, cost what it may. If I have unjustly wrested a plank from a drowning
man, I must restore it to him though I drown myself.[5] This, according to
Paley, would be inconvenient. But he that would save his life, in such a case,
shall lose it.[6] This people must cease to hold slaves, and to make war on
Mexico, though it cost them their existence as a people.

---

[4] Rev. William Paley, *Principles of Moral and Political Philosophy* (1785), a text Thoreau is
known to have studied at Harvard College.

[5] Cited by Cicero, *De Officiis*, III, a text Thoreau knew at college.

[6] Luke 9:24; Matthew 10:39.

In their practice, nations agree with Paley; but does any one think that   10
Massachusetts does exactly what is right at the present crisis?

A drab of state, a cloth-o'-silver slut,
To have her train borne up, and her soul trail in the dirt.[7]

Practically speaking, the opponents to a reform in Massachusetts are not a
hundred thousand politicians at the South, but a hundred thousand merchants and farmers here, who are more interested in commerce and agriculture than they are in humanity, and are not prepared to do justice to the
slave and to Mexico, *cost what it may.* I quarrel not with far-off foes, but with
those who, near at home, coöperate with, and do the bidding of, those far
away, and without whom the latter would be harmless. We are accustomed to
say, that the mass of men are unprepared; but improvement is slow, because
the few are not materially wiser or better than the many. It is not so important that many should be as good as you, as that there be some absolute
goodness somewhere; for that will leaven the whole lump.[8] There are thousands who are *in opinion* opposed to slavery and to the war, who yet in effect
do nothing to put an end to them; who, esteeming themselves children of
Washington and Franklin, sit down with their hands in their pockets, and
say that they know not what to do, and do nothing; who even postpone the
question of freedom to the question of free trade, and quietly read the prices-
current along with the latest advices from Mexico, after dinner, and, it may
be, fall asleep over them both. What is the price-current of an honest man
and patriot today? They hesitate, and they regret, and sometimes they petition; but they do nothing in earnest and with effect. They will wait, well
disposed, for others to remedy the evil, that they may no longer have it to
regret. At most, they give only a cheap vote, and a feeble countenance and
God-speed, to the right, as it goes by them. There are nine hundred and
ninety-nine patrons of virtue to one virtuous man. But it is easier to deal
with the real possessor of a thing than with the temporary guardian of it.

All voting is a sort of gaming, like checkers or backgammon, with a   11
slight moral tinge to it, a playing with right and wrong, with moral questions; and betting naturally accompanies it. The character of the votes is not
staked. I cast my vote, perchance, as I think right; but I am not vitally
concerned that that right should prevail. I am willing to leave it to the
majority. Its obligation, therefore, never exceeds that of expediency. Even
voting *for the right* is *doing* nothing for it. It is only expressing to men feebly
your desire that it should prevail. A wise man will not leave the right to the
mercy of chance, nor wish it to prevail through the power of the majority.

---

[7] The *Revenger's Tragedy,* a play published anonymously in 1607 and recently attributed to
Thomas Middleton.

[8] Corinthians 5:6.

There is but little virtue in the action of masses of men. When the majority shall at length vote for the abolition of slavery, it will be because they are indifferent to slavery, or because there is but little slavery left to be abolished by their vote. *They* will then be the only slaves. Only *his* vote can hasten the abolition of slavery who asserts his own freedom by his vote.

I hear of a convention to be held at Baltimore, or elsewhere, for the   12
selection of a candidate for the Presidency, made up chiefly of editors, and men who are politicians by profession; but I think, what is it to any independent, intelligent, and respectable man what decision they may come to? Shall we not have the advantage of his wisdom and honesty, nevertheless? Can we not count upon some independent votes? Are there not many individuals in the country who do not attend conventions? But no: I find that the respectable man, so called, has immediately drifted from his position, and despairs of his country, when his country has more reason to despair of him. He forthwith adopts one of the candidates thus selected as the only *available* one, thus proving that he is himself *available* for any purposes of the demagogue. His vote is of no more worth than that of any unprincipled foreigner or hireling native, who may have been bought. O for a man who is a *man*, and, as my neighbor says, has a bone in his back which you cannot pass your hand through! Our statistics are at fault: the population has been returned too large. How many *men* are there to a square thousand miles in this country? Hardly one. Does not America offer any inducement for men to settle here? The American has dwindled into an Odd Fellow— one who may be known by the development of his organ of gregariousness, and a manifest lack of intellect and cheerful self-reliance; whose first and chief concern, on coming into the world, is to see that the almshouses are in good repair; and, before yet he has lawfully donned the virile garb, to collect a fund for the support of the widows and orphans that may be; who, in short, ventures to live only by the aid of the Mutual Insurance company, which has promised to bury him decently.

It is not a man's duty, as a matter of course, to devote himself to the   13
eradication of any, even the most enormous, wrong; he may still properly have other concerns to engage him; but it is his duty, at least, to wash his hands of it, and, if he gives it no thought longer, not to give it practically his support. If I devote myself to other pursuits and contemplations, I must first see, at least, that I do not pursue them sitting upon another man's shoulders. I must get off him first, that he may pursue his contemplations too. See what gross inconsistency is tolerated. I have heard some of my townsmen say, "I should like to have them order me out to help put down an insurrection of the slaves, or to march to Mexico;—see if I would go"; and yet these very men have each, directly by their allegiance, and so indirectly, at least, by their money, furnished a substitute. The soldier is applauded who refuses to serve in an unjust war by those who do not refuse to sustain the unjust government which makes the war; is applauded by those whose own act and

authority he disregards and sets at naught; as if the state were penitent to that degree that it hired one to scourge it while it sinned, but not to that degree that it left off sinning for a moment. Thus, under the name of Order and Civil Government, we are all made at last to pay homage to and support our own meanness. After the first blush of sin comes its indifference; and from immoral it becomes, as it were, *un*moral, and not quite unnecessary to that life which we have made.

The broadest and most prevalent error requires the most disinterested virtue to sustain it. The slight reproach to which the virtue of patriotism is commonly liable, the noble are most likely to incur. Those who, while they disapprove of the character and measures of a government, yield to it their allegiance and support are undoubtedly its most conscientious supporters, and so frequently the most serious obstacles to reform. Some are petitioning the State to dissolve the Union, to disregard the requisitions of the President. Why do they not dissolve it themselves—the union between themselves and the State—and refuse to pay their quota into its treasury? Do not they stand in the same relation to the State that the State does to the Union? And have not the same reasons prevented the State from resisting the Union which have prevented them from resisting the State? 14

How can a man be satisfied to entertain an opinion merely, and enjoy it? Is there any enjoyment in it, if his opinion is that he is aggrieved? If you are cheated out of a single dollar by your neighbor, you do not rest satisfied with knowing that you are cheated, or with saying that you are cheated, or even with petitioning him to pay you your due; but you take effectual steps at once to obtain the full amount, and see that you are never cheated again. Action from principle, the perception and the performance of right, changes things and relations; it is essentially revolutionary, and does not consist wholly with anything which was. It not only divides States and churches, it divides families; ay, it divides the *individual*, separating the diabolical in him from the divine. 15

Unjust laws exist: shall we be content to obey them, or shall we endeavor to amend them, and obey them until we have succeeded, or shall we transgress them at once? Men generally, under such a government as this, think that they ought to wait until they have persuaded the majority to alter them. They think that, if they should resist, the remedy would be worse than the evil. But it is the fault of the government itself that the remedy *is* worse than the evil. *It* makes it worse. Why is it not more apt to anticipate and provide for reform? Why does it not cherish its wise minority? Why does it cry and resist before it is hurt? Why does it not encourage its citizens to be on the alert to point out its faults, and *do* better than it would have them? Why does it always crucify Christ, and excommunicate Copernicus and Luther, and pronounce Washington and Franklin rebels? 16

One would think, that a deliberate and practical denial of its authority was the only offence never contemplated by government; else, why has it not 17 assigned its definite, its suitable and proportionate, penalty? If a man who has no property refuses but once to earn nine shillings for the State, he is put in prison for a period unlimited by any law that I know, and determined only by the discretion of those who placed him there; but if he should steal ninety times nine shillings from the State, he is soon permitted to go at large again.

If the injustice is part of the necessary friction of the machine of government, let it go, let it go: perchance it will wear smoothly—certainly the machine will wear out. If the injustice has a spring, or a pulley, or a rope, or a crank, exclusively for itself, then perhaps you may consider whether the remedy will not be worse than the evil; but if it is of such a nature that it requires you to be the agent of injustice to another, then, I say, break the law. Let your life be a counter friction to stop the machine. What I have to do is to see, at any rate, that I do not lend myself to the wrong which I condemn. 18

As for adopting the ways which the State has provided for remedying the evil, I know not of such ways. They take too much time, and a man's life will be gone. I have other affairs to attend to. I came into this world, not chiefly to make this a good place to live in, but to live in it, be it good or bad. A man has not everything to do, but something; and because he cannot do *everything*, it is not necessary that he should do *something* wrong. It is not my business to be petitioning the Governor or the Legislature any more than it is theirs to petition me; and if they should not hear my petition, what should I do then? But in this case the State has provided no way: its very Constitution is the evil. This may seem to be harsh and stubborn and unconciliatory; but it is to treat with the utmost kindness and consideration the only spirit that can appreciate or deserves it. So is all change for the better, like birth and death, which convulse the body. 19

I do not hesitate to say, that those who call themselves Abolitionists should at once effectually withdraw their support, both in person and property, from the government of Massachusetts, and not wait till they constitute a majority of one, before they suffer the right to prevail through them. I think that it is enough if they have God on their side, without waiting for that other one. Moreover, any man more right than his neighbors constitutes a majority of one already. 20

I meet the American government, or its representative, the State government, directly, and face to face, once a year—no more—in the person of its tax-gatherer; this is the only mode in which a man situated as I am necessarily meets it; and it then says distinctly, Recognize me; and the simplest, the most effectual, and, in the present posture of affairs, the indispensablest mode of treating with it on this head, of expressing your little satisfaction with and love for it, is to deny it then. My civil neighbor, the tax-gatherer, is the very man I have to deal with—for it is, after all, with men and not with parchment that I quarrel—and he has voluntarily chosen to be an agent of the government. How shall he ever know well what he is 21 and does as an officer of the government, or as a man, until he is obliged to consider whether he shall treat me, his neighbor, for whom he has respect, as a neighbor and well-disposed man, or as a maniac and disturber of the peace, and see if he can get over this obstruction to his neighborliness without a ruder and more impetuous thought or speech corresponding with his action. I know this well, that if one thousand, if one hundred, if ten men whom I could name—if ten *honest* men only—ay, if *one* HONEST man, in this State of Massachusetts, *ceasing to hold slaves,* were actually to withdraw from this copartnership, and be locked up in the county jail therefore, it would be the abolition of slavery in America. For it matters not how small the beginning may seem to be; what is once well done is done forever. But we love better to talk about it; that we say is our mission. Reform keeps many scores of newspapers in its service, but not one man. If my esteemed neighbor, the State's ambassador,[9] who will devote his days to the settlement of the question of human rights in the Council Chamber, instead of being threatened with the prisons of Carolina, were to sit down the prisoner of Massachusetts, that State which is so anxious to foist the sin of slavery upon her sister— though at present she can discover only an act of inhospitality to be the ground of a quarrel with her—the Legislature would not wholly waive the subject the following winter.

Under a government which imprisons any unjustly, the true place for a   22 just man is also a prison. The proper place to-day, the only place which Massachusetts has provided for her freer and less desponding spirits, is in her prisons, to be put out and locked out of the State by her own act, as they have already put themselves out by their principles. It is there that the fugitive slave, and the Mexican prisoner on parole, and the Indian come to plead the wrongs of his race should find them; on that separate, but more free and honorable, ground, where the State places those who are not *with* her, but *against* her—the only house in a slave State in which a free man can abide with honor. If any think that their influence would be lost there, and their voices no longer afflict the ear of the State, that they would not be as an enemy within its walls, they do not know by how much truth is stronger than error, nor how much more eloquently and effectively he can combat injustice who has experienced a little in his own person. Cast your whole vote, not a strip of paper merely, but your whole influence. A minority is powerless while it conforms to the majority; it is not even a minority then; but it is irresistible when it clogs by its whole weight. If the alternative is to keep all just men in prison, or give up war and slavery, the State will not hesitate which to choose. If a thousand men were not to pay their tax-bills

---

9 In 1844, Samuel Hoar, the statesman of Concord, was sent to Charleston, South Carolina, on behalf of African-American seamen from Massachusetts threatened with arrest and slavery on entering the port, and was rudely expelled from Charleston.

this year, that would not be a violent and bloody measure, as it would be to pay them, and enable the State to commit violence and shed innocent blood. This is, in fact, the definition of a peaceable revolution, if any such is possible. If the tax-gatherer, or any public officer, asks me, as one has done, "But what shall I do?" my answer is, "If you really wish to do anything, resign your office." When the subject has refused allegiance, and the officer has resigned his office, then the revolution is accomplished. But even suppose blood should flow. Is there not a sort of blood shed when the conscience is wounded? Through this wound a man's real manhood and immortality flow out, and he bleeds to an everlasting death. I see this blood flowing now.

I have contemplated the imprisonment of the offender, rather than the   23 seizure of his goods—though both will serve the same purpose—because they who assert the purest right, and consequently are most dangerous to a corrupt State, commonly have not spent much time in accumulating property. To such the State renders comparatively small service, and a slight tax is wont to appear exorbitant, particularly if they are obliged to earn it by special labor with their hands. If there were one who lived wholly without the use of money, the State itself would hesitate to demand it of him. But the rich man—not to make any invidious comparison—is always sold to the institution which makes him rich. Absolutely speaking, the more money, the less virtue; for money comes between a man and his objects, and obtains them for him; and it was certainly no great virtue to obtain it. It puts to rest many questions which he would otherwise be taxed to answer; while the only new question which it puts is the hard but superfluous one, how to spend it. Thus his moral ground is taken from under his feet. The opportunities of living are diminished in proportion as what are called the "means" are increased. The best thing a man can do for his culture when he is rich is to endeavor to carry out those schemes which he entertained when he was poor. Christ answered the Herodians according to their condition. "Show me the tribute-money," said he;—and one took a penny out of his pocket;— if you use money which has the image of Caesar on it, and which he has made current and valuable, that is, *if you are men of the State*, and gladly enjoy the advantages of Caesar's government, then pay him back some of his own when he demands it. "Render therefore to Caesar that which is Caesar's, and to God those things which are God's"—leaving them no wiser than before as to which was which; for they did not wish to know.

When I converse with the freest of my neighbors, I perceive that,   24 whatever they may say about the magnitude and seriousness of the question, and their regard for the public tranquillity, the long and the short of the matter is, that they cannot spare the protection of the existing government, and they dread the consequences to their property and families of disobedience to it. For my own part, I should not like to think that I ever rely on the protection of the State. But, if I deny the authority of the State when it presents its tax-bill, it will soon take and waste all my property, and so harass me and my children without end. This is hard. This makes it impossible for a man to live honestly, and at the same time comfortably, in outward respects. It will not be worth the while to accumulate property; that would be sure to go again. You must hire or squat somewhere, and raise but a small crop, and eat that soon. You must live within yourself, and depend upon yourself always tucked up and ready for a start, and not have many affairs. A man may grow rich in Turkey even, if he will be in all respects a good subject of the Turkish government. Confucious said: "If a state is governed by the principles of reason, poverty and misery are subjects of shame; if a state is not governed by the principles of reason, riches and honors are the subjects of shame." No: until I want the protection of Massachusetts to be extended to me in some distant Southern port, where my liberty is endangered, or until I am bent solely on building up an estate at home by peaceful enterprise, I can afford to refuse allegiance to Massachusetts, and her right to my property and life. It costs me less in every sense to incur the penalty of disobedience to the State than it would to obey. I should feel as if I were worth less in that case.

Some years ago, the State met me in behalf of the Church, and com- 25 manded me to pay a certain sum toward the support of a clergyman whose preaching my father attended, but never I myself. "Pay," it said, "or be locked up in the jail." I declined to pay.[10] But, unfortunately, another man saw fit to pay it. I did not see why the schoolmaster should be taxed to support the priest, and not the priest the schoolmaster; for I was not the State's schoolmaster, but I supported myself by voluntary subscription. I did not see why the lyceum should not present its tax-bill, and have the State to back its demand, as well as the Church. However, at the request of the selectmen, I condescended to make some such statement as this in writing:—"Know all men by these presents, that I, Henry Thoreau, do not wish to be regarded as a member of any incorporated society which I have not joined." This I gave to the town clerk; and he has it. The State, having thus learned that I did not wish to be regarded as a member of that church, has never made a like demand on me since; though it said that it must adhere to its original presumption that time. If I had known how to name them, I should then have signed off in detail from all the societies which I never signed on to; but I did not know where to find a complete list.

I have paid no poll-tax for six years. I was put into a jail once on this 26 account, for one night; and, as I stood considering the walls of solid stone, two or three feet thick, the door of wood and iron, a foot thick, and the iron grating which strained the light, I could not help being struck with the foolishness of that institution which treated me as if I were mere flesh and blood and bones to be locked up. I wondered that it should have concluded

---

[10] Thoreau's first act on returning to Concord after leaving college was to "sign off" from the Church.

at length that this was the best use it could put me to, and had never thought to avail itself of my services in some way. I saw that, if there was a wall of stone between me and my townsmen, there was a still more difficult one to climb or break through before they could get to be as free as I was. I did not for a moment feel confined, and the walls seemed a great waste of stone and mortar. I felt as if I alone of all my townsmen had paid my tax. They plainly did not know how to treat me, but behaved like persons who are underbred. In every threat and in every compliment there was a blunder; for they thought that my chief desire was to stand on the other side of that stone wall. I could not but smile to see how industriously they locked the door on my meditations, which followed them out again without let or hindrance, and *they* were really all that was dangerous. As they could not reach me, they had resolved to punish my body; just as boys, if they cannot come at some person against whom they have a spite, will abuse his dog. I saw that the State was half-witted, that it was timid as a lone woman with her silver spoons, and that it did not know its friends from its foes, and I lost all my remaining respect for it, and pitied it.

Thus the State never intentionally confronts a man's sense, intellec- 27
tual or moral, but only his body, his senses. It is not armed with superior wit or honesty, but with superior physical strength. I was not born to be forced. I will breathe after my own fashion. Let us see who is the strongest. What force has a multitude? They only can force me who obey a higher law than I. They force me to become like themselves. I do not hear of *men* being forced to live this way or that by masses of men. What sort of life were that to live? When I meet a government which says to me, "Your money or your life," why should I be in haste to give it my money? It may be in a great strait, and not know what to do: I cannot help that. It must help itself; do as I do. It is not worth the while to snivel about it. I am not responsible for the successful working of the machinery of society. I am not the son of the engineer. I perceive that, when an acorn and a chestnut fall side by side, the one does not remain inert to make way for the other, but both obey their own laws, and spring and grow and flourish as best they can, till one, perchance, overshadows and destroys the other. If a plant cannot live according to its nature, it dies; and so a man.

The night in prison was novel and interesting enough. The prisoners in 28
their shirt-sleeves were enjoying a chat and the evening air in the doorway, when I entered. But the jailer said, "Come, boys, it is time to lock up"; and so they dispersed, and I heard the sound of their steps returning into the hollow apartments. My room-mate was introduced to me by the jailer as "a first-rate fellow and a clever man." When the door was locked, he showed me where to hang my hat, and how he managed matters there. The rooms were whitewashed once a month; and this one, at least, was the whitest, most simply furnished, and probably the neatest apartment in the town. He naturally wanted to know where I came from, and what brought me there;

and, when I had told him, I asked him in my turn how he came there, presuming him to be an honest man, of course; and, as the world goes, I believe he was. "Why," said he, "they accuse me of burning a barn; but I never did it." As near as I could discover, he had probably gone to bed in a barn when drunk, and smoked his pipe there; and so a barn was burnt. He had the reputation of being a clever man, had been there some three months waiting for his trial to come on, and would have to wait as much longer; but he was quite domesticated and contented, since he got his board for nothing; and thought that he was well treated.

He occupied one window, and I the other; and I saw that if one stayed there long, his principal business would be to look out the window. I had soon read all the tracts that were left there, and examined where former prisoners had broken out, and where a grate had been sawed off, and heard the history of the various occupants of that room; for I found that even here there was a history and a gossip which never circulated beyond the walls of the jail. Probably this is the only house in the town where verses are composed, which are afterward printed in a circular form, but not published. I was shown quite a long list of verses which were composed by some young men who had been detected in an attempt to escape, who avenged themselves by singing them. 29

I pumped my fellow-prisoner as dry as I could, for fear I should never see him again; but at length he showed me which was my bed, and left me to blow out the lamp. 30

It was like travelling into a far country, such as I had never expected to behold, to lie there for one night. It seemed to me that I never had heard the town clock strike before, nor the evening sounds of the village; for we slept with the windows open, which were inside the grating. It was to see my native village in the light of the Middle Ages, and our Concord was turned into a Rhine stream, and visions of knights and castles passed before me. They were the voices of old burghers that I heard in the streets. I was an involuntary spectator and auditor of whatever was done and said in the kitchen of the adjacent village inn—a wholly new and rare experience to me. It was a closer view of my native town. I was fairly inside of it. I never had seen its institutions before. This is one of its peculiar institutions; for it is a shire town. I began to comprehend what its inhabitants were about. 31

In the morning, our breakfasts were put through the hole in the door, in small oblong-square tin pans, made to fit, and holding a pint of chocolate, with brown bread, and an iron spoon. When they called for the vessels again, I was green enough to return what bread I had left; but my comrade seized it, and said that I should lay that up for lunch or dinner. Soon after he was let out to work at haying in a neighboring field, whither he went every day, and would not be back till noon; so he bade me good-day, saying that he doubted if he should see me again. 32

When I came out of prison—for some one interfered, and paid that 33 tax—I did not perceive that great changes had taken place on the common, such as he observed who went in a youth and emerged a tottering and gray-headed man; and yet a change had to my eyes come over the scene—the town, and State, and country—greater than any that mere time could effect. I saw yet more distinctly the State in which I lived. I saw to what extent the people among whom I lived could be trusted as good neighbors and friends; that their friendship was for summer weather only; that they did not greatly propose to do right; that they were a distinct race from me by their prejudices and superstitions, as the Chinamen and Malays are; that in their sacrifices to humanity they ran no risks, not even to their property; that after all they were not so noble but they treated the thief as he had treated them, and hoped, by a certain outward observance and a few prayers, and by walking in a particular straight though useless path from time to time, to save their souls. This may be to judge my neighbors harshly; for I believe that many of them are not aware that they have such an institution as the jail in their village.

It was formerly the custom in our village, when a poor debtor came out   34
of jail, for his acquaintances to salute him, looking through their fingers, which were crossed to represent the grating of a jail window, "How do ye do?" My neighbors did not thus salute me, but first looked at me, and then at one another, as if I had returned from a long journey. I was put into jail as I was going to the shoemaker's to get a shoe which was mended. When I was let out the next morning, I proceeded to finish my errand, and, having put on my mended shoe, joined a huckleberry party, who were impatient to put themselves under my conduct; and in half an hour—for the horse was soon tackled—was in the midst of a huckleberry field, on one of our highest hills, two miles off, and then the State was nowhere to be seen.

This is the whole history of "My Prisons."   35

I have never declined paying the highway tax, because I am as desirous   36
of being a good neighbor as I am of being a bad subject; and as for supporting schools, I am doing my part to educate my fellow-countrymen now. It is for no particular item in the tax-bill that I refuse to pay it. I simply wish to refuse allegiance to the State, to withdraw and stand aloof from it effectually. I do not care to trace the course of my dollar, if I could, till it buys a man or a musket to shoot one with—the dollar is innocent—but I am concerned to trace the effects of my allegiance. In fact, I quietly declare war with the State, after my fashion, though I will still make what use and get what advantage of her I can, as is usual in such cases.

If others pay the tax which is demanded of me, from a sympathy with   37
the State, they do but what they have already done in their own case, or rather they abet injustice to a great extent than the State requires. If they pay the tax from a mistaken interest in the individual taxed, to save his property, or prevent his going to jail, it is because they have not considered wisely how far they let their private feelings interfere with the public good.

This, then, is my position at present. But one cannot be too much on   38
his guard in such a case, lest his action be biased by obstinacy or an undue

regard for the opinions of men. Let him see that he does only what belongs to himself and to the hour.

I think sometimes, Why, this people mean well, they are only igno- 39
rant; they would do better if they knew how; why give your neighbors this pain to treat you as they are not inclined to? But I think again, This is no reason why I should do as they do, or permit others to suffer much greater pain of a different kind. Again, I sometimes say to myself, When many millions of men, without heat, without ill will, without personal feeling of any kind, demand of you a few shillings only, without the possibility, such is their constitution, of retracting or altering their present demand, and with-out the possibility, on your side, of appeal to any other millions, why expose yourself to this overwhelming brute force? You do not resist cold and hunger, the winds and the waves, thus obstinately; you quietly submit to a thousand similar necessities. You do not put your head into the fire. But just in proportion as I regard this as not wholly a brute force, but partly a human force, and consider that I have relations to those millions as to so many millions of men, and not of mere brute or inanimate things, I see that appeal is possible, first and instantaneously, from them to the Maker of them, and, secondly, from them to themselves. But if I put my head deliberately into the fire, there is no appeal to fire or to the Maker of fire, and I have only myself to blame. If I could convince myself that I have any right to be satisfied with men as they are, and to treat them accordingly, and not according, in some respects, to my requisitions and expectations of what they and I ought to be, then, like a good Mussulman and fatalist, I should endeavor to be satisfied with things as they are, and say it is the will of God. And, above all, there is this difference between resisting this and a purely brute or natural force, that I can resist this with some effect; but I cannot expect, like Orpheus, to change the nature of the rocks and trees and beasts.

I do not wish to quarrel with any man or nation. I do not wish to split 40
hairs, to make fine distinctions, or set myself up as better than my neighbors. I seek rather, I may say, even an excuse for conforming to the laws of the land. I am but too ready to conform to them. Indeed, I have reason to suspect myself on this head; and each year, as the tax-gatherer comes round, I find myself disposed to review the acts and positions of the general and State govern-ments, and the spirit of the people, to discover a pretext for conformity.

We must affect our country as our parents,
And if at any time we alienate
Our love or industry from doing it honor,
We must respect effects and teach the soul
Matter of conscience and religion,
And not desire of rule or benefit.[11]

---

[11] *The Revenger's Tragedy.*

I believe that the State will soon be able to take all my work of this sort out of my hands, and then I shall be no better a patriot than my fellow-countrymen. Seen from a lower point of view, the Constitution, with all its faults, is very good; the law and the courts are very respectable; even this State and this American government are, in many respects, very admirable, and rare things, to be thankful for, such as a great many have described them; but seen from a point of view a little higher, they are what I have described them; seen from a higher still, and the highest, who shall say what they are, or that they are worth looking at or thinking of at all?

However, the government does not concern me much, and I shall 41
bestow the fewest possible thoughts on it. It is not many moments that I live under a government, even in this world. If a man is thought-free, fancy-free, imagination-free, that which *is not* never for a long time appearing *to be* to him, unwise rulers or reformers cannot fatally interrupt him.

I know that most men think differently from myself; but those whose 42
lives are by profession devoted to the study of these or kindred subjects content me as little as any. Statesmen and legislators, standing so completely within the institution, never distinctly and nakedly behold it. They speak of moving society, but have no resting-place without it. They may be men of a certain experience and discrimination, and have no doubt invented ingenious and even useful systems, for which we sincerely thank them; but all their wit and usefulness lie within certain not very wide limits. They are wont to forget that the world is not governed by policy and expediency. Webster[12] never goes behind government, and so cannot speak with authority about it. His words are wisdom to those legislators who contemplate no essential reform in the existing government; but for thinkers, and those who legislate for all time, he never once glances at the subject. I know of those whose serene and wise speculations on this theme would soon reveal the limits of his mind's range and hospitality. Yet, compared with the cheap professions of most reformers, and the still cheaper wisdom and eloquence of politicians in general, his are almost the only sensible and valuable words, and we thank Heaven for him. Comparatively, he is always strong, original, and, above all, practical. Still, his quality is not wisdom, but prudence. The lawyer's truth is not Truth, but consistency or a consistent expediency. Truth is always in harmony with herself, and is not concerned chiefly to reveal the justice that may consist with wrong-doing. He well deserves to be called, as he has been called, the Defender of the Constitution. There are really no blows to be given by him but defensive ones. He is not a leader, but a follower. His leaders are the men of '87. "I have never made an effort," he says, "and never propose to make an effort; I have never countenanced an

---

[12] Daniel Webster (1782–1852), constitutional lawyer and orator from New Hampshire.

effort, and never mean to countenance an effort, to disturb the arrangement as originally made, by which the various States came into the Union." Still thinking of the sanction which the Constitution gives to slavery, he says, "Because it was a part of the original compact—let it stand." Notwithstanding his special acuteness and ability, he is unable to take a fact out of its merely political relations, and behold it as it lies absolutely to be disposed of by the intellect—what, for instance, it behooves a man to do here in America today with regard to slavery—but ventures, or is driven, to make such desperate answer as the following, while professing to speak absolutely and as a private man—from which what new and similar code of social duties might be inferred? "The manner," says he, "in which the governments of those States where slavery exists are to regulate it is for their own consideration, under their responsibility to their constituents, to the general laws of propriety, humanity, and justice, and to God. Associations formed elsewhere, springing from a feeling of humanity, or any other cause, have nothing whatever to do with it. They have never received any encouragement from me, and they never will."[13]

They who know of no purer sources of truth, who have traced up its   43
stream no higher, stand, and wisely stand, by the Bible and the Constitution, and drink at it there with reverence and humility; but they who behold where it comes trickling into this lake or that pool, gird up their loins once more, and continue their pilgrimage toward its fountainhead.

No man with a genius for legislation has appeared in America. They   44
are rare in the history of the world. There are orators, politicians, and eloquent men, by the thousand; but the speaker has not yet opened his mouth to speak who is capable of settling the much-vexed questions of the day. We love eloquence for its own sake, and not for any truth which it may utter, or any heroism it may inspire. Our legislators have not yet learned the comparative value of free trade and of freedom, of union, and of rectitude, to a nation. They have no genius or talent for comparatively humble questions of taxation and finance, commerce and manufactures and agriculture. If we were left solely to the wordy wit of legislators in Congress for our guidance, uncorrected by the seasonable experience and the effectual complaints of the people, America would not long retain her rank among the nations. For eighteen hundred years, though perchance I have no right to say it, the New Testament has been written; yet where is the legislator who has wisdom and practical talent enough to avail himself of the light which it sheds on the science of legislation?

The authority of government, even such as I am willing to submit to—   45
for I will cheerfully obey those who know and can do better than I, and in many things even those who neither know nor can do so well—is still an

---

[13] These extracts have been inserted since the lecture was read. [Author's note.]

impure one; to be strictly just, it must have the sanction and consent of the governed. It can have no pure right over my person and property but what I concede to it. The progress from an absolute to a limited monarchy, from a limited monarchy to a democracy, is a progress toward a true respect for the individual. Even the Chinese philosopher was wise enough to regard the individual as the basis of the empire. Is a democracy, such as we know it, the last improvement possible in government? Is it not possible to take a step further towards recognizing and organizing the rights of man? There will never be a really free and enlightened State until the State comes to recognize the individual as a higher and independent power, from which all its own power and authority are derived, and treats him accordingly. I please myself with imagining a State at least which can afford to be just to all men, and to treat the individual with respect as a neighbor; which even would not think it inconsistent with its own repose if a few were to live aloof from it, not meddling with it, nor embraced by it, who fulfilled all the duties of neighbors and fellow-men. A State which bore this kind of fruit, and suffered it to drop off as fast as it ripened, would prepare the way for a still more perfect and glorious State, which also I have imagined, but not yet anywhere seen.

Questions for Study and Discussion

1. What, according to Thoreau, is the purpose of government? What does he believe government should do? What does he think government can do? What does he believe government can't do?

2. Why was Thoreau jailed? Even though jailed, why did he consider himself free?

3. What, according to Thoreau, should people do about laws they consider unjust? What other alternatives are available? Do governments have a conscience? Should they have a conscience?

4. What is Thoreau's tone in this essay? Who is his audience? What is his attitude toward his audience?

5. What is Thoreau's purpose in this essay? Is he merely trying to rationalize his own behavior or does he have a deeper purpose?

6. On what grounds does Thoreau find fault with Daniel Webster? Do you agree with his assessment?

7. What types of evidence does Thoreau use both to support and to document his claims?

Writing Topics

1. Thoreau wrote, "Under a government which imprisons any unjustly, the true place for a just man is also a prison." Using examples from recent history, argue for or against the validity of Thoreau's statement.

2. Write an essay in which you attempt to reconcile individual conscience with majority rule.

3. Read "Letter from Birmingham Jail" by Martin Luther King, Jr. (pp. 591–604), and write an essay in which you discuss the influences of Thoreau's "Civil Disobedience" on King's thinking.

ELIZABETH CADY STANTON

Elizabeth Cady Stanton (1815–1902), American reformer and leader of the women's rights movement, was born in Johnstown, New York. She was admitted to the Johnstown Academy, an all-male institution, by special arrangement. Stanton excelled in Greek and went on to study at the Emma Willard Academy in Troy, New York, graduating in 1832. Emma Willard was the best school Stanton could attend; all other degree-granting institutions at the time excluded women. After college Stanton studied law with her father, but again, because of her sex, was not able to gain admission to the bar.

Influenced by the legal restrictions placed upon women and the discrimination shown against them, Stanton also showed early interest in the temperance and antislavery movements. In 1840 she married Henry Brewster Stanton, an abolitionist and journalist, but in a not uncharacteristic fashion refused to "obey" him or be referred to as Mrs. Stanton. After a brief period in which the couple lived in Boston, they moved to Seneca Falls, New York, where in July of 1848 the Seneca Falls Convention, which she helped to organize, was held. At the convention, generally regarded as the beginning of the women's movement, Elizabeth Cady Stanton read her "Declaration of Sentiments," a list of grievances against existing laws and customs that restricted the rights of all women. Because of her pioneering work and tireless efforts on behalf of women, Stanton was elected president of the National American Woman Suffrage Association in 1890.

Declaration of Sentiments and Resolutions

Adopted by the Seneca Falls Convention,
July 19–20, 1848

When, in the course of human events, it becomes necessary for one 1 portion of the family of man to assume among the people of the earth a position different from that which they have hitherto occupied, but one to which the laws of nature and of nature's God entitle them, a decent respect to the opinions of mankind requires that they should declare the causes that impel them to such a course.

We hold these truths to be self-evident: that all men and women are 2 created equal; that they are endowed by their Creator with certain inalienable rights; that among these are life, liberty, and the pursuit of happiness; that to secure these rights governments are instituted, deriving their just powers from the consent of the governed. Whenever any form of government becomes destructive of these ends, it is the right of those who suffer from it to refuse allegiance to it, and to insist upon the institution of a new government, laying its foundation on such principles, and organizing its powers in such form, as to them shall seem most likely to effect their safety and happiness. Prudence, indeed, will dictate that governments long established should not be changed for light and transient causes; and accordingly all experience hath shown that mankind are more disposed to suffer, while evils are sufferable, than to right themselves by abolishing the forms to which they are accustomed. But when a long train of abuses and usurpations, pursuing invariably the same object, evinces a design to reduce them under absolute despotism, it is their duty to throw off such government, and to provide new guards for their future security. Such has been the patient sufferance of the women under this government, and such is now the necessity which constrains them to demand the equal station to which they are entitled.

    The history of mankind is a history of repeated injuries and usurpations   3
on the part of man toward woman, having in direct object the establishment of an absolute tyranny over her. To prove this, let facts be submitted to a candid world.

    He has never permitted her to exercise her inalienable right to the   4
elective franchise.

    He has compelled her to submit to laws, in the formation of which she   5
had no voice.

    He has withheld from her rights which are given to the most ignorant   6
and degraded men—both natives and foreigners.

    Having deprived her of this first right of a citizen, the elective fran-   7
chise, thereby leaving her without representation in the halls of legislation, he has oppressed her on all sides.

    He has made her, if married, in the eye of the law, civilly dead.   8

    He has taken from her all rights in property, even to the wages she   9
earns.

    He has made her, morally, an irresponsible being, as she can commit   10
many crimes with impunity, provided they be done in the presence of her husband. In the covenant of marriage, she is compelled to promise obedience to her husband, he becoming to all intents and purposes, her master— the law giving him the power to deprive her of her liberty, and to administer chastisement.

    He has so framed the laws of divorce, as to what shall be the proper   11
causes, and in case of separation, to whom the guardianship of the children shall be given, as to be wholly regardless of the happiness of women—the law, in all cases, going upon a false supposition of the supremacy of man, and giving all power into his hands.

    After depriving her of all rights as a married woman, if single, and the   12
owner of property, he has taxed her to support a government which recognizes her only when her property can be made profitable to it.

    He has monopolized nearly all the profitable employments, and from   13 those she is permitted to follow, she receives but a scanty remuneration. He closes against her all the avenues to wealth and distinction which he considers most honorable to himself. As a teacher of theology, medicine, or law, she is not known.

He has denied her the facilities for obtaining a thorough education, all colleges being closed against her. 14

He allows her in Church, as well as State, but a subordinate position, claiming Apostolic authority for her exclusion from the ministry, and, with some exceptions, from any public participation in the affairs of the Church. 15

He has created a false public sentiment by giving to the world a different code of morals for men and women, by which moral delinquencies which exclude women from society, are not only tolerated, but deemed of little account in man. 16

He has usurped the prerogative of Jehovah himself, claiming it as his right to assign for her a sphere of action, when that belongs to her conscience and to her God. 17

He has endeavored, in every way that he could, to destroy her confidence in her own powers, to lessen her self-respect, and to make her willing to lead a dependent and abject life. 18

Now, in view of this entire disfranchisement of one-half the people of this country, their social and religious degradation—in view of the unjust laws above mentioned, and because women do feel themselves aggrieved, oppressed, and fraudulently deprived of their most sacred rights, we insist that they have immediate admission to all the rights and privileges which belong to them as citizens of the United States. 19

In entering upon the great work before us, we anticipate no small amount of misconception, misrepresentation, and ridicule; but we shall use every instrumentality within our power to effect our object. We shall employ agents, circulate tracts, petition the State and National legislatures, and endeavor to enlist the pulpit and the press in our behalf. We hope this Convention will be followed by a series of Conventions embracing every part of the country. 20

[The following resolutions were discussed by Lucretia Mott, Thomas and Mary Ann McClintock, Amy Post, Catharine A. F. Stebbins, and others, and were adopted:] 21

WHEREAS, the great precept of nature is conceded to be, that "man shall pursue his own true and substantial happiness." Blackstone[1] in his Commen- 22

---

[1] Sir William Blackstone (1723–1780): The most influential of English scholars of the law. His *Commentaries of the Laws of England* (4 vols., 1765–1769) form the basis of the study of law in England.

taries remarks, that this law of Nature being coeval[2] with mankind, and dictated by God himself, is of course superior in obligation to any other. It is binding over all the globe, in all countries and at all times; no human laws are of any validity if contrary to this, and such of them as are valid, derive all their force, and all their validity, and all their authority, mediately and immediately, from this original; therefore,

Resolved, That such laws as conflict, in any way, with the true and 23
substantial happiness of women, are contrary to the great precept of nature and of no validity, for this is "superior in obligation to any other."

Resolved, That all laws which prevent women from occupying such a 24
station in society as her conscience shall dictate, or which place her in a position inferior to that of man, are contrary to the great precept of nature, and therefore of no force or authority.

Resolved, That woman is man's equal—was intended to be so by the 25
Creator, and the highest good of the race demands that she should be recognized as such.

Resolved, That the women of this country ought to be enlightened in 26
regard to the laws under which they live, that they may no longer publish their degradation by declaring themselves satisfied with their present position, nor their ignorance, by asserting that they have all the rights they want.

Resolved, That inasmuch as man, while claiming for himself intellec- 27
tual superiority, does accord to woman moral superiority, it is preeminently his duty to encourage her to speak and teach, as she has an opportunity, in all religious assemblies.

Resolved, That the same amount of virtue, delicacy, and refinement of 28
behavior that is required of woman in the social state, should also be required of man, and the same transgressions should be visited with equal severity on both man and woman.

Resolved, That the objection of indelicacy and impropriety, which is so 29
often brought against woman when she addresses a public audience, comes with a very ill-grace from those who encourage, by their attendance, her appearance on the stage, in the concert, or in feats of the circus.

Resolved, That woman has too long rested satisfied in the circumscribed 30
limits which corrupt customs and a perverted application of the Scriptures have marked out for her, and that it is time she should move in the enlarged sphere which her great Creator has assigned her.

Resolved, That it is the duty of the women of this country to secure to 31
themselves their sacred right to the elective franchise.

Resolved, That the equality of human rights results necessarily from the 32
fact of the identity of the race in capabilities and responsibilities.

---

[2] Coeval: existing simultaneously.

Resolved, therefore, That, being invested by the Creator with the same   33
capabilities, and the same consciousness of responsibility for their exercise, it
is demonstrably the right and duty of woman, equally with man, to promote
every righteous cause by every righteous means; and especially in regard to
the great subjects of morals and religion, it is self-evidently her right to
participate with her brother in teaching them, both in private and in public,
by writing and by speaking, by any instrumentalities proper to be used, and
in any assemblies proper to be held; and this being a self-evident truth
growing out of the divinely implanted principles of human nature, any
custom or authority adverse to it, whether modern or wearing the hoary
sanction of antiquity, is to be regarded as a self-evident falsehood, and at war
with mankind.

[At the last session Lucretia Mott[3] offered and spoke to the following   34
resolution:]

Resolved, That the speedy success of our cause depends upon the zeal-   35
ous and untiring efforts of both men and women, for the overthrow of the
monopoly of the pulpit, and for the securing to women an equal participation with men in the various trades, professions, and commerce.

Questions for Study and Discussion

1. The opening paragraphs of the Seneca Falls declaration closely parallel
those of the Declaration of Independence. Why do you suppose Stanton chose to
start in this manner?
2. What is a parody? Is Stanton's essay a parody of the Declaration of
Independence? Why or why not?
3. What is it that Elizabeth Cady Stanton and the other women at the
Seneca Falls Convention want?
4. What is the "elective franchise"? Why is it so fundamental to Stanton's
argument?
5. What does Stanton mean when she says, "He has made her, if married,
in the eye of the law, civilly dead"?
6. In paragraphs 4 through 18 Stanton catalogs the abuses women suffer.
Who is the "He" referred to in each of the statements? What is the rhetorical
effect of listing these abuses and starting each one with similar phrasing?
7. At what audience is Stanton's declaration aimed? What in the declaration itself led you to this conclusion?

---

[3] Lucretia Mott (1793–1880): One of the founders of the 1848 convention at which these
resolutions were presented. She is one of the earliest and most important of the feminists
who struggled to proclaim their rights. She was also a prominent abolitionist.

8. What is the function of the resolutions that conclude the declaration? What would have been gained or lost if Stanton had concluded the declaration with paragraph 20?

9. Is there anything in the style, tone, or voice of this document that would lead you to call it "feminine" or "female"? Explain.

Writing Topics

1. Write a report updating Stanton's declaration. What complaints have been resolved? Which still need to be redressed? What new complaints have been voiced by women in the last twenty years?

2. Write an essay in which you compare and contrast the Declaration of Independence with Stanton's declaration. You should consider such things as purpose, audience, and style.

PRETTY SHIELD

Pretty Shield, a wise woman of the Crow tribe, gave this eyewitness account of a Crow–Lacota battle to her biographer, Frank B. Linderman. Pretty Shield's biography was published in 1932. This story was most recently republished in *Spider Woman's Granddaughters: Tradition Tales and Contemporary Writing by Native American Women* (1989), an anthology compiled by Paula Gunn Allen.

The following text is Linderman's translation of Pretty Shield's story.

A Woman's Fight

Once, when I was eight years old, we moved our village from The-mountain-lion's-lodge [Pompey's Pillar] to the place where the white man's town of Huntley now stands. There were not many of us in this band. Sixteen men were with us when the women began to set up their lodges, and one man named Covered-with-grass was sent out as a wolf. I could see him on the hill when my mother was setting up her lodge-poles. I was dragging the poles of my play-lodge to a nice place that I had selected when I saw Covered-with-grass, the wolf on the hill, signal, "The enemy is coming." 1

Instantly two men leaped upon the backs of horses, their war-horses, that were always kept tied near lodges, and rode out on the plains to drive the other horses into camp. 2

There was great excitement, much running about by the women, who left their lodges just as they happened to be when the signal came. Some of the lodges had but a few poles up. Others, whose owners were quicker, had their lodge-skins tied, hanging loosely from the skin-poles. 3

Men, watching the hills, stationed themselves, one between every two lodges. Mothers, piling packs and parfleches into breast-works, called their children; and horses whinnied. Then I saw the horses that had been out on 4

588

the plains coming fast, their hoofs making a great noise and much dust. I must get out of the way.

Dragging my poles, a load beneath each arm, I ran between two lodges 5 whose lodge-skins were flapping in the wind, my own little lodge yet on my back. In came the horses, more than a hundred, sweeping into the camp between two lodges that were far apart, too far apart, I thought. And this thought gave me an idea. Why not close that wide gap between those two lodges? Why not set up my little lodge between the two big ones, and shut this wide place up?

While yet the horses were running around within the circle of the 6 camp I dragged my poles to the spot, and quickly pitched my lodge there. I heard my mother calling me. I had to work very fast to shut up that wide place, believing that my little lodge would keep our horses from getting out, and the Lacota from getting in; but I did not finish pegging down my lodge-skin, not quite. Corn-woman found me. "Ho! Ho!" she cried out, "here is a brave little woman! She has shut the wide gap with her lodge. Ho! Ho!"

But just the same she picked me up in her arms and carried me to my 7 mother, as though I were a baby. Corn-woman told this story every year until she died.

Now I shall have to tell you about the fighting, a little, because it was a 8 woman's fight. A woman won it. The men never tell about it. They do not like to hear about it, but I am going to tell you what happened. I was there to see. And my eyes were good, too. [. . .]

Yes [. . .] a woman won that fight, and the men never tell about it. 9 There was shooting by the time my play-lodge was pitched. A Lacota bullet struck one of its poles, and whined. Arrows were coming among the lodges, and bullets, when Corn-woman carried me to my mother, who made me lie down behind a pack. I saw what went on there.

Several horses were wounded and were screaming with their pain. One 10 of them fell down near my mother's lodge that was not yet half pitched. Lying there behind that pack I did not cover my eyes. I was looking all the time, and listening to everything. I saw Strikes-two, a woman sixty years old, riding around the camp on a gray horse. She carried only her root-digger, and she was singing her medicine-song, as though Lacota bullets and arrows were not flying around her. I heard her say, "Now all of you sing, 'They are whipped. They are running away,' and keep singing these words until I come back."

When the men and even the women began to sing as Strikes-two told 11 them, she rode out straight at the Lacota, waving her root-digger and singing that song. I *saw* her, I *heard* her, and my heart swelled, because she was a woman.

The Lacota, afraid of her medicine, turned and ran away. The fight was 12 won, and by a woman.

Questions for Study and Discussion

1. Pretty Shield's narrative consists of two separate but related stories. In the first she tells of how she "shut the wide gap with her lodge." Although Pretty Shield never tells us the reason, why do you think "Corn-woman told this story every year until she died"? How is this story related to the one about Strikes-two that follows?

2. What is Pretty Shield's purpose in telling this story? What is her own role in the incident?

3. From the context of the story, what do you think the expression "sent out as a wolf" means?

4. Why do you suppose Pretty Shield tells us that she "was there to see"? Why did she feel the need to add, "And my eyes were good, too"?

5. How was the old woman Strikes-two able to drive away the Lacota? Why do you suppose the Crow men are unwilling to tell of her success?

6. What does Pretty Shield mean when she says, "I *saw* her, I *heard* her, and my heart swelled, because she was a woman"?

7. From what Pretty Shield tells us in her story, how would you describe the relationship between men and women in Crow society?

Writing Topics

1. What came to mind when you first read Pretty Shield's title, "A Woman's Fight"? How do you feel about women fighting? How are fighting women often portrayed in America? Write an essay in which you explore the idea of women and fighting. Is it appropriate behavior for women in America? Should the question of appropriateness even be raised? Why, or why not? Why do you suppose so many Americans have trouble with the idea of women in combat?

2. Have you ever witnessed a heroic act? If so, what happened? Who was the hero? What effect did this person's deed have on you? Do you believe that it is important for people, especially young people, to witness, hear about, or read about heroic acts?

3. Madeleine Kunin, deputy secretary of education in the Clinton administration, has said, "Women have to tell their stories. They have to tell about the journey—the obstacles, the triumphs, the defeats. If you don't describe that, nobody else can follow it or learn from it." Write an essay in which you examine the significance for later generations of stories like Pretty Shield's.

MARTIN LUTHER KING, JR.

Martin Luther King, Jr., was born in 1929 in Atlanta, Georgia. The son of a Baptist minister, he was himself ordained at the age of eighteen and went on to study at Morehouse College, Crozer Theological Seminary, Boston University, and Chicago Theological Seminary. He first came to prominence in 1955, in Montgomery, Alabama, when he led a successful boycott against the city's segregated bus system. As the first president of the Southern Christian Leadership Conference, King promoted a policy of massive but nonviolent resistance to racial injustice, and in 1964 he was awarded the Nobel Peace Prize. He was assassinated in Memphis, Tennessee, in 1968.

Dr. King dated his landmark letter from Birmingham Jail April 16, 1963. He appended the following note to the published version:

> This response to a published statement by eight fellow clergymen from Alabama (Bishop C. C. J. Carpenter, Bishop Joseph A. Durick, Rabbi Hilton L. Grafman, Bishop Paul Hardin, Bishop Holan B. Harmon, the Reverend George M. Murray, the Reverend Edward V. Ramage and the Reverend Earl Stallings) was composed under somewhat constricting circumstances. Begun on the margins of the newspaper in which the statement appeared while I was in jail, the letter was continued on scraps of writing paper supplied by a friendly Negro trusty, and concluded on a pad my attorneys were eventually permitted to leave me. Although the text remains in substance unaltered, I have indulged in the author's prerogative of polishing it for publication.

Letter from Birmingham Jail

My Dear Fellow Clergymen:

While confined here in the Birmingham city jail, I came across your recent statement calling my present activities "unwise and untimely." Seldom do I pause to answer criticism of my work and ideas. If I sought to answer all criticisms that cross my desk, my secretaries would have little time for anything other than such correspondence in the course of the day, and I would have no time for constructive work. But since I feel that you are men of genuine good will and that your criticisms are sincerely set forth, I want to try to answer your statement in what I hope will be patient and reasonable terms.

I think I should indicate why I am here in Birmingham, since you have been influenced by the view which argues against "outsiders coming in." I have the honor of serving as president of the Southern Christian Leadership Conference, an organization operating in every southern state, with headquarters in Atlanta, Georgia. We have some eighty-five affiliated organizations across the South, and one of them is the Alabama Christian Movement for Human Rights. Frequently we share staff, educational, and financial resources with our affiliates. Several months ago the affiliate here in Birmingham asked us to be on call to engage in a nonviolent direct-action program if such were deemed necessary. We readily consented, and when the hour came we lived up to our promise. So I, along with several members of my staff, am here because I was invited here. I am here because I have organizational ties here.

But more basically, I am in Birmingham because injustice is here. Just as the prophets of the eighth century B.C. left their villages and carried their "thus saith the Lord" far beyond the boundaries of their home towns, and just as the Apostle Paul left his village of Tarsus and carried the gospel of Jesus Christ to the far corners of the Greco-Roman world, so am I compelled to carry the gospel of freedom beyond my own home town. Like Paul, I must constantly respond to the Macedonian call for aid. 3

Moreover, I am cognizant of the interrelatedness of all communities and states. I cannot sit idly by in Atlanta and not be concerned about what happens in Birmingham. Injustice anywhere is a threat to justice everywhere. We are caught in an inescapable network of mutuality, tied in a single garment of destiny. Whatever affects one directly, affects all indirectly. Never again can we afford to live with the narrow, provincial, "outside agitator" idea. Anyone who lives inside the United States can never be considered an outsider anywhere within its bounds. 4

You deplore the demonstrations taking place in Birmingham. But your statement, I am sorry to say, fails to express a similar concern for the conditions that brought about the demonstrations. I am sure that none of you would want to rest content with the superficial kind of social analysis that deals merely with effects and does not grapple with underlying causes. It is unfortunate that demonstrations are taking place in Birmingham, but it is even more unfortunate that the city's white power structure left the Negro community with no alternative. 5

In any nonviolent campaign there are four basic steps: collection of the facts to determine whether injustices exist; negotiation; self-purification; and direct action. We have gone through all these steps in Birmingham. There can be no gainsaying the fact that racial injustice engulfs this community. Birmingham is probably the most thoroughly segregated city in the United States. Its ugly record of brutality is widely known. Negroes have experienced grossly unjust treatment in courts. There have been more unsolved bombings of Negro homes and churches in Birmingham than in any other city in the nation. These are the hard brutal facts of the case. On the basis of these conditions, Negro leaders sought to negotiate with the city fathers. But the latter consistently refused to engage in good-faith negotiation. 6

Then, last September, came the opportunity to talk with leaders of 7

Birmingham's economic community. In the course of the negotiations, certain promises were made by the merchants—for example, to remove the stores' humiliating racial signs. On the basis of these promises, the Reverend Fred Shuttlesworth and the leaders of the Alabama Christian Movement for Human Rights agreed to a moratorium on all demonstrations. As the weeks and months went by, we realized that we were the victims of a broken promise. A few signs, briefly removed, returned; the others remained.

As in so many past experiences, our hopes had been blasted, and the   8
shadow of deep disappointment settled upon us. We had no alternative except to prepare for direct action, whereby we would present our very bodies as means of laying our case before the conscience of the local and the national community. Mindful of the difficulties involved, we decided to undertake a process of self-purification. We began a series of workshops on nonviolence, and we repeatedly asked ourselves: "Are you able to accept blows without retaliating?" "Are you able to endure the ordeal of jail?" We decided to schedule our direct-action program for the Easter season, realizing that except for Christmas, this is the main shopping period of the year. Knowing that a strong economic-withdrawal program would be the by-product of direct action, we felt that this would be the best time to bring pressure to bear on the merchants for the needed change.

Then it occurred to us that Birmingham's mayoral election was coming   9
up in March, and we speedily decided to postpone action until after election day. When we discovered that the Commissioner of Public Safety, Eugene "Bull" Connor, had piled up enough votes to be in the run-off, we decided again to postpone action until the day after the run-off so that the demonstrations could not be used to cloud the issues. Like many others, we waited to see Mr. Connor defeated, and to this end we endured postponement after postponement. Having aided in this community need, we felt that our direct-action program could be delayed no longer.

You may well ask, "Why direct action? Why sit-ins, marches, and so   10
forth? Isn't negotiation a better path?" You are quite right in calling for negotiation. Indeed, this is the very purpose of direct action. Nonviolent direct action seeks to create such a crisis and foster such a tension that a community which has constantly refused to negotiate is forced to confront the issue. It seeks so to dramatize the issue that it can no longer be ignored. My citing the creation of tension as part of the work of the nonviolent-resister may sound rather shocking. But I must confess that I am not afraid of the word "tension." I have earnestly opposed violent tension, but there is a type of constructive, nonviolent tension which is necessary for growth. Just as Socrates[1] felt that it was necessary to create a tension in the mind so that

---

[1]The greatest of the ancient Greek philosophers, Socrates was sentenced to death because he persisted in raising difficult questions of authority.

individuals could rise from the bondage of myths and half-truths to the unfettered realm of creative analysis and objective appraisal, so must we see the need for nonviolent gadflies to create the kind of tension in society that will help men rise from the dark depths of prejudice and racism to the majestic heights of understanding and brotherhood.

The purpose of our direct-action program is to create a situation so   11 crisis-packed that it will inevitably open the door to negotiation. I therefore concur with you in your call for negotiation. Too long has our beloved Southland been bogged down in a tragic effort to live in monologue rather than dialogue.

One of the basic points in your statement is that the action that I and   12 my associates have taken in Birmingham is untimely. Some have asked: "Why didn't you give the new city administration time to act?" The only answer that I can give to this query is that the new Birmingham administration must be prodded about as much as the outgoing one, before it will act. We are sadly mistaken if we feel that the election of Albert Boutwell is a much more gentle person than Mr. Connor, they are both segregationists, dedicated to maintenance of the status quo. I have hoped that Mr. Boutwell will be reasonable enough to see the futility of massive resistance to desegregation. But we will not see this without pressure from devotees of civil rights. My friends, I must say to you that we have not made a single gain in civil rights without determined legal and nonviolent pressure. Lamentably, it is an historical fact that privileged groups seldom give up their privileges voluntarily. Individuals may see the moral light and voluntarily give up their unjust posture; but, as Reinhold Niebuhr[2] has reminded us, groups tend to be more immoral than individuals.

We know through painful experience that freedom is never voluntarily   13 given by the oppressor; it must be demanded by the oppressed. Frankly, I have yet to engage in a direct-action campaign that was "well timed" in the view of those who have not suffered unduly from the disease of segregation. For years now I have heard the word "Wait!" It rings in the ear of every Negro with piercing familiarity. This "Wait" has almost always meant "Never." We must come to see, with one of our distinguished jurists, that "justice too long delayed is justice denied."

We have waited for more than 340 years for our constitutional and   14 God-given rights. The nations of Asia and Africa are moving with jetlike speed toward gaining political independence, but we still creep at horse-and-buggy pace toward gaining a cup of coffee at a lunch counter. Perhaps it is easy for those who have never felt the stinging darts of segregation to say, "Wait." But when you have seen vicious mobs lynch your mothers and

---

[2]Niebuhr (1892–1971), an American theologian, attempted to establish a practical code of social ethics based in religious conviction.

fathers at will and drown your sisters and brothers at whim; when you have seen hate-filled policemen curse, kick, and even kill your black brothers and sisters; when you see the vast majority of your twenty million Negro brothers smothering in an airtight cage of poverty in the midst of an affluent society; when you suddenly find your tongue twisted and your speech stammering as you seek to explain to your six-year-old daughter why she can't go to the public amusement park that has just been advertised on television, and see tears welling up in her eyes when she is told that Funtown is closed to colored children, and see ominous clouds of inferiority beginning to form in her little mental sky, and see her beginning to distort her personality by developing an unconscious bitterness toward white people; when you have to concoct an answer for a five-year-old son who is asking, "Daddy, why do white people treat colored people so mean?"; when you take a cross-country drive and find it necessary to sleep night after night in the uncomfortable corners of your automobile because no motel will accept you; when you are humiliated day in and day out by nagging signs reading "white" and "colored"; when your first name becomes "nigger" your middle name becomes "boy" (however old you are) and your last name becomes "John," and your wife and mother are never given the respected title "Mrs."; when you are harried by day and haunted by night by the fact that you are a Negro, living constantly at tiptoe stance, never quite knowing what to expect next, and are plagued with inner fears and outer resentments; when you are forever fighting a degenerating sense of "nobodiness"—then you will understand why we find it difficult to wait. There comes a time when the cup of endurance runs over, and men are no longer willing to be plunged into the abyss of despair. I hope, sirs, you can understand our legitimate and unavoidable impatience.

You express a great deal of anxiety over our willingness to break laws. 15 This is certainly a legitimate concern. Since we so diligently urge people to obey the Supreme Court's decision of 1954 outlawing segregation in the public schools, at first glance it may seem rather paradoxical for us consciously to break laws. One may well ask: "How can you advocate breaking some laws and obeying others?" The answer lies in the fact that there are two types of laws: just and unjust. I would be the first to advocate obeying just laws. One has not only a legal but a moral responsibility to obey just laws. Conversely, one has a moral responsibility to disobey unjust laws. I would agree with St. Augustine[3] that "an unjust law is no law at all."

Now, what is the difference between the two? How does one determine 16 whether a law is just or unjust? A just law is a manmade code that squares with the moral law or the law of God. An unjust law is a code that is out of

---

[3]An early bishop of the Christian church, St. Augustine (354–430) is considered the founder of theology.

harmony with the moral law. To put it in the terms of St. Thomas-Aquinas[4]: An unjust law is a human law that is not rooted in eternal law and natural law. Any law that uplifts human personality is just. Any law that degrades human personality is unjust. All segregation statutes are unjust because segregation distorts the soul and damages the personality. It gives the segregator a false sense of superiority and the segregated a false sense of inferiority. Segregation, to use the terminology of the Jewish philosopher Martin Buber, substitutes an "I-it" relationship for an "I-thou" relationship and ends up relegating persons to the status of things. Hence segregation is not only politically, economically, and sociologically unsound, it is morally wrong and sinful. Paul Tillich[5] has said that sin is separation. Is not segregation an existential expression of man's tragic separation, his awful estrangement, his terrible sinfulness? Thus it is that I can urge men to obey the 1954 decision of the Supreme Court, for it is morally right; and I can urge them to disobey segregation ordinances, for they are morally wrong.

Let us consider a more concrete example of just and unjust laws. An 17 unjust law is a code that a numerical or power majority group compels a minority group to obey but does not make binding on itself. This is *difference* made legal. By the same token, a just law is a code that a majority compels a minority to follow and that it is willing to follow itself. This is *sameness* made legal.

Let me give another explanation. A law is unjust if it is inflicted on a 18 minority that, as a result of being denied the right to vote, had no part in enacting or devising the law. Who can say that the legislature of Alabama which set up that state's segregation laws was democratically elected? Throughout Alabama all sorts of devious methods are used to prevent Negroes from becoming registered voters, and there are some counties in which, even though Negroes constitute a majority of the population, not a single Negro is registered. Can any law enacted under such circumstances be considered democratically structured?

Sometimes a law is just on its face and unjust in its application. For 19 instance, I have been arrested on a charge of parading without a permit. Now, there is nothing wrong in having an ordinance which requires a permit for a parade. But such an ordinance becomes unjust when it is used to maintain segregation and to deny citizens the First Amendment privilege of peaceful assembly and protest.

I hope you are able to see the distinction I am trying to point out. In no 20 sense do I advocate evading or defying the law, as would the rabid segrega-

---

[4] The wide-embracing Christian teachings of medieval philosopher St. Thomas Aquinas (1225–1274) have been applied to every realm of human activity.

[5] Tillich (1886–1965) and Buber (1878–1965) are both important figures in twentieth-century religious thought.

tionist. That would lead to anarchy. One who breaks an unjust law must do so openly, lovingly, and with a willingness to accept the penalty. I submit that an individual who breaks a law that conscience tells him is unjust, and who willingly accepts the penalty of imprisonment in order to arouse the conscience of the community over its unjustice, is in reality expressing the highest respect for law.

Of course, there is nothing new about this kind of civil disobedience. It was evidenced sublimely in the refusal of Shadrach, Meshach, and Abednego to obey the laws of Nebuchadnezzar,[6] on the ground that a higher moral law was at stake. It was practiced superbly by the early Christians, who were willing to face hungry lions and the excruciating pain of chopping blocks rather than submit to certain unjust laws of the Roman Empire. To a degree, academic freedom is a reality today because Socrates practiced civil disobedience. In our own nation, the Boston Tea Party represented a massive act of civil disobedience.   21

We should never forget that everything Adolf Hitler did in Germany was "legal" and everything the Hungarian freedom fighters[7] did in Hungry was "illegal." It was "illegal" to aid and comfort a Jew in Hitler's Germany. Even so, I am sure that, had I lived in Germany at the time, I would have aided and comforted my Jewish brothers. If today I lived in a Communist country where certain principles dear to the Christian faith are suppressed, I would openly advocate disobeying that country's antireligious laws.   22

I must make two honest confessions to you, my Christian and Jewish brothers. First, I must confess that over the past few years I have been gravely disappointed with the white moderate. I have almost reached the regrettable conclusion that the Negro's great stumbling block in his stride toward freedom is not the White Citizen's Counciler[8] or the Ku Klux Klanner, but the white moderate, who is more devoted to "order" than to justice; who prefers a negative peace which is the absence of tension to a positive peace which is the presence of justice; who constantly says, "I agree with you in the goal you seek, but I cannot agree with your methods of direct action"; who paternalistically believes he can set the timetable for another man's freedom; who lives by a mythical concept of time and who constantly advises the Negro to wait for a "more convenient season." Shallow understanding from people of good will is more frustrating than absolute misunderstanding from people of ill will. Lukewarm acceptance is much more bewildering than outright rejection.   23

---

[6]When Shadrach, Meshach, and Abednego refused to worship an idol, King Nebuchadnezzar had them cast into a roaring furnace; they were saved by God. (See Daniel 1:7–3:30.)

[7]In 1956 Hungarian nationalists revolted against Communist rule, but were quickly put down with a violent show of Soviet force.

[8]Such councils were organized in 1954 to oppose school desegregation.

I had hoped that the white moderate would understand that law and order exist for the purpose of establishing justice and that when they fail in this purpose they become the dangerously structured dams that block the flow of social progress. I had hoped that the white moderate would understand that the present tension in the South is a necessary phase of the transition from an obnoxious negative peace, in which the Negro passively accepted his unjust plight, to a substantive and positive peace, in which all men will respect the dignity and worth of human personality. Actually, we who engage in nonviolent direct action are not the creators of tension. We merely bring to the surface the hidden tension that is already alive. We bring it out in the open, where it can be seen and dealt with. Like a boil that can never be cured so long as it is covered up but must be opened with all its ugliness to the natural medicines of air and light, injustice must be exposed, with all the tension its exposure creates, to the light of human conscience and the air of national opinion, before it can be cured.

In your statement you assert that our actions, even though peaceful, must be condemned because they precipitate violence. But is this a logical assertion? Isn't this like condemning a robbed man because his possession of money precipitated the evil act of robbery? Isn't this like condemning Socrates because his unswerving commitment to truth and his philosophical inquiries precipitated the act by the misguided populace in which they made him drink hemlock? Isn't this like condemning Jesus because his unique God-consciousness and never-ceasing devotion to God's will precipitated the evil act of crucifixion? We must come to see that, as the federal courts have consistently affirmed, it is wrong to urge an individual to cease his efforts to gain his basic constitutional rights because the quest may precipitate violence. Society must protect the robbed and punish the robber.

I had also hoped that the white moderate would reject the myth concerning time in relation to the struggle for freedom. I have just received a letter from a white brother in Texas. He writes: "All Christians know that the colored people will receive equal rights eventually, but it is possible that you are in too great a religious hurry. It has taken Christianity almost two thousand years to accomplish what it has. The teachings of Christ take time to come to earth." Such an attitude stems from a tragic misconception of time, from the strangely irrational notion that there is something in the very flow of time that will inevitably cure all ills. Actually, time itself is neutral; it can be used either destructively or constructively. More and more I feel that the people of ill will have used time much more effectively than have the people of good will. We will have to repent in this generation not merely for the hateful words and actions of the bad people, but for the appalling silence of the good people. Human progress never rolls in on wheels of inevitability; it comes through the tireless efforts of men willing to be coworkers with God, and without this hard work, time itself becomes an ally of the forces of social stagnation. We must use time creatively, in the knowledge that the time is always ripe to do right. Now is the time to make real the promise of democracy and transform our pending national elegy into a creative psalm of brotherhood. Now is the time to lift our national policy from the quicksand of racial injustice to the solid rock of human dignity.

You speak of our activity in Birmingham as extreme. At first I was   27
rather disappointed that fellow clergymen would see my nonviolent efforts as those of an extremist. I began thinking about the fact that I stand in the middle of two opposing forces in the Negro community. One is a force of complacency, made up in part of Negroes who, as a result of long years of oppression, are so drained of self-respect and a sense of "somebodiness" that they have adjusted to segregation; and in part of a few middle-class Negroes who, because of a degree of academic and economic security and because in some ways they profit by segregation, have become insensitive to the problems of the masses. The other force is one of bitterness and hatred, and it comes perilously close to advocating violence. It is expressed in the various black nationalist groups that are springing up across the nation, the largest and best-known being Elijah Muhammad's Muslim movement. Nourished by the Negro's frustration over the continued existence of racial discrimination, this movement is made up of people who have lost faith in America, who have absolutely repudiated Christianity, and who have concluded that the white man is an incorrigible "devil."

I have tried to stand between these two forces, saying that we need   28
emulate neither the "do-nothingism" of the complacent nor the hatred and despair of the black nationalist. For there is the more excellent way of love and nonviolent protest. I am grateful to God that, through the influence of the Negro church, the way of nonviolence became an integral part of our struggle.

If this philosophy had not emerged, by now many streets of the South   29
would, I am convinced, be flowing with blood. And I am further convinced that if our white brothers dismiss as "rabble-rousers" and "outside agitators" those of us who employ nonviolent direct action, and if they refuse to support our nonviolent efforts, millions of Negroes will, out of frustration and despair, seek solace and security in black-nationalist ideologies—a development that would inevitably lead to a frightening racial nightmare.

Oppressed people cannot remain oppressed forever. The yearning for   30
freedom eventually manifests itself, and that is what has happened to the American Negro. Something within has reminded him of his birthright of freedom, and something without has reminded him that it can be gained. Consciously or unconsciously, he has been caught up by the *Zeitgeist*,[9] and with his black brothers of Africa and his brown and yellow brothers of Asia,

---

[9]*Zeitgeist:* German word for "the spirit of the times."

South America, and the Caribbean, the United States Negro is moving with a sense of great urgency toward the promised land of racial justice. If one recognizes this vital urge that has engulfed the Negro community, one should readily understand why public demonstrations are taking place. The Negro has many pent-up resentments and latent frustrations, and he must release them. So let him march; let him make prayer pilgrimages to the city hall; let him go on freedom rides—and try to understand why he must do so. If his repressed emotions are not released in nonviolent ways, they will seek expression through violence; this is not a threat but a fact of history. So I have not said to my people, "Get rid of your discontent." Rather, I have tried to say that this normal and healthy discontent can be channeled into the creative outlet of nonviolent direct action. And now this approach is being termed extremist.

But though I was initially disappointed at being categorized as an   31
extremist, as I continued to think about the matter I gradually gained a measure of satisfaction from the label. Was not Jesus an extremist for love: "Love your enemies, bless them that curse you, do good to them that hate you, and pray for them which despitefully use you, and persecute you." Was not Amos an extremist for justice: "Let justice roll down like waters and righteousness like an ever-flowing stream." Was not Paul an extremist for the Christian gospel: "I bear in my body the marks of the Lord Jesus." Was not Martin Luther an extremist: "Here I stand; I cannot do otherwise, so help me God." And John Bunyan: "I will stay in jail to the end of my days before I make a butchery of my conscience." And Abraham Lincoln: "This nation cannot survive half slave and half free." And Thomas Jefferson: "We hold these truths to be self-evident, that all men are created equal. . . ." So the question is not whether we will be extremists, but what kind of extremists we will be. Will we be extremists for hate or for love? Will we be extremists for the preservation of injustice or for the extension of justice? In that dramatic scene on Calvary's hill three men were crucified. We must never forget that all three were crucified for the same crime—the crime of extremism. Two were extremists for immorality, and thus fell below their environment. The other, Jesus Christ, was an extremist for love, truth, and goodness, and thereby rose above his environment. Perhaps the South, the nation, and the world are in dire need of creative extremists.

I had hoped that the white moderate would see this need. Perhaps I was   32
too optimistic; perhaps I expected too much. I suppose I should have realized that few members of the oppressor race can understand the deep groans and passionate yearnings of the oppressed race, and still fewer have the vision to see that injustice must be rooted out by strong, persistent, and determined action. I am thankful, however, that some of our white brothers in the South have grasped the meaning of this social revolution and committed themselves to it. They are still all too few in quantity, but they are big in quality. Some—such as Ralph McGill, Lillian Smith, Harry Golden, James McBride

Dabbs, Ann Braden, and Sarah Patton Boyle—have written about our struggle in eloquent and prophetic terms. Others have marched with us down
nameless streets of the South. They have languished in filthy, roach-infested
jails, suffering the abuse and brutality of policemen who view them as "dirty
nigger-lovers." Unlike so many of their moderate brothers and sisters, they
have recognized the urgency of the moment and sensed the need for powerful
"action" antidotes to combat the disease of segregation.

Let me take note of my other major disappointment. I have been so   33
greatly disappointed with the white church and its leadership. Of course,
there are some notable exceptions. I am not unmindful of the fact that each
of you has taken some significant stands on this issue. I commend you,
Reverend Stallings, for your Christian stand on this past Sunday, in welcoming Negroes to your worship service on a nonsegregated basis. I commend the
Catholic leaders of this state for integrating Spring Hill College several years
ago.

But despite these notable exceptions, I must honestly reiterate that I   34
have been disappointed with the church. I do not say this as one of those
negative critics who can always find something wrong with the church. I say
this as a minister of the gospel, who loves the church; who was nurtured in
its bosom; who has been sustained by its spiritual blessings and who will
remain true to it as long as the cord of life shall lengthen.

When I was suddenly catapulted into the leadership of the bus protest   35
in Montgomery, Alabama, a few years ago, I felt we would be supported by
the white church. I felt that the white ministers, priests, and rabbis of the
South would be among our strongest allies. Instead, some have been outright
opponents, refusing to understand the freedom movement and misrepresent-
ing its leaders; all too many others have been more cautious than courageous
and have remained silent behind the anesthetizing security of stained-glass
windows.

In spite of my shattered dreams, I came to Birmingham with the hope   36
that the white religious leadership of this community would see the justice of
our case and, with deep moral concern, would serve as the channel through
which our just grievances could reach the power structure. I had hoped that
each of you would understand. But again I have been disappointed. . . .

There was a time when the church was very powerful—in the time   37
when the early Christians rejoiced at being deemed worthy to suffer for what
they believed. In those days the church was not merely a thermometer that
recorded the ideas and principles of popular opinion; it was a thermostat that
transformed the mores of society. Whenever the early Christians entered a
town, the people in power became disturbed and immediately sought to
convict the Christians for being "disturbers of the peace" and "outside agitators." But the Christians pressed on, in the conviction that they were "a
colony of heaven," called to obey God rather than man. Small in number,
they were big in commitment. They were too God-intoxicated to be "astro-

nomically intimidated." By their effort and example they brought an end to such ancient evils as infanticide and gladitorial contests.

Things are different now. So often the contemporary church is a weak, 38
ineffectual voice with an uncertain sound. So often it is an arch-defender of the status quo. Far from being disturbed by the presence of the church, the power structure of the average community is consoled by the church's silent—and often even vocal—sanction of things as they are.

But the judgment of God is upon the church as never before. If today's 39
church does not recapture the sacrificial spirit of the early church, it will lose its authenticity, forfeit the loyalty of millions, and be dismissed as an irrelevant social club with no meaning for the twentieth century. Every day I meet young people whose disappointment with the church has turned into outright disgust.

Perhaps I have once again been too optimistic. Is organized religion too 40
inextricably bound to the status quo to save our nation and the world? Perhaps I must turn my faith to the inner spiritual church, the church within the church, as the true *ekklesia*[10] and the hope of the world. But again I am thankful to God that some noble souls from the ranks of organized religion have broken loose from the paralyzing chains of conformity and joined us as active partners in the struggle for freedom. They have left their secure congregations and walked the streets of Albany, Georgia, with us. They have gone down the highways of the South on torturous rides for freedom. Yes, they have gone to jail with us. Some have been dismissed from their churches, have lost the support of their bishops and fellow ministers. But they have acted in the faith that right defeated is stronger than evil triumphant. Their witness has been the spiritual salt that has preserved the true meaning of the gospel in these troubled times. They have carved a tunnel of hope through the dark mountain of disappointment.

I hope the church as a whole will meet the challenge of this decisive 41
hour. But even if the church does not come to the aid of justice, I have no despair about the future. I have no fear about the outcome of our struggle in Birmingham, even if our motives are at present misunderstood. We will reach the goal of freedom in Birmingham and all over the nation, because the goal of America is freedom. Abused and scorned though we may be, our destiny is tied up with America's destiny. Before the pilgrims landed at Plymouth, we were here. Before the pen of Jefferson etched the majestic words of the Declaration of Independence across the pages of history, we were here. For more than two centuries our forebears labored in this country without wages; they made cotton king; they built the homes of their masters while suffering gross injustice and shameful humiliation—and yet out of a

---

[10]*Ekklesia*: word referring to the early Church and its spirit; from the Greek New Testament.

bottomless vitality they continued to thrive and develop. If the inexpressible cruelties of slavery could not stop us, the opposition we now face will surely fail. We will win our freedom because the sacred heritage of our nation and the eternal will of God are embodied in our echoing demands.

Before closing I feel impelled to mention one other point in your   42 statement that has troubled me profoundly. You warmly commended the Birmingham police force for keeping "order" and "preventing violence." I doubt that you would have so warmly commended the police force if you were to observe their ugly and inhumane treatment of Negroes here in the city jail; if you were to watch them push and curse old Negro women and young Negro girls; if you were to see them slap and kick old Negro men and young boys; if you were to observe them, as they did on two occasions, refuse to give us food because we wanted to sing our grace together. I cannot join you in your praise of the Birmingham police department.

It is true that the police have exercised a degree of discipline in han-   43 dling the demonstrators. In this sense they have conducted themselves rather "nonviolently" in public. But for what purpose? To preserve the evil system of segregation. Over the past few years I have consistently preached that nonviolence demands that the means we use must be as pure as the ends we seek. I have tried to make clear that it is wrong to use immoral means to attain moral ends. But now I must affirm that it is just as wrong, or perhaps even more so, to use moral means to preserve immoral ends. Perhaps Mr. Connor and his policemen have been rather nonviolent in public, as was Chief Pritchett in Albany, Georgia, but they have used the moral means of nonviolence to maintain the immoral end of racial injustice. As T. S. Eliot has said, "The last temptation is the greatest treason: To do the right deed for the wrong reason."

I wish you had commended the Negro sit-inners and demonstrators of   44 Birmingham for their sublime courage, their willingness to suffer, and their amazing discipline in the midst of great provocation. One day the South will recognize its real heroes. They will be the James Merediths,[11] with the noble sense of purpose that enables them to face jeering and hostile mobs, and with the agonizing loneliness that characterizes the life of the pioneer. They will be old, oppressed, battered Negro women, symbolized in a seventy-two-year-old woman in Montgomery, Alabama, who rose up with a sense of dignity and with her people decided not to ride segregated buses, and who responded with ungrammatical profundity to one who inquired about her weariness: "My feets is tired, but my soul is at rest." They will be the young high school and college students, the young ministers of the gospel and a host of their elders, courageously and nonviolently sitting in at lunch counters and will-

---

[11]In 1961 James Meredith became the first black student to enroll at the University of Mississippi, sparking considerable controversy and confrontation.

ingly going to jail for conscience's sake. One day the South will know that when these disinherited children of God sat down at lunch counters, they were in reality standing up for what is best in the American dream and for the most sacred values in our Judaeo-Christian heritage, thereby bringing our nation back to those great wells of democracy which were dug deep by the founding fathers in their formulation of the Constitution and the Declaration of Independence.

Never before have I written so long a letter. I'm afraid it is much too   45 long to take your precious time. I can assure you that it would have been much shorter if I had been writing from a comfortable desk, but what else can one do when he is alone in a narrow jail cell, other than write long letters, think long thoughts, and pray long prayers?

If I have said anything in this letter that overstates the truth and   46 indicates an unreasonable impatience, I beg you to forgive me. If I have said anything that understates the truth and indicates my having a patience that allows me to settle for anything less than brotherhood, I beg God to forgive me.

I hope this letter finds you strong in the faith. I also hope that circum-   47 stances will soon make it possible for me to meet each of you, not as an integrationist or a civil-rights leader but as a fellow clergyman and a Christian brother. Let us all hope that the dark clouds of racial prejudice will soon pass away and the deep fog of misunderstanding will be lifted from our fear-drenched communities, and in some not too distant tomorrow the radiant stars of love and brotherhood will shine over our great nation with all their scintillating beauty.

> Yours for the cause of Peace and Brotherhood,
> MARTIN LUTHER KING, JR.

Questions for Study and Discussion

1. Why did King write this letter? What was he doing in Birmingham? What kinds of "direct action" did he take there and why? What did he do that caused him to be jailed?

2. King says that he "stand[s] in the middle of two opposing forces in the Negro community." What are those forces, and why does he see himself between them?

3. What does King find wrong with the contemporary church as opposed to the early Christian church?

4. What specific objections to his activities have been presented in the statement that King is responding to? How does he answer each objection?

5. What does King call upon the clergy to do? What actions does he wish them to take and what beliefs to hold?

6. King says that he advocates nonviolent resistance. What does he

mean? In his letter he notes that the Birmingham police department has been praised for its nonviolent response to demonstrations. What is King's response to this claim?

7. King's letter was written in response to a published statement by eight fellow clergymen. While these men are his primary audience, he would appear to have a secondary audience as well. What is that audience? How does King show himself to be a man of reason and thoughtfulness in his letter of response?

Writing Topics

1. Write an essay in which you discuss how both Martin Luther King's actions and his "Letter from Birmingham Jail" exemplify Thoreau's principle of civil disobedience (pp. 563–80).

2. King advocates nonviolent resistance as a way of confronting oppression. What other means of confronting oppression were available to him? What are the strengths and weaknesses of those alternatives? Write an essay in which you assess the effectiveness of nonviolent resistance in the light of its alternatives.

W. H. AUDEN

Wystan Hugh Auden was born in York, England, in 1907, and was educated at Oxford University. While a student at Christ Church College there, he began to write the poems that brought him attention as an original, modern voice in English letters. During the 1930s, Auden developed his special kind of direct, often political poetry and also wrote plays, a movie script, and books that grew out of journeys to Iceland and China with such friends and fellow writers as Louis MacNeice and Christopher Isherwood. At the end of the thirties, he left England for the United States, later to become an American citizen. As he grew older, his poetry became more introspective, less "public" and political. He died in 1973.

Many countries have monuments dedicated to their "unknown soldier," a soldier killed on the battlefield who symbolizes the ideals of national service and sacrifice. "The Unkown Citizen" suggests what might be written on a monument for a symbolic civilian, who represents his society's peacetime values.

The Unknown Citizen

(To JS/07/M/378
This Marble Monument
Is Erected by the State)

He was found by the Bureau of Statistics to be
One against whom there was no official complaint,
And all the reports on his conduct agree
That, in the modern sense of an old-fashioned word, he was a saint,
For in everything he did he served the Greater Community.   5
Except for the War till the day he retired
He worked in a factory and never got fired,
But satisfied his employers, Fudge Motors, Inc.
Yet he wasn't a scab[1] or odd in his views,
For his Union reports that he paid his dues,   10
(Our report on his Union shows it was sound)
And our Social Psychology workers found
That he was popular with his mates and liked a drink.
The Press are convinced that he bought a paper every day
And that his reactions to advertisements were normal in every way. 15
Policies taken out in his name prove that he was fully insured,

---

[1]A strike breaker.

And his Health-card shows he was once in hospital but left it cured.
Both Producers Research and High-Grade Living declare
He was fully sensible to the advantages of the Installment Plan
And had everything necessary to the Modern Man,   20
A phonograph, a radio, a car and a frigidaire.
Our researchers into Public Opinion are content
That he held the proper opinions for the time of year;
When there was peace, he was for peace; when there was war, he went.
He was married and added five children to the population,   25
Which our Eugenist says was the right number for a parent of his
    generation,
And our teachers report that he never interfered with their education.
Was he free? Was he happy? The question is absurd:
Had anything been wrong, we should certainly have heard.

Questions for Study and Discussion

1. Do the words in this poem literally express Auden's own views? What makes you think so? If not, whose views are they meant to express?

2. Why do you think Auden presents this poem as an inscription on a public monument? What is the advantage of this choice? Why would a society erect a monument to its "unknown citizen"?

3. What does the poem tell us about the unknown citizen? What doesn't it tell us? What do its inclusions and omissions reveal about the state's official attitudes and values? How do these attitudes and values compare with Auden's? How do you know?

4. Look at the inscription following the title. What can you say about its content and style? How does it affect your understanding of the poem?

5. Comment on Auden's use of capitalization, citing examples from the poem. How does it affect the poem's meaning?

6. How do you think Auden meant readers to respond to this poem? Cite evidence from the poem to support your answer. How do you respond to it? Why do you respond that way?

Writing Topics

1. Auden wrote his poem in 1939. Using whatever information you think relevant, write an essay in which you describe the "unknown citizen" of today.

2. Suppose that in the year 2000 the state were to erect a monument to you, and that you could write the inscription yourself. What would you want your monument to say? Write your own inscription, limiting yourself to 500 words.

3. The United States government relies heavily on statistical information about its citizens, information that depersonalizes them in various ways. What

sort of information does the government collect? What are the advantages and uses of having such information? What are the disadvantages and abuses? What information—to your knowledge—has the government collected about you? Write an essay in which you discuss the pros and the cons of extensive information-gathering by the government.

SHIRLEY JACKSON

Shirley Jackson (1919–1965), a novelist and writer of short stories, is considered a master of gothic horror and the occult. The settings of her stories, in contemporary, familiar surroundings, make them more immediate and hence more frightening. "The Lottery," for instance, which was first published in 1948 in the *New Yorker*, is set in a small New England town in the present. In fact, it was written while Jackson was living in Bennington, Vermont. The story generated more mail than anything published in the magazine until then. According to one critic, "The Lottery" embodied Jackson's belief that "humankind is more evil than good."

Her husband, Stanley Edgar Hyman, said critics who saw in Jackson's stories a playing out of her own neurotic fantasies misunderstood her work: "They are a sensitive and faithful anatomy of our times, fitting symbols of the concentration camp and the bomb." Among her many other works are *We Have Always Lived in a Castle* (1953) and *The Haunting of Hill House* (1959). "The Lottery" tells the story of a town that conducts a cruel, annual ritual made crueller for being repeated even though no one remembers why it is being done.

The Lottery

The morning of June 27th was clear and sunny, with the fresh warmth of a full-summer day; the flowers were blossoming profusely and the grass was richly green. The people of the village began to gather in the square, between the post office and the bank, around ten o'clock; in some towns there were so many people that the lottery took two days and had to be started on June 26th, but in this village, where there were only about three hundred people, the whole lottery took less than two hours, so it could begin at ten o'clock in the morning and still be through in time to allow the villagers to get home for noon dinner.

The children assembled first, of course. School was recently over for the summer, and the feeling of liberty sat uneasily on most of them; they tended to gather together quietly for a while before they broke into boisterous play, and their talk was still of the classroom and the teacher, of books and reprimands. Bobby Martin had already stuffed his pockets full of stones, and the other boys soon followed his example, selecting the smoothest and roundest stones; Bobby and Harry Jones and Dickie Delacroix—the villagers pronounced this name "Dellacroy"—eventually made a great pile of stones in one corner of the square and guarded it against the raids of the other boys. The girls stood aside, talking among themselves, looking over their shoulders

1

2

at the boys, and the very small children rolled in the dust or clung to the hands of their older brothers or sisters.

Soon the men began to gather, surveying their own children, speaking 3 of planting and rain, tractors and taxes. They stood together, away from the pile of stones in the corner, and their jokes were quiet and they smiled rather than laughed. The women, wearing faded house dresses and sweaters, came shortly after their menfolk. They greeted one another and exchanged bits of gossip as they went to join their husbands. Soon the women, standing by their husbands, began to call to their children, and the children came reluctantly, having to be called four or five times. Bobby Martin ducked under his mother's grasping hand and ran, laughing, back to the pile of stones. His father spoke up sharply, and Bobby came quickly and took his place between his father and his oldest brother.

The lottery was conducted—as were the square dances, the teen-age 4 club, the Halloween program—by Mr. Summers, who had time and energy to devote to civic activities. He was a round-faced, jovial man and he ran the coal business, and people were sorry for him, because he had no children and his wife was a scold. When he arrived in the square, carrying the black wooden box, there was a murmur of conversation among the villagers, and he waved and called, "Little late today, folks." The postmaster, Mr. Graves, followed him, carrying a three-legged stool, and the stool was put in the center of the square and Mr. Summers set the black box down on it. The villagers kept their distance, leaving a space between themselves and the stool, and when Mr. Summers said, "Some of you fellows want to give me a hand?" there was a hesitation before two men, Mr. Martin and his oldest son, Baxter, came forward to hold the box steady on the stool while Mr. Summers stirred up the papers inside it.

The original paraphernalia for the lottery had been lost long ago, and the 5 black box now resting on the stool had been put into use even before Old Man Warner, the oldest man in town, was born. Mr. Summers spoke frequently to the villagers about making a new box, but no one liked to upset even as much tradition as was represented by the black box. There was a story that the present box had been made with some pieces of the box that had preceded it, the one that had been constructed when the first people settled down to make a village here. Every year, after the lottery, Mr. Summers began talking again about a new box, but every year the subject was allowed to fade off without anything being done. The black box grew shabbier each year; by now it was no longer completely black but splintered badly along one side to show the original wood color, and in some places faded or stained.

Mr. Martin and his oldest son, Baxter, held the black box securely on 6 the stool until Mr. Summers had stirred the papers thoroughly with his hand. Because so much of the ritual had been forgotten or discarded, Mr. Summers had been successful in having slips of paper substituted for the chips of wood that had been used for generations. Chips of wood, Mr. Summers had argued, had been all very well when the village was tiny, but now that the population was more than three hundred and likely to keep on growing, it was necessary to use something that would fit more easily into the black box. The night before the lottery, Mr. Summers and Mr. Graves made up the slips of paper and put them in the box, and it was then taken to the safe of Mr. Summers' coal company and locked up until Mr. Summers was ready to take it to the square next morning. The rest of the year, the box was put away, sometimes one place, sometimes another; it had spent one year in Mr. Graves's barn and another year underfoot in the post office, and sometimes it was set on a shelf in the Martin grocery and left there.

There was a great deal of fussing to be done before Mr. Summers   7
declared the lottery open. There were the lists to make up—of heads of families, heads of households in each family, members of each household in each family. There was the proper swearing-in of Mr. Summers by the postmaster, as the official of the lottery; at one time, some people remembered, there had been a recital of some sort, performed by the official of the lottery, a perfunctory, tuneless chant that had been rattled off duly each year; some people believed that the official of the lottery used to stand just so when he said or sang it, others believed that he was supposed to walk among the people, but years and years ago this part of the ritual had been allowed to lapse. There had been, also, a ritual salute, which the official of the lottery had had to use in addressing each person who came up to draw from the box, but this also had changed with time, until now it was felt necessary only for the official to speak to each person approaching. Mr. Summers was very good at all this; in his clean white shirt and blue jeans, with one hand resting carelessly on the black box, he seemed very proper and important as he talked interminably to Mr. Graves and the Martins.

Just as Mr. Summers finally left off talking and turned to the assembled   8
villagers, Mrs. Hutchinson came hurriedly along the path to the square, her sweater thrown over her shoulders, and slid into place in the back of the crowd. "Clean forgot what day it was," she said to Mrs. Delacroix, who stood next to her, and they both laughed softly. "Thought my old man was out back stacking wood," Mrs. Hutchinson went on, "and then I looked out the window and the kids were gone, and then I remembered it was the twenty-seventh and came a-running." She dried her hands on her apron, and Mrs. Delacroix said, "You're in time, though. They're still talking away up there."

Mrs. Hutchinson craned her neck to see through the crowd and found   9
her husband and children standing near the front. She tapped Mrs. Delacroix on the arm as a farewell and began to make her way through the crowd. The people separated good-humoredly to let her through; two or three people said, in voices just loud enough to be heard across the crowd, "Here comes your Missus, Hutchinson," and "Bill, she made it after all." Mrs. Hutchinson reached her husband, and Mr. Summers, who had been waiting, said cheerfully, "Thought we were going to have to get on without you, Tessie." Mrs.

Hutchinson said, grinning, "Wouldn't have me leave m'dishes in the sink, now, would you, Joe?" and soft laughter ran through the crowd as the people stirred back into position after Mrs. Hutchinson's arrival.

"Well, now," Mr. Summers said soberly, "guess we better get started, 10 get this over with, so's we can go back to work. Anybody ain't here?"

"Dunbar," several people said. "Dunbar, Dunbar." 11

Mr. Summers consulted his list. "Clyde Dunbar," he said. "That's 12 right. He's broke his leg, hasn't he? Who's drawing for him?"

"Me, I guess," a woman said, and Mr. Summers turned to look at her. 13 "Wife draws for her husband," Mr. Summers said. "Don't you have a grown boy to do it for you, Janey?" Although Mr. Summers and everyone else in the village knew the answer perfectly well, it was the business of the official of the lottery to ask such questions formally. Mr. Summers waited with an expression of polite interest while Mrs. Dunbar answered.

"Horace's not but sixteen yet," Mrs. Dunbar said regretfully. "Guess I 14 gotta fill in for the old man this year."

"Right," Mr. Summers said. He made a note on the list he was holding. 15 Then he asked, "Watson boy drawing this year?"

A tall boy in the crowd raised his hand. "Here," he said. "I'm drawing 16 for m'mother and me." He blinked his eyes nervously and ducked his head as several voices in the crowd said things like "Good fellow, Jack," and "Glad to see your mother's got a man to do it."

"Well," Mr. Summers said, "guess that's everyone. Old Man Warner 17 make it?"

"Here," a voice said, and Mr. Summers nodded. 18

A sudden hush fell on the crowd as Mr. Summers cleared his throat and 19 looked at the list. "All ready?" he called. "Now, I'll read the names—heads of families first—and the men come up and take a paper out of the box. Keep the paper folded in your hand without looking at it until everyone has had a turn. Everything clear?"

The people had done it so many times that they only half listened to 20 the directions; most of them were quiet, wetting their lips, not looking around. Then Mr. Summers raised one hand high and said, "Adams." A man disengaged himself from the crowd and came forward. "Hi, Steve," Mr. Summers said, and Mr. Adams said, "Hi, Joe." They grinned at one another humorously and nervously. Then Mr. Adams reached into the black box and took out a folded paper. He held it firmly by one corner as he turned and went hastily back to his place in the crowd, where he stood a little apart from his family, not looking down at his hand.

"Allen," Mr. Summers said. "Anderson . . . Bentham." 21

"Seems like there's no time at all between lotteries any more," Mrs. 22 Delacroix said to Mrs. Graves in the back row. "Seems like we got through with the last one only last week."

"Time sure goes fast," Mrs. Graves said. 23

"Clark . . . Delacroix." 24

"There goes my old man," Mrs. Delacroix said. She held her breath   25
while her husband went forward.

"Dunbar," Mr. Summers said, and Mrs. Dunbar went steadily to the   26
box while one of the women said, "Go on, Janey," and another said, "There
she goes."

"We're next," Mrs. Graves said. She watched while Mr. Graves came   27
around from the side of the box, greeted Mr. Summers gravely, and selected a
slip of paper from the box. By now, all through the crowd there were men
holding the small folded papers in their large hands, turning them over and
over nervously. Mrs. Dunbar and her two sons stood together, Mrs. Dunbar
holding the slip of paper.

"Harburt . . . Hutchinson."   28

"Get up there, Bill," Mrs. Hutchinson said, and the people near her   29
laughed.

"Jones."   30

"They do say," Mr. Adams said to Old Man Warner, who stood next to   31
him, "that over in the north village they're talking of giving up the lottery."

Old Man Warner snorted. "Pack of crazy fools," he said. "Listening to   32
the young folks, nothing's good enough for *them*. Next thing you know,
they'll be wanting to go back to living in caves, nobody work any more, live
that way for a while. Used to be a saying about 'Lottery in June, corn be
heavy soon.' First thing you know, we'd all be eating stewed chickweed and
acorns. There's *always* been a lottery," he added petulantly. "Bad enough to
see young Joe Summers up there joking with everybody."

"Some places have already quit lotteries," Mrs. Adams said.   33

"Nothing but trouble in *that*," Old Man Warner said stoutly. "Pack of   34
young fools."

"Martin." And Bobby Martin watched his father go forward. "Over-   35
dyke . . . Percy."

"I wish they'd hurry," Mrs. Dunbar said to her older son. "I wish they'd   36
hurry."

"They're almost through," her son said.   37

"You get ready to run tell Dad," Mrs. Dunbar said.   38

Mr. Summers called his own name and then stepped forward precisely   39
and selected a slip from the box. Then he called, "Warner."

"Seventy-seventh year I been in the lottery," Old Man Warner said as   40
he went through the crowd. "Seventy-seventh time."

"Watson." The tall boy came awkwardly through the crowd. Someone   41
said, "Don't be nervous, Jack," and Mr. Summers said, "Take your time,
son."

"Zanini."   42

After that, there was a long pause, a breathless pause, until Mr. Sum-   43
mers, holding his slip of paper in the air, said, "All right, fellows." For a
minute, no one moved, and then all the slips of paper were opened. Sud-

denly, all the women began to speak at once, saying, "Who is it?" "Who's got it?" "Is it the Dunbars?" "Is it the Watsons?" Then the voices began to say, "It's Hutchinson. It's Bill," "Bill Hutchinson's got it."

"Go tell your father," Mrs. Dunbar said to her older son. 44

People began to look around to see the Hutchinsons. Bill Hutchinson 45
was standing quiet, staring down at the paper in his hand. Suddenly, Tessie Hutchinson shouted to Mr. Summers, "You didn't give him time enough to take any paper he wanted. I saw you. It wasn't fair."

"Be a good sport, Tessie," Mrs. Delacroix called, and Mrs. Graves said, 46
"All of us took the same chance."

"Shut up, Tessie," Bill Hutchinson said. 47

"Well, everyone," Mr. Summers said, "That was done pretty fast, and 48
now we've got to be hurrying a little more to get done in time." He consulted his next list. "Bill," he said, "you draw for the Hutchinson family. You got any other households in the Hutchinsons?"

"There's Don and Eva," Mrs. Hutchinson yelled. "Make *them* take 49
their chance!"

"Daughters draw with their husbands' families, Tessie," Mr. Summers 50
said gently. "You know that as well as anyone else."

"It wasn't *fair*," Tessie said. 51

"I guess not, Joe," Bill Hutchinson said regretfully. "My daughter draws 52
with her husband's family, that's only fair. And I've got no other family except the kids."

"Then, as far as drawing for families is concerned, it's you," Mr. Sum- 53
mers said in explanation, "and as far as drawing for households is concerned, that's you, too. Right?"

"Right," Bill Hutchinson said. 54

"How many kids, Bill?" Mr. Summers asked formally. 55

"Three," Bill Hutchinson said. "There's Bill, Jr., and Nancy, and little 56
Dave. And Tessie and me."

"All right, then," Mr. Summers said. "Harry, you got their tickets 57
back?"

Mr. Graves nodded and held up the slips of paper. "Put them in the box 58
then," Mr. Summers directed. "Take Bill's and put it in."

"I think we ought to start over," Mrs. Hutchinson said, as quietly as she 59
could. "I tell you it wasn't *fair*. You didn't give him time enough to choose. *Everybody* saw that."

Mr. Graves had selected the five slips and put them in the box, and he 60
dropped all the papers but those onto the ground, where the breeze caught them and lifted them off.

"Listen, everybody," Mrs. Hutchinson was saying to the people around 61
her.

"Ready, Bill?" Mr. Summers asked, and Bill Hutchinson, with one 62
quick glance around at his wife and children, nodded.

"Remember," Mr. Summers said, "take the slips and keep them folded 63
until each person has taken one. Harry, you help little Dave." Mr. Graves
took the hand of the little boy, who came willingly with him up to the box.
"Take a paper out of the box, Davy," Mr. Summers said. Davy put his hand
into the box and laughed. "Take just *one* paper," Mr. Summers said. "Harry,
you hold it for him." Mr. Graves took the child's hand and removed the
folded paper from the tight fist and held it while little Dave stood next to
him and looked up at him wonderingly.

"Nancy next," Mr. Summers said. Nancy was twelve, and her school 64
friends breathed heavily as she went forward, switching her skirt, and took a
slip daintily from the box. "Bill, Jr.," Mr. Summers said, and Billy, his face
red and his feet over-large, nearly knocked the box over as he got a paper
out. "Tessie," Mr. Summers said. She hesitated for a minute, looking around
defiantly, and then set her lips and went up to the box. She snatched a paper
out and held it behind her.

"Bill," Mr. Summers said, and Bill Hutchinson reached into the box 65
and felt around, bringing his hand out at last with the slip of paper in it.

The crowd was quiet. A girl whispered, "I hope it's not Nancy," and 66
the sound of the whisper reached the edges of the crowd.

"It's not the way it used to be," Old Man Warner said clearly. "People 67
ain't the way they used to be."

"All right," Mr. Summers said. "Open the papers. Harry, you open 68
little Dave's."

Mr. Graves opened the slip of paper and there was a general sigh 69
through the crowd as he held it up and everyone could see that it was blank.
Nancy and Bill, Jr., opened theirs at the same time, and both beamed and
laughed, turning around to the crowd and holding their slips of paper above
their heads.

"Tessie," Mr. Summers said. There was a pause, and then Mr. Summers 70
looked at Bill Hutchinson, and Bill unfolded his paper and showed it. It was
blank.

"It's Tessie," Mr. Summers said, and his voice was hushed. "Show us 71
her paper, Bill."

Bill Hutchinson went over to his wife and forced the slip of paper out 72
of her hand. It had a black spot on it, the black spot Mr. Summers had made
the night before with the heavy pencil in the coal-company office. Bill
Hutchinson held it up, and there was a stir in the crowd.

"All right, folks," Mr. Summers said. "Let's finish quickly." 73

Although the villagers had forgotten the ritual and lost the original 74
black box, they still remembered to use stones. The pile of stones the boys
had made earlier was ready; there were stones on the ground with the
blowing scraps of paper that had come out of the box. Mrs. Delacroix
selected a stone so large she had to pick it up with both hands and turned to
Mrs. Dunbar. "Come on," she said. "Hurry up."

Mrs. Dunbar had small stones in both hands, and she said, grasping 75
for breath, "I can't run at all. You'll have to go ahead and I'll catch up with
you."

The children had stones already, and someone gave Davy Hutchinson 76
a few pebbles.

Tessie Hutchinson was in the center of a cleared space by now, and she 77
held her hands out desperately as the villagers moved in on her. "It isn't fair,"
she said. A stone hit her on the side of the head.

Old Man Warner was saying, "Come on, come on, everyone." Steve 78
Adams was in the front of the crowd of villagers, with Mrs. Graves beside
him.

"It isn't fair, it isn't right," Mrs. Hutchinson screamed, and then they 79
were upon her.

Questions for Study and Discussion

1. At what point in the story do you first begin to suspect that something
terrible is going to happen? When do you figure out what it is?
2. What kinds of details does the author use in her story to create a sense
of normality? To create a sense of horror? Support your answer with examples.
3. Describe the ritual in your own words. What is the terrible irony of this
ritual? What other ironies are there in the story?
4. What different attitudes toward the ritual are expressed by Old Man
Warner, Tessie, Mr. Summers, Nancy's friend? Did those attitudes remain fixed
or did they change? Explain. Which person do you think speaks for most of the
town?
5. How believable is Jackson's story? What effect does that believability
have on the impact of the story?
6. The townspeople continue to live in their town knowing that yearly
they risk either killing each other or being killed. Why do they stay? What point
about society is Jackson trying to make in her story?

Writing Topics

1. What do you know about "scapegoat" rituals such as the one depicted
in Jackson's story? What is a scapegoat? What was the intention of these rituals?
Do some research to find out more about them. In what kinds of cultures were
they practiced? Have any of these cultures survived into the present?
2. Consider some of the religious or fraternal rituals you, your community,
or your friends observe. During which rituals are you or your friends aware of the
meaning each time you participate? Which rituals have you repeated without
thought to their meaning? Are you surprised at your answers? In what way do
your answers enhance or detract from your understanding of Jackson's story?

Glossary

Abstract: See *Concrete/Abstract.*

Action is the series of events in a narrative. It is also called the story line. See also *Plot.*

Alliteration: See *Sound.*

Allusion is a passing reference to a person, place, or thing. Often drawn from history, the Bible, mythology, or literature, allusions are an economical way for a writer to convey the essence of an idea, atmosphere, emotion, or historical era. Some examples of allusion are "The scandal was his Watergate," "He saw himself as a modern Job," and "The campaign ended not with a bang but a whimper." An allusion should be familiar to the reader; if it is not, it will neither add to the meaning of a text nor enrich an emotion.

Analogy is a special form of comparison in which the writer explains something unfamiliar by comparing it to something familiar: "A transmission line is simply a pipeline for electricity. In the case of a water pipeline, more water will flow through the pipe as water pressure increases. The same is true of electricity in a transmission line."

Analysis is a type of exposition in which the writer considers a subject in terms of its parts or elements. For example, one may analyze a movie by considering its subject, its plot, its dialogue, its acting, its camera work, and its sets. See also *Cause and Effect, Classification, Process Analysis.*

Anecdote. An anecdote is a brief story told to illustrate a concept or support a point. Anecdotes are often used to open essays because of the inherent interest of a story.

Antagonist. An antagonist is a character who struggles against the central character, or protagonist, in a conflict. Chillingworth in *The Scarlet Letter* is a villainous antagonist; Jim in *The Adventures of Huckleberry Finn*, a virtuous antagonist. See also *Protagonist.*

Aphorism. An aphorism is a short, concise statement embodying a general truth.

Appropriateness: See *Diction.*

Argument is one of the four forms of discourse. (Narration, description, and exposition are the other three.) To argue is to attempt to persuade a reader to agree with a point of view or to pursue a particular course of action by appealing to the reader's rational or intellectual faculties. See also *Deduction, Induction, Logical Fallacies,* and *Persuasion.*

Assonance: See *Sound.*

Assumptions are things one believes to be true, whether or not their truth can be proven. All writing includes many unstated assumptions as well as some that are stated, and an active reader seeks to discover what those assumptions are and to decide whether they are acceptable.

Attitude is the view or opinion of a person; in writing, the author's attitude is reflected in its tone. See also *Tone.*

Audience is the expected readership for a piece of writing. For example, the readers of a national weekly newsmagazine come from all walks of life and have diverse interests, opinions, and educational backgrounds. In contrast, the readership for an organic chemistry journal is made up of people whose interests and education are quite specialized.

Cause and Effect is a form of analysis that answers the question *why.* It explains the reasons for an occurrence or the consequences of an action. Determining causes and effects is usually thought-provoking and quite complex. One reason for this is that there are two types of causes: (1) *immediate causes,* which are readily apparent because they are closest to the effect, and (2) *ultimate causes,* which are somewhat removed, not so apparent, or perhaps even obscure. Furthermore, ultimate causes may bring about effects that themselves become causes, thus creating what is called a *causal chain.* For example, the immediate cause of a flood may be the collapse of a dam, and the ultimate cause might be an engineering error. An intermediate cause, however, might be faulty construction of the dam owing to corruption in the building trades.

Character. A character is a person in a story. Characters are generally regarded as being one of two types: flat or round. A flat character is one who exhibits a single trait, such as the devoted husband, the kind grandmother, or the shrewd businessman; such a character is stereotypic, unwavering, and thoroughly predictable. A round character, on the other hand, displays various traits and is complex and at times unpredictable—in short, very much like most of us. The chief character in a story is often called the *protagonist,* whereas the character or characters who oppose the protagonist are the *antagonists.*

Classification, sometimes called classification and division, is a form of exposition. When classifying, the writer sorts and arranges people, places, or things into categories according to their differing characteristics. When dividing, the writer creates new, smaller categories within a large category, usually for purposes of classification. For example, a writer might divide the large category *books* into several smaller ones: textbooks, novels, biographies, reference books, and so on. Then specific books could be classified by assigning them to these categories.

Cliché. A cliché is a trite or hackneyed expression, common in everyday speech but avoided in most serious writing.

Climax. In a work of fiction or drama, the climax is the point of highest tension, sometimes identical with the turning point of the narrative.

Coherence is a quality of good writing that results when all sentences, paragraphs, and longer divisions of an essay are naturally connected. Coherent writing is achieved through (1) a logically organized sequence of ideas, (2) the repetition of key words and ideas, (3) a pace suitable for the topic and the reader, and (4) the use of transitional words and expressions. See also *Organization, Transitions.*

Colloquial Expressions: See *Diction.*

Comparison and Contrast is a form of exposition in which the writer points out the similarities and differences between two or more subjects in the same class or category. The function of any comparison and contrast is to clarify—to reach some conclusion about the items being compared and contrasted. The writer's purpose may be simply to inform, or to make readers aware of similarities or differences that are interesting and significant in themselves. Or, the writer may explain something by comparing it to something very familiar, perhaps explaining squash by comparing it to tennis. Finally, the writer can point out the superiority of one thing by contrasting it with another—for example, showing that one product is the best by contrasting it with all its competitors.

Conclusion. The conclusion of an essay is the sentences or paragraphs that sum up the main points and suggest their significance or in some other way bring the essay to a satisfying end. See also *Introduction.*

Concrete/Abstract. A concrete word names a specific object, person, place or action: *bicycle, milkshake, building, book,* John F. Kennedy, Chicago, or *hiking.* An abstract word, in contrast, refers to general qualities, conditions, ideas, actions, or relationships that cannot be directly perceived by the senses: *bravery, dedication, excellence, anxiety, stress, thinking,* or *hatred.* Although writers must use both concrete and abstract language, good writers avoid too many abstract words. Instead, they rely on concrete words to define and illustrate abstractions.

Conflict in a story is the clash of opposing characters, events, or ideas. A resolution of the conflict is necessary in order for the story to conclude.

Connotation/Denotation refer to the meanings of words. Denotation is the literal meaning of a word. Connotation, on the other hand, is the implied or suggested meaning of a word, including its emotional associations. For example, the denotation of *lamb* is "a young sheep." The connotations of *lamb* are numerous: *gentle, docile, weak, peaceful, blessed, sacrificial, blood, spring, frisky, pure, innocent,* and so on. Good writers are sensitive to both the denotations and connotations of words.

Consonance: See *Sound.*

Contrast: See *Comparison and Contrast.*

Deduction is a method of reasoning from the general to the particular. The most common form of deductive reasoning is the *syllogism,* a three-part argument that moves from a general statement (major premise) and a specific statement (minor premise) to a logical conclusion, as in the following example:
   a. All women are mortal. (major premise)
   b. Judy is a woman. (minor premise)
   c. Therefore, Judy is mortal. (conclusion)

The conclusion to a deductive argument is persuasive only when both premises are true and the form of the syllogism is correct. Then it is said that the argument is sound.

Definition is a statement of the meaning of a word, or of an idea or even an experience. A definition may be brief or extended, the latter requiring a paragraph of an essay or even an entire essay. There are two basic types of brief definitions, each useful in its own way. The first method is to give a *synonym*, a word that has nearly the same meaning as the word you wish to define: *dictionary* for *lexicon*, *nervousness* for *anxiety*. No two words ever have exactly the same meaning, but you can, nevertheless, pair a familiar word with an unfamiliar one and thereby clarify your meaning. The other way to define quickly, often with a single sentence, is to give a *formal definition:* that is, to place the term to be defined in a general class and then to distinguish it from other members of that class by describing its particular characteristics. For example:

WORD	CLASS	CHARACTERISTIC
A *canoe*	is a *small boat*	that has *curved sides* and *pointed ends* and is *narrow, made of lightweight materials,* and *propelled by paddles.*
A *rowboat*	is a *small boat*	that has a *shallow draft* and usually a *flat* or *rounded bottom,* a *squared-off* or *V-shaped stern,* and *oarlocks* for the *oars with which it is propelled.*

Denotation: See *Connotation/Denotation.*

Denouement is the resolution or conclusion of a narrative.

Description is one of the four basic forms of discourse. (Narration, exposition, and argument are the other three.) To describe is to give a verbal picture of a person, a place, or a thing. Even an idea or a state of mind can be made vividly concrete, as in, "The old woman was as silent as a ghost." Although descriptive writing can stand alone, description is often used with other rhetorical strategies; for instance, description can make examples more interesting, explain the complexities of a process, or clarify a definition or comparison. A good writer selects and arranges descriptive details to create a *dominant impression* that reinforces the point or the atmosphere of a piece of writing.

Objective description emphasizes the *object* itself and is factual without resorting to such scientific extremes that the reader cannot understand the facts. *Subjective* or *impressionistic description*, on the other hand, emphasizes the *observer* and gives a personal interpretation of the subject matter through language rich in modifiers and figures of speech.

Dialogue is the conversation that is recorded in a piece of writing. Through dialogue writers reveal important aspects of characters' personalities as well as events in the plot.

Diction refers to a writer's choice and use of words. Good diction is precise and appropriate—the words mean exactly what the writer intends and are well suited to the writer's subject, intended audience, and purpose in writing. There are three main levels of diction, each with its own uses: formal, for grand occasions; colloquial, or conversational, especially for dialogue; and informal, for most essay writing. See also *Concrete/Abstract, Connotation/Denotation, Specific/General.*

Discourse, Forms of. The four traditional forms of discourse, often called "rhetorical modes," are narration, description, exposition, and argument. Depending on the purpose, a writer may use one or more of these forms in a piece of writing. For more information see *Argument, Description, Exposition,* and *Narration.*

Division: See *Classification.*

Dominant Impression: See *Description.*

Draft. A draft is a version of a piece of writing at a particular stage in the writing process. The first version produced is usually called the rough draft or first draft and is a writer's beginning attempt to give overall shape to his or her ideas. Subsequent versions are called revised drafts. The copy presented for publication is the final draft.

Editing. During the editing stage of the writing process, the writer makes his or her prose conform to the conventions of the language. This includes making final improvements in sentence structure and diction and proofreading for wordiness and errors in grammar, usage, spelling, and punctuation. After editing, the writer is ready to type a final copy.

Effect: See *Cause and Effect.*

Emphasis is the placement of important ideas and words within sentences and longer units of writing so that they have the greatest impact. In general, the end has the most impact, and the beginning nearly as much; the middle has the least. See also *Organization.*

Essay. An essay, traditionally, is a piece of nonfiction prose, usually fairly brief, in which the writer explores his or her ideas on a subject. Essays come in many forms including personal narratives and scientific and theoretical inquiries, as well as critical, humorous, and argumentative pieces. The word *essay* presently is used fairly loosely to include not only personal writing but most short nonfiction prose pieces.

Evaluation of a piece of writing is the assessment of its effectiveness or merit. In evaluating a piece of writing, one should ask the following questions: What does the writer have to say? Are the writer's ideas challenging or thought-provoking? What is the writer's purpose? Is it a worthwhile purpose? Does the writer achieve the purpose? Is the writer's information sufficient and accurate? What are the strengths of the essay? What are its weaknesses? Depending on the type of writing and the purpose, more specific questions can also be asked. For example, with an argument one could ask: Does the writer follow the principles of logical thinking? Is the writer's evidence convincing?

Evidence is the data on which a judgment or argument is based or by which proof or probability is established. Evidence usually takes the form of statistics, facts, names, examples, illustrations, and opinions of authorities, and always involves a clear indication of its relevance to the point at issue.

Example. An example is a person, place, or thing used to represent a group or explain a general statement. Many entries in this glossary contain examples used in both ways. Examples enable writers to show and not simply to tell readers what they mean. The terms *example* and *illustration* are sometimes used inter-changeably. See also *Specific/General.*

Exposition is one of the four basic forms of discourse. (Narration, description, and argument are the other three.) The purpose of exposition is to clarify, explain, and inform. The methods of exposition are analysis, definition, classification, comparison and contrast, cause and effect, and process analysis. For a discussion of each of these methods of exposition, see *Analysis, Cause and Effect, Classification, Comparison and Contrast, Definition,* and *Process Analysis.*

Fallacy: See *Logical Fallacies.*

Figures of Speech are words and phrases that are used in an imaginative rather than literal way. Figurative language makes writing vivid and interesting and therefore more memorable. The most common figures of speech are:

 Simile. An explicit comparison introduced by *like* or *as:* "The fighter's hands were like stone."

 Metaphor. An implied comparison that uses one thing as the equivalent of another: "All the world's a stage."

 Personification. The attributing of human traits to an inanimate object: "The engine coughed and then stopped."

Hyperbole. A deliberate exaggeration or overstatement: "I am so hungry I could eat a horse."

Metonymy. A type of comparison in which the name of one thing is used to represent another, as in the words *White House* used to represent the president of the United States.

Synecdoche. Another comparison in which a part stands for the whole, as in the word *crown* used to represent a king or the word *sail* to represent a ship.

See also *Symbol.*

Focus. Focus is the limitation that a writer gives his or her subject. The writer's task is to select a manageable topic given the constraints of time, space, and purpose. For example, within the general subject of sports, a writer could focus on government support of amateur athletes or narrow the focus further to government support of Olympic athletes.

General: See *Specific/General.*

Genre. A genre is a type or form of literary writing, such as poetry, fiction, or the essay; the term is also used to refer to more specific literary forms, such as an epic poem, novel, or detective story.

Hyperbole: See *Figures of Speech.*

Illustration: See *Example.*

Imagery is the verbal representation of a sensory experience: sight, hearing, touch, smell, taste, even the sensations one feels inside one's own body. Writers use imagery to create details in their descriptions. Effective images can make writing come alive and enable the reader to experience vicariously what is being described.

Induction is a method of reasoning that moves from particular examples to a general statement. In doing so, the writer makes what is known as an *inductive leap* from the evidence to the generalization, which can never offer the absolute certainty of deductive reasoning. For example, after examining enrollment statistics, we can conclude that students do not like to take courses offered early in the morning or late in the afternoon. See also *Argument.*

Introduction. The introduction of an essay consists of the sentences or paragraphs in which the author captures the reader's interest and prepares for what is to come. An introduction normally identifies the topic, indicates what purpose the essay is to serve, and often states or implies the thesis. See also *Conclusion.*

Irony is the use of language to suggest other than its literal meaning. *Verbal irony* uses words to suggest something different from their literal meaning. For example, when Jonathan Swift writes in *A Modern Proposal* that Ireland's population problem should be solved through cannibalism, he means that almost any other solution would be preferable. *Dramatic irony,* in literature, presents words or actions that are appropriate in an unexpected way. For example, Oedipus promises to find and punish the wrongdoer who has brought disaster on Thebes, then discovers that the criminal is himself. *Irony of situation* involves a state of affairs the opposite of what one would expect: a pious man is revealed as a hypocrite, or an athlete dies young.

Jargon refers to specialized terms associated with a particular field of knowledge. Also, it sometimes means pseudotechnical language used to impress readers.

Logic, in writing, is the orderly, coherent presentation of a subject. As a subdivision of philosophy, logic is both the study and the method of correct reasoning, using the techniques of deduction or induction to arrive at conclusions.

Logical Fallacies are errors in reasoning that render an argument invalid. Some of the more common logical fallacies are:

Oversimplification. The tendency to provide simple solutions to complex problems: "The way to solve the problem of our high national debt is to raise taxes."

Non sequitur ("It does not follow"). An inference or conclusion that does not follow from the premises or evidence: "He was a brilliant basketball player; therefore, he will be an outstanding Supreme Court justice."

Post hoc, ergo propter hoc ("After this, therefore because of this"). Confusing chance or coincidence with causation. Because one event comes after another one, it does not necessarily mean that the first event caused the second: "I know I caught my cold at the hockey game, because I didn't have it before I went there."

Begging the question. Assuming in a premise that which needs to be proved: "Government management of a rail system is an economic evil because it is socialistic."

Either/or thinking. The tendency to see an issue as having only two sides: "America—love it or leave it."

Metaphor: See *Figures of Speech.*

Meter: See *Sound.*

Metonymy: See *Figures of Speech.*

Modes, Rhetorical: See *Discourse, Forms of.*

Mood is the emotional effect or feeling that a literary work evokes in the reader.

Narration is one of the four basic forms of discourse. (Description, exposition, and argument are the other three.) To narrate is to tell a story, to tell what happened. Whenever you relate an incident or use an anecdote to make a point, you use narration. In its broadest sense, narration includes all writing that provides an account of an event or a series of events.

Objective/Subjective. Objective writing is impersonal in tone and relies chiefly on facts and logical argument. Subjective writing refers to the author's personal feelings and conveys his or her emotional response to the subject. A writer may modulate between the two within the same essay, according to his or her purpose, but one or the other is usually made to dominate.

Opinion. An opinion is a belief or conclusion not substantiated by positive knowledge or proof. An opinion reveals personal feelings or attitudes or states a position. Opinion should not be confused with argument.

Organization is the plan or scheme by which the contents of a piece of writing are arranged. Some often-used plans of organization are *chronological order,* which relates people and events to each other in terms of time, for example, as one event coming before another, or two conditions existing simultaneously; *spatial order,* which relates objects and events in space, for example, from far to near or from top to bottom; *climactic order,* which presents ideas and evidence in order of increasing importance, power, or magnitude to heighten emphasis; and its opposite, *anticlimactic order.*

Paradox. A paradox is a self-contradictory statement that yet has truth in it, for example: "Less is more."

Paragraph. The paragraph, the single most important unit of thought in an essay, is a series of closely related sentences. These sentences adequately develop the central or controlling idea of the paragraph. This central or controlling idea, usually stated in a topic sentence, is necessarily related to the purpose of the whole composition. A well-written paragraph has several distinguishing characteristics: a clearly stated or implied topic sentence, adequate development, unity, coherence, and an appropriate organizational strategy.

Parallelism. Parallel structure is the repetition of word order or form either within a single sentence or in several sentences that develop the same central idea. As a rhetorical device, parallelism can aid coherence and add emphasis. Roosevelt's statement "I see one third of the nation ill-housed, ill-clad, and ill-nourished" illustrates effective parallelism.

Persona, or speaker, is the "voice" you can imagine uttering the words of a piece of writing. Sometimes the speaker is recognizably the same as the author, especially in nonfiction prose. Often, however, the speaker is a partly or wholly fictional creation, as in short stories, novels, poems, and some essays.

Personification: See *Figures of Speech.*

Persuasion is the effort to make one's audience agree with one's thesis or point of view and thus accept a belief or take a particular action. There are two main kinds of persuasion: the appeal to reason (see *Argument*) and the appeal to an audience's emotions; both kinds are often blended in the same piece of writing.

Plot is the sequence or pattern of events in a short story, novel, film, or play. The chief elements of plot are its *action,* the actual event or events; *conflict,* the struggle between opposing characters or forces; the *climax,* the turning point of the story; and the *denouncement,* the final resolution or outcome of the story.

Poetry is a rhythmical, imaginative, and intense form of expression. Poetry achieves its intensity by not only saying things in the fewest possible words but also in relying more heavily than other forms of literature on such language devices as metaphor, symbol, connotation, allusion, sound repetition, and imagery.

Point of View, as a technical term in writing, refers to the grammatical person of the speaker in a piece of writing. For example, a first-person point of view uses the pronoun *I* and is commonly found in autobiography and the personal essay; a third-person point of view uses the pronouns *he, she,* or *it* and is commonly found in objective writing. Both are used in the short story to characterize the narrator, the one who tells the story. The narrator may be *omniscient*—that is, telling the actions of all the characters whenever and wherever they take place, and reporting the characters' thoughts and attitudes as well. A less knowing narrator, such as a character in the story, is said to have a *limited,* or restricted, point of view.

Prewriting. Prewriting is a name applied to all the activities that take place before a writer actually starts a rough draft. During the prewriting stage of the writing process, the writer will select a subject area, focus on a particular topic, collect information and make notes, brainstorm for ideas, discover connections between pieces of information, determine a thesis and purpose, rehearse portions of the writing in the mind and/or on paper, and make a scratch outline.

Process Analysis answers the question *how* and explains how something works or gives step-by-step directions for doing something. There are two types of process analysis: directional and informational. The *directional* type provides instructions on how to do something. These instructions can be as brief as the directions for making instant coffee printed on a label or as complex as the directions in a manual for building your own home computer. The purpose of directional process analysis is simple: The reader can follow the directions and achieve the desired results. The *informational* type of process analysis, on the other hand, tells how something works, how something is made, or how something occurred. You would use informational process analysis if you wanted to explain to a reader how the human heart functions, how hailstones are formed, how an atomic bomb works, how iron ore is made into steel, how you selected the college you are attending, or how the Salk polio vaccine was developed. Rather than giving specific directions, the informational type of process analysis has the purpose of explaining and informing.

Protagonist. The protagonist is the central character in the conflict of a story. He or she may be either a sympathetic character (Hester Prynne in *The Scarlet Letter*) or an unsympathetic one (Captain Ahab in *Moby-Dick*).

Publication. The publication stage of the writing process is when the writer shares his or her writing with the intended audience. Publication can take the form of a typed or oral presentation, a dittoed or photocopied copy, or a commercially printed rendition. What's important is that the writer's words are read in what amounts to the final form.

Purpose. The writer's purpose is what he or she wants to accomplish in a particular piece of writing. Sometimes the writer may state the purpose openly, but sometimes the purpose must be inferred from the written work itself.

Revision. During the revision stage of the writing process, the writer determines what in the draft needs to be developed or clarified so that the essay says what the writer intends it to say. Often the writer needs to revise several times before the essay is "right." Comments from peer evaluators can be invaluable in helping writers determine what sorts of changes need to be made. Such changes can include adding material, deleting material, changing the order of presentation, and substituting new material for old.

Rhetoric is the effective use of language, traditionally the art of persuasion though the term is now generally applied to all purposes and kinds of writing.

Rhyme: See *Sound*.

Rhythm: See *Sound*.

Satire is a literary composition, in prose or poetry, in which human follies, vices, or institutions are held up to scorn.

Setting is the time and place in which the action of a narrative occurs. Many critics also include in their notion of setting such elements as the occupations and life-style of characters as well as the religious, moral, and social environment in which they live.

Short Story. The short story, as the name implies, is a brief fictional narrative in prose. Short stories range in length from about 500 words (a short short story) to about 15,000–20,000 words (a long short story or novella).

Simile: See *Figures of Speech.*

Sound. Writers of prose and especially of poetry pay careful attention to the sounds as well as the meanings of words. Whether we read a piece aloud or simply "hear" what we read in our mind's ear, we are most likely to notice the following sound features of the language:

Rhythm. In language, the *rhythm* is mainly a pattern of stressed and unstressed syllables. The rhythm of prose is irregular, but prose writers sometimes cluster stressed syllables for emphasis: "Théy sháll nót páss." Much poetry is written in highly regular rhythms called *meters,* in which a pattern of stressed and unstressed syllables is set and held to: "Th' ĕxpénse / ŏf spír / ĭt iń / ă wáste / ŏf sháme." Even nonmetrical poetry may sometimes use regular rhythms, as in this line by Walt Whitman: "I célĕbráte mўsélf aňd síng mўsélf."

Assonance, Consonance, and Rhyme. The repetition of a consonant is called *consonance,* and the repetition of a vowel is called *assonance.* The following line of poetry uses consonance of *l* and *d,* and assonance of *o:* "Roll on, thou deep and dark blue ocean—roll!" When two nearby words begin with the same sound, like *deep* and *dark* above, that sound pattern is called *alliteration.* And when two words end with whole syllables that sound the same, and one of those syllables is stressed, the result is called *rhyme,* as in strong / along and station / gravitation.

Specific/General. General words name groups or classes of objects, qualities, or actions. Specific words, on the other hand, name individual objects, qualities, or actions within a class or group. To some extent the terms *general* and *specific* are relative. For example, *dessert* is a class of things. *Pie,* however, is more specific than *dessert* but more general than *pecan pie* or *chocolate cream pie.* Good writing judiciously balances the general with the specific. Writing with too many general words is likely to be dull and lifeless. General words do not create vivid responses in the reader's mind as concrete specific words can. On the other hand, writing that relies exclusively on specific words may lack focus and direction, the control that more general statements provide. See also *Example.*

Style is the individual manner in which a writer expresses his or her ideas. Style is created by the author's particular selection of words, construction of sentences, and arrangement of ideas. A skillful writer adapts his or her style to the purpose and audience at hand. Some useful adjectives for describing styles include literary or journalistic, ornamental or economical, personal or impersonal, formal or chatty, among others. But these labels are very general, and an accurate stylistic description or analysis of a particular author or piece of writing requires consideration of sentence length and structure, diction, figures of speech, and the like.

Subjective: See *Objective/Subjective.*

Symbol. A symbol is a person, place, or thing that represents something beyond itself. For example, the eagle is a symbol of the United States, and the cross a symbol of Christianity.

Synecdoche: See *Figures of Speech.*

Theme is the central idea in a piece of writing. In fiction, poetry, and drama, the theme may not be stated directly, but it is then presented through the characters, actions, and images of the work. In nonfiction prose the theme is often stated explicitly in a thesis statement. See also *Thesis.*

Thesis. The thesis of an essay is its main idea, the point it is trying to make. The thesis is often expressed in a one- or two-sentence statement, although sometimes it is implied or suggested rather than stated directly. The thesis statement controls and directs the content of the essay. Everything that the writer says must be logically related to the thesis. Some therefore prefer to call the thesis the *controlling idea.*

Tone. Comparable to "tone of voice" in conversation, the tone of a written work reflects the author's attitude toward the subject and audience. For example, the tone of a work might be described by such terms as friendly, serious, distant, angry, cheerful, bitter, cynical, enthusiastic, morbid, resentful, warm, playful, and so forth.

Transitions are words or phrases that link sentences, paragraphs, and larger units of a composition to achieve coherence. These devices include connecting words and phrases like *moreover, therefore,* and *on the other hand,* and the repetition of key words and ideas.

Unity. A well-written essay should be unified: that is, everything in it should be related to its thesis, or main idea. The first requirement for unity is that the thesis itself be clear, either through a direct statement, called the thesis statement, or by implication. The second requirement is that there be no digressions, no discussion or information that is not shown to be logically related to the thesis. A unified essay stays within the limits of its thesis.

Writing Process. The writing process consists of five major stages: prewriting, writing drafts, revision, editing, and publication. The process is not inflexible, but there is no mistaking the fact that most writers follow some version of it most of the time. Although orderly in its basic components and sequence of activities, the writing process is nonetheless continuous, creative, and unique to each individual writer. See also *Draft, Editing, Prewriting, Publication,* and *Revision.*

Acknowledgments Continued

"Inaugural Address" by William Jefferson Clinton, January 20, 1993.

"Sexual Correctness: Has It Gone Too Far?" by Sarah Crichton. From *Newsweek*, October 25, 1993. © 1993, Newsweek, Inc. All rights reserved. Reprinted by permission.

"Propaganda: How Not to Be Bamboozled" by Donna Woolfolk Cross. From *Speaking of Words: A Language Reader.* Reprinted by permission of the author.

"Talking in the New Land" by Edite Cunha. Reprinted by permission of the author.

"I'm nobody! Who are you?" by Emily Dickinson. Reprinted by permission of the publishers and the Trustees of Amherst College from *The Poems of Emily Dickinson,* Thomas H. Johnson, ed., Cambridge, Mass.: The Belknap Press of Harvard University Press, Copyright © 1951, 1955, 1979, 1983 by the President and Fellows of Harvard College.

"Why Worry About the Animals?" by Jean Bethke Elshtain from *The Progressive,* March 1990. Reprinted by permission from *The Progressive,* 409 East Main Street, Madison, Wisconsin 53703.

"A Tale of Two Gravies" by Karen P. Engelhardt. Copyright © by Karen P. Engelhardt. Reprinted by permission of the author.

"Confessions of a Working Stiff" by Patrick Fenton from *New York Magazine,* 1971. Copyright 1993, Patrick Fenton. Reprinted by permission of the author.

"Advertising's Fifteen Basic Appeals" by Jib Fowles. Reprinted from ETC. Vol. 39, No. 3, Fall 1982, with permission of the International Society for General Semantics, Concord, California.

"The Road Not Taken" from *The Poetry of Robert Frost,* edited by Edward Connery Lathem. Copyright 1944 by Robert Frost. Copyright 1916, © 1969 by Henry Holt and Company, Inc. Reprinted by permission of Henry Holt and Company, Inc.

"Shame," from *Nigger: An Autobiography* by Dick Gregory. Copyright © 1964 by Dick Gregory Enterprises, Inc. Used by permission of Dutton Signet, a division of Penguin Books USA Inc.

"Our Son Mark" from *Through the Communication Barrier* by S. I. Hayakawa. Reprinted with permission of the Estate of S. I. Hayakawa.

"Those Winter Sundays" is reprinted from *Angle of Ascent, New and Selected Poems,* by Robert Hayden, by permission of Liveright Publishing Corporation. Copyright © 1975, 1972, 1970, and 1966 by Robert Hayden.

"Heritage" by Linda Hogan. Reprinted by permission of the author and Greenfield Review Press.

"How Far She Went" from *How Far She Went* by Mary Hood. Copyright © 1984 by Mary Hood. Reprinted by permission of the publisher, the University of Georgia Press.

"All Happy Clans Are Alike: In Search of the Good Family" from *Families* by Jane Howard. Copyright © 1978 by Jane Howard. Reprinted by permission of Simon & Schuster, Inc.

"Salvation" from *The Big Sea* by Langston Hughes. Copyright © 1940 by Langston Hughes, renewed © 1968 by Arna Bontemps and Georges Houston Bass. Reprinted by permission of Hill and Wang, a division of Farrar, Straus & Giroux, Inc.

"Theme for English B" by Langston Hughes. Reprinted by permission of Harold Ober Associates Incorporated. Copyright 1951 by Langston Hughes. Copyright renewed 1979 by George Houston Bass.

"How It Feels to Be Colored Me," from *I Love Myself When I Am Laughing* by Zora Neale Hurston. Used by permission of Lucy Ann Hurston.

"The Lottery" from *The Lottery* by Shirley Jackson. Copyright © 1949 by Shirley Jackson. Copyright renewed 1977 by Laurence Hyman, Barry Hyman, Mrs. Sarah Webster, and Mrs. Joanne Schnurer. Reprinted by permission of Farrar, Straus & Giroux, Inc.

"Unfair Game" by Susan Jacoby. Originally appeared in *The New York Times,* 1978. Copyright © 1978 by Susan Jacoby. Reprinted by permission of Georges Borchardt, Inc., for the author.

"Letter from Birmingham Jail" by Martin Luther King, Jr. Reprinted by arrangement with The Heirs to the Estate of Martin Luther King, Jr., c/o Joan Daves Agency as agent for the proprietor. Copyright 1963 by the Estate of Martin Luther King, Jr. Copyright renewed 1991 by Coretta Scott King.

"The Human Cost of an Illiterate Society" from *Illiterate America* by Jonathan Kozol. Copyright © 1985 by Jonathan Kozol. Used by permission of Doubleday, a division of Bantam Doubleday Dell Publishing Group, Inc.

"A Woman's Fight" from *Red Mother* by Frank B. Linderman. Copyright 1932 by Frank B.

Linderman. Copyright renewed 1960 by Norma Waller, Verne Linderman, and Wilda Linderman. Reprinted by permission of HarperCollins Publishers, Inc.

"Can the American Family Survive?" by Margaret Mead and Rhoda Metraux from *Aspects of the Present.* Copyright © 1980 by Catherine Bateson Kassarjian and Rhoda Metraux. By permission of William Morrow & Company, Inc.

"On Friendship" by Margaret Mead and Rhoda Metraux from *A Way of Seeing.* Copyright © 1961–1970 by Margaret Mead and Rhoda Metraux. By permission of William Morrow & Company, Inc.

"Summer Job," from *Mary* by Mary Mebane. Copyright © 1981 by Mary Elizabeth Mebane. Used by permission of Viking Penguin, a division of Penguin Books USA Inc.

"Immigrants" by Pat Mora is reprinted with permission from the publisher of *Borders* (Houston: Arte Publico Press—University of Houston, 1986).

"The Looting of Language," Nobel Lecture 1993 by Toni Morrison. © The Nobel Foundation 1993.

"Mommy, What Does 'Nigger' Mean?" by Gloria Naylor. Originally appeared in *The New York Times,* 1986, and titled "The Meaning of a Word." Reprinted by permission of Sterling Lord Literistic, Inc. Copyright © 1986 by Gloria Naylor.

"Sexism in English: A 1990's Update" by Alleen P. Nilsen. © Alleen Pace Nilsen, Professor of English, Arizona State University, Tempe, AZ 85287–0302.

"In the Region of Ice" by Joyce Carol Oates from *The Wheel of Love and Other Stories.* Copyright © 1970 by Joyce Carol Oates. Reprinted by permission of John Hawkins & Associates, Inc.

"On the Subway" from *The Gold Cell* by Sharon Olds. Copyright © 1987 by Sharon Olds. Reprinted by permission of Alfred A. Knopf, Inc.

"Politics and the English Language" by George Orwell, copyright 1946 by Sonia Brownell Orwell and renewed 1974 by Sonia Orwell. Reprinted from his volume *Shooting an Elephant and Other Essays* by permission of Harcourt Brace & Company and the estate of the late Sonia Brownell Orwell and Martin Secker & Warburg.

"Shooting an Elephant" from *Shooting an Elephant and Other Essays* by George Orwell, copyright 1950 by Sonia Brownell Orwell and renewed 1978 by Sonia Pitt-Rivers. Reprinted by permission of Harcourt Brace & Company and the estate of the late Sonia Brownell Orwell and Martin Secker & Warburg.

"Fear in a Handful of Numbers" by Dennis Overbye from *Time,* October 9, 1989. Copyright 1989 Time Inc. Reprinted by permission.

"Androgynous Man," by Noel Perrin. Copyright © 1984 by The New York Times Company. Reprinted by permission.

"Rope" from *Flowering Judas and Other Stories,* copyright 1930 and renewed 1958 by Katherine Anne Porter, reprinted by permission of Harcourt Brace & Company.

"Abortion Is Too Complex to Feel All One Way About," originally titled "Hers," by Anna Quindlen. Copyright © 1986 by The New York Times Company. Reprinted by permission.

"Active and Passive Euthanasia" by James Rachels, *The New England Journal of Medicine,* Vol. 292, pp. 78–80, 1975. Copyright 1975. Reprinted by permission.

"Homosexuality: One Family's Affair" by Michael Reese and Pamela Abramson. From *Newsweek,* January 13, 1986. © 1986, Newsweek, Inc. All rights reserved. Reprinted by permission.

"The Endless Streetcar Ride Into the Night, and the Tin Foil Noose" from *In God We Trust, All Others Pay Cash* by Jean Shepherd. Copyright © 1966 by Jean Shepherd. Used by permission of Doubleday, a division of Bantam Doubleday Dell Publishing Group, Inc.

"One Last Time" from *Living Up the Street* by Gary Soto, 1985. Reprinted by permission of the author.

"A Brother's Murder," by Brent Staples. Copyright © 1986 by The New York Times Company. Reprinted by permission.

"The Recoloring of Campus Life" by Shelby Steele. Copyright © 1989 by *Harper's Magazine.* All rights reserved. Reprinted from the February issue by special permission.

"The Importance of Work" from *Outrageous Acts and Everyday Rebellions* by Gloria Steinem. Copyright © 1983 by Gloria Steinem. Copyright © 1984 by East Toledo Productions, Inc. Reprinted by permission of Henry Holt and Company, Inc.

"'I'll Explain It to You:' Lecturing and Listening" by Deborah Tannen from *You Just Don't*

Understand. Copyright © 1990 by Deborah Tannen. By permission of William Morrow & Company, Inc.

"On Being White, Female, and Born in Bensonhurst" by Marianna de Marco Torgovnick, Professor of English at Duke and author of *Gone Primitive: Savage Intellects, Modern Lives* (1990) and *Crossing Parkway: Readings by an Italian American Daughter* (1994). Reprinted by permission of the author.

"A Sense of Shelter" from *Pigeon Feathers and Other Stories* by John Updike. Copyright © 1959, 1960, 1961, 1962 by John Updike. Reprinted by permission of Alfred A. Knopf, Inc.

"Harrison Bergeron" by Kurt Vonnegut, J., from *Welcome to the Monkey House* by Kurt Vonnegut, Jr. Used by permission of Delacorte Press/Seymour Lawrence, a division of Bantam Doubleday Dell Publishing Group, Inc.

"The Unromantic Generation," by Bruce Weber. Copyright © 1987 by The New York Times Company. Reprinted by permission.

"Miss Duling." Reprinted by permission of the publishers from *One Writer's Beginnings* by Eudora Welty, Cambridge, Mass.: Harvard University Press, Copyright © 1983, 1984 by Eudora Welty.

"A Worn Path" from *A Curtain of Green and Other Stories*, copyright 1941 and renewed 1969 by Eudora Welty, reprinted by permission of Harcourt Brace & Company.

"Last Day" from *Charlotte's Web*, copyright 1952, by E. B. White. Renewed © 1980 by E. B. White. Reprinted by permission of HarperCollins Publishers.

All pages from "Once More to the Lake" from *One Man's Meat* by E. B. White. Copyright 1941 by E. B. White. Reprinted by permission of HarperCollins Publishers, Inc.

"In Search of Bruce Lee's Grave." Copyright © 1990 by Shanlon Wu. All rights reserved.

"Let's Tell the Story of All America's Culture" by Ji-Yeon Mary Yuhfill from *The Philadelphia Inquirer*, 1991. Reprinted with permission from *The Philadelphia Inquirer*.

Index of Authors and Titles